Advance Praise for *Career Dharma:*
The Natural Art of Work

Career Dharma beautifully shows that meditation practice is not just about silent sitting, it is also about how we live and work. This impressively comprehensive book details a way of choosing one's career, and acting within one's career, that brings the principles of a meditative life into one's work. Doing that helps us tap into a wellspring of joy within us. The advice on working without egoism and lethargy is particularly wonderful.

 — Chade-Meng Tan
  Bestselling author of *Search Inside Yourself* and *Joy on Demand*

This book is fascinating, deep, accurate, insightful and much needed! Drs Best and Datta have been able to give solutions to today's challenges with finding our purpose through the lens of practical ancient wisdom. This is probably the most comprehensive, practical, ethical, universal and detailed analysis of careers I've come across. I have already recommended it to many.

 — Dr. Chetna Kang MB BS MRCPsych
  Consultant Psychiatrist
  Executive Committee Member, Royal College of Psychiatrists
   Spirituality and Psychiatry SIG

In the *Bhagavad-gita*, a classic on yoga wisdom, Krishna tells the warrior Arjuna (and by extension us, the reader) that we can never escape action; even when we choose not to act, we're engaged in a form of action. The real question, then, becomes, "What is the best way to act? How do we act with skill?" This Krishna defines as yoga, "skill in action" (*yogah karmasu kaushalam*). In this ground-breaking work, *Ca-*

reer Dharma: The Natural Art of Work*, Urmila Edith Best and Ruchira
S. Datta take the ancient insights of the *Bhagavad-gita* and other yoga
texts and apply them to the field of work and career.

While we can spend so much of our life fighting ourselves, Krishna
counsels Arjuna to be true to his nature. We're each born with a particular nature, which allows us to make a unique contribution in the
world. *Career Dharma* comes at a time when the majority of us feel
unfulfilled at work, alienated from our nature, and in search of guiding purpose. Best and Datta artfully combine ancient wisdom with
contemporary research in human psychology and sociology to help us
navigate and thrive in the arena of work and career. *Career Dharma* is
predicated on the idea that ancient texts and traditions carry genera-
tional insights that can help us better navigate the complexities of life
and live more effectively. Ultimately, this is a book about yoga — the
yoga of work — that is sure to inspire and reshape lives.

    — Simon Haas
       International bestselling author of *The Book of Dharma: Making
          Enlightened Choices* and *Yoga and the Dark Night of the Soul*

As is well known, the wisdom philosophies and spiritual practices
of Eastern traditions have increasingly permeated western culture,
particularly since the 60's counter-culture. Most of these influences,
however, have been directed at spiritual, meditational and enlightened health practices - in other words, they are mostly transcendent
additions to the more prosaic realities of professional life. It is thus
a sign of the deepening influence of India's sacred traditions to encounter a book applying principles from one of the most prominent
of these, the Bhagavata tradition, to the this-world career aspects of
embodied existence. Bringing social science research into dialogue
with texts such as the *Bhagavad Gita* and *Bhagavata Purana*, Best and
Datta apply devotionally imbued wisdom insights to our every-day
civic interactions and professional attitudes. *Career Dharma* is thus
indispensable reading for all stripes of yogis seeking guidance in
how to navigate the nitty-gritty demands of the 9-5 workplace as
practitioners, and an enlightening read for the intellectually curious
wondering how Yogic philosophy might be relevant to the real world.

    — Edwin Bryant
    Professor of Hindu Religion and Philosophy
    Rutgers University

Career Dharma is magnificent; the breadth of research and the depth of insight combined with the relevance of the topic and the accessibility of the analysis make it an irresistible read. It is by far the best book I have read that gives a contemporary presentation of the *Gita*'s social teachings.

    — Chaitanya Charan
    The Spiritual Scientist
    Author of more than 25 books on the *Bhagavad-gita*, *Ramayana*,
        and related topics

Most people will spend almost 100,000 hours at work in a given lifetime, which is roughly a third of the average person's lifespan. It makes sense, therefore, to carefully look at whether or not our employment is appropriate to our nature and exactly how we approach what we do — is it satisfying and effective, or not? Likely to become the bible on 'nature and work,' this mammoth and comprehensive text, written by two experts in the field, Drs. Urmila Edith Best and Ruchira S. Datta, is a pragmatic and unrelenting look at why we do what we do, how it impacts our day-to-day life, and what we bring to the task. Drawing on a wealth of academic studies, insightful reflections, and sacred literature both East and West, the authors offer painstaking analyses that will be of value to readers worldwide, whatever these readers happen to be doing for a living. *Career Dharma: The Natural Art of Work* will be a valuable addition to your library, but don't let it just sit on your bookshelf; wade through it and let it work for you, enveloping your daily actions with intention and joy.

    — Steven J. Rosen (Satyaraja dasa)
      Author of numerous books on Indic spirituality and founding
        editor of the *Journal of Vaishnava Studies*

Finding one's inner calling is sometimes hard to achieve and often seems beyond hope. In *Career Dharma: the Natural Art of Work*, Urmila Best and Ruchira Datta explain to those interested in their own internal psychological workings how one can identify and act according to one's own nature and realize a flourishing and satisfying career. They explore methods of work that are in line with a person's natural talents, and they open up the reader's emotional and spiritual dimensions, leading them toward greater appreciation of the factors that restrict people from experiencing a fulfilling and joyful career. In an easily accessible writing style, Best and Datta explain techniques that can assist a person in finding their dharma, something that may have previously felt unknowable. *Career Dharma* will remain a vital reference and guide for those seeking sound career advice from both timeless ancient wisdom and contemporary empirical research.

— Gopal Gupta
Associate Professor
Joe Dunham Distinguished Professorship in Ethics
Aurora University
Editor, *Journal of Hindu-Christian Studies*[1]

Best and Datta take a fresh approach to questions of career choice, career satisfaction, and work more generally, in their accessibly written *Career Dharma*. In this book, readers are taken along a set of broad inquiries and vignettes about work, guided by the authors' reflections on texts such as the *Bhagavad-Gītā*, the *Bhāgavata Purāṇa*, and more. For readers interested in understanding the ways that religious principles can be adapted to answer contemporary questions related to work, this book will not disappoint.

— Nicole Karapanagiotis, Ph.D.
Associate Professor of Religion, Rutgers University, Camden
Author of *Branding Bhakti: Krishna Consciousness and the Makeover of a Movement*

We all want peace and prosperity in the world and in our own lives. Yet most people find their jobs unfulfilling and their prosperity disappointing in both amount and kind. Drawing from the ancient wisdom of the *Bhagavad-gita* and *Bhagavata Purana* as well as current research, in *Career Dharma: The Natural Art of Work* Best and Datta detail how we can each find a career that will be satisfying and will yield a rich, meaningful life. They also give a big picture of how society works when individuals follow these principles of career dharma, and testimonies give concrete examples. Anyone looking for their ideal career can benefit from the wisdom found in this book.

— Giriraj Swami
Author of *Many Moons*, *Watering the Seed*, and *I'll Build You a Temple*

It is said that if you find a job you love you will never have to do a day's work. In *Career Dharma*, Urmila and Ruchira expertly show us how to align with our true nature to find that sometimes elusive occupation that deeply fulfils us. The self-help guru Stephen Covey called this connecting with your "inner yes", what you were born to do. Drawing on ancient wisdom integrated with modern science, the authors take it even further, guiding us in making our work a joyful experience that gives us purpose, direction and meaning. Highly recommended for anyone trying to decide on their vocation or who may have found themselves stuck in a 'dead-end' job they wake up dreading every day.

 — Krishna Dharma
  Best-selling author including the Brilliant as the Sun series; publisher and speaker

With apologies to Lewis Carroll, while reflecting on present-day Western society's fragmentation in light of Best and Datta's book: Now I know why all the king's horses and all the king's men couldn't put Humpty together again. So much more than a "career guide," *Career Dharma* offers the thoroughly grounded, research-based vision that could be the basis for creation of truly alternative, integrated communities of any size, in which we neither labor, nor work, but where we have *livelihoods* that are rooted truly in following our *calling*. Best and Datta provide all the necessary conceptual tools for making such dreams into realities that bypass the many traps of utopian ideas and experiments, making it possible to get the Humpty Dumpty of meaningful life back on his feet and running.

 — Kenneth Valpey, Ph.D
  Author of *The Bhagavata Purana: Sacred Text and Living Tradition*, and *Cow Care in Hindu Animal Ethics*
  Research Fellow, Oxford Centre for Hindu Studies

The wheel of dharma, as seen on the cover, holds the key to a life of success and harmony. That key is: "If you protect dharma, dharma will always protect you." In *Career Dharma*, authors Best and Datta highlight the truth of our relationship with dharma — our essential nature and the natural laws governing it — in terms of what we spend the majority of our time doing: earning our livelihood. Readers will discover which types of prosperity are not personally destructive and learn how to protect them. They will also gain an awareness of that field of work which resonates with their individual nature, and how to protect the authenticity of that field. Most importantly, *Career Dharma* links our way of working with the path of self-realization and thus with ultimate satisfaction. By citing evidence both from ancient wisdom and empirical research, this book shows the benefit of finding our purpose beyond the cycle of frustration and shades of ego in a way that enables work to add real value to ourselves and to others. Having established the path of personal satisfaction and meaning in careers, Best and Datta describe an ideal society in terms of sustainable prosperity. Their model of mathematical eco-sociology, and their example of an *ahimsa* farm, offer rational guidance to society's leaders and thinkers. *Career Dharma* is an insightful and valuable read for those looking for an alternative to today's failing consumerism and decaying societal models. Reading it is time well spent.

> — Sivarama Swami
> Author of many books on *bhakti* yoga, such as *Suddha Bhakti Cintamani*, and *Nava-vraja-mahima* in 9 volumes

This book convincingly shows how the universal principles of social organization discovered by the ancient sages work even now, and how important it is to consciously apply them in our life to achieve happiness and innner satisfaction.

> — Bhaktivijnana Goswami, Ph.D
> Author of books on spirituality in Russian, including *The Arrow of Grace, Parallels,* and *Deep Healing Prayers*

Meaningful work has become a hot-button issue. What career suits me? How should I "slot in"? Will the workplace fulfill me? Consider data for the USA: just 66 percent of college graduates are in jobs requiring a college degree. What's more, only 27 percent found jobs related to their college major.

Add to this crisis in career-preparation the staggering financial burden, and the camel's back shatters. From 1989 to 2016, college tuition and fees went up by 98 percent (adjusted for inflation).

Clearly we need a more prudent and enlightened approach to workforce sanity and satisfaction. The erudite team of Drs. Best and Datta offer a profound guidebook for choosing a career as well as for conducting oneself along the chosen career path. *Career Dharma* uniquely combines the best of contemporary analytical knowledge with the precious insights of ancient wisdom.

> — Devamrita Swami
> Author of *Hiding in Unnatural Happiness* and *Searching for Vedic India*

Dr. Urmila Best and Dr. Ruchira Datta present us an exceptional, invaluable book on a most important topic. Unless one finds a natural, satisfying career in life, happiness often proves to be elusive. Indeed, a natural, satisfying career even grounds many people in their spiritual practice and family duties. An inspiring career brings personal satisfaction.

Unfortunately, in today's extremely over-complicated, ever-mutating world, many people, including spiritual practitioners, find it hard to settle on their natural career, their true calling in life. Dr. Best and Dr. Datta have come powerfully to the rescue with a comprehensive, thoughtful, authoritative, user-friendly guide to career choice. They cover all the bases.

I sincerely hope that this important book will reach the hands and eyes of many people, for many people actually need it.

— H D Goswami, PhD

Author of *A Comprehensive Guide to Bhagavad-gita* and *Enlightenment by the Natural Path*

Being a professor of food engineering and advisor of the Bhakti Yoga Club at Southern Illinois University, and a father of two daughters who graduated from this university, I have faced constant challenges on how to guide my students and children to choose their right career so that they enjoy and feel happy about what they are doing. It is very challenging for most students to figure out what is best for them. Even though students do job shadowing and learn about different professions, many students change their majors while in college. And more challenges come when they start working and they find out that is not what they wanted to do. Once a graduate advisee asked me if she could take theatre and music courses. I asked her why she is thinking about those courses while being in food engineering major. She replied, because she wanted to be a Hollywood star! I simply laughed at what she said but she was serious about her decision, and she changed her major to theatre. Now this book is a great relief to me. Drs Best and Datta have done a great job to help students, parents, teachers, advisors, professors and career counselors to not only find their right career but to find their goal of life – purpose of life. Drawing from time-tested Vedic literatures, they give a framework for choosing one's career based on one's nature. This book is the most comprehensive book I have ever come across in the field of career counselling. I like the collection of case studies and testimonies on different professions. For me, the most eye-opening part of this book was to learn that we are not our jobs. According to the four stages of life, the first quarter should be used for study and preparation of career and only the second quarter of our life should be used in career. Ideally the remaining two should be used in gradual withdrawal, retirement and preparation for death. I highly recommend this book to all parents, teachers, students, professors and career counselors. This book will help everyone to find the right path for themselves or their dear ones.

    — Ruplal Choudhary, Ph.D
    Professor of Food Engineering and Technology
    Southern Illinois University, Carbondale, IL

Career Dharma: The Natural Art of Work says it all. This book reveals a fascinating, innovative and pragmatic approach to career or vocation ('one's calling'), with wisdom gleaned from the ancient Vedic civilization of India. This great culture recognized the profound connection between a person's natural work, based on their inherent psycho-physiological makeup, and one's peace, fulfillment, and even enlightenment. The authors are eminently qualified, both scholarly and experientially, to provide such a groundbreaking and empowering perspective on work to people of all personalities and lifestyles. The current state of dissatisfaction among workers in general should make *Career Dharma* a cutting-edge offering to a wide audience. I can highly recommend this book to anyone looking to find a career with heart and personal meaning, as well as organizations wanting to maximize performance and satisfaction among their managers and staff.

    — J. Phillip Jones, LMHC
    Director of *Pathways for Life* at Pacific Pathways
    Associate Publisher/Wellness Manager, Mandala Publishing
    Author, *Transcendence: Finding Peace at the End of Life*

Career Dharma by Dr. Urmila Edith Best and Dr. Ruchira S. Datta is an eye opener! They have presented an efficient framework which sheds light on the known and many unknown dynamics of the art of work. The knowledge presented here can resolve any work-related issue, across all fields, time and place.

    — Ramesh Goel
    Professor and Graduate Director
    Director, Environmental Engineering and Microbiology Lab
    Civil & Environmental Engineering
    University of Utah

Any intelligent person that has spent some time debating nature vs. nurture generally comes to the conclusion that our temperament, happiness or success is a mix of both. If we logically extend this idea, it becomes apparent that in order to be happy and/or successful, it may be a good idea to nurture our nature. But how? If nature is personal, how do we know if we have identified it correctly? And how can we be sure we are cultivating and nurturing it properly?

Luckily there is a body of wisdom that has explored these concepts for thousands of years. This is the wisdom of 'Dharma'. The philosophy of Dharma shortcuts our journey of happiness, success and mastery by letting us in on a secret. Our difficulties are not ours alone.

Throughout all of history, humanity has gone through different versions of the same basic struggles that we are going through. The guidelines of Dharma protect and support us on this journey. Dharma says, "Nature or temperament is categorized into *buckets*." As are the 3 *shades of ego* that influence our being. Understanding these universal principles of nature empowers us to pinpoint our own.

Once we are clear on our unique nature, destiny & purpose, the tasks are then to cultivate and nurture these. The philosophy of Dharma again guides us in this nurturing. However, the ideas of Dharma, though practical, are trapped in cryptic texts and archaic cultures.

That is why I am so happy to endorse and support the printing of this book *Career Dharma: The Natural Art Of Work*. This book uncovers and translates the core principles of Dharma for the modern world. It specifically guides us in living a happy, successful, and uplifting career. It is not some modern self-help fluff, but a deep exploration of some of the greatest wisdom in history. I could not think of a better team to write this book. The authors not only have exceptional careers of their own, but are deeply versed in the wisdom of Dharma.

— Vishnu Swami — The Maverick Monk
Author of *Eternal Dharma: How To Find Spiritual Evolution Through Surrender & Embrace Your Life's True Purpose*

CAREER DHARMA

The Natural Art of Work

Urmila Edith Best
&
Ruchira S. Datta

Nine Islands
MEDIA

Nine Islands Media
A Division of Datta Enterprises LLC
65 E. Wilson Bridge Road, Suite 307
Worthington, Ohio 43085

Illustrations & Cover Art: Padma Gopi Walsh
Photographs: Ruchira S. Datta

Library of Congress Control Number: 2023936302
ISBN 979-8-9872753-1-3 (paperback)
ISBN 979-8-9872753-2-0 (ebook)
ISBN 979-8-9872753-3-7 (audiobook)

18 17 16 15 14 13 12 11 10 9 8 7 6 5 4 3

Publisher's Cataloging-in-Publication Data
provided by Five Rainbows Cataloging Services

Names: Best, Edith Elizabeth, 1955– author. | Datta, Ruchira Sreemati, 1973– author.
Title: Career dharma : the natural art of work / Urmila Edith Best [and] Ruchira S. Datta.
Description: Worthington, OH : Nine Islands Media, 2023. | Includes index.
Identifiers: LCCN 2023936302 (print) | ISBN 979-8-9872753-1-3 (paperback) | ISBN 979-8-9872753-2-0 (ebook) | ISBN 979-8-9872753-3-7 (audiobook)
Subjects: LCSH: Career development. | Success in business. | Self-realization. | Dharma. | Yoga. | Illustrated works. | BISAC: BUSINESS & ECONOMICS / Careers / General. | BUSINESS & ECONOMICS / Motivational. | RELIGION / Eastern. | RELIGION / Spirituality.
Classification: LCC HF5381 .B47 2023 (print) | LCC HF5381 (ebook) | DDC 650.1– dc23.

To our teachers, our students, and our readers.

namo gurubhyaḥ namaḥ

Contents

Foreword

Career Dharma: The Natural Art of Work is an important contribution to the subject of natural work as a pathway to maximising human potential, individual satisfaction, and social well-being. It is part of an emerging awareness that the world's wisdom traditions offer us a possible resource for inspiring new ways of thinking about the challenges and complexities of the modern world. This wisdom-inspired approach aims to create a new quality of solution that is natural, sustainable, and without adverse consequences.

Following suit, *Career Dharma* takes its inspiration from the ancient Vedic and Puranic traditions of India. The authors translate Sanskrit *sutras* or aphorisms into a set of tools and guidelines that, with some reflection and practice, the reader can use to explore how the "personal signature" of their nature is ideally suited to different types and qualities of work according to their psychological and emotional temperaments, as well as their aspirations, skill sets, and talents. The text offers a thorough overview of work itself, categorizing work using a novel Vedic taxonomy that offers new perspectives on how we think about work and vocation. This new way of looking at the nature of work and people offers the reader some insight into how to find the work most suited to them and perhaps why people in the modern world often find themselves misplaced and in unsatisfying occupations.

As you might expect from a work that draws from wisdom teachings, *Career Dharma* makes the case for a holistic worldview, in which we are all connected in a great web of life and nature, where each of us has a meaningful purpose to find and express in our lives. When we are aligned to our innate *personal signature*, we then flow more naturally toward optimal work and the satisfaction that comes from a job well done as a vital part of society — and the greater web of life. Optimal work is achieved by understanding our unique orientation, proclivity, and temperament, which express themselves in different values and views of wealth that the authors delineate in the text. Thus, the text suggests that the evolution of work and the prosperity it creates is dependent on the evolution of the individual which is achieved through awareness, reflection, and mindful practice. As such, work is much more than labour, but is an expression of our inner spirit out into the external realm of our day-to-day. When the two align, we achieve optimal work. The implication is that we do well when we consider the inner reality as an important, if not primary, area of concern in developing our professional roles. The authors suggest that people often find themselves in unsatisfying work because they have failed to address their inner spirit as the basis of what would make them truly happy.

Career Dharma supports the reader in their journey to optimal work by providing guidance, exercises, and true stories that engagingly illustrate the role that our inner development can play in our outer success. While the text is accessible and easy to read, it is also philosophical and thought-provoking. Aided by excerpts from various thinkers, authors, and life coaches, it calls on the reader to consider that the deeper meaning of the art of work is also *the art of being*. The quality of our being determines the quality of our work. Many of us are driven by a Do-Have-Be model of thinking, whereas the wisdom of dharma suggests we take the more satisfying and reliable path of Be–Do–Have.

There is something for everyone in this book. The scholarly background of the authors is evidenced in its thorough analysis of the various aspects of work, including considerations on how to make career choices ideally suited to our natures; how we can conduct ourselves to achieve optimal outcomes in our chosen fields; and broader considerations of work from a systems point of view on how individuals can co-operatively thrive as groups. There is good reason to recommend this book to a wide audience. It is valuable to anyone at the early stages of their career, as well as those considering a course correction in search of work that is meaningful, purposeful, and nourishing to the spirit. It is also a useful reference for educators, guidance counselors, sociologists, and anthropologists. Policymakers would benefit greatly from the strategic meta-vision of work that it provides — especially in its call to value people and their full potential.

What I enjoyed most was the call to awaken the spirit in all of us, to achieve wholeness, balance, connection, and harmony with ourselves, each other, nature, and all that we hold sacred. To quote from the text:

A principle of the natural art of work involves regular recognition of the whole and the source from which we come, because harmony with truth will make us happy, and disharmony with truth will bring frustration. One of the keys to a satisfying career — and life — is something unique to human beings among all of Earth's creatures: a regular, deliberate conscious connection with our source, the whole of which we are a part....

When we consciously, deliberately, and regularly acknowledge the source of everything, and dedicate our work to that source, then we become aware of the harmony and plan underlying what we experience. We become aware of our own place, the real and valuable contribution we can make, and the subjective feeling of our own value and worth.

This inspires in me a recollection that life is magical, and that work becomes play when our inner being is nourished, free to express itself, and truly satisfied by its sacred creative propensities. Work as divine play is a prosperity of a different kind, a wealth of a different quality. It is the byproduct of tasting a natural satisfaction within us, something the authors call *rasa*, a Sanskrit *sutra* for an inner fulfilment that is not dependent on the course of ordinary circumstances and is therefore sustainable and without adverse effects.

In essence, *Career Dharma: The Natural Art of Work* is a well-researched, well-written, informative manual that offers us a new way of thinking about work and our relationship to it. It gently raises our awareness of a better way of doing things and offers practical steps on how to get there. It is ancient time-tested wisdom adapted to people's needs in today's world.

Dr. Michael Geary
Living Wisdom Foundation (UK)

Why Another Book On Career?

The Natural Art of Work: Introduction

Why do some people love their work while others slog through drudgery, struggling through various careers in an effort to find satisfaction? Do those who truly enjoy their work know a winning formula? Did they just luckily stumble upon a different kind of life? Was their career satisfaction mostly the result of a privileged family and upbringing?

"This work is perfect!" the graphics designer smiles. "The nature of the work, the team, the management structure, the working environment: they are all just what I need. Everything that I love — playing with ideas, solving intellectual puzzles, lots of freedom, and creating something people will find useful — are all here. I get so absorbed in what I'm doing that I lose track of time and forget about eating and sleeping. I'm loving this moment to moment. In my other jobs, I was trudging through the work, hoping I'd enjoy a result later like a good paycheck although I didn't like the process itself."

"I spent eight years of education to become a lawyer just to discover that I find no joy in working in law," a young woman confided. "My parents are furious that I'm not using my education at all, and I'm still not sure what I want to do. My present job is just a way to make money."

In Chapel Hill, North Carolina, USA, a professor addresses his class: "When I was 19, a visiting speaker to my class told us a formula for becoming a school superintendent by age 33, instead of the more common 55. I followed his formula exactly, and it worked! The only problem was that I discovered I hated being a school superintendent. My wife hated our lifestyle so much she divorced me. Eventually I returned to my real love — teaching. Before you invest years of your life into a field of work, make sure it's what you really want to do."

A young college student loves his class in communication with a focus on the healing professions. "I think I want to be a doctor, as I really enjoy helping people and everything about medicine fascinates me," he tells his family. When family members point out that he can't remember any of the names and functions of body parts from his anatomy class in secondary school, he's not deterred. "If I can remember everything from my favorite computer game, I'm sure I could do it," he insists, while his parents sigh.

"I'm so grateful to be working from home," the young mother says as she encourages her two-year-old to have another apple, and separates her quarreling five- and seven-year-olds. "While this job uses only a bit of my talents, interests, and education, I can set my own hours and my boss deals directly with the customers. I don't want the customer part of the job." She carries her daughter to the sink to wash her face. "Also, I'm getting good experience I can bring with me into business management once all the children are in school. I'm getting exposure to a wide range of business situations, which I would rarely get in most jobs."

The above are real-life examples as told to the authors. This book is for anyone who wants to find or improve their way of making a living, so as to feel personally satisfied and fulfilled by their contribution to society. Finding happiness in our work is not something that can be left to chance. Most of us spend as much time in work as in eating, fun, time with family and friends, physical care, and learning combined. Work occupies half or more of our waking hours during the years of our life when we are most filled with energy, hopes, dreams, and an ability to learn. Some think that maintaining life is intrinsically a struggle, and only the lucky find it otherwise. Perhaps the fact that many find life difficult comes from chance, random forces shaping us, or the curse of an unfriendly or disinterested creator. If we consider the option that the basis of the universe is harmony and preservation of life, then we would expect our means of making a living to be filled with the exuberance of life.

However, while the vast majority of people need to work in order to have food, shelter, and life's necessities, in 2013, 87% of workers worldwide were apathetic or dissatisfied with their jobs.[2] To put the remaining 13% of satisfied workers into perspective, consider these analogies: imagine being a doctor. A patient comes and complains that everything hurts and is stiff — except the left arm and hand. Or imagine having a car where the windows can't go up all the way, the brake pedal sticks, the lights suddenly stop working and then start again, the wipers smear the windows, and the wheels keep turning to the left. In fact, all that works in the car is the speed indicator and the glove compartment. Perhaps it seems we need to resign ourselves to spending half or more of our waking hours in necessary work — a word synonymous with labor, toil, or slog — as just the way life is. Or perhaps we plan to be part of that mysterious 13% whose experience reflects the word *livelihood*: work that is really lively, making us full of life. When we call our job "making a living" we would hope that our time spent at work genuinely feels like living — full of vitality.

So Much Advice

Have you ever been told to "Do what you're best at," "Follow your passion," "Solve an important problem," "Find a need and fill it," or the like? Unfortunately, this sort of advice is so general that it can seem meaningless.

If we want career advice that's more tailored to our specific temperament and aptitudes, there are a variety of assessments available that indicate both what our inclinations are and what careers would be most suitable. For instance, the popular Myers-Briggs Type Indicator classifies people according to whether one's propensity is Sensing (S) or Intuitive (N), Thinking (T) or Feeling (F). For example:

> ST people focus their attention on facts and handle these with impersonal analysis. They tend to be practical and matter-of-fact, and they successfully use their abilities in technical skills dealing with facts, objects, and money. [Besides accounting, finance, and commerce,] STs also do well in production, construction, applied science, and law....
>
> –Isabel Briggs Myers with Peter B. Myers, *Gifts Differing: Understanding Personality Type*[3]

Do What You Are by Paul Tieger, Barbara Barron, and Kelly Tieger gives detailed advice on career choice based on this system. Another system, the Enneagram, classifies people into nine types, which tend to be associated with particular occupations. For example, the Helper and Peacemaker types might go into nursing, whereas an Individualist type might be a creative artist. Following yet another system, the Johnson O'Connor Research Foundation has spent decades developing a refined program for testing a wide variety of career aptitudes through actual tasks rather than filling out questionnaires.

An example that is widely used among professional career counselors is John Holland's RIASEC system (aka "Holland Codes"). Many colleges and universities advise students to take self-assessments that integrate Holland Codes with a broad range of other information, to help students decide what careers they might want to go into, and correspondingly, to choose a major.

With so much advice already available, some of which might be conflicting, those setting out to make their way in the world may well feel perplexed and overwhelmed by having to choose from among so many different sets of guidelines.

Why So Many Viewpoints?

How did we get into this situation? Well, for millennia, children have become adults who need their own livelihood. So we might think that the solution would be already well-established. For instance, people have wished to untangle their hair and make it look neat for thousands of years. Combs from 7 millennia ago look essentially the same as combs we can buy in the corner store today, however different the materials and means of manufacture. Even in today's world of endless discussions on every topic imaginable, how to untangle hair seems to be settled knowledge. It's not something that every generation has to decide anew. But unlike hair combing, many of us face so much uncertainty and dissatisfaction about how to make our living. Why has it taken so long to solve this vital issue?

One reason is that livelihood has always depended on setting. So countless viewpoints exist, each of which applies in distinct settings and thus may be confusing. Additionally, in some ways this is an unprecedented period in history. The variety of options individuals might personally encounter has mushroomed. The greater burden of choice springs from a greater palette of possibilities.

Often what we think of as an established truth is overturned, such as what diets are best or what behaviors or medicines are likely to prevent disease. How do we know what to believe? How do we know what is valid and what to question? This concern is not simply a matter for academic discussion. Until we have a yardstick with which to judge how much to trust any particular perspective and thus to winnow the options down, the plethora of possibilities will continue to grow.

Different Strokes for Different Folks

How to choose and conduct a livelihood depends on circumstances. For instance, we may be constrained by our financial, familial, social, and other resources and obligations as to how far we can physically move in pursuit of our livelihood. In that case, we are restricted to livelihoods in geographic regions where it is feasible for us to live. We may have different requirements, such as a flexible schedule or regular, fixed hours. We each have differing capacities for physical endurance and exertion, for sustained mental focus and for rapid responsiveness, for solitude and for continual public interaction. We rank these considerations to find criteria for choosing a livelihood. Furthermore, we may conduct our livelihood differently depending on whether we are a rank-and-file employee, a business owner, a middle manager, a consultant, and so forth. Combining all these concerns leads to a multitude of possibilities.

On the other hand, simply saying "Everyone is different and we each have to find our own way" doesn't really give us any useful guidance in itself when we're deciding how to make our living. Each individual out of eight billion people does not need to come up with a new solution.

A New Framework

In this book, instead of trying to outfit you with a jumble of one-size-fits-all guidelines, we give you a coherent set of principles that work together and support one another as a framework: a guidance *system*. This framework is flexible enough to adjust to different individuals in different times, places, and circumstances, while also providing enough structure to be genuinely useful in decision making. It need not be adopted wholesale, but can be tried out piecemeal, and elements can be incorporated into working life as they prove useful.

Many books focus solely on the initial choice of career, as if once this is properly settled everyone will "live happily ever after" (at least as far as work is concerned). Other books focus solely on getting along in the workplace, without acknowledging that sometimes the underlying issue is that a shift in roles is needed. The framework in this book supports and guides us *both* in choosing a career *and* in how to conduct ourselves along our chosen career path. In Part I we focus primarily on the choice of career, in Part II we focus on how we conduct our work as individuals, and in Part III we focus on work among groups.

These principles don't just come from the latest flavor-of-the-month study, whose methodology most people are not in a position to evaluate. While we do cite recent studies that corroborate these principles, the principles themselves emerge from time-tested ancient wisdom. Along the way, we provide plenty of examples to illustrate how to put these principles into practice.

Our approach is also based on a more nuanced definition of the word "work". For the purpose of this book, we are defining "work" as activity to sustain bodily life, whether directly as in growing food one will eat, or indirectly as in getting paid for work at a job and using the money to purchase food.[*]

When we understand how to work as a natural art, distinctions between work and play somewhat blur, as all that we do can fill us with joy and purpose, which are together the real essence of "productivity."

The concept of a "natural art" stems from the term dharma. Dharma refers to the intrinsic nature of something. The dharma of sugar, for example, is sweetness. Dharma can also refer to a way of being and acting in harmony with nature in general, or of aligning our own inherent self with the systems of the universe.[†] Thus, one's career dharma refers to a way of working that is natural both for the individual and for the individual's relationship to the cosmos.

In order to bring together the somewhat complex nuances of the natural art of work, we shall use a metaphor for work throughout this book. We compare each type of work to a kind of tree, and we com-

---

[*] We realize that such a definition in and of itself creates some difficulties, as summarized by this quote:

> In viewing labor as a kind of activity, the metaphor assumes that labor can be clearly identified and distinguished from things that are not labor. It makes the assumptions that we can tell work from play and productive activity from nonproductive activity....[4]

[†] The word dharma is often translated as "ethical code." On the other hand, it is also translated as "intrinsic nature," e.g., the dharma of water is to be wet, and the dharma of fire is to be hot. Since in this world, people are often alienated from their innermost natures, these two meanings appear to be at odds with each other. Dharma is related to the Sanskrit verbal root *dhr*, "to hold." One's dharma is that which one can hold steadily, and which holds one steady.

pare the worker to a tree keeper. As a tree gets its vitality from water, minerals, and sunlight, each type of work gains its ability to provide a livelihood for the worker from sources such as customers and skills. As the fruits of wealth are what the tree produces, such as leaves, fruits, flowers, oxygen, wood, sap, resin, bark, pollen, nectar, and so forth, so our tree of work provides varieties of ways of enriching our lives such as money and knowledge. Our tree of work is also part of an ecosystem made up of similar and dissimilar trees and plants, as well as the environment in general.

The Basis for this Book

Many aspects of the challenges to career choice and path even in modern society spring from basic truths about humans and how we interact with the natural world. Despite today's rapid pace of change, we do indeed have much in common with our ancestors. We can therefore turn to ancient wisdom for help with this challenge. Timeless truths offer an anchor that can keep us from getting lost in a sea of unmoored viewpoints. We may then wonder which parts of ancient wisdom hold principles that we can apply today, and which parts were only useful in their own time.

Given that the fundamental truths of human nature are timeless, it makes sense to give a fair hearing to the wisdom that our forebears lived by. We can use their valuable legacy, while setting aside whatever may pertain only to a particular time, place, and circumstances that are not our own. Humanity progresses because each generation, rather than inventing everything from scratch, builds on what has gone before. Retaining for ourselves what is most useful from timeless older wisdom can save us a lot of time and trouble.

Our own primary source for the natural art of work presented in this book is the ancient *Bhagavad-gita*. We also draw on the classic *Bhagavata Purana* (which elaborates upon the *Vedanta-sutra*) and the *Upanishads*. You may have heard of some or all of these as the foundational texts for yoga philosophy.

For those familiar with the *Bhagavad-gita* (sometimes called just the *Gita*), a little reflection reveals that it's primarily focused on career guidance. One of the main protagonists, named Arjuna, feels that his career is no longer satisfying, incapable of providing happiness in the present or the future. He wants to leave the world of work entirely and retire. By the end of the *Gita*, Arjuna has learned, at least in a summary way, all the principles of career fulfillment we discuss in parts I and II of this book. The *Bhagavad-gita* presents such principles of work as part of yoga, or connection, and describes this process as an "art," or *kaushalam*.[5] Such work is an art, as it requires a sense of the interplay between people and society as a whole, as well as between ourselves and the natural world. The *Bhagavata Purana* greatly expands on those topics, as well as directly and indirectly explaining the topics in Part III, where we delve into the systems of interrelationship among careers.

These ancient texts are of course a slice of ancient wisdom, something that spans many centuries and the entire globe. These particular texts are useful and relevant, with much to say, and we feel familiar enough with them to be able to draw sound suggestions from them. The two of us have each been studying them for many years, within a lineage of accomplished masters going back centuries. We've been striving to put them into practice in our own lives, and teaching from them as well.

However, if you haven't heard of these texts, or didn't realize that yoga has anything to do with this subject, we'll explain everything as we go along. Furthermore, we'll be including plenty of empirical evidence, as well as real-life examples and support from a range of different traditions, so that you can judge for yourself how it all hangs together and makes sense. We ourselves are both PhDs who have worked in the sciences (one of us in hard science, the other in social science), and analytical thinking is ingrained in each of our natures.

Readers who have heard of various isms and ideologies may read some of what we present and think, "That sounds like X-ism." While it may be natural for the mind to take shortcuts by labeling ideas in relation to familiar ones, especially when we present contemporary or historical examples that may also be familiar, please note that this timeless wisdom predates these isms and ideologies. The latter may include many associated ideas that don't necessarily bear any relation to our framework. So it will be useful to keep an open mind and take a fresh look at what we present, on its own merits.

What we ask is that you start with enough of an open mind to understand what we're presenting. We fully expect you to engage your critical thinking faculties in checking whether what we say is coherent, is consistent with your own and others' experience, and is corroborated by empirical evidence. There is also anecdotal evidence, especially in the form of testimonials throughout the book. Please note that all the testimonials were largely unedited. Therefore, some terminology in those testimonials may be inconsistent with the book as a whole. We also include examples other than the testimonials, embedded in the text. Many of those are of real people or composites of real people. In some of the cases of examples embedded in the text, we have changed the names and identifying details to protect the subjects' privacy. Many readers will find the testimonials helpful, as they bring the points in the book to life. However, they can be skipped entirely without loss of continuity. The chapters labeled "additional thoughts" can also be skipped.

Some people have an instinctive negative reaction to ancient writings that many consider sacred — a reaction of "I only accept knowledge based exclusively on scientific evidence." We suggest that readers who feel that way start by turning to Chapter 37, where we demonstrate the value of integrating ancient wisdom with modern knowledge for practical application. We hope that anyone who reads this chapter will be prepared to approach our presentation with an open mind.

While the two of us are quite far apart on various social issues, this book represents areas where we overlap. We've been heartened in finding this common ground. We're optimistic that just as we've been able to cooperate in producing this book, despite the ways in which our perspectives are very different, so a variety of readers will also be able to draw benefit from this book, extracting what is most useful and helpful to each of you.

We both feel blessed beyond measure by the impact that this ancient wisdom has made on us as we integrated it into our lives. We would like to share it with you in a spirit of gratitude. We hope that you'll find this new way of thinking gives you meaningful aid at different turning points in your life across the years.[*]

---

[*]Note to readers: To avoid cluttering the text, full citations are in references at the back of the book. Only parenthetical remarks are in footnotes. Longer parenthetical remarks are in endnotes. Translations of Sanskrit and Bengali verses in this text are our own unless otherwise specified. We use our own translations in order to have terminology consistent with what we use in the rest of the text.

Part I

One's Natural Work

Chapter 1

Work and Nature

All humans — perhaps all life — long for happiness and vitality. Many of us have experienced, at least from time to time, a kind of expanding inner happiness in which we have less awareness of the constrictions of time and our socially projected self, with full absorption in what we are doing at that moment. While many people find such situations in games, sports, entertainment, hobbies, and so forth, the *Bhagavad-gita* tells us we can, ideally, achieve this state in our work. Imagine so many hours a day in such a state of fulfilling happiness! Mihályi Csíkszentmihályi called such an experience flow, where an important component is the match between the activity itself and the ability and interest of the actor.[6]

We could describe such a state as being more fully and authentically who we are, doing what we are most suited to do, in a way that perfectly challenges us.

If matching our work with our abilities and interests is a key factor in fulfillment and a flow experience, why isn't working according to our nature the norm for everyone? Why is it so common to find people who've been working in jobs that suck the life out of them, for years or even decades? One reason is that mismanagement of organizations and businesses can result in "making a virtue out of necessity." These situations often start quite innocently — the group's goals genuinely don't match the current members' interests and talents. For example, let's say the need of a group is to have an accountant, but all the current members are "people persons" who focus on the big picture rather than details, and thrive on variety and change. If all the current group members want or need to stay and there aren't funds to hire someone new, then a current member who is particularly honest and good at math could be pressed into long-term accounting work. A slightly better strategy would be if the leadership could very temporarily allocate the existing participants to positions that get that job done as well as possible, while seeking both resources and people outside the group to fill the gaps. This strategy is only slightly better, because supposedly temporary "fixes" can persist for a long time, as anyone who has something duct-taped or rubber-banded in their home can attest. As long as workers seem to be doing a "good job," leadership may not have an incentive to situate people ideally according to their natures. A person whose nature is opposed to their work may be able to produce good results in an external sense, while feeling that they're drying up inside.

The ideal strategy is for organizations and businesses to make matching people's nature to tasks a top priority. Then, when a need arises that no one currently in the group can meet, the fact that the group is made up of satisfied people will attract others with the requisite desires and skills to fill the gaps. Matthew Kelly, in his book *The Dream Manager*, tells how by helping its employees to achieve their dreams, a janitorial business reduced turnover nearly to nil and had a waiting list of people wanting to work for the company. This is his philosophy:

> An organization can only become the best-version-of-itself to the extent that the people who drive that organization are striving to become better-versions-of-themselves. This is universally true whether the organization is a business, a school, a government, a nonprofit, or a sports team. To the extent that a CEO, an executive team, and a group of managers and employees explore their potential as individuals, so too will an organization explore its potential.
> –Matthew Kelly, *The Dream Manager*[7]

The worst situation is when leaders attempt to insist on or force people to work for long periods in an area of group or corporate need not matched to their individual nature. Those leaders easily end up justifying their policies with appeals to loyalty, teamwork, cooperation, and so forth. Ideological organizations such as governments, religions, and non-profits may add concepts such as *service, surrender,* and *love* to their appeals. Ironically, in some spiritual and religious traditions, conceptions of discipline and surrender are tied to intentionally accepting work that is disliked, unsuitable, or both. Such practices are often based on philosophies that say there is no self beyond the socially projected one. One goal of such systems is to deny and dissolve this artifice through increasing the pain of ego to the point that a person will renounce it. "Dying to self" or "dying to live" can sometimes be interpreted to mean an intentional immersion in work that is unsuitable to one's nature. Other philosophies put a high value on self-flagellation, figuratively and sometimes literally beating oneself up (the word suggests a many-stranded whip with sharp tips intended to cause pain). According to the *Bhagavad-gita*, however, self-torture is self-deluding and counter-productive.[8] Some workplace career paths, without directly alluding to any of these philosophies, have entry-level or junior employees do work that goes against their nature as a way for them to supposedly "pay their dues." Others expect some extraordinary accomplishment from employees before they "get to" do work that is congenial.

Max Perkins spent decades as an influential and highly successful editor at Charles Scribner's Sons, cultivating long-term relationships with several authors who shaped American literature in the twentieth century. His father had died without leaving any savings when Max was a boy of sixteen. Although Max was well-connected and his relatives sent him to Harvard, his father's death left him on a marginal financial footing. His biographer A. Scott Berg writes:

> Max chose to study economics. He did so, [his friend Van Wyck] Brooks believed, because Max "did *not* like to know about railway rates and fire-insurance statistics." The choice was an extension of one of his grandfather Evarts's aphorisms: "I pride myself on my success in doing not the things I like to do, but the things I don't like to do." That kind of Yankee thinking, which found virtue in hardship, enabled Max to move upstairs at the [literary club, the] Stylus, into a tiny attic with a table and a cot, and often to study through the night. Years later Perkins realized, "I threw away my education though by majoring in political economy which I hated, on some theory that for that very reason it was good discipline and that whatever courses in literature which I would have loved could give me, I would get

in the natural course of things." Max never read all he would have liked. Throughout his career, for example, he was embarrassed about his shallow knowledge of Shakespeare's works.

–A. Scott Berg, *Max Perkins: Editor of Genius*[9]

In this example, the cultural emphasis on finding "virtue in hardship" led to misused time, though fortunately Max did eventually find his calling.

The natural art of work, on the other hand, takes an opposite and delightful approach. This approach is logical, and harmonious with four views of reality. If we believe that life and the structure of the universe or biosphere are the results of random chance favoring survival, then matching work to desires and skills would be the best fit for survival and thriving. For example, in the non-human world, we see a match between the forms and abilities of various organisms and their environments, food sources, and so forth. The same principles would apply to the human world. On the other hand, if we believe that an impersonal force is the ultimate reality, or if we perceive the universe itself as a great organic form with the creator as its cosmic soul, we would also draw the same conclusion — that each part of reality, each being, would be best engaged in doing work for which he or she is best suited. And finally, if we believe in a personal God, then logically God would want us to use the gifts we have in the intersection of our happiness and our abilities, and in ways that would enhance both ourselves and God's purposes.

Considering all the above, we do well to take what we like, what we are good at, what gives us a sense of accomplishment, and what both engages and stretches our skills, and find a matching livelihood. Such a match is not enough for life's happiness, but it is an essential first step.

We want to clearly acknowledge that every job and every career will sometimes, perhaps even often, include tedious and/or unpleasant tasks. While we advocate that one work according to one's nature, this is not equivalent to saying "only and always do what you feel like doing."

We can think of this first step of finding a matching livelihood as similar to planting and maintaining a tree that one really likes. Some trees provide beauty, some provide shade, some provide fragrance in their flowers, and some provide medicine or fragrance in their resin.

A tree keeper who prefers apples would do well to plant and tend an apple tree. This seems obvious when planning a landscape, so why not for the work that yields the "fruit" of one's life? A tree will respond better to the care of someone who has both love and talent for tending it, and the whole ecosystem will flourish if persons work where their heart and skill lie. The same holds true for any enterprise — having people work in areas that combine their interests and skills will not only result in a happier workforce but better products and services.[10]

1.1   Overcoming Obstacles

One objection to having work that fits our tastes and abilities is practical: such work may not be available, it may not pay enough, or both. In one sense, this objection has to do with an entire system of society and work, and therefore a full solution may be out of the reach of a particular individual. An individual's natural work may also not be available because the training and education are financially prohibitive, or at odds with the individual's family and social responsibilities. For example:

Chris Langan showed, at an early age, many signs of brilliance in math and science. But, not only was his family very poor, they also lacked the skills to navigate through getting financial aid so Chris could attend college. When his car broke down, he was unable to negotiate with his advisor to change his schedule so he could travel to school by bus. Although he was writing academic papers in his area of interest and talent, without a degree or academic connections, he could not get them published. Instead, he was working as a bouncer in a bar (pub).[11]

Some cultures, such as some Orthodox Jewish sects and the Amish, only approve and facilitate a limited range of career choices for their children.[12] Even devoted members of such communities say "many spend a frustrated life of unfulfilled potential."[13] In both these examples, the main way in which careers are limited is through restricted educational and training opportunities. The intent is to keep members away from lifestyles opposed to religious rules.

Of course, it's also worth remembering that there is often a trade-off when we work against our nature in order to avoid obstacles. For instance, if it may seem to be a choice between getting what we want and earning enough money, motivational speaker Jay Shetty reminds us that we need to sacrifice to get what we want. If we're not willing to do that, we end up sacrificing anyway — by losing the very thing we want entirely.[14]

When there appear to be insurmountable obstacles between our ideal career and our nature, there is usually a solution. Not everyone will find the way to their dream career through the process we suggest. But, for most people who follow it, external obstacles will not be as substantial as they might have appeared at first. Let's use an analogy: in some forms of martial arts, even a beginner is taught to break wood with the side of the hand by focusing on the goal of where the hand needs to end up rather than on the obstacle of the wood.[15] For those of us who have broken boards in this way, in some cases even with no martial arts experience at all, the truth of overcoming obstacles becomes clear.

Let's expand on that analogy with a much bigger idea. Imagine for a moment the universe, or this one planet — the biosphere — as a great body. In our own body, health means that each cell of each organ and part is doing the specific job for which it is best suited, and doing it well. Furthermore, when a cell or organ does the job for which it's best suited, that job itself helps keep the organ alive. It's hard to say that an individual cell or organ is "happy" when its means of living is in accord with its nature, of course, but the analogy can still help us. Just as we feel overall vitality when all the parts, organs, and cells of our body do the job for which they are most suited — the job that fills them most with life and literally nourishes them — so does the great body of the earth or the whole universe function optimally when each part — each of us — gains its life from doing the work for which it is most suited by temperament and ability. The very structure of the universe, therefore, supports efforts by the individual parts to nourish their own lives by doing what is a clear match with their nature. Even if we perceive the planet or universe as a machine rather than an organism, a machine works best when all the parts are acting according to their function.

On the other hand, suppose that reality goes beyond the universe as machine or a great organism. Even a neutral universal intelligence would naturally tend towards each being and part being optimally engaged.

We will make the working assumption in this book that the universe is benevolent, and that it responds to people. Such an idea may seem strange or even absurd if we think of the cosmos as a cold, impersonal machine. Many of the principles of the art of work will still work for those who have the latter view. And, perhaps a playful openness to the concept of a responsive benevolent cosmos will prove both fun and enriching. "A playful attitude includes a willingness to let one's presuppositions and hypotheses be challenged and changed by the encounter."[16]

A benevolent universe would actively assist in such an ideal arrangement. According to the *Bhagavad-gita*, God responds to our desires.[17] Such is also stated in the Isopanishad[18] and in the Katha Upanishad.[19]

As a result, we can surmise an overall reality or truth that is in accord with our individual desire to match our nature with our life. Any movement in that direction, therefore, is likely to meet with ultimate success. In situations where having a career in accord with one's nature seems fraught with obstacles, we suggest having a fixed goal and strong vision of such a career, and then taking incremental, practical steps towards that vision.

Adrian Granzella Larssen offers a good example of the successful application of this approach. She made a career change with small steps, some that worked and some that didn't, and eventually reached her goal of becoming a nationally recognized "career expert." She suggests a variety of different types of small steps a person could make to change career, and most would be equally applicable to starting a new career when there are obstacles.[20]

Barbara Sher's book *Wishcraft* gives many examples of how to map out such incremental practical steps, as well as suggestions for overcoming obstacles, toward any major life goal and vision. Even if the small steps seem very small, perhaps even useless in and of themselves, little drops of water wear away stone, and we may find ourselves achieving our dream even after we thought it all but impossible.[21] How, specifically, does that work?

A growing popular movement suggests that intention and desire, held strongly enough, are sufficient to remove obstacles.[22] We can find stories where such seems to be the case, but for most of us such a system leads us merely to unfulfilled hopes and dreams. We may then be told we simply need more firm belief or more concentrated visualization to manifest what we want, but this is not always helpful.[23]

Another example of removing obstacles is the school superintendent mentioned in the Introduction who, by sheer determination, followed a career trajectory to achieve his dream job. The moral at first seemed to be: have tremendous determination, strength, and cleverness to smash and bash all the obstacles, with an attitude of: I will win!

I will not be stopped by anything! However, he found to his dismay that what he thought was a dream job was actually a nightmare and was in opposition to his nature.

In fact, though, the mindset of "bash and smash all obstacles" and the opposite idea of "just desire and believe strongly enough" reflect the duality of ego and indolence, respectively, neither of which fills us with, or leads to, the state of joy and purpose that is the whole point of matching our enjoyable talents with our career in the first place! The means of finding our ideal work and preparing for it can be congruent with the goal — matching what we like and are good at with the job we do. In other words, the process can become as natural and joyful as the result.

1.2   Journey to a Calling

If we suppose there is a neutral or beneficent universal intelligence, then the process can be understood as a relationship between that universal presence and our own self. Formulas cannot adequately describe a relationship, yet we can delineate the process in a general way. The first step is to have a vision and desire that are in harmony with the function of the universe, or, if you prefer, the intention of a personal God. Such a desire is not a difficult or mystical thing. If we desire to have our occupation be filled with joy and purpose for the most part, that particular desire is also the will of the universe!

You might ask why, if our having a source of livelihood that matches our enjoyment and talents were the natural will of the universal intelligence, do some of us find it so difficult to make that match? There is, in one sense, a different answer to this question for each individual who finds him or herself confronting this problem. Answers may include the need for a person to learn another preliminary lesson before finding success. Sometimes, for some of us, the lesson to be learned can be simple and amazing, and the process of overcoming obstacles can be almost magical! At other times, the lessons can be as hard-won as in an epic adventure tale.

After the first step of connecting a desire and vision of what we love and what we are good at with how we earn our livelihood, the next thing to do is to take steps towards that desire frequently, as often as possible. Even if we spend only a few minutes a day practicing a skill, studying something, getting experience, or cultivating sub-skills, we both move towards our goal and clearly communicate, both to ourselves and to the universe, that our desire is strong enough for us to match with effort.

Stephen M.R. Covey writes the following in his book *The Speed of Trust*:

> When trust is high, the dividend you receive is like a performance multiplier, elevating and improving every dimension of your organization and your life. High trust is like the leaven in bread, which lifts everything around it....
>
> With regard to having trust in self, it often begins with the little things. I remember one extremely busy time in my life where for about a five-month period I was staying up until 2:00 or 3:00 A.M. every night to finish a project. I'd wake up to my alarm clock in the morning (which I had set quite early so I could exercise) only to reach over, turn it off, and go back to sleep....
>
> After I had done this for a time, I started thinking, Why am I setting this alarm so early?...Not only had this repeated behavior weakened my self-confidence, it had become a self-fulfilling prophecy. When I set the alarm, I didn't believe I was going to get up; instead, I believed I was going to rationalize why I shouldn't. Setting the alarm had become a joke.
>
> Finally, I decided to change my approach. I determined that instead of using the ringing alarm each morning as a decision point, I would make a decision the night before and set my alarm when I really intended to get up....Whatever decision I made when I set the alarm, I wanted my commitment to be clear and to act with integrity. Otherwise, I would continue to lose trust in my ability to do what I had made a personal commitment to do. While this may seem like a somewhat trivial example, it turned out to be very meaningful to me in terms of building self trust....
>
> What's the net result of repeated failure to make and keep commitments to ourselves? It hacks away at our self-confidence. Not only do we lose trust in our ability to make and keep commitments, we fail to project the personal strength of character that inspires trust....

> Behavior #12 — Keep Commitments — is the "Big Kahuna" of all behaviors. It's the quickest way to build trust in any relationship — be it with an employee, a boss, a team member, a customer, a supplier, a spouse, a child, or the public in general. Its *opposite* — to break commitments or violate promises — is, without question, the quickest way to destroy trust.
> —Stephen M.R. Covey, *The Speed of Trust: The One Thing That Changes Everything*[24]

We would go beyond this to say that our commitment to taking incremental steps communicates itself not just to those around us or the public in general, but also to the universe. Those incremental steps, even if seemingly insignificant, attract the universal power to respond. After all, we are moving towards what this essence of the universe wants us to be doing! The response may come in the form of meeting the right people, getting the right book, or a host of other synchronistic events. Sometimes, it may appear that things are going in the opposite direction, but in the long run one will find that "in the end everything will be okay; if it's not okay, it's not the end."

Of course, one problem with zeroing in on a livelihood that matches our nature is the difficulty we may have with identifying our nature — as if we don't really know ourselves. We may like what we have little talent for, have talent in areas of little interest, or have so many talents and interests that we are stumped trying to choose among them. We explore the topic of recognizing our nature in the next few chapters. Throughout the remainder of the book, we help crystallize the vision of what working in harmony with both our own nature and the will of the universe would look like. Keeping this whole picture in mind, we can continually compare our present life to it and see what small, doable step we can take at each point to bring our livelihood into greater alignment with it, like filling in the next piece of a jigsaw puzzle.

Chapter 2

What is My Nature: Six Kinds of Wealth

Most of us find knowledge about ourselves to be fascinating. Newspapers and magazines have daily astrology predictions based on sun signs, which people use to try to find out not only their destiny, but also what category of person they are. As we write this in 2019, we can take numerous "tests" on social media sites to determine what kind of person we are and in what category we belong. Socrates said "know thyself." But it's doubtful that quizzes that purport to answer the questions "Which Disney character are you?" or "What do your shoes reveal about your personality?" are actually helpful.

Some personality tests are, however, relevant to aiding us in finding a suitable career . These include Myers-Briggs, "I Just Get Myself," Personality Insights' DISC system, Anthony Gregorc's mind styles, Enneagram, and many more. All indicators of nature or personality are measured on a continuum, so a person will score somewhere between, for example, absolutely risk-seeking to absolutely risk-averse. There are also specific career aptitude tests, some of which attempt to identify a set of personal characteristics and then match those to a list of possible careers. Many people have found that such tests, especially when administered and evaluated with the help of a trained career counselor, provide useful information and guidance. Additionally, there are books such as *Finding Your Element*[25] that explain a series of principles along with self-tests for understanding and application. We will not attempt here to list all such tests or evaluate them.

Rather, we would like to share a somewhat different, ancient perspective on the relationship between career, individual psychology, and talents that can hopefully add to our ability to know ourselves.

First, let us consider the concept of wealth. Generally, people think of wealth mostly in relationship to money, and objects that cost a lot of money to buy or replace, such as land, homes, vehicles, and so forth. However, classics such as the *Bhagavata Purana* list various categories of wealth or prosperity. These categories can help us discover how to find a career in which we both draw from, and increase, kinds of prosperity that energize us and inspire us to describe our lives as "rich." As a "rich life" can mean a life filled with satisfaction and quality of various kinds, there are various kinds of "riches."

Let's explore that further. You may be familiar with Howard Gardner's model of multiple intelligences.[26] Because the majority of schools teach mostly language and mathematics, people have a tendency to think of intelligence as being only in those areas. But Gardner suggests that some people are intelligent in, for example, music or interpersonal relationships. There is also the research of Daniel Goleman into the understanding of emotional intelligence as compared to intellectual intelligence. In a similar way, our point is that there can be several types of wealth, not just money; and most people like to get and share various different types of wealth, with one or two dominating what they define as a rich life.

We will list the categories of richness in the ancient language of Sanskrit, as doing so will allow us to explore a broader range of meaning. All six categories are represented in a hexagonal diagram (see figure).

2.1   The Six Kinds of Wealth

First let's look at *aisvarya*. The literal meaning of this word would be the wealth of power and control. Leadership is implied (as in leaders of countries, armies, businesses, etc.), but this wealth could also mean having autonomy in one's life. Some of us like to start and manage our own projects, businesses, etc. We might be energized by caring for many people in the sense of engaging them in meaningful work and providing them with what they need. Those who thrive on the richness of *aisvarya* may also generate this wealth for others. In other words, some people help others to gain power, control, and autonomy, as well as other kinds of wealth and richness.

Figure 2.1: Six Kinds of Richness

The six kinds of richness arranged as points of a six-pointed star.

For example, the coach of a high school rugby team, Larry Gelwix, could tell that the players were not practicing enough to build their strength and endurance. The coaches were going to order the team to follow a particular program, but felt that doing so would detract from the players' practice time devoted to rugby itself. Larry and the other coaches took the problem to the team captains: it would take six weeks to build the players' stamina and strength, and six weeks was all the time they had until the tournament. The captains voluntarily took up the challenge and, consulting with the coaches, came up with their own system to allocate responsibility to sub-group leaders for targeted strength-building sessions that they would manage separately from rugby practice times. Larry's encouragement of the captains helped those captains to grow in leadership, wisdom, and authority.[27]

Aisvarya can also be defined literally as money, so those who are energized by this kind of richness might be those who enjoy making, investing, managing, and increasing money. The term "wealth" can also apply to items and environments associated with wealth and luxury. There is some implication in *aisvarya* of wanting to be the lord of the world and to enjoy all that it contains, and so this form of prosperity can imply the epitome of material enjoyment and supremacy.

The kind of richness next to *aisvarya* is *virya*. *Virya* literally means vitality and strength. It is closely associated with muscle strength. It can also mean sexual virility and potency for anyone, but particularly males. *Virya* is associated with strength, energy, determination, vigor, courage, and so forth. This kind of richness can refer to power in sports, warfare, dance, and careers that require physical strength and endurance. It is the wealth of health and is, therefore, closely connected to the healing professions. It is also a key ability needed for control of the mind in meditation and yoga. Therefore, *virya* refers to mental strength as well. It is the potency that brings endeavors to fruition and sustains the process from seed to fruit in our tree of work.

Next to *virya* is *yasa* — fame. This is the richness of honor, glory, renown, praise, and respect. The root of the word *yasa* means to spread, and can also indicate beauty. We may recall the Beatles' song, "Baby, You're A Rich Man" about "the beautiful people," those whose fame spread everywhere. Here is richness of community and society, family and friends, filled with gratitude and appreciation. A personality named *Yasa* is said to be the son of *Kirti* and her husband, Dharma.[28] These names in turn have meanings. *Kirti* refers to spoken words of praise and honor. Dharma is a complex word. To recap, it refers to the essence of something, its nature, and what gives it its identity: e.g., "the dharma of sugar is sweetness." Dharma can be roughly translated as cosmic order, and what is "right" in the sense of what is real and true. *Yasa*, then, is the prosperity that spreads from our own virtuous merits and deeds, which others appreciate. There is a kind of satisfaction, a feeling of having a "rich" life, when we act virtuously according to our roles, designations, and responsibilities in society. *Yasa* is also the satisfaction we gain when honoring others for their right actions and intentions.

Next to *yasa* is *sri*. *Sri* is often used synonymously with fortune or prosperity in general, and is a name for a divine being, Lakshmi, who personifies fortune, prosperity, wealth, or resources. So, in one sense, *sri* is all-encompassing for all six types of wealth. Its core meaning has to do with giving off light or radiance, and can mean beauty, grace, and splendor. The word *sri* is often used as a title for both men and women in India, meaning respectable, and is also joined with various names of the Supreme, as in *Sri* Bhagavan, or *Sri* Rama. Conjoined with names for God in that way, *sri* denotes both respect and the concept that God is the source and protector of all riches. *Sri* can connote majesty and ruling power, thus having a relationship to leadership. This leadership occurs due to the leader's attractive qualities, rather than due to the control and organizational abilities of the wealth of *aisvarya*. As the counterpoint of *virya*, *sri* also means feminine beauty and romantic love, as well as general affection and care. *Sri* is the realm of aesthetics such as painting, sculpture, music, dance, theater, architecture, landscaping, and so forth, when those arts enhance respect and are enlightening.

Next to *sri* on the hexagonal figure is *jnana*, which can be translated as intelligence, philosophy, science (both hard and soft), and the process of learning and understanding. Ultimately, the richness of *jnana* is one of knowing the essence of things, the meanings of events, and the principles or truths of life. But, in a general way, *jnana* can also refer to all the levels of Bloom's taxonomy,[29] which are:

- knowing information;

- understanding what one knows so as to be able to explain it;

- applying what one knows so as to be able to use it;

- analyzing what one knows, so as to have understanding on a deeper level in terms of the categories and sub-parts;

- synthesizing what one knows, so as to be able to apply it on a broader level, using creativity to use the knowledge in a variety of ways; and

- evaluating what one knows along a spectrum such as good/bad, useful/useless, attractive/repulsive, etc.

Jnana is a counterpoint to *aisvarya* because the former deals primarily with one's mind and intelligence, while the latter deals primarily with others and the external world. Also, any learning starts with recognizing that one does not already know (practical humility), whereas exercising power and control implies that one believes one knows what is good for oneself and others. As with *aisvarya*, *jnana* suggests a love for both learning and increasing others' intelligence and knowledge.[30]

The last of the six types of prosperity, and the most mysterious, is *vairagya*: equanimity and peacefulness. *Vai* means "without" and *raga* means attachment, passion, interest, and emotion. *Vairagya* is not repression or suppression, but an inner state of equanimity and freedom from attachment and aversion. It is also a state of inner identity separate from all the labels, titles, designations, and corresponding expectations and duties of this world. A person who enjoys the richness of *vairagya* experiences him or herself as an observer of body, mind, society, family, and world rather than identifying directly with them. Someone who finds pleasure in receiving and giving *vairagya* feels enriched by a lack of ego, an ease of forgiveness, humility, compassion, and a sense of non-dependence on circumstances or others' approval for security or happiness. Of all the six forms of life's riches, *vairagya* lends dignity to the others. In fact, the others are not fully attractive without some *vairagya*. No matter how beautiful, strong, acclaimed, learned, and powerful someone is, if those riches are mixed with conceit and a disdain for others, the attractiveness of those forms of wealth is cut short. At least a little sense of honest humility must be added to all other types of prosperity for them to be truly attractive. The wealth of *vairagya* is also distinct from the other five, as only *vairagya* cannot be lost through external circumstances or the actions of others. In addition to an inner state of equilibrium, *vairagya* can also mean the wealth of being satisfied with simplicity and functionality in one's home, dress, and so forth.

These types of prosperity are not interchangeable. For example, Microsoft for a while had their own ebook format, but it was never profitable. In 2019 they decided to stop supporting these books, so that those who purchased them would no longer be able to open and read the books on their electronic devices. Any notes and highlighting they had made would also be lost. To compensate for this disturbance, Microsoft offered its customers a monetary refund. But people complained that cash is not equivalent to having a book to which one can refer and that had one's notes within it — these are different types of value.

Consider the six types of prosperity:

- *Aisvarya*: organizational leadership, money, and luxury.

- *Jnana*: knowledge.

- *Virya*: strength, power, and health.

- *Sri*: splendid beauty, gracefulness; charismatic leadership.

- *Yasa*: meritorious fame and community.

- *Vairagya*: equanimity and freedom.

Each of us can ask ourselves: which of these forms of wealth express my most basic sense of a worthwhile life, and which are less important to me? Which of these do I think about, worry about, gravitate towards, and want to increase? Which do I want not only to have for myself but also generate for those I care about? Which ones do I naturally bring to a situation?

2.2   The Kinds of Wealth and Careers

Let us look at some actual examples of the relationship between career and the six types of wealth. Mike is a traveling musician, who, with his wife, writes and performs songs about philosophy. That work provides the wealth of *jnana* through the songs' messages, *sri* in the beauty of the music itself, and *vairagya* in their traveling, minimalistic lifestyle.

Chris helps businesses set up management software. He customizes the software package for their needs and trains people within the company to use that software themselves for increased management effectiveness and efficiency. His career brings him a top salary and a position of leadership, also helping others to become leaders and increase their profit. Chris has some degree of autonomy in his work, and has an expanding customer base. So, primarily, he is enjoying *aisvarya*. He is also constantly learning and helping others to learn, which brings him the wealth of *jnana*.

Nar runs an organic farm that includes a compassionate, no-kill dairy. He's constantly learning about crops and farming techniques, and enjoys having visitors to teach in person as well as sharing his knowledge online. He's very muscular, and gets a good workout from the physical labor of farm work. Nar loves selling milk and produce to the community, and has regular community gatherings in his large home. The prosperity of his career is mostly in *virya*, the wealth of physical strength, health, and vitality. To some extent, Nar also enjoys *yasa* and *jnana*.

Vati is a web designer and artist. She works from home on a flexible schedule, keeping track of her hours and billing customers. She mostly works for non-profits, friends, and family members. The primary ways in which her career brings her prosperity are *sri* through the aesthetics of her work and *vairagya* for the freedom and flexibility of the job. To a lesser degree, she gains the richness of *yasa* through doing good work in her community.

Chuck is studying to be an astronomer. He loves working at the visitor center for one of the best telescopes in the world. He especially enjoys the appreciation of the guests when he teaches about the night sky outside with a laser. In the visitor center itself, one can see many of Chuck's stunning photographs of various astronomical phenomena. Having a scientific career naturally includes the richness of *jnana*, though the primary way in which Chuck's career gives him a sense of prosperity is in the praise of community, *yasa*, as well as the beauty of nature and his photographs of it, *sri*.

Champa teaches classical East Indian dancing. Any dance form involves physical strength and endurance, *virya*, combined with beauty and grace, *sri*. She not only teaches dance, but uses dance to teach traditional stories and philosophy to both her students and the community in general. Therefore, *jnana* and *yasa* add to the richness of her career.

Each type of work uses some particular kinds of wealth in the worker, and generates a particular kind of richness for the worker and others. A job that requires physical strength, for example, such as building houses, may also help maintain and develop physical strength. However, it is possible for a job to require a particular kind of wealth, such as beauty, but to deplete the very kind of wealth it requires. For example, fashion models may be on diets and travel schedules that speed physical aging. Doctors who work in hospitals may give health and strength to others at the cost of their own health, which is damaged by their erratic schedule, sleep deprivation, and poor diets. Jobs that are not regenerative are inherently unsustainable and possibly even exploitative. (We discuss sustainable work further in Chapter 21.)

The six types of wealth are like six kinds of products we can get from the trees of work, such as bark, medicines, fruits, resins, sap, flowers, shade, oxygen, and so forth. Having considered what kind of wealth we want to earn and share, we will now consider in the next chapter the analogy of in what geographical regions we want to grow our trees of work.

Because practice right after learning something is the best way to solidify understanding, please turn now to Appendix A. For each item, please do the first part: put a check mark next to the main form(s) of prosperity that this occupation provides to the worker. Please ignore the options for the field of work for now; we will describe these fields in subsequent chapters.

Chapter 3

What is My Nature: Fields of Work

In the previous chapter, we considered six ways to have a rich life, as a way of understanding our nature in relationship with work. The six types of wealth relate to the kind of rich life we want to enjoy and share. Using our metaphor of our work being a tree, we compared the types of prosperity to the varieties of valuable products one can get from a tree. Thus, when we understand the ways in which we feel rich, we can use that knowledge to choose a career, just as if we want to get fragrant resin we can understand what kind of tree to plant and nurture.

Here, we will look at another ancient model of matching nature and career that is related to the six types of prosperity. Continuing with our metaphor, if we decided, for example, that we most enjoy dealing with the fragrant resin of trees, then not only would we plant certain trees, such as myrrh, but we would also need to plant those trees in a suitable geographical region: in the case of myrrh, one that is hot and dry. Those people who love hot and dry climates as well as enjoy myrrh know instinctively what kind of tree to plant. Similarly, when we know both the geographical region of work we enjoy as well as the type of wealth we want from our work, the combination of those two preferences indicates which jobs would suit us best.

Because in English we often speak of similar types of work as being in the same field, we will use the term *field* for these general types of work, rather than the more awkward *geographical regions*. The model of four fields of work that we present in this chapter will run through the rest of the book.

Please note that our use of *field* in terms of career refers to similarities in mood, disposition, and societal role among many careers. For instance, our "Field of Artistry" includes people who work to create beauty, whether they be engineers, janitors, or artists. In other words, common uses such as, "I'm in the music field," or "the medical field," describe an entirely different way of grouping types of work.

In texts such as the *Bhagavad-gita*, all possible careers can be grouped into four very broad fields.[*] In comparison, modern classifications are usually more diverse and often consist of subcategories of those four. For example, the job website Monster lists several dozen categories of jobs, such as: accounting, banking, customer service, energy, business, legal, science, real estate, media, logistics, and so forth. UC Berkeley lists thirteen career categories, such as sciences, law, international, and environment. In one sense, having only four fields into which to fit hundreds of thousands of specific jobs means that within each of those fields the scope and type of work will vary considerably. Yet, the simplicity of a four-category system hones in on the deepest, most general level of types of work. Also, as we mentioned in the Introduction, there is research that strongly suggests having fewer choices makes the process of choosing not only easier but more likely to occur. For example, people are ten times more likely to purchase jam when there are six choices than when there are twenty-four.[32] Certainly, if we start by choosing a general field of work rather than a specific job within a field, the entire process of career choice is less daunting.

One reason to use the ancient model of four career fields is that in all but the simplest human societies, no matter the specific job titles that people have and how those specific jobs have changed through the industrial and technological revolutions, those four broad types are always present: 1) some people produce food and other necessities from natural resources, 2) some keep the system functioning and

---

[*] We do not use the Sanskrit terms for these fields to avoid any preconceptions some readers may associate with these words. The longer one has known about these Sanskrit terms, the more difficult and important it may be to let go of preconceptions.

> The mind unlearns with difficulty what it has long learned.
>   –Seneca[31]

However, like the Sanskrit words for the six types of wealth, the traditional names are deeply nuanced and complex. Thus, finding a single English equivalent has its own challenges. After much study and deliberation, we chose the following English words to label these ancient and intricate concepts: the Field of Ideas, the Field of Government, the Field of Resources, and the Field of Artistry. Our use of these phrases is specific to this book and defined in this chapter.

containing a sense of beauty, 3) some educate, and 4) some govern society. Therefore, another reason for looking at four general fields rather than many specific categories is that the availability of in a specific category or job can wax and wane over time, sometimes dramatically, while these fields don't. For example, in much of the world today, blacksmiths are not in demand, and the job of "computer engineer" did not exist a hundred years ago; yet these are both in the Field of Artistry. In some places at any given time one might find a surplus of doctors, and in other places or at other times a lack. However, these four general fields do not fluctuate like this: they are perpetually inherent and needed in any organized society. Thus, while we may find that life requires flexibility from us, adapting to a changing environment by shifting between specific jobs, we can still derive the benefits of working according to our nature in the same general field.

The four categories also describe something important yet often subtle about work. In each of these divisions, the dharma is different. What is helpful, useful, satisfying, and even principled in work within one of these categories may be harmful and frustrating in another. This crucial aspect of the ancient divisions of work is described in Chapter 5 and Chapter 6.

Finding the field of work that matches our nature leads to a feeling of satisfaction. This feeling can be illuminated by referring to a traditional system (presented in the ancient Sanskrit text *Natya Shastra* attributed to Bharata Muni) and its use of a concept called *rasa*. Roughly speaking, *rasa* can mean "flavor" or "taste."

This system sets out how life's purpose is best expressed and experienced through relationships and emotions. Persons who follow career dharma have a life infused with this essential sustenance.

The word *rasa* is used in different but related contexts. In the sense of the body, it's an Ayurvedic (traditional Indian medicine) word meaning the liquid that carries nourishment throughout the body. *Rasa* is not only the liquid that nourishes us and gives us the facility to have pleasure, but in Ayurveda *rasa* also refers to the tastes on the tongue itself: sweet, salty, bitter, pungent, sour, and astringent. Without these tastes, food would still be functional in the sense of bodily survival, but eating it would not cause us to experience much happiness. Similarly, another definition of *rasa* has it describe a state of emotion in relationships: feelings of friendship, joy, surprise, and so forth, are types of *rasa*. Once again, without *rasa*, life is poor and meaningless.

Careers where the worker, the work, or both, are out of harmony with dharma may give the worker and society a shadow or reflection of *rasa* without the concomitant satisfaction, like an unfulfilled promise, or a carrot hanging from a stick that is always just out of reach. Genuine *rasa* easily removes any attraction for, or interest in, its shadow. As is stated in the *Bhagavad-gita*, as one experiences greater *rasa*, taste for lesser *rasa* fades away.[*]

Sometimes people are advised to "do what you love" or "follow your passion," as we noted in the Introduction. Our advice to "work according to your nature" may sound superficially similar to this. However, within each of the four general fields of work there are many specific jobs. In selecting among these, there is much more room for compromise in balancing what we love doing with what is needed by those around us or what compensates us adequately. Thus, our advice leaves considerably more leeway for moderation and flexibility.

We will explain in Chapter 5 and Chapter 6 how the concerns and dispositions of these four fields are fundamentally distinct, and why it is best for society and individuals that each person stays in the field that best suits his or her temperament, rather than crossing between fields.

3.1   Field of Artistry

We're going to discuss the fields in order of increasing abstraction and decreasing numbers of people who are attracted to that field. First, let's look at the field considered to be the foundation of the others, the Field of Artistry. This is the largest field, with the greatest variety of trees of work, and encompasses what most people call *work*. In this field, people provide for both beauty and function in society, with varying emphases on each. Some workers in the Field of Artistry have careers that directly and clearly provide the main means through which society in general experiences pleasures — what gives "beauty" to each and all of the senses.

---

[*]The original Sanskrit is:

> *viṣayā vinivartante nirāhārasya dehinaḥ*
> *rasa-varjaṃ raso 'py asya paraṃ dṛṣṭvā nivartate* [33]

The Field of Artistry also includes jobs where beauty and function are very intertwined, providing both pleasures and practical needs. Such jobs include:

- jobs that make our environment clean and beautiful, such as garbage collection, landscaping, janitorial work, and laundry;

- crafts involved in buildings, such as construction, plumbing, or working as an electrician;

- assisting in communications, such as through secretarial work, clerical work, proofreading, printing, or public relations;

- supporting the exchange of money, such as by working as a cashier, bookkeeping, or working as a bank teller;

- work with machines, such as operating, assembling or repairing them, as well as other objects, driving various vehicles, or working in a ship's crew;

- working outdoors, such as by picking fruit, baling hay, mowing lawns, pruning trees, and so forth;

- working in service establishments such as collecting tickets or ushering; assisting in retail through serving customers, ringing up sales, and restocking shelves; or serving or cooking in restaurants;

- many types of technical work, such as engineering, drafting, or working as an architect;

- working with metals, such as pipefitting, crafting jewelry, or welding; and

- caregiving, such as day care, licensed practical nursing in the US, bodywork, caring for individuals with special needs or the chronically ill, or elder care.

The above list is not meant to be comprehensive, but is intended to give some idea of the range of careers within the Field of Artistry.

It's important to remember that there's frequently a link between artistry and practicality. In some fields of medicine, such as certain kinds of surgery, doctors characterize their own work as being similar to plumbing or carpentry: in other words, a kind of artistry. Discovering or remembering that there is artistry — grace or efficacy in motion or emotion — involved in each of these careers is a key ingredient to finding fulfillment in them. These days it is also key to job stability, since work of this kind done without any artistry is work that can potentially (and soon will) be done by a robot.

Indeed, machines can do more in the Field of Artistry (without producing the *rasa* of this field) than in the other fields, because this field has the least "abstraction." Work in Artistry has clearly defined and objective standards of excellence and often equally clearly defined processes for achieving excellence. For example, a dance form such as ballet or a craft such as furniture making has firm boundaries of what works, and well-established means of training. In contrast, what defines and produces excellence in the other fields is more nuanced and has softer "edges."

This field is sometimes compared to the legs of the universe, which support and move everything. In the *Bhagavata Purana*, it is stated that God personally oversees the work of the figurative legs in the universe [34] because of the importance of this work to the overall goals of life. For those familiar with yogic philosophy, in the subtle body the foundational chakras are the *Mula* (function, physical needs) and *Svadhisthana* (beauty, sweetness, emotions).

3.2   Field of Resources

The next field of career is filled with the trees of work that provide the resources for human society. Those in the Field of Resources are concerned with expanding wealth and profit. They are absorbed with how to use resources effectively and efficiently, and with the distribution of products. Here we find careers such as farming, business, finance, and trade. The essence of this field is directing the flow of raw materials from earth, water, air, fire, plants (including actual trees!), and animals through the processes of harvesting and refinement to the people who finally use or consume them. People in the Field of Resources may have people in the Field of Artistry working with them. For example, a farmer who owns land and makes fruit available to the public works in the Field of Resources, but those the farmer hires to pick the fruit work in the Field of Artistry.

There is more "abstraction" in this field than in Artistry. Concepts of an ideal worker in this field vary considerably from one culture to another, and even within cultures, the measure of a successful career in this field has some variance. The variations are more subtle and abstract than variations in technique or taste. For example, is it preferable to run a business like a family or with more emotional distance? To what extent is it desirable for owners and managers to involve subordinates in decision making? Is it a better choice to solve problems by executive decisions, changing rules, or more collaboration? Various cultures answer these questions quite differently.[35] There are many schools of thought as to the process for becoming skilled in the Field of Resources, as well.

When people in the Field of Resources are successful in their work, they tend to accumulate more money and power, *aisvarya*, than they need. Ideally, they would then be inclined to charity and philanthropy on a large scale. They also help sustain those who work in the Field of Artistry, by employing such persons, as well as consuming the products and services they provide through transforming raw materials. A person in the Field of Resources may, for example, work with mining or distributing the pigments from earth that constitute paint. That same person may then purchase paintings made by a person in the Field of Artistry using those pigments.

Analogously, in the universal body, the Field of Resources is considered the digestive system, responsible for providing essential nutrients to all parts of society. It is ideally the energy source for society as a whole, giving vigor, strength, and fuel for basic survival as well as the ability to focus on the finer things of life. The digestive system interacts with living beings outside the body, and those in the Field of Resources may be the means for trade between societies and nations. They may provide the drive by which strangers come together to form a coherent society in the first place.

In our bodies, our gut sometimes is called a "second brain." Digestive health and emotions affect each other.[36] Chemicals and friendly microbes in our digestive system impact our overall decisions.[37] In a similar way, those who directly provide for economic stability and prosperity have great power to affect the feelings, desires, and "wants" of the rest of society. Just as it's difficult for a hungry person to appreciate philosophy or art, or even to be in a good mood, it's hard for a resource-poor population to give its attention to the best of human society and civilization. In the subtle body, the chakra connected with the abdomen is *Manipura* (vitality).

3.3 Field of Government

As human beings are social animals, anything more than a very small group of humans requires some system of defense and oversight of the group as a whole, and this is the focus of the Field of Government.[a] Even the most seemingly independent groups tend to need some form of "governance" after a time:

> The event [Burning Man] began in 1986 as a rejection of rules: There was no central authority, no prohibitions, no assigned camping spots. In the early years on the Black Rock Desert, after the event outgrew Baker Beach in San Francisco, people brought fireworks and guns. They raced through the desert night with headlights off. They fired hunting rifles from moving vehicles at vacant cars. "A lot of people — and I was one of them — thought that Burning Man was about this crazy feeling you could have, being with really creative people that are all anarchists, and there is no order, and it's just amazing what can come out of that," said Harley K. Dubois, who attended those early years. "And what came out of that was some people getting hurt." In 1996, a man on a motorcycle playing chicken with a large vehicle was killed. Then a rave set up two miles north of the main camp got out of hand. Three people inside tents were run over and seriously injured. The Bureau of Land Management kicked the event off public land. Longtime participants split over whether a more organized Burning Man could be Burning Man at all. Today, the event's six "founders" are the people who reconstituted Burning Man after 1996, including Ms. Dubois. The anarchists drifted away. And the founders created a street grid, an early version of what would become a semicircular city with all arterial roads converging on a giant, flammable human figure in the center.
>
> They "invented a sense of superordinate civic order — so there would be rules, and structure, and streets, and orienting spaces, and situations where people would feel a common purpose together; where people could become real to one another," Larry Harvey, one of the founders, recounted in an oral history

before his death last year. "It had gone beyond a bit of
pranksterism in the desert," he said. "We had made a
city, and no one wanted to take responsibility for it."

To Mr. Romer, this was a teachable moment. "An-
archy doesn't scale!" he said.

–Emily Badger, *A Nobel-Winning Economist Goes to
Burning Man*[38]

A key distinction between government and the management of an
enterprise such as a corporation is that government is responsible for
the interests of everyone in a domain, whereas an enterprise focuses on
the interests of a small subset of people and can eliminate problems by
simply excluding the people associated with them. For example, a privately run school can admit only students who are most likely to excel
according to its criteria, whereas many governments in the modern
world legally have to educate all children.

It's easy to understand how this field is more "abstract" than the
Field of Resources when considering how many different forms of
government exist in the world today. Concepts and measurements
of excellence in this field, as well as the means to become personally
excellent, are very context-specific. It is harder to measure success
in business than in gymnastics, and yet harder to measure success in
government than in business.

Government careers do not necessarily mean just anyone whose
pay comes from a government agency, but those jobs directly involved in governing. Trees of work in this field include protection
from internal or external threats, creation and maintenance of rules
and order, and providing large-scale services and infrastructure.
Those who protect a social group from internal and external threats
naturally work as police, firefighters, or in military jobs. Creating
and maintaining rules and order includes jobs in law and courts,
legislatures and parliaments, and top executives such as cabinet min-
isters and presidents. Providing infrastructure, of course, involves
jobs that oversee the planning, construction, and maintenance of
roads, bridges, and any widely provided government service, such as
public health and education in many modern countries. The Field
of Government is responsible for stewardship of non-agricultural
nature, such as urban green space, parks, commons, and wild lands,
including caring for the well-being of the plants (such as trees!) and
animals there.

It might seem like this field only involves careers in official governments of villages, cities, states, and nations. However, people can work in this field if they are part of organizations that do work similar to that of government. On a large scale, such work might involve careers in NATO, the United Nations, or Interpol. On a very small scale, work as a security officer for a business, or as a landlord of an apartment building, is part of this field.

Leadership roles within each of the other fields may appear to be in the Field of Government, but in fact are not. Those leadership roles may involve some government-type functions and thus seem to fit in more than one field of work. However, the temperament and focus of someone actually in the Field of Government, versus those taking leadership roles within their own fields, are different, as we discuss in Chapter 4. Each field needs leaders who have the temperament of that field, and not the temperament or the role of the Field of Government. Sometimes, those leaders work with, or alongside, government as advisors or in some similar capacity. We might wonder why there needs to be a Field of Government at all if each field has its own leaders. Yet, those working in the Field of Government provide a viewpoint and services that make a unique contribution and use a nature at odds with the natures of leaders of other fields. We discuss this concept in more detail in Chapter 6.

By way of allegory, in the universal body the Field of Government is compared to the arms. As government includes military and other forms of protection, it is interesting that the word arms is often used as a synonym for weapons. But arms are not only for the protection of the body: they are also for providing what the body requires. They collect some of the wealth received by those in the Field of Artistry and generated by those in the Field of Resources — as taxes and fees[*] — and redistribute them for the benefit of society in general. Those in this field of work are the main persons who ensure that peace, order, care, and so forth occur within the circle of their protective arms. Perhaps, then, it is fitting that in the subtle body, it is the *Anahata*, or chakra of care and compassion, that is closest to the arms.

---

[*]Governments collect wealth through various mechanisms: taxes, penalties, fines, fees, tolls, tariffs, and so forth. It is a complex, dynamic balancing act to assess these different levies in a way that is as just and fair as possible, and is something which goes far beyond the scope of this book. Throughout the rest of this book, we use the word "tax" as a catchall term to indicate any of these levies that produce revenue for the government. Our use of this word does not imply any preference for one particular kind of government levy over others.

3.4 Field of Ideas

The last of the four fields of work, in order of increasing abstraction, is the Field of Ideas: the realm of the intellect. Here are jobs that provide wisdom, guidance, truth, and education to society. These trees of work are in research and study and can include teaching anything at any level. Counseling and therapeutic jobs are in this category, as are those who lead others in religious instruction, training, ritual, and worship. Here also are writers, journalists, speakers, and scientists, including those in medicine. Jobs in this category can be in pure mathematics and philosophy, where academics and scholars research, write about, and discuss their subjects mostly among themselves, and only a few of their findings trickle into the rest of society. Others in this field may guide and instruct within society in general.

Some may work as advisors to those in the Fields of Government, Resources, or Artistry. Peter Drucker's use of the term "knowledge workers"[39] conveys a similar, though not completely identical, concept. For example, some software developers have more in common with an automotive designer or a chemical engineer than with a mathematics professor. As with the Fields of Resources and Government, assistants to those in the Field of Ideas are, themselves, in the Field of Artistry.

Broad-based education for each field of work, as opposed to training for specific tasks or crafts, is done by people in the Field of Ideas. Many of us have experienced trying to learn something from someone who is quite skilled at what they are teaching, yet is not able to convey that skill to us. This happens because the skill of teaching is distinct from the skill that one is teaching. Effective teaching requires thinking abstractly about how what is being taught can be broken down in different ways suitable to the backgrounds of different students. So, generally, teaching falls into the Field of Ideas.

However, just because one field of work focuses on the realm of the intellect does not mean that all intelligent people would work in this field. Every field of work uses intelligence and can benefit from as much intelligence as we can bring to bear. Intelligence is certainly not the monopoly of intellectuals.

We also want to make clear that work in the Field of Ideas is not necessarily limited to being expressed in words. Sometimes ideas are expressed through song, gesture, painting, and so forth. The question arises, how does this work differ from art made in the Field of Artistry?

The distinction is that in the Field of Ideas the truth of what is being expressed is paramount, whereas in the Field of Artistry the aesthetics are paramount.

The wisdom of those in the Field of Ideas shapes the rest of society. In the universal body, this field is the head, the brain. Those who work here guide government officials to rule fairly and wisely — indeed, they help define fairness and wisdom. They establish ethics and honest practice for those in the Field of Resources, and design models for uplifting both the producers and consumers of function and beauty. This guidance of the other fields may be done indirectly through publishing or teaching to society in general, or through jobs in those sectors in a role of guidance. Those who work in the Field of Ideas, as the head, are supposed to provide vision and direction for the rest of the social body. This role requires a degree of neutrality and detachment that working in any of the other fields would preclude. We will have more to say about this in Chapter 6.

The chakras in the subtle body that correspond to the head are the *Visuddha* (speech) and *Ajna* (wisdom).

3.5   Personal Taste

Identifying which field best suits us for our career boils down to our personal taste. Just as some children's favorite toys are trains and others love their blocks, our career inclinations are evident in what we like to "play" with:

- The Field of Ideas: Some of us love to toy with ideas, taking them apart and putting them together as if they were interlocking colored blocks. We may love teaching, and discovering new ways of understanding as we teach others.

- The Field of Government: Some of us love caring for others and making sure that people have all their needs covered. We find it fun and satisfying to protect them. Or we may relish fighting for just causes, even putting our life and health on the line for ethical, moral, and social justice principles and practices.

- The Field of Resources: Some of us love to start and run businesses and to "play" with money. Or we may enjoy working with natural resources in farming. We have an insatiable thirst to expand, improve, and increase profit, yield, and efficiency.

Figure 3.1: Different Fields of Work in a School

Organizational chart of a school, including workers from various fields of work

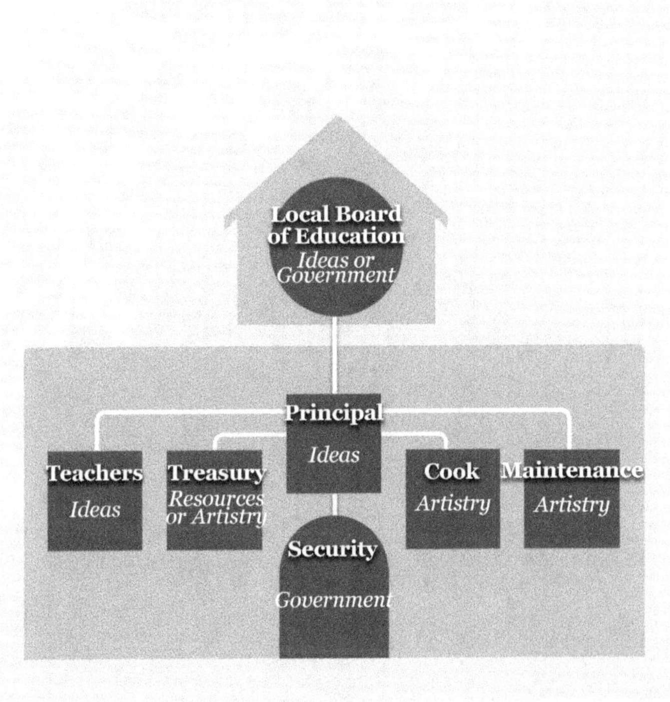

- The Field of Artistry: Some of us love the fine arts, or service careers, or jobs where we get to hone a craft. We may love being able to literally move in the world in a way that people find useful or inspiring.

What we like to play with is evident in what kinds of things we do unprompted and for which no one pays us. The areas to which we gravitate show our natural field. Let's hone our understanding further by combining the six ways of being rich with the fields of work.

On the basis of everyday observation, it seems that certain forms of wealth are, to a large extent, naturally produced in certain fields, just as particular types of trees grow more abundantly in specific geographical regions. Each of the six types of wealth is enjoyed in all

Figure 3.2: Different Fields of Work in a Law Firm

Organizational chart of a law firm, including workers from various fields of work

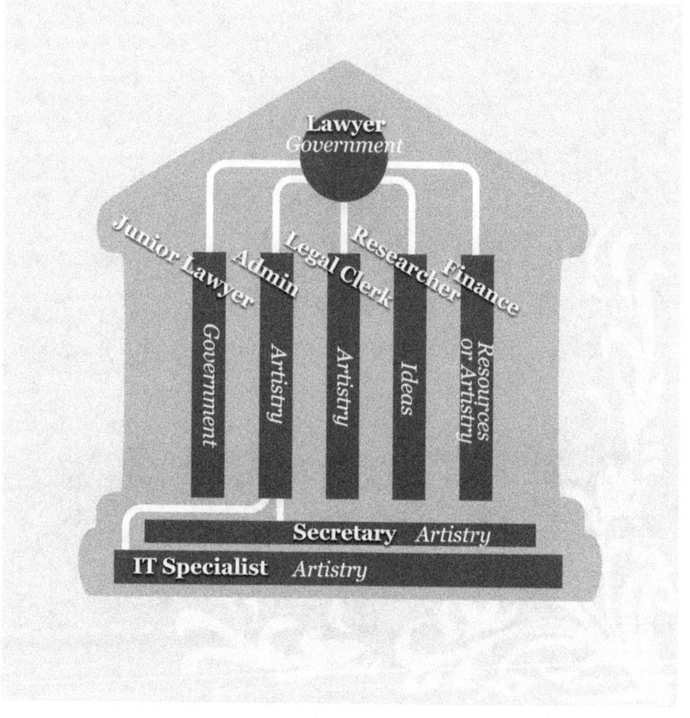

fields, distributed throughout society from the field where it is produced. Additionally, anyone in any field can add value to a form of wealth and increase it. However, some forms of wealth are naturally especially related to certain fields. We suggest that the wealth of *sri* (splendid beauty, gracefulness, charismatic leadership) is mainly the product of the Field of Artistry, and the wealth of *aisvarya* (organizational leadership, money, luxury) is the primary product of those in the Field of Resources. Those in the Field of Government distribute and organize *aisvarya*. They also produce *virya* (strength, power, health) in the sense of community protection from crime and foreign enemies, through their own heroism and valor, as well as public works that provide virtual and physical infrastructure for society as a whole. *Jnana* (knowledge) is naturally the product of the Field of Ideas. *Yasa*

Figure 3.3: Fields of Work and the Six Kinds of Richness

Diagram showing six kinds of richness and the four fields of work that naturally produce them

(meritorious fame, community) is mainly the product of the Field of Government, connected with the highest expression in all fields. *Vairagya* (equanimity, freedom) is primarily a product of those in the Field of Ideas, which is then used in the Field of Government and Field of Resources, as persons in both those fields are expected to distribute money and resources rather than keeping them all for themselves. *Vairagya* that those in the Field of Ideas generate finds its use in the Field of Artistry when workers feel inspired to be satisfied with their craft.

To understand how to match our nature to our career, we can combine the six ways to feel rich with the four fields of action in terms of what we naturally enjoy. We can then narrow down our career choices within a field.

Let's look at two forms of wealth — *virya* (strength, power, health) and *vairagya* (equanimity, freedom) — in connection with each of the four fields, as a sample. The wealth of *virya* could combine with the Field of Artistry in careers as a builder, athlete, or dancer. *Virya* and the Field of Government could yield the occupation of soldier, firefighter, or police officer. In the Field of Resources, the wealth of *virya* could mean a career as a farmer or a businessperson dealing with health products. Combining *virya* with the Field of Ideas might mean a career as a teacher of martial arts or yoga. *Vairagya* and the Field of Ideas can mean living as a member of the religious clergy, or a medical professional in an area of poverty. *Vairagya* can combine with the Field of Government in a career as a judge. *Vairagya* and the Field of Resources could combine in a job where a business gives the bulk of its profits to charity. *Vairagya* in the Field of Artistry might be found in the job of a mountain guide, or builders who design houses out of discarded items and containers. While any form of wealth can combine with any field of work to indicate specific careers, generally those who like to "play" in specific fields tend to also have a strong taste for the kind of richness that naturally grows in that field. In fact, one indication that one is in the proper field is liking the dominant form of prosperity in that field.

3.6   Outside the Fields

Are there people who work outside of these four broad fields of career? First, as we mentioned briefly earlier, there are some societies that are organized in such a simple way that they have no division of labor. Such societies are mostly found among a small subset of indigenous groups. Sometimes individuals or small groups leave modern society, attempting to copy such simple communities. While these groups exist outside of the bulk of modern human interaction, they generally live lightly on the planet. Such communities usually resist integration into larger societies. Unfortunately, in recent history many of these groups have been enslaved, exploited, and artificially assimilated.

Within an organized society, another obvious group outside the four fields of work is those who are disabled. Additionally, as we discuss in Chapter 29, in the normal human life cycle, most of us in childhood and older age do not engage in a career. However, some people remain as long-term students or seekers of truth, not settling into any career early on, or sometimes for their entire lives. These people can remain in one place associated with an established school, for example, or travel as intentional nomads, doing odd jobs to survive rather than to have regular work. Other people go from childhood directly into a kind of retirement from worldly life and never have a career in the general sense of the term. Often such people are motivated by intellectual or spiritual desires or realizations.

Society does well to respect and honor all these categories of persons. We can call them commensals, an ecological term, literally meaning "sharing a table." A commensal derives benefits, but neither harms nor helps. Though commensals don't help society directly or in the short term, they do not harm it either. They can, therefore, be allowed to have independence and autonomy. Sometimes society may benefit from their special viewpoint and skills as well. We will highlight some of their essential roles in later chapters.

In summary, in this chapter, we have looked at the ancient categorization of work into four fields in terms of their overall characteristics. Our view has been mostly of their positive aspects. In the next chapter, we will examine the psychology of each field.

Chapter 4

What is My Nature: Temperaments of Those in the Four Fields of Work

In the previous chapter, we discussed four metaphorical "geographical regions," or fields, of work. In each field there are a large variety of specific metaphorical trees of work, each of which yields one or more of the six fruits, or varieties of wealth. The four fields are the Field of Artistry, the Field of Resources, the Field of Government, and the Field of Ideas. Having looked at the work each field offers society, we will now turn to the psychology of those who work in each field.

For each field of work, we are going to look at two levels of the corresponding nature of workers. The first level is the qualities that indicate a disposition towards work in that field, i.e., that show a relationship between potential worker and type of work. For those considering what career to take up, or thinking of a career change, this level of our nature sometimes does not seem to bear a resemblance to its matching career, just as a lemon seed bears little resemblance to the lemon tree. Yet it is possible to identify the potential tree from the configuration of the seed. The second level is the qualities of those who have become experts in their work. This kind of expertise, in terms of the *Bhagavad-gita* and *Bhagavata Purana*, does not just refer to the skill set the work demands. Expertise in the ancient sense also means understanding and applying the principles of the natural art of work. One could say that the second level of qualities show the goal, or ideal, of workers in each of the four fields. The ideal is important as it provides a guide against which to measure our progress from novice to expert, from seed to plant. Knowing the goal can also inspire us to continue when things are difficult. Finally, knowing the ideal of each field of work also yields a vision of the ideal way all fields can interact in society at large, on which we elaborate in Part III. In Chapter 7, we discuss the process of progressing from novice to expert.

As we go through the descriptions of the ideal persons in each of the fields, some of us may be incredulous, thinking, "That's not how those working in those fields behave! Their behavior is the opposite." Such a situation points to the need for the ancient wisdom of not just matching work and nature, but also understanding the *principles* of work, which we detail in parts II and III of this book.

4.1 Field of Artistry

> It looked like a sculpture, with its beautiful silver metal parts and intricate black iron body, only it was even better because it was a machine with parts that moved. I was the sort of child who loved machines because I was fascinated with how things worked; I took everything from dolls to bicycles apart to see how they were made.
>
> I spent hours playing with my grandmother's sewing machine. I was a shy, quiet child, and I'd play in that magical space beneath it, in the cool quiet dark away from the household clamor....I explored and moved each of that sewing machine's belts, pulleys, cogs, and circular spinning parts, sometimes pretending it was a magical vehicle, and always wondering what that machine could do.
>
> –Isabel Toledo, *Roots of Style: Weaving Together Life, Love, and Fashion*[40]

The quality that indicates a disposition to the Field of Artistry is enjoyment in "playing" with what pertains to function and beauty in society. Some of us love making fine art, or performing services, or exercising a craft. We may love working with a particular medium, such as wood or clay. We may love working with a particular tool, such as a blowtorch or paintbrush, or using our own body as a tool, as in soccer or ballet. We may love working with our hands and being able to point to our handiwork: "I made that," "I fixed that," "I cleaned that." We may love the solid sense that we've helped someone after we've shifted them into their hospital bed or shown them where to get what they need at a shop. Those who love to produce a beautiful painting that will hang in the house of another or in a public building, those who are happy to see others wearing the clothes they have designed or sewn, and those who are happy to see clean streets where they've properly disposed of the trash will find their hearts joyful here.

Those who have achieved expertise in the Field of Artistry according to the principles of the natural art of work serve others authentically and honestly. In fact, honesty is the most valued and essential quality in all fields of work, but is most obvious and appreciated in the arts, crafts, and service areas. Persons who represent their product or service accurately, and are satisfied with receiving a fair price or salary in exchange, bring happiness both to themselves and to those who use the product or service.

In this field, people ideally find great satisfaction in the work itself. In fact, the phenomenon of flow, in which a worker finds joy in getting completely immersed in work, is particularly evident in the Field of Artistry. As an example of such happy absorption, the *Bhagavata Purana* describes an arrow maker who was so engrossed in making a completely straight arrow that he did not even see or notice the king himself, who was passing right next to him with a large and noisy retinue. [41] In fact, many people who work in the Field of Resources, the Field of Government, or the Field of Ideas take up hobbies or leisure time activities in areas otherwise in the Field of Artistry, just to find this sense of flow. When work in this field is properly matched with an individual's nature, the worker would not like to trade places with those whose work may bring them far more money or fame.

Csíkszentmihályi (who described the phenomenon of flow) stresses that finding the artistry in one's job may in some cases require active engagement:

> ...small adjustments can turn a routine job...into a professional performance one can look forward to with anticipation each morning. First, one must pay attention so as to understand thoroughly what is happening and why; second, it is essential not to accept passively that what is happening is the only way to do the job; then one needs to entertain alternatives and to experiment with them until a better way is found.
>
> –Mihályi Csíkszentmihályi, *Finding Flow: The Psychology of Engagement with Everyday Life*[42]

We'll have more to say about this in Chapter 7.

The love of one's craft, the satisfaction of giving a needed, essential service, and the dignity of a job well done result in a kind of natural humility ideally found in the Field of Artistry. Workers in these jobs tend to be happy with loving relationships, secure homes, and using their abilities to help others.[43] They get joy from service. The fundamental questions they continually ask themselves about their work are: Is it supportive? And: Is it beautiful?

As this field has the least "abstraction," those who excel in the skills of their craft feel a level of comfort with less uncertainty. In other words, knowing objectively and specifically what excellence means and how to achieve it means a focus on following a well-defined path to a well-defined goal rather than chalking out one's own way. Anders Ericsson and Robert Pool researched what they termed the "science of expertise" and found a system by which workers could achieve mastery in their careers. But this system of becoming expert only works for some occupations, all in the Field of Artistry. Here are Ericsson and Pool's criteria for the careers where the system of what they term "Deliberate Practice" will be effective:

> These fields have several characteristics in common. First, there are always objective ways — such as the win/loss of a chess competition or a head-to-head race — or at least semiobjective ways — such as evaluation by expert judges — to measure performance. This makes sense: if there is no agreement on what good performance is and no way to tell what changes would improve performance, then it is very difficult — often impossible — to develop effective training methods. If you don't know for sure what constitutes improvement, how can you develop methods to improve performance? Second, these fields tend to be competitive enough that performers have strong incentive to practice and improve. Third, these fields are generally well established, with the relevant skills having been developed over decades or even centuries. And fourth, these fields have a subset of performers who also serve as teachers and coaches and who, over time, have developed increasingly sophisticated sets of training techniques that make possible the field's steadily increasing skill level. The improvement of skills and the development of training

techniques move forward hand in hand, with new training techniques leading to new levels of accomplishment and new accomplishments generating innovations in training.

—Anders Ericsson & Robert Pool, *Peak: Secrets from the new science of expertise*[44]

When people in this field are interested in the riches of *yasa* (meritorious fame, community) and *aisvarya* (organizational leadership, money, luxury), such interest can be in the simple ways of having the respect of their community, and a sense of mastery of their craft. In modern times, the leaders in the Field of Artistry — especially in the categories of music, theater/film, and sports — do, indeed, get *yasa* and *aisvarya* to a degree that only those in the highest government posts did in the past. However, we sometimes find that such riches cheapen the integrity of this field, as they beguile workers into aiming for acclaim and power rather than the quality of their craft. Their work suffers, like a tree forced to grow in an unsuitable climate. We discuss these issues more in Chapter 6. On the other hand, it is difficult for persons in the Field of Artistry to reach the ideal of contentment with their work when others, instead of appreciating this quality, try to take advantage of it to squeeze more and more out of them, exploiting them. We'll have more to say about the relationships between people in different fields in Part III.

4.2 Field of Resources

I went to work when I was just out of grammar school. I got a job as quotation-board boy in a stock-brokerage office. I was quick at figures…As quotation-board boy I posted the numbers on the big board in the customers' room….

…Those quotations did not represent stock prices to me, so many dollars per share. They were numbers. Of course, they meant something. They were always changing. It was all I had to be interested in — the changes….

That is how I first came to be interested in the behavior of prices. I have a very good memory for figures. I could remember in detail how the prices had acted the previous day….

> That is how I first came to take an interest in the message of the [stock ticker] tape. The fluctuations were from the first associated in my mind with upward or downward movements....
>
> ...I didn't think of anything except that I could keep on proving my figuring was right. That's all the fun there is — being right by using your head.
>
> —Edwin Lefevre, *Reminiscences of a Stock Operator*[45][*]

The main quality of those inclined to the Field of Resources is a love of "playing" with care of resources such as land, crops, and animals, or money, which represents those resources. Such persons enjoy continually staying on top of upcoming ways to earn more money. [46] They tend to be ambitious and want to increase their own wealth. In fact, they are rarely satisfied with their successes, but always think of how to improve and expand, in quality, quantity, or both. In order to do so, they are willing to take risks. They have drive to achieve their goals, and like to be always active. They tend to be goal-oriented rather than process-oriented, with some preliminary intuitive grasp of the flow of resources.

Those who have achieved expertise in this field, following the natural art of work, become "systems thinkers," albeit confined to their own specific "tree" of work. If they are working, for example, with the land and animals, they can feel and understand the whole system of the seasons, natural production schedules of plants and animals, their competitors in the marketplace, and so forth, as a whole. The flows they can understand and grasp are of natural resources and money. They want to re-direct those flows and increase them so that they themselves can tap into them. The fundamental questions they continually ask themselves about their work are: Is it sustainable? And: Is it regenerative?

It's worth elaborating a bit what we mean here by "sustainable" and "regenerative". Centuries ago, most people in the Field of Resources were farmers (specifically, those farmers who produced a surplus beyond their own subsistence). In that context, continuous intensive farming of the same field every year would have depleted the

---

[*]The journalist Edwin Lefevre wrote this fictionalized autobiography of the well-known stock trader Jesse Livermore, which appeared in 1923. Apparently Livermore preferred to disguise his identity, rather than appear as author of the book with Lefevre.

soil of nutrients, so that the yield of crops would dwindle year by year, perhaps even to nothing. In other words, such a yield could not be sustained. Instead, farmers would let the field lie "fallow" during certain years, not planting it with crops, allowing the nutrients to be replenished before planting again the next year. This was an example of a sustainable practice. In allowing the soil to renew itself, the farmers were cherishing their source of wealth (about which we say more in Chapter 21). Similarly, since the dawn of agriculture, farmers haven't allowed their entire harvest of grain to be consumed. They reserve some as seed for the next year's harvest. Thus the stock of grain, which is depleted during the winter, is regenerated over the course of the following year. Under-consuming the harvest and reserving the seed grain closes the circuit so that the cycle of sowing and reaping can continue indefinitely in tune with the cycle of seasons. Working in tune with this cycle is the essence of what it means to be "regenerative".

In the 21st century, the words "sustainable" and "regenerative" have come to be associated with "green" and "environmentally friendly." However, in this book we are using these words in a broader sense. A couple of examples will illustrate what we mean. First, to understand the broader sense of "sustainable", let's take a look at one aspect of how the brothers George and John Hartford ran their grocery chain, the Great A&P, during the 1930s:

> John was especially annoyed that some unit managers had adopted the strategy of selling selected products below cost and raising prices on other items to make up the difference....When the chairman of the Southern Division told his division president to slash prices to build business, he offered one caveat: "But there is one thing and it is most important: do not advertise a standard brand of coffee at cost, or 1 cent above cost. I think you understand that Mr. George Hartford feels very strongly against this sort of thing."...Auditors advised headquarters whenever they found a store selling merchandise below cost, and John personally reprimanded offenders.
>
> –Marc Levinson, *The Great A&P and the Struggle for Small Business in America*[47]

Individual store managers wanted to sell particular items below cost to draw customers away from other stores. Selling below cost was an anti-competitive practice that was illegal in many states of the US. (We talk more about the value of competition in Chapter 32.) More to the point here, selling below cost is antithetical to maintaining one's income: it is *unsustainable*. While individual store managers were tempted to do this, the Hartfords considered the profitability of every single sale to be an inviolable principle, which they continually took pains to uphold.

People whose nature is to work in the Field of Resources have a natural sense of how best to direct effort and resources, something that is key to their enterprises being sustainable. While explaining the safety procedures on an airplane, flight attendants regularly tell us that oxygen masks will drop down from overhead if the cabin loses pressure, and say, "If you are traveling with small children or people who need help putting on their oxygen mask, put your own oxygen mask on first before helping them." The reason for this is that if you become disabled by lack of oxygen, then you will no longer be able to put your own oxygen mask on, nor will you be able to help others. The person whose nature is to work in the Field of Resources instinctively keeps this sort of consideration in mind.

To understand better how this works, let's visualize a geyser: a hot spring that sometimes boils up into a tall column of water, which then gushes into the surrounding area, creating a natural fountain (Strokkur in Iceland is one example). Imagine that a person, a geyserkeeper, could stand in the middle of the geyser with a long spade and partially regulate this natural process, stoking the spring to get it to surge, and shoveling the surrounding soil to channel the flow. The geyserkeeper would be responsible for ensuring the local area gets all its water needs met by the geyser. Such geyserkeepers would first focus on ensuring the geyser is erupting plentifully right where they're standing. Similarly, persons in the Field of Resources will naturally focus first on ensuring a healthy flow of resources to themselves. The geyserkeepers would next focus on the areas where the water pools, adjacent to the main column. Similarly, persons in the Field of Resources will also focus on the overflow spilling out to the closest surrounding circles, such as their teams, their enterprises, and so forth. Beyond this, the geyserkeepers would take care to ensure the water flows or seeps into the surrounding wetlands. After their teams and enterprises are taken care of, persons in the Field of Resources will focus on channeling the abundant stream of resources so that it expands to the surrounding society, perhaps through charity and taxes and perhaps through other side benefits. Like farmers, they understand at a deep level that the strength of their own position is interdependent with that of their surroundings. However, they understand just as deeply that it is their responsibility and duty to take care of the flow to themselves first, to ensure that the whole fountain is *sustainable*.

Suppose two investments are under consideration: a wind farm generating renewable energy, and a clothing retailer. Which of these is the more sustainable? A person who has a sentimental dedication to "green" investing might automatically assume that it is the wind farm. However, nature is not sentimental, nor are persons whose nature is to work in the Field of Resources. Such a person would look closely at the specifics of each possible investment, such as cash flow, oncoming pitfalls, and possibly unreliable dependencies, and see whether all aspects suggest a continued or expanding flow of resources — one that is *sustainable* in the entire sense that we mean here. They will see whether each business can robustly withstand expected downturns and steadily renew itself through all pertinent cycles. Which business turns out to be more sustainable in the final analysis will depend on the details of the specific situation:

> Building and maintaining a [wind] turbine requires heavy equipment that damages tiles under [agricultural] fields, which affects drainage in surrounding fields. Drainage problems can hurt crop yields and even stop a farmer from being able to plant it in the first place. A turbine also makes it more difficult, or sometimes impossible, for crop dusters to fly over fields around it in order to spray pesticides that protect their crops. Farmers also have concerns about their own safety, and the safety of the people they hire. Reports of turbines catching fire and throwing ice, even blades breaking off, cause farmers to worry. There are also issues of shadow flicker and the noise turbines can make, which are not just annoying — they can even make people feel sick.
>
> –Leah McBride Mensching, *Wind Energy Isn't A Breeze*[48]

Next, to understand the broader sense of "regenerative", we'll walk through an example based on an investment theory: the sector rotation model.[*]

In this model, broad categories of businesses are grouped into sectors. Some examples of sectors might be Consumer Staples, Utilities, Technology, or Consumer Discretionary. Each sector contains multiple types of business; for instance, Utilities might include power generation and internet service, whereas Consumer Discretionary might include jewelry and golf. According to the sector rotation model, businesses in different sectors do well in different phases of the *business cycle*. These phases can be likened to seasons of the year. So, for example, the Utilities and Consumer Staples sectors may do well in a "cool" (slow-moving) business cycle phase akin to the winter season, whereas the Technology and Consumer Discretionary sectors may do well in a "warm" (fast-paced) business cycle phase akin to the summer season. Just as spring follows winter, etc., and eventually winter comes around again in the course of a year in a temperate climate, so these phases also follow one another and eventually cycle around.

Now imagine a time and place where the sector rotation model holds, and consider an expert in the Field of Resources who specializes in the jewelry business. As the "warm" business cycle phase begins and ripens, this person may find business to be booming, and so may invest capital in opening jewelry shops in several new locations. When the expert sees the signs that the "warm" business cycle phase will soon come to a close, however, she or he will pull some of the previously invested capital out of the jewelry business, perhaps selling off some of the shops, display cases, etc. Then she or he will save that capital, perhaps by investing it in businesses belonging to the next sector in the rotation (e.g., a power company, if the next phase favors utilities), or perhaps by investing it in gemstones. Then the next time the "warm" business cycle phase rolls around, the expert has savings available to take advantage of the new opportunities for the jewelry business.

As we mentioned above, farmers don't consume the entire harvest, and instead reserve some seed grain for the next planting season. Similarly, our hypothetical expert does not use all the profits the jewelry business made during the hottest business cycle phase to consume

---

[*]Disclaimer: We are not recommending this as an investment strategy, or saying anything about whether it works, which is beyond our expertise. Even if it did work in a particular time and place, that would not imply that it works in any other time, place, or context. We're just using it as an illustrative example.

to the hilt, nor to try desperately to keep all the jewelry shops open when the "warm" phase is ending. Rather, the expert in the Field of Resources saves some of those profits for the next "warm" phase. This expert's running of the jewelry business is *regenerative*: it can keep going through multiple business cycles because it's aligned with the changes in its context in different phases.

Of course, our use of the words *sustainable* and *regenerative* is not unconnected with the usual use of the word "green" in the early 21st century. Ensuring that relationships with the broader environment are stable and robust is a significant aspect of ensuring a business is sustainable, just like relationships with suppliers, employees, trading partners, and so forth. This is an aspect of cherishing the sources of wealth, which we discuss more in Chapter 21. Designing products, services, and business models to be in tune with natural cycles is a significant aspect of keeping a business regenerative, just as with other kinds of cycles affecting businesses. We will discuss this a bit more in Chapter 37.

Experts in the Field of Resources value education, though mostly in practical areas, and will often try creative and innovative ways to be more profitable or efficient. As it is the persons in this field who generally fund charities, the arts, and religion, these people like to preserve and nourish tradition in their communities. Thus, they grow to want not only greater wealth for themselves but also more prosperity for society in general. In other words, they are earning first for themselves, but allowing their prosperity to overflow and benefit people more widely. They are generally decisive in doing so.

Those in the Field of Resources are concerned not only with their work in and of itself but with how to make that work profitable. People who do well in the Field of Resources are often most energized by independently gaining their own income through sales commissions, running their own business, or managing their own farm. In this way, they have more control over their money and the ability to increase it.

A prime example of the nature of a person in the Field of Resources is illustrated in this story:

> Long ago, in Kolkata, Mr. Nandi asked a friend, "Please give me a little capital, so I can start some business."
>
> His friend replied, "You are a businessman?"
>
> "Yes."

"If you are really a businessman, why are you asking
money from me? Money's on the street. You can find it
yourself."

Mr. Nandi said, "I don't see anything."

"You don't see anything? Look at that, the dead
mouse over there. That is your capital."

At that time there was a plague in Kolkata. The government had declared that anyone who brought a dead
mouse to the municipal office would be paid two annas, a
tiny sum. So Mr. Nandi took that dead mouse to the municipal office to collect two annas. With those two annas
he purchased some betel nuts that he washed and sold for
four annas. In a similar way, over and over again, buying
and selling, that man became very rich.

–AC Bhaktivedanta Swami[49]

Such is the enterprising spirit of the accomplished person in the
Field of Resources.

4.3 Field of Government

Pat sometimes found it advantageous to flaunt his
toughness off the gridiron as well. When larger boys
menaced him, Pat responded by instantly going on the
offensive, forcing the aggressors to either throw down
or back away. Caught off guard by the puny kid's utter
lack of fear, sometimes his adversaries would elect to
retreat, but when they wouldn't, Pat wasn't shy about
exchanging blows....

Despite Pat's quickness to resort to his fists, he was
in many ways the antithesis of a bully. As a matter of
principle, he fought only with kids who were bigger than
he was, and on several occasions he intervened to rescue
nerdy classmates who were being hassled by older, larger
tormentors. But when Pat fought, he fought to win and
never capitulated, which earned him the reputation at
Leland and beyond as a guy not to be trifled with.

–Jon Krakauer, *Where Men Win Glory: The Odyssey
of Pat Tillman*[50]

People inclined to the Field of Government are concerned about fairness and rules. They are interested in people and want to make them happy. Their "play" involves heroism in caring for or protecting other people. They may tend to argue or fight easily, especially if they believe some higher principle is at stake. Courage and a "tough skin" are fairly typical of such persons. In some cases, a tendency towards leadership, or at least a "take charge" mentality, will be evident.

Those who have become expert in the principles of the natural art of work in the Field of Government become, like those in the Field of Resources, goal-oriented, decisive, determined, and systems thinkers. But, rather than awareness of the flows of the natural world, they are aware of the flows in human society. They intuitively understand and grasp emerging trends and needs throughout the section of society they govern, whether it's the apartment complex they rent out, the community they patrol as a police officer, the area of government they administer, or the entire picture as a legislator or upper government executive. Sensing the system, they are resourceful and know how to use and move those resources to increase the happiness and prosperity of society in all six areas of richness.

The *Bhagavad-gita* lists the qualities of those who work expertly in this field as: heroism, power, determination, resourcefulness, courage in battle, generosity, and leadership. The *Bhagavata Purana* gives a similar list: dynamic power, bodily strength, determination, heroism, tolerance, generosity, great endeavor, steadiness, high regard for those in the Field of Ideas, and leadership.

An example of heroism is that firefighters and other first responders run towards danger — a fire or other crisis — rather than away from it. This propensity for running towards danger is notably different from the propensity we discussed in the previous section on the Field of Resources to "put your own oxygen mask on first." Note that one propensity is not strictly better than the other. If everyone ran towards a fire, this would often result in the tragedy of more needless victims, as some of the people who did so would themselves be injured or killed. If no one ran towards a fire, this would also result in more needless victims, as people trapped in the fire would be injured or killed when they could have been safely rescued. So it's best that there's a mix of people with different propensities in society, for example, some people in the Field of Resources and some people in the Field of Government.

Another angle from which to look at this example is with respect to the different kinds of richness. The firefighter running towards the fire generates *yasa*, righteous fame, and *virya*, heroism. The merchant prudently moving away from the fire has a healthy sense of self-preservation, so as to be in a position to continue to generate *aisvarya*, or wealth for all of society. These are different dimensions of what makes for a good life, and both are needed and valuable in society as a whole. Of course, at any particular fire, some individual firefighters may also stay away to conserve their strength for another fire another day. At the same time, a merchant may run into the fire, e.g., to save a child. If either of these situations were to become a general trend, however, we may question whether the person concerned is in the right line of work.

While heroism is a key trait of both novices and experts in the Field of Government, it is important to note that the latter, in practicing the natural art of work, certainly don't manufacture, engineer, or in any way precipitate crises in order to get the opportunity for heroism. That would be egoism, about which we say more in Chapter 25. Rather, as servant leaders, these people are willing to invest a lot of time and effort in prevention of such crises as well as continuous preparation for them. Other members of society well-versed in these principles respect and appreciate such servant leaders for their skill in avoiding crises, even though this work is less showy. Such servant leaders know or have learned:

> The highest he could raise himself to was to die gloriously for something; now he rises to something greater: to live humbly for something.
> –Otto Ludwig, *Gedanken Otto Ludwigs*[51]

No matter what government work a person in this field does, he or she inspires others and commands respect. There is a sort of charisma and positive outlook that draws others to trust and follow those who work in this field. While they show their strength to protect innocent people and combat evil, their overall nature is ideally tolerant and generous. Thus, they will only use force and power when all other means fail. In a similar way, although they collect money in tax revenue (or rent), they also redistribute the majority of it for the benefit of those in their domain. The fundamental questions they continually ask themselves about their work are: Is it just? And: Is it honorable?

People in this field value education, and many are highly educated and trained. They tend to be interested in studying history, law, politics, martial arts, morals, ethics, and justice. They want to protect the weak. Furthermore, their study is not just theoretical — they will fight tirelessly for their principles, regardless of personal cost.

While every field of work provides something of value to people in general, and can thus be understood as including some elements of a parental role, those in government careers have traditionally been viewed as fathers and mothers of the country. Taking a position in government means to cherish the citizens just as parents cherish their children. As parents love their children equally, so those in government fields care for all citizens, weak and strong, famous and obscure. They take responsibility not only for human citizens, but also for animals and plants, as much as in any family the adults have responsibility for any animals or vegetation in their care.

4.4 Field of Ideas

> ...there in the attic...were stored the lithographed lecture notes of Academician Ostrogradsky's course on differential and integral calculus, which my father had attended as a very young army officer. And it was these sheets which were used to paper the walls of my nursery.
>
> I was then about eleven years old. As I looked at the nursery walls one day, I noticed that certain things were shown on them which I had already heard mentioned by Uncle. Since I was in any case quite electrified by the things he told me, I began scrutinizing the walls very attentively. It amused me to examine these sheets, yellowed by time, all speckled over with some kind of hieroglyphics whose meaning escaped me completely but which, I felt, must signify something very wise and interesting. And I would stand by the wall for hours on end, reading and rereading what was written there.
>
> –Sofya Kovalevskaya, *A Russian Childhood*[52]

An inclination to work in the Field of Ideas can be evident in the desire to "play" with language or mathematics in pursuit of truth. Persons so inclined tend to be insatiably curious and to want to know what is true and real. They are often good at breaking ideas and projects into smaller components. They see the patterns in ideas, relationships, and systems. Often such people like to teach others. Some people with a proclivity for the Field of Ideas prefer to work on their own, delving into their research and study.

Regarding those who are expert in applying the principles of the natural art of work to the Field of Ideas, the *Bhagavad-gita* lists the associated qualities as: peacefulness, self-control, austerity, purity, tolerance, honesty, knowledge, wisdom, and religiousness. The *Bhagavata Purana* adds satisfaction, simple straightforwardness, devotion to God, and mercy. The Sanskrit word used here for peacefulness can also be translated as quiet of mind or stoicism. We might also find people in this field of work who are devoted to truth and philosophy, but not necessarily to God in the sense of any particular religion. The fundamental questions people in this field continually ask themselves about their work are: Is it true? And: Is it wise?

People who enjoy the Field of Ideas may be dedicated to assisting others mentally and emotionally by helping them to understand life and how things work. They also may be dedicated to understanding themselves, or to seeking higher states of clarity, insight, and awareness. They may take pleasure in helping people physically through medicine and through teaching physical skills. In general, people in this field like to collect knowledge, understand it, use it, and share it. Sometimes they can "live in their heads" without much concern for their own body and with little awareness of the world around them. Scientists and religionists are in this group, so there is often a strong interest in finding the essence of reality. Writing and speaking, when they are used to communicate philosophy, science, spirituality, values, and principles of life, are part of this field of work.

Some people in this field focus on minutiae such as the literary ornaments in poetry or the eating habits of bears. Others give their attention to systems and the big picture of interrelationships. However, unlike those in the Fields of Resources and Government who absorb themselves in their intuitive understanding of systems in order to control those systems, in the Field of Ideas systems people seek to discern patterns and links that may guide persons in the Fields of Resources and Government in the preservation of harmony. The main motives of experts in this field are balance, harmony, peace, and equilibrium. They tend to feel themselves beyond the fray of life in general. It's as if they are sports commentators who watch and report on a game, but do not play it themselves. As detached observers, they tend to grow to be self-controlled, austere, and tolerant people. The ups and downs of life do not affect them so much.

While experts in the Field of Ideas have a quiet inner determination to remain balanced and detached, lacking is the kind of external goal-driven action distinctly evident in the Field of Resources and Field of Government. Instead, like those in the Field of Artistry, they are satisfied with simple and basic things in life. Another such commonality is contentment with whatever living standard is achieved as a fair by-product of their work. And, in both fields (Artistry and Ideas), there is a tendency to be satisfied with the work itself rather than financial profit. However, the Field of Ideas is primarily an internal pursuit, while the Field of Artistry is typically external work. An idea maker defines or explains a new concept or theory, rather than crafting a beautiful chair, for example. He or she is satisfied with external simplicity because he or she has a very active and fulfilling internal life of the mind and intellect. An Artistry worker is satisfied with external simplicity because he or she is not interested in controlling or managing big things or many people.

4.5   An Illustration of the Four Fields

To illustrate the four fields and how they work together, we present an example of producing a new medicine. Work on new medicines involves all four fields. We mentioned in Chapter 3 that scientists, including those in medicine, are generally in the Field of Ideas. On the other hand, some people may get science degrees and work in medicine in some of the ways we list below, in other fields of work.

To produce new medicines requires answering questions. Is the candidate medicine likely to have the desired therapeutic effect without inducing unacceptable adverse side effects? Neutral, detached persons in the Field of Ideas go through all stages of answering this question with more and more confidence, while remaining objective. Another question is whether and how our new medicine would be effectively integrated into healing in different cultures and subcultures. Some people in the Field of Ideas specializing in medical anthropology investigate this type of social question. Some other questions are: How much of the medicine would patients take, and how often? If the medicine treats a contagious condition, how many people would need to be treated for the condition to peter out? You will remember that the driving questions of the Field of Ideas are: "Is it true? Is it wise?" The questions about the medicine relate to the second of these in particular.

One type of question in the Field of Ideas is: How does some group of agents — people, organisms, cells — do something? Scientists such as sociologists, anthropologists, ecologists, microbiologists, epidemiologists, physiologists, or immunologists may investigate such questions, which may turn out to be applicable in creating, producing, and distributing the new medicine.

There are many other concerns when producing a new medicine and this is where people from the other fields come in. For instance, it's important to ask how the medicine can be produced and distributed efficiently. This is a question for the Field of Resources (and may involve quite a bit of math). The driving questions of the Field of Resources are "Is it sustainable? Is it regenerative?"

How can *everyone* who needs it get the medicine? This is a question of public health, which is in the Field of Government. The driving questions of the Field of Government are "Is it just? Is it honorable?" Note that there is often a tension between these questions and the questions driving the Field of Resources. For many diseases, the answer to "Is it regenerative?" would probably be "No" without government subsidies in many countries. The question of what fraction of the population *needs* the medicine can become politically fraught, so objective answers would more likely come from people in the Field of Ideas than from people in the Field of Government (who would tend to think more about fairness and implementability).

Finally, many technical aspects of actually getting the medicine into production require people in the Field of Artistry: collecting or producing the components of the formulation, mixing ingredients, packaging them, keeping everything sterile, etc. The main questions in the Field of Artistry are: "Is it supportive? Is it beautiful?" In this case, the first question is the most relevant. Any kind of massive effort in the physical world requires solving practical, physical problems one after the other. In this case, solving some of them correctly requires knowing a lot of science. Conducting basic science can also require some people in the Field of Artistry. Some biologists describe their day-to-day efforts as "transferring very small amounts of liquid from one place to another." Scientific experiments often require constructing some apparatus, perhaps using a great deal of ingenuity. Many careers in the Field of Artistry require a lot of inventiveness and creativity, and work in the Field of Artistry often requires a certain kind of endurance and hardiness. These qualities would be needed to complete the endeavor.

From this example, we can see how the different fields can work together, even in an enterprise that on first glance might appear to only involve one of them (the Field of Ideas).

4.6 Choosing Between the Fields

At this point, we've explained what temperament is suitable to each of the four fields, as well as begun to sketch the ideal worker in each field. This understanding of the ideal worker gives us one piece of the answer to what field is most suitable for us. As we mentioned in each grouping above, ideal workers in each field continually examine their work in the light of a pair of fundamental questions:

- Field of Artistry: Is it supportive? Is it beautiful?

- Field of Resources: Is it sustainable? Is it regenerative?

- Field of Government: Is it just? Is it honorable?

- Field of Ideas: Is it true? Is it wise?

Of course, every human being is concerned, to some extent and in some way, with all four pairs of questions. And any sort of career may intersect with any and all of those concerns more or less. At the same time, our career or vocation will tend to predominantly serve as a concrete answer to one of those pairs. One can think, "If I have to choose among those pairs, which pair of questions do I *most* want my career to offer to myself and society?" In other words, a way to have those questions help direct you to a field in line with your nature is to discern which pair of questions resonates with you the most in terms of what you want the career part of your life to answer.

If both the pair from the Field of Artistry and a pair from another field equally draw you in terms of career, then the Field of Artistry may be most suitable, as it will allow you to support those in the other field that appeals to you. After all, one way of working in the Field of Artistry is to continually ask "Is it supportive?" to a particular person with whom you are interacting directly. Then, if that person is driven by one of the other questions, you also help answer that question in the affirmative by supporting that person. For instance, when you support a person who is driven by the question "Is it wise?" then you're indirectly contributing to greater wisdom in society. When you support a person who is driven by the question "Is it sustainable?" then you're indirectly contributing to greater sustainability in society, and so forth. So, for instance, you indirectly contribute to justice if someone who directly contributes to justice in the Field of Government, perhaps as a public servant, a humanitarian coordinator, or a political activist, is at the end of the chain of people you support. The same holds for the other questions.

If all four pairs seem equally urgent to you in terms of career, the Field of Artistry may be most suitable to supporting the public in general. As we mentioned in Chapter 3, the Field of Artistry generally contains the most people, followed in decreasing order by the Field of Resources, the Field of Government, and the Field of Ideas.

Let's look at some examples of the Field of Artistry. As a person in the Field of Artistry, if you work as an orderly in a hospital or in customer service at a general store, you may help people in all four fields over the course of a week. If you support different persons in different fields while working in the Field of Artistry — perhaps over the course of a day or perhaps from year to year — then you may end up indirectly contributing to the greater good in all these different ways.

If only one pair of questions seems to draw you, but you are also particularly drawn to another field of work (though not to its driving pair of questions), you could work in the former field while cooperating with the latter. For instance, if you are driven to continually ask, "Is it true? Is it wise?" and the subject matter that particularly interests you is transit management, you could teach transit management principles or advise those in the Field of Government who make the decisions and who are driven by questions of fairness and honor. For example, you might foresee and warn about future challenges arising from transit solutions that currently work well for most people. We talk more about cooperation among fields in Chapter 33.

At this point in the book, some readers may have a pretty good idea of which of these four fields is most suitable to their nature. For such persons, we still suggest going through all the rest of the book, rather than skipping those parts focusing on fields other than their own. All of us interact with people in each of the four fields at various points in the course of our lives, and it's helpful for each of us to be able to put ourselves in the shoes of people in fields other than our own, to try to understand their perspectives, and to respect and appreciate them.

Other readers may still feel ambivalent between two or more fields. We expect that as we continue to flesh out different aspects of these four fields in the following chapters, these people will gradually arrive at a better sense of which field they find most congenial.

A reader may also find repeated feelings that sections of the book dealing with particular fields are too long, too involved, of questionable relevance, not interesting, etc. Later in the book, we have testimonies from people in various fields, and the same kinds of feelings may arise. Such feelings may indicate that those sections deal with fields that are not the reader's own.

In the next chapter, we explain how dividing workers into these specific four fields helps society to run smoothly and well. Because practice right after learning something is the best way to solidify understanding, please turn now to Appendix A. For each item, do the second part: put a check mark next to the field of work of that occupation.

Chapter 5

Why Fence Off Four Fields? General Considerations

Good fences make good neighbors.
–Robert Frost, *Mending Wall*[53]

In the *Bhagavad-gita* it is said:

> Don't jump onto someone else's path, even if it seems so much easier and better than yours. It is better to endure the difficulties of your own path, because to walk a path meant for another is very dangerous.
> –Vraja Kishor, *A Simple Gita*[54]
>
> — *Bhagavad-gita* 3.35

In previous chapters, we discussed some reasons why it's better to work according to our own nature. That being said, it's also in the nature of some of us to be versatile. In terms of the broad division into four fields we've been working with, it may be possible for some of us to work in more than one field, perhaps sequentially over the course of our lives, or in parallel on multiple projects — indeed, while you were reading you may well have thought that you yourself have worked in more than one field! It may be possible for a particular individual to fill the requirements of more than one field with complete technical competence: as the *Bhagavad-gita* says above, more easily and better. But, throughout this book, we discuss many aspects of the four fields that go beyond technical competence.

No matter how much technical competence we can exhibit in an unsuitable field, the above *Gita* quote suggests that there is significant reason for caution when working in ways that do not match our temperament. In this section, we'll describe specifically how the requirements of working in one field can be at odds with that of another field. Mixing the fields in an individual's career can lead to frustration and even corruption, as well as compromising the overall functioning of society. Thus, we give caveats to be vigilant about when individuals cross fields. It's worth noting that conflicts among fields involve fundamental, tacit aspects of our ways of work. Therefore, the problems those conflicts cause can percolate beneath our level of awareness for a long time before rising to the surface.

Working well in another field may require consciously adopting a different persona, much as an actor "becomes" different people in playing different roles. Just as not all of us are talented actors, not all of us are genuinely suited to the difficult and dangerous task of crossing fields for more than a brief time. Even talented actors revert to their own ways of being and would find it an unbearable strain to stay in character constantly. In a similar way, even an expert at playing the role required for another field will at the very least feel strained and will eventually revert to his or her own true nature in whole or part.

5.1   The Importance of Working in One's Natural Field

As we have been describing throughout this book, and as the above *Bhagavad-gita* quote also makes clear, it is best that each individual works according to his or her own nature. However, there are many reasons why people may have spent time working in a field that is at variance with their nature. In such cases, it is advisable that they leave the incompatible field of work — even if they may have considerable education and experience there — to enter a field of work that accords with their nature.

There are a number of reasons people are in fields at variance with their nature. In many cases, these reasons represent a tension between one's own nature and pressure from others. One cause might be because it was the field their parents or other family members worked in. Even if it was natural for the parents, it may not be natural for each of their children. Another reason is that when they were teenagers or young adults, the field might have been one their close friends went into. Or, it might be a field that seemed to them, or to those close to them, the most lucrative or prestigious that they could enter. It also might be a field they were expected to enter due to social prejudices about their race, gender, ethnic background, etc. Sometimes people take up an unsuitable career in the mood of "paying one's dues to family or society." Another reason is that it might be that they are very intelligent, and in their social circle all intelligent people were expected to enter a particular field of work, e.g., the Field of Ideas ("You're so smart, it's best you spend all your time thinking"), the Field of Artistry ("You're so smart, you can make this machine work"), the Field of Government ("You're so smart, you should be in charge"), or the Field of Resources ("You're so smart, you should be rich"). As we've noted before, every field of work needs and benefits from intelligence.

Throughout this book, we describe how the benefits of working according to one's own nature, from the psychophysical perspective, the social perspective, and the spiritual perspective, run deep and wide. Over the long run they far outweigh any of the above reasons for entering an unnatural field. Even if persons have never had a chance to work in their natural field, we will use the term "crossing fields" when they work in a field that is at variance with their nature. When individuals work in fields out of line with their natures, not only do those individuals have to bear continual grating friction, but at the very least society also misses out on the greater contributions those individuals could have made by becoming experts in their more suitable fields. So, at any point in one's working life one can begin taking steps to enter one's natural field of work, and to practice the natural art of work. This change doesn't necessarily have to be sudden. As we noted in Chapter 1, Barbara Sher's book *Wishcraft* gives practical suggestions for how to develop and implement a plan with small, doable steps for making this kind of change.[55]

It's good to keep in mind that if we've been trained and are perhaps working in one field of work, then when we start working in another field of work, even though it's our natural one, we may well find ourselves initially less competent than in the field where we have education and experience. In terms of our metaphor of trees and fields of work, suppose we move from a cold field where we'd been tapping maple trees for their syrup, to a hot field where we climb coconut trees to harvest coconuts, as we prefer this fruit and have noticed that we are more suited to warm climes. Initially, we may not have the arm strength necessary to climb trees at all — we'll need to build it up. If we're past the student phase of life, where a lack of competence is the norm, we may feel uncomfortable being a novice again. Having to learn new skills may result in some apparent loss of status in our own mind, or garner criticism from people around us. People in our lives may feel uncomfortable that we're stepping outside the categories in which they thought they knew us. If we're prepared for this discomfort, however, we can recognize it when we encounter it, which can help us keep up our enthusiasm and go through it.

On a more practical level, we may at first face a substantial loss of income. If we have heavy financial obligations, such as paying off a student loan or a mortgage, or supporting a family, these obligations can make switching to our natural field seem out of the question. If we've already invested substantial time and money in an educational credential such as a college degree, we may feel that work in our natural field would be a "waste" of our degree. Often, this kind of thinking is an example of the "sunk-cost fallacy," more colloquially known as throwing good money (or time, or energy) after bad. This mindset is a way of trying to avoid a loss by not acknowledging it.

If, for example, our school degree is not serving our needs, then that in itself is some kind of loss, and the wisest course would be to stop compounding that loss by continuing along an unsuitable path. We may also think that switching to our natural field would require another degree, for which the cost in time and money would be prohibitive. In reality, however, things are not so black-and-white. Many aspects of whatever education we already have may turn out to be useful in our natural field, far beyond what we can imagine when just starting to make the change. Furthermore, while learning to work in our natural field may require some training and support, it may not require an entirely new degree. In a 2017 *New York Magazine* post, Charlotte Cowles gives practical advice about how to shift incrementally to a more suitable field, taking into account financial constraints.[56] And the payoff from switching to our natural field will be well worth the trouble, as we shall see below.

The change may not be as drastic as we first feared. We may be able to change to a different one of the four fields while remaining in the same general industry, although it may require taking on a different role with a different emphasis. For example, education and experience in nursing can enable work in any of the four fields. The Field of Artistry may mean a role with more direct patient interaction, or specializing in, e.g., inserting intravenous lines with the fewest pricks and the least pain. In the Field of Resources, the role could involve a business transporting licensed practical nurses to patients' homes, or distributing medical devices. In the Field of Government, one could work to establish healthcare infrastructure in developing countries, or work on disaster preparedness and disaster relief. In the Field of Ideas, one could follow in the footsteps of the founder of modern nursing, Florence Nightingale, who made significant innovations in the discipline of statistics (which itself was just getting started) as well as nursing itself. Thus, those who are in the wrong field in nursing can switch fields while retaining the value of their education and experience.

On the other hand, for some people this process of change may be as drastic as, or even more drastic than, they feared. Those going through such a transformation may take comfort in the fact that what looks like disintegration, including the dismantling of many of the assumptions and structures that they thought they could rely on in life, may simply be remodeling. During metamorphosis, a caterpillar's innards liquefy, yet miraculously this sets the stage for the butterfly to emerge.[*]

For example, the Silicon Valley chef Mirit Cohen explains how she took a radical turn in life:

> This morning while doing my physical therapy exercises and deep breathing, a story from my past popped into my head. When I was 23 I was at the top of my game, poised to get everything I had asked for. In my 2nd year of a PhD program in Developmental Psychology at Stanford University, I had just secured a coveted NIH grant. I was in discussions with the Max Planck Institute in Germany about collaborating with them to bring primatology into my doctorate, since that was my true passion. It was a Friday and I was preparing a major presentation of my research for the following Monday. The problem was, something was wrong. I was falling asleep. A LOT. When writing at my desk…asleep, when reading journal articles on the sofa…asleep, when attempting to force myself to do it in the hot sun while sitting on a stone bench…asleep, when in a small class of only 3 people…asleep. I didn't have narcolepsy. I was deeply unhappy. I went home, cried to my boyfriend (now husband) that I wasn't going back. That's exactly what I did. I was a no-show that Monday when I was

---

[*]Dabrowski's Theory of Positive Disintegration gives one roadmap for these transformations.[57]

meant to present to the faculty. I took a leave of absence and, on a hunch, pursued my pipe dream of becoming a chef. I thought it was just a diversion. It's hard to fall asleep while handling knives and fire. Two years later, I realized I was doing what I loved, and I wanted more. Eighteen years later, and I'm in my dream job, designing workplace experiences that help people live and work better. Was I a quitter? To face potentially achieving greatness in my field, and simply walk away? Or was I courageous enough to listen to my own body (which was telling me something important about my mental health and well-being), and ultimately lead a life where I get to spend my time doing what I love? There are many ways our bodies send us signals that we are unmoored, have lost our path, and it's time to head for safety, no matter the stakes. I didn't fully understand it at the time, but I'm so grateful for the power my body's signals had to help me chart a better course for my life.
    –Mirit Cohen[58]

As we patiently strive to take our natural place, ultimately nature also comes to our aid (which we discussed in Chapter 1). As we move toward harmony with the universal body, we find that the universe also moves toward harmony with us. In the Bible it is said:

Draw near to God, and He will draw near to you.

–James 4:8

The Lord says in the *Bhagavad-gita*:

Whoever steps towards Me, however far, I also correspondingly step towards them.

— *Bhagavad-gita* 4.11

In a Hadith, the Prophet Muhammad says:

It is said that when you take only one step toward Him, He advances ten steps toward you. But the complete truth is that God is always with you.

— *Essential Sufism*[59]

5.2 Dangers of Working in an Unsuitable Field

Let's now turn to the dangers of people suited for one field working in other fields unsuitable for them. For anyone crossing into an unsuitable field, perhaps the most obvious danger is a lack of job satisfaction. Key factors of inner job satisfaction are the nature of the work itself, a sense that one is advancing or gaining in mastery, and a sense of responsibility or feeling needed. Working in an unsuitable field diminishes these internal motivators to the point that we are likely to feel dependent on external factors for satisfaction, such as pay, company policy, relationships with colleagues, job security, quality of supervision, working conditions, and so forth.[60] At the beginning of this chapter we quoted the *Bhagavad-gita*,[61] which says that doing unsuitable work is "dangerous." The Sanskrit literally says that our work becomes a "vehicle of fear." Thus, rather than being absorbed in our work because it generates inner happiness, we worry about, fear, complain about, and attempt to adjust the externals, hoping that doing so will substitute for what is intrinsically out of sync. Our work may be a vehicle of fear metaphorically, in the sense that trying to drive a car in water or a skateboard on a highway (motorway), or a bicycle in the sky would be scary and dangerous.

In the *Bhagavad-gita*,[62] Krishna states that one's nature cannot be repressed, even if one is wise, and that if we don't use our nature in the ideal way, we will exhibit it anyway, just in ways not helpful to ourselves and others. In Chapter 7, we discuss how children often exhibit their nature inappropriately due to lack of training and foresight on the part of parents or teachers. But the problem can persist into adulthood for those who work in incompatible fields. For example, a person who is naturally suited for the Field of Government but who acts in another field may spend time and energy arguing uselessly with others about issues of fairness and morality because of not having the proper outlet for creating these practically in society. A person suited for Resources with no compatible occupational outlet may try to engage family and friends in various schemes to "get rich quick."

On a broader societal level, when people work in the wrong fields, opportunity is lost for both individuals and society. On an individual level, one feels the frustration of not being able to give to society one's unique qualifications and talents. "I'm doing something that others could do as well or better than I can, and I'm not doing the work that no one is doing well." When people not qualified for a field fill the available job openings, those with the inclinations and qualifications may be forced to work unsuitably just to maintain themselves. Thus, some people working in the wrong field can send ripples through society that force others into wrong positions. Not only do all those individuals lose opportunities, but society loses by not having the most qualified people in the right places. If doctors are driving trucks and truck drivers are performing surgery, society in general is the loser.

In addition to the above dangers any time a person does unsuitable work, there are some specific problems between pairs of fields. We'll look at some of those in the next chapter, comparing and contrasting the traits and dispositions needed for each.

Subtle ways of crossing fields

Atmosphere

A situation that can be confusing is when we are sure we have the right career in the right field, but we feel uncomfortable or unmotivated, or we just plain don't like our work. We may feel conflicted and doubt what we know to be true about our own nature. Such circumstances can occur when elements at odds with a field of work so permeate a particular work environment that the field is compromised. In Chapter 23, we write about the importance of keeping all parts of a field in harmony with that field's function and the psychology of its natural workers. However, sometimes management structure, rules and procedures, supervision style, working schedules, organizational culture, or other areas of the work atmosphere are so out of harmony with the field to which the work itself belongs that those who work there feel they are in the wrong field.

For a real-life example, someone we'll call Kevin had worked as a manager in two different businesses. He had significantly grown a natural foods business and worked in ways that touched upon all areas of the business — finance, inventory, quality control, human resources, building management, vendors, sales, distribution, and so forth. He felt at home with this work, which lay squarely in the Field of Resources. Due to a change in ownership and restructuring, he got a job as a finance manager at another company. Although managing finance was in the Field of Resources and therefore might be expected to be a good "fit" for him, the overall structure of the new company was a very strict hierarchy with firm times to work, and no provision to do anything outside of one's designated area. So, when Kevin could see ways to save the company significant amounts of money, he would be told that such thinking was the province of another department and his input was not wanted. When he finished his work hours before closing time, he was not permitted to leave, nor to do anything else for the company, nor even to engage in study to improve his talents. Thus, after some time working there he felt bored and constricted. About a year later he went to another job that gave him freedom to observe and channel the flow of resources that is integral to this field. Although all three of Kevin's jobs were in the same field, his experience of them varied based on their atmosphere.

Livelihood or hobby

Some people despair of being able to maintain themselves by working in their own field, and thus get an income from an inappropriate field. They then take up a hobby in their own field in order to express their natural tendencies. Such a strategy may be needed in the short term, for example, for those who are switching from an incompatible field to their own field. But, as a long-term way of life, the harms of crossing fields are likely to appear in one's life with this type of "adjustment." Some specific problems tend to arise in this situation. For example, the psychological disharmony felt in one's livelihood is likely to affect the rest of one's time and make it difficult to "switch" to the mood that is integral to one's natural work. Also, there may not be the time and energy needed to do the hobby to the level of quality and satisfaction desired by both the worker and society or to get trained in one's field. If a person does devote as much time as the hobby would need to be of real value, there may be little time left for proper sleep, meals, exercise, recreation, time with family, spiritual practices, and all the various aspects of life. Such an unbalanced life will affect one's ability to practice all aspects of dharma in one's career.

5.3 Summary

Crossovers between fields cause harm to society in general, and the individuals involved will feel conflicted and torn. Persons acting outside of their natural field will be told that the attributes they hold most dear are wrong or inappropriate, and, indeed, such will be the case, as they are out of their environment, as we might call it "wrong" for a fish to attempt to breathe through gills on land — a fish out of water. For example, while exacting justice is essential for society when done in the Field of Government, that behavior becomes objectionable when done in the other fields, as it can become personal vengeance. Such a situation would cause great angst to an ill-placed person, who is acting according to the ideals of a different field.

This extreme caution is not to say that we are proposing an absolute rule against individuals crossing between the four fields of work. Work may need to be done by whoever is available in a time of emergency. Also, individuals, in times of difficulty, may sometimes have to work outside their field. With that said, even in emergencies, it is good to be aware of the issues that can arise.

Furthermore, the recommendation that each person stay in one of the four fields throughout their career need not preclude social mobility. There are occupations with vastly different pay and prestige *within* each field. A person in the Field of Artistry may go from waiting tables or taking out the trash to working as a cardiac surgeon, a world-renowned musician, or a highly paid software engineer. A person in the Field of Resources may go from operating a small organic farm to heading a national chain of grocery stores. A person in the Field of Government may go from working as a security guard for an office building to becoming a head of state. A person in the Field of Ideas may go on from teaching kindergarten to becoming an Ivy League professor.[*]

The above examples suggest why someone might try to move not only within a field, but also cross between fields, in the hope of gaining greater prestige. However, such a move is fraught with danger beyond what we've already outlined in the chapter. While sometimes a field in general is held in relative prestige, this type of calculation can also vary greatly among different times, places, and subcultures. In terms of time, there are numerous examples from just the last century or two, in various places, where society suddenly changed such that those working in a particular field were reviled and became objects of contempt. Sometimes those working in that field found their lives in danger just because of the kind of work they did. Stalin's purges of scholarly and military persons are one example of such occurrences. While this situation would always be tragic for anyone to be in, consider how much more tragic it would feel if that work had not even been natural to those people in the first place! So, in general when we

---

[*]The pairs of examples we just listed each differ greatly in prestige and pay in the United States, at the time of our writing; perhaps in another time, place, or culture it would be perfectly obvious that people can make these kinds of changes.

are at a crossroads in our career, switching fields would be a very shaky bridge to social mobility, as it can be nearly impossible to determine how each field will be treated in the future. Furthermore, if one seeks to cross into an unsuitable field primarily to climb the social ladder, it's important to point out that the pursuit of prestige will be in general unfulfilling if it's at the cost of one's values (for reasons we discuss more in Part II).

In the next chapter, we look at scenarios where people cross from the specific field suitable to them into another specific field and describe some of the problems and dangers that arise.

Chapter 6

Why Fence Off Four Fields? Specific Mixtures

6.1 Dangers of Working in an Unsuitable Field

We turn in this chapter to the dangers of crossing between specific pairs of fields (i.e., when those suited to work in one specific field work in a specific other one instead). With four fields, there are six possible combinations, so this chapter is inevitably long. However, the discussion of these dangers helps to delineate the definitions and values of each of the four fields. We suggest that on a first reading, if you feel at this point that you know which field is most suitable for you, you just read the three sections about crossing between your field and each of the other ones. If you are still confused between two fields, you can read the section about that pair of fields first. This will highlight the differences and can help you settle which one suits you best.

The dangers of crossing between pairs of fields do affect people in all four fields; for example, the dangers of one person crossing between the Field of Government and the Field of Resources can have a big impact on other individuals in the same society who work in the Field of Artistry or the Field of Ideas. Also, knowing these dangers is useful for parents and teachers to help identify a child's most suitable field. So we do suggest that all readers read the entire chapter at some point, and definitely before proceeding to Part III. However, the order of reading the sections is not significant.

Crossing Government and Resources

While both the Fields of Government and Resources focus on providing for large numbers of people, Government redistributes the people's own wealth, and Resources creates new wealth, or turns natural resources into usable wealth. Because of this difference, people in Resources often think those in Government are foolishly "generous" and Government people often think those in Resources are too profit-minded.

When people suited for the Field of Resources instead work in the Field of Government:

People suited for the Field of Resources tend to focus on the special interests of their particular industry, rather than on the general interests of society as a whole. When working in their own field, they rightfully strive to increase the flow of specific resources, needing laser-like focus on the special interests of their enterprises. The mood of the Field of Government, on the other hand, is different.

Government is supposed to work in the long-term public interest. The entire society is the responsibility of government; it cannot get rid of problems by shifting responsibility to another entity, or by excluding specific people from its domain:

> The buck stops here.
> –Harry Truman[63]

Unfortunately, the mood of concentrating on their own flow of resources rather than the overall picture of society may lead such people to focus directly on lining their own pockets. Less brazenly, they may make decisions with a view towards helping their industry, with an eye towards reentering it. Some may hope to reenter their area with a new role of special pleading, through the connections and know-how they've formed in government. Such behavior, the so-called "revolving door in government," means that the main concerns for working in the Field of Government, namely fairness and justice for all, can be overlooked.

A related phenomenon is "regulatory capture." As we describe in Chapter 35, workers in the Field of Government ideally promulgate and enforce standards that prevent exploitation of any segment of society by any industry. (Note that agriculture is a specific example of an industry; in terms of career dharma, it is not qualitatively separate from other kinds of enterprise.) If the people who are supposed to be looking out for all of society identify with a favored industry, they may create standards to protect that industry's interests rather than the public interest. Later, in Chapter 32, we describe the benefits of competition within a field. When people from industry enter government and write the regulations, they can use these rules to exclude competitors, enabling a small group within the industry to form a cartel that colludes to exploit the public. Or, they can weaken or eliminate regulations that inconvenience their industry yet protect the public. We shall look at some specific examples of these exploitative practices in Chapter 33. All these problems arise even when those in the Field of Resources get too much control over those in the Field of Government. When people working in the Field of Government actually have the nature to work in the Field of Resources, the difficulty is compounded.

A prime example of how the mood of the Field of Resources is incompatible with work in the Field of Government is in the running of prisons. Ideally, persons in the Field of Government act for the benefit of all of society and keep the long-term interests of all people at heart, with fairness and justice as highly prized values. Their roles include protecting the people in general from crime, for example by imprisoning criminals. The criminals are also among the people under their care, so running prisons includes preventing crime within the prisons, i.e., preventing prisoners from perpetrating further crimes while incarcerated and protecting prisoners from being victimized by other prisoners. Running prisons also includes reforming the prisoners, both for their own upliftment and for preventing additional harm and violence to society at large at the time of their release.

When persons whose nature is in the Field of Resources run prisons, on the other hand, they are not intrinsically motivated to focus on preventing crime within the prisons, since doing so does not affect resources one way or the other. Financially, they have no incentive to reform the prisoners, but quite the opposite: if the released prisoners go on to commit more crimes and are again sent to prison, this greater recidivism (perhaps due to criminals being traumatized, hardened, trained in crime, and/or making new criminal contacts while in prison) helps the "business" of running prisons to be sustainable and regenerative! Persons focused on resources may also be tempted by considerations of efficiency to use prisoners as cheap and involuntary labor for other enterprises, lining their own pockets in the process. In all these ways, such persons significantly undermine the role of prisons in promoting justice in society.

Indeed, those in the Field of Resources running prisons may directly push for more people to be in prison:

> After three inmates escaped Arizona's Kingman prison in 2010, operated by the private Management & Training Corp. (MTC), the state pulled 238 high-risk prisoners out of the facility over what it called lax security. That put the number of prisoners in Kingman below the 97 percent threshold stipulated by contract. Despite the security concerns, MTC threatened to sue the state. Arizona paid more than $3 million for empty beds, according to a 2011 Arizona Republic report.[64]
>
> —Reid Wilson, *Are governments incentivizing longer prison terms?*[65]

A 2013 report found that 65% of private prison contracts reviewed included such occupancy quotas.[66] In the Field of Resources, wanting more customers for an honest business that provides real value is laudable. With this natural inclination of those suited for Resources, pushing for more people in prison may appear to make business sense for these companies. However, when applied to work that is firmly in the Field of Government, the effects on the larger society can be devastating.

On a personal level, those working in the Field of Government whose nature is in the Field of Resources may feel frustrated and impatient with being called upon to take into account so many varied considerations, dealing with the needs of every part of society. They feel more at home being able to say, "That's not my business" for concerns outside of a limited sphere. They may react by trying to fabricate rationales for why they should be able to ignore much of what they're being asked to consider. If nevertheless they can't escape what they see as an endless stream of conflicting demands, they may be overwhelmed and start to feel they are in an impossible position.

When people suited for the Field of Government instead work in the Field of Resources:

Those suited for the Field of Government tend to prioritize care of people as more important than the project or profits. Such a situation might sound attractive and desirable. However, in the Field of Resources, if the project doesn't thrive and generate profits, then the people who work there will ultimately suffer through the collapse or downsizing of the business. Additionally, one of the main concerns of people naturally suited to the Field of Government is *yasa*. Fame that comes from righteousness and builds community is the primary wealth they generate for society at large. Honor, fairness, and justice predominate in persons who exemplify the ideal of those in government. Indeed, they are willing to give their lives for the sake of these principles. But, to be successful in the Field of Resources, one is generally expanding profit for one's own company, not justice in society in general. The concern of persons in the Field of Resources is to increase the overall prosperity of their enterprises through a focus on efficiency and leverage. They are on guard against overreach and overextension draining resources beyond what the activities of their enterprise can sustain and replenish.

Anita Roddick started the famous Body Shop brand with a focus on social and environmental causes, both typical concerns of government:

> However, as The Body Shop's profits and name-recognition grew, the Roddicks began paying more attention to social causes than their business, launching an array of environmental projects rather than revamping the company's aging product line. Better-run imitators, such as The Bath & Body Works, ate into The Body Shop's customer base. And critics on the left who were once Body Shop allies suddenly started attacking the company for "hypocritical practices," generating a wave of negative press. As a result, sales fell and profits dulled.
>
> By 1996, it was clear that a change was needed. The Roddicks stepped back from running day-to-day operations and installed managing director Stuart Rose, who promptly restructured the company, bringing in other professional managers, installing tighter inventory control and streamlining processes.
>
> — *Anita Roddick: Cosmetics With A Conscience*[67]

Protecting the environment as a whole is a typical concern of the Field of Government: as we have inherited the earth from our ancestors, it is only fair and just that we cherish it to pass along to generations to come. On the other hand, as we explained in Chapter 4, a person in the Field of Resources approaches sustainability while keeping themselves and, by extension, their own enterprises, as their central focus. According to the quote above, the degree of attention the Roddicks were paying to social causes was *not sustainable* in terms of The Body Shop's financial health.

The Body Shop has undergone an acquisition and multiple changes in management since then. Like many such companies, eventually the business side dominated as the brand became successful, and those naturally in the Field of Resources took over running the company.

In general, someone ideally suited to the Field of Government is likely to define a "fair price" for the customer in such a way as to lead to failure of the enterprise. One can say that those most ideally suited for the Field of Government have inner principles that are often at odds with the goals of the Field of Resources. There is, indeed, the need for a tight relationship between these two fields, such that concern for people, justice, and fairness regulates and moderates the urge for expanding projects and profits. We discuss this relationship in Chapter 35.[*]

Crossing Resources and Ideas

Those in the Field of Ideas and those in the Field of Resources may frequently fail to understand one another. To those in the Field of Ideas, work in the Field of Resources may appear self-centered and materialistic, and thus unpalatable, when the reality is simply that the Field of Resources operates ideally under a *practical* system of ethics. Work in the Field of Ideas may appear theoretical and useless to those in the Field of Resources, who consider it unethical for anyone to be spending money paying for research, study, and teaching about topics for which there is no discernible benefit (in their eyes).

When people suited for the Field of Ideas work in the Field of Resources:

A person whose nature is to work in the Field of Ideas focuses on truth foremost, taking a neutral, detached perspective. The very nature of work in the Field of Resources is not to be neutral or objective, but to focus on increased flows of resources for the profit of one's

---

[*] A groundbreaking urban planning theorist, Jane Jacobs, has detailed the distinct dharmas (which she calls "moral syndromes") of people in the Field of Government and people in the Field of Resources in her book *Systems of Survival*, arguing that they are fundamentally incompatible. Her book offers interesting further reading for this section.[68]

enterprise and family. Thus, people whose nature is to work in the Field of Ideas but who work in the Field of Resources may find that bias creeps into their habits of mind without their being aware of it for some time:

> It is difficult to get a man to understand something, when his salary depends on his not understanding it!
> –Upton Sinclair, *I, Candidate for Governor: And How I Got Licked*[69]

The person may gradually feel frustration and dissatisfaction as exemplified by the well-known writer Michael Lewis describing how he left his position as a bond trader at Salomon Brothers:

> I left Salomon Brothers in 1988, but not for any of the obvious reasons. I didn't think the firm was doomed. I didn't think that Wall Street would collapse. I wasn't even suffering from growing disillusionment (it grew to a point, still bearable, then stopped). Although there were many perfectly plausible reasons to jump ship, I left, I think, more because I didn't need to stay any longer.
>
> My father's generation grew up with certain beliefs. One of those beliefs is that the amount of money one earns is a rough guide to one's contribution to the welfare and prosperity of our society....
>
> ...When you sit, as I did, at the center of what has been possibly the most absurd money game ever and benefit out of all proportion to your value to society (as much as I'd like to think I got only what I deserved, I don't), when hundreds of equally undeserving people around you are all raking it in faster than they can count it, what happens to the money belief? Well, that depends. For some, good fortune simply reinforces the belief. They take the funny money seriously, as evidence that they are worthy citizens of the Republic. It becomes their guiding assumption — for it couldn't possibly be clearly thought out — that a talent for making money come out of a telephone is a reflection of merit on a grander scale....

For me, however, the belief in the meaning of making dollars crumbled; the proposition that the more money you earn, the better the life you are leading was refuted by too much hard evidence to the contrary. And without that belief, I lost the need to make huge sums of money. The funny thing is that I was largely unaware how heavily influenced I was by the money belief until it had vanished.

It is a small piece of education, but still the most useful thing I picked up at Salomon Brothers.
 –Michael Lewis, *Liar's Poker*[70]

Eventually, as with any crossing of fields, the person may come to feel depressed, and take to intoxication in an effort to escape. For example, Carl Bosch, one of the inventors of the Haber-Bosch process for fixing nitrogen, loved to work in the Field of Ideas. His employer Farben and the German government, however, kept pressuring him to increase his involvement in the business side of the process, which crossed him into the Field of Resources:

It is not surprising that after 1935, some of the fight went out of Bosch. He started drinking in earnest. He had always enjoyed alcohol; it provided him with a safety valve, a fast way to decompress. Now it increasingly provided him with an escape. Those around him began noticing that his occasional bouts of depression were becoming more frequent and lasting longer. Some people said he started taking painkillers. He came to the offices in Frankfurt less frequently, holed up in his Heidelberg villa more, took fewer meetings, and slowly became something of a solitary, tended by [his wife] Else, surrounded by his collections, staying up all night and snapping photographs of the stars.
 –Thomas Hager, *The Alchemy of Air*[71]

When such persons do become aware of how bias and personal profit affect their neutrality, they are likely to feel disgusted with themselves. Their concept of fairness and transparency may be such that they are inclined to give things away, and either feel conflicted by profit-minded work or abandon it. Sometimes such a situation results in businesses that focus on giving away large amounts of profits or in some way promoting research. Such businesses may reach a point where the founders see profit and marketing overwhelming ideals, and they sell the business to those suited for the Field of Resources or close it entirely, as in the following example:

> Lawrence [not his real name] holds a master's in social work and taught a twenty-one hour, certified course on counseling techniques. Although he loved sharing his ideas, he closed the course as soon as it got big enough to have become a business. He gave as his reason the fact that he was spending as much time marketing as teaching, and doing so negated his happiness in teaching. Lawrence regretfully said that the business of securing a venue large enough for the growing number of students, promoting the courses, and managing the finances, had so much soured his experience that he moved into just writing and personal counseling.
> — *personal communication*[72]

While people suited for the Field of Ideas may love to have their own garden, they tend to lose interest and enthusiasm if their garden expands into an agribusiness. Such people do not enjoy, or even understand, the relentless thirst for bigger and better which must drive those in the Field of Resources in order to be successful. In practice, this lower intensity of drive may eventually lead them to "take their eye off the ball," overlooking something that turns out to be crucial for their own business.

When people suited for the Field of Resources work in the Field of Ideas:

Perhaps the most obvious problem with this specific crossover is the increased likelihood of corruption in the Field of Ideas for society in general. For example, when pharmaceutical companies fund drug tests about their own potentially profitable medicine, the temptation to skirt the standards of responsible research will be strong, and patients can wind up being hurt. A similar problem ensues when individuals whose natural leanings are to maximize profits and increase the flow of resources work in jobs that require a strong sense of detachment, and a disinterest in having personal luxuries. Such people may distort truth to facilitate their natural wealth of *aisvarya*. If they can adhere to the principles of their job, they may find themselves dispirited and unmotivated by the lack of money and leadership opportunity in what is optimally a job where people share, or even completely abjure, personal credit.

It is expected that those suited to the Field of Resources prioritize "selling" and, in doing so, would often present a one-sided or distorted view of their product or service in order to increase their business. Customers are aware of this nature of Resources, and often internally adjust for it, or do some independent research. When such a mentality enters the Field of Ideas, however, a person may work at "selling" a religion, or an ideology, or a scientific theory, through generalization, distortion, selective presentation of information, and so forth. However, people do not expect those in the Field of Ideas to be salespeople, and tend to have a more open faith in their objectivity. If and when such tactics come to light, people in general may lose faith in science, religion, or objective truth overall. Thus, the function of the Field of Ideas as the guiding beacon of society is compromised. People in general seek to find truth and guidance without recourse to those most suitable to helping them do so.

Additionally, because people whose nature is to work in the Field of Resources are likely to find the Field of Ideas to be full of impractical pie-in-the-sky concerns, they may neglect such concerns entirely. This situation is a loss both to the individual and society, because the work in the Field of Ideas remains undone or is poorly done.

For these reasons, various institutions have taken steps to enforce clear boundaries between the Field of Ideas and the Field of Resources. For example, during some periods, a number of US newspapers have instituted a "wall" between those working in the newsroom (i.e., in the Field of Ideas) and those cultivating relationships with advertisers (i.e., in the Field of Resources):

> [The] wall, between the journalistic and business-oriented functions of a news organization, is one of the foremost professional markers of journalism, a principle that is reinforced most strongly in the central sites of its socialization — journalism schools, textbooks, and reviews, not to mention thousands of newsrooms large and small....

...journalists have constructed and enshrined a border between themselves and their organizations' business operations primarily as a way to safeguard their professional autonomy, or journalists' ability to exercise judgment and control their work process....

Journalists have developed a variety of tools to defend their jurisdiction from commercial interests. Though boundary work is fundamentally a rhetorical process, one key strategy is more organizational than rhetorical – the distinctly bifurcated structure of news organizations...with the news and business departments operating independently from each other and often at odds....This organizational separation has historically manifested itself most materially in the physical separation between newsroom and advertising departments, an arrangement that reinforces the boundary both physically and symbolically. Longtime *Chicago Tribune* publisher, Robert McCormick, famously enforced this physical divide with separate elevators for journalists and those in the business operation, the latter of which did not stop on the newsroom floor....

Aside from organizational divides, most of the journalists' work in defining and defending the news-business boundary has been accomplished rhetorically. The professional values regarding independence from business are most formally encoded at the organizational level in news organizations' written guidelines and at the professional level in codes of ethics....

–Mark Coddington, *The wall becomes a curtain: Revisiting journalism's news-business boundary*[73]

A longer version of this extract appears in the endnotes.[b] US journalists implemented this wall because they understood their primary function to be public service, and their primary asset to be credibility. Thus, for journalists to uphold and reinforce the boundary between news and business is part of cherishing their field of work (Ideas) and their source of wealth (*jnana*, here most closely related to truth), which we discuss more in Chapter 21 and Chapter 23.

Crossing Ideas and Artistry

Both these fields use the wealth from the Field of Resources in various ways. Those in both Ideas and Artistry tend to feel satisfied when basic needs are met. Yet, those in Artistry tend to be more externally focused, and those in Ideas more absorbed in their internal state of awareness.

We will describe in Chapter 33 that people in the Field of Artistry do many kinds of work to assist those in education. For example, experts in design bring a publication to life with illustrations, layout, and typography. This is natural and normal, since work in the Field of Artistry is needed to make everything run well and beautifully. However, doing Artistry-type work to *assist* those in the Field of Ideas is distinct from working directly *in* the *Field* of Ideas. The work of Ideas often involves fully integrating a broad vision of concepts into one's work. Artistry, on the other hand, usually involves work involving detail and quality in a narrower and more tangible sphere.

When people suited for the Field of Artistry work in the Field of Ideas:

For people in the Field of Artistry, the realm of Ideas may seem like it is full of abstractions with as much meaning as crossword puzzles — something whose role in their life is as an occasional idle pastime rather than as serious work. So a person whose nature is in the Field of Artistry but who ends up in the Field of Ideas may neglect to put energy into a broad view of society and its long-term interests. The most essential aspects of the work will then be neglected. Or such persons may end up mentally "checking out," simply going through the motions and remaining personally unfulfilled.

Those suited for the Field of Artistry ideally have a mood of service to others' desires and needs. While those who cherish the field (see Chapter 23) do maintain the standards of their craft over the whims of customers, their concern is to please others. But the worker in the Field of Ideas serves others with wisely applied and understood truth that may sometimes feel like bitter medicine or painful procedures. When those suited for Artistry work in Ideas they will feel an inner conflict between the detached guidance they need to give society and their predominant desire to please. They may thus neglect doing the research to find possibly unpleasant truths, or distort the information they disseminate. For example, sometimes pharmaceutical researchers provide drug companies distorted results that justify marketing a medicine, or military intelligence personnel give incomplete or distorted information to governement officials. If the motive is a desire to please those to whom one reports, the cause of such situations may be that those working in the Field of Ideas are actually suited for the Field of Artistry.

Those suited for Artistry are often easily satisfied with expertise in their craft and a simple life of "creature comforts." While simplicity in life is also common in Ideas, the satisfaction comes from taking pleasure in the mind and intellect, or in spirituality. Those naturally suited for Ideas are harder to corrupt because the externals of the world hold little interest. This relative freedom from being compromised is essential in the work of the dissemination of wisdom. Conversely, those suited for Artistry are highly susceptible to corruption once they work in the Field of Ideas. They have little natural love for the intrinsic purity of the field itself, as such things are not their source of enjoyment. On top of that, if someone offers them a life of security and comfort in external things in exchange for a lack of rigor in their work, they can be strongly tempted to accept. The combination of the desire for an externally comfortable life along with the tendency to want to please others creates an exceptionally volatile situation for the fire of corruption when brought to the Field of Ideas.

In Chapter 3 and Chapter 4, we mention how the Field of Artistry is the least abstract field. The comfort with clear objectives for both result and process that is natural for those in the Field of Artistry thus often translates into bureaucratic[c] procedures when brought to the other fields. That bureaucratic tendency often found in the Field of Artistry is most stifling for individuals and society when brought to the Field of Ideas. Freedom is key to the Field of Ideas, and persons working there require both the literal and figurative space to allow for discussion and exploration that may seriously challenge the status quo. Bureaucrats, on the other hand, are devoted to upholding the status quo. Thus there is a conflict. Furthermore, those in the Field of Artistry are concerned with the beauty and function of society in the sense of tangible, tactile work. But the Field of Ideas is one of abstractions. When those suited for Artistry work in Ideas, they often miss subtlety and context in knowledge and information. They may, thus, present facts, quotes, and truths out of context, in isolation, with the aim of preserving or creating functionality in a limited sphere.

A contribution Artistry makes to society, as explained previously, is supplying pleasure. This enjoyment is generally of a practical or sensory nature — clean streets, well-manicured parks, attractive haircuts, tasty food, music to engage emotions and movement, packages delivered intact and on-time, or well-run appointment systems at an office. When persons with such inclinations work in Ideas, they may bring sensuality to sciences hard and soft, to religion and spirituality, and to the pedagogy of educators. An example of such sensuality, that may be due to crossing fields, would be the chemists who have created, glorified, and facilitated the use of harmful and dangerous intoxicants. One example is American chemist Alexander Shulgin. He invented many drugs himself, and produced bestselling manuals explaining to the public how to produce drugs such as MDMA, also known as "ecstasy." This drug is like a combination of a narcotic, amphetamine, and psychedelic that is

> fusing the cerebral and the sensual
> —Ben Westhoff, *Fentanyl Inc*[74]

the very definition of crossing Ideas with Artistry. He propounded a doctrine that such drugs would enhance peoples' lives, although in fact people can die of overdoses and experience various unwanted effects.[75] Shulgin described many of the drugs in his popular manuals without conducting any large-scale studies of safety. Another possible example is that the science of the harms of alcohol to individuals and society[76] has been drowned out by the alcohol industry, which has introduced other framings and funded research to support them, to promote the widespread, general use of alcohol.[77][78] This spirit of pleasure that is nourishing in its own Field of Artistry twists the very nature of Ideas, which is the field where detached wisdom flourishes. Well-known examples of the value of those with detached wisdom in this field are Socrates and Galileo. Mixing Artistry and Ideas is as if salt and spices — needed for food to be palatable and well-digested in the mouth and stomach — were instead rubbed in the eyes. The clear vision the Field of Ideas should provide is thus impeded with tears and irritation.

When people suited for the Field of Ideas work in Field of Artistry:
Working in the Field of Artistry usually entails dependence on specific patrons, customers, or employers. This dependence naturally creates a special interest in pleasing that particular sub-segment of society, which will feel very awkward to people whose nature is in the Field of Ideas, who place a high value on autonomy. Furthermore, focus on specific projects naturally shortens the time frame of one's thinking so that it fits within project windows. Both constraints, of deadlines and whom to please, run the risk of taking precedence

over large-scale considerations of research, and long-term or abstract thinking. Thus, such persons feel conflicted. The inner conflict may show itself in insubordination, procrastination, and failure to meet deadlines.

Integrity and honesty are important in all fields of work, but are most prominent in Ideas and Artistry, albeit in very different ways. In Ideas, the content of one's work is saturated with truth and wisdom. But that work is best done in its own way and own time, according to the inner inspiration of the worker, perhaps in a kind of "dance" of mutual adjustment with other workers in the field. In Artistry, integrity is crucial in doing work to concrete expectations, specifications, and formulas without "cutting corners" or compromising on quality. Integrity is crucial in being on-time and reliable. But a worker naturally suited to Ideas often feels the integrity of Artistry to be an unbearable and, as explained above, unattainable constraint. With integrity at their very core, such Ideas persons may feel inner conflict at failing to be able to consistently have the different kind of integrity that Artistry needs. In this failure, such persons not only struggle with inner dissonance but also harm the Field of Artistry itself. Artistry is what makes society function on the most elemental and physical levels. If the workers there need so much creative, intellectual, or personal freedom that they cannot be reliable on a practical level, things literally will not "work."

Those naturally suited for the Field of Ideas may chafe at seeing their work in Artistry as providing sensory pleasures for society. Their natural tendency towards detachment and equilibrium often comes with a disdain towards pleasures they may categorize as "worldly" or "demeaning." While the Field of Ideas provides its natural workers with their own type of satisfactions in the abstract realm, they may not recognize the deep need of the rest of society (and often themselves, as well) for healthy, nourishing, and spiritually uplifting pleasures on the physical platform. Thus, they may suck their career in the Field of Artistry dry, leaving their work as bare function without beauty.[*] The essential purpose of the field is thus subverted. Or, on a personal level, they may get "sucked in" to the sensory nature of the work they are doing in Artistry. While such pleasures are the natural "food" for those suited to Artistry, for those suited to Ideas they are like poison. Those suited for Ideas may not have an innate sense of how to engage

---

[*]Some developments in the early 20th century, such as brutalism, or atonal music, may fall into this category.

in, and propagate, such enjoyments for the good of themselves and society. If they equate the sensory with the superficial, they may consider it to have no intrinsic value anyway and thus may become careless about its manipulation. They may, thus, use their knowledge to turn these pleasures into the darkest realms of exploitation. Some examples are food scientists who use knowledge of taste and texture to create artificially designed and processed foods meant to induce people to overeat, or psychologists who design advertisements that appeal to our basest desires in order to sell products.

Just as those in Artistry can have hobbies such as crossword puzzles in Ideas, so those in Ideas may take up hobbies such as gardening or painting. Such activities are done to please themselves (and the Divine) but not a customer, unlike those in Artistry whose joy is in having their painting hang on another's wall. Certainly, those in Ideas often appreciate doing such hobbies as a way to allow their minds and intellect contemplative space while they do physical work. However, if their main occupation is only working with concrete, tangible areas, they may turn to unhealthy outlets for the mental activity they can't express: whether it be intoxication, as the fictional Sherlock Holmes would do when bereft of any interesting cases, risky schemes, or even nefarious or criminal pursuits.

The early life of Steven Czifra, who spearheads educational opportunities for those leaving prison, is an example of someone who belongs to the Field of Ideas turning to such pursuits:

> The idea of going to college did not even cross Czifra's mind when he was growing up....His father was Hungarian: he fled the crackdown after the Hungarian uprising, in 1956, when he was sixteen, and ended up as a roofer in [Los Angeles, California]....[Czifra said of his mother,] "She didn't finish high school, and my dad was illiterate. They were both partyers." His parents fought violently all the time. "Where I come from, if you're mad at somebody you throw boiling water on them," he told someone later....
>
> Czifra reacted to all this by going wild. He broke into a house when he was eight or nine, and started doing drugs. In fifth grade, he was bored in school, so he stopped going. He joined a...gang....One evening when

he was fourteen or fifteen, [he carjacked a truck while drunk.] He was promptly arrested and sentenced to ten years.

Because of his age, he was sent to the California Youth Authority, C.Y.A....

...He was in solitary from when he was sixteen to when he was twenty — a kind of solitary where you couldn't even shout to the person next door.

The one good thing about solitary in Y.A. was a big box there containing hundreds of books. He read until all that was left was a volume of Shakespeare, with four plays in it. At first, he found the language nearly impossible to understand, but he had nothing else to do, so he kept at it. He gradually realized it was better than anything he had read before, and he looked for more. He decided that his favorite play was "Richard II," because of the way it forced you to confront a disagreeable man-child who ruined his life and killed people, and yet, by the end, made you feel compassion for him. When he finished with the Shakespeare, he wrote to a librarian, who sent him ancient-Greek literature in translation. He read Milton and Wordsworth and Dickens.

[Due to continued misbehavior, Czifra was transferred from Y.A. to prison, where he again got in trouble. He was finally released when he was nearly thirty.]

After a while, he heard that if you went to community college you could qualify for a federal Pell Grant, worth a little over five thousand dollars, and nine thousand more in loans. That was more than enough for him to live on, so...he signed up. He didn't make the connection between community college and the reading he did in prison — he just needed the cash. But when he got to college and looked at a literature syllabus he realized that he'd read almost everything on it. One...teacher taught him how to read "Paradise Lost" like a literary critic — how to analyze it, how to take it apart — and Czifra realized that this was his thing, this was what he wanted to do.

–Larissa MacFarquhar, *Building a Prison-to-School Pipeline*[79]

The article goes on to describe how Czifra went on to UC Berkeley and co-organized the Underground Scholars Initiative, for students who had been in prison, with another ex-convict student, Daniel Murillo, and the help of several Berkeley students and faculty. After graduating, Czifra went to work for the program.

It is good to remember that people in the Field of Ideas may communicate truth and wisdom through a variety of media such as music, painting, sculpture, and dance, in addition to language and mathematics. Therefore, at least some workers in the fine arts are in the Field of Ideas, not Artistry. When such persons have to produce their art for commercial employers or sponsors, they are crossing into Artistry and will have the types of difficulties outlined in this section.

In the *Bhagavata Purana*, this particular crossing of fields is strongly discouraged, even in emergency situations.

Crossing Artistry and Government

Those in Government tend to want to expand, whereas those in Artistry tend to be more easily satisfied. Those in the Field of Government embrace danger to protect others, and those in the Field of Artistry want a secure and protected life. Those in Government think of everyone's work, and those in Artistry are focused on their own craft.

As is true for Artistry and Ideas, we will describe in Chapter 33 that people in the Field of Artistry do many kinds of work to assist those in government. However, doing Artistry-type work to assist those in the Field of Government is distinct from working directly *in* the *Field* of Government. While more practical than that of Ideas, the work of Government often involves taking a broad perspective of society as a regular, continual part of one's work. Artistry, on the other hand, generally involves work that requires attention to detail and quality in a much more defined way of serving others.

When people suited for the Field of Artistry work in the Field of Government:

For some people in the Field of Artistry, the constant focus on the interplay of people needed to work in Government may feel like a draining distraction from what they prefer to do: focus on honing and exercising their own skills. They will often refer to this interplay of people as "politics!" in a pejorative way. So a person whose nature is in the Field of Artistry but who ends up in the Field of Government may end up neglecting to take a broad view of society and its long-term interests, in favor of the aspects of their work that are more suited to Artistry. They may put aside, therefore, some of the most needed aspects of their work.

The mood of those inclined towards the Field of Government is that of running towards danger, with a willingness to sacrifice their health, limbs, and even life for the safety and security of those they protect. While historically many in Government live luxurious lifestyles, those who follow the dharma of that field accept luxury to encourage patriotic feelings of awe for the pomp, ceremony, and opulence of their community, not for their own hedonistic life. The Roman Emperor and well-known Stoic Marcus Aurelius illustrates this well in describing his own palace:

> Marcus also asked the senate for money from the public treasury, not because such funds were not already at the emperor's disposal, but because he was wont to declare that all the funds, both these and others, belonged to the senate and to the people. "As for us," he said, in addressing the senate, "we are so far from possessing anything of our own that even the house in which we live is yours."
> –Cassius Dio, *Roman History*[80]

Indeed, the willingness of ideal workers in the Field of Government to sacrifice everything for the good of the constituents reveals their inner resolve and detachment. But those who are naturally attracted to the Field of Artistry have a love of a secure life of comforts, which they may hesitate to sacrifice for what to them are intangibles such as justice and ethics. Their natural role in their own field is also to produce beauty and pleasure for society and to delight in such themselves. Such persons are prime candidates for corruption by the perks of a job in Government (which would not be the case if they worked in their own Field of Artistry). They may become enamored with the adulation and respect, along with access to resources and side benefits.

People in the Field of Artistry may assist those in Government as bureaucrats, whose role it is to carry out well-defined procedures that have been specified in law. These roles are very important to the functioning of a complex society, even though bureaucracy has developed a poor reputation among people in general, perhaps partly because when a citizen interacts with a bureaucrat, they may expect a level of discretion (hewing to the spirit of the law over the letter of the law) that the bureaucrat does not exercise. This is often not entirely fair, because exercising discretion is not the role of the bureaucrat, who may sometimes not even have the autonomy to do so — and it is generally the case that those whose nature accords with the Field of Artistry may adhere to their role quite rigidly and bureaucratically. We can immediately understand, then, how when those naturally suited to the Field of Artistry work not as bureaucrats but fully in the Field of Government, which really does require strategy and shrewd discretion in decision making, they may mar the work by doing it in the bureaucratic fashion natural to them.

In Chapter 3 and Chapter 4, we mention how the Field of Artistry is the least abstract. There is more definition about what to do and how to do it than there is in other fields. Those in the Field of Artistry have more difficulty embracing uncertainty in the what and how of their work than do those in Government. For example, both the ability and the thrill of functioning in the "Fog of War"[81] is natural to those in the Field of Government but would likely be uncomfortable to those in the Field of Artistry. The comfort with clear objectives for both result and process that is natural for those in the Field of Artistry thus often translates into bureaucratic procedures when brought to the other fields.

When people suited for the Field of Government work in Field of Artistry:

Those in the Field of Government direct society and are practical leaders, whether as firefighters or Secretary of Education. But, in Artistry they need to take the role of follower. Rather than be the rule makers and enforcers, they are the rule obeyers. They thus may often find themselves chafing under such regulation, and seeking to reform the system that employs them. Such an attitude may, for different reasons than for those in Ideas who work in Artistry, similarly lead to insubordination, procrastination, and failure to meet deadlines. They may find themselves frequently attentive to the business of others rather than their own. They may feel constant frustration that they lack the time and energy to focus on justice and public interest. They may simply become agitators and complainers without a positive outlet. Without any platform or power to take responsibility for enacting justice in a full-fledged way, they may become focused on vilification, vengeance, and vigilanteism, rather than on actual justice and honor. As we discuss in Chapter 23, work that is in the Field of

Government requires a big-picture systems view, taking both short-term and long-term considerations into account, which those working outside the field do not have the knowledge, means, or standing to take.

On a societal level, when workers who have the nature of Government work in the Field of Artistry, their greater concern with working conditions and care of workers than with the work itself can cause the quality of work in this field to suffer. Also, their finding personal energy in quick, decisive, and sometimes dangerous work can damage a field that requires detailed care about quality and function. Those who thrive on risk-taking are not a good fit to be the accountants, plumbers, and furniture makers of society! Nor will those who thrive on public acclaim be satisfied with work where the worker is often in the background of the finished product or service. And, while a person suited for the Field of Government will certainly care, when working in Artistry, how his or her work will help others, the focus will not be on the creation of pleasures and beauty. Thus, such workers may diminish or restrict the flow of joy in society. Their mood of service will, additionally, be more like that of a parent than that of an assistant, and thus their relationships with those they serve will be incompatible with the type of service they are rendering.

As in other combinations of the fields, there is certainly room for cooperation between these fields. For example, those in the Field of Government may gain some expertise in the craft of acting in order to add to the effectiveness of their role of public leadership.

Crossing Government and Ideas

> Power tends to corrupt and absolute power corrupts absolutely.
> —John Emerich Edward Dalberg-Acton, *Historical Essays and Studies*[82]

> Quis custodiet ipsos custodes?
> —Juvenal, *Satire VI*[83]

> [Who will watch the watchers themselves?]

Both Government and Ideas people are concerned with long-range vision and whole systems. But the focus of those in the Field of Ideas can often seem impractical to those in Government, and Government concerns can seem too harsh or hastily arrived at for those absorbed in Ideas.

When people suited for the Field of Ideas work in the Field of Government:

We explain in Chapter 35 how it's the function of people in the Field of Ideas to advise people in the Field of Government, taking a neutral, detached perspective and calling out abuses. This mechanism can be disrupted when people whose nature is to be in the Field of Ideas instead work in the Field of Government. They may lose the perspective to offer this service. In general, short-term crises may compromise their natural long-term, overall perspective. Furthermore, in the Field of Government, justice, fairness, and law rightly predominate, but in the Field of Ideas, forgiveness, equanimity, tolerance, and detachment are the ideal. Someone whose nature is in the Field of Ideas may appear, when working in the Field of Government, to be soft on domestic crime and enemy nations. In addition, their own natural detachment from concepts of fame and honor may make it hard for such persons to energize and lead citizens patriotically. Truth will need to be sacrificed for diplomacy, which will be agonizing and difficult for the person whose nature is to be in the Field of Ideas. Sometimes persons in the Field of Ideas may fall prone to "analysis paralysis," spending more effort on collecting and integrating information than is practical for efficient decision making.

Work in the Field of Government may pose a particular problem for those in the Field of Ideas who are naturally inclined to careers at the extreme end of theoretical and "pure" knowledge rather than "applied" knowledge. Such persons are sometimes denigrated as "ivory tower intellectuals." Having people in society who investigate and perhaps teach with little or no concern for anything other than the knowledge itself is essential in society. Unfettered by almost any constraint, such people sometimes inadvertently contribute much good to society. However, when working in Government, the immediate and long-term effects of research and recommendations are primary, rather than knowledge for its own sake. Benefit to society has to be the main consideration, not just a constraint, for work in the Field of Government. Those who stay detached from any such considerations may cause havoc in the area they govern. An ancient example of this situation is found in the *Bhagavata Purana*[84] in the story of King Vena, where persons in the Field of Ideas supported a despot without due consideration for the full scope of the results for the citizens.

We want to make it clear that it is normal for people in the Field of Ideas to work alongside those in government, *as advisers*. Their role is to present the objective truth to those working in the Field of Government and to take the long view. On the other hand, it is the role of those working in the Field of Government to collate all this advice and make decisions for which they are responsible. The need to continually make many decisions with the information and advice at hand, however limited, is fundamentally at odds with the continuous deep, detached study required for the Field of Ideas. Those suited to the Field of Ideas generally want to research and study issues thoroughly before responding, but in government, swift action is often needed. An ill-placed person may feel pressured about decisions, and then agonize over the results.

When people suited for the Field of Government work in the Field of Ideas:

This crossover can result in the politicization of a specific field of knowledge. Knowledge can be bent for political purposes. People's immediate needs, and motives of righteous fame, may dominate over truth. Those who work in the Field of Ideas do best with systems of "mutual adjustment" where the organizational form and hierarchy is fluid.[85] When those with a nature attuned to Government work in the Field of Ideas, they may tend to impose the more hierarchical structure with which they feel comfortable, but such a form stifles the free flow of knowledge. They may also find it difficult to be energized by *vairagya*, and long for their native wealth of *yasa*. They can thus be swayed by acclaim and community biases that swerve them from truth. Interestingly, those suited for the Field of Government may love to "play" with ideas, but the focus of that play is practical action for community development and protection. Areas such as pure mathematics will be neglected as frivolous.

Crossing Resources and Artistry

Both Resources and Artistry deal with the practical needs of society. But those in Artistry tend to focus on craft, quality, and the satisfaction of a job well done, and those in Resources tend to focus on profit, expansion, and quantity.

When people suited for the Field of Resources work in the Field of Artistry:

It is not uncommon for those in the Field of Resources to do some work in the Field of Artistry as part of their own education and apprenticeship, for the simple reason that they often manage people in the Field of Artistry and benefit from practical experience with that work. However, when those whose nature is in Resources work in Artistry as their career, their innate drive for expansion of profit and goods tends to emphasize quantity over quality. Thus, a lot of the *artistry* in the Field of Artistry becomes lost to automation and mechanization. This loss affects the other artisans, people working in the right field, who may end up having to sacrifice the quality of their work in order to compete and survive. When those in the Field of Artistry are pushed to automation, it's as if the very soul of their work is gone. Becoming unhappy and unfulfilled, such persons may resort to intoxicants to ease their pain.

The loss also affects society in general, as low quality products become the norm. Some examples of low quality in the Field of Artistry are fast foods, clothing that becomes fashionably obsolete or falls apart quickly, plastic items replacing metal and glass, entertainment that titillates with gratuitous violence and sex rather than inspiring reflection through plots and character development, and drug-fueled sports. There are several adverse consequences when people become accustomed to low quality in their food, clothing, objects such as furniture, entertainment, and services. One is that the wealth of *sri* in the Field of Artistry diminishes and is no longer distributed in society. People no longer understand or appreciate beauty and splendor. Thus, people in general experience reduced *rasa* in their life.

If someone inclined to the Field of Resources works in the Field of Artistry without having the means to strive for things that are bigger and better, such a person will feel dissatisfied. The drawback is mainly the temperamental differences between people in the two fields. People in the Field of Artistry are generally satisfied with simple living, preferring to focus on honing the quality of their craftsmanship or fulfilling their personal artistic vision rather than on constant expansion.

Generally, people from the Field of Resources who keep working in the Field of Artistry will eventually feel frustrated and dissatisfied because their nature is not given scope to express itself.

When people suited for the Field of Artistry work in the Field of Resources:
When people from the Field of Artistry work in the Field of Resources, perhaps driven to such work because of the career paths within a firm, they will feel frustrated when their superiors relentlessly drive them to keep finding new ways to expand the business, which they are not intrinsically motivated to do.

On the societal level, this crossover is likely to result in waste and inefficiency. Those whose nature is in the Field of Artistry find it tiring to focus on optimal flows of resources over the long haul. A more subtle societal problem with this crossover is due to the laudable tendency of those in the Field of Artistry to be satisfied with the simplest, most direct, and immediate way of fulfilling their needs. In the Field of Resources, however, sustainability of the enterprise depends on cherishing our sources of wealth and field of work, a topic we discuss in Part II. Cherishing natural resources as a whole requires a kind of long-term thinking and big-picture view where ecology, sustainability, and renewal are prioritized at the expense of immediacy. It is irksome for those naturally inclined to the Field of Artistry to have to have such priorities and such a viewpoint. This crossing of fields is one of the reasons for depletion and pollution of natural resources — poor outcomes for humanity and the planet.[*]

6.2   Conclusion

We have outlined only some of the societal and individual harms of crossing fields. The harms help highlight the similarities within each of the four fields, and the differences between them. We hope this description helps one to appreciate the ancient wisdom of the division of the numerous types of careers into four (rather than another number) and into these specific categories of Ideas, Government, Resources, and Artistry. Each category has its own glory, beauty, and ideals that in another category become disqualifications. We propose that this

---

[*]Another reason is that people whose nature *is* to be in the Field of Resources do that work while heavily veiled with the shades of ego, which we discuss in Chapter 8, and without striving to become expert in the art of work, which we discuss in parts II and III.

ancient way of defining broad areas of work provides crucial keys for individuals to have their work contribute to society while aligning that work with their own natures.

It may seem natural when understanding broad categories of people, and especially when understanding what happens when people work and act contrary to their nature, to apply such insight in a negative way to criticize others. After all, this chapter has dealt with the harms of crossing fields, so it may seem the logical next step is to be critical of individuals we may know who have done so! In one sense, seeing how the points in this chapter practically apply to the individuals and society with which we are familiar solidifies our understanding. We may then be filled with respect for the ancient wisdom from which this chapter springs. Part of the natural art of work, however, is healthy and practical humility and compassion. Those who are working in the wrong field — and that might include oneself — will be experiencing some kind and degree of difficulty. They may also have some awareness of how their unnatural situation adversely affects others. But, they may not be aware of the deep cause or the solution. Even after knowing about the four fields, it can be quite tricky to recognize one's own natural field, and those who know a person well for many years can sometimes be mistaken. It is best, therefore, to refrain entirely from finding fault with the character and motives of individuals who have crossed fields. Rather, the knowledge in this chapter can lead us to see that the faults exhibited when one is in the wrong field become glorious qualities when a person is in their natural place. Using this knowledge to see that much suffering for individuals and society is often due not to something intrinsically evil in people, but to unnatural situations, can bring us increased respect for others. Analogously, we can understand that an apple tree cannot produce tasty fruit in the tropics, nor will blueberries thrive in alkaline soil.

Of course, for us to truly take advantage of this ancient wisdom, it is vital to first understand and nourish our own nature. This is what we'll explore in the following chapter.

Chapter 7

Nourishing Our Nature

It is a true calamity in modern society that few people successfully match their work to their nature, and many are not even sure what their nature is! Some people, the lucky ones, circumstantially fall into a career that fits their nature, but for most of us several factors need to fall into place. First, that we recognize that every individual has a way of working and being that is like a personal signature. Second, that we know that all natures are originally value-neutral but can be trained either to benefit or to harm. Third, that we recognize our own nature, and this is best done with others' help, ideally before we reach the prime of life and our main working years. Fourth, both recognition of our nature and the positive use of it generally depend on formative experiences and training.

7.1   Our Personal "Signature"

There is an ongoing debate about what aspects of our nature are inherent rather than conditioned, and to what degree. Various studies emphasize one aspect or the other. At the same time, there are certainly some characteristics of our nature that are a hard-wired part of our genetic makeup. That fact is obvious to parents of several children as they notice the differences between siblings raised in the same environment; and it is clear in the studies of identical twins separated at birth[86][87] where common traits defy the differences in upbringing:

> In 1979, University of Minnesota psychologist Thomas Bouchard and his colleagues chronicled the fates of about 60 pairs of identical twins raised separately. Some

of the pairs had scarcely met before Bouchard contacted them, and yet the behaviors and personalities and social attitudes they displayed in lengthy batteries of tests were often remarkably alike. The first pair Bouchard met, James Arthur Springer and James Edward Lewis, had just been reunited at age 39 after being given up by their mother and separately adopted as 1-month-olds. Springer and Lewis, both Ohioans, found they had each married and divorced a woman named Linda and re-married a Betty. They shared interests in mechanical drawing and carpentry; their favorite school subject had been math, their least favorite, spelling. They smoked and drank the same amount and got headaches at the same time of day....They both had sons whom one named James Alan and the other named James Allan.
  –Lorna Reiko, *Identical twins who were separated at birth: Amazing similarities*[88]

When thinking about what our personal "signature" might be, we notice — as we've examined in the previous chapters — that some of us find life richer when we have freedom and detachment, and some when we have leadership and responsibility for others. Some of us love to work in the Field of Ideas and some in the Field of Resources. Additionally, some of us feel more energized working with people, and others feel more alive when getting projects done alone. As parents and teachers well know, each person exhibits certain traits and tendencies from an early age that keep surfacing regardless of circumstances, and that resist punishment or rewards. Indeed, a study that followed people from childhood over the courses of their careers found:

The participants' passions, preferences and values, already present and measurable at age 13, when weighted and combined with SAT scores, accurately predicted the types of careers in which they would make their mark.

"Prior research has documented that those with higher ability are more likely to achieve eminence," Lubinski said. "But this is the first study to show that qualitatively different *types* of eminence can be pre-

> dicted as early as age 13, by combining information on
> the pattern of abilities and interests, across a 35-year
> time span."
>
> — *Research News*[89][*]

Children may face a problem: parents, teachers, and society imposing upon them a nature that is not their own. Often, such imposition is well-intentioned. Adults want to steer children into lucrative or high-status careers, thinking this will make their children happy. For example, 36% of Harvard graduates go into careers in business consulting or finance, highly prestigious jobs that they often find unfulfilling in the long term.[92] In addition, within some communities, only a handful of careers are considered acceptable, leaving a wide swathe of natures unfulfilled. Sometimes people are pushed into careers because there is a perceived lack. For example, if there are not enough teachers to serve the current population, then government and teachers may strongly encourage students to take up teaching without regard for people's natures. Then, after some delay, there may be an oversupply of people in that line of work. Young people need protection from such early "pigeonholing."

Part of this protection consists in exposing all children to work in all four fields. Not only will this exposure help them find their own place, but it will also give them a healthy respect for fields that are not their own. Besides, as mentioned before, sometimes we all need to do some unsuitable work in emergencies. Moreover, it's likely that most of us will need to use some of the skills from each of the four fields in our own household or family lives as adults at some point.

In general, modern education focuses almost entirely on subjects and instructional methods that are most appropriate to the Field of Ideas, such as analyzing classical poetry. This type of education does not encourage, and to some degree suppresses, many students' personal "signature." Such curricula and methods also imply that everyone can or should go into the Field of Ideas, and that it is the aim of education to achieve this, and the fault of education if it doesn't happen.

---

[*]Readers may note that this study specifically followed children who had been identified as "precocious" according to standardized tests. However, their answers to the Study of Values questionnaire varied independently of the test scores that identified them as "precocious," and it is those values that predicted their fields. The same values may be found in other individuals regardless of precocity — indeed, the questionnaire was not designed for precocious children[90] — although perhaps these values become firm at a different age.[91]

This mindset becomes a pernicious excuse that results in justifying exploitation. If people in the Field of Artistry are facing a constant struggle just to get by and meet their basic needs for food, shelter, heat, and medical care, one paycheck or emergency away from disaster, for instance, it is claimed it must be their own fault for not being educated, or the education system's fault for not educating them. Those doing the exploiting can deny having anything to do with the problem.

7.2 All Natures Are Neutral and Can Benefit or Harm

An important point made twice in the *Bhagavad-gita* is that while we exhibit our nature instinctively, we do not automatically use it in beneficial ways.[93] In fact, children and youth so often misuse their natures that in many cases we can discover our natural work by considering what our parents or teachers most frequently criticized in us![94] For example, during childhood a natural leader may repeatedly hear, "Mind your own business," from exasperated parents and siblings. Natural inventors may be told as children, "Can't you follow instructions?" Scholarly children inclined to solitary reading may be chided to socialize more and get away from their books. Children with desires for the performing arts may be criticized for always wanting to "take center stage." Clint Pulver tells the story of frequently getting into trouble in school as a child for tapping his fingers on his desk. One teacher instead offered him drumsticks and told him to learn drumming. Clint went on to become not only a professional and widely acclaimed drummer, but also a comedian and motivational speaker.[95]

When Richard Rodriguez delved into study in ways that didn't resonate with his family, he found the very qualities that would be most helpful to his future career as a non-fiction writer were a source of confusion for his family:

> Teachers would say to the rest of the class, "I only wish the rest of you took reading as seriously as Richard obviously does." But at home I would hear my mother wondering, "What do you see in your books?" (Was reading a hobby like her knitting? Was so much reading even healthy for a boy? Was it the sign of "brains"? Or was it just a convenient excuse for not helping around the house on Saturday mornings?) Always, "What do you see...?"
>
> –Richard Rodriguez, *Hunger of Memory*[96]

Children with unrecognized or unappreciated inclinations are so often berated and shamed for their natures that many of them struggle through life trying to repress or "fix" the very aspects of themselves they would do best to cultivate.

Therefore, we do well, both with regard to our own nature and to others' natures, to avoid any type of evaluative ranking. Anyone's particular nature is, by definition, best suited to that person as it is an expression of themself. With that said, we can certainly evaluate how a person's nature is *used* in terms of whether and how they *apply* their innate tendencies. Each individual's nature is something like a tool. One can only comparatively rank how "good" tools such as hammers, pliers, wrenches, drills, and screwdrivers are in relation to fitness for particular jobs, not in isolation. One can rank the one who uses a tool in terms of discrimination in applying the tool to appropriate jobs, as well as both skill and motive. If someone misuses a tool, it is the misuse that needs adjustment, not the tool itself.

There are several ways in which we commonly come to recognize our nature. People who know us well and have training in identification of people's natures may inform and guide us. We may take tests specifically designed to reveal our nature. And some situations or people in life may create an impression upon us which give us an "Aha!" type of experience. All those avenues — with the addition of training and practice — can also be ways in which we learn how to use our nature for our highest good and happiness.

7.3   Written or Computer-Based Exams to Decide on Propensity

There are many exams available that attempt to guide us in the right career direction. Undoubtedly, many of these are worthwhile. However, the personal observations of a qualified, unbiased, and helpful teacher, mentor, coach, or parent can often be even more valuable than an impersonal test. We also do well to remember that particular attributes in a person can match a variety of trees of work in a particular field of work. When we use such tests we can, therefore, use them as one part of information among many to help us decide on a career.

There are also, as we mentioned early in the book, many tests to determine not only career but personality style. While many of these tests and categories can be extremely helpful and informative, we are each our own unique individual with a singular combination of traits in various degrees. Therefore, any system of broad personality categorizations will not be sufficient to distinguish precisely what work will be most suitable for us. If, like tests of vocational aptitude, we take personality tests as one piece of valuable information among many, then such tests can serve us well in choosing a career.

One important note about personality categorizations is that all broad types — no matter what system of grouping is used — exist in each of the four fields of work, though not for every specific tree of work. For example, one personality type is "an outgoing people person." People of this type like to be with large groups of people, tend to speak out in such groups, and like activity and change. They tend to be inspirational and fun people. In the Field of Ideas, such persons could be, among many other specific careers, a teacher or professor who teaches more through field trips and activities than lectures. In the Field of Government, such a person could have a career organizing large social gatherings. In the Field of Resources, such a person might manage a human resources department, and in the Field of Artistry a suitable career might be a performer in the entertainment industry.

Finally, we briefly mention intelligence tests such as Stanford-Binet IQ tests. Most educational systems and tests today primarily value and test a narrow definition of intelligence. Furthermore, as we mentioned in Chapter 5, there are often ill-founded assumptions that people with high levels of intelligence should all go into a narrow range of careers, or only work in the Field of Ideas.

The research shows, however, that while people with high IQs tend to have an early advantage in some careers, average IQ persons who engage in intensive, long-term deliberate practice can outpace that advantage:

> Research has also shown that skilled adult chess players — even grandmasters — do not have systematically higher IQs than other adults with similar levels of education. Nor is there any correlation between the IQs of highly skilled chess players and their chess ratings. [p. 228]....In the long run it is the ones who practice more who prevail, not the ones who had some initial advantage in intelligence or some other talent.
>
> —A. Ericsson and R. Pool, *Peak: Secrets from the New Science of Expertise*[97]

Even regarding what is stereotypically most associated with high IQ, namely "genius," the research does not support such a tight association:

> ...although psychologists have often defined genius in terms of exceptional intelligence, the actual empirical relationship between the two phenomena is more ambiguous. No doubt a certain minimal level of intelligence seems necessary to demonstrate significant levels of creative behavior. That is, there exists some threshold level of IQ below which it is virtually impossible to claim any distinctive level of creativity. Although the exact location of this threshold is not known, there is no well-documented case of an eminent creator having a below-average intelligence. Even so, a high level of intelligence by itself cannot guarantee that a person will display an impressive degree of creativity. There are plenty of people with high IQs, for example, who do not seem any more creative than individuals with average or even low IQ scores.
>
> –Dean Keith Simonton, *The Origins of Genius*[98]

Additionally, all the fields of work need people of high intelligence for a prosperous society overall. A highly intelligent farmer, for example, would be able to get higher yields with less land and less work, while nourishing the soil. The optimal course is to take up a career that suits our tastes and what we love, and then apply our intelligence there, rather than seeing intelligence in isolation as an indicator of career.

Such a recommendation was one conclusion of the study we cited earlier that followed children from age 13 for decades over the course of their careers:

> "People stereotype precocious kids, particularly if they have mathematical talent, by assuming they are going to be a scientist," said David Lubinski,[99] co-director of the Study of Mathematically Precocious Youth (SMPY)[100] at Vanderbilt's Peabody College of education and human development.[101] "It's like saying if you're tall you're going to be a basketball player.

> "There are a lot of tall kids who don't want to play
> basketball. It's the same with academic talents. We need
> to really encourage kids to get in touch with not only
> their gifts, but what they are passionate about," he said.
>
> — *Research News*[102]

7.4 Life Impressions That Awaken Our Nature

Sometimes as if by chance we awaken to a new understanding — "Hey,
I like this, I'm good at it, and it is useful!" Such an awakening may
come about by meeting someone — perhaps a teacher — who notices
something positive in us. Or we might find ourselves in a situation
where we get a chance to practice or display our nature in a positive
way. Such life impressions can mark the start of a true calling in life.

The *Bhagavata Purana* tells us that in ancient history, families often planned formal ceremonies and events as a key part of revealing
and then nurturing children's inherent tendencies. The Sanskrit word
for these formal ceremonies and the impressions they create for the
children is *samskara*. Unfortunately, some of these rites, in whatever
culture or tradition, can become over-ritualized to the point that they
lose their original function. The principle of intentional impressions
to help reveal and nurture career tendencies remains important, despite abuse.

Today we refer to people, activities, and situations that are intimately connected with our emotional states as "triggers." While the
word is often used pejoratively, triggers can also be positive. Exposing
our children — and ourselves — to a variety of positive experiences can,
indeed, trigger the awakening of our nature, which may have been
dormant, or even mistakenly repressed, due to our thinking it was a
liability.

Considering the importance of impressions in awakening our nature, and the lack of qualified people to recognize the natures of children and youth, one logical conclusion would be to expose children to
as broad a range of impressions as possible. The hope is that one of
those impressions will resonate with the child. The concept of broad
exposure is part of the basis behind the kind of liberal arts education
seen in most of the world's schools today. It's probably safe to say that
the way in which this education is delivered at the moment renders
it of limited use. One reason for much of education's irrelevance is
that we are broadly exposed not to practical impressions that could

awaken our nature, but simply to a slew of information. Few of us use, on any level, much of what we learned in school. Indeed, we often forget it immediately after the exam, and may feel we are none the worse for that. We propose that a better system would, by age twelve or fourteen, give young people a chance to experience at least some kinds of work in all four fields, and to spend time with people whose lives are filled with all six types of wealth (*sri* or splendid beauty, *jnana* or knowledge, *virya* or strength and health, *yasa* or meritorious fame and community, *vairagya* or equanimity and freedom, and *aisvarya* or leadership, money, and luxury). Unfortunately, modern schools generally give one-size-fits-all education and training, not starting with targeted career classes until age 16, and in many cases age 20. While some specialized training, and opportunities for experience, exist in some schools for younger students, those opportunities are often extra-curricular.

It's rare, if not nearly impossible, for classroom-type education to give young people the range of impressions needed to nourish their natures. Real-world and apprenticeship experiences make a significant difference. Whether in a classroom or on-the-job, teachers also need training to uncover and nurture the hidden tendencies of their students. It is best that such training not only be a required part of teachers' education, but also be given, at least on a basic level, to everyone in adolescence so they can help their own future children.

While growing up in a family, parents' or other older family members' careers certainly give children impressions and a chance to practice particular skills. However, such advantages don't necessarily translate into a successful career suiting the children's natures if those impressions aren't compatible. For example, parents who work in the Field of Resources indirectly — and often intentionally as well — give all their children impressions related to their own field. However, their children may have a personal "signature" in a different field. Such impressions from the family will not, therefore, help them, and may even confuse them. In perhaps an ironic twist, such incompatible impressions may sometimes help us discover our nature by experiencing what we don't want.

7.5   Training to Nurture Nature Positively

Life impressions are often necessary to first awaken an understanding of our nature, much like a seed awakens in water and warmth. But to mature into a healthy plant, the seed needs ongoing nourishment. Eric Windhorst references a number of sources (such as Hillman and Dabrowski) to compare the nurturing of our nature to the growth of an acorn into an oak tree. He reminds us 1) the path to a full expression of our nature takes patience and is often fraught with obstacles, 2) even through difficulties, having a sense of an inner calling can give us resilience, 3) our development to our own nature is ultimately personal and individual, 4) a need for support and nourishment is life-long, not just in an initial period of training, 5) each individual has an essential contribution he or she can make to overall existence, and 6) development, like all else in nature, has times of development and times of rest.[103] In a similar way, training grows a person's nature, which impressions have awakened. The kind of training varies significantly depending on the respective field of work, and even on the individual tree of work. But for all trees of work, training encompasses three areas: values, skills, and information.

Training in career-specific values

In every field of work, and for every tree of work (specific career), people need training in the values specific to that work. As we discussed in earlier chapters, the ideal ethics for each field can be summarized in the following questions. In the Field of Artistry, they ask: Is it supportive? Is it beautiful? In the Field of Resources, they ask: Is is sustainable? Is it regenerative? In the Field of Government, they ask: Is it just? Is it honorable? In the Field of Ideas, they ask: Is it true? Is it wise? On the flip side, for each field, we do well to learn how to recognize the particular ethical and moral challenges of our work, both in specific behaviors and in types of egoistic thinking. We discuss the corresponding shades of ego to which people in specific fields particularly fall prey in Chapter 8. For any type of work in any field, it is wise if at first people make a point of philosophically examining the situations they encounter in terms of the values of their field as well as their more generally held values. This may require a regular practice of journaling or group discussion, perhaps with like-minded peers and mentors.

Eventually, these concerns will become so ingrained that inner guidance by these values will become nearly automatic. We discuss these overall pitfalls and remedies in Part II.

Training in career-specific skills

Perhaps the most obvious area of training is in the skills needed in each field of work. At one extreme are jobs where it is common to train and practice skills for the entire length of one's career. Trees of work in the Field of Artistry such as dance, music, fine arts, athletics, and so forth, are some of the most typical examples. In the book *Peak*, authors Ericsson and Pool[104] detail the experiences of people who undertake a lifetime of painstaking practice for hours each day. Those who are outstanding in their careers have usually already put in 10,000 hours of practice (specifically, as the book describes, "deliberate practice," which we'll describe in greater detail later in this chapter) by the age of 18. That's 20 hours a week over 10 years! While most people in such careers may be satisfied with achieving and maintaining a lower level of excellence than those at the top, a sense of dedication to training is important. It's also worth mentioning that some skills, again perhaps mostly in the Artistry Field, have windows of opportunity for training. For example, perfect pitch can be trained, generally speaking, only between the ages of 2 and 6.[105]

> If ballet dancers are to develop the classic turnout — the ability to rotate the entire leg, beginning at the hip, so that it points directly to the side — they must start early. If they wait until after their hip and knee joints calcify — which typically happens between the ages of eight and twelve years — they'll probably never be able to get a full turnout. The same sort of thing is true for the shoulders of athletes, like baseball pitchers, whose sport requires them to throw a ball with an overhead motion. Only those who start training at an early age will have the requisite range of motion as adults, with the throwing arm able to be stretched well back behind the shoulder to produce the classic wind-up. And something similar holds true with the motion tennis players use when serving — only those who start young have the full range of the serving motion.

–Ericsson, Anders; Pool, Robert, Peak: Secrets from
the New Science of Expertise[106]

There is also a sensitive period between 6 and 12 months of age for infants to hear the sounds of more than one language. If they only hear the sounds of a single language during this period, then their brain's auditory processing becomes specialized to distinguish only the phonetic categories that exist in their native language.[107] In that case, their ability to understand even speakers of their native language who speak with foreign accents, let alone to understand or speak a foreign language, becomes impaired, limiting their educational and career opportunities later in life. Other sensitive periods have been found related to other aspects of language acquisition, visual processing, and musical training.

At the other end of the spectrum is what we commonly term "unskilled labor," which also generally resides in the Field of Artistry. While such workers usually require a modicum of skills training in the beginning, that training period is short, there's rarely a "window of opportunity," and the level of competency required is low. No one has a global reputation for expertise in, for example, trash collecting or ditch digging.

Between the intensive career-long practice and training required for a top-level chess player and the brief, cursory skills training required for a janitor or fast-food cook, are most of the trees of work that can be classified as *semi-skilled* such as a flight attendant, or *skilled*, such as a nurse. Skills that need training fall into five categories:

- motor, such as how to play a violin or secure a food cart;

- sensory, such as how to judge when various foods are properly cooked or how to discern how likely it is that a particular visual presentation will help students achieve optimum learning;

- emotional, such as how to listen empathically or stay focused in a hospital emergency room;

- mental, such as how to memorize large amounts of information, how to compute answers to simple math problems, or how to operate software and apps; or

- intellectual, such as how to analyze information into categories and then resynthesize that information into another format, or how to evaluate arguments using rules of logic.

Most careers require some combination of these types of skills, and many skills are transferable from one tree of work to another, particularly within the same field.

Training in career-specific information

In addition to training in values and skills, there is training in knowledge or information. We may gather knowledge just about our own tree of work. We may learn about a wider area of the field, or we may learn how the trees and fields cooperate and compete, topics we discuss in Part III of this book. In certain trees of work in the Field of Government and the Field of Resources, comprehensive knowledge about the interrelationships among specific careers and overall fields is essential to the job. By definition, many trees of work in the Field of Ideas require a base of knowledge, whether specific, broad, or both. The more a career involves working with systems, the broader the knowledge base needs to be. In all cases of knowledge training, if we stay on the level of only memorized information, we will never approach expertise in our work. At the very least, it's best to get to the level of assimilation or understanding of that information, so that we can translate the information into a form that includes our personal realization.

Information we cannot apply through skills rarely helps anyone, and most values and skills require at least a modicum of information and understanding. So, there is an interrelationship among these three areas of training. At the same time, each career requires its own balance of the three, with commensurate training in each. For example, training in cooking, swimming, and teaching will be incomplete if it's only or mostly information-based.

Unfortunately, some education systems focus almost entirely on information training, and teachers often don't even ensure that learners understand that information.[108] However, dynamic, increasing mastery is one of the main components of job satisfaction[109][110] An increasing sense of mastery and advancement depends on training. Therefore, both initial and ongoing training beyond memorized, unassimilated information is essential to the natural art of work.

Role of teacher or coach

Most careers require training under a coach or teacher of some sort, especially in the beginning. Ericsson and Pool[111] have thoroughly explained, particularly for highly skill-based careers, a system of what they term *deliberate practice* as differentiated from simply doing the same thing over and over again. In sum, deliberate practice comprises:

- developing skills that others have done, for which there is effective training, under an expert teacher;

- always pushing beyond one's current abilities with almost maximum effort, which may not be fun;

- clear and specific interim goals with full conscious attention to them;

- modification in response to feedback, at least initially from an expert teacher;

- having effective mental representations of success overall and for each level; and

- building on top of existing skills.[112]

Relationships with teachers can be especially crucial when people have a nature and career inclinations that significantly differ from their families, as in this account of a "scholarship boy" from a "working class family" (i.e., somebody who could not afford an expensive education without a scholarship) who became a journalist and editor:

> He [the scholarship boy] cannot afford to admire his parents. (How could he and still pursue such a contrary life?) He permits himself embarrassment at their lack of education. And to evade nostalgia for the life he has lost, he concentrates on the benefits education will bestow upon him. He becomes especially ambitious. Without the support of old certainties and consolations, almost mechanically, he assumes the procedures and doctrines of the classroom. The kind of allegiance the young student might have given his mother and father only days earlier, he transfers to the teacher, the new figure of authority....I came to idolize my grammar school teachers.

> I began by imitating their accents, using their diction, trusting their every direction. The very first facts they dispensed, I grasped with awe. Any book they told me to read, I read – then waited for them to tell me which books I enjoyed. Their every casual opinion I came to adopt and to trumpet when I returned home. I stayed after school "to help" – to get my teacher's undivided attention.
>
> –Richard Rodriguez, *Hunger of Memory*[113]

While there is ample empirical evidence that most people can become very good at almost anything through tens of thousands of hours of teacher-directed, intensive, focused, and somewhat painful regular practice, the *Bhagavad-gita* and *Bhagavata Purana* have an additional perspective.

Looking first at the relationship between teacher and student, gaining of expertise goes beyond training in values, skills, and understanding from someone more expert. In the *Bhagavad-gita*, Krishna explains that a teacher needs literally to perceive, or see, underlying universal principles and truths of what is being taught.[114]Ideally, a teacher of anything would be a person in the who can directly perceive underlying patterns and the big picture of ultimate reality, not just the small piece he or she is teaching. Before accepting any teacher, prospective students do well to carefully test and examine that teacher's qualifications in order to avoid blindly following them. During this time of testing, students' questions to the teacher help to ascertain whether or not to accept that teacher as an authority.

Accepting a qualified teacher does not entail merely a mechanical transfer of values, skills, and information. There is a kind of energy, in Sanskrit called *shakti*, that empowers and enthuses an authentic teacher-student relationship. This energy is a kind of enthusiasm enlivening the connection from teacher to students, so that the student is graced with this wisdom and insight. This enthusiasm is not necessarily spectacular or showy, but a discerning observer or participant can perceive a deep wellspring flowing from teacher to student:

> Students gravitate toward teachers with whom they have forged a connection. Learning is an emotional experience, and mentorship is rooted in the intimacy of intellectual exchange. Something important passes between

you, something almost sacred…great teaching…reaches deep inside you. It satisfies desires that you didn't know you had. It makes the world feel newly large and meaningful.…The other thing that students say about their favorite teachers is "he changed my life."
                        –William Deresiewicz, *Excellent Sheep*[115]

Just as the teacher's ideal qualifications include being able to perceive the deeper overall principles of what is taught, so the student's ideal qualification according to the *Bhagavad-gita* is to take a position of teachable humility. This humility is demonstrated through practical assistance to the teacher in a mood of willing giving, and through asking questions. Questions reveal doubts, clarify points, and express eagerness to learn. Questions after having tested and accepted a teacher are generally not aimed at challenging the teacher's authority. The ideal student does not disrupt the learning process by continually or persistently bringing up irrelevant or far-fetched points.

Looking next at the purpose and mood of practice, the *Bhagavad-gita*[116] defines practice in relationship with establishing a connection. If, for example, in the Field of Resources we are practicing how to chart and influence the flow of money and goods, we want to do so with a feeling of connection to the people who create and consume the goods, to the source of the goods such as the Earth, and ultimately to the source of everything. If in the Field of Government we are practicing protecting the community, we want to do so with a feeling of connection and service to those we protect and to the land itself, as well as a sense that we are mere stewards on behalf of the divine guardian of all. Ideally, practice done in this way brings as much joy as performance, and such joy increases with time and expertise.

7.6   Practice as a Type of Impression

Identifying a career and practicing the skills needed for that career have an interesting relationship. Whether in the areas of values, skills, or information, some sort of deliberate practice is essential, both as part of initial training, and to maintain or increase a competency. Beyond playing those roles, getting some experience with deliberate practice for a particular career can also be a good indicator of whether that career truly matches our nature.

In *Decisive*, Chip and Dan Heath suggest something they call "reality testing" whenever we are faced with a decision — and what career to choose is certainly a major decision. Part of reality testing is something they call *ooch*, meaning "to conduct a small experiment to test your hypothesis."[117] In other words, if someone feels that being a technician in a hospital's pathology lab is the right job, it is wise to spend some time in volunteer or apprenticeship positions in such a lab before deciding on extensive classroom or formal training in that career. It can also be helpful to ask people who have been in that career for a long time, and especially to ask people who tried that career and switched to a different one, what they find to be the biggest upsides and downsides to working in that career. The upsides and downsides they feel may be quite different from what we would feel, due to their different natures. However, they have a perspective on aspects of the work that only become apparent over the long term, which may be valuable for us to take into account. Keep in mind that while it's wise to stay in the overall field corresponding to our nature, a variety of "trees of work" or specific occupations exist within each field of work and we may switch among these trees within the same field over the course of our lives.

We suggest, in addition to directly testing how one likes the work itself, that one get a sense of how much enjoyment there is in the ongoing deliberate practice of what is needed for the job. Often a key indication of whether a job matches our nature is how easy and joyful the initial practice is. But more important is how we feel when the practice regularly pushes us out of our comfort zone and becomes hard work requiring steady determination. While we may never find that kind of practice to be fun in the sense of relaxing entertainment, the right kind of career gives us the pleasure of expressing ourselves and what we are meant to be.

When practice intensely and regularly pushes us out of our comfort zone to the point where it becomes a drain and a chore, then either we have reached the highest level of expertise that we desire, or it may be time to change direction entirely. A change of direction might be to a similar tree of work in the same field, where our skills are also useful. Or a change might mean relegating a career to a hobby, or to the trash.

A final consideration about practice: suppose a person circumstantially does a particular kind of work without much direction or training. Without training and practice in the values, skills, and information connected with a particular career, it might be hard to do that job well. Even a person whose nature is to work in that career might find untrained work boring and uninspiring in such a situation, and not recognize his or her own latent nature in it.

7.7 Sample Ideas of Specific Training for Each Field

Young people who are inclined to the Field of Ideas do well to study classic literature, systems of logic, and debate, with emphasis on skills related to research, writing, calculating, and speaking. They can write for student publications and engage in peer counseling, peer advising, or peer tutoring. They might benefit from taking the initiative to start learning about cognition, by the end of secondary school if possible. For example, *Make It Stick: The Science of Successful Learning* succinctly presents counter-intuitive notions that significantly enhance learning, teaching, and communication.[118] Developing their own word problems (at whatever level of mathematics they are studying), and solving them together with their peers in all fields, is a helpful practice that strengthens logical faculties, structures thinking, and highlights ambiguities in the mappings between words and reality. This practice also helps mathematical concepts become *instruments de pensée*, or tools for thought. If these young people take advantage of every opportunity to apply mathematics (of whatever level) in real-life situations, sooner or later they will inevitably have the singularly edifying experience of seeing a seemingly logical argument fall apart when confronted with data. Such an experience will help highlight gaps in their thinking and prod them to find and question hidden assumptions. In this way, they will develop discernment of the power and limitations of logic, language, observation and experience, learning to balance trust and skepticism in each — key ingredients of wisdom. They may also take advantage of opportunities to learn about public speaking, such as the Toastmasters International Youth Leadership Program. They need to understand at least the basics of philosophy, especially epistemology (or theory of knowledge), and the basics of linguistics, especially semantics and pragmatics. (Otherwise they would end up using an epistemology and semantics built from unsound foundations that would continually trip them up.) Integrating cognitive science into philosophy is a strong advantage to develop; the philosopher Paul Thagard, for instance, practices such integration.

Those inclined to the Field of Government can take part in organizations such as secondary school student government, though often students in these programs do not have enough authority in their schools to gain actual practice. There are also forensics competitions (speech and debate tournaments), at least in the USA, called student congress, which gives some familiarity with the work of the American legislator (though without direct power over anything). Similarly, the Model UN gives simulated practice in international relations. Exposure, perhaps through film and role-play, to a diverse set of tactics and strategies for preventing, calming, smoothing, and otherwise settling quarrels is crucial. Real-life practice is ideal for developing intuition about the efficacy, time horizons, tradeoffs, and limitations of these various tactics and strategies. The methods described in the books *Difficult Conversations*[119] and *Crucial Conversations*[120] comprise some of these tactics and strategies. Taking advantage of any opportunities to organize camps, outings, community service, etc. would be ideal for youth inclined to the Field of Government. They also do well to learn about leadership, finances, law, history, political theory, debate, oratory, persuasion, rules of order, game theory, emotional intelligence, and possibly martial arts. Travel is particularly helpful.

Those in the Field of Resources can benefit from running businesses or projects according to what is suitable for their age, learning about leadership and motivation, studying flows in economics and the natural world, learning the basics of accounting, and perhaps getting training in entrepreneurship and agriculture. *The Fifth Discipline*, for example, presents counter-intuitive insights that will be profitable for people in the Field of Resources to learn, such as taking the time to get genuine enthusiasm for ideas from one's subordinates rather than merely communicating one's own vision. Another example involves getting the best out of teams in business, in this instance smoothing out tension between the "two cultures" of R&D (Research & Development) and Marketing. (We note that members of these departments often come from the Field of Ideas and the Field of Resources respectively. Each department would also include members from the Field of Artistry.) When John MacCarthy became president of the innovative hard drive manufacturer DataQuest Drives, he brought together members of the management team, including Joe Grauweiler, head of R&D, and Charlie Smyth, head of Marketing and Sales. These two departments had been at odds for thirty years.[d121]

The book details the groundwork that facilitated a fruitful dialogue among the management team, and how it led to greater cooperation within the company. (We discuss cooperation between fields of work within society, mirrored here as different departments within a firm, in Chapter 33 in Part III.)

A helpful training practice for the Field of Resources is to trace the full life cycle of products and services that people in the Field of Resources encounter in life: what labor and materials came through what routes, how the products or services are used, and what happens to the laborers, component materials, and routes afterward. Different kinds of cycles can be correlated on calendars or more sophisticated charts. Visits to ports or hubs through which cargo is shipped can be helpful. Young people can also learn about the rise and fall of larger enterprises through reading memoirs and history, through hearing from mentors who are, or have been, engaged in such enterprises, and through investing in real or fantasy portfolios.

The Field of Artistry contains the widest variety of trees of work. With exposure to many, one or more of these types of work are likely to catch and hold the interest of the child inclined to the Field of Artistry. Those in the Field of Artistry do well to receive early impressions and practice in the areas of their interest, focusing on achieving automaticity of skills. As we've mentioned, while such early training is very helpful, the choice of a particular tree of work is not set in stone; people in the Field of Artistry can continue to shift to different trees of work within that field throughout their lives, as their own interests, and demand within society, shift. The cultivated discipline required to achieve automaticity of skills is itself a kind of meta-skill, which the person in the Field of Artistry can continue to reuse in different contexts. Deliberate practice, as we alluded to above, is a key factor in this cultivated discipline.

7.8   Scenarios

Let's consider some hypothetical scenarios for people in each of the four fields. Please keep in mind the multiplicity of trees in each field of work! Each of these scenarios applies only to persons in a portion of each field.

Field of Resources:

Ren's father has a university degree in science and runs his own computer business. His mother runs a tutoring business. Ren taught himself basic arithmetic. When he was in primary school, he decided that his mother's students might need some office supplies. He convinced his father to help him source high-quality supplies like pencils and so forth at wholesale prices, which he then sold to the students for a small profit. (Other children often start by trading candy, stickers, and so on.) Ren loved to play games, mostly ones that involved strategy and memorization, and he was very competitive and hated to lose. Ren used to get in trouble with his parents and teachers for refusing to follow rules and wanting to do things his own way. Adults also often got annoyed with him because he would tell them how to manage things better. He started a food business while in primary school, making frozen treats from fresh juice and selling them to his father's customers. He helped in his father's business while still a child, at first getting paid to collect the trash, and later learning how to build and repair computers, as well as doing accounting. Ren started working regular jobs when he was in secondary school, and in his twenties, he was managing a textile company while he got a university degree in business. Ren gradually learned about various aspects of running a company, until he became a general consultant to many kinds of business. That work enabled him to work from home part-time and help his wife with child care, but it also involved some travel.

In this scenario, we find Ren has a natural joy in finding opportunities for moving the flow of resources to help others and gain financial benefit for himself. He was fortunate to gain experiences in production and business, which left favorable impressions upon him, though he also irritated his family and teachers with his strongly held views on improving systems of resource flow.

Field of Ideas:

Lei's father was a computer programmer, and her mother did social work. Lei was always cheerful and responsible, and kept to herself. As a child, she would spend many hours writing stories and researching areas of science and history. Lei often got so absorbed in her reading, research, and writing that she lost track of time. Her parents frequently admonished her for being unaware of her surroundings and uninvolved in family matters. Lei also got in trouble for asking endless questions, especially at around age twelve. When she took up an area of study, she would carefully read the books on the topic, and put into practice what she was studying. Lei often went to the library, and took out only books on science. When she was a teenager, her family moved to an area near the ocean. In the local university, she took an introductory class on marine biology, where she loved the professor's interactive teaching style and extensive fieldwork. By the time Lei was twenty-seven, she had a career along with her husband doing field research for the university in marine biology, in ways she could also involve their children.

In this scenario, Lei as a child demonstrates her taste for research, study, and writing, along with some social detachment. As a teenager or young adult she was able to gain direct impressions of a scientific career. Again, we note that her tendencies attracted some criticism from family members during childhood.

Field of Artistry:

Tua grew up in a big city where his mother was the administrator of a science museum, and his father a professor of ecology. Tua would regularly stay at his mother's museum after school. He liked to sit near the displays and sketch pictures, particularly of the animal scenes. While his mother taught classes to school groups at the museum, he would sketch her points as if illustrating a book. Tua was always in trouble in school for drawing pictures of nature instead of paying attention to the class. There were frequent disciplinary meetings between his teachers and parents, and at one point his parents removed all his art supplies for two months as a punishment. When he was ten, Tua started to learn the flute after school, and he would practice daily for many hours. As a teenager, he became interested in film creation. His parents felt he was wasting his time in film and refused to get him any equipment. They were mostly concerned about his failing grades in English and math. Tua finally found some film classes he could take after school without his parents' knowledge, where he would have access to equipment for editing film. He stopped his formal education after high school and apprenticed with various filmmakers until he started experimenting with nature documentaries that combined photography, his own nature paintings, and background flute music. By the time Tua was thirty, he was able to work almost entirely from home, other than when he was doing photography or drawing in nature.

In this scenario, we find a situation where the nature of the child is quite different from the nature of the parents, which elicits strong disapproval from both his family and teachers. He had to arrange for his own training against his parents' wishes, and got his experiences mostly through working on his own desires when he was expected to be doing other things.

Field of Government:

Ziar's parents were dairy farmers near a small town. Ziar loved to play chess from the time she was five and often played against a computer as her parents were not expert. She would watch the History Channel on television and read books on history. She often got into trouble for complaining about things being unfair. "Life's not fair," was something she heard many times a week. By the time Ziar was twelve, she was involved in collecting petitions to change the way cattle were treated in her area, and she volunteered in the local homeless shelter. As a teenager, she joined the high school debate team and student congress and got elected as vice president in the student government. Ziar would complain to the school principal and even the school board about unfair grading and attendance practices. Her parents didn't approve of her activism and kept telling her not only that life was unfair, but to mind her own business and be satisfied with her lot. Ziar took a year off after secondary school to work in a pro bono law office, got a university degree in history, married a man who became a court judge, and served on the city council of the area when she was raising a family.

In this scenario, we again find a difference between the nature of child and parents, with the parents trying to change the child to be more like themselves. Her interest in fairness and happiness in aiding social justice are key indicators of her nature. She arranged for her own experiences and also took advantage of formal educational opportunities.

Conclusion

In each of the above scenarios, we find evidence of a person's nature from childhood. However, unless perhaps their own nature is similar, parents and teachers are likely to find the child's nature irritating at times, and may even attempt to squelch it completely. Through a combination of impressions and training, each person was able to find, as an adult, a career that matched his or her nature.

However, life doesn't stop when we find the right career! There are still problems that can arise and that ancient wisdom can help us navigate. This will be the focus of the rest of Part I.

Because practice right after learning something is the best way to solidify understanding, please turn now to Appendix B, which will help you understand your own nature with respect to the six kinds of richness and the four fields of work.

Chapter 8

Fields of Work and the Shades of Ego

Much career advice stops at the point of matching one's work to
one's nature. While such a match is crucial to happiness in work,
the strengths and talents inherent in our nature also contain intrinsic faults that can trip us up. In this and the following chapter, we
examine two of those faults — the shades of ego and the cycle of frustration. Here, we examine the former, which prevent us from gaining
satisfaction through our work.

8.1   Prosperous Pleasure or Shrouding Shades

We have been looking at matching our nature and career in terms of
the ancient categorization of four fields of work. All these metaphorical fields, each containing a large variety of trees of work, are situated
in the greater ecosystem of the world. In the *Bhagavad-gītā*, we learn
that the energy of this universe is divine and spiritual.[122] In ordinary
conversation, we often refer to Earth and Nature as if to the consort
of God — Father God and Mother Earth or Mother Nature. As a divine and spiritual force, Nature is the energy of prosperity and all six
types of richness. Ultimately, this energy epitomizes the pleasure of
loving *rasa*. When we deal with Mother Nature properly, we get prosperous pleasure. Mothers care for their children with affection, but
they can also, out of affection, correct and reprimand their children.
Even a very loving mother might tell the school authorities or police
if her child is stealing and being violent. In a similar way, how we re-

late to the total universal energy determines whether we experience a spiritual loving energy in our work and our lives or a restraining and punitive one.

In this chapter, we will summarize ancient knowledge of the three degrees or kinds of coverings of nature we face when our work is out of harmony with cosmic truth. We often find ourselves feeling restrained by thoughts and actions that do not serve our interests and happiness. These thoughts and actions can throw us out of alignment with our work, leading to dissatisfaction both in ourselves and in those we interact with in our career. Such a situation means a type of shade covers our awareness and satisfaction, which we call a shade of ego (or equivalently, ego shade).

Ultimately, one mistake switches our experience with Nature from prosperous pleasure to shades of ego. That fundamental mistake is imagining that we are the center of existence. Thoughts, feelings, and actions based on this idea immediately put us out of harmony with reality. We may think of reality as a universe or biosphere governed by mathematical and scientific laws, or we may conceive of reality as a neutral energetic living force, or a beneficent Supreme Being. Regardless of which understanding we embrace, we are left with the logic that harmony with truth will make us happy and disharmony with truth will bring frustration. And, the fact of the matter is that none of us is at the center of reality. Life is not about us. We are not the most important being there is.

Imagine a complex dance performance with many dancers each playing their own role, sometimes synchronized, but always harmoniously supporting each other. Sometimes a particular dancer dances at center stage, or even alone. Always, however, each dancer contributes to the whole performance as a unit. If a dancer decided to take center stage outside of the normal choreography of the dance, there would be chaos. Our bodily cells are supposed to function in the same way. Each has its role to play as part of an organ or a system — our body. Sometimes a part of our body takes metaphorical center stage, but in a healthy body the emphasis is always on unity and coordination. When bodily cells decide to take center stage outside of the normal functioning of the body, that condition is called cancer. The same is true of individuals in the universal body. We may not be consciously aware that we are attempting to be #1. We unconsciously mask our desires with quiet justifications. Logically and rationally we all know we are insignificant and are on this Earth for a brief blip of time, so it can be difficult to understand how our thoughts, feelings, and behaviors aim for center stage.

8.2 The Three Ego Shades

What are the shades of ego that distort our perception and prevent prosperous pleasure? Several chapters of the *Bhagavad-gita* give an analysis of the shades of ego. Self-centered egotistical mindsets exist on a continuum, which can be roughly divided into three forms.

Imagine a room with one large window, and a sunny day outside. Clear glass in the window allows a person to see almost as well as being outside, but the glass is rarely completely clean, and it has a limiting frame around it. If there is translucent glass in the window (as commonly found in shower or toilet rooms), then light and vague shapes can be seen outside. If the window has thick curtains across it, then the outside can't be seen at all. In this analogy, the outside represents complete and unfiltered reality, where we gain the full prosperous pleasure of a match between our nature and our career. The clear glass window represents a thin ego shade and is called *sattva*. A translucent glass window represents a moderate ego shade and is called *rajas*. A thick curtain represents a dark ego shade and is called *tamas*.[*]

We are using the Sanskrit terms because they describe subtle concepts, and often using just one word as an English translation communicates only part of the concept, but we'll define these terms further in a moment. What's important is the idea that shades of ego, by distorting reality, also interfere with the connection between our nature and the happiness we derive from our work, just as windows and window coverings interfere with our connection with the outside — and the darker the shade, the worse the effect.

Let's look at the different shades of ego. It's important to note that the following descriptions of them may in some cases seem natural or desirable. However, pay attention to the words "I," "me," and

---

[*]Some readers may be familiar with polyvagal theory, which delineates three bodily states. These states may be loosely designated as "socially engaged," "fight-or-flight," and "freeze." They correspond to different patterns of neuroendocrine activation, each associated with a neuroanatomical complex: the ventral vagal complex (VVC), the sympathetic nervous system (SNS), and the dorsal ventral complex (DVC).[123] Researchers have suggested that the VVC state corresponds to *sattva*, the SNS state corresponds to *rajas*, and the DVC state corresponds to *tamas*.[124] The details of polyvagal theory are far beyond the scope of this book, and readers who are interested can explore further.

"mine" while reading the descriptions, as an indirect indication of the degree to which one imagines oneself to be the center of existence is the frequency with which these words crop up in one's language. We can pay attention to our own use of these words to become aware of the sometimes very subtle ways that the fundamental mistake of self-centeredness creeps in.

Sattva is related to the Sanskrit word *sat* (pronounced *sut* to rhyme with *hut*) and means that which is authentic, lasting, and beneficial. It is often translated as goodness, or as illumination. The *Yoga-sutras* describe *sattva* as "illumination" while the *Sankhya-karika* describes it as "light" (as opposed to "heavy") and "luminous."[*] The ego shade of *sattva* is: "I am wonderful because I am in balance and harmony . I am equipoised. I am peaceful. I forgive because of the wonderful feeling I get from being full of forgiveness and equanimity. I don't care for the praise of the world or outward things. My inner happiness, peace, and equilibrium are superior to the striving and desires of most people. I can generate my own happiness within. I see everyone equally. I do not create enemies."

Rajas indicates a mood of energetic, external striving for bigger and better things of this world, both for the body and the mind. It is often translated as passion or attachment. The *Yoga-sutras* describe *rajas* as "activity" while the *Sankhya-karika* describes it as "exciting" and "mobile."[†] For the body, a person in *rajas* wants expansive sensual pleasures, and for the mind a person in *rajas* wants praise, honor, and acknowledgment. The ego of *rajas* is: "I am wonderful because I am a dutiful and responsible person. I am a moral citizen and (maybe) a religious person. I contribute to the world by giving charity and many good works through a lot of sacrifice and energy. I support forms of philosophy, art, and culture. I'm concerned with moral and ethical principles, justice, and fairness.[130] I see a diversity of persons and species and work hard for their rights and privileges. I'm strong and defeat my enemies in a fair contest. Others will respect me for all I've done in the world. I've increased and expanded good works for myself, my loved ones, and others."

---

[*] The *Yoga-sutras* comprise a guidebook for practitioners of solitary, exclusive meditation and use the Sanskrit word *prakāśa*.[125] The *Sankhya-karika* describes analytical ontology and uses the Sanskrit words *laghu* and *prakāśaka*.[126] The latter word also appears in the description of *sattva* in *Bhagavad-gita*[127]

[†] The *Yoga-sutras* use the Sanskrit word *kriyā*[128] and the *Sankhya-karika* uses the Sanskrit words *upaṣṭambhaka* and *chala*.[129]

Tamas can mean darkness, ignorance, and delusion. It is a kind of complacency. The *Yoga-sutras* describe *tamas* as "steadiness, immovability, or inertia,"[131] and the *Sankhya-karika* describes it as "heavy" and "enveloping."[*] Like *rajas*, *tamas* relates to pleasures of the senses and pride rather than to the inner satisfaction of *sattva*. But, unlike *rajas* and *sattva*, there is not much drive to accumulate or earn these pleasures. Those in *sattva* have unbreakable determination to achieve inner peace, and those in *rajas* have strong determination to achieve external things as long as success looks possible. On the other hand, the determination in *tamas* is for external things that can be easily gained today and now. The ego of *tamas* is: "I am wonderful because I am satisfied with my family, my work, and having the basic good things in life. I know how to do my work and that's enough. I do what I can to be a good person, at the same time being practical. If something makes me and the people I like happy right now, I don't worry much about the consequences. I'm not very ambitious to do something great in the world. I'm good at focusing my concern on my own circle, my own tribe, my own territory, and keeping others separate. I'm really good at getting even with my enemies and putting them in their place."

Sattva dominates the celestial plane, *rajas* the earthly realm of humans, and *tamas* the natural world of animals, plants, and objects. However, all three tend to be present to some degree in a mixture in almost all persons. (We, the authors, also continue to find each of these shades arising in us in the course of our lives.)

A careful study of human psychology may lead to an understanding similar to that which the *Bhagavad-gita* presents. For example, various thinkers label ego in terms of *having* (corresponding to *tamas*), *doing* (corresponding to *rajas*), or *being* (corresponding to *sattva*).[133] One in a "having" ego consciousness defines identity and self-worth in terms of possessions. In the "doing" ego consciousness, one's identity and value is understood in terms of one's external achievements, and in the "being" ego consciousness, one defines identity and worth in terms of inner qualities such as love, kindness, and so forth.[134]

---

[*]The *Yoga-sutras* use the Sanskrit word *sthiti* and the *Sankhya-karika* uses the Sanskrit words *guru* and *varanaka*.[132]

8.3   The Shades of Ego and Fields of Work

No matter what our field of work and our specific tree of work may be, we can get overcome by self-centeredness anywhere along the continuum of egocentric mindsets. However, for each of the four fields of work, a particular shade of ego poses a particular pitfall for people in that field, like an occupational hazard. For one thing, it's easiest to draw the energy and motivation needed to do work in the particular field from one or perhaps two of the shades of ego. For another thing, the process of doing the work of that field itself may foster some of the self-concepts associated with that shade of ego. We could say that the ego shade that a field of work is likely to encourage is the "dark side" of the intrinsic value of that field.

For example, the Field of Government emboldens the ego shade of *rajas* in those who work there. Recall from Chapter 4 that the driving questions of the Field of Government are: "Is it just? Is it honorable?" We can see how easy it is to slip from making these questions the center of one's active hours, to making "I'm concerned with moral and ethical principles, justice, and fairness" a central part of one's identity and deriving ego satisfaction in this way. Furthermore, the Field of Government naturally generates *yasa*, or righteous fame, characterized by praise, honor, and acknowledgment from others. Tasting that recognition can naturally lead to wanting it to continue and even increase. Both this identification of oneself as a moral citizen and this thirst for prestige are characteristic of the ego shade of *rajas*. The Field of Government is concerned with public service and can be the most essentially other-centered of the four fields. So it's particularly ironic that this self-centered mistake, the ego shade of *rajas*, can so insidiously creep in and partially or wholly replace the focus on others in one's motives and decision making. Not only may one not be aware that this shift has happened, it may even be difficult to recognize within oneself when someone else points it out. So taking time for reflection and self-examination is essential. Since the public always has many needs to be met, it's easy to let time for introspection fall by the wayside as one continually engages in frenzied activity (another characteristic of the ego shade of *rajas*). However, prioritizing and committing to self-reflection is essential for ensuring one's activities are well-directed and efficacious. This precaution can also help avoid the many problems that arise from the ego shade of *rajas*, some of which we'll describe further in Part II.

Those who love the Field of Artistry tend to be naturally satisfied with a basic life. The complacency and inertia of the ego shade of *tamas* can be a negative aspect of that otherwise laudable quality. As we described in Chapter 3, work in the Field of Artistry can provide immediate feedback and directly provide pleasures. One sees the relief or pleasure on the face of the person one has helped; one sees the increased beauty of the place one has cleaned up or the art one has made; one sees the object one has fixed working well. This direct and instant gratification can facilitate the state of flow, as we mentioned in Chapter 4, leading to fulfillment and satisfaction with one's work. However, the flip side is that one can easily fall into the mental habit: "If something makes me and the people I like happy right now, I don't worry much about possible long-term consequences. I'm good at focusing my concern on my own circle, my own tribe, my own territory, and keeping others separate." Such mental habits characterize the ego shade of *tamas*.

In the Field of Resources, a mix of the ego shades of *rajas* and *tamas* tends to emerge. As we described in Chapter 3, those in the Field of Resources have an insatiable thirst to increase profit, yield, and efficiency. To motivate ourselves to engage in this in an expert way, and as a result of doing so, it is easy, almost natural, to fall into thinking: "I contribute to the world with charity and many good works through a lot of sacrifice and energy. Others will respect me for all I've done in the world. I've increased and expanded good works for myself, my loved ones, and others." Such thinking characterizes the ego shade of *rajas*. Moreover, working in the Field of Resources requires intense concentration on what is going on in one's own enterprise, immediate environment, and surrounding trends, something we described in Chapter 4. It is easy to fall from such concentration into thinking in the ego shade of *tamas*: "If something makes me and the people I like happy right now, I don't worry much about the consequences. I'm good at focusing my concern on my own circle, my own tribe, my own territory, and keeping others separate."

The Field of Ideas tends to encourage the ego shade of *sattva*. To work expertly in the Field of Ideas requires objectivity. The Field of Ideas naturally generates *vairagya*, or detachment. This detached, neutral perspective in turn leads one to a sense of being balanced in one's thinking and one's life. It's all too easy to go from such a state of balance to thinking: "I am wonderful because I am in balance and harmony. I am equipoised." This is a kind of pride in *vairagya*. Pride in *yasa*, or righteous fame, can be pierced directly by others' criticism (from which there is no escape in this world), and pride in other kinds of richness can be pierced when they are taken away, by others or by circumstance. However, since *vairagya* cannot be taken away by anything outside oneself, and great *vairagya* includes indifference to the praise or criticism of others, pride in *vairagya* is particularly difficult to get rid of. This pride is one of the drawbacks of renunciation that we go on to describe in Chapter 21.

Besides *vairagya*, the Field of Ideas requires *jnana*, or knowledge, and generates more *jnana*. With one's mind constantly fixed on the realm of pure ideas and knowledge, one can easily slip into thinking: "I don't care for the praise of the world or outward things. My inner happiness, peace, and equilibrium are superior to the striving and desires of most people." These kinds of thoughts characterize the ego shade of *sattva* and can be quite tricky to avoid. Yet there is an obvious tension, bordering on a contradiction, between thinking "I see everyone equally" and "My state of mind is superior to that of most people." This fundamental mistake separates us from integrity and our connection with reality.

So, here we see the danger that the work that suits us may also bewilder us. We suggest regular introspection and self-reflection as a key means to avoid these ego traps in each field. While such a regular practice is essential, it is often not sufficient. We discuss further guidelines throughout Part II, particularly in Chapter 25 and Chapter 27. Our recommendations for achieving egolessness — a state beyond the shades of ego — constitute safety precautions against the occupational hazards posed by the shades of ego associated with particular fields of work.

8.4   The Relationships Among the Shades

Though we described the shades of ego as simply and directly corresponding to fields, the three shades of ego combine into millions of mixtures, just as the three primary colors combine into millions of hues. To make matters more complicated — ouch! — as we alluded to above, the three forms of self-centeredness are not only associated with fields of work. From times of day, to types of food, to how we speak — all can be analyzed as under the influence of these three shades of ego. They compete for supremacy in all spheres of life on Earth. Returning to the metaphor of a window, we can perhaps more easily remember that these shades exist on a continuum. In other words, each tree of work tends to engender different degrees of obstruction and clarity of consciousness. Also, the shades are nearly always mixed. One could have a window that is partially clear, partially translucent due to dirt or other factors, and partly covered by a curtain. Still, there is a general connection between the kind of work one does and the particular egocentric way in which one may tend to perceive the world.

Therefore, one may be tempted to use one's current dominant shade of ego as a diagnostic for what work one is suited to do. It is more accurate, however, to say that particular shades of ego pose occupational hazards of specific fields of work rather than that they indicate one's choice of work. It is also problematic to use one's current inclination to a shade of ego as a diagnostic for one's field. The reason is that any shade of ego can arise in and affect people in any field of work. Indeed, those who work expertly in their own natural fields are better able to avoid the shades of ego that are occupational hazards of those fields than those who work in unsuitable fields.[135] It may be that in our own natural field we are better able to metaphorically use the "tools" of the field without getting injured in the process. In any case, the shades of ego cause problems no matter when and where they arise. The *Bhagavad-gita* says:

> Sometimes *sattva* becomes predominant, surpassing *rajas* and *tamas*. Sometimes *rajas* surpasses *sattva* and *tamas*, and sometimes *tamas* surpasses *sattva* and *rajas* . In this way the shades of ego are always competing with one another for supremacy.
>
> — *Bhagavad-gita* 14.10

So the shades of ego tend to come in waves, one succeeding the other. Though in a particular person at one point in life, one shade of ego may be more predominant more of the time, in general as time passes all the shades of ego play a part in a person's life. Since the influence of the shades of ego may dramatically change in one's life due to factors unrelated to one's work, determining or changing one's field of work based on the shade of ego that is predominant at a given time is not practical. Generally it is best that people stay in the same choice of the four fields of work, the one that best suits their temperament, throughout their career, for the reasons we explained in Chapter 6.

Regardless of one's field of work, some long-term behaviors can change what shade of ego tends to predominate in a person's life. For instance, various types of food and entertainment tend to increase one shade of ego or another. Most chemical intoxicants increase either *tamas*, *rajas*, or a combination of those, and the regular use of any intoxicant has a profound influence, in general, on how deeply one's awareness is in the shade of egoistic perspective rather than the light of reality.

Going one step further, how do the shades of ego apply to people whose "career" involves criminal activity? Deep in the lower echelons of the ego of *tamas* are persons who are so attached to the idea of easy results without caring for consequences that they sometimes become involved in criminal activities. Or they seek *rasa* primarily in things that only vaguely imitate *rasa*, such as intoxicants and some types of video games. In terms of livelihood, no matter what ego shades or mixture influence a person, criminal or harmful means of livelihood generally have an influence of the darker portions of *tamas* in the mix. Criminal activities are usually a misuse of any of the four fields of work, or a mixture of more than one field. (So two steps in reforming criminals would be to identify their proper field of work and to reduce their shades of ego — the same process recommended for the rest of us.)

The complacency, inertia, and lack of clear perception associated with the ego of *tamas* may cause a person to begin or continue to follow a boss to the detriment of oneself and/or others. Such bosses may require their subordinates to do anything from cutting corners to engaging in dishonest, corrupt, or illegal activities in the course of their work. These bosses may also require the subordinates to work in ways that have a high likelihood of causing them long-term injury or burning them out. Such bosses may also cheat their subordinates in additional ways.

A good thing to keep in mind is that if we see that our supervisors don't care to be honest or considerate of others in general, then our supervisors probably aren't being honest or considerate with us either, even if they occasionally take steps to persuade us otherwise in order to get us to keep working for them. The idea that "My boss is honest, considerate, and fair with me, despite not being honest, considerate, and fair to others," i.e., "My boss treats me specially," is inherently an egocentric idea. At some point it may be relatively true, perhaps because the boss considers the employee as part of the circle of extended ego centering on the common tribe. However, the fundamental mistake, whether in the boss or in the employee, is that the idea that "My boss treats me specially" is an illusion, and to rely on its persisting in the same form is like building one's house on sand. Whenever the going gets tough, such bosses may narrow their egocentric circle so the employee suddenly finds themselves on the outside. Though at that point they may feel betrayed, at a deep level they would have participated in setting that situation up, by buying into the joint egocentric illusion. Or, the boss and employee may go down together, having jointly cut themselves off from the whole by their tribalistic (i.e., extended egocentric) mentality. In any case, this egocentrism would all along have separated the employee from greater possibilities for finding meaning in their work, through serving the greater whole rather than exploiting some parts of it.

Of course, one can also unfortunately be forced by circumstances to work for such an exploitative boss. Regardless of how one gets into such a situation, it drains away some of one's possible fulfillment in work. Such a situation can also itself heighten *tamas*, sometimes leading to a vicious cycle. While the remedy for a particular situation may be tricky to find and to execute, moving toward the greater clarity of *sattva* can be an important first step.

8.5 Three Kinds of Determination

The ego shades are not confined to obviously negative states.

In every line of work, no matter how closely aligned it is with our nature, there will be tasks that we definitely don't feel like doing. These tasks may be tedious, unpleasant, or even dangerous. They may occur regularly and we may have to spend many hours on them.

Depending on our upbringing and circumstances, our entry into the world of work may be the first time in our lives when we are faced with this aspect of reality. Many of us as children say, "I can't wait to grow up so then I can do what I want!" It's only once we do grow up that the reality hits us like a bucket of cold water: we are bound as responsible adults to spend much more time and energy on tasks we don't feel like doing than we did as children.

How, then, can we have every moment of our work be fulfilling? Many people would suggest that the only way to get through these kinds of tasks is through determination.

Intuitively, when we hear the word "determination," it sounds like it must be a positive quality. It certainly can be, yet a common theme in the *Bhagavad-gita* is that seemingly positive qualities can be lightly or heavily darkened by the shades of ego. Indeed, this insight is one of the most powerful, and at the same time most accessible, in the *Bhagavad-gita*. This theme will come up several times as we describe the art of work. In particular, let's look at the three kinds of determination:

> Darkened [determination] is foolish and cannot break free from dreams, fears, lamentation, melancholy, and delusion.
> –Vraja Kishor, *A Simple Gita*[136]
> — *Bhagavad-gita* 18.35

This is determination, darkened by the heaviest shade of ego, *tamas*. In the context of this book, persisting in a field of work that is not aligned with one's nature is the premier example of a situation that, over the long term, requires this "darkened determination" and, concomitantly, further darkens our determination.

Determination darkened by the medium shade of ego, *rajas*, is described in the *Bhagavad-gita* as follows:

> [Feverish determination] latches on to materialistic results, motivated by attachment and desire for specific rewards.
> –Vraja Kishor, *A Simple Gita*[137]
> — *Bhagavad-gita* 18.34

Intuitively, this sort of determination seems reasonable. However, in modern terms, this state is what is called extrinsic motivation. In Daniel Pink's book *Drive*, he details research on what inspires and motivates us, especially in our work. There he highlights that this kind of external motivation, while it can work in short bursts, is not sustainable over the long term.

Finally, we have the form of determination darkened by the lightest shade of ego, *sattva*:

> O Arjuna, that determination which is unbreakable and which, through the practice of yoga [connection], firmly holds the mind, vital force, senses, and deeds, is determination in *sattva*.
> — *Bhagavad-gita* 18.33

This determination comes not from without, but through connecting with the Source within. The natural arts of work we detail in parts II and III increase this type of inner steadiness and joy in work holistically, as one of the ways to combat the shades.

8.6 Ways to Combat the Shades

Considering the role of the shades as occupational hazards that we described earlier, one may ask, "Why should a person do work that may tend to increase a shade of self-centered ego to which they are already predisposed? Won't that work simply increase their self-centeredness?" The simple answer is that it is true such a danger exists. Indeed, if persons try to find happiness only by matching their nature to a type of work, they risk solidifying the preexisting stranglehold of one ego-centered shade on them. As Janis Joplin sang long ago, "Why is love like a ball and chain?" People who recognize this problem often use three ways to attempt to avoid it, none of which we recommend in general. Let's see what these are.

The first alternative is to find a way to live without having a career at all. Indeed, some people take such a path. We discussed such persons, commensals, in Chapter 3. For most of us, however, we want both a regular source of income and satisfying work, so this alternative will not be suitable.

The second alternative sometimes presented is that one should intentionally work in a field that doesn't correspond to one's nature, and thus will not feed one's ego-centeredness. Although certain philosophical traditions adopt this approach, acting in this way would be painfully trying to be what we are not. Aside from all the points we have made so far about the good of matching nature to livelihood, one definition of *our nature* is how we will act even if we try to repress it. Defined in that way, not acting according to our nature is impossible. For example, if we don't use our nature in our work, we may use it in a hobby. If we have no positive outlet at all in which to express our nature, we will express it negatively. The *Bhagavad-gita* directly links thinking one will act against one's nature with ego-centeredness.[138] We can see that putting energy into maintaining a false self-concept is ultimately self-centered, even if the identity we are trying to assume may itself be other-centered. (In general, this can be a subtle issue, and guidance from the outside perspective of a mentor can help detect it.)

Yet a third alternative is to try and move one's dominant type of ego to a lighter shade on the continuum, or to switch to a shade that is not the associated occupational hazard of our particular field of work. Indeed, most of what humans do to improve life individually and collectively is simply moving along the spectrum of ego shades or combining them in various ways. Because the shades exist on a continuum and as mixtures, people in *tamas* will, indeed, experience an increase in their quality of life if they add more *rajas* to their life. As another example, simply changing one's diet to fresh, organically grown, lovingly-cooked, violence-free vegetarian food will increase *sattva* in a person's life. Learning how to organize one's life and mind to be more productive will increase *rajas*. Avoiding entertainment that idolizes theft and violence will decrease *tamas*. These practices, as well as others we describe later in this book and practices from other traditions, are intended to reduce the shades of ego or remove them altogether.

We will find partial and temporary value in the categories of ego shades that give us greater clarity. But, even people in *sattva* will experience waves of *rajas* and *tamas* that overwhelm them sometimes, and *sattva* itself is a type of egocentric shade. It's a fairly common experience to feel we had increased the goodness in ourselves and then be surprised when we act, speak, or even think in ways we regret. So, while it is overall a good idea to have *sattva* dominant in our life, full satisfaction only exists when one is beyond the shades of ego entirely. After all, even if we try to feel satisfied with temporary, partial, and unstable progress, we will find that moving along the continuum, or changing their mixture, we remain egocentric to various degrees, and therefore out of sync with reality, as already discussed.

We've looked at ways people may try to separate their naturally corresponding field of work from the shade of ego to which they are predisposed in an effort to be less ego-centered. Each of those ways — not having a career at all, working in a field whose occupational hazards differ from the shade of ego we tend to, or changing our shade of ego — has difficulties. The answer is perhaps counter-intuitive. We will be cured of our egocentric mood if we work in our own natural field while following certain principles. Those principles remove the shades entirely, leaving us metaphorically in the full light of the sun with no intermediate window at all. In such a situation, each field brings out our ideal corresponding qualities rather than inflaming the egoistic "dark side" of those qualities.

Chapter 9

What is my nature: Goals of life

As explained previously in Chapter 3, the impetus or drive for any activity — whether in what we call work or anything else — is to experience varieties of pleasure and relationships, called *rasa*. Everyone's work is motivated by a desire or hope of enjoying *rasa*. To use our tree analogy, a particular tree may produce oranges. When the tree keeper eats that orange, he or she experiences the *rasa* of physical sweetness and perhaps of emotional appreciation. Metaphorically, our specific tree of work produces some fruit, or result, that we enjoy and that gives us a reason to continue working. Thus we experience *rasa*. As explained in previous chapters, those results will be one or more of the six types of richness, and the opportunity to spend time in the areas of life we enjoy "playing" with.

Ancient texts describe that, generally, human beings go through four steps in an attempt to experience *rasa* through the richness of the fruits of their work. The first is called dharma, which, as we mentioned earlier, is a complex word, difficult to define. Dharma can mean the essential definition or quality of something without which that something loses its identity. Some examples are the saltiness of salt, and the sweetness of sugar. Similarly, each work has its dharma, whether we consider individual trees of work, or the four broad fields of work. In terms of the fields, the dharma of the Field of Artistry is beautiful help for those they serve. The dharma of the Field of Resources is regenerative sustainability of resources. The dharma of the Field of Government is honorable justice for all those under their care. The dharma of the Field of Ideas is truthful wisdom for the world.

We do the dharma of our work to gain benefit, or in Sanskrit, *artha*. Again, a complex word, *artha* means something of value. Ideally, if we are in the right field of work and are cultivating a congenial tree of work in the proper way, the products of that tree will be the kinds of richness we like, and we will experience *rasa*. If, on the other hand, we work hard to maintain a tree of work that is not congenial to our nature, then we may exchange that work's products for money, which we then use to purchase our preferred form of riches elsewhere. While the latter situation is less desirable for many reasons, either way we procure some or all of the six forms of riches (*artha*) through doing our work properly (dharma). The result, *rasa*, satisfies our mind and senses. The Sanskrit word for such satisfaction is *kama*. *Kama* can also mean desires or even lust. We work, get riches, use those riches to fulfill our desires, and in that process experience *rasa*. This is the natural process of life.

However, as we have all experienced, that three-step process of work to riches to satisfaction is far from certain. Such is the case even if we are in the right field for our nature, even when we are nurturing a tree of work that perfectly uses and challenges our skills and generally yields the right combination of the kinds of richness we desire in order to experience *rasa*. Symptoms are that doing our work is frustrating or boring instead of putting us in a state of flow, or that our tree of work produces little or no riches, or the kinds of riches it produces do not inspire us. Most ironic of all is when everything is perfect but we are still not satisfied — due to the temporary, transitory, and difficult nature of the world. For example, when we have the perfect career in all respects, there may be an underlying fear of loss of one or all aspects of it. That fear undermines our pleasure.

Therefore, the last natural step for most people after work-wealth-pleasure is freedom. In the fourth stage of this process, we may seek freedom from the specific job, or even from the desires that propel us to live and work at all. The Sanskrit word for this goal of life is *moksha*, liberation. Those who are frustrated trying to enjoy *rasa* in this world may get involved in political and social liberation movements. Or they may try to "liberate themselves" from the particular job, location, relationships, and so forth, which comprise their life at any particular moment. Or, they may take to a form of religion or spirituality to find a form of transcendent relief.

However, attempts at liberation often fail wholly or partly, and a person decides to try again to earn riches and *rasa* through worldly duties. Thus, liberation can lead right back to the same cycle of duties: duties-wealth-happiness-liberation-duties, etc. Thus, the hope to become fulfilled through matching nature to career becomes instead a cycle of frustration. For example, the United States is one of the most religious and charitable democracies. After WWII, America was a wealthy superpower and the population used its wealth for the luxuries of life. But the generation born into such pleasures sought a type of freedom from work, family, education, and a "normal life" in the counter-culutre movement (sometimes called the hippie movement). The vast majority of those who decided to "tune in, turn on, drop out" found their "freedom" disappointing and returned to the world of duties, wealth, and pleasure-seeking.

On an individual level, we see this cycle of frustration play out over the lifespan of some people who, after working, gaining wealth, and enjoying that wealth, retire to find freedom. Retirees may find that they become bored with their freedom, however, and yearn to return to the workforce. Such is especially the case when people retire young – perhaps because they no longer need to work for an income – but the phenomenon can happen even when retirement occurs in old age.[139]

On a small scale, we may experience the cycle of frustration when we work hard at school, enjoy the prosperity of knowledge and the honor of our community, and then find freedom in a long summer break or a gap year. After looking forward to the time away from work, we may find ourselves soon longing to get back into work.

The ancient sources suggest a fifth goal of life that can help us out of our frustration – love. Srinath Chakravarti, in his 16th-century book *Chaitanya-mata-manjusha* – a commentary on the *Bhagavata Purana* – wrote in an oft-cited verse that to achieve natural love of God is the highest perfection of human life.[*] This was also taught by Jesus Christ:

> "Which commandment is the first of all?" Jesus answered, "The first is:…'you shall love the Lord your God with all your heart, and with all your soul, and with all your mind, and with all your strength.' The second is this: 'You shall love your neighbor as yourself.' There is no other commandment greater than these."
>
> –Mark 12:28–31

---

[*]The original Sanskrit is: *prema pumārtho mahān.*

Indeed, we find much career advice telling us to choose work that not only matches our nature but which also both expresses and increases love in ourselves and others. Loving relationships are an essential element of *rasa*, without which we get a shadow, but not the substance, according to the *Bhagavad-gita*,[140] as we mentioned in Chapter 3.

Love, specifically spiritual love, takes us out of the cycle of frustration, as well as removing the shades of ego. Learning to incorporate love in our work, as well as the principles to make work an art, make up the rest of this book.

Chapter 10

The Priest and the Shoemaker

In thinking about the four goals of life, and how love supersedes them all, this traditional instructive story is illuminating. One person is constantly engaged in supposedly spiritual pursuits, and the other apparently just does his work, but who's actually the more spiritual and satisfied? The story is as follows…

The sage among the angels, Narada, flew in the sky and was dancing as he flew from the Kingdom of God to Earth. While he danced, Narada played his veena (a sitar-like stringed instrument) and sang about God.

Narada landed and began walking. There a priest saw him. Every day this priest prayed to God for people who paid him, asking the Lord to give them wealth, health, and whatever they wanted, including liberation from *samsara*, the cycle of birth and death. He took three ritual baths a day to be very clean, and studied many holy books in great depth with much care. He performed all his priestly rituals exactly according to the scripture he studied.

The priest asked Narada, "I know you are going soon to meet the Lord. Would you please ask him when I'm going to get liberation? I want to be free from *samsara*."

"All right," Narada agreed. "I'll ask him."

As Narada walked on, he met a shoemaker who was sitting under a tree across the street from his shop. The shoemaker's work involved strong dyes and leather, which meant that his apron and clothes were always stained, and therefore he could not follow the strict rituals of cleanliness. He had never gone to college, nor had he gotten any formal education in holy books. His spiritual practice was simple — he liked to sing all day about God, and he did his best work making and repairing shoes to make people happy.

When Narada walked by, the shoemaker asked him, "Are you going to see the Lord? Will you please ask him when will I be with him in his kingdom?" Narada gave assurance that he would ask.

When Narada Muni went to the kingdom of God, he did as he promised and asked the Lord about the priest and the shoemaker.

The Lord replied, "After his body dies, the shoemaker will come here to me."

"What about the priest?" Narada asked.

"He will have to stay there for many more births and deaths. I do not know when he is coming," the Lord said.

Narada contemplated this answer for a long time, and couldn't understand it. Then he said, "Please explain this mystery."

The Lord smiled, "You will understand soon. When they ask you what I am doing in my own kingdom, tell them that I am putting an elephant through the hole in a needle."

When Narada went back to Earth, he went to the priest's house. The priest asked, "Have you seen the Lord? When did he say I will get liberation?"

Narada answered, "He said he does not know, but it will be many births and deaths."

"Hmph!" scoffed the priest. "What was he doing?"

"He was putting an elephant through the hole in a needle," Narada answered.

"I don't believe such rubbish," the priest shouted. "I don't think you really saw him at all!"

Narada then left and went on to the shoemaker, who asked him, "Have you seen the Lord? Would you please tell me what he was doing?"

"He was putting an elephant through the hole in a needle," Narada replied.

The shoemaker began to cry in love for God, "Oh, my Lord is so wonderful. He can do anything."

"Do you really think that the Lord can push an elephant through the hole of a needle?" Narada asked.

"Why not?" the shoemaker said, "Of course I think it is true."

"How could it be true?" asked Narada.

"You can see that I am sitting under this giant banyan tree," the shoemaker answered, "and you can see that so many fruits are falling every day. In each seed there is a banyan tree like this one. So we see that the Lord put a big tree within a small seed. Is it hard to understand that the Lord is pushing an elephant through the hole of a needle, too?"

Narada started to dance. "The Lord said you will go to his kingdom at the end of this life," he said, and the shoemaker danced with him.

Part II

The Art of Work: Individuals

/ Chapter 11

Honest Work of Value

"Strive for yoga [connection], which is the art of all work."
— *Bhagavad-gita* 2.50

The four ways [to have work of value] are earning to give,
advocacy, and research, as well as direct work.
—Benjamin Todd, *80,000 Hours: Find a fulfilling career
that does good*[141]

 In this endeavor there is no loss or diminution, and a little
advancement on this path can protect one from the most
dangerous type of fear.
— *Bhagavad-gita* 2.40

From the moment that human beings first stared into the sky,
contemplated their place in the universe, and tried to create
something that bettered the world and outlasted their lives,
we have been purpose seekers.
—Daniel Pink, *Drive: The Surprising Truth About What
Motivates Us*[142]

In Part I, we explored ancient wisdom about the benefit of linking our
nature to what we do for a livelihood and some ideas for how to make
that link. We also discussed the pitfalls that can trip up even those
whose work matches their nature — in particular, the cycle of frustration and the shades of ego. Now in Part II we discuss some ways
in which, as individuals, we can gain truly prosperous pleasure while
avoiding those pitfalls. The first aspect is to have work that is of real,
felt value for oneself and others. It's useful to keep in mind, as we

set out in Chapter 2, that value goes beyond money and that different types of value are not completely interchangeable. A very basic reason to do valuable work is that doing so provides the worker with much greater satisfaction. For example, in Pink's research,[143] he lists "purpose" as one of the three key elements of fulfilling work — along with autonomy and mastery:

> On average, our pool of American workers said they'd be willing to forego 23% of their entire future lifetime earnings in order to have a job that was always meaningful. The magnitude of this number supports one of the findings from Shawn's recent study on the Conference for Women. In a survey of attendees, he found that nearly 80% of the respondents would rather have a boss who cared about them finding meaning and success in work than receive a 20% pay increase. To put this figure in perspective, consider that Americans spend about 21% of their incomes on housing. Given that people are willing to spend more on meaningful work than on putting a roof over their heads, the 21st century list of essentials might be due for an update: "food, clothing, shelter — and meaningful work."
>
>   –Shawn Achor, Andrew Reece, Gabriella Rosen Kellerman & Alexi Robichaux, *9 Out of 10 People Are Willing to Earn Less Money to Do More-Meaningful Work*[144]

Frederick Herzberg's research[145] uncovered a similar key category of job satisfaction, which he called "responsibility." In short, we are satisfied with our work when we have practical evidence that whether or not we do our job, and do it well, makes a real difference to the quality of life for ourselves and others. In his well-known book *Flow*, Mihályi Csíkszentmihályi[146] devotes a long chapter to how to have a satisfying life both during and outside our working hours, through finding meaning in what we do.

Conversely, a singularly painful experience is the disappointment, sadness, or even bitterness we feel when our need for meaning and value is not met. For example, when we work for hours or days on something that never gets used, or gets criticized, we wonder why we "wasted our time." If we got paid for our work, at least the money symbolized that someone assigned some degree of value to what we did. But Herzberg's research shows that payment alone is not enough.

However, we then face a very peculiar question — what do we mean by meaning? How do we know our work has value? As W.H. Auden wrote in his 1947 essay *Squares and Oblongs*:

> The poet is capable of every form of conceit but that of the social worker: — "We are all here on earth to help others; what on earth the others are here for I don't know."
>
> –Wystan Hugh Auden, *The Complete Works of W. H. Auden: Prose. 1939–1948.*[147]

11.1   What Makes Honest Work

The first step in meaningful work is to make sure our work is honest. Perhaps the most obvious tenet of honesty is that what we receive in various forms of wealth for our work represents the real worth of that work in the ordinary sense of *worth*.

There is a general human tendency to assume that the price of an object or service accurately represents its quality, worth, or value. Thus, expensive placebos are more likely to produce relief or cure than are inexpensive ones.[148] However, deciding on the value of our work by what we charge for it is not a reliable measure.

> When value is determined by price (rather than vice versa), the level and distribution of income seem justified as long as there is a market for the goods and services which, when bought and sold, generate that income. All income, according to this logic, is earned income: gone is any analysis of activities in terms of whether they are productive or unproductive.
>
> Yet this reasoning is circular, a closed loop. Incomes are justified by the production of something that is of value. But how do we measure value? By whether it earns income. You earn income because you are productive and you are productive because you earn income. So with a wave of a wand, the concept of *unearned income* vanishes. If income means that we are productive, and we deserve income whenever we are productive, how can income possibly be unearned?
>
> –Mariana Mazzucato, *The Value of Everything*[149]

In the broadest sense, honest work is fair to the worker, the consumer, the employer, and so forth. In contrast, dishonest work is hoping to get wealth with no giving of commensurate goods or services. A gross form of such dishonesty is outright theft, and a subtle form is gambling in games of pure chance. Those whose view of reality is obscured by the thick curtain of *tamas*, as explained in Chapter 8, may be particularly inclined to gain an unfair advantage in work, or even inclined to criminal activities.

While the concept of fairness is universal,[150] how the concept is understood can vary widely:

> There is more than one way to decide who is deserving of what. One is by need: Some people have more than they need, and others need more than they have. Even when liberal leaders describe policies that are beneficial to everyone, they make it clear that the most important beneficiaries are those whose needs are most urgent....Still, there are other ways of judging what's fair. Conservatives tend to value equity, or proportionality, and they see unfairness when people are asked to contribute more than they should expect to receive in return, or when people receive more than they contribute.
>
> –Dan Meegan, *Conservatives Have a Different Definition of 'Fair'*[151]

For the second step in meaningful work, we can turn to researchers such as Abraham Maslow,[152] who presented what he termed a hierarchy of needs, and others such as Marshall Rosenberg, who gave a list of human needs[153] as well as emotions that accrue if those needs are either met or unmet. Looking at Maslow's needs, we can find a connection between needs and the fields of work. For example, he lists physical needs for food, water, moderate temperature, etc. There are also needs for safety, which includes law and order. We have needs for community, autonomy, and, ultimately, being fully who we are, dynamically, in the service of the greatest whole of which we are a part. When our work meets ultimate needs — which in their highest expression deal with the spirit — then our work is also meaningful in an ultimate sense.

Combining these two steps, we can say that our work is honest when it is both fair and directly provides for the needs of ourselves and others, as when we contribute to produce food, build houses, enforce societies' laws, enhance relationships, increase wisdom, and ultimately nourish the spirit's needs for love, freedom, joy, vitality, and understanding. We can also provide for these needs indirectly through sharing the various forms of wealth that result from our work, as we describe in Chapter 14.

11.2 Work That Harms Directly or Indirectly

However, if our work produces or supports something completely frivolous that leads to undesired results, or that fills what are often termed "manufactured needs," then we can categorize our work as less valuable even if it's fair. Manufactured needs are actually new desires created by advertising in order to make us feel lacking and extract money from our pockets:

> The consumer *champion* is seen as a rational maximizer, expressing their rights and freedoms in the marketplace (and in society more widely), fulfilling basic and higher order needs. In contrast, the consumer *dupe* is a forlorn figure, manipulated and controlled by the corporate marketing and advertising machine. They are viewed as unthinking automatons swayed by the fickle superficial dictates of fashion, forever comparing themselves to others in the race to fulfill manufactured needs, surrounding their lives with superfluous material items and leading a largely meaningless life because of it.
> –Matthew McDonald, Stephen Wearing, *Social Psychology and Theories of Consumer Culture: A Political Economy Perspective*[154]

Beyond the lack of meaning when our work contributes to "manufactured needs," we will certainly not find meaning in our work if, directly or indirectly, we have a career that *deprives* others of their needs, such as doing work that appears to offer something to meet needs when it does the opposite.

An example of this would be the promotion of diamond engagement rings costing one or two months' salary. "Three-quarters of American brides wear a diamond engagement ring, which now costs an average of $4,000."[155] The De Beers company, through an aggressive advertising campaign with the ad agency N. W. Ayer, begun in

1938 (in the midst of the Great Depression), changed the cultural customs of engagement and marriage to convince people that spending a month's salary for a diamond was a "need" whereas previously millions of people had married without any idea that such a financial sacrifice for a gem was required or even desirable:[156]

> In the 1980s, De Beers ran a campaign to reset the norm to two months' salary. The ads said things like, "Isn't two months' salary a small price to pay for something that lasts forever?" The story from the campaign stuck, and De Beers' "two months' salary rule" is still widely accepted in the US today.
>
> –Lindsay Kolowich Cox, *The Engagement Ring Story: How De Beers Created a Multi-Billion Dollar Industry From the Ground Up*[157]

Another example would be manufacturing cigarettes or working in other industries that damage public health:

> Internal documents from a major tobacco company show that executives struggled with whether to disclose to the Surgeon General what they knew in 1963 about the hazards of cigarettes, at a time when the Surgeon General was preparing a report saying for the first time that cigarettes are a major health hazard.
>
> The executives of the company, the Brown & Williamson Tobacco Corporation, chose to remain silent, to keep their research results secret, to stop work on a safer cigarette and to pursue a legal and public relations strategy of admitting nothing.
>
> –Philip J. Hilts, *Tobacco Company Was Silent on Hazard*[158]

"Needs" created by addiction to harmful products are the clearest cases of manufactured needs. A person feels that manufacturing needs, or producing harmful "goods" or "services," is a fit way to work when they are at least partially under the *tamas* ego shade.

The situation becomes more complex when we consider not just the products and forms of wealth our work produces but the means of production. For example, if we produce food by torturing animals or destroying the rainforest, it causes harm to society and internal harm to ourselves. When clothes are manufactured in factories that expose workers to unsafe conditions, the work's value is decreased both in terms of fairness and harm. The process of work is best when it is also valuable in the sense that both the process and result are meeting our own and others' needs throughout the work chain, from conception to consumption.

To detect and avoid any direct or indirect harm our work might cause requires consulting with a variety of others. We all tend to have blind spots about people from various groups or circumstances with which we're not personally familiar. We not only don't know how different aspects of our work might affect them, we don't even necessarily know *that* different aspects of our work might affect them. In other words, we don't know what we don't know. So, ensuring the full value of our work requires intentionally making an effort to include people who ordinarily lie at the periphery of our consciousness — i.e., are marginalized — and asking them whether and how they are affected.

For example, in the summer of 2015 and again in the summer of 2017, videos were published showing that automatic soap dispensers in public restrooms that functioned for people with lighter skin would not function for people with darker skin. It's easy to understand how this could have happened. When engineers were designing and testing the sensors that detect hands under the soap dispenser, nobody involved in design or testing had dark skin, so none of them noticed the problem before these soap dispensers were manufactured and deployed on a massive scale.

The soap dispensers, obviously, being inanimate objects, don't "intend" to exclude dark-skinned people. If we asked individual engineers involved in the design or testing, they also could honestly say, "I didn't intend to exclude dark-skinned people. It was an inadvertent omission." Clearly, not intending to exclude them was insufficient. To avoid situations like this requires us to intend *not* to exclude them, i.e., to intend to include them (and whoever might be marginalized in a given context), and to take efficacious action to put those intentions into practice.

It is also desirable to look at both short- and long-term value versus harm. If both the process and results of our work help us and others to meet needs in the present but "sow the seeds of further suffering"[159] then the work is not a meaningful contribution overall. Therefore, work has value when both the process and results of that work in the short and long term meet needs of the worker and others in the society, without concomitant harm to anyone else's needs. It is not necessary, or generally possible, to eliminate absolutely all harm from both processes and results, however. The *Bhagavad-gita* states that there is always some fault in all types of work, in the same way that there is some amount of smoke present wherever there is fire.[160]

When considering both the processes of our work and the forms of wealth it produces, our motives are almost as important as our actions, though actions are primary. We can note that even seemingly valuable work, when done out of malice, envy, pride, vengeance, greed, and so forth, may not honestly meet anyone's needs. For example, junk food manufacturers appear to be creating value by producing food, but they've intentionally engineered food that induces people to overeat, without providing much nutritional value.

When we discussed the ego shades (in Chapter 8) of *tamas*, *rajas*, and *sattva*, we mentioned the idea of clarity of consciousness. When we are but slightly covered by the ego shade of *sattva*, we can clearly understand the long-term results of what we are doing, and we are keenly aware of our own motives. As we descend into *rajas* and *tamas*, that clarity becomes increasingly obscured and distorted. We then rationalize our need to harm, if we are even aware that we are doing harm. For example, company managers may rationalize skimping on worker safety as a necessity for profitable productivity. Someone with clarity of consciousness, however, understands the opposite to be true. As an example, when Paul O'Neill took over Alcoa Aluminum, he emphasized having zero injuries for all workers as the company's primary focus:

> O'Neill never promised that his focus on worker safety would increase Alcoa's profits. However, as his new routines moved through the organization, costs came down, quality went up, and productivity skyrocketed. If molten metal was injuring workers when it splashed, then the pouring system was redesigned, which led to fewer injuries. It also saved money because Alcoa lost less raw materials in spills. If a machine kept breaking down, it was replaced, which meant there was less risk of a broken gear snagging an employee's arm. It also meant higher quality products because, as Alcoa discovered, equipment malfunctions were a chief cause of subpar aluminum.
>
> –Charles Duhigg, *The Power of Habit: Why We Do What We Do in Life and Business*[161]

This example shows how avoiding harm can bring positive effects that might at first seem counter-intuitive; although this endeavor to protect workers would have been worthwhile even had it not improved productivity.

11.3 Avoiding Harm

In reading this chapter, it may be immediately obvious that some ways of determining meaningful work are straightforward but others could be confusing, such as whether or not our work meets intangible, spiritual needs. While the execution requires some finesse, the formula for ensuring our work meets ours and others' spiritual needs is fairly simple and can be done in any career that is fair and not harmful. The formula is as follows: in every dealing with other living beings and objects, aim to please the divine whole, in both action and motive, while remaining detached from the external results. According to the *Bhagavad-gita*[162] and the *Bhagavata Purana*,[163] the divine whole can be understood in four ways: as the form of the universe, as an undifferentiated oneness of being, as the Soul of the Universe, or as the Supreme Being. We understand what action and motives please the divine whole through the relative clarity that comes from *sattva* (or better yet, transcendence), from sacred ceremony (as we will discuss in Chapter 17), from sacred writings, and from teachers who have practically realized spiritual wisdom. As an example of what we can find from sacred writings, here is a list from the *Bhagavad-gita* describing what a person who continuously pleases the divine whole is like:

> One who is not envious but is a kind friend to all living entities, who does not think oneself a proprietor and is free from false ego, who is equal in both happiness and distress, who is tolerant, always satisfied, self-controlled....a person by whom no one is put into difficulty and who is not disturbed by anyone, who is equipoised in happiness and distress, fear and anxiety....not dependent on the ordinary course of activities, who is pure, expert, without cares, free from all pains, and not striving for some result....One who is equal to friends and enemies, who is equipoised in honor and dishonor, heat and cold, happiness and distress, fame and infamy.
>
> — *Bhagavad-gita* 12.13-19

Yes, the above list is a high bar, but the point is to strive for such dealings, with others, with objects, and with our environment. Regarding how to try to please the Divine with detachment from the results, we give more details in Chapter 25. In summary here, we can say we achieve the deepest sense of meaningful work when we aim to please our source purely out of love and are not discouraged when our best efforts to do so don't also result in the separate pleasure of others, or in a measurement of success in the ordinary sense.

> For, in the end, it is impossible to have a great life unless it is a meaningful life. And it is very difficult to have a meaningful life without meaningful work.
> —Jim Collins, *Good to Great: Why Some Companies Make the Leap… and Others Don't*[164]

Chapter 12

Additional Thoughts: Going Deeper into Esoteric Understandings of Meaningful Work

In the last chapter, we defined meaningful work as that which involves both fair exchanges and the meeting of real needs of everyone involved at all steps of the process, without causing harm. For those who wish to go deeper and who are open to more esoteric concepts, we would like to suggest that when we strive to meet spiritual needs as we have just described, then meaningful work has yet another dimension.

When we carefully consider all the ways in which we think of meaning and value, we quickly notice that meaning has to do with making things better. We want to "better" someone or something in the world, and perhaps if possible, do something that goes beyond our lifetime. We ascribe meaning to action when it helps people live longer, get a better education, eradicate or alleviate more diseases, have better relationships that last longer, communicate faster, have more choices, and so forth. For example, one way of measuring whether work has value is: "The number of people whose lives you improve, and how much you improve them."[165]

In other words, we strongly associate meaning and value with some sort of positive increase — whether of time, numbers of people, or quality. We seek meaning in making something good go on for longer — how long the organization, building, medical procedure, knowledge, theater act, or relationship lasts. The longer it lasts, the more meaningful we deem it. We seek meaning in increasing numbers of people — how many people receive an education who were previously illiterate, how many people are cured from serious diseases, how many people are freed from human trafficking. We seek meaning in increases in quality — how much betterment there is in health, talent, opportunity, knowledge, and so forth. Value is understood when there is increase.

12.1 The universe's balance

We may remember learning in school that neither matter nor energy is ever created or destroyed. For every action there is an equal and opposite reaction. Balance will reassert itself. Therefore, when we aim to have our work be meaningful in terms of creating an increase of the duration, quantity, or quality of something good, some sort of counter-balancing decrease tends to occur. Laws of conservation have broad application even beyond physics. Antibiotics increase health on the one hand by curing many infections, but have also decreased health by depleting essential digestive flora and encouraging "super-bugs." Social media increases our connection to those at a distance while decreasing our connection to the person sitting next to us.

The tendency towards equilibrium that we see in the laws of physics is also evident, albeit on a subtle level, in what some philo-sophical systems call the "law of karma." According to karmic law , everyone reaps the results of the seeds they sow. What goes around comes around. In other words, persons getting an increase at present gave up something in the past, or will pay in the future. Karmic law thus implies fairness rather than increase — others can not add to or subtract from what I have earned for myself. If others were able to give me something good beyond what I karmically deserve, then they would also be able to do harm to me beyond karmic justice. Therefore, by the law of karma, my work can be, at best, a means to enable others to receive the results they paid for themselves. I can, so to speak, be the delivery person for their package. However, I'm not providing an absolute increase for them. I'm storing up a credit in my karmic account, which will be canceled in the future when I enjoy the results, or which is itself canceling a debit from the past — in either case, going back down to zero. The enjoyable results, meanwhile, are temporary and themselves will also be finished. So even for myself I don't end up with an absolute increase.

What about an increase over time? Is there really more meaning to a business or charity or school or whatever that lasts twenty years rather than twenty minutes? Compared to the age of our universe, our lifetime can be measured in billionths of a second. Everything is lost eventually. For example, centuries ago, smiths in Damascus forged incredibly strong, intricately patterned blades out of Wootz steel. Various Damascus steel blades were reported to have sliced through rocks, tree trunks, rifle barrels, and weaker steel blades. Today, that technology is lost (though some modern bladesmiths call their blades "Damascus steel" in order to burnish their reputation). Experimental archaeologists trying to replicate the process note that it may be dependent on specific sources of ore that are themselves no longer extant.[166] Eventually all knowledge, advancements, and so forth pass from human society, and then perhaps reappear. Taking the above into consideration, it's rather arbitrary to think 2,000 years rather than 200 years, or 20 years, or 20 minutes, is a real increase in an ultimate sense. Regardless of how long something lasts, anything that is an increase in one area of life necessitates a balancing decrease in another. The length of time that balancing act is in place does not represent genuine increase.

So, at one level it could be argued, nothing is created or destroyed. An apparent increase or decrease may manifest or unmanifest, but balance is maintained. Creation only involves changing energy to matter or matter to energy, or changing the form of either or both. If defining meaningful work as creating an absolute increase is a contradiction of nature's laws, perhaps we must content ourselves with finding meaning in work that is as meaningful as is possible in a transactional sense. Does such an attitude leave us with cynicism and despair about our work really making the world a *better* place? We turn to the sacred writings of the ancients for the way out.

12.2 Infinite increase of the good, but not necessarily the goods!

In line with our analysis above, the *Bhagavad-gita* states that ordinary transactional work — under any of the shades of ego — has no absolute value now or in the future.[167] On the other hand, the *Bhagavad-gita* also states that there is another energy beyond that of equal and opposite reactions, beyond that of only illusions of increase, beyond that where we find nearly total disinterest in work, even in our complex

Figure 12.1: Balanced Yet Ever-Expanding

River branching over time

modern world.[168] That other energy is of the nature of absolute increase with no concomitant decrease. The invocation of the Iso Upanishad describes this other energy as being infinite, beyond transactions and balance. One can subtract infinitely from infinity and still have infinity. The infinite can, therefore, give infinitely and still remain infinite. There can be absolute increase without a corresponding decrease.

One indication of the truth of an energy of infinite, genuine increase is the universal belief in absolute increase in our ordinary life, despite the clear evidence that our planet has limits. Why would we all seek absolute increase, unless it exists somehow and somewhere? Humans are thirsty in a desert because we are meant to consume water, whereas creatures who can live without drinking do not feel thirst.

On the other hand, one could make a similar argument regarding balance. If in this other energy there is ever-expanding increase without equal decrease, whence comes our yearning for the balance that takes the form of justice and fairness in this world? Yes, a dynamic kind of balance and fairness could at least theoretically exist in an expanding infinite energy, if that energy were free from malice and envy.

Every ancient spiritual tradition — at least in its original form — describes the nature of this other energy as beyond laws of physics (or even laws of karma). It is, unfortunately, true that over time, adherents translate the concepts of this other energy into more familiar ideas of good behavior or transactional honesty. It is also unfortunately true that some adherents translate the concepts of this other energy into thinking that they will get any desired amount of any of the six kinds of richness for themselves by some deadline. Over time, "spirituality" comes to mean merely living a good and moral life in worldly terms. Authentic spiritual energy, however, suggests love, mercy, and grace. These words point to a flow of pure giving, even with nothing whatsoever to balance that giving. The 16th-century holy man Krishnadasa Kaviraja defined this transcendent love as finding happiness solely in the happiness of the other.[169] One could describe grace this way: "The infinite's own happiness increases by increasing our happiness and thus there is absolute increase." By definition, the infinite is not giving love to meet a need on the part of the infinite, as the infinite always overflows without lack. As there is no way we can pay for this gift, it is mercy or grace.

A legitimate argument may be made that all genuine spiritual and religious traditions do, indeed, seem to demand various forms of payment in the shape of voluntary difficulty and deprivation such as fasting or other practices of self-restraint, times of ritual connection, and so forth. Even in traditions that teach the concept of unearned grace, adherents are encouraged to engage in regular prayer and scripture reading, for example. In Chapter 17, we describe these practices of mind and action, which are, indeed, part of the natural art of work. However — and this point is essential — none of these practices can repay or balance out infinite grace. Rather, their purpose is to increase receptivity to that love, express gratitude, and engage in a loving exchange.

As an example, we can consider that when small children make handmade cards and gifts for their parents, the parents usually feel moved and overjoyed. In general, the cards or gifts are all made from materials that belonged to the parents in the first place. The quality of the cards or gifts is such that they're not the most functional tools and there's no way the parents could trade them to someone else for goods and services. The parents are happy because their children are expressing love through their actions, not because this expression repays or balances out everything the parents are giving the children.

Ironically, ancient wisdom teaches that an obstacle to being receptive to infinite love and grace is the very concept that we can be an independent source of meaning and value in our work.[170] We may fancy that by our cleverness, hard work, caring, learning, connections with others, power, responsibility, good character, and so forth, we can create absolute value. This mood and way of thinking keeps us squarely in the realm of fair transactions rather than grace. Then, when love and mercy come to us, we may be suspicious of them ("there ain't no such thing as a free lunch") or even unaware of them. With suspicion or unawareness, we may push grace away, as a small child refuses parental help, wishing to be in control. Thus, there is a strong urge in an egotistical being to resist unearned increase. Rather, we treasure the voluntary and involuntary sacrifices we make in the form of hard work, deprivation, self-discipline, and so forth, as we see them as legitimizing our claims to having earned and created our good fortune. Even when we clearly haven't earned something in the conventional sense — as when acquaintances, friends, or relatives give us unexpected large gifts — we may feel we deserve the bounty because of our overall character and behavior (or if not, we may feel so uncomfortable that we reject the gifts). This tendency exists in various degrees and types in all three ego shades.

When we've let go of the idea of being the sole source of our prosperity, which is the fruit of our work, then we are open to mercy that fills us with

> love, joy, peace, patience, kindness, generosity, faithfulness, gentleness, and self-control
>
> —Galatians 5:22–23

as gifts of grace. The *Bhagavad-gita* describes that in this state of grace we

> feel boundless happiness, relish and rejoice in ourselves, have full detachment from all material miseries, and cannot imagine any greater gain.
>
> — *Bhagavad-gita* 6.20-23

A few paragraphs ago, we noted that in the world of equal and opposite reactions, no one can really be the creator of someone else's happiness or distress. We are, at best, a kind of delivery channel for what others have earned, not the cause of others' fortune or misfortune. Our mentality and actions that seem to do others good or bad are really just ricocheting back to us. Therefore, neither in relation to others nor to ourselves can work be truly making anything better in mundane affairs. Even the most apparently honest and meaningful work is just like shuffling air pockets around under a rug.

But here's the most amazing part about boundless love: with grace from an infinite source filling us, metaphorically our cup overflows, as David says in Psalm 23 of the Bible. We can thus continually remain full and yet keep giving the surplus to others. Then, just as we received unearned grace, we can choose to give it as well in the form of meeting others' spiritual needs. In this way, when it comes to sharing the love and grace of the infinite with others, not only is the love and mercy real, but our agency is also real. We can direct the flow and nature of that energy and be an agent of genuine increase for others through our work.

What about the receptivity of those to whom we help direct, through our work, this transcendent flow of increase? Just as we need to be receptive, don't they, as well? And, if their receptivity is essential, then isn't it their receptivity and not our choice that brings grace to them? It is true that we are directed not to throw pearls in front of swine who will simply trample them[171] or to give unreceptive persons knowledge of spiritual benefits that they will only criticize or reject.[172] However, we can look for something in others that is not exactly true receptivity but a precursor state, such as an effort to do honest work, or curiosity about something beyond the ordinary. When, by our effort to meet their needs spiritually, they sense the slightest fragrance of authentic increase, that experience is so qualitatively different from ordinary transactional pleasure that the "free sample" itself starts to create receptivity. In addition, people who are overflowing with the causeless mercy of the infinite are the agents of awakening it in others simply through their presence and intention.

The ultimate magic, perhaps, is that real agency to generate real increase in others can operate in any field of work, with any tree of work. While some people might assume that certain specific vocations have a more obvious external connection with infinite grace, there is no greater inherent connection with grace in one kind of work than another. Within the framework of everyday honest work in any field, a person who is overflowing with authentic increase is always doing meaningful work. In this way such people resolve the apparent tension between mystical experience and worldly activism. We may know someone who can increase others' calm, clarity, and courage just through their own demeanor and bearing. When we work in alignment with truth, our sense of fearlessness and grace not only pervades our own lives but also tangibly benefits others. The *Bhagavata Purana* states that persons who have inner peace bring sanctity even to already sacred places, just by their very presence.[173]

As we continue in this book, we'll describe practical ways of living and working that enable us to receive and share the absolute increase of a higher reality, and thus give real value and meaning not only to our work but to every moment of our lives.

Chapter 13

Testimony: Investment Banker

On December 15, 2020, one of the authors, Ruchira Sreemati Datta (RSD), interviewed Charles Vishwambhar Towle (CVT) via video-conference. We've edited the transcript for length and clarity.

Authors' Note: As an investment banker, CVT naturally discusses investments, which comprise his day-to-day work. Our inclusion of this interview is not meant to endorse any specific types of investments or practices described, which we are not qualified to evaluate. We include the interview as an example of a person in the Field of Resources applying the natural art of work, not as financial advice.

All footnotes, as well as text in square brackets, are our editorial insertions to clarify, explain, or elaborate on what was said in the interview.

RSD Maybe we can begin by you introducing yourself?

CVT Charles Vishwambhar Towle, managing partner at US Capital Global. We manage corporate, foundation, and individual money for a minimum investment size of $3 million per entity. Generally our average entities that we manage are $10 million, $12 million per account. We put that capital to work in companies. We originate loans for companies throughout the globe that are interested in either developing health technologies or financial technologies, or growing their existing businesses. So early-stage to late-stage businesses. Our discipline is size of transaction. So we provide financing for either early-stage or late-stage companies, minimum transaction size $5 million, up to half a billion. So that's what I do all day long: I handle people's money and allocate it for enterprises, for businesses. What we are about: wider access to wealth creation and wealth distribution for those companies, foundations, and investors, and also for the CEOs, founders, and entrepreneurs that have existing businesses, that want to grow. And capital is where both those entities intersect for a win-win. That's what we do as an agent, and as a principal, we'll also manage funds for the benefit of those investors.

RSD All right. I understand that you use a specific set of dharma-based principles in your work. Could you list these principles?

CVT I worked closely with Dr. Michael Geary, the principal of Cranmore Foundation, Living Wisdom Foundation. They take ancient technologies from the Puranas, *Isopanishad* [an Upanishad], *Bhagavata Purana, Bhagavad-gita*, and then they translate that culturally for application into businesses. My business partners and I retained Michael Geary, over three years. And he co-created this dharma model with his partners and advisors, and they consulted with my firm, US Capital, and Breakwater. That's another group. That's another business. We manage their fund; it was a fund strategy that we were managing, a private equity fund strategy that we managed, and we actually had a successful exit.

It's an example partnership that US Capital had, that successfully exited its partnership. Michael Geary consulted with that partnership that had a successful exit, and also US Capital back then, over ten years ago, and basically applying this dharma model, and the core principles, I think it was from *Isopanishad*: *satya*, which is truth, knowing thyself, *ahimsa*, respect, relationship. You know thyself so you can interact with your stakeholders, if it's your clients, your investors, or regulators. *saucha*, standards, or compliance. You interact with others, in a respectful way, in relationships, *ahimsa*, that doesn't have friction. What standards are you using in that, on the compliance side, for a service industry? And then the actualization of that: *tapasya*, effort. So those are the four principles that Michael Geary consulted with us on, consulted with our group, and basically we developed, we upgraded our entire mission statement, and we upgraded the way we operated with all of our stakeholders, by first doing our "Know thyself." So, truth. That's the first thing that we figured out: Who are we? What are we about? What we determined was: wider access. That's what we're about. Wider access to what Goldman, Moelis, and the big banks had, in a coveted way, we broke that open and gave wider access. That was our truth. And he coached us to utilize this dharma model.

RSD Could you say, had he been developing this model for some years previous to consulting for you? Were you among his first clients, or had he developed this for some years prior to that, do you know?

CVT He was working on it prior to this. But we were one of the first firms that he was able to apply it. We took it, and we applied it to our company.

RSD Right. So since it starts from the basis of truth, could you give some examples of how you've used that principle of truth, which you are phrasing as "Know thyself," or however else you phrase it?

CVT Every time we bring on any new partners, or any new staff, whatever they're at, from entry-level to partner-level, what we require is commitment. And any interaction or relationship, in order to be committed, even a husband or wife, the husband or partner needs to know themselves. What are their drivers, what are their motivations? As an example, with our staff, we seek to extract their commitment, but we acknowledge that the only way they can be committed is if they know their truth. Because finance is a business that is constantly dynamic and demanding. It's not something where you check in, check out. You never kind of check out. It's very much integrated. We want to make sure that our staff know what their motivations are. If their motivations are to a Wall Street kind of culture: trade, make big bucks, then exit — We are *not* a trading culture. Our culture is, we've had clients now for — well, Jeff has had clients for decades. I've had clients for a decade. And my turnover is very low with my clientele, because of this commitment that goes both ways, and this trust.

RSD Yes, trust.

CVT And that's because of the person I am naturally, I "know thyself" to be — by nature, I'm an asset manager. I'm a custodian. I'm a fiduciary. I look at, if it's an asset that's real estate, a temple, museum, hotel, whatever it may be, who is it benefitting? If it's a museum, it's for the benefit of the public. If it's a hotel, for the benefit of the hotel guests, right? But also the investors of that hotel, the creditors of the hotel, right? The food and safety board, that is providing oversight and compliance to that hotel, for the restaurants, the nightclub. Whatever it may be — and I'm going into a hotel as an example, because right now we're dealing with some hotels in this COVID, restructuring them, and we have to be very conscious of *all* the stakeholders: labor, potential guests—what are the new guest standards, in terms of cleanliness. So, knowing thyself: as a fiduciary, the asset is not mine to enjoy. I'm very careful, if I'm going to that hotel of which I'm an investor, or if I'm going to a temple of which I'm a trustee, or if I'm going to a museum that I sit on the board of or am treasurer, I don't want perks. We learned that, from our spiritually minded parents, what's on the altar — literally or figuratively — is sacred. And capital, wealth, is God's energy. We're very careful of not taking it for our separate enjoyment.

RSD Maybe you could elaborate a little bit on what the energy means to you. Especially since you are dealing with it all the time, you may have a more practical realization of what it is.

CVT Fortune is the energy that stimulates creation. And the creator — we have, as individuals, we have both potentials. We have the potential to create, to co-create; and we have the potential to be stimulated to create. And banking is very much like this. Capital is a stimulant of creation. People say capital causes creation. Actually no, it's ideas that are the ultimate cause. The entrepreneur's *ideas*, the inventors, or the ideas people, they're the ones that speak. Capital then stimulates that spoken word to take form. That's the stimulant. So God manifests as both the creator and the stimulant. The energy, actually, is stimulating, which is Lakshmi. In co-creating, we may remember God as the source, or forget God as the source, but in either case, the stimulant comes from God.

RSD Right.

CVT The same thing, in terms of me being an agent: I'm not the "creator." Or a co-creator! I'm not an entrepreneur, in terms of an inventor. I'm not a scholar. But I'm also not the energy. I'm an agent. So in banking, I know my truth to be as an agent, to facilitate great CEOs, CTOs, or inventors, that have that creation ability, but that also need that stimulus, that energy, that causes the spark.

RSD So what about the next foundation, that is respect. So, first you had "know thyself," and then respect, in relationship with others, once you know yourself, so could you give —

CVT Respect is manifested, in the grossest way in a relationship, in a business, through client feedback. Investors: are they upset, or are they happy? If they're happy, you're doing good. If they're upset, you're not doing good. That's pretty much the grossest way, how *ahimsa*, or respect, is manifesting.

RSD So in this case the most challenging thing might be if you have to pull out of some relationship because, for whatever reason, it's no longer a fit.

CVT Well here's the thing though. Am I pulling out, or is the capital pulling out, and I'm the agent, or the doctor, that's delivering the bad news: that this capital, or as a doctor, this drug, is not functioning.

And you know this in your cancer research and working with oncologists or whatever: certain things may not work with the patient. The doctor needs to deliver the bad news.

RSD Yes.

CVT The way the doctor, as a professional, measures his or her *ahimsa*, is with the patient. How does he or she deliver the message that the drug is not functioning, is not mixing well or doing its job? Or the body, the host, is not reacting well to the drug? That's not in the doctor's control. The doctor has prescribed XYZ, the patient has taken XYZ, it's not functioning. Does the patient hate the doctor? Well, if the patient hates the doctor the patient probably needs to go to a mental doctor. That's a separate issue.

RSD Well, it is a very emotional thing.

CVT It is! It's an emotional thing.

RSD That's one reason why it is very difficult for doctors to deliver such news, because, since it has such a traumatic impact on the patient's life, they can become emotional and take their upset out on the doctor, even though, as you mentioned, the doctor is just delivering the news.

CVT Exactly.

RSD That's a situation where it's very tricky to maintain —

CVT I have to do it respectfully. I have to do it in a nonviolent way: *ahimsa. Ahimsa* is to be as frictionless as possible, to not cause that violence. I could easily come to my CEO and tell the CEO, "Look, you don't qualify for the $20 million credit decision. You *think* you qualify for it. Sorry. We're moving on." One way to deliver. Or another way is, "The capital markets have determined that the risk, the stage that the business is at, the collateral and cash flow that the business has, the ingredients and the variables that the host company has, is not fitting and matching well for the capital markets to appreciate. So the credit facility, the $20 million, that we initially structured, it's not working. It's not working for the capital markets, and it's not going to work for your business. It's not you, it's the capital markets not appreciating the risk. There is capital available — there's always capital available, but the thing is, is it appropriate or not? And are you willing to take it?" So this is what I have to do, tell them that the $20 million that they initially wanted, is not matching them. The client then has two options: to react in a very pissed-off way, or to accept some bad news. But the way I inform them, my style and tone, will have an impact on their reaction. I could do it nonchalantly: "Hey, you don't qualify for $20 million. Move on. See you later. Sayonara." Which is a really

Wall Street way, I could easily do that. I mean, trust me, you see those movies, and you see it all the time: "Sorry, $20 million, off. Done. Shot. Move on." Very New York way. That's effective. Very efficient. I have to hand it to them, that's an efficient way to do it. I'd probably be a lot more rich if I did certain things like that. But look, we take the time, we'll go through and explain it to them.

Because for us, our truth is wider access. Our truth is not to make, is not just to be rich. I want to be rich with class. So, wider access. Because my background, I come from a family with class, and also a high-class spiritual family.

RSD Thank you. So, yes, so those are some examples of truth and respect, and then the next principle you mentioned is standards. So standards, as a translation of *saucha*, I would think of as, you know, in terms of, like, specific rules of practice and so forth.

CVT In a financial environment, to uphold standards as a financial group, means you are licensed, regulated, you don't have dings on your record. I have a public record, a public license. You can look it up on the SEC[*] website, FINRA[†]. I'll give you my brokerage ident actually. Nothing negative. No red flags, not even a speeding ticket. You have to publicize, actually, your speeding tickets, or if you had a DUI[‡]. All that stuff appears on a financial advisor's record. Because a financial advisor, they are, since they're handling people's money, they're kind of a quasi-public office, it's so regulated. So to do well in a regulated environment, the standards that we measure by are what the regulatory bodies have established. If we're able to do well within the framework of the regulatory bodies, we remain licensed, plus we want wider access for these assets.

In order to give wider access, what we have done is we have implemented and utilized a lot of President Obama's JOBS Act[§]. Regulation D, General Solicitation 506(c), Reg. A[◇]. So we're able to publicize — that which has only been coveted and private for millionaires, we made public. So a credit fund, our credit fund is exactly the limits, the credit funds of Apollo, of Ares, of White Oak. But you can't get, nobody can get access to White Oak, or Ares, or Apollo,

---

[*] The Securities and Exchange Commission, a US governmental body regulating securities markets

[†] The Financial Industry Regulatory Authority, a private standards body regulating member brokerage firms and exchange markets in the US.

[‡] Driving Under the Influence (of alcohol or drugs), a traffic offense in the US.

[§] The Jumpstart Our Business Startups Act, a US law passed in 2012.

[◇] SEC regulations.

unless it's on the public market. But the public markets, what they give, is not what they give to CalPERS*. It's not what they give to the sheikhs. It's not what they give to SoftBank.

A little dirty secret about finance, which many people know, is what's on the public markets is not what's on the private markets. And Yale, I think Yale Endowment Fund, as an investment philosophy they have, has said, "We're going majority private, less public." Yale's the first one to break open that open secret.

Now the public assets are not where the money's at. The money is in the private assets: private equity, private credit. But private equity, private credit, you have to have a minimum of $20 million to invest in that in one deal. That means you have to have a minimum of $100 million of liquidity to throw. How many investors are like that? That's less than 2,000. Or actually, less than 5,000. Five thousand investors that are like that, they can throw around $100 million. That's what private investment is for. That's what VC's for. VC funds get oversubscribed, by few investors. If you are Charles Vishwambhar or Ruchira, and you're an accredited investor, you don't get access to those things. You don't get access to those things. There's not wider access.

And so the regulators have a framework of licensing that discourages the wider access. However, President Obama, in public policy, has opened it up. And so we're just utilizing regulatory technology to break that open.

RSD As far as I understand, the rationale they put out, is that only if you have that much liquidity are you able to sustain the risk. There's a risk from any investment, and they —

CVT Well, President Obama threw that away with the JOBS Act. He said, "No no no no." And Trump is actually building up on that, and I think Biden's going to close the loop. There's a push, really — to your point, there's this *perception* that only those with liquidity can take on the risk. But if you do it in a responsible way, if you have $20,000, and you're able to put $1,000 into SpaceX and $19,000 into other places *appropriately*, then you can mimic the endowment investment model, the Yale endowment investment model.

I mean Yale's been pushing this. And I think this is why the public policy's getting to that point. But finance is moving slow, the regulators are moving slow, so with regards to standards and infrastructure, it's in the Stone Age. Those are the standards. As a firm, what we do

---

*The California Public Employees' Retirement System is a large institutional investor.

in terms of measuring our standards, and as a principal, myself, is: licensing. As long as we maintain clean licensing, because we're very innovative, and there's a lot of tech companies that are also innovative, that don't have licensing. They don't have standards. We're not a tech finance firm; we're a financial tech firm. So finance is first. In regard to the regulations, the governing codes that govern the financial markets, we don't just follow the letter of the codes, but also the spirit.

RSD Yes, that's very tricky. I feel like, you mentioned Wall Street, that in many cases, what some firms do is try to find the loopholes that were not written into the letter of the law, because people didn't think of every possible loophole, and violate the spirit. That's a way to make money, if you can find something that wasn't written into the letter, because people just didn't think of every possible thing.

CVT Exactly, exactly. And that — my business partner and I, since we're yogis, when we look at, when we read these laws, we also look at who co-wrote or sponsored those laws. What were their motivations? And then discover — what's the *satya*? We apply the dharma model on those laws, so that we can develop reg tech products and services. And that's why we're able to exercise innovative financial products, and then maintain clean licensing with the SEC and FINRA. Because now we are informing them — I mean, I'm on a call with, I think it was sixteen regulators at one point, from DC, Chicago, San Francisco offices, and they were questioning us on our investment platform, how we were operating it, and how we were able to do that on the basis of the JOBS Act. And I could see that they were basically taking notes, it was like a workshop for them. They're learning from what we're doing.

RSD I wanted to get to the question of, can you describe any cases? You sort of have, a little bit, but specific cases where multiple principles came into play. Do you have any specific examples that you want to go into?

CVT Oh, that was, that's our corporate culture. That's our corporate culture and our principle of wider access to wealth creation, that interacts — okay, two examples. One is our corporate culture.

So, as I told you, our corporate culture, we basically translate into four principles, in the form of commitment, which is truth, collaboration, which is *ahimsa*, integrity, which is *saucha* or standards, and excellence.

So what we tell our corporate staff, is: first be committed: to your-self, to our product. Quality. That's one-on-one. Next, the way you express your commitment, is, what are your standards? You know what the job function is? Can you fulfill it, yes or no? If something outside the job function comes, could you expand your job function, yes or no? Have integrity, what you can and cannot do. So first be committed, have integrity, and then, once you have integrity, what you can and cannot do, you can work in teams. And everything we do is in teams. It's two to four people, minimum, teams. Up to six.

And when you work in collaboration, when you're working in teams, now you're combining these different elements of individuals and professionals, to work together, to exhibit first-class service for our clients. Right? And then therefore, what's our first-class service, how is that exhibited? That's through *tapasya*, that's that effort, that's that excellence. That affects our work product, the quality of service.

In our corporate culture, we're always measuring our people's commitment, integrity, collaboration with each other, and their ex-cellence, and we have subsets for each item. It's really cool, the way we treat our staff. That's one thing in our corporate culture, that we're constantly talking about.

Now, in regards to our transactions, and wealth creation — wealth creation and wealth distribution. The last fifty years of this modern economy of Wall Street has been mainly driven by wealth creation. The next fifty years, we're moving into wealth distribution. There are still going to be elements of wealth creation, obviously. But there also needs to be equitable wealth distribution. Equitable not just for peo-ple, I'm talking equitable for other conscious beings, like the environ-ment. Our food industry. Protein. Animals. Land use. Water. So wealth distribution could be another way of making an investment. How do we apply this within our company, wealth creation, ? How we are applying multi [i.e., seeking wins for multiple parties], the *ahimsa* principle, the *satya* principle, is the following.

We have as an example, clients that need money; we have investors that want to invest their money. So already now we have two stake-holders I have to deal with in a deep way.

The client has a dream that they've invented, they want to grow. A client has a health tech solution that they want to bring to fruition, because, their wife passed away from poor detection of mammograms. How to do mammograms. He wants to use sound technology to bet-ter detect, and test more regularly, as a substitute for X-ray mammo-grams, using sound technology. That's his dream. He's a professor, who was the head of oncology at UCSF. This is a deal that's about to become public. He's invested his own wealth, $50 million of his own wealth, in this technology. Very passionate about it. Now as a personal story of his, which we'll talk about in a few weeks, he needs capital. He's put $50 million of his own capital, he needs an additional $20 million to take this technology from stage A to stage B: licensing, etc. And CE marking,[*] FDA[†] approval of tests. So he needs an additional $20 million.

I have clients, investors, that want returns on equity, but also want to make impact investment. Here's a health tech that has a good return on equity and is also an impact investment. So I got both. So now, what's the *satya* of this client? The truth of this client is a solution that's very personal, that he wants to share with the marketplace, that he himself is the inventor, he's the patented inventor of. My investors want to feel good by doing well. So those are these two interests.

How do I express that in a way that's respectful to both parties? Wall Street, I could just say, you know what, doctor? You take a back seat. You shouldn't run the show. Let me put this patent into a patent troll entity, [which just holds patents for the chance to sue others developing similar technology, without developing the patented inventions itself,] sell it to these investors. They make their money. Do they feel good? No. Does he? Do his dreams get met? Maybe not. This now becomes a licensing troll, a patent troll, that just — it maybe has some value in the future, and maybe Microsoft, Amazon, or Johnson & Johnson, will take a piece of it and have it go — it gets lost. It may or may not become a good or service in the future.

As a banker, I do well, but do I meet my truth of wider access to wealth creation that is not just for corporates and a quick buck for my investors.

RSD And I notice that the patent troll solution, it also makes the transaction a bit more impersonal, right?

CVT It does. Very much it does.

RSD It takes the personal out of the equation.

CVT It totally takes away my relationship with the client. I deliver on my investors, but I don't deliver on my investors' impact investment needs. So everything I'm doing as a finance professional, I have to be careful of my stakeholders. What do the stakeholders want? What's

---

[*]CE marking indicates that a product meets health and safety standards of the European Economic Area.

[†]The US Food and Drug Administration also regulates medical devices and electronic products that emit radiation.

the integrity? And so I structured an investment vehicle that protects the interests of my investors, but also delivers enough financing capability so that the doctor could see his technology get to life. Or get to the next stage. I think it's a stage two of three kind of scenario. It's not going to go to market yet. That's a separate transaction.

That's an example, where we're applying, deeply, we're applying *satya*, *ahimsa*, combined. We're also applying, deeply, *tapasya*. Because, in order to achieve this with two stakeholders — actually, three stakeholders, because I'm a stakeholder too. I don't make money unless there's a trade. So sometimes one could argue I'm conflicted, because the quicker the trade, the better. However, the trade needs to have impact, and longevity, and be sustained. Dharmic.

RSD Yes. Sustainable.

CVT It needs to be dharmic. Because, if it's a quick trade and I make a quick buck, I could maybe get the reputation that it's adharmic, it's not sustained, and when something breaks, you see firms like Lehman Brothers, hundred-year-old plus firm [that collapsed in the 2008 financial crisis]. I guess this is why Michael Geary was very excited to apply this dharma model, this technology, on our firm. And then naturally, we're always applying, two, three, four principles, with our clients, if it's health tech, with our investors, impact investors, equity investors, and then ourselves as the third stakeholder.

RSD How has using these principles affected your success and prosperity at work? How do you feel that, going into this firm where you have applied these principles, this has worked out for you compared to whatever other options you had ten years ago when you were starting out?

CVT What's that *Bhagavad-gita* verse about equipoised?

RSD There're so many!

CVT In our business, we lend money all the time. But sometimes when we lend money, the borrower, as a tactic, if it's going to go into a renegotiation, which a lot of deals right now, during COVID, are going through review, there's a little stress. Any review. Any test, there's a little stress. And so sometimes, our clients under stress will engage an attorney to negotiate, and the attorneys then get a little hostile.

RSD Hostile. Oh goodness, yeah.

CVT Well, it's finance. It's all hostile. You deal with money, imagine. So my attorney said, "Charles, how are you so calm?" You're dealing with…the regulators are always asking you questions about this, this, and that. Every month, you're getting some legal questions from the attorneys. So your compliance has to deal with regulators. Then you got general counsel that has to collect money on foreclosures, so you're dealing with litigation. Then you have to redo the notes themselves.

The investors are happy. We never have investor lawsuits, knock on wood. But occasionally, the investors get a little agitated, because they didn't get the full amount of check they hoped for. Because, they're also dealing with stress. They are also investors, maybe, in restaurants, that are having to undergo collapse or restructuring, so whatever liquidity they can get from our own deals, it's never going to be enough. Even though, getting over 10% for certain funds for this year [2020], in my opinion is great, but for some investors it's not good enough. So then my compliance, my legal guy, said, "How do you deal with it?"

And when that question came, immediately I thought about you, about the dharma, it's so natural. I truly realize that everything I have, and everything I do not have, is by divine grace. So there's this verse, I guess Krishna tells Arjuna, about the different factors of happiness and distress, hot and cold, whatever cases they are in materialistic life, to be detached, a way of life–

RSD The one about, the touch of the sense objects, they are coming:

> *mātrā-sparśās tu kaunteya*
> *śītoṣṇa-sukha-duḥkha-dāḥ*
> *āgamāpāyino 'nityās*
> *tāṃs titikṣasva bhārata*

> *— Bhagavad-gita* 2.14

Like, you know, heat and cold, happiness and distress, they're just coming, and you just have to tolerate them.

CVT That's it! That's it. That's right. So I live, that's the way I sustain myself. Especially this year of exaggerated chaos [2020]. Exaggerated chaos. I don't get "intoxicated" by the happiness, neither do I get overly distressed on the distressed portions. My *satya*, what my truth is, is best efforts, and whatever comes and does not come is as a result of divine grace.

The next thing is, the relationship side of *ahimsa*, a big lesson I've learned in dealing with professionals is you get a lot more with softness, which is a devotional sentiment of *bhakti* (loving devotional service), than you do with hardness. With regards to *ahimsa*; that firm discipline, having the standards, *saucha*; but also exhibiting in an *ahimsa*-like way, and knowing your truth, in any relationship you're in; being conscious of your truth, and exhibiting that.

Exhibiting that, requires *tapasya*, requires that fire of love, that action. If I do that, then I'm inspired. And if I'm inspired, that's the standard by which I measure my success. One way you know the Divine is reciprocating — is inspiration.

Professionally, if you've got that standard of being inspired in continuing to work, you're doing something right. But if you're not inspired to do the work, to do the banking, to do one's spiritual service and practice, then something's off. Your relationships are off. You're not aligned with your truth. You're not actualizing that truth in the fire of *tapasya*. So that's how I know, personally that I'm aligned. That's how I know professionally too.

RSD Could you speak a bit about your work-life balance? Does dharma help you with this? And if so, how does it help you?

CVT The principles in my business partnership are very much interwoven, actually, with *bhakti* yoga. My partnership was founded in the holy place of Govardhan. Before that, my senior partner and his partners already had a finance firm in Montecito, that was doing well, and is doing well. And then when he connected with people practicing *bhakti*, his vision changed. Devotional life has a way of broadening one's vision, which is actually great for business. So instead of thinking about the body, you're thinking about your consciousness, soul. Then, automatically, you're broadening your vision. Becoming more conscious is very good for one's success. Taking his business from a Montecito-based firm, Santa Barbara/Montecito-based firm, to a global firm, is what happened in Govardhan. It went from being one office with a few professionals, to being multinational with over 100 professionals, institutional firm. That's vision.

Work-life balance is actually integrated. Because now we, as a finance firm, we're assisting devotional projects around the globe, regardless of affiliation, from a financial and legal perspective. If it's to build temples, help publish books, the bank is doing that. At root, we're a devotional bank. We're helping devotional projects. Not just a bank for those in the yoga tradition. We financed a Christian angel group out in Texas and Nevada. We work with a few sheikhs in terms of compliant investment structures involved in gold. So we're very much in a globalist conscious mood. Our firm as a finance firm, organically helps, in our business, finance spiritually motivated projects. We love that. For me it's not segregated, it's integrated.

RSD What about your family, how much time you have to dedicate to your family, when you're in this work that can suck up all your time and energy?

CVT It's a very good question, because work-life balance is not just about you personally, but also how is your relationships with your wife, and your kids, because they're part of your life. I have an investment in *seva*, service — like this week, I'm taking my two sons, with the blessings of my wife, to a rural community to deliver gifts for all the children. So I very much integrate my children to be a part of the charitable aspect, the devotional aspect of my life. They are my partners in that. And I talk to my children about the business. They're young. Eight years old, six, three — my daughter's still too young. But my sons, I'm taking them tomorrow to a rural community in central California with a bunch of gifts we're going to wrap up and deliver to all the children over there, and we're very happy about that. That devotional service, my children are a part of that. I took them in India to deliver gifts of clothing and medicine. My relationship with them is very much integrated in the way I express my charity. Just the way my mother and father did too. They integrated me very much in devotional life.

And I see that, as you invest in service like that, actually what happens is you get *sukriti*, you get good luck. That good luck, the result of that is good association, and good association gives you great direction, great mentors. And with that great association, those great mentors, it brings to life the contents in books that, you know — I'm reading with my children, *Bhagavata Purana*. Every night we read *Bhagavata Purana*. Because that coincides with — the books, the *Upanishads*, the *Gita*, the *Bhagavata Purana*, this knowledge is for the philosopher-kings. And, actually, everybody's a philosopher-king. It's not just, there's one philosopher-king in California and everybody: bow down to them! We're each the philosopher-kings of our own internal reality. If we're a carpenter, if we're a plumber, if we're a chef, if we're a banker, if we're President of the United States, if we're the head of a department, if we're the Health Secretary, if we're a general, a policeman—we're each philosopher-kings. And these books, in their essence, it's for the philosopher-kings, it's for our highest self.

RSD So you're using the phrase "philosopher-king" as "one who is doing their work in the saintly consciousness." Is that how you're defining it?

CVT Exactly. And one who's doing their work in an excellent way is themselves, in their own right, a king. Right? And so the contents of the books come to life with great mentors.

RSD And, how about your wife?

CVT Oh, we have fun. I mean with a wife, you have to have loving play, you've got to keep it sweet. My dharma, as a husband, is to be a provider and a good father, however, there's a tagline. The tagline is, you'd better have play. To have play, you'd better have a counter for your play. You have to have a counter, you know, a yin-yang, to have good play. So yes, of course, my wife's in every decision, everything I do, business, spiritual practices, and the children. She's a partner. Central. She's pivotal to my life.

RSD How has integrating dharma into your work affected your spiritual well-being in general? It sounds like you always focused on spiritual well-being, so it may be a little difficult to say…

CVT In work, whatever work you're doing, you're basically committing more than half your life to something. More than half your life is spent to maintain your body. So how in your doing that, in your acting in that capacity, how does it benefit your consciousness? How do you invest in an area of your life that can also impact your consciousness, is the key point. First, you've got to eat well.

Prasada [pure vegetarian food offered in spiritual ceremony], is what you take.

Especially those that want to apply yoga beyond three times a week or beyond the mornings, how do I apply that yoga, that union, at work? What union? You know, start asking those questions. And then, how do I see them — my customers, my teammates at work, my work product, as an expression of union? How do I see — just by asking those questions, deep, that activity of deep breathing or deep concentration, you're already starting there.

That's why mantra meditation's so important. It's important to slow down. You see people, they're losing their vitality, and I see in Wall Street finance, they lose their vitality quickly. *He snaps his fingers.* It's quick: Up, burn. Up, burn. That's why analysts, they burn out so quickly. They burn out so quickly because they don't have good guides, they don't have good mentors, they don't have good resources. A good guide and a good resource, like the book that you're compiling and putting together, will be an excellent resource for people to then, "Oh, what is my yoga," start asking those questions. If they can start asking those questions, then they can start growing at work.

I think, what questions I asked, what would I ask at work: Why am I so lucky, or unlucky? Why is this happening to me? What did I do to deserve this, good or bad? When I started asking those questions, I started realizing that I'm not in control. I started then adopting this equipoised mood.

And then association, I do, I take guidance, I take mentorship, from people like Michael Geary, and also some *bhakti* practitioners you know like Uma Didi and others, about my business and how to resolve certain issues, and those droplets of wisdom, that you could find in books or in living guides, have been extremely helpful in growing to integrate the yoga system I grew up in, into my work. I think it's guides, guides and books, which people can use, and classes.

RSD How do you integrate spirituality beyond dharma, for example, *bhakti*, into your work? So *bhakti* is more specifically the relationship with the Supreme Person, your connection with the Supreme Person. It goes beyond those four principles.

CVT That's a good question. Your relationship with the Supreme Person is multi-faceted. You have to live *bhakti* also in relationships as a father, brother, husband, co-worker. So, I encourage and teach at the office, that beyond the dharma model, to have a *bhakti* view. The *bhakti* view are some of the devotional sentiments.

As an example we have somebody that is, not unstable but a little hyper at the office. And another person that's very sober, and not hyper. There's a disconnect, but they have to interact. And that interaction may cause friction in the office. And both sides just want to blow up. I coach each side to have more—one side, the sober side, to have more empathy, to have more tolerance. And the volatile, hyper side, to have more *sattva*. Qualities, of grace, of beauty, of don't be fast, slow it down. Hyper? Be graceful. Sober? Be tolerant. I mostly try to give the *qualities* of *bhakti*, so when co-workers are interacting, they can interact better. They're improving themselves, in their interactions. By improving themselves in their interactions, as co-workers, or as husband and wife, or as brother and sister, whatever it is, then your relationship with the Supreme Being also is exhibited with those same qualities. But if you just have a relationship with the Supreme Being, but you're being a complete prick with everybody else, what's the use of that?

Look at Prabhupada. Prabhupada was, how he was with everybody, and how he was with Radha-Damodara [the Divine Couple]. He's an example.

The *bhakti* principle, in my opinion, the devotional principle, is exhibited with the relationships at home. You can't disregard that. Or at the workplace.

RSD Well, yes, this has been great. A lot of fascinating stuff that I think will be very, very valuable for the readers, and making what we've said real. You are actually making it real and putting it into practice. So, do you have any parting words of your own, that you wanted to say that we maybe hadn't covered?

CVT Seek teachers and mentors. I want to make sure that that's very clear. You have your books and your case studies. I have a *Bhagavad-gita*, at my office. I have myself. How do I integrate this? A good guide or mentor is able to extract the integration between your workplace, your ideals, and where you're at. Your ideals may be *Bhagavad-gita*. You know where you're at or you kind of know where you're at. And you're in a workplace 50% of the time or 60% of the time, and you're at home 30% of the time. How do I harmonize these three different pieces of my life? That's what a guide does.

That's Supersoul, so internally you may have a guide. Sometimes it's your friends: your peers following spiritual practices. I know there's that story in the *Bhagavata Purana*, in the Eleventh Canto, there's a tree and a bird...

RSD Yes, 24.*

---

*Throughout this book we have been referring to the *Bhagavad-gita*, the famous conversation between Krishna and Arjuna. A less well-known conversation, between Krishna and his friend Uddhava, called the *Uddhava-gita*, forms part of the *Bhagavata Purana*. Therein, Krishna tells Uddhava the story of King Yadu's encounter with an *avadhuta* (eccentric mendicant). The *avadhuta* said:

> 33–35. In summary, O King, I have taken shelter of twenty-four extraordinary teachers, who appear in the following forms: the earth, air, sky, water, fire, moon, and sun; also, I accept as guru the pigeon and the python, as well as the sea, the moth, the honeybee, the elephant and the one who steals honey; add to these entities the deer, the fish, the prostitute Pingala, the *kurara* (hawk) bird and the child, as well as the young girl, the arrow maker, the serpent, the spider and the wasp. My dear King, by studying the actions of these people, entities, and phenomena, I have learned the science of the self.
>
> — *Bhagavata Purana* 11.7.33–35

> *Commentary*...The *avadhuta* is making an important point about how a sincere soul can learn from everyone and everything around him, and, when properly guided by purified intelligence, can even accept these people, creatures, and phenomena as teachers, of sorts, from whom or from which one might receive knowledge and guidance.
>
> –Steven J. Rosen, *Krishna's Other Song: A New Look at the Uddhava Gita*[174]

CVT Different guides. Be conscious of those guides. The tree can be your guide.

RSD It's pretty widely accepted that in business, it's good to have mentors.

CVT It's universal. In certain industries, you don't need it. In finance, you're not going to get a book unless you ritually worship the investment banker.

They laugh

RSD So, what do you mean by a "book" in this context?

CVT Oh, the book of deals and relationships in investing, right? Every banker has their book of deals. I have my top twenty clients, they only pick up the phone call from me. If I have somebody junior who comes and says, "Charles, can I get a piece of your book?" That's like, "Wait, why would I do that? You should be a student of mine, learn the way I treat my book of business, my clients, the way they enjoy working with me. Based on how you learn that, then obviously you'll get a piece of the book."

So in banking it's quite normal to get, you know, the book, of the bank.

But you know what, what's happening now is the, this last year, there's been moves by UBS — Barclays and UBS have made certain moves with bankers, requiring them to update and submit their book to their compliance departments, and recategorize them as corporate. And then, they're requiring each banker to have a +2, and make introductions to their book.

RSD Have a +2?

CVT Basically, if I was in a bank like Barclays, I have my book, they'd say, "Charles, you and two others need to be in touch with your book." Right? So they're breaking people's books. They're trying to homogenize the role of the mentor banker. It's interesting. So to your point, actually, there is a little bit of war of impersonalism, and break the mentoring down. Even in banking. I see that happening.

RSD Yes, I mean basically, the personal is more personal but on the other hand there's more possibility of corruption and exploitation, so then, I mean —

Interested readers can find out what the *avadhuta* learned from each of these teachers in Steven J. Rosen's book *Krishna's Other Song*.

CVT Let's homogenize it, make it impersonal, and just make it ruled by standards. Okay. We'll see how that works for expanding family life and making loving relationships. That's not going to do well. But, I get where they're going. I see that.
RSD Thank you so much.
CVT Thanks.

Chapter 14

Work on the Plane of Dedication

One of the simplest and most immediately joyful ways of making our work more fulfilling is to share the fruits of our work with others. Indeed, the Sanskrit word for "a kind of wealth" is *bhaga*, which comes from the root word *bhaj*, meaning "to divide or share." We might begin by sharing our wealth with our own family. Beyond this, we can give some of our earned wealth in charity. In this chapter, we'll discuss how charitable giving can help bring fulfillment to our working life. However, not just any kind of giving is automatically uplifting to the giver, as we'll explain.

14.1   The Joy of Giving

The Golden Rule tells us to do unto others as we would have them do unto us, if we were in their shoes. (That is, we are to take into account their circumstances; if someone is starving, we don't give them a gadget just because we ourselves like to get gadgets.) This principle is widespread among traditions and cultures all over the world, going back to ancient times. It is practical for almost everyone. After all, most of us find ourselves temporarily weakened at some point in life. At those points, a hand up can help us get back on our feet and continue to live out our full potential. Therefore, one corollary of the Golden Rule is that we give in charity, and many traditions and cultures urge charity as a regular practice to strengthen society in general.

On a personal level, studies have shown that when people are given money and asked to spend it on themselves, they are not as happy after spending it as people who are given money and asked to spend it on others. Furthermore, when asked to reflect on previous spending, people savor the happiness of past purchases made for someone else much more than past purchases made for themselves.[175] These experiments are corroborated by extensive statistics, in which charitable giving as a proportion of income is correlated with measures of happiness across nations, even for donors who lacked sufficient food or money for themselves.[176]

Giving brings joy, no matter one's circumstances.

14.2 Failing to Give Fills the Heart with Petty Anxieties; One Who Gives is Strong at Heart

Taking into account what we've just said about how giving is such a certain and long-lasting avenue of happiness, what keeps this practice from becoming universal? One reason is feeling a lack of capacity. How can we give when we ourselves feel so insecure? We then confront a deeper issue, however. What defines our capacity to give? To keep things simple, in this section we'll stick to discussing giving money. Some of us, some of the time, are genuinely completely broke and can't make ends meet: there's "too much month at the end of the money." For example, if the rent is already past due, we're short of the money, and we have no idea where it's going to come from, this situation is a pretty solid basis for saying that giving *any* money in charity is beyond our capacity at the moment. Unfortunately, this sort of situation is common for too many people, all too often.

However, a large number of us are not in such dire situations. So, let's ask: which persons are wealthy enough that giving some money in charity is *definitely* within their capacity?

The Institute for Public Policy Research (IPPR) conducted one-on-one interviews and focus groups in various neighborhoods of London, England, in 2002. One of the interviewees spoke of how much charity he or she gave. This person was not named in the report. For the sake of discussion, let's give the person a pseudonym: Richard. Richard had an annual income of more than £80,000 per year, and was in the category of research participants who stated from the beginning that they never or rarely gave to charity, had given less than £30 in the previous 3 months, and also never or rarely volunteered with a charity. To put this into perspective, in the Greater London area in 2002, a loaf of bread cost £0.74, the average salary was £17,953, the average car cost £13,100, and the average house cost £154,478.[e][177] And this is how Richard answered the question of what level of assets defines "wealthy:"

> Wealthy? It's £50 million and upwards as far as I'm concerned. £50 million is the point at which you don't have to panic anymore.
> —Laura Edwards, *A Bit Rich: What the wealthy think about giving*[178]

So apparently, Richard was waiting until he accumulated £50 million before he would feel he was in a position to give any charity. Was Richard correct? Would someone with £50 million truly not have to panic any more?

Let's take a look at history. In February 2002, when these interviews were conducted, £1 was worth about $1.43, so the amount in question was $71.5 million (in 2002 US dollars).[f] But it's possible to find examples of people who once had wealth equivalent to $71.5 million in 2002 going broke.

In the 1920s, the economist Irving Fisher talked up the wisdom of investing in the US stock market, and he put his money where his mouth was:

> In the late nineteen-twenties Fisher went heavily into the stock market and in the Crash lost between eight and ten million dollars. This was a sizable sum, even for an economics professor.
> —John Kenneth Galbraith, *The Age of Uncertainty*[179]

Using the US Consumer Price Index to convert 1929 dollars (CPI 17.2) to 2002 dollars (CPI 179.9), we find that this loss would have been equivalent to between $83.7 million and $104.6 million in 2002; and indeed, Fisher lost everything.

Nelson Bunker Hunt, a Texas financier and oil baron, invested in silver together with his brother W. Herbert Hunt. Between January and March of 1980, the brothers collectively lost $1.7 billion. Bunker Hunt is said to have remarked, "A billion dollars isn't what it used to be." In 1986, when he declared bankruptcy, Bunker Hunt claimed $100 million in assets and $500 million in debts, i.e., he had gone $400 million beyond broke.[180] Again, using the US Consumer Price Index to convert 1986 dollars (CPI 109.6) to 2002 dollars (CPI 179.9), this $400 million in 1986 would have been equivalent to $656.6 million in 2002.[*]

On March 5, 2008, Forbes magazine estimated the Irish businessman Seán Quinn's personal wealth at $6 billion.[181] On November 14, 2011, he was declared bankrupt, admitting debts of €194 million that he could not pay (the amount was in dispute, with various parties claiming it was far higher).[182] For consistency, we will again convert these amounts to 2002 dollars. Using 2008 CPI (215.3), Quinn's 2008 fortune would have been equivalent to $5.013 billion in 2002. Using an exchange rate of $1.36 to €1 and 2011 CPI (224.9), his acknowledged 2011 debts would have been equivalent to $211 million in 2002 — for a net loss of $5.224 billion, in 2002 dollars.

So we can sympathize with Richard. Though he felt he needed £50 million not to "have to panic anymore," we see here that he might have to panic even with more than seventy times that amount. All the people we just described had not only a lot of wealth, but also a lot of financial savvy; yet despite that, they sustained severe financial losses.

So is there any amount of money such that, once we've gotten that much, we can be absolutely, 100% certain that we won't by some turn of fortune again go completely broke? Having gone through these examples, we can only conclude: no, there is not.

On the other hand, some people with less than £50 million may not be panicking about money to the same extent as Richard. Here's what another person said in the same IPPR report that brought us Richard:

> I think money is there to be enjoyed but also to be used
> for others' benefit who maybe do not have as much.
> —Laura Edwards, *A Bit Rich: What the wealthy think
> about giving*[183]

We'll give this person the pseudonym Alfred. Alfred was in the category of research participants who earned between £34,000 and £60,000 a year, and had given at least £60 to charity in the prior three months, or estimated they gave at least £240 in a year and/or volun-

---

[*]As we don't know Bunker Hunt's prior individual net worth, we're only counting the loss below zero here, not the loss relative to that earlier large positive figure.

teered regularly, at least four hours per month.[*] Alfred is speaking of money in terms of enjoyment and benefit, rather than panic, even though Alfred has a lower income than Richard.

It turns out that this anecdotal evidence of Richard and Alfred is not exceptional. In 1982, psychologists Kent Yamauchi and Donald Templer identified factors describing people's attitudes towards money, two of which are particularly relevant to charity: Anxiety and Distrust.[†]

14.3 Charity's Challenge: Anxiety

To understand what those psychologists mean by Anxiety with a capital "A," in the case of Richard as described above, the word "panic" suggests the factor Anxiety. A few of the survey items give the flavor of Anxiety with a capital "A":

> - I show signs of nervousness when I don't have enough money.
> - I show worrisome behavior when it comes to money.
> - I worry that I will not be financially secure.
>
> –Kent T. Yamauchi & Donald I. Templer, *The Development of a Money Attitude Scale*[184]

Most particularly, Yamauchi and Templer found that "these attitudinal factors are essentially independent of a person's income."

These attitudes aren't completely in line with objective reality. Such attitudes are, therefore, "cognitive distortions," which can develop from previous experiences, or be learned at impressionable stages of development.

Cognitive distortions are also known as thinking errors or twisted thinking. These are thoughts accompanying emotional distress, that:

---

[*]We're inferring that Alfred had less than £50 million at the time, because even if he had simply invested £50 million at merely 1% per year, this would yield a purely passive income of £500,000 per year.

[†]The names of these factors give us some intuitive idea of what they mean; each factor is a measure of how strongly people respond to a group of survey items. While the name is suggestive of what we mean by the everyday word "anxiety," the psychologists don't necessarily mean exactly the same thing. For one thing, this assessment was only about money, whereas "anxiety" can be about many things.

Seem believable at the time but which on closer scrutiny are not always consistent with objective reality and are unhelpful....They are common to humankind but proliferate with emotional distress.

–Berni Curwen, Stephen Palmer & Peter Ruddell,
Brief Cognitive Behaviour Therapy[185]

The stories of Irving Fisher, Bunker Hunt, and Seán Quinn demonstrate that this Anxiety is not completely baseless. Nevertheless, is there a way to keep such Anxiety from controlling us?

As for those who in the present age are rich, command them not to be haughty, or to set their hopes on the uncertainty of riches, but rather on God who richly provides us with everything for our enjoyment. They are to do good, to be rich in good works, generous, and ready to share, thus storing up for themselves the treasure of a good foundation for the future, so that they may take hold of the life that really is life.

–1 Timothy 6:17–19

Here, the Apostle Paul locates the problem in "setting our hopes on the uncertainty of riches." When we rely on a foundation that is, as we've seen, inherently unreliable, we're setting ourselves up for Anxiety. The Apostle Paul is counseling people to be "generous, and ready to share," the opposite of how they would act if they "set their hopes on the uncertainty of riches."

A general strategy to help us overcome a cognitive distortion is to do a "behavioral experiment": to act counter to what the distortion would demand. When we see what actually happens, it can help us bring our overly anxious thoughts more in line with reality. At least it helps us learn that we have the power to act despite our anxiety.

One such behavioral experiment would be to give money in charity, even, or perhaps especially, when we don't *feel* "rich," which can help us courageously move away from anxiety and towards healthy self-empowerment through connection with others and ultimately with the whole biosphere or universe. Since this strategy is counterintuitive, it is helpful that many of the world's ancient spiritual traditions make specific prescriptions about giving in charity. The duty of charity is prescribed for Christians in the above quote, among many others. For Jews, this duty is called *tzedakah*; for Muslims, it is called *zakaat*; for Hindus, and Buddhists, it is called *daan*; and so forth.

The *Bhagavata Purana*, for example, says:

> A person who divides accumulated wealth for five aims: *dharma* (aligning our own inherent self with the systems of the universe), *yasa* (righteous fame), *artha* (richness), *kama* (personal desires), and one's own family members, enjoys both in the present and in the future.
>
> — *Bhagavata Purana* 8.19.37

> It is the duty of every living being to perform welfare activities for the benefit of others with one's life, wealth, intelligence, and words.
>
> — *Bhagavata Purana* 10.22.35

> One who fails to distribute one's wealth to the proper shareholders — higher beings, sages, forebears, and ordinary living beings, as well as one's immediate relatives, extended family, and own self — is maintaining one's wealth simply like a Yaksha [a miserly being] and will fall down [from one's position in society].
>
> — *Bhagavata Purana* 11.23.24

Of the five aims, the first two — dharma and *yasa* — are generally considered "charity" in English. What we're describing in this chapter as "charity" means giving richness compassionately to help other living beings in need such as the poor, the sick, children, the elderly, the creatures of the Earth, the ignorant, those who are suffering, and so forth. Traditional examples of charity include digging wells and planting trees for the public.

Conversely, in this book, richness given as a deliberate offering to the whole is considered one type of sacred ceremony, which we discuss in Chapter 17. For example, giving toward the construction, operation, and maintenance of spiritual gathering places is such a way of sacred connection,[*] rather than "charity."[†]

There is an intimate relationship between giving in charity and the effectiveness of engaging in sacred ceremonies to connect with the Divine. Jiva Gosvami has this to say in his learned commentary on the *Bhagavata Purana*:

> Performing sacred ceremonies along with dharma, one cannot attain perfection without being merciful to living beings: "There will be anxiety great as death for the person who makes distinction between his own belly and the bellies of others."[‡][186] The person sees difference between his own and others' bellies. He does not see the Lord equally in every being. He thinks only of his own stomach when he feels hunger. For the person who sees difference the Divine appears like death, and gives anxiety and entanglement. This is further explained: "On the other hand, the soul in all beings, who has taken shelter in all beings, is to be worshipped with respect and gifts, treating all beings as equal friends."[187]
> –Jiva Gosvami, *Bhakti Sandarbha*[188]

It might seem like the best way to overcome this Anxiety is to save or to hoard,[§] but counter-intuitively, charitable giving can be an excellent antidote. The very act of letting go of the results of one's work brings a sense of detachment,[189] and it is attachment that is the root of worry and fear.

---

[*]Notably, the Sanskrit word *vira-bhakti-rasa* specifically refers to an ecstatic state of an enlightened soul who, out of love, surrenders to God as an act of charity and refuses to take any blessings from God. Such souls have a mood of caring for the Lord in a protective way. Such ecstasies of enlightened saints are not applicable for people in general, and therefore donations to God are technically sacred ceremony, not charity.

[†]Notably, the Sanskrit word *daan* specifically does *not* describe donating to a temple, which may be for *nirmalya* or *yajna*.

[‡]The original Sanskrit is: *ātmanaś ca parasyāpi yaḥ karoty antarodaram tasya bhinna-dṛśo mṛtyur vidadhe bhayam ulbaṇam*

[§]We have been talking about the psychological research that is specifically about money. We may keep objects around that may be difficult to replace in case of need, e.g., because they're not easily available or because we don't have the financial means to buy them new.

14.4   Charity's Challenge: Distrust

Among the factors the psychologists Yamauchi and Templer used to describe people's attitudes towards money, Distrust with a capital "D" is another challenge that may keep people from giving in charity. Here are a few survey items to give the flavor of Distrust with a capital "D":

- I argue or complain about the cost of the things I buy.

- After buying something, I wonder if I could have gotten the same for less elsewhere.

- I automatically say, "I can't afford it," whether I can or not.

- When I make a major purchase, I have the suspicion that I have been taken advantage of.

  –Kent T. Yamauchi & Donald I. Templer, *The Development of a Money Attitude Scale*[190]

Again, such Distrust is not baseless. There are people who try to take advantage of others in the name of charity (as we'll discuss in more depth later in this chapter). While acknowledging this fact, we still have several ways of giving charity despite feeling Distrust:

- We can directly care for infants, tend to animals, take developmentally disabled adults on outings in nature, or provide companionship to a person with dementia. This way the recipients of our charity don't have the mental capacity to take advantage of us.

- We can diligently investigate the trustworthiness of one or more charitable undertakings, before participating in or donating to them.

- We can give to a diverse set of recipients with a wide variety of needs, accepting that some rate of fraud is worth the trouble we save on investigation, and feeling confident that enough of the recipients are genuinely needy.

In this way, Distrust (which may be reasonable depending on our local environment) need not rob us of the opportunity for fulfilling connection represented by charity.

Yet another reason for people to feel they have little capacity for giving charity is that they may consider charity only in terms of money. In this book we've highlighted the six kinds of richness, and we discuss means of charity besides giving money in the next section. With more ways to give, more people have the capacity to give.

14.5   What Do We Give in Charity?

You might be wondering what, specifically, we are suggesting to give in order to engage in the natural art of work. Must we give a certain amount or proportion of money, or work for a nonprofit or in the public sector? While charitable donations of money (sacrificing the fruits of one's labor) and any kind of public service are valuable means of charity (and may sometimes have an immediate effect in the world), let's examine the power of charity in line with one's own nature. The fulfillment that comes from this kind of charity is inherently sustaining. This kind of charity can be less circuitous and more direct than giving money that is used to purchase services.

As we discussed in Chapter 2, each of us is naturally drawn to certain kinds of richness more than others. We listed these categories of wealth as *aisvarya*, "power and control;" *sri*, "beauty, grace, and splendor;" *virya*, "vitality and strength;" *jnana*, "intelligence, philosophy, science (both hard and soft), and the process of learning and understanding;" *yasa*, "honor, glory, renown, praise and respect;" and *vairagya*, "equanimity and peacefulness." We also described how each of the kinds of richness is enhanced by a little bit of renunciation.

So in the natural art of work, we may choose to offer some of the specific kind (or kinds) of wealth we find personally enriching for the benefit of something greater than ourselves. Let us consider examples of giving each of the six types of wealth to our local community. If we feel enriched by *aisvarya*, we might organize community festivals or sit on the local civilian review board overseeing the police. If we feel enriched by *jnana*, we might tutor local children or research what ideas from elsewhere can have a positive social or environmental impact on our community. If we feel enriched by *virya*, we might volunteer for disaster preparedness and relief, or act as a lifeguard at the public pool. If we feel enriched by *sri*, we might paint murals celebrating our neighborhood, or sing in a choir or *kirtan* (call-and-response singing praise of the Lord). If we feel enriched by *yasa*, we may headline fundraisers for community causes, or help talented people gain recognition and advancement opportunities. If *vairagya* is what enriches us, we can help in a charity drive encouraging people through our own example to donate unused clothing, non-perishable food, furniture, and so forth; share techniques for simple living; or teach classes in topics such as forgiveness. In this way, whatever kind of wealth brings the greatest feeling of richness to our lives, we can lovingly contribute to others to enrich their lives also.

We may be able to enrich others' lives with the six types of prosperity in ways different from our main career, as when a banker volunteers as a lifeguard. Often, we will find it even more satisfying when our charity is an extension of both our career and the way we feel prosperous, as when an architect who relishes *vairagya* and *virya* donates his or her expertise to design structures that support the health of the inhabitants and the local ecosystem. When we can be charitable in these ways, the joy of giving infuses our work, which can bring us greater fulfillment:

> The simple Truth is that richness is determined by what I do with what I have. It does not matter how much money I have or what my talents may be. Use determines whether I am a rich and purposeful person. If I use the money and the talents I have only for my benefit, I am not rich. The truly rich reach out to the world. They make it a better place by what they do and who they are. Look at what you have — your financial resources, your time, and your talents. How much of each is used on yourself and how much of your time, talents, and resources is used for the common good?
>
> –Jim Rosemergy, *Even Mystics Have Bills to Pay: Balancing a Spiritual Life and Earthly Living*[191]

14.6 To Whom Do We Give?

Charity often begins at home, literally, in the sense of sharing our various types of wealth with our immediate family. Indeed, many species of animals share with their immediate family and possibly with their herd or pack. This behavior has an advantage in that we can directly see what is needed and how our sharing benefits others. We may also give to extended family, then to a broader circle of community. We may define "community" geographically as those who live close to us and share in our daily lives. We may define community in terms of shared nationality, religious beliefs, ethnicity, shared political views, or other areas of commonality. We then extend the spirit of charity beyond our local community to a greater circle, such as our country or even the entire planet, by cultivating a broad vision. Those who risk their lives in battle sometimes imagine their whole country as filled with people like their neighbors — including children, the elderly, and the sick, who cannot defend themselves — or the army as filled with people just like their comrades. Those who abjure eating meat sometimes contemplate factory farms as filled with animals who would like to live and run and play, just like their own pets. Those who work to save endangered species sometimes envisage the planet as filled with a rich variety of life, of which they can appreciate a small sliver at their local zoo.

While on a spiritual level we have commonality with all life, we may perceive the world in terms of those like us, and those who are different. Giving to those we identify as like ourselves may give us a sense that we are all looking out for one another. In other words, if we are in need, those whom we helped are likely to help us in return. Our charity thus provides us with a kind of security in a community of mutual shared giving. We may also prefer to give to those whom we can relate to and identify with because we have a better sense of where there is a real need and can directly see how our charity has benefited others. Giving charity beyond however we define our community has some advantages as well. Such giving may help us to understand what we do, indeed, have in common, despite our differences, which may be easier to see. This can help us gradually extend our sense of connection across greater and greater differences, to cover the whole Tree of Life. We also may be inclined to give without considering any benefit for ourselves. And the greatest needs may exist beyond our community. In fact, we may take many of our privileges so much for granted that we need to make an effort to educate ourselves on needs that exist beyond our horizon.

As we can see, there is a vast range of people to whom to give and convincing reasons to do so. However, the shades of ego can creep into our charitable giving, and this is what we shall turn to in the next chapter. We'll go into the specifics of just *how* we can share, such that our sharing and giving will genuinely help take us to prosperous pleasure.

Chapter 15

How Charity Can Cover us with the Shades of Ego

What of the times when generosity is not uplifting either to the donor or to the recipient? Many of us may have had such experiences where giving or receiving charity left us with regret or disappointment. In order to give hard-earned riches in charity in ways that round out the natural art of work, it's helpful to consider the relationship between charity and the shades of ego.

15.1 Charity in the Ego Shade of *Tamas*

In the *Bhagavad-gita*, it is said:

> Charity given at the wrong place and the wrong time, to
> the wrong person, or in a disrespectful and insulting way,
> covers one with the ego shade of *tamas*.
>
> — *Bhagavad-gita* 17.22

The nature of the ego shade of *tamas* is complacency. It restricts our outlook and our options, inclining us to be shortsighted or impulsive, not wanting to make the effort to think things through.

Often, a person deep in *tamas* will revel in being really good at insulting, or getting even with, enemies and putting them in their place. In this mood, one might give charity in a disrespectful and insulting way, perhaps with some sarcastic comments thrown in.

Suppose Sam's cousin Derek is addicted to a drug that is ruining his life. Thanks to his addiction, Derek has lost the job Sam helped him get; Derek's wife, who's Sam's good friend, has left him; and Derek is living on the street. Derek keeps coming around and asking Sam for money, which Sam knows from previous experience he'll just spend on his favored drug. So finally Sam throws some money in Derek's face and yells at Derek to go away and stop bothering him. Technically, this was an act of charity: Sam gave to a person in need. At this time and place, though, Derek was the wrong person to give to, and Sam knew it. Sam did this just to get Derek to go away and make Sam's own life easier. Either Sam didn't think through how the gift would actually harm Derek, or Sam bore him too much contempt to care. Sam was thinking only of his own most immediate needs — a hallmark of the shade of *tamas*.

Any contemptuous charity either results from *tamas*, or will tend to cover us with *tamas* anew, even if all other aspects of the charity are worthy. Such contempt can be just a matter of our frame of mind, or might extend to giving at inappropriate places and times. Conversely, respectfully giving to people and causes that result in harm is also an indication of *tamas*.

Ultimately, this kind of charity is also disrespectful to the riches themselves and to our own work to get these riches, so if done repeatedly, it undermines our fulfillment in the natural art of work.

15.2   Charity in the Ego Shade of *Rajas*

With regard to *rajas*, the *Bhagavad-gita* says:

> Charity given with the expectation of some return from
> the recipient or of some other reward, and charity given
> grudgingly, cover with the ego shade of *rajas*.
>
> — *Bhagavad-gita* 17.21

A gift with strings attached isn't really a gift; the other end of the string with which we think we're binding the recipient also entangles us. When we give to enhance our image in others' eyes or even in our own, such giving is a key way for the shade of *rajas* to inflate our egos. The expectation of a reward even in heaven or an afterlife also has this effect.

We think, "I'm a good, charitable, moral person who works hard to help others." *Rajas* ego thus places us at the center of reality. We see ourselves at the center of a circle of giving, justice, or simply reputation. This simple falsehood distorts everything connected with our charity.

For example, suppose we belong to a club that participates in a half marathon every year to raise funds for sick children. For many years we've worked hard on this event, designing T-shirts and organizing training runs. At the club meeting after the event, the club president announces how much money was raised, to a chorus of cheers. Then the club vice president asks for a big thank-you to each individual who helped and says what they did. The whole club erupts into applause for each person's hard work.

This year, however, we are listening to the list of helpers and applauding happily, until we realize the vice president has gone through the whole list without ever mentioning us. We can't help but wonder, "Wait, what about me? All that work, and not even a thank-you!" We may even start wondering if someone in the club has it in for us and deliberately left our name off the list.

At the reception after the meeting, we casually make our way over to the club vice president. After chatting for a bit, we say, "You know...I was just wondering...was there a reason why the T-shirts were left off the acknowledgments?"

The vice president looks blank for a moment, then says, "Oh my gosh, did I forget? I'm sooo sorry!" and then continues apologizing profusely, assuring us it was an accidental oversight. We say of course we understand; it's no big deal.

Still, an ashen aftertaste lingers. We don't feel in much of a mood to hang around the reception; in fact, we feel a little unwell. We hastily make our farewells and head home for an early night.

In this example, the charity we gave covered us with the shade of *rajas*, perhaps only partially. The acknowledgment we had been getting meant quite a lot to us and was a key part of the happiness from our charitable giving.

Another aspect of charity given in the shade of *rajas* is when we give grudgingly, perhaps at the urging of some superior. In such situations, we are more concerned about our position than the act of giving and the receiver. For example, sometimes our boss or a general company drive might canvass us to give to one particular charity. If we give when we really would rather not, to avoid looking bad or because we fear negative consequences at work, then our charity covers us with the shade of *rajas* and will not enhance our satisfaction with our work. (As a side note, in this example we're not focusing on whether or not the person canvassing us assumed we'd say yes or no as we felt, or whether the person was keeping personal tabs on who gave what and will remember it in making decisions to promote or lay off. In general, we can't know for sure what's going on in other people's heads, nor control or manipulate what they do. Here we're describing how we as individuals can engage in the natural art of work, regardless of how others act.)

It may happen that we engage in regular ongoing charity that suits our means, until at one point our circumstances change. If at this point continuing to give would put us in an unsustainable situation, yet at the same time we feel obligated due to expectations others have formed, we may begin to give grudgingly. In that case, the continued level of charity covers us with some admixture of the shade of *rajas*. This covering with the shade of *rajas* may also have started previously, when we developed a taste for our reputation as a generous person, which we may now be somewhat loath to give up, creating mixed feelings.

This grudging giving can be a subtle issue that takes self-examination or an outside perspective to notice. On one hand, the *Bhagavata Purana* does give inspiring examples of persistent, heartfelt charity, such as King Rantideva. Once, King Rantideva had fasted for several weeks and was finally about to take some food and water to break his fast. One by one, guests unexpectedly arrived from various fields of work, which people in general treated with greater or lesser degrees of respect. Seeing each of the guests equally as members of the universal family, King Rantideva respectfully gave each of them a share of his food. One guest came along with a pack of dogs, so King Rantideva bowed down and respectfully gave all his remaining food to the guest and his dogs. King Rantideva only had one glass of water left. At that moment, a poor person, who was a pariah in society, arrived and begged for a drink of water. Seeing his condition, the king was aggrieved, and spoke as follows:

> I do not pray for mystic powers or salvation. I wish I could remain taking the distress of this person, and every living being, upon myself so that they could be free from suffering. By offering my water to maintain the life of

this poor being, who is struggling to live, all my hunger,
thirst, fatigue, trembling, abjection, distress, lamentation, dejection, and bewilderment are extinguished.

> — *Bhagavata Purana* 9.21.12-13

With these words, the kindhearted king, who was on the verge of
death himself due to thirst, respectfully gave away his last drink of
water without hesitation. At this point, the guests revealed themselves
as powerful divine beings who had come in disguise to test the king.
Though the king offered them respect, he did not ask any favors from
them, for he was filled with love of the universal shelter, the Divine
Person. Even those who followed the principles of King Rantideva,
let alone King Rantideva himself, became the best of yogis.[192]

The story of King Rantideva may touch our hearts and move us.
On the other hand, it may take some honest self-reflection to see
whether we are ready yet for that level of generosity. Such readi-
ness usually doesn't happen all of a sudden. In the yogic process, as
in much of life, knowing where we are helps us determine how to
progress. Until we arrive at the stage of King Rantideva, resentment
may arise in our heart if a charitable request genuinely goes beyond
our capacity.

Engaging our hard-earned wealth in charity that covers us with
the ego shade of *rajas* is risky. We are investing our riches in a self-
image the foundation of which is external, and therefore shaky. Any
number of incidents of ill fortune can overturn it completely in a moment. Before investing too much in our good name, no matter in
how select a circle (even only in our own minds), we can ponder these
words:

> Here lies One Whose Name was writ in Water.
> –John Keats[193]

The gifted poet Keats requested that these words be engraved on
his tombstone as he was dying of tuberculosis, which killed him at the
age of twenty-five. While Keats's fame has grown in subsequent centuries, as far as he was concerned his aspirations for name and fame
ended in nothingness. Various life situations can erase our fame and
good name at any time, despite whatever we may do to protect ourselves. We would be wiser to work towards something more lasting.

15.3 Charity in the Ego Shade of *Sattva*

The *Bhagavad-gita* says regarding *sattva*:

> Charity given at the right time and place, in the right circumstances, to the right person, without expecting a return, simply because it is right to give, covers us with the ego shade of *sattva*.
>
> — *Bhagavad-gita* 17.20

Here we are giving simply because giving itself directly brings us joy and inner peace (not indirectly via our self-image). We do not care whether the recipient or any other person knows that we gave the gift, and we ourselves may forget each particular gift shortly after giving it; what we remember is how good it feels to give.

For example, we might donate money to a charitable foundation that gives gifts to foster children on their birthdays. We don't know who the foster children are and certainly don't expect anything in return from them or anyone else. It simply makes us happy to think that they are getting gifts.[8] As discussed above, this feeling of happiness is usually more lasting than that from money we spend on ourselves. So this inner satisfaction is also a fulfilling reward for our work.

Sounds appealing, doesn't it? The covering of *sattva* is so light that it often doesn't seem like our awareness is impeded at all. However, *sattva* is still an impediment to fully unfettered awareness.

Consider how many times the word "right" occurs in the *Bhagavad-gita*'s definition of charity in *sattva*. Because we are not at the center of reality, we simply cannot always have the perspective to see what is right. The gift we give with the aim of helping others may have consequences we don't intend. It may not help them overall; it may even harm them. While the broader perspective we give in Part III may help avoid this unintended consequence to some extent, any particular situation involves so many complexities that it's usually impossible to foresee the exact results of our charity.

More importantly, in charity in *sattva* we still find ourselves at the center of this act. We are giving to make ourselves feel good. While this internal sense is more stable than one based on externals in *rajas* or on the impulses of the moment in *tamas*, it is still me-centered and distorts reality. This is a rather subtle problem, and to avoid it we can go beyond ordinary charity.

Regardless of its pitfalls, in ancient writings charity in *sattva* is recommended over *rajas* and *tamas*, as a pivotal part of enhancing our fulfillment in the natural art of work.

15.4 Going Beyond Charity

Now that we've seen the *Gita's* wake-up call regarding how charity can cover us with shades of ego, we can consider going beyond any kind of egocentric charity. We'll start with rethinking expanding our giving beyond our local community to larger causes, such as the nation, or the planet. All these levels of giving have their limitations. Our local community might not offer opportunities for giving that really satisfy us. A larger body is more likely to have a need somewhere for each of us to fill. Still, the possibility remains even at higher levels that, if we try to give charity in *sattva*, we won't always be able to find "the right person at the right time and place, in the right circumstances" to whom to give, or we may encounter a situation wherein misspending may be easier to hide in larger organizations. Furthermore, even if we do find an ideal situation at a particular time, we need to remain alert to inevitable changes.

A still broader outlook is to consider that we are each simply cells in a universal body, so to speak, and it is for this Universal Ideal that we give (or rather, give back). Imagining our place in the universal form or biosphere can help bring us a sense of proportion. It helps us cultivate a healthy sense of equilibrium regarding our work and charity.

We can then consider our motives for giving. Jim Rosemergy analyzes what he calls "rites of passage" of giving in our life as follows:

1) We do not give. 2) We give out of a sense of guilt. 3) We give out of a sense of duty. 4) We give in order to receive. 5) We give because it is our nature.[194]

We can go a step beyond giving "because it is our nature:" we can give charity to suitable recipients, as far as we can determine, with the aim of pleasing our ultimate source. While our external actions may appear like charity in *sattva*, it is the movement of our heart that transcends. This is the greatest possible extension of our charity. This Supreme Entity is the fountainhead of all varieties of wealth, so we can give our riches as a grateful acknowledgment of their source. As stated in the *Bhagavata Purana*:

> By giving respect and giving charity, by acting as a friend
> and by seeing all as alike, one should try to please Me,
> [the one] who abides in all creatures as the Self of their
> self.
>
> — *Bhagavata Purana* 3.29.27

When we sincerely try to please the universal entity, the universal entity is pleased simply by knowing our intention to please. (On the other hand, if we're being insincere, even with ourselves, the universe has ways of letting us know.) Our ultimate source is the most loving and well-wishing friend, who is willing and able to reciprocate with us. Often called God, our Divine Source appreciates our diverse natures and reciprocates with our loving offerings.[*] This loving relationship can grow without bounds, as the complete whole is unlimited. By cultivating a personal relationship with the Divine, we can turn the natural art of work into the yoga of love.

---

[*]Therefore, when we give just to please the source, we also become happy (unlike the philanthropists described by Kant in the previous endnote, acting out of duty). According to the *Bhagavad-gita*, action purely enlightened by yogic knowledge is "joyfully performed."[195]

Chapter 16

Play of the Shades of Ego in Charity

16.1   The Fable of Beth

❧   ❧   ❧

Beth is a practical nurse. Six days a week she works the day shift from 8am to 4:30pm in a nursing home. Usually another nurse, Melinda, arrives at 4pm to relieve Beth, and the shift change goes on from 4 to 4:30pm. On June 1, it's 4:30pm and Melinda still hasn't shown up. Beth calls Allison, the day nurse coordinator at headquarters, to find out what to do. Allison asks Beth to stay on at the nursing home while Allison tries to find out what happened to Melinda. Half an hour later, Allison calls Beth back to say that Melinda has been in a bad car accident. A truck ran a red light and plowed into Melinda's car, so now she's in the hospital. Allison explains that Melinda's shift (the swing shift) usually goes from 4pm to 12:30am. Allison says she'll try to get hold of the night nurse Fiona, who usually arrives at 12am, and ask her to come earlier. Allison requests that Beth please hang in there. Beth understands that this is an emergency. Knowing the elderly people she is taking care of may come to harm if no nurse is available, Beth agrees to stay on. Fiona finally arrives at 8pm and Beth is at last able to leave at 8:30pm. Though she's completely exhausted, Beth is filled with concern and sympathy for Melinda, and doesn't resent the extra hours she put in this evening.

When Beth arrives for work at 8am the next morning, she sees Fiona as usual. Beth is surprised and asks Fiona if she's been on duty the whole time. Fiona says, "Yes, and I have a message for you. The night nurse coordinator Angela called and said they don't know how

209

long Melinda will be in the hospital, it looks pretty bad. So she asked me to come in again at 8pm tonight. She wanted me to ask you also, if you could please stay till 8:30pm again. I definitely can't come before 8pm, I'm exhausted."

Beth can see that and doesn't feel it would be reasonable to ask Fiona to come before 8pm. So she agrees, and again works from 8am to 8:30pm.

Days go by and the arrangement remains the same. On her day off, Beth is very busy taking care of the household chores and errands that have piled up in the meantime. She rearranges her daily routine, and begs off of some evening gatherings she usually attends. She explains that with the situation at work she's too exhausted.

After a week goes by with no change, Beth calls Allison again, and asks, "Do you know how Melinda is doing?"

Allison says sadly, "She has a compound fracture in her left arm, both legs are broken and her pelvis was crushed. She also has internal injuries. It's really awful. It will be a long road to recovery."

Beth says, "Oh my God, that's terrible! I can't imagine how much pain she must be going through."

Allison says, "She has yet another surgery next week. We'll send a get-well card for her over to the nursing home, you can sign it before we send it out."

"Yes, I'll definitely want to wish Melinda a full and speedy recovery." Beth feels a bit hesitant to bring it up in the midst of this dire situation, but finally asks, "So, will you be hiring another swing shift nurse? If you have a job ad posted, I can let some of my friends know."

Allison says, "I'm afraid the budget won't support a whole extra nurse. I'll ask Rose or Hilda if they can take some additional shifts to give you guys a break."

Beth knows Rose and Hilda from shift changes: Rose has been working the swing shift on Melinda's day off, and Hilda has been working the night shift on Fiona's day off. Allison continues, "Thank you for being a trooper, we really appreciate it."

After hanging up, Beth feels a bit dismayed at not knowing how long this situation will go on. On the other hand, she's glad that Melinda is on paid leave while she's in the hospital. At least Melinda doesn't have to worry about how to pay the bills on top of everything else.

The extra shifts by Rose and Hilda don't materialize. When Beth asks, Allison explains that Rose already works a retail job and Hilda works in a hospital, so neither of them are available for more shifts at the nursing home.

Three weeks later, Beth has somewhat adjusted her daily rhythms to her new schedule, though it's still draining. She receives her paycheck for June 1 to June 14 and gets an unpleasant surprise. Beth calls Allison again.

Beth says, "Between June 1 and June 14 I was working twelve and a half hours a day, four days a week, and eight and a half hours a day, two days a week. That comes to 134 hours during those two weeks. There are only 120 hours listed on my pay stub. Can you please explain this?"

Allison replies, "I'm sorry, we can only afford to pay you for 60 hours a week."

Beth says, "What do you mean? I've been working 67 hours a week!"

Allison explains, "There are a lot of costs involved in running a nursing home and if we paid you more we'd have to cut somewhere else. You know, some of our patients have no relatives and no means whatsoever to help pay for their care. Let me look up your facility…Charlene and Clara are pro bono patients. Be thankful we don't have to throw them out on the street!"

Clara is particularly sweet, and the thought makes Beth's eyes well up for a moment. Still, she says, "That would be awful! They're so frail and have nowhere to go! But what the pay stub is recording simply isn't true. That's not how many hours I worked. It just doesn't seem right…."

Allison says, "Well, if it makes you feel better we can lower your pay rate by 10%, then put 67 hours on the pay stub. Would you prefer that instead? It's totally up to you."

Allison's tone sounds reasonable and understanding. Beth thinks for a minute. If she's ever looking for a job in the future, they might ask her rate of pay at this one. She decides her current rate of pay would sound better. Anyway, it's just till Melinda comes back. "No, thank you. I guess we can leave it this way for now."

At least Beth's paycheck is bigger than before. Beth resolves that whenever the day's toll is getting her down, she'll remember that she's doing it for Clara and Charlene. That will keep her going.

Keeping Clara and Charlene in mind works for a while. By mid-July, though, the grueling schedule is really getting to Beth. Resentment wells up and is getting harder and harder to ignore. She didn't ask for this. All her free time goes into catching up with errands, household chores, and sleep. She hardly ever has time to take walks in nature or cook healthy meals, as used to be her habit. Her yoga and meditation practices have completely gone out the window. To make matters worse, she's not finding time to meet with her friends. Beth calls Allison and explains that she's getting stretched too thin.

Allison says, "Well it isn't just you, Fiona is doing the same. She's really just the salt of the earth, don't you think?"

Beth says, "Yes, I've often admired Fiona's quiet competence." She and Fiona used to talk more during shift changes before Melinda's accident. Nowadays whichever one of them is going off shift is usually so bone-tired, their conversation has been pared down to essentials.

Allison continues, "In fact we had a similar situation at one of our other facilities last spring, the nurses there have been doing twelve-and-a-half-hour shifts too. I know nursing can be tough, but you know you're really making a difference in the lives of your patients. How many people get to say that about the work they do every day?"

After she gets off the phone, Beth wonders glumly if she's really cut out for nursing. It seems like everyone else is doing this amount of work with no problem. Anyway, she really needs this job.

A couple of weeks later Allison sends out an email inviting all the nurses who are available to the Staff Appreciation Dinner on August 10. Beth feels a moment of irritation that this falls on her day off, when she has so many things to do. She feels like she's falling behind with everything. She's had to drink more and more coffee just to stay alert throughout her shifts, and now she's up to a pot a day. On the bright side, at least the nursing home provides free coffee. Beth considers that after all, it's nice of them to put on this dinner, and she resolves to enjoy it.

During the dinner, supervisors highlight the contributions of various staff. Beth appreciates being part of an organization with such remarkable people, and wants to see if she can get a chance to talk with some of them after the meal. Allison takes the mike.

"Now I'd like to highlight one of our shining stars....Beth has gone above and beyond the call of duty, time after time. Here are some of the testimonials we keep getting about her work. Last November, I got this letter from Dana, the daughter of one of our patients:

"'Whenever I visit my mother Cecilia, she has something new to tell me about how wonderful Beth is. Beth always arranges her tray just the way she likes it, Beth is the best at helping her get out of bed,

Beth brought her some wildflowers, and on and on. Beth is her favorite nurse! I'm so glad my mother is in such good hands. I just want to make sure you know what a gem you have in Beth.'

"And here's another letter I got last March from our patient Caroline:

"'I want to let you know how special Beth is. She remembers which is my good arm and always helps me so gently. Sometimes I feel tired of life, but whenever Beth's around she puts a smile on my face and makes me glad I've seen another day.'

"These letters speak for themselves. Let's hear it for Beth!"

After the applause dies down, Allison continues, "As a small token of our appreciation, we're naming Beth as Gold Star Nurse of the Year, and presenting her with three 60-minute massage coupons. Beth, please come forward."

The audience continues applauding as Beth goes up to receive her award. Feeling a bit shy about everyone looking at her, Beth smiles for the camera as she is presented her certificate. After going home, Beth feels a warm glow for the rest of the evening. Most of all she feels touched by the appreciation from her patients and their loved ones. The work is hard, but moments like this make it all worthwhile.

A couple of weeks later, Beth calls Allison. "When are you going to get another cleaning staff person to our facility? It's been a week since Linda got sick, and Maria just can't keep up by herself. Today I found two plastic sandwich bags lying on the floor in the hallway. It's lucky I saw them before someone slipped on them. You know some of our patients aren't such steady walkers in the best of circumstances. If they fall and break a hip, sometimes they don't recover. Can't you just get someone from a temp agency?"

Allison replies, "Whoa, whoa, whoa. Slow down and take a breath. What is this barrage? You don't need to lecture me about how elderly people might have trouble walking. I've been running nursing homes for years, I think I know that much by now."

"I'm sorry, I didn't mean to come across that way. I'm just worried about the patients."

"Yes, so we all are. We know about the situation and we're working on it. How about you worry about doing your job, and I'll do mine. Fiona told me you've been twenty minutes late twice in the last week."

"Yes, I'm really sorry about that. I'll do my best not to let it happen again."

"Please see to it, thanks. Bye now."

Beth hangs up, feeling frustrated. Her apartment has gotten very messy and twice she's had to spend time searching for something in the morning — once it was her cellphone, once it was her car keys. She feels annoyed that just because it happened twice, Fiona felt the need to report it to Allison.

Then again, Beth knows how exhausted she feels at the end of her own twelve-and-a-half-hour shifts. Sometimes she'll be counting the minutes until Fiona arrives, and every minute seems like forever. She can understand why Fiona would be dismayed by repeated lateness. Beth resolves to be more vigilant about setting her keys and cell phone on the shelf she calls her "launching pad," regardless of how exhausted she feels whenever she gets home.

Beth is still fuming at Allison's tone, though. The conversation keeps replaying itself in her head, and retorts she feels like making swirl around. *The way I'm doing my job is not endangering patients. I have a right to be angry about this utter negligence. You were just evading my question. Every time I talk to you I just get the run-around. Is this the way to talk to "Gold Star Nurse of the Year?" So much for that, I can't get even a little bit of slack. One day I'll just quit, and then you'll see what a mess you have on your hands.*

Beth realizes that this kind of thinking isn't going to get her anywhere. Besides, she has to get to the drugstore, which is closing in less than half an hour. Beth puts Allison out of her mind and gets on with her errands.

On the last day of August, Beth brings a dinner tray to her patient Clara. Suddenly Clara upsets the tray, spilling beet soup all over her gown, her bed, and the floor.

"Now look what you've done to yourself!" Beth yells. "How could you be so clumsy! Everything is filthy! And there's no one here to clean up your mess but me! Why can't you be more careful?"

"I'm so sorry! I didn't mean to!" Clara's hands are shaking even more than before, and a tear leaks from the corner of one eye.

Suddenly Beth hears a voice from behind her. "Beth, what's gotten into you? You know she couldn't help it!"

Beth turns around and sees Mrs. Danforth-Stiles frowning at her. Beth had forgotten that she's here visiting another patient, her mother Christine. Without another word, Mrs. Danforth-Stiles grabs a bunch of paper towels, hands Beth some, and kneels down to wipe the beet soup from the floor. Beth thinks to herself, *Wow, that dress looks so expensive, and she doesn't mind getting it dirty!* Swiftly followed by, *What a silly thought at a time like this. You really messed up big time!*

Beth turns back to Clara. "I'm so sorry! I know it was just an accident. I had a rough night, I couldn't sleep even though I was so tired. Please forgive me for getting so upset. It's not a big deal, we'll get this taken care of in no time."

Clara nods and says quietly, "I see. It's okay."

After Mrs. Danford-Stiles finishes wiping the floor she gets up and leaves without another word. Beth turns her attention to changing Clara's gown and bed linens. Beth feels her heart contract as Clara keeps watching her silently with eyes full of fear, as if she doesn't know what Beth will do next. Beth wonders how to set Clara back at ease, she can hardly bear to see Clara looking at her this way. As the following day is her day off, Beth resolves to get Clara something special.

The next day, however, Allison calls Beth and asks her to come into Allison's office. Beth goes in with a feeling of dread, bracing herself. Allison begins, "As you've probably guessed, Mrs. Danforth-Stiles told me about your explosion yesterday. This kind of outburst is completely unacceptable."

"I know, I'm really sorry. I won't let it happen again."

"It definitely won't happen again. Your behavior was abusive, and you know that we have a zero-tolerance policy for abuse. I'm sorry to have to tell you that your position is terminated, effective immediately."

"What?!" Beth is stunned. She had expected a severe dressing down and perhaps some kind of penalty, but not this. "I know it was terrible, but it was just one incident. Can't I get another chance?"

"I'm afraid my hands are tied. This is our policy, it's not up to me."

"But…won't it take you a while to find a replacement? And then to train that person…at least let me stay on a few days, even without pay. There are so many little details about all the patients that a new person wouldn't know."

"Thank you for offering, however that won't be necessary. Melinda has recovered and will be coming back to work. I've already spoken to her, she will be taking over your shift."

Beth feels as if her head is spinning. Melinda. Wasn't everything supposed to get better when Melinda got back? Now Beth can't remember exactly why. "I see…"

"We do recognize all the good work you've done, and I'm sincerely sorry to have to let you go. I'll give you a good reference, and truly wish you the best in your next endeavors. Take care."

There's nothing left to say; it looks like that's the end of that. Beth says weakly, "Thank you," and quickly walks out before any tears can escape.

When she gets home, Beth is still in shock, her head whirling. Just like that! After all the extra hours she put in, the award, and everything! She can't believe it!

Beth looks around her messy apartment and decides to go take a walk in the park. She has plenty of time on her hands, she might as well.

After an hour in the park watching the ducks, Beth feels a bit better, and a deep sense of relief washes through her. The schedule had been just killing her. Now she feels like she can finally breathe.

She deeply regrets her outburst at Clara, though. Perhaps she can visit some time soon and try to make things right. At the moment, though, she has to figure out what she's going to do now.

Beth feels lucky that she has some money saved up. As her paycheck got bigger, she hasn't really had time to spend the extra money. She was eating out a lot more, since she felt too exhausted to cook after her twelve-and-a-half-hour shifts. On her days off she'd been going to a nice restaurant because she felt like treating herself. Plus she'd been spending more on coffee at home. Still, the new expenses added up to less than the extra money she was making.

She hasn't even had time to use any of those massage coupons they gave her. Beth decides to go get a massage: she definitely needs one!

A few days later, Beth is in the produce section at the grocery store, pondering where she needs to cut back while she's out of a job, when suddenly she spots Fiona. And who's that by the oranges — Melinda! Melinda's face looks drawn, and as she slowly walks toward the vegetables, Beth judges that there's something slightly off about her gait.

For a moment Beth feels like hiding. They both must know how she was fired. There's nowhere to go, though. Anyway, she had decided just yesterday that the "zero-tolerance policy" was a crock. She's going to take pride in all the good work she did. After all, she'd better, if she's going to find another job. Anyway, Beth really does want to know how Melinda is doing, she still doesn't look completely well. Beth decides to seize the moment.

"Hey Fiona! And Melinda! Funny meeting you here. I don't think the three of us have ever all been in the same place at the same time before!"

Fiona turns first and starts wheeling her cart over. "Oh yeah! It's the annual worker appreciation day, so they gave us all the day off."

The date had escaped Beth's mind since she's been out of work. Melinda turns toward Beth, looking embarrassed. Fiona continues, "Say, why don't the three of us get some lemonade and go catch up with each other on the patio? It's a beautiful day. My treat!"

They agree and go ahead. As they sit sipping their lemonade and making small talk, Beth feels some tension flow out of her. Fiona and Melinda aren't treating her any differently because she got fired. If anything, Fiona seems particularly friendly and sympathetic. Beth turns to Melinda.

"I was so sorry to hear about your accident. From what Allison told me it sounded like a long, painful road to recovery. I'm glad to see you're better!"

Melinda says quietly, "Yes, I've come a long way. I'm still in a bit of pain, but it's way less than before and I'm grateful." Melinda pauses and takes a breath, "Beth, Allison gave me to understand I replaced you. I feel bad about that. I didn't really have any choice. I blew through all my savings and maxed out my credit cards from being out of work while in the hospital. I don't feel I'm even completely ready to come back to work myself, and I've had to cut down on my physical therapy, against the doctor's recommendation. I just really needed the job; I'm so sorry."

Beth answers, "Oh, of course I understand, it's not your fault at all. Your paid leave ran out? That must have been so rough on top of all the healing you needed to do."

Melinda gives a little laugh. "Paid leave? I only had three days' sick leave saved up and that was it! Toward the end Allison was telling me even my unpaid leave was going to run out soon."

Three days? Beth wonders. *Didn't Allison tell me Melinda was on paid leave?* Beth tries to think back to when Allison was talking about Melinda. *Actually I don't remember her ever mentioning the words "paid leave," I can't remember why I thought Melinda was on paid leave this whole time. Oh well, whatever.*

Melinda goes on. "When Allison told me the shifts are twelve and a half hours now, I could hardly believe it! She said that's been the standard at our facility for a while now, and gradually they're rolling it out across all the facilities. You all must be made of stern stuff. I'm still not fully recovered, and frankly, I'm finding it really tough."

Fiona says, "Oh yeah, it can get tough all right, even in the best of circumstances," and Beth murmurs agreement. The three are distracted as some birds fly down to peck at crumbs on the patio, and the conversation turns to other topics.

A while later Beth asks, "Say, Fiona, were they paying you for sixty hours instead of sixty-seven too? Allison gave me this line about how the budget couldn't support more."

Fiona looks taken aback. "I don't know. I saw my paycheck was a lot bigger after they changed the shift length, I just figured they knew how to do the math." Fiona names the figure on her regular paycheck.

Beth says, "Yes, that's the same as what I was getting. Anyway, I suppose if we were being paid the same, at least that's fair."

The three chat for a while longer before going back in to finish their shopping.

Later that evening, Beth begins to wonder, *Why couldn't the budget support paying full wage for two nurses working twelve-and-a-half-hour shifts a day? That's twenty-five staff hours a day. When three nurses were working eight-and-a-half-hour shifts a day, that was twenty-five and a half staff hours a day. It's not like they were still paying Melinda.*

Something's fishy, Beth thinks. *Anyway, whatever. It's a blessing that I'm out of there. Better focus on moving forward and figuring out what to do next.*

At the end of September, Aria, the regional manager for those nursing homes, reviews the quarterly numbers. She notes that Allison and Angela have reduced costs at the facilities for which they're responsible. Aria pays them each a substantial quarterly bonus. It's only fair that they share in the savings. Aria feels a sense of satisfaction at once more having controlled costs while maintaining standards. She runs a tight ship, and expects to be getting a substantial raise at the end of the year as a reward for her competence.

❧   ❧   ❧

16.2 Analysis of the Fable

As the story is mainly from Beth's perspective, we'll start here with what Allison did, which forms the context. While the situation began as an emergency, Allison took advantage of the opportunity to control costs by changing the nursing home from three nurses per day to two nurses per day. Furthermore, she was less than forthcoming about the change being permanent, so by the time the nurses realized it was more than an emergency variance, the policy had already become "standard."

Controlling costs is indeed an important ingredient of keeping an operation sustainable, which Aria, the regional manager, is focusing on. However, controlling costs is only one of the means to that end, not an end in itself. Depleting the employees on a daily basis more than they can recover from is itself unsustainable, so the whole aim of sustainability is defeated in the long run. Failing to communicate directly and forthrightly about the change with the employees may have avoided some difficult conversations. However, this kind of failure erodes trust and damages relationships with the employees. Depleting these assets, of trust and good relationships, is also unsustainable in the long run.

Overall, the way Allison implemented the policy change was rather impersonal, speaking of what "the budget" would support without considering the impact on the nurses' overall lives. We sometimes equate being impersonal with being professional, and contrast the professional with the personal. We may think being impersonal is the same as being neutral and fair, and try to mollify someone who is upset with a policy by saying "it's nothing personal." However, acting impersonally is merely a cheap impersonation of fairness, which may in reality serve to cloak systematic unfairness. In our story, Allison was instituting systematic wage theft. In the US, 60% of workers in nursing homes are victims of wage theft, and employers in many different industries steal upwards of $19 billion of workers' wages every year.[196]

In the story, Aria is in the Field of Resources, and we have left open whether Allison is in the Field of Resources or is in the Field of Artistry supporting Aria. We have left open the degree of autonomy that Allison had in executing the policies she did. While it may be easiest for Beth to point fingers at Allison for instituting wage theft, it may be Aria who had the authority to order this. So, Aria certainly bears more responsibility. On the other hand, Aria would not be able to execute these orders without the cooperation of Allison, Angela, and so forth. So they may also bear some degree of responsibility.

The above story, which happens in some form in all too many places, illustrates two points. First, that charity often takes forms other than that of directly giving money. Beth was giving the charity of her time, energy, and care, along with giving money in the form of getting paid less than she worked. Second, that charity in the ego shades of *tamas* and *rajas* is not truly satisfying to the giver, receiver, or others involved. In fact, in the above example, the harm extended to the future nurses they would hire. We do well to consider these points in our perhaps instinctive urge to give to others, and our asking others to give some form of charity.

Let's look into the story in a little more depth. First of all, it's important to understand that this story, and most situations involving work, are part of a wider system and that there is a chain of connections. We can start with the manager. Allison could do better at cherishing the sources of wealth, specifically the workers, while running the nursing home. We'll have much more to say about the principle of cherishing the sources of wealth in Chapter 21. Of course, Allison herself is part of a system. She may be under pressure from Aria, Aria may be under pressure from someone else, and so forth. Several years in the future, Allison's replacement may learn to continue the same policy as simply "the way things are done here." Nevertheless, we're each responsible for how the time and energy we put in helps form a system and keep it going. We'll be discussing how the natural art of work applies to systems in Part III.

We didn't specify whether the nursing home is run by a business, a government, or a charity. Exploitative tactics in the name of charity are a dynamic of human behavior that can appear in any sector or indeed, under any ideology or ism. Addressing systematic problems is always going to be challenging, but as a general point, having more people who more thoroughly practice the natural art of work, taking its principles to heart, lifts the ego shades under which exploitative desires fester, preventing these tactics, just as sunlight-killing pathogens prevents disease.

All that being said, let's get back to Beth, who, like most of us, works in a system over which she feels she has little influence, whatever its flaws. At the beginning of the story, Beth has been working according to her nature and is generally in the ego shade of *sattva*, which is balanced, sustainable, and productive. Over the course of the story, the ego shade of *rajas*, which is characterized by activity beyond balance, creeps in more and more. (On the other hand, the ego shade of *tamas* is characterized by inertia beyond balance.) Allison's prodding leads Beth to take on more activity than she personally is able to sustain, in the name of charity (and perhaps also teamwork). Like all the ego shades, *rajas* is a syndrome, comprising many symptoms that go together and reinforce each other. In particular, when we are covered by the ego shade of *rajas*, we tend to create "solutions" to problems that eventually create more problems themselves. Each of the ego shades can be contagious. Here, in one sense, *rajas* spreads from Allison to Beth.

However, it's extremely rare that we're able to work in an environment with no influence of *rajas* or *tamas*. We each have tools to help immunize ourselves from these influences, which inevitably come our way in the course of work.

The first tool is neutral awareness and connection with the truth of what's happening, to whatever extent we are able. Allison implied that Beth's extra hours taking care of Clara, Charlene, and the other patients were a form of charity toward them, helping keep them off the street. From the Beth-centered perspective, Beth was a hero whose volunteering was making a difference to Clara and Charlene. However, from the objective perspective, Clara and Charlene were also being taken care of when three nurses were working eight-and-a-half-hour shifts. Now they were receiving the same amount of nurse-hours of care as before the change, and the quality of some of those hours was degraded by the increased length of the shifts. So Beth's extra hours weren't really providing additional direct care as a charity toward those patients. As Beth found out at the end of the story, the nursing home was not also paying Melinda, and the nursing home's expenses for that facility had not gone up, so Beth's donated hours weren't a form of charity towards Melinda either. Beth's extra hours were effectively a monetary donation into the nursing home organization as a whole. Whether they were going to any charitable purpose was not knowable to Beth.

When we're caught up in an ego-centered perspective, neutral awareness of reality can be difficult to achieve. The second tool is association with others in the ego shade of *sattva*, or beyond ego altogether. Early on in the story, Beth became isolated from her usual associates. Another characteristic of *rajas* (and *tamas* even more so) is that the set of options we see as available to us tends to narrow.

A detached perspective from outside the situation, especially from a wise friend or mentor, could have helped Beth see how she was going astray and what she might do differently to adjust her balance.

The third tool is to engage in practices specifically aimed at increasing *sattva*, or transcending ego altogether. Over the course of the story, Beth almost completely gave up on her previous practices of cooking healthy meals, taking walks in nature, yoga, and meditation. Some other characteristics of *rajas* (and *tamas* even more so) are taking all-or-nothing views, discounting the importance of *sattva*, and perhaps feeling some disinclination towards it. While the changed circumstances necessitated adjusting the time spent on practices in *sattva* and perhaps in the manner in which they were practiced, eliminating them altogether went overboard (as *rajas* tends to do). The growing lack of order in Beth's apartment indicated that *tamas* was accumulating, as it tends to do somewhere in life when *rajas* has been predominating (since *rajas* is inherently unsustainable). A characteristic of *sattva* is the ability to adjust to constraints, and even a short practice that induces *sattva* can have a great qualitative effect. This is one reason why regular, deliberate connection with the whole is a key ingredient of the natural art of work, as we'll discuss in Chapter 17. The regularity holds firm against the buffeting of *rajas* and *tamas* that may be swirling in our environments and our minds.

Had she used these tools, Beth might have found other options available to her. She might have communicated with Fiona, and perhaps other nurses such as Rose and Hilda. They might have gone in together to meet with Allison and voiced their concerns with the new arrangement. Or, Beth might have considered leaving as a more serious option, rather than simply an angry retort. This way she might have left on her own terms, before she got so depleted and before taking actions that she later regretted. She might work for a different nursing home organization. She might start her own nursing home. She might go into a slightly different line of work, such as becoming a visiting or live-in home health aide. She might go into a new line of work altogether, while remaining in the Field of Artistry. Instead, during the course of the story Beth got caught up on a treadmill, wound up by the ego shade of *rajas*. Never was this truer than when Beth received the award at the Staff Appreciation Dinner, as she was drawn in by the momentary fulfillment of *rajas*, obscuring her other, healthier options.

Beth's fable illustrates the complex interactions between charity and the various shades of ego, and ways in which one's situation can swiftly become unsustainable. As we move forward in the book, we shall explore ways to help escape these traps.

Chapter 17

Regular, Deliberate Connection with the Whole

A principle of the natural art of work involves regular recognition of the whole and the source from which we come, because harmony with truth will make us happy, and disharmony with truth will bring frustration. One of the keys to a satisfying career — and life — is something unique to human beings among all of Earth's creatures: a regular, deliberate conscious connection with our source, the whole of which we are a part. Why connect with our source? Everything in our field of work has an origin outside of ourselves. Looking honestly at our work, with a little reflection, we find that our nature mysteriously seems to be a part of us. Did it come from our genes? Past lives? The will of a creator? Because certain basic elements of our nature are present from a very young age and do not normally change over our lifetime, it's hard to say we are fully responsible for our talents, abilities, and inclinations. Yes, we can work hard through intentional deliberate practice to become expert in some field. Yet, the opportunities for such deliberate practice are not fully under our control. First of all, there are some "windows of opportunity" for certain types of training, and most of those "windows" occur while we're still under the care of our parents and family. Additionally, we are born in a certain community and situation where some opportunities abound and some are absent. Also, the life impressions that continue to shape our nature are only somewhat under the control of our overt desires and planning.

The raw materials we turn into wealth or desirable objects, the animals from whom we may get products such as labor, the people whom we manage and care for — none are our creation nor fully under our control. Our memory and intelligence are areas we can significantly develop and train, but we are not their origin. Even our body is not really ours in one sense. It was developed by our mother in the womb, and subsequently by our parents. Furthermore, that development was dependent on food, water, and so forth that they did not create out of nothing. Additionally, any of those — our nature, expertise through training, expertise through impressions, our body, mind, intelligence, materials, other life forms — can be lost in a moment without our consent. Clearly, something or someone greater than ourselves is running the show. So, to acknowledge and harmonize with this truth, first we consider the concept of connection with our source, and then four ways of understanding the nature of our source. Finally, we describe general and specific ways of having a regular connection.

In the natural world, connection with and giving back to the source happens automatically. For example, the sun nourishes trees. The trees transform the solar energy into their various products that we enjoy. When we eat the fruit of a tree, the energy of the fruit, derived from sunlight, gives us energy. If our body is burned after death, that solar energy is released again in the form of fire. In this natural cycle, we find not just a movement towards equilibrium, but a movement towards giving back to the source. For all life forms, this process is built-in. However, in the human form, we can also choose to deliberately, voluntarily, and regularly give back.

Does our source, the whole — however we understand what that means — need us to voluntarily give back? No, not at all. All we have been given will again be taken. From dust to dust, from sun to sun, from water to water. For those who do not give voluntarily, death forcibly takes. Death is the means by which it becomes obvious we were never really the owners of anything. Why, then, do all human societies have a concept of dedication to the source, if we give anyway by nature?

Edith's mother in her later years used to regularly say, "Better to give with a warm hand than a cold hand," meaning she preferred to voluntarily engage in dedication to the source during life than to be forced at death. As a great king stated in the *Bhagavata Purana*:

> All the varieties of material wealth of this world are certainly separated from their possessor at death. Therefore, why not please God [in life] with the riches one is destined to lose at death?"
>
> — *Bhagavata Purana* 8.20.6

17.1 Benefits of Regular Connection to Our Source

In Chapter 11, we discussed having our work be truly meaningful. When we consciously, deliberately, and regularly acknowledge the source of everything, and dedicate our work to that source, then we become aware of the harmony and plan underlying what we experience. We become aware of our own place, the real and valuable contribution we can make, and the subjective feeling of our own value and worth. Analogously, a tiny screw may be swept up with the rest of the rubbish when on its own, but when it's in its rightful place as part of a machine, it is valuable indeed. When we try to estimate our value and meaning independently, we can become overwhelmed by our insignificance in the vastness of space and time. Connecting with the whole immediately reveals a true and eternal value in each of us, and we "relish and rejoice in the self."[197] This connection is one of love.

The catch is that knowing how our lives are meaningful and our work has value is not something we can fully grasp while preoccupied in the fields of work themselves, though we can take that wisdom with us into the fields. It's more effective to have times when we stop our normal activities and refocus on our true value in the greater scheme of things. Taking these regular breaks revitalizes our sense of self most deeply, just as sleep and recreation restore our body and mind. Such times help us to be more productive when we are working. This productivity is not just in the sense of "getting things done," like a hamster running in a wheel in a cage, but knowing what to get done when and in what order.[198] The understanding we gain in these focused times of connection is beyond our mind, or even our intuition. After all, we can hear about our place in reality from books and wise persons, but the real knowing can only come from direct experience.[199]

We could go through life hoping that perhaps one day a special experience of realizing our value in relation to our source will just...happen. Indeed, there are people who have an extraordinary mystical experience without doing anything in particular to attract it. Living with that kind of hope, though, is something like banking on a great-great aunt we've never heard of leaving us a fortune in her will. Better to intentionally carve some time and space out of our life. Just as we work continually, it's best that our connection with the wellspring that recharges and revitalizes us also happen continually.

17.2   Ways of Understanding Our Source

What are the ways in which we might understand the whole, the origin from which we come? The *Bhagavata Purana* gives us four different conceptions, as outlined in brief in Chapter 11. All four describe the same truth, but from different angles of vision.

First, is the understanding of our source as the biosphere or universe itself, conceived of as a gigantic body with awareness and senses. We mentioned this conception earlier. Here is a similar description of the universe as the Supreme Form:

> The rivers are the veins of the gigantic body, the trees are the hairs of his body, and the air is the breath of that omnipotent form. The passing ages are his movements...the clouds that carry water are the hairs on his head, the terminations of days or nights are his dress, and the supreme cause of material creation is his intelligence. His mind is the moon, the reservoir of all changes.
>
> *— Bhagavata Purana 2.1.33-34*

Second, is the understanding of the whole as *brahman*, the great formless luminosity in which there is absolute oneness. The *Bhagavad-Gita* describes *brahman* as: "immortal, imperishable, eternal, and the constitutional position of ultimate happiness."[200]

Third, one can understand our source as the Soul of the Universe, the Soul of all souls, the Lord of the heart. Here are several descriptions from various parts of the *Bhagavad-gita* :

- He is the goal, the sustainer, the master, the witness, the abode, the refuge, and the most dear friend; the creation and the annihilation, the basis of everything, the resting place and the eternal seed.[201]

- The Supersoul is the original source of all senses, yet He is without senses. He is unattached, although He is the maintainer of all living beings. He transcends the shades of ego, and at the same time He is the master of all the shades of ego.[202]

- He is the source of light in all luminous objects. He is beyond the darkness of matter and is unmanifested. He is knowledge, He is the object of knowledge, and He is the goal of knowledge. He is situated in everyone's heart.[203]

Finally, we can relate to our source and the complete whole as the Supreme Being, God as the ultimate entity. In the *Bhagavad-gita* and *Bhagavata Purana*, the Supreme Person automatically includes the three previous understandings. "He is most charming to look at, and His serene aspect gladdens the eyes and souls of the devotees who behold Him. The Lord is eternally very beautiful, and He is worshipable by everyone in the universe. He is ever youthful and always eager to bestow His blessing upon His devotees."[204]

17.3 Four General Systems to Connect with Our Source

The Bhagavad-Gita describes four ways to connect with the Source, and we can analyze all traditions of divine connection as one or a combination of these. They are devotion, action, knowledge, and mastery. Each of these types of traditions has sacred ceremonies of connection.

Most spiritual and religious organizations and traditions are more or less in the category of devotion. Connection and dedication are based on learning about, worship of, dedication to, and love for the Supreme Being. Usually, there is also some form of active service. The principle behind devotional connection systems is that our ego-centeredness and sense of disconnection come from a lack of love and devotion to our root relationship with the Supreme Entity. We reconnect by awakening that devotion.

The system of action connection is often mixed with the system of devotional connection, though some traditions stress one or the other as their primary method. Action connection is a way to take the activities we already do in the world for survival and pleasure and dedicate the processes and results to the primal source. Those with any of the four understandings of our source (universal form, luminous oneness, Soul of the Universe, or personal entity) may work in this system. Often, the fruits of work are explicitly given a way to create freedom, and peace.[205] The principle is that all forms of action originate in the source, but our self-centered desire to enjoy the results of our work distorts reality. By foregoing the results while continuing the work, we refocus on true source-centered reality.

Knowledge connection is primary in only a few religious or spiritual traditions of the modern world. However, it may be the main process for those whose idea of our source is the universe itself, perhaps understood as a unified organism. It is also sometimes the primary practice in traditions where ultimate truth is understood as formless and impersonal. Many action and devotion connection systems also include important aspects of knowledge. When knowledge, understanding, and philosophy are means to increase devotion connection or inform action connection, they are not strictly the knowledge connection system at all. A knowledge connection *system* usually involves learning about both the phenomenal and numinous, temporary and eternal, mundane and transcendent, with the aim of detachment from the former and absorption in the latter. The principle behind knowledge connection is that our suffering comes from a misconception of separation from the whole, leading us to grasp at the transient. Changing our point of view and overcoming ignorance, we are again connected.

Mastery connection is well known as part of the Eastern traditions, though it has also played a role in the Abrahamic religions, where it is mostly limited to relatively small enclaves or to religious ascetics such as monks and nuns. However, the other connection systems may also use some elements of mastery connection in their practices, such as fixing the mind in a call to grace, especially repetitive prayer. The technique of mastery connection — though usually just a fragment of it — is gaining in popularity as mindfulness, yoga, and meditation. While those within any of the four understandings of our source have favored mastery connection, today it's mostly used by those who conceive of our source as the abstract formless oneness, or as the Soul of the Universe. Mastery connection usually involves ways of bodily movement, breathing, and stilling the mind to gradually experience connection to the whole. The principle is that the natural design of the body and mind are to be in a state of connection and transcendent awareness. Putting the body and mind in their default settings allows us to access this pure consciousness.

17.4 Specific Practices We Can Do Regularly

If we are already part of a tradition of religion or spirituality, we may already be familiar with some daily ceremonies or practices such as worship, reading of sacred writings, prayer, or meditation. Setting aside a time early in the morning before the demands of the day rush in upon us can be very helpful. Others may prefer evenings, when our schedule lightens up, though the brain and body may be more tired. Many traditions tie moments for dedication to our source to sunrise, noon, and sunset. These can be times to punctuate our other activities and devote our energy to transcendence. If we live with others, we might be able to schedule group time for singing prayers, mantras, or hymns, or for study and discussion. It's usually helpful to have some sort of support from one's community (in Sanskrit: *sanga*) for ways and times of dedication. In the modern age, we can also participate in virtual communities for this purpose.

An opportunity where the sacrifice of time and energy is most effective is in relation to food. Those who understand our source to be the Supreme Being can cook for God's pleasure, and offer the food to him before they eat it themselves. Acting in this way recognizes God as the master of our lives. Just as it's natural that a friend first offers food to an honored guest, so a personal conception of God fits well with sanctifying food through offering. Those who conceive of the source as the universal Soul, or the formless oneness of peace and happiness, can thank their source for nourishment before eating. If we think of our source as the universe itself, then before eating we can meditate on how all we eat is a transformation of sunlight, water, and minerals in an amazing process that almost mystically nourishes our body. Such offering, sanctifying, or meditation related to food can become a daily sacred ceremony of connection.

In addition to daily ceremonies of dedication and connection, our work benefits from regularly setting aside an entire day for making a deliberate connection. In Christianity and Judaism there is a weekly Sabbath. While Muslims do not have a weekly day of rest, on Fridays they have noon prayers congregationally in a mosque, when there is also frequently a sermon. Many Hindus observe a day of prayer and fasting twice every lunar month. Buddhists have the Uposatha days each month for special dedication. Then, of course, in every tradition there are many sacred holidays throughout the year for celebration and focus on the divine. Making an individual commitment to regular offerings of practical spiritual service is also most helpful.

Our suggestion can be as simple as taking some regular time each day to connect oneself with the source, whether that be through prayer, saying grace or sanctification of food, reading or singing sacred texts, or any number of other rituals.

Cautions

In most traditions, dedication to the Supreme Source is linked to dedication to a prominent teacher or teachers of the tradition. The principle of respecting and pleasing the teachers of truth is as important as, if not more important than, respecting the teachers of valuable topics within the mundane sphere. At the same time, sectarianism regarding specific teachers of truth is generally counter-productive for connection with truth. And, sometimes, respect and worship for teachers of truth eclipses connection with truth itself.

Another danger involves ritual. Deliberate, regular conscious contact with our source and intentionally dedicating our work to that source are part of all human cultures. Over time, however, such experiences can tend to become ritualized and stripped of their dynamic meaning and power. Therefore, it is important to focus not only on the external behaviors of such connection, but especially on the thoughts, emotions, and desires involved in this dedication and connection.

17.5 Connection Mood—Avoiding the Shades of Ego!

The ideal mood, intention, and emotion that pervades a genuine connection between ourselves and our source are gratitude, admiration, respect, and love. The aim is that we connect simply because the part is in its rightful place when integrated with the whole. If we want nothing other than the connection itself, and we come to serve the source that gives us everything, that mood is perfect.

Unfortunately, many humans approach divine connection while covered by a shade of ego. When someone ostensibly engages in activities of connection but is envious, proud, angry, or divisive (and maybe even violent), and is not trying to reduce egocentric interests, the connection gets mixed with the darkness of *tamas*.[206] Such people may think that God only exists in their own place of worship but not everywhere else. They may become sectarian, claiming that their way is the only true way and their teacher the only valid teacher. Unable to recognize symptoms of spiritual realization in others, their treatment of other living beings remains selfish.[207] Any attempt at connection is helpful to such a person, but in this case the effects will be slow and very gradual.

When the mood is impacted by the ego shade of *rajas*, then the motive for worship, sacred study, prayer, and service is to win the praise of others in this world, to get money, or just for the pride of being a righteous person[208] Those whose motivation is in the ego shade of *sattva* worship the Supreme and sacrifice the results of their activities in order to become free from the difficulties of material life and to achieve inner harmony.[209]

> When a ritual begins to feel empty, stale and even oppressive, the likely explanation is that it has lost its connection to deeply held values. To keep rituals alive and vibrant requires a delicate balance. Without the structure and clarity they provide, we are forever vulnerable to the urgent demands in our lives, the seductions of the moment and the limits of our conscious will and discipline. On the other hand, if our rituals become too rigid, unvarying and linear, the eventual consequence is boredom, disengagement and even diminished passion and productivity.
>
> –Jim Loehr & Tony Schwartz, *The Power of Full Engagement: Managing Energy, Not Time, is the Key to High Performance and Personal Renewal*[210]

If we are careful to have a loving mood during the times we have a ceremony to focus on connection, then gradually our mind will be spontaneously attracted to transcendence. Just as the water of a river flows naturally towards the ocean, an ecstasy of spiritually prosperous *rasa* (the state of emotion in relationships, and the essential principle of nourishment and pleasure), uninterrupted by material distractions, will flow towards the infinite.[211] Ultimately, the happiness, peace, clarity, and compassion that we experience during these times of connection will seep into the rest of our lives, so that eventually every moment we will feel the joyous value of ourselves and our work in relation to the Divine.

17.6 Interplay Between Life, Work, and Times of Regular Connection with the Divine

The focus in this chapter has been on how having regular ceremonies to connect with the whole, our source, is part of our transformation of career. At the same time, how we work affects our time of dedicated connection. We probably all know someone who has regular and dedicated spiritual or religious practice that doesn't seem to bring them happiness or satisfaction in life overall. One reason might be that such practices remain a separate or somewhat isolated part of their life. Yet, when every part of our life is in awareness of our connection to the whole, then the part of our days and weeks we dedicate exclusively to that connection will bear fruit:

> For one who is linked and engaged during eating, sleeping, work, and recreation, the process of connection with the Divine becomes the destroyer of suffering.
>
> — *Bhagavad-gita* 6.16–17

Chapter 18

Additional Thoughts: Example Sacred Ceremony

We expect that many readers can draw on sacred ceremonies that are already dear to their hearts for their regular, dedicated practice. For anyone who may be looking for some new elements, we present the following daily prayers: one for the morning, one for beginning the workday, and two possibilities for ending the day. These prayers were composed by Srimati Dasi of Vrindavan, India, and are used here with her permission. She addresses these prayers to "Ṭhākurajī," a way of addressing one's object of worship with love and reverence.[*] Readers can substitute any form of address they prefer. For instance, the early American inventor and Founding Father Ben Franklin used to rise early and address "Powerful Goodness." If possible, dedicating sacred space for this practice (at least enough for one to sit or kneel) can be helpful, though it is not required.

Explanatory footnotes are our editorial insertions.

18.1   "Good Morning" by Srimati Dasi

> Good morning, Ṭhākurajī! — it's so wonderful to see
>   You.
> Your playful eyes and laughing smile
> Are the mercy giving sunrise that
> Illumines, enlivens and nourishes my heart.

---

[*] The "Th" is pronounced like the *th* in "ho*th*ead." With that caveat, the whole word is pronounced thaah-koor-jee.

Thank You for today.
It's another chance to love and serve You.
Today is called the present because it's a gift from You.
      And I am so grateful — but I need Your help to
      use it wisely.
I don't know what's going to happen today.
Or how much of my plan I'll get done
— But You do!
And so I now gift this day back to You.
Today I'm also entrusting myself to You.
My body is Yours. My mind is Yours.
Everything I am is Yours.
May we all work together to bring You joy!
Ṭhākurajī, please increase my unflinching faith in You.
Help me experience Your active presence in my day.
      Please deepen my desire to consciously cooper-
      ate with You.
— I really do want to love and serve You!

18.2   "Go To Work" by Srimati Dasi

Ṭhākurajī, it's time for me to go to work.
In the quiet of *bhajana**, I often feel Your presence.
But when out in the world, I forget You.
Why do I so easily lose connection with You?
Please don't let me forget You, Ṭhākurajī.
So many things will demand my attention today.
I need Your help — please give me focus and clarity.
Protect me from careless thoughts, words, and deeds.
May the work I do today, and the way I do it,
Bring faith, joy and, a smile to everyone.
Don't let me lose my way in the dark.
Use me as a beacon of Your loving kindness and care.
Today, throughout the day, please help me remember
I belong to You — I am Your eternal servant.
I know Your love for me is not based on my achieve-
      ments.
But still, may all I do truly serve You and Your purpose.
— Most of all, may it please You! —

---

*Dedicated sacred practice.

18.3   "End of Day" by Srimati Dasi

Ṭhākurajī, this morning I entrusted myself and my day
to You.
You took my words as real — and accepted them.
And what an incredibly blissful and busy day it's been.
— You showed me what it really means to be Your
servant — AMAZING!
Thank You for being with me through the day.
And for keeping me completely in tune with Your plan.
This has really strengthened my faith in You — and in
me!
— And increased my desire to be forever Your servant.
Ṭhākurajī, how can I come closer to You?
How can I best see Your plan for me in my daily life?
Please help me — I really do want to serve You.
— Please draw me ever closer to You in love.
Yes, the world goes on, and I still have many things to do.
But right now it's just You and me — and that's wonder-
ful!
I am feeling so grateful and satisfied to be Your servant
— Please empower me to live every day just for You!
— Thank You —

18.4   "Time to Rest (for Difficult Times)" by Srimati Dasi

Ṭhākurajī, I feel exhausted and stressed.
It's been a very long and tough day for me.
So many trials and challenges — no success today!
— I found it so hard even to take shelter of You.
But right now I'm in Your presence.
It's just You and me — and I can breathe again.
I place my troubled mind and heart before You.
— Please calm my anxiety, and free me from all fear.
Ṭhākurajī, when my plan fails, let me trust Yours.
And let me see the opportunities, not the inconve-
niences.
When I'm confused and indecisive, please guide me.
— And let me see why I failed, and how I can best suc-
ceed.

Ṭhākurajī, please forgive my foolishness today.
So often I acted and spoke without taking Your shelter.
These are moments I'd rather forget — but still they are
    special.
— They opened my eyes to Your very forgiving and lov-
    ing nature.
Ṭhākurajī, thank You for the way You led me through
    today.
You have convinced me that You are my only strength
    and solace.
Tomorrow I'll have another chance to serve You.
Please lovingly guide me — for I am Your eternal servant.
— Thank You —

Chapter 19

Additional Thoughts: Every Act a Ceremony: An Essay by Charles Eisenstein

Note: The following essay has been edited slightly for length. Reprinted by permission of the author.

19.1   Every Act a Ceremony: An Essay by Charles Eisenstein

I met a woman a few weeks ago who works with a Kogi *mama*, or shaman, from the Sierra Nevada of Colombia. He came to California a few years ago and performed extensive ceremonies on a particular spot of land. He said, "You'd better do a ceremony here regularly, or there will be serious fires." No one did the ceremonies, and the next year there were forest fires. He came back afterward and repeated his warning. "If you don't do the ceremonies, the fires will be even worse." The next year, the fires were worse. He came again and issued his warning a third time: "Do the ceremonies or the fires in this part of the world will be worse still." Soon after that, the Camp Fire devastated the region.

Later, the woman found out that the spot the Kogi shaman identified was the site of a genocidal massacre of the indigenous people who lived there. He was somehow able to perceive that. In his understanding, a horrifying trauma like that affects the land in addition to human beings. It will be angry, out of balance, unable to maintain harmony until it is healed through ceremony.

Two years ago I met some Dogon priests and asked them about their views on climate change. Like the Kogi, the Dogon have kept ceremonial practices intact for thousands of years. The men said, "It isn't what you people think. The biggest reason that the climate is going crazy is that you have removed sacred artifacts from the places where they belong, the places where they were placed with great deliberation and care, and removed them to museums in New York and London." In their understanding, these artifacts and the ceremonies that surrounded them maintain a covenant between humans and the Earth. In exchange for the payment of beauty and attention, Earth provides an environment fit for human habitation.

19.2   Ritual, Ceremony, and Materiality

How are we to understand such stories? The politically correct modern mind wants to respect other cultures, but hesitates to seriously adopt the radically different view of causality they hold. The ceremonies I speak of are in a different category from what the modern mind considers to be practical action in the world. Thus, a climate conference might begin by inviting an indigenous person to invoke the four directions, before moving on to the serious business of metrics, models, and policy.

In this essay, I will explore another view of what modern people can draw from the ceremonial approach to life, as practiced by what Orland Bishop calls "cultures of memory" — traditional, indigenous, and place-based peoples, as well as esoteric lineages within the dominant culture.

This alternative is not a substitute for the rational, pragmatic approach to solving personal or social problems. Nor does it stand alongside but separate from the pragmatic approach. Nor is it a borrowing or importation of the ceremonies of other people.

It is a reunion of the ceremonial with the pragmatic built upon a profoundly different way of seeing the world.

Let's start with a provisional distinction between ceremony and ritual. Though we may not recognize them, modern life is replete with rituals. Swiping a credit card is a ritual. Standing in line is a ritual. Medical procedures are rituals. Signing a contract is a ritual. Clicking "I agree" to the "Terms and Conditions" is a ritual. Filing taxes is a complicated ritual that for many people requires the aid of a priest — initiated in arcane rites and rules, fluent in a special language that the layperson can barely understand, and distinguished by the addition of honorific letters to his or her name — to properly complete. The CPA [Certified Public Accountant] helps you execute this ritual that allows you to remain a member in good standing of society. Rituals involve the manipulation of symbols in a prescribed manner or sequence in order to maintain relationships with the social and material world.

By this definition, ritual is neither good nor bad, but merely a way that humans and other beings hold their reality together.

A ceremony, then, is a special kind of ritual. It is a ritual done in the knowledge that one is in the presence of the sacred, that holy beings are watching you, or that God is your witness.

Those whose worldview has no place for the sacred, holy beings, or God will see ceremony as superstitious nonsense or, at best, a psychological trick, useful maybe to calm the mind and focus the attention.

Now hold on. In a worldview that does have a place for the sacred, holy beings, or God, isn't it true that He or She or They are always watching us, watching everything we do? Wouldn't that make everything a ceremony?

Yes it would — if you were constantly in the felt presence of the sacred. How often is that? And how often would you, if asked, merely profess to know holy beings are watching, without actually in the moment knowing it through and through? With vanishingly few exceptions, the religious people I know don't seem to act most of the time as if they thought God were watching and listening.

The exceptions transcend any specific faith. One recognizes them through a kind of gravity they carry. Everything they say and do carries a kind of moment, a weight. Their gravitas permeates beyond solemn occasions to their laughter, their warmth, their anger, and their ordinary moments. And when such a person performs a ceremony, it is as if the gravity changes in the room.

Ceremony is not an escape from the messy world of matter into a hocus-pocus realm of spirituality. It is a fuller embrace of the material. It is practice in paying due respect to materiality, whether as sacred in and of itself, or sacred because it is God's masterwork. At the altar, one places the candles just so. I have an image in my mind of a man from whom I learned the meaning of ceremony. He is deliberate and precise; not rigid yet neither sloppy. Paying attention to the necessity of the moment and the place, he makes an art of each movement.

In a ceremony, one attends fully to the task at hand, performing each action just as it should be. A ceremony is therefore a practice for all of life, a practice in doing everything just as it should be done. An earnest ceremonial practice is like a magnet that aligns more and more of life to its field; it is a prayer that asks, "May everything I do be a ceremony. May I do everything with full attention, full care, and full respect for what it serves."

19.3   Practicality and Reverence

Clearly then, the complaint that all those days in ceremony would have been better spent planting trees or campaigning against the logging industry misses something important. Steeped in ceremony, the tree planter will attend to the proper placement of each tree and the right choice of tree for each microclimate and ecological niche. She will take care to plant it at the right depth and to ensure that it will receive the proper protection and care thereafter. She will strive to do it just right. Similarly, the campaigner will distinguish what really needs to be done to stop the logging project, and what might instead gratify his crusader's ego, martyr complex, or self-righteousness. He will not forget what he serves.

It is nonsense to say of an indigenous culture, "The reason they have lived sustainably on the land for five thousand years has nothing to do with their superstitious ceremonies. It is because they are astute observers of nature who think seven generations in the future." Their reverence for and attention to the subtle needs of a place is part and parcel of their ceremonial approach to life. The mindset that calls us to ceremony is the same mindset that calls us to ask, "What does the land want? What does the river want? What does the wolf want? What does the forest want?" and then pays close attention to the clues. It holds land, river, wolf, and forest in a status of beingness — counting them among the holy beings that are always watching, and who have needs and interests entwined with our own.

What I am saying might seem contrary to theistic teachings, so for those who believe in a creator God, I will offer a translation. God is peeking out from every tree, wolf, river, and forest. Nothing was created without purpose and intent. And so we ask, "How may we participate in the fulfillment of that purpose?" The result will be the same as asking, "What does the forest want?" I will leave it to the reader to translate the rest of this essay into theistic language.

I personally cannot claim to be someone who knows that holy beings are always watching him. In my upbringing, holy beings such as the sky, the sun, the moon, the wind, the trees, and the ancestors were not holy beings at all. The sky was a collection of gas particles petering out into the void of space. The sun was a ball of fusing hydrogen. The moon was a chunk of rock (and a rock an agglomeration of minerals, and a mineral a bunch of unliving molecules...). The wind was molecules in motion, driven by geomechanical forces. The trees were columns of biochemistry and the ancestors were corpses in the ground. The world outside ourselves was mute and dead, an arbitrary melee of force and mass. There was nothing out there, no intelligence to witness me, and no reason to do anything better than its rationally predictable consequences could justify.

Why should I keep the candle on my altar positioned just right? It is just wax that oxidizes around the wick. Its placement exercises no force on the world. Why should I make my bed when I'll just sleep in it again the next night? Why should I do anything better than it has to be done for the grade, the boss, or the market? Why should I ever exert any effort to make something more beautiful than it needs to be? I'll just cut some corners — no one will know. In my childish imagination, the sun and wind and grass may see me, but come on, they aren't really seeing me, they don't have eyes, they don't have a central nervous system, they are not beings like I am. That is the ideology I grew up in.

The ceremonial view does not deny that one can usefully see the sky as a bunch of gas particles or the stone as a composite of minerals. It just doesn't limit the sky or the stone to that. It holds as true and useful other ways of seeing them, not privileging their reductionistic composition to be what they "actually" are. Therefore, the alternative to the worldview of my upbringing is not to abandon practicality for some kind of ceremonial aesthetic. The divide between practicality and aesthetics is a falsity. It stands only in a causal account of life that denies its mysterious and elegant intelligence. Reality is not as we have been told. There are intelligences at work in the world beyond the human, and causal principles besides those of force. Synchronicity, morphic resonance, and autopoesis, while not antithetical to force-based causality, can expand our horizons of possibility. Accordingly, it is not that a ceremony will "make" different things happen in the world; it is that it tugs and molds reality into a form where different things happen.

Living a life devoid of ceremony leaves us without allies. Shut out of our reality, they abandon us to a world without intelligence — the very image of modernist ideology. The mechanistic worldview becomes its own self-fulfilling prophecy, and we are indeed left with nothing but force by which to affect the world.

The transition that traditional people like the Kogi or Dogon offer is not to adopt or imitate their ceremonies; it is to a world view that holds us humans companioned in the world, participating in a colloquy of intelligences in a universe bursting with beings. A ceremony declares a choice to live in such a universe and to participate in its reality-formation.

19.4   Ceremony in Environmental Healing

Practically speaking — wait! Everything I have said is eminently practical already. Instead, let me speak of extending the ceremonial mind to the realm of environmental policy and practice. That means to do right by each place on Earth, to understand it as a being, and to know that if we treat each place and species and ecosystem as sacred that we will invite the planet into sacred wholeness as well.

Sometimes, the actions arising from seeing each place as sacred fit easily into the logic of carbon sequestration and climate change, such as when we stop a pipeline to protect the sacred waters. Other times, the logic of the carbon budget seems to run contrary to the instincts of the ceremonial mind. Today, forests are being removed to make way for solar mega-arrays, and birds are being killed by gargantuan wind turbines that tower over the landscape. Furthermore, anything that doesn't easily exhibit an influence on greenhouse gases is becoming invisible to environmental policymakers. What is the practical contribution of a sea turtle? An elephant? What does it matter if I place my candle sloppily on the altar?

In a ceremony, everything matters and we attend to every detail. As we approach ecological healing with a ceremonial mind, more and more becomes visible for our attention. As science reveals the importance of formerly invisible or trivialized beings, the scope of the ceremony expands. Soil, mycelia, bacteria, the forms of waterways…each demands its place on the altar of our agricultural practices, forestry practices, and all relationships with the rest of life. As the subtlety of our causal reckoning deepens, we see for example that butterflies or frogs or sea turtles are crucial for a healthy biosphere. In the end, we realize that the ceremonial eye is accurate: that environmental health cannot be reduced to a few measurable quantities.

I am not suggesting here to abandon remediation projects that might be based on a coarser understanding of the beingness of the world: i.e., that might be mechanistic in their conception of nature. We have to recognize the next step forward in the deepening of a ceremonial relationship. Recently I've been corresponding with Ravi Shah, a young man in India who is doing breathtaking work regenerating ponds and their surrounding land. Following the example of Masanobu Fukuoka, he exercises the most delicate attention, placing some reeds here, removing an invasive tree there, trusting in the innate regenerative powers of nature. The more he minimizes his interference, the greater its effect. That is not to imply zero interference would be the most powerful of all. It is that the finer and more precise his understanding, the better able he is to align with and serve nature's movement, and the less he needs to interfere to accomplish that. The result is that he has created – or more accurately, served the creation of – a lush and verdant oasis in a deteriorating landscape: a living altar.

Ravi is understandably impatient with large-scale water restoration projects like those I described in my book: Rajendra Singh's work in India and the Loess Plateau restoration in China, which come nowhere near to his degree of reverence and attention to micro-local detail. Those projects arise from a more conventional, mechanistic understanding of hydrology. "Where is the sacredness?" he asks. "Where is the humbling to the exquisite wisdom of interdependent ecosystems unique to each place? They're just building ponds." "Maybe so," I said, "but we must meet people where they are, and celebrate each step in the right direction." These mechanistic hydrological projects also carry within them a reverence for water. Ravi's project can offer a glimpse of what might be, without indicting the work that represents the first of many steps to get there.

I would add to that, that for land to heal it needs an example of health, a reservoir of health from which to learn. The oasis of ecological health he has established can radiate outward through the social and ecological surroundings, transmitting health to nearby places (for example, by providing refuge and spawning grounds for plants and animals) and transmitting inspiration to other earth healers. That is why the Amazon is so crucial, especially its headwaters region, which

is possibly the largest intact reservoir and font of ecological health in
the world. It is where Gaia's memory of health, of a past and future
healed world, still resides intact.

Ravi's earth repair work functions exactly as a ceremony. One
could say, "Don't make special ceremonies — every act should be a ceremony. Why single out those ten minutes as special." In the same way,
one could insist that every place on Earth be immediately treated as
Ravi treats his. Most of us though, like society as a whole, are not ready
for such a step. The chasm is too great. We cannot expect to undo our
techno-industrial systems, social systems, or our deeply programmed
psychology overnight. What works for most of us is to establish one
oasis of perfection — the ceremony — as best we are able, and then to
allow it to ripple out across our lifescape, progressively bringing more
attention, beauty, and power into every act. To make every act a ceremony begins with making one act a ceremony.

19.5   Ceremony from First Principles

Bringing some part of life into ceremony does not cast the rest into
the category of the mundane or unceremonious. In performing the
ceremony, we intend that it radiate through our day or week. It is a
touchstone amidst life's sturm and drang. So also, we are not to merely
preserve a few wild places, sanctuaries, or national parks, or restore a
few places to pristine condition; rather, these places are lodestars: examples and reminders of what is possible. As people like Ravi steward
such places, we are called to bring a bit of them, and then more and
more of them, to all places. As we establish a tiny moment of ceremony in our lives, we are called to bring a bit of it, and then more and
more of it, to all moments.

How do we reintroduce ceremony in a society from which it is
nearly absent? I said already that it is not to imitate or import the
ceremonies of other cultures. Nor is it necessarily to resuscitate the
ceremonies of one's own bloodline, an endeavor that, while avoiding
the appearance of cultural appropriation, risks the appropriation of
one's own culture. Ceremonies are alive though; attempts to imitate
or preserve them bring us just their effigy.

What option is left then? Is it to create our own ceremonies?
Strictly speaking, no. Ceremonies are not created, they are discovered.

Here is how it might work. You start with a rudimentary ceremony, perhaps lighting a candle each morning and taking a moment to meditate on who you want to be today. But how do you light the candle perfectly? Maybe you pick it up and tilt it over the match. Then where do you put the match? On a little plate perhaps, kept off to the side. And you put the candle back down just right. Then maybe you ring a chime three times. How long between rings? Are you in a hurry? No, you wait until each tone fades into silence? Yes, that is how to do it...

I'm not saying that these rules and procedures should govern your ceremony. To discover a ceremony, follow the thread of "Yes, that is how to do it," that mindfulness reveals. Watching, listening, concentrating the attention, we discover what to do, what to say, and how to participate. It is no different than how people like Fukuoka learn right relationship with the land.

The candle may grow into a small altar and its lighting into a longer ceremony of caring for that altar. Then it radiates outward. Maybe soon you organize your desk with the same care. And your home. And then you put that same care and intentionality into your workplace, your relationships, and the food you put into your body. Over time, the ceremony becomes an anchor point for a shift in the reality that you inhabit. You may find that life organizes itself around the intention behind the ceremony. You might experience synchronicity that seems to confirm that, indeed, a larger intelligence is at work here.

As that happens, the feeling swells that numberless beings accompany us here. The ceremony, which only makes sense if holy beings are watching, draws us into an experiential reality in which holy beings are indeed present. The more present they are, the deeper the invitation to make more acts, indeed every act, a ceremony done with full attention and integrity. What would life be then? What would the world be then?

Full attention and integrity takes different forms in different circumstances. In a ritual it means something quite different than it does in a game, a conversation, or cooking dinner. In one situation it might demand precision and order; in another, spontaneity, daring, or improvisation. Ceremony sets the tone for each act and word being aligned with what one truly is, what one wants to be, and the world in which one wants to live.

Ceremony offers a glimpse of a sacred destination, the destination of:

Every act a ceremony.
Every word a prayer.
Every walk a pilgrimage.
Every place a shrine.

A shrine connects us with the sacred that transcends any shrine and includes every shrine. A ceremony can make a place into a shrine, offering a lifeline to a reality in which everything is sacred; it is the outpost of that reality or that world-story. In the same way, a healed piece of ground is an outpost of those remaining oases of Earth's original vitality, such as the Amazon, the Congo, and a scattering of undisturbed coral reefs, mangrove swamps, and so on.

The beings we have excluded from our reality, the beings we have diminished in our perception into non-beings, they are still there waiting for us. Even with all my inherited disbelief (my inner cynic, educated in science, mathematics, and analytic philosophy, is at least as strident as yours), if I allow myself a few moments of attentive quiet, I can feel those beings gathering. Ever hopeful, they draw close to the attentiveness. Can you feel them too? Amid the doubt, maybe, and without wishful thinking, can you feel them? It is the same feeling as being in a forest and suddenly realizing as if for the first time: the forest is alive. The sun is watching me. And I am not alone.

Chapter 20

Testimony: Plumber

On June 10, 2022, one of the authors, Urmila Edith Best (UEB), interviewed Saradi[*] Devi dasi (SDd) and Catu[†] dasa (Cd) via videoconference. They live in the Flemish-speaking part of Belgium. Catu's English is a bit better than his wife's, so he participated in the interview to help her with the language. We've edited the transcript for length and clarity.

All footnotes, as well as text in square brackets, are our editorial insertions to clarify, explain, or elaborate on what was said in the interview.

UEB What job are you doing right now?

SDd Plumber![‡]

UEB What are the different jobs that you've done?

SDd Before this, I was working at the campsite.

UEB What were you doing at the campsite?

SDd Everything.

UEB Everything! Like what, what kind of everything?

SDd Reception, cleaning, gardening, I think. Everything.

UEB And before that?

SDd Ah, the hotel. Cleaning and concierge. Concierge means when there was a phone call after 5pm, and we have to answer it. Most of the time our guests want to come inside, or there was something.

UEB And then what before that? I remember you were a gardener at one point.

one point.

---

[*]Pronounced: SAH-ruddy

[†]Pronounced: CHAH-too

[‡]In the United States, the kind of work Saradi Devi dasi currently does would be done by an HVAC technician.

SDd Yeah, I was going to school for that, but I didn't do it, because it was not working with my knees.

UEB But being a plumber works with your knees?

SDd Yeah, I am standing the whole day, eight hours a day, and I clean the heating system.

Cd Gas, and gasoline?

SDd We call that gas kettles, something like —

Cd Gas convector.

SDd Something like that.

Cd The heating system that's usually in the cellar, it's heating the building. She's cleaning the heating system. It's the burner which is heating the house.

UEB You have to clean those out.

Cd She's maintaining the machine. Gasoline and diesel.

UEB What else do you do as a plumber?

SDd That's all. As for me, that's my job now.

UEB You just focus on cleaning the heating system.

SDd And sometimes I have to repair something.

UEB So you don't install sinks and toilets and that kind of thing?

SDd No, no, no.

Cd Installation, no.

SDd I did it before, but I don't do it now.

UEB So why did you decide to focus on just the cleaning and maintenance part of plumbing?

SDd Because the other side is too heavy. I did it before. I put bathrooms, I did — solar cells and floor heating. But it's too heavy. And at my age, I need an easy job.

Cd Yeah, she's getting older now.

UEB Yeah, that happens to all of us.

SDd But no, the work's too heavy.

UEB What are all the different kinds of licensure and certifications — you got certified in a number of things, right? You have different kinds of certification.

SDd Yes. I have the gas — that I have a certification; I have gasoline; I have electricity; I have VCA —

Cd VCA, that's like security, to work secure. You get this kind of test —

SDd A test, yes.

Cd That you can work safely.

SDd When you have to go on the roof, the top of the roof, that you know how to do it, and what you can do. On the top you have to stay 4 meters away from the side, and a lot of rules.

And they have four of the same type of test, for example in electricity, but those are more complicated.

UEB Which of your various trainings did you like the best?

Cd Gardening?

SDd No, this one! This I like!

Cd She likes this, you know!

SDd Yes, this is very nice! I meet a lot of people, I have a lot of talks. Two weeks ago I met a devotee [a fellow practitioner of devotion connection]. It was very surprising because he is in a relationship with a Muslim, and that was very complicated.

UEB So what did you like about your training? What parts of it did you really like?

SDd I think, everything! It's nice to know what you have to do. We do a lot. We say it's an easy job, but sometimes it's very complicated. When there is something wrong with the heat system, I have to look what is wrong, and then you have to do electricity, metering —

Cd Measuring.

SDd Measuring, we have to —

Cd Measure the pressure, because these things are complicated. And they have to work properly, otherwise you have a problem; it's gasoline.

SDd But everything I have to learn now, it's very interesting, I think there is nothing that I don't like.

UEB So what sort of things do you find particularly interesting?

They laugh

SDd Everything!

Cd There are no difficult questions!

SDd No! I think it's not so easy to choose one. I mean, everything is interesting, because when you do it, or when you learn it, it's like, you can understand how the heating system is working, and you need — everything that I learned, I need in some way, every day.

UEB Oh, wow.

Cd So you find it fascinating.

SDd Yeah. It's very fascinating.

UEB Yes, yes. And why do you find work so satisfying? What's satisfying about it for you?

SDd I think, when you do your job very well, the people are very happy.

UEB There's a sense of satisfaction that grows, yes? That you're making people happy?

SDd You make people happy, and especially in the wintertime, that they have a very good heater, and that they don't have problems of cold during the winter. We are doing, we are making sure that they have the heating, and warm water, and I think that's the part of my job that I like, because people depend on you. When I do something wrong, people don't have warm water or they don't have heating.

Cd I think you also like the social contact.

SDd Yeah, the social contact is also — because, I have, my part of the job, in Belgium you call that, social —

Cd Social welfare.

SDd Something like that.

Cd These houses are from social welfare.

UEB Oh.

Cd So people can rent it cheaper, because there are so many people who don't have enough money to live in big houses. So these are special houses.

SDd Most of the people don't have a job, or they're sick and — coming out of jail, last week, someone.

UEB I see. Is that what you do exclusively? You only work in these sorts of buildings?

SDd Yes, yes.

UEB Ah, so you work for the government then.

SDd No, no. It's —

Cd The company was from the government before. Before it was Electrabel and now it's Equans. They became bigger.

SDd I don't know if you see it, but that's my…*she shows the company logo on her shirt*…that's my company.

UEB Very nice, very nice.

SDd My company is working for another company, who is renting the houses to people, that don't have so much money.

Cd But I think they are still connected to the government.

SDd Yeah.

UEB And how do you see your work as being spiritual service?

SDd I think that is a little bit complicated because the thing that I do for Krishna is for the people that are warm during wintertime. Most of the time also, we are talking with people, and people are telling their whole life story. Most of the time we are there one hour or two hours, and they are talking to us like we're family or friends. Most of the time I hear their whole story about what they have before, and when they were a child. I think, we are listening to the people. We can't say, "You have to do this or that," but I think it's important that they can speak to us, and that we are listening to them.

UEB And you really feel that that's something you're doing to please Krishna, to be someone that they can speak to?

SDd Yeah, I think so. Because last month, I had someone, who heard, I think, the day before, that she has cancer, and really, she wanted to speak to me, and I was there for, I think, three hours.

UEB Wow.

SDd Working, I think, thirty minutes on the heater, and the rest, we were sitting together and she was talking to me like, "What do I have to do?" and "What can I do?" And I think that's also important, what you can do, like, helping people in that moment.

UEB Wow.

SDd Or, to be there, for them.

UEB Right, so you're providing not only that they have heat and hot water, but you're providing a friend, you're being kind of a friend, someone that they can talk to.

SDd I think 90% of the time it is like that, they are talking to us. Most of the time we are working and talking together.

Cd At the same time.

SDd At the same time. Sometimes I have to say, "Okay, I'll do first the heater and then I can sit down," and we are talking about life.

UEB So you think that this is an important way that you're pleasing Krishna, by helping people like this.

SDd I think so.

UEB Very nice. That's beautiful.

And how did you decide that you wanted to be a plumber? What made you decide that this was what you wanted to do for your work?

SDd The landlord before, we were —

Cd Where we were living before, he proposed to her to work with him, and that's how it started.

UEB And so you just kind of tried it and discovered that you really liked it.

Very nice. And what is it that you are doing, every day, as part of like a ceremony to connect with the Lord, with the Divine? What do you do every day as part of your connection?

Cd [A worship ceremony for the Lord as] Giriraja.

SDd Giriraja! That's the first thing that I do in the morning. And chanting. And when I'm working and people are not talking, most of the time I'm listening to some lecture on spiritual topics, that I have on my cellphone at that time.

UEB So worship and chanting and listening to lectures on the job.

And is there anything else that you'd like to speak about that might be helpful for people in similar kinds of occupations, as to how they could spiritualize their occupation?

Cd Oh yes. She's really talking to Giriraja. She's — He's a person, of course, but she's really treating Him as a person. Everything she wants to say, she tells Him. So I think for her that's very important.

to SDd

She's speechless now!

laughter

UEB I'm just thinking how wonderful that is.

Cd I am witnessing, because while she's doing the worship, I'm not talking to her, we are not talking to each other, I let her do what she's doing. But I observe, and she's really — before, I was not favorable, doing this before going to work, because she has to go to work early. She gets up early in the morning, and she does her worshiping, and she does it every day, without forgetting any time.

UEB That's wonderful.

And are you still driving a truck?

Cd I'm still driving a truck, for at least one and a half more years.

UEB How many years have you been driving a truck?

Cd If I stop driving a truck in one and a half years, I'll have been driving a truck for fifty years.

UEB Wow.

Cd All sorts of trucks, not only one kind. All sorts of trucks. Everything on wheels!

SDd On big wheels!

Cd On big wheels!

UEB So, how do you feel about having a plumber for your wife?

Cd Well, she's doing it! It's amazing, every time she wants to do something. I was thinking, oh no, this is not something for her. Specifically, I was thinking she has to do something else like working on a desk or a bureau or whatever. And yeah, she's doing it! Days and days and days and days she's into papers, looking for — she's learning, about this plumbing.

SDd holds up a blueprint

She's interested, so —

UEB Oh, look at that blueprint!

SDd Electricity.

UEB That's electricity.

SDd Yeah.

UEB So how are you feeling about her work?

Cd I admire her. I admire her spirit for it. Because I am not interested in these kinds of things. Not for me. But everyone is different, so —

What I feel about it…you know, she's 16 years younger. There will come a time when I'm not here any more, probably, if everything goes the normal way, then I will be leaving my body and she will still be here. Because women live longer, they say.

UEB So she'll still be here fixing the pipes.

Cd So she can maintain herself. She doesn't need any support for anything, she can be self-sufficient.

UEB Very nice.

Cd It takes a lot of time of her. It takes, I think, in a day, in 24 hours, it is taking 12 hours from her. Same with me. I'm a truck driver, I am driving a truck for 12 hours a day. For now I have to do it. In one and a half years…

UEB Do you have some of your spiritual program in the morning together?

SDd No.

Cd Together, no. Not together. I'm just watching her when she's doing worship.

UEB So you do your chanting and everything while you're driving.

Cd I start already when I go in the car, I go to the company. I have to drive, like, half an hour. I start already in the car. And then I continue in the truck. Sometimes it's one and a half hours, sometimes it's two hours, it depends.

UEB So if you both work so many hours, how do you have time to cook and take care of the house and everything?

SDd In the evening.

Cd The evening, and the weekends.

SDd When we are not at Radhadesh [a nearby *bhakti* yoga center].

UEB And you go to Radhadesh sometimes, and you still do some service there.

Cd It has been a while.

UEB With COVID and everything?

SDd Yeah, with COVID.

Cd And also, we don't go like before, for three days or one week any more. Normally we go one day. Just a day visit. And then, we arrive there ten o'clock. Maybe are already gone at two o'clock. So we are there four hours. Just for one day.

UEB Thank you so much for giving me your time.

Chapter 21

Cherishing Our Sources of Wealth

21.1   A Story from *Panchatantra*

Legend has it that there once was a farmer who, despite much toil, could not get crops to grow in his field. One day, he noticed a magical cobra by an anthill at the edge of his field. He thought to himself that this cobra might have the power to help him, so he brought the cobra a bowl of milk. The next day, he went to the anthill and found a gold coin. The farmer happily started up a friendship with the cobra, bringing a bowl of milk every day and getting a gold coin in return.

One day, the farmer learned he had to leave his village for a few days. He called his ten-year-old son and told him to be sure to set out a bowl of milk for the cobra by the anthill every day while the farmer was gone.

The first day, the farmer's son set out a bowl of milk as he had been told. The next day, he went to the anthill and found a gold coin.

That anthill must be full of gold coins! This cobra must be guarding them, thought the boy. *Let me kill the cobra so I can dig all the gold coins out of the anthill.*

The boy went and found a forked stick. He then ran up to attack the cobra. The cobra reared up and bit the farmer's son. The boy was able to escape and go home, but died shortly thereafter.

When the farmer returned, he was grief-stricken to learn from the villagers that his son had died. A few days later, the farmer once more took a bowl of milk to the cobra. The cobra told the farmer what his son had done and bade him farewell, leaving a single diamond.

21.2 Digging Up the Roots of Our Tree of Work

In hindsight, we see that attacking the cobra to get more gold not only put an end to the flow of gold, it also resulted in the death of the farmer's son. Stories like this are told in many cultures; some of us may be familiar with the story of the farmer who killed the goose that laid the golden egg. If we look at the fruits of our tree of work and think the tree must be pulling fruit out of the ground, we might try digging up the soil all around the roots of the tree. Not only would we not find any fruit there, we may topple the tree, killing it and ourselves.

Such stories are common folklore because many of us do indeed undermine the sources of our own wealth. Every one of us has run into a situation where we have a pressing short-term goal. What seems to us like "laser-like focus" on that goal may inadvertently turn into tunnel vision. In that frame of mind we may not think through the broader, longer-term impacts of what we're doing.

To steward the sources of our wealth is not only our responsibility, it's in our own best interest. Trying to ruthlessly exploit those sources risks bringing the flow of richness to an end. Rather, in the natural art of work we carefully nurture and protect the sources of our wealth. Let's look at some examples of how we can do this.

21.3 Stewarding Our Psychophysical Complex

We do our work through our body and mind. Thus, taking care of our physical and mental health is an integral part of the natural art of work. We need to take care of our psychophysical complex, just as we would maintain a car that a company had lent us for conducting its business. While taking care of our body and mind may sound obvious in theory, in practice it's easy to get so caught up in urgent matters that we never notice how we're neglecting our health until a crisis arises. So, many of us would do well to firmly prioritize habitual healthy behaviors such as regular exercise, especially green exercise (exercise outdoors in nature). Regular recreation is also important for our mental health. Sometimes we may want to take a step back in order to choose recreation that is truly restorative:

> ...computer and video game designers intentionally manipulate the reward system to keep players hooked. The promise that the next level or big win could happen at any time is what makes a game compelling. It's also what makes a game hard to quit. One study found that playing a video game led to dopamine increases equivalent to amphetamine use — and it's this dopamine rush that makes both so addictive. The unpredictability of scoring or advancing keeps your dopamine neurons firing, and you glued to your seat...the most effective stress-relief strategies are exercising or playing sports, praying or attending a religious service, reading, listening to music, spending time with friends or family, getting a massage, going outside for a walk, meditating or doing yoga, and spending time with a creative hobby....Because they aren't exciting like the dopamine releasers, we tend to *underestimate* how good they will make us feel.
>
> –Kelly McGonigal, *The Willpower Instinct*[212]

The unpredictability of encountering something we like in a social media feed also has the same effects as described here for video games. In general, these effects tend towards the *rajasic*, whereas what McGonigal described above as "most effective stress-relief strategies" tend to have more *sattva* in the mix.

Part of caring for our physical and mental health is maintaining a high level of self-integrity:

> [Self trust] is about developing the integrity, intent, capabilities, and results that make you believable, both to yourself and to others. And it all boils down to two simple questions: 1) Do I trust myself? and 2) Am I someone others can trust?
>
> ...
>
> Research shows that many of us don't follow through on the goals we set or don't keep the promises and commitments we make to ourselves. For example, while almost half of Americans set New Year's resolutions, research shows that only 8 percent actually keep them.
>
> What happens when we do this time after time? What's the net result of repeated failure to make and keep commitments to ourselves? It hacks away at our

self-confidence. Not only do we lose trust in our ability to make and keep commitments, we fail to project the personal strength of character that inspires trust. We may try to borrow strength from position or association. But it's not real. It's not ours…and people know it.…

The lack of self trust also undermines our ability to trust others. In the words of Cardinal de Retz, "A man who doesn't trust himself can never really trust anyone else."

The good news in all of this is that every time we do make and keep a commitment to ourselves or set and achieve a meaningful goal, we become more credible. The more we do it, the more confidence we have that we *can* do it, that we *will* do it. The more we trust ourselves.

–Stephen M. R. Covey & Rebecca R. Merrill, *The Speed of Trust: The One Thing That Changes Everything*[213]

21.4   Stewarding Those Who Work Under Us

People were 59 percent more willing to share information, 72 percent more likely to seek advice and 57 percent more likely to seek information from the civil person as compared to the uncivil behaving person. The civil person also inspired people to work 71 percent harder. Participants were 73 percent more likely to want to do well for this (civil) person and 1.22 times more likely to recommend him (for a job) compared with the uncivil person.

–Christine L. Porath and Alexandra Gerbasi, *Does Civility Pay?*[214]

Whatever field of work we are in, we may sometimes have people working for us or under us. These people are one of the most important sources of our wealth, and nurturing and protecting them is a key part of stewarding our field of work. The *Bhagavata Purana* says:

We deal suitably with all living beings by being kind, merciful, and compassionate to those under us; cultivating friendship with peers; and treating those above us with respect, modesty, and civility.

— *Bhagavata Purana* 11.3.23

The working relationships we cultivate with those under us become a resource that continues to bring dividends over time, both as we are able to work smoothly with the same people over multiple projects and because those people may recommend others they know to come work with or under us. Thus, caring for these relationships leads to a self-renewing network of people we can draw on, who may have a variety of talents that become useful in different contexts.

Our kindness and patience while training those under us will usually be rewarded many times over when they become fully competent and able to take responsibility. Just as we steward our own psychophysical complexes, so we are responsible for being mindful of those under us, and not pressuring or compelling them into going beyond their capacity. While pressuring them may appear to lead to increased productivity for a short time, doing so soon leads to burnout, from which there may be a long and difficult recovery period. Our relationship with overworked employees may be permanently damaged, and they may never work to their former capacity again. Furthermore, people under ongoing strain are more prone to make costly mistakes and even fatal flaws in their work, as we illustrated in the Fable of Beth in Chapter 16. "People pleasers" who feel awkward saying "no" are especially vulnerable to psychophysical damage under pressure from those above them. It may be easy to push these people past their limits long-term simply because they do not communicate that they are struggling to function beyond their own capacity. A process in which all workers are pushed to the max has little resiliency, so unexpected events can easily lead to critical failures. If we are pushing people inappropriately because those above us are in turn pressuring us with unrealistic expectations, it is our responsibility to respectfully and firmly inform those above us of what is actually feasible.

The importance of keeping our word and our commitments is *especially* important towards those working under us. When we set out clear expectations and hold ourselves accountable for keeping our commitments, then it's more likely those we supervise will reciprocate, leading to smooth productivity of the team.

It's important to note that cherishing the people we work with — especially those whom we supervise — involves recognizing that they may find joy in work that bores or frustrates us. Sometimes we may falsely take up the pain of doing work we find unpleasant out of fear of exploiting others. While none of us can avoid all unpleasant aspects of our jobs, we may be surprised that there are those who genuinely enjoy what we find onerous or, for that matter, those who find onerous what we enjoy. A great way to care for ourselves, our tasks, and others is to find the persons who are suited to a particular kind of work and let them do it happily.

Importantly, we can apply, support, and recommend the principles of the natural art of work described throughout this book to those working under us, as far as is possible and appropriate. We want to take care, as stated above, that we do this kindly. Any pressure or compulsion would be self-defeating since, after all, this art of work is *natural*. Indeed, one of the most fundamental tasks we have as supervisors is to recognize the different natures of those working under us and do our best to assign work accordingly. Ideally such assessment is done when someone first starts to work under us, so their nature and situation match from the beginning. But, in some cases, we will want to move people from their existing situation and arrange for additional training for these subordinates to help them get a role suited to their natures (as we touched on in Chapter 7). Such an investment of our time and resources can yield great rewards both in their future productivity as well as in our relationships with them.

It generally seems much easier to perceive the shades of ego in others than in ourselves. However, it is almost never useful to tell others, whether our peers, subordinates, or superiors, our perceptions about their shades of ego or indeed about their states of mind in general. Our perceptions of others are colored by our own states of mind, so even if, in any instance, those perceptions happen to be correct, it is easy for others to disregard or criticize our observations as merely stemming from our biases. Since shades of ego can also be contagious, often the most useful thing to do with a perception of a shade of ego in someone else is to look for that ego shade in oneself.

The following story took place in India in the early part of the 20th century:

> Once, many years ago, Puri Gosvami went to his home in Ganganandapur. At that time his family there had two cows. One was an old cow, the other was a young cow who gave milk. Puri Gosvami used to stay on the veranda of the temple room. From there he overheard his mother telling her daughter-in-law (Puri Gosvami's younger brother's wife), "Bouma, take good care of the

milk-giving cow. If you cannot take such good care of the other one, that is all right." Hearing this, Puri Gosvami told his sister-in-law, "Yes, Bouma, in our house also there is an old lady who cannot do a lot of work. It is not necessary to take good care of her either." Hearing this, his mother thought he had a point, and she was embarrassed by what she had said.

> –Devamayi Dasi, *A Life of Devotion: The Holy Biography of Om Visnupad Srila Bhakti Pramod Puri Gosvami Maharaj*[215][*]

Through his sarcastic comment (which was so unthinkable as to be ridiculous), Puri Gosvami nudged his mother to see more of the old cow's perspective and apply the Golden Rule. Cherishing our subordinates includes adjusting to natural variation in their working capacity over the course of their careers, rather than exploiting them to the breaking point and then discarding them (let alone consuming them). Of course, we can expect this natural variation to culminate in retirement at some point in life. We touch on the life cycle in Chapter 29.

21.5 Stewarding Air, Water, and Land

The air we breathe, the water we drink and wash with, the land we live and work on, as well as the public spaces we gather in or traverse are all fundamental to our physical and mental health as well as our ability to work. Thus it is the responsibility of all of us to keep our air, our water, and our homes, workplaces, and public spaces clean. Steps to avoid unnecessarily fouling the environment, and to clean up after ourselves, are an intrinsic part of a responsible work process.

21.6 Cherishing the Six Kinds of Richness

We often use the riches we receive in the course of our work to enhance our future work, either directly or indirectly. It is natural for those working with a particular kind of richness to grow in that kind of richness, which becomes a source of further wealth. Part of cherishing our particular kind of wealth is protecting it from being used in

---

[*]In the book, the story was relayed by a speaker who referred to Puri Gosvami as "Srila Guru Mahārāj," since he is Puri Gosvami's disciple. We have replaced all these references with "Puri Gosvami" here for clarity and smoothness of reading.

the wrong situations or in the wrong way. In a general sense, any type of prosperity can be an excuse for pride and arrogance – signs that instead of cherishing our wealth, we are misusing it and may thus lose it or at least lose the joy it can bring us.

So, a danger that applies to each kind of richness is hubris. We may come to rely on our richness and think that it can help in every situation. For instance, though we may be rich in *virya*, a microscopic virus can quickly bring down the strongest. If one gets into a car accident or other freak accident, in a split second it can:

- damage one's health, destroying *virya*;

- lead to expenses and loss of income, destroying *aisvarya*;

- disable one from doing an activity that had put one in the spotlight, destroying *yasa*;

- dull or destroy one or more senses, diminishing one's ability to experience some aspects of *sri*; or

- injure one's head, destroying *jnana*.

When looking at specific forms of wealth, every strength can become a weakness and every virtue a vice in certain situations. Thus, stewarding our wealth includes guarding against the specific pitfalls of the kinds of riches we accumulate. Let's look at these in turn.

If we are drawn to *virya* (strength or vigor), we may come to overestimate our own strength and underestimate the contribution of others and other kinds of wealth. We may genuinely not understand what it's like to be weak, so we may accidentally hurt or neglect those without the gift of strength. Most obviously, we may use our strength to exploit or harm others rather than to protect and inspire them. The cherishing of *virya* is especially important for those in the Field of Resources. Cherishing *virya* means producing healthy food, fabric, and medicines even if it's somewhat less profitable in the short run to do so. Of course, the proper dharma for those in the Field of Government is to take special care to use the strength of weapons and law for the good of others and not for oppression. For those who are professional athletes, cherishing this wealth means building and using one's natural strength and skill without resorting to chemical enhancements that give one an unfair advantage while destroying health in the long run.

If we are drawn to *sri* (radiant fortune, resources, beauty, grace, or splendor), one danger is that it is the most naturally ephemeral of all types of prosperity. If we keep chasing something that keeps escaping, we may lose the opportunity to work for something lasting. Earlier, we had mentioned that *sri* is a name of a goddess, Lakshmi. She is described as *chanchala*, "swiftly-moving." As they say, Lady Luck is fickle. When we possess beauty or charm we can misuse it to bewilder others through their lust and envy. There is much evidence that attractive people are deemed more trustworthy, make more money, get more help, and are more likely to secure employment. However, it's best to guard against using beauty to gain unfair advantages, which can often culminate in a backlash.[216] One danger is that one who has physical beauty may not be taken seriously:

> When patients perceived as attractive – ergo healthy – complained about pain, their pain was regarded as less severe and taken less seriously than complaints about pain from unattractive patients.
> –Tonya K. Frevert & Lisa Slattery Walker, *Physical Attractiveness and Social Status*[217]

Extremely beautiful people may be seen as less competent, as if their attractiveness is the sum total of their talents.[218] One might also use the wealth of beauty to falsely give an impression of high quality to otherwise shoddy material or work, in order to deceive others. On the other hand, cherishing *sri* is fundamentally linked with generosity, which also tends to increase it. One value of cherishing this source of wealth is especially evident in the Field of Artistry. Those in this field who treasure *sri* in their work will be able to withstand pressures to cut corners and sacrifice craft for the sake of mass production. Thus they preserve traditional skills in their specific area.

If we are drawn to *aisvarya* (controllership: wealth or power), we do well to keep in mind that not all problems can — or should — be solved with wealth or influence over other people. Connection, understanding, and negotiation towards win-win solutions will often yield longer and more solid results. Furthermore, *aisvarya* can be isolating. It is particularly easy for people with *aisvarya* to grow and maintain the ego of being at the center of reality. We may genuinely not understand what it's like to be poor and/or powerless, so we may hurt or neglect those without *aisvarya*. Both those in the Field of Resources and those in the Field of Government especially have responsibilities to distribute wealth appropriately, as we discuss in Chapter 14, and to be inspirational servant leaders. The cherishing of *aisvarya* means nurturing and empowering others to gain mutual prosperity. Such leaders make others feel smart, instead of impressing them with the leaders' own competence and intelligence.[219]

If we are drawn to *yasa* (righteous fame), we may forget that fame always brings with it increased scrutiny and criticism, which often lead to infamy (whether deserved or undeserved). We also may find fame comes between us and other people. Many people say, "Please don't reduce me to a label," yet if we become famous, our name itself may become a symbol that people use to label an experience, a group, a concept — whatever phenomenon people associate with or remember about us. Whether they invoke that label positively or negatively, many people may use a mental model that is a caricature of us, rather than seeing us as whole persons. A large number of people may regard famous people as a public resource and make demands that go beyond their capacity. The famous persons may then act to please others in order to maintain their fame, rather than do what's right. We, therefore, want to guard against using our reputation, status, and high regard to insist that others show us deference even when we are wrong. That reputation, status, and high regard can also shade us with *rajas*, as we mentioned in Chapter 8. While *yasa* can greatly facilitate our doing good in the world, it can also deafen us to the needs and concerns of those we could help. Particularly for those in the Field of Government, *yasa* is best used to build strong communities and a sense of gratitude without demeaning other jurisdictions and communities. Rejoicing in the strengths of one's community can be inspiring to others rather than a way to disparage others.

One of the most fundamental ways to cherish *yasa*, regardless of our field of work, is in terms of our personal and professional integrity. Integrity includes being honest, maintaining our own ethical and professional standards, keeping our commitments, and maintaining consistency among our thoughts, words, and actions. All of these behaviors allow others to have trust in us. Trust is the foundation and lubrication of any kind of interaction, so being able to trust and be trusted boosts our flow of work.

The Speed of Trust by Stephen M. R. Covey and Rebecca R. Merrill highlights the impact of trust:

When trust goes down, speed will also go down and costs will go up. When trust goes up, speed will also go up and costs will go down. It's that simple, that real, that predictable....

Once you really understand the hard, measurable economics of trust, it's like putting on a new pair of glasses. Everywhere you look, you can see the impact — at work, at home, in every relationship, in every effort. You can begin to see the incredible difference high-trust relationships can make in every dimension of life.

The serious practical impact of the economics of trust is that in many relationships, in many interactions, we are paying a hidden low-trust tax right off the top — and we don't even know it!

...

Once you know where and what to look for, you can see these taxes show up everywhere — in organizations and in relationships. They're quantifiable. And they're often extremely high.

...

As bestselling author Francis Fukuyama has said: "Widespread distrust in a society...imposes a kind of tax on all forms of economic activity, a tax that high-trust societies do not have to pay." [Fukuyama, *Trust: The Social Virtues and the Creation of Prosperity*, 1995, pp. 27–28] I contend that this low-trust tax is not only on economic activity, but on all activity — in every relationship, in every interaction, in every communication, in every decision, in every dimension of life.

I also suggest that, just as the tax created by low trust is real, measurable, and extremely high, so the *dividends* of high trust are also real, quantifiable, and incredibly high....

When trust is high, the dividend you receive is like a performance multiplier, elevating and improving every dimension of your organization and your life. High trust is like the leaven in bread, which lifts everything around it. In a company, high trust materially improves communication, collaboration, execution, innovation, strategy, engagement, partnering, and relationships with all stakeholders. In your personal life, high trust signifi-

cantly improves your excitement, energy, passion, creativity, and joy in your relationships with family, friends, and community. Obviously, the dividends are not just in increased speed and improved economics; they are also in greater enjoyment and better quality of life.
>   –Stephen M. R. Covey & Rebecca R. Merrill, *The Speed of Trust: The One Thing That Changes Everything*[220]

The Speed of Trust gives many specific examples as well as practical steps for building trust within an organization, starting with oneself. Many of these are also *sattvic* practices, and in general, increasing *sattva* can help build trust.

If we are drawn to *jnana* (knowledge), we may tend to overestimate our knowledge overall, or the reach of whatever knowledge we do have. We do well to remember that some of what we think we know may be mistaken, and we may not even know to what extent or in what area we are wrong. This is especially true when we are just starting to learn about some area regardless of how knowledgeable we may be about other areas — in fact, inapplicable knowledge can trip us up. As they say, a little learning is a dangerous thing:

> …what is commonly known as the Dunning-Kruger effect [is] that those who perform the worst overrate their skills the most. The effect is found by giving a group of people a task to do and then asking them how well they think they've done on the task. Poor performers overestimate how well they've done; strong performers often underestimate their performance….And Dunning has collected an impressive amount of evidence that the reason it happens is that those who lack skills also lack the knowledge of what skills they're missing….The unskilled just don't know what they don't know.
>   –Steven Sloman & Philip Fernbach, *The Knowledge Illusion: Why We Never Think Alone*[221]

The Dunning-Kruger Effect straightforwardly follows from the illusion to which we are all prone, shading our egos: "I am the center of reality." Imagine the knowledge that exists in the world about some subject could be objectively measured as, say, 5,000 units. Suppose I start out knowing 0.01 unit and after a little learning, I know 0.5 unit. However, I don't know any of these measurements: 0.01, 0.5 or 5000.

All I know is that relative to myself, *I now know fifty times more than I did before! That's 5000%! Wow, that's a lot! How much more could there possibly be to know, anyway?* The shading of ego also suggests that whatever I know must be the most important or relevant part, since it is now associated with me.[h] On the other hand, when I know 100 units, and the same amount of effort gets me from 100 to 100.5, I know this is just 0.5% of even what I myself already know about the subject, so it doesn't seem like much. By this point I may also know that there are at least 5,000 units available, so I know that what I know is just 2% of what there is to be known. If I've been applying the knowledge along the way, then I may also have experienced firsthand the ill effects of whatever I *didn't* know or was mistaken about at each point or even whatever is not known at all by humanity, as well as the difficulty of translating between theory and practice.

Knowing about the Dunning-Kruger effect itself can help us avoid this particular mistake. Beyond this, we can seek the perspectives of experts in each area of knowledge as mentors or coaches. To figure out who the experts are, it would be good to learn what training it takes to become an expert in that area. Otherwise, we may end up mistakenly thinking someone who has read some internet blogs is an expert! We can start by asking the real experts about the foundation of their area of knowledge. Cherishing *jnana* includes dealing respectfully with experts in each domain, keeping in mind the time and energy they have put into study and practice.

Additionally, when we are rich in *jnana*, it may be frustrating trying to communicate clearly with those who don't grasp information that is second nature and seems obvious to us. Furthermore, it is said that every philosopher and scientist has to present a new perspective in order to survive, but trying to establish ourselves as presenting a unique view may blind us to established truths and be mostly about inflating our sense of importance. Finally, we can get carried away in the realm of ideas and miss out on the emotional side of life. Being rich with *jnana* may particularly be a hindrance in situations such as diplomatic negotiation where intuitive emotional intelligence is called for. Cherishing *jnana* ideally means to love understanding, clarity, and insight for how they help ourselves and others. Especially for those in the Field of Ideas, ensuring that *jnana* leads to beneficial wisdom is crucial.

Another way of cherishing *jnana* is to value the community of learned experts in our area of knowledge. Historically, sometimes the learned consensus about what constitutes a correct paradigm turns out to be mistaken, sometimes to a large degree. In such cases, it is the mavericks who bring truth and understanding. However, for most of us, most of the time, the guidance and wisdom of community helps to guard against our accepting erroneous and possibly harmful ways of understanding.

Last, if we are drawn to *vairagya* (equanimity and freedom), at first it may seem that already means we are sacrificing rather than enjoying a particular type of wealth. This point is a little bit subtle. The *Bhagavata Purana* says:

> When one gives up the selfish conception by which one thinks, "This is my property, and that is another's," and when one is no longer concerned with the pleasures of one's own material body or indifferent to the discomforts of others, one becomes fully peaceful and satisfied. One considers oneself simply one among all the living beings who are equally part and parcel of the Supreme Lord. Such a satisfied soul is considered to be at the highest standard of service in devotion.
>
> — *Bhagavata Purana* 11.2.52

The key distinction is that one whose renunciation is in the spirit of healthy sacrifice does not become indifferent to the discomforts of others. Practicing renunciation as an end in itself is called "dry renunciation," which has a few drawbacks:

- It can engender pride in oneself and foster looking down upon those who renounce less.

- It can lead to a buildup of fiery energy that forces a release through bursts of anger.

- It can be difficult to balance and hard to sustain.

- One may facilitate this kind of renunciation by numbing one's senses, becoming less attuned to sensory experience. In this case a person may honestly not even perceive what causes discomfort to others, as one has drawn a veil of ignorance over one's awareness.

There are some things to remember about these points. Regarding the second point, apparent renunciation can be disguised aversion rather than neutrality. Regarding the third point, when real renunciation is based entirely on neutrality, it can "tip" into either enjoying (first, by contemplating on a mental level[222]) or hating what one is renouncing. Either way, falling under the sway of anger destroys the freedom of renunciation itself, and one's renunciation has denied one other types of pleasures. A metaphor for this unfortunate situation is found in the *Bhagavata Purana*, where it states that although detachment allows a person to cross an ocean of difficulties, persons without compassion and love for the Divine are likely to drown in a tiny puddle of their own anger, making all their renunciation useless.[*]

The thought process behind dry renunciation is essentially self-centered. By contrast, renunciation in the spirit of sharing is called "engaged renunciation." It is other-centered rather than self-centered: one is sacrificing for the sake of one's beloved ideals. The essence of engaged renunciation is not denial, but giving, ultimately to the greater whole. One of the functions of those in the Field of Ideas is especially to set an example for society in terms of cherishing *vairagya*. Indeed, love of truth is essential for the functioning of the Field of Ideas, so those in this field who are experts in dharma are prepared to give up other things when they come in conflict with truth. Thus *vairagya* is also essential for the functioning of the Field of Ideas.

A misuse of *vairagya*, which in some cases can also apply to *yasa*, is to develop an attitude of moral superiority. People who are happy and feel prosperous with their renunciation are often unmoved by what tempts most others into morally compromised situations. And those whose life is rich with the fame that comes from being upright and ethical may have developed deeply embedded strategies to preserve their moral and ethical standing. When detached persons see others lapse from standards they maintain with little or no effort, a mood of self-righteous condemnation can result. Such a contemptuous attitude is indicative of the shade of *tamas*, which then damages our detachment. To cherish *vairagya*, then, means to temper it with empathy and compassion and, with that mood, to help uplift others appropriately.

Vairagya is different from the others, as it cannot be taken away without some cooperation from us. Nevertheless, sufficient temptation may destroy *vairagya*.

Next, in Chapter 23, we discuss caring for our field of work as a whole.

---

[*]See *Bhagavata Purana* 11.4.11[223] with context from the preceding verse. The commentator Sridhara Swami elaborates that just as drowning persons helplessly discard whatever treasures they had been carrying on their heads, so these dry renunciates throw away their richness of *vairagya* when they speak ill words to hurt others out of anger.

Chapter 22

Testimony: Internal Medicine Physician

My legal name is Venugopal Damerla.

My designation is MD: I am an Internal Medicine Physician at the Veterans Affairs Medical Center in the Denver area. My American board certifications are in internal medicine and integrative medicine, and I am Fellowship Trained in Hematology-Oncology.

For further info, you can follow a link to my website.[224]

The teaching that the Divine is equally present in everyone, as in the hearts of all people who seek me out for help, gives me a very crucial clue to interact with and accept them without judgment. God is our eternal loving companion, witnessing our desires, pains, sufferings, pleasures, and all actions. Then I realized if I sincerely make an internal shift — by requesting Him within — then He might be graceful enough to grant me an understanding of what mattered for my patient for better health and well-being.

On the contrary, when I exclude the important step of connecting with a patient through the medium of the Divine, I am often perceived as cowardly, insecure, distracted, artificial, and leading a life of double standards. The process of applying medical knowledge for healing the body in one part of my life and performing external acts of a spiritual or religious practice in another part of my life is mechanical and superficial. In my experience, this disconnect does not bring out the best of what I can offer, but is only a strategy for survival and *not con-*

scious living. Empathetic listening, to understand others on a personal level and make them feel heard, is the most important element to enter into a partnership. Doing that is not about being "nice."

Daily spiritual practices inject new life power with which I courageously introspect and constantly improve myself as an instrument of the Divine. When I am conscious of the guiding voice within, loving and caring naturally surface and cut through all barriers, creating a healing touch for my patients. Now, I don't live constantly with a sense of urgency, but am capable of taking a pause before I see every patient. I can calmly create an internal sacred space for every person in front of me with an unconditional heartful intention to help. I also make less errors, and complaints from patients are a rarity — which is quite perplexing to my colleagues! God ceases to be someone confined to the walls of a temple, or someone far out there in space. For me, God is for real — right there in between me and the patient, to create our trusting bond and harmony. During a patient encounter I am able to come from a place of authenticity, with a higher degree of self-awareness to relate with them (and everyone in general) in a manner that awakens their own insight and intuition. This creates an environment where "healing" is able to unfold and grow…and disease-promoting habits or thought patterns are bound to have less power over them.

When the point of trust is reached, I advise my patients that the underlying principle is that things go from the internal to the external. What this practically means is that the extent to which one is in clean, healthy consciousness will manifest as strong, auspicious emotional and physical health. I have had many of my patients become curious about my spiritual path and introduce them to mantra meditation as a code to relaxation as a spiritually based clinical intervention based on our recently published original research in a peer-reviewed US medical journal.[225]

What all this adds up to is: devotional connection is not a lazy or monotonous endeavor even for one moment — it is an adventure of making continuous internal shifts to align with the will of the all-pervading Divinity. When I see medicine as not different from that spiritual connection, it stops being a "job." It is an ever-enlivening quest, capable of providing a direction to explore and fulfill things I love to do for the common good of all. I firmly stand on a platform of being myself, while an efficient harmonious flow of wisdom from all sides of my being has a positive emotional influence on my patients, family, and friends.

Chapter 23

Cherishing Our Field of Work

In Chapter 21, we discussed ways that we can keep our individual careers vital and viable through stewardship of the sources of our prosperity. We are most likely to have prosperous pleasure both as individuals and throughout society when we also steward our field as a whole. In Chapter 6, we explored the value of the specific ancient division of Fields of Artistry, Resources, Government, and Ideas in terms of the harm that accrues to individuals and society when people work in unsuitable fields. Another way of appreciating the wisdom of these particular four categories of work is to note that workers in each field — regardless of the specific job — share a specific responsibility in common that differs from those in other fields. That responsibility, metaphorically speaking, is to maintain the viability and "fertility" of the field by attending to the upkeep of the overall principles there. Some of the points for each field might seem obvious in theory. However, the difficulty for each of us is to steward the principles of our field even when doing so seems disadvantageous for us in the short term.

23.1 Stewarding the Field of Artistry

In the Field of Artistry, the key principle is keeping society beautiful and smoothly functioning in a mood of service. We serve the people for whom we are creating beauty and function: our customers, patrons, and/or employers. When we treat these people courteously, respectfully, and professionally, then in general they will remember us for future projects and recommend us to others. If we go the extra

mile to be kind, to fix problems, and to add little extra touches of quality, then we will be particularly memorable in this impersonal day and
age.

Unfortunately, we'll run into some people who are dissatisfied no
matter what we do. Nevertheless, over the long term, professionalism will become our solid asset. As a professional reputation is something that takes a long time to build or repair, yet can be damaged
very quickly, we would be wise to guard it carefully, especially when
it seems difficult in the moment.

When we work in the Field of Artistry, our skills and our craftsmanship are the wellspring of our work. We honor those wellsprings
by doing work to a high level of quality. While meeting the customer's
constraints as to time and price can itself be an art, if a customer makes
demands that would keep us from doing the job well, then honoring
our craft may require refusing politely and firmly. We can work
with customers to suggest alternatives that could meet their needs
and make them happy, even if these alternatives are not what the
customers initially asked for. Educating the customers in this way is
part of stewarding our field of work. Still, it's best to be ready to lose
an occasional customer.

We may think working hastily and cutting corners to reduce costs
will bring us more money through more customers. Disregarding
long-term consequences is characteristic of the ego shade of *tamas*,
which, as we mentioned in Chapter 8, is an occupational hazard of
the Field of Artistry. If we do this, we're shooting ourselves in the
foot. Aiming low may work for a while, but eventually either our
shoddy work will come back to bite us in the form of costly and time-
consuming repairs and unhappy customers, or someone will undercut
us. In fact, with robotic automation of more and more functions in
more and more areas, there will soon be no way for humans to compete on speed and price. The human care with which we accomplish
our craft may soon be not just our best asset, but our only one.

For those who deal primarily with beauty, aesthetic sense is the
foundation of work. Dealing with patrons can be even more challenging in jobs that focus on beauty than in jobs that primarily deal
with function, since tastes differ. However, our strong personal flavor is precisely what brings the most value to our creations. As far as
technical skills go, artificial intelligence is taking great leaps forward
as far as replicating those, even going so far as to applying a painter's
brushstroke style to a photograph or other image. While what is most
unique and authentic about an artist may be off-putting to one patron,

it is precisely what will attract others. Being true to ourselves is what we can sustain, and what will sustain us, in the natural art of work. We can thus try to please the customer, but within the framework of our own artistry.

Of course, personal flavor used to be inherent and unavoidable in the Field of Artistry:

> During the 1880s, inventors developed new machinery that made flow production possible in the manufacture of soap, cigarettes, matches, breakfast cereals, canned goods, and many other products. As a result, factories could process massive batches of raw materials.
>
> New techniques for national marketing emerged in tandem with the mass-produced products they promoted....the very idea of chewing gum and flashlights had to be introduced to a population accustomed to goods made at home or by craftspeople....the creators of the first national market for manufactured consumer products...faced a further task. A population accustomed to homemade products and unbranded merchandise had to be converted into a national market for standardized, advertised, brand-named goods in general.
>
> –Susan Strasser, *Satisfaction Guaranteed*[226]

This conversion started in the 1880s and was accomplished over the early part of the 20th century. Now the sensitivities of many of those who consume mass-marketed goods and services have been dulled by the world of hastily, cheaply produced commodities, which are designed to be soon tired of and discarded so that more of them can be sold (as described in Giles Slade's book *Made to Break*[227]). Those who work in the Field of Artistry can help reeducate the tastes of customers by maintaining high standards of quality. In certain parts of this field, techniques and skills have been passed down through generations. As of 2021, there are still certain geographical regions or groups of people who specialize in certain crafts, and who excel in specialized techniques of those crafts. For example, only in Iran can one find the highest quality of hand-knotted wool and silk rugs. Beyond keeping these ancient traditions and crafts alive and flourishing, each person's development of a personal "signature," so to speak, in the craft is also part of cherishing this field.

It is true that modern factory goods have advantages of standard-ized, interchangeable parts, accessible from numerous geographical regions. Relying fully on hand-crafted items is practical mainly in a society where animals are the primary means of transport, and one lives near the craftsperson who both created and can repair one's items. Rather than a call to return to preindustrial times, we can consider how to use technological advancements to further the satis-faction of workers in the Field of Artistry as well as those who use the goods and services from this field. For example, sites such as Etsy con-nect shoppers with artisans who sell hand-crafted items. Musicians can schedule tours to places where they already know from social media that there are a significant number of people who appreciate their music. Putting a high value on using technological advance-ments to further cherish the skills, beauty, and personal touch of the workers in this field is essential to avoid having the negative uses of industrialization and technology overwhelm us.

Of course, all of this discussion goes hand-in-hand with what we talked about earlier in the section: treating our customers, patrons, and employers with courtesy, respect, and professionalism. Indeed, our customers, patrons, and employers will generally respect our professionalism more when we maintain our standards, politely and firmly. Such is service in action.

23.2   Stewarding the Field of Resources

For those who work in the Field of Resources, the key principle is keeping society flourishing in a healthy and sustainable way. To ac-complish this, it is useful to remember that one key part of this field, directly or indirectly, may be other living beings, including plants and animals. We mentioned earlier that the Golden Rule asks us to treat others as we would like to be treated, if we were in their shoes. We also mentioned treating those who work under us with kindness, compassion, and mercy. This includes cows from whom we get milk, sheep from whom we get wool, and so forth. We can easily relate to their needs and wishes, which are much like our own: to live and run and play, along with others of their own kind. So these animals who work under us deserve not to be overworked or mistreated (let alone killed!), just like humans who work under us. Beyond individual animals upon whom we may depend, we also have a special interest in the health of the entire species. For instance, those who keep bees would advocate protecting bees in general from insecticides, which are often sprayed indiscriminately from the air over wide areas and are likely to harm them.

Those who literally keep trees or grow crops do well to remember that plants are also living beings to be treated with kindness and respect. We can proactively continue to learn about how plants and trees react and interact, regardless of whether we can see any immediate effect on fruit or crop yield. For instance:

> Students at the Institute for Environmental Research at RWTH Aachen discovered something amazing about photosynthesis in undisturbed beech forests. Apparently, the trees synchronize their performance so that they are all equally successful. And this is not what one would expect. Each beech tree grows in a unique location, and conditions can vary greatly in just a few yards. The soil can be stony or loose. It can retain a great deal of water or almost no water. It can be full of nutrients or extremely barren. Accordingly, each tree experiences different growing conditions; therefore, each tree grows more quickly or more slowly and produces more or less sugar or wood, and thus you would expect every tree to be photosynthesizing at a different rate.
>
> And that's what makes the research results so astounding. The rate of photosynthesis is the same for all the trees. The trees, it seems, are equalizing differences between the strong and the weak. Whether they are thick or thin, all members of the same species are using light to produce the same amount of sugar per leaf. This equalization is taking place underground through the roots. There's obviously a lively exchange going on down there. Whoever has an abundance of sugar hands some over; whoever is running short gets help. Once again, fungi are involved. Their enormous networks act as gigantic redistribution mechanisms. It's a bit like the way social security systems operate to ensure individual members of society don't fall too far behind.
>
> –Peter Wohlleben, *The Hidden Life of Trees: What They Feel, How They Communicate*[228]

Additionally, we have a responsibility to nurture and renew the soil. For instance, certain types of chemical fertilizers may appear to rapidly increase yield, while degrading the soil. On the other hand, using manure for fertilizer deposits a balanced mix of nutrients back into the soil, resulting in a sustainable steady-state cycle:

> There is a biological basis for the central role soil organic matter plays in growing healthy crops and sustaining bountiful harvests. Fertility isn't only about chemistry and physics. Soil ecology and nutrient cycling driven by microbial life also matter. So even when standard soil chemistry tests say you need to add fertilizers, the right soil life – if present and abundant – may be able to supply what plants need. Growing evidence shows that synthetic fertilizers work like agricultural steroids, propping up short-term crop yields at the expense of long-term fertility and soil health. Consider fertilizers and agrochemicals as like antibiotics – a godsend if you really need them, but foolish to rely on for regular use....
>
> In hindsight, we know that our dependence on the plow and fertilizers to pump up crop yields depleted soil organic matter and disrupted the beneficial fungi that extract crucial micronutrients from rocks and deliver them to crops. When we take out mycorrhizal fungi – eliminating or limiting their role in nutrient acquisition – and compromise microbial roles in pest and pathogen control, we have to replace them with fertilizers and pesticides.
>
> But we can reverse this by cultivating beneficial microbial life. And the key to doing this seems to be practices that build soil organic matter – feed them and they will come.
>
> –David R. Montgomery, *Growing A Revolution: Bringing Our Soil Back To Life*[229]

Turning now to those who facilitate exchanges between suppliers and customers, cherishing this field of work includes treating customers with respect, courtesy, and professionalism, much as in the Field of Artistry. In the Field of Resources, however, the emphasis is also on building sustainable working relationships with suppliers, treating them fairly and honoring commitments.

Some in the Field of Resources work directly with money, in finance or accounting. We can keep in mind where any real increase in an investment comes from:

> Now, consider for a moment a world in which wealth consisted only of inert matter, and production was only working this inert matter into different shapes. Such things have no reproductive power of their own. If I put away hammers or barrels or money, they will not increase.

> But…suppose I release a swarm of bees. At the end of a year, I will have more bees, as well as the honey they have made. Or suppose I put cattle out on the range. At the end of the year, I will, on average, also have an increase.

> What provides the increase in these cases is something distinct and separate from labor. Though it generally requires labor to make use of it, we can readily distinguish it from labor. It is the active power of nature — the principle of growth, or reproduction, which characterizes all forms of what we call life.

> It seems to me that this is the true cause of interest — that is, the increase of capital over and above that due to labor. Certain powers in nature — with a force independent of our own efforts — help us turn matter into forms we desire. In other words, they aid us in producing wealth.

> Both types of things are included in the terms wealth and capital — things that have no innate power of increase, and things that yield over and above what can be attributed to labor. With inanimate things, labor alone is the efficient cause. When labor stops, all production stops. But in these other modes, time is an element. The seed grows whether the farmer sleeps or works.

> Furthermore, there are also variations in the powers of nature and of people. Through exchange, these variations can be used to obtain an increase in net output. This somewhat resembles the increase produced by the vital forces of nature.

> …

In short, then, when we analyze production, it falls into three modes:

- *Adapting* — Changing natural products, in form or place, to fit them to satisfy human desire.

- *Growing* — Utilizing the vital forces of nature, as in raising vegetables or animals.

- *Exchanging* — Increasing the general sum of wealth by exploiting local variations in the forces of nature, or variations among human forces due to situation, occupation, or character.

...

Thus, interest springs from the power of increase given to capital by the reproductive forces of nature, or by the analogous capacity of exchange.
   —Henry George, *Progress and Poverty*[230]

Those who work in the Field of Resources do well to protect the sustainability of this field in a holistic way. As Dan Ariely explains:

Some special companies see trust as a public good (like clean air and water), and customers return the trust. One company in which I personally have a lot of faith is Timberland, the maker of outdoor clothing. I once attended a talk by Jeff Swartz, the CEO, in which he detailed many of the ways that Timberland is trying to reduce CO_2 emissions, recycle, use sustainable materials, and treat its employees fairly. At the end of Jeff's talk, another CEO asked him, "What are the returns on these investments?" Jeff answered that he has been trying to find an economic return for these actions but that he had not yet found it in the data. He further added that it would be nice if being environmentally and socially responsible was also financially rewarding but that he didn't really feel it was necessary. He simply wanted to make sure that his company followed the moral principles he wanted his kids to live by. After hearing this, I went and bought my first pair of Timberland shoes.
   —Dan Ariely, *Predictably Irrational, Revised and Expanded Edition*[231]

The underlying basis for real growth in finance is the labor, growth, or reproduction of other living beings. To steward our finances includes unearthing exactly what this underlying basis is. Cherishing the Field of Resources includes taking care to nurture and protect those other living beings who are the sources of our wealth, no matter how many layers of indirection and abstraction obscure those sources. Of course, in this process we would also be checking that this underlying basis is sound, sustainable, and regenerative. It is often the influence of the ego shade of *tamas* that induces us to think more about a limited circle, and the ego shade of *rajas* induces us to think about what will bring us praise and glory, which may sometimes be at odds with what is good for the field.

Cherishing any field includes keeping one's work honest and free of criminal elements. This is particularly important in the Field of Resources:

> Someone once asked Slick Willie Sutton, the bank robber, why he robbed banks....Sutton looked a little surprised...."I rob banks because that's where the money is."
> –Robert M. Yoder, *Someday They'll Get Slick Willie Sutton*[232]

To protect the Field of Resources from criminal elements may involve very deep dedication to the health of one's work, never more so than when one's own family are the Mafia! In this regard, we can consider Giovanni Impastato. His brother Peppino is more famous (subject of at least one film and a separate book). Their father was a Sicilian mafioso; however, Peppino refused to join the Mafia. Instead he campaigned against it and eventually was murdered. Giovanni has continued this campaign. Giovanni is in the Field of Resources, bravely running a business while at the same time defying the powerful Sicilian Mafia and publicly urging others also to do so. The Mafia often acts as a de facto parallel yet corrupt government, or infiltrates government.[233][234]

Peppino, who likely was in the Field of Government himself, was standing for election when he was murdered. A person in the Field of Resources is not in a position to oppose the Mafia by trying to supplant them, as an honest worker in the Field of Government could. Yet persons in the Field of Resources can also stand against the Mafia's power by continuing to conduct their business honestly. Giovanni Impastato faced threats:

> ...in late November [2002] Giovanni remembers: 'They even daubed red paint on the white walls of our shop, in the form of rivulets of blood flowing from a bullet wound.' [His wife] Felicetta adds: 'I can tell you they looked very realistic.' In June 2007 the attacks resumed: twice in two days acid was thrown at the front door of the family house....
> —Tom Behan, *Defiance*[235]

This kind of intimidation had been going on for decades in the town, Cinisi, where the Impastati lived:

> One of the victims was Gaspare Cucinella, an old man who ran a corner shop on the Corso, selling flour and beans. 'Binardinu' Palazzolo and his brothers had been demanding protection money but Cucinella had refused to pay. Then one day in 1937 when Cucinella was out in the country side he saw the Palazzolos coming and knew what they meant to do, but they got the first shot in and — *ammazzarono* [they murdered him].
> —Tom Behan, *Defiance*[236]

Though Giovanni Impastato knew the Mafia was not making empty threats, he continued to conduct his business in accordance with the principles of trade, in which money is exchanged for goods and services, not extorted. In this way he was cherishing the Field of Resources.

23.3 Stewarding the Field of Government

For those in the Field of Government, the key principle is caring for and protecting people. They are especially attuned to:

- the needs of *all* the people in their jurisdiction, not just some of them;

- fairness and justice;

- showing mercy in a holistic perspective; and

- the long-term as well as the short-term benefit.

We may need to go out of our way to steward *all* the people, with many different kinds of interests. Otherwise, some traps we may easily fall into, because they may feel natural, are:

- paying more attention to those whom we perceive as more related to us;

- paying more attention to those whom we perceive as more similar to us;

- paying more attention to those who are able to do more for us personally;

- paying more attention to those with more of one or more kinds of richness; or

- paying more attention to those who are more vocal about their needs.

Recall that the ego shade of *rajas* is the occupational hazard of the Field of Government. Considering ourselves and our own circle more important because we think we are just and honorable, and wanting to garner prestige from others, relate to *rajas* and can lead us into the above traps.

We can proactively look into the needs of people who are not in any of these groups, speak with them and actively listen to them, and reach out to them. Although this may not be easy at first, when people are touched by our sincerity they will reciprocate. Traveling to different neighborhoods of our jurisdiction and walking around can be an important element of getting to know all our people.

We benefit from being particularly on guard against the natural tendencies within ourselves to favor particular groups in regards to upholding fairness and justice. Of particular concern is to keep the interests of absent persons in mind:

> One of the most important ways to manifest integrity is to *be loyal to those who are not present.* In doing so, we build the trust of those who are present. When you defend those who are absent, you retain the trust of those present. [Emphasis in original.]
> —Stephen R. Covey, *The 7 Habits of Highly Effective People: Powerful Lessons in Personal Change*[237]

While what Covey describes is an important principle for everyone, this aspect of honorable behavior is absolutely essential to the functioning of the Field of Government.

For example, in a murder case, family members of the victim may sometimes be desperate for some resolution. However, instead of prosecuting the first person we find who might have committed the murder, it is important to keep in mind that our primary duty is to absent persons: the murder victim, potential future victims of the real murderer, and potential victims of any murderers in our jurisdiction. Our duty to all these persons is to catch and prosecute the real murderer, not the first suspect we find, even though during the time it takes to do that the family of the victim may undergo additional distress.

As punishing innocent people undermines the whole basis of community and society in trust, good faith, and neighborliness, it is easy to see why the *Bhagavata Purana*[238] and other ancient traditions also describe such punishment as a particularly heinous act:

> To impose a fine on the innocent is not right, or to flog
> the noble for their integrity.
>
> —Proverbs 17:26

These principles remind us to also be fair to those who are suspected of crimes. Such fairness means, among other things, reminding ourselves that innocent people can be suspects, and that we have probably been unfairly accused in everyday life. Fairness means to assiduously avoid dealing with suspects in ways that could be "punishing them" without due process. Such concerns relate to how persons are accused, apprehended, physically restrained, and so forth.

In fact, fairness and justice extend even to those who are criminals. Justice and fairness refer to implementing specific consequences for specific actions. They do not entail labeling people as enemies and treating them as categorically distinct from the rest of the people. In the *Bhagavata Purana*, the ancient prince Prahlada says:

> Making distinctions among oneself, one's friends, and
> one's enemies is disastrous.
>
> — *Bhagavata Purana* 7.5.12

Those who are duly convicted of crimes are still among our people. Stewarding the people includes endeavoring to reform criminals and help them become law-abiding citizens.

Each government's police force — both the ethos of the force as a whole as reflected in training and policies, and the actions and mood of individual officers — is protecting citizens in general rather than seeing them as enemies or potential enemies. Even in war zones, high-quality military training includes rules of engagement to avoid injuring innocent people and noncombatants as far as possible, as well as other war crimes. Such training includes de-escalation techniques. The very term "law enforcement" may tend to pollute this aspect of the Field of Government, as it can suggest a position of antagonism rather than prevention and protection. When the police see the general citizenry as potential or actual criminals, then a military-type mood can grow, leading to brutality. The best policing models that cherish the field involve working to root out causes of crime, connecting regularly with local communities in genuine bonds of friendship and trust.

A related but perhaps surprising way to degrade the Field of Government are attempts to temper the natural tendency of those suited for this field to run towards danger. Many workers in this field are in intrinsically dangerous situations regularly, such as those faced by police officers and firefighters. If such workers neglect their own safety nearly or completely, injuries and fatalities may decimate the workforce to levels dangerous for society as a whole. Therefore, in some places there is systematic training to attempt to moderate workers against the natural tendency of their field. While such training may be well-intentioned, the results can pollute this field of work:

> They're also trained to prioritize their own safety over others'. "Police training starts in the academy, where the concept of officer safety is so heavily emphasized that it takes on almost religious significance," writes Seth W. Stoughton, a former cop and current researcher for The Atlantic. This mentality is so ingrained, he says, that it's often called the "first rule of law enforcement." That's why cops are given such latitude to use force when they feel it's needed — they're, quite literally, trained to put themselves first. To stoke this belief, Stoughton reports that cops are often shown "painfully vivid, heart-wrenching dash-cam footage of officers being beaten, disarmed or gunned down after a moment of inattention or hesitation." Then, they're told that the "primary culprit isn't the felon on the video, it's the officer's lack of

> vigilance." That kind of programming puts the onus on them to quickly parse right from wrong — it's their job, they're taught, to always be on. After all, as they're often trained to believe, cops are in danger. Hands-on exercises have them react to a variety of situations in which the suspect attacks them with a gun or knife first, and they learn to finesse their split-second reaction times to eliminate the threat. And if their reaction to that threat is a mistake? Well, cops have a saying for that: "Better to be judged by twelve than carried by six."
>
> —Isabelle Kohn, *The Secret Lives of Police Wives — and the Abuse They Suffer in Silence*[239]

The result of such training can be brutality with the public and even domestic violence when the heroism, strength, and courage natural to this field is used to protect the members of the field from society rather than to protect society at the risk of cost to oneself. Of course, foolish risk-taking and courage may look similar, and to know the difference, training in self-preservation is needed. The sanctity of this field is damaged when the self-preservation natural to the Field of Resources becomes the main guiding principle in Government, rather than the honor and justice that are its real central principles. Indeed, one reason for this type of degradation can be an undue influence of Resources in Government.

This discussion brings us to the subject of kindness and mercy. As stewards of the people, it is naturally within our jurisdiction to look for those in need and find ways to help them. Kindness is an integral part of our mandate. It is important that we remain alert to the broader trends to which individual cases of mercy may aggregate, as, again, it is easy for us to be more merciful to particular groups of people, perhaps without even being consciously aware of it. It's best to be vigilant, keeping mercy as the guiding principle at the level of designing and setting up whole systems, and making fairness and justice our top priority when handling individual cases within the already existing system.

We may also need to go out of our way to understand what affects our people as a whole. Just as we don't usually notice the air we're breathing (provided it's clean) since it constantly surrounds us, similarly we may not recognize what views are shared by all our people, since often they are an implicit or perhaps unconscious part of the culture we've all been immersed in since childhood. Learning about and keeping up with how governments in other jurisdictions do things, and perhaps even visiting them, can help broaden our perspective. Doing so can help suggest practices that we might implement in our own jurisdiction.

Cherishing the Field of Government often involves long-term thinking regardless of short-term needs. However, human beings in general are subject to a cognitive illusion called "hyperbolic discounting." If someone asks us if we want $100 one year from now or $120 a year and one day from now, we will choose to wait an extra day and get an extra $20. But if someone asks us if we want $100 now or $120 tomorrow, often many of us will choose $100 now, even if we have no urgent bills to pay. Whenever we have to make a decision regarding something immediate, by default a different part of our brain geared towards short-term thinking kicks in. These two systems are described in *Thinking Fast and Slow*.[240] It may take willful effort for us to override the fast system with the more reflective one. Since this cognitive illusion is common to human beings, an entire mass of people may tend towards shortsightedness. So those in the Field of Government have a special responsibility to look out for long-term threats and opportunities, and take action while enough time is available for that action to be completed.

As those in government have to deal with the whole of society, they are often engaged in tricky balancing acts with many tradeoffs. The constraints of decision making within specific time frames can limit how deeply they can attend to all the considerations above. So getting help from those in the Field of Ideas can often be useful. We'll discuss the interplay of these Fields more in Chapter 33.

An area of government we may wish we didn't need is the military. But most nations understand that the possible — and sometimes actual — use of force is sometimes needed for peace and security. Cherishing this aspect of this field ideally involves keeping military action among those who volunteer for this work. Such would include the avoidance of conscription (the "draft") and keeping battles out of civilian areas completely. Weapons that cause civilians harm long after the war has ended, such as nuclear bombs and landmines, would never be used. The codes and ethics of war among the combatants are principles of honor among those who cherish this field. Government leaders who have the title of "commander-in-chief" but who sit comfortably in protected bunkers while they send others into harm's way damage this field of work because they may then be prone to trivialize the fighters' sacrifice. If leaders believe that war is absolutely necessary as a last resort to combat real evil, then they demonstrate personal sacrifice by visiting the troops, living austerely themselves, and so forth.

Keeping the Field of Government wholesome also involves how wealth is collected. Government can levy taxes, and impose fines for those not in obedience to the law. In other times, "booty" won in battle would also be collected. This field gets corrupted when taxes are too high or disproportionate, or fall more lightly on groups such as those who are related to us, similar to us, more vocal about their needs, and so forth. Income from bribes, kickbacks, and other such "favors" also pollutes this field in general.

Cherishing this field also means keeping the principle of serving people uppermost and not trying to use our position for personal gain at the expense of the public's trust. In the United States, The Code of Federal Regulations calls this problem "Misuse of Position" in four areas — use of public office for private gain, use of nonpublic information, use of government property, and use of official time.[241]

Using public office for private gain includes expediting licensing and permits for friends, or appearing to have one's agency endorse something it in fact does not. Off-duty police officers who show their badges to get out of traffic citations, or even distribute get-out-of-citation passes to their relatives so that they can do the same, also fall into this category. Misusing nonpublic information includes using knowledge about business contracts and bidding for personal financial gain or to aid one's friends and family. Government equipment and spaces are not to be used to conduct personal business, nor are one's own paid time or the paid time of government employees under one's direction to be used for one's personal business. If such behaviors are common in government, they sabotage the justice and honor that form the core of this field and the whole field is spoiled, both for the workers in the field and the people in general. In general, one cherishes the Field of Government by using the field solely to protect and maintain those in need.

Related to giving special preference to friends is the danger for those in this field to put loyalty as a value above all else, to the extent that the field itself becomes compromised and spoiled. An emphasis on loyalty tends to be naturally strong among those drawn to this field and can support some helpful form of civic spirit in the sense of grateful service to the jurisdiction that sustains and protects us. But when loyalty becomes an end in and of itself, or the main measurement of personal worth, situations such as the following may result:

> Lenin's one-party state was based on different values. It overthrew the aristocratic order. But it did not put a competitive model in place. The Bolshevik one-party state was not merely undemocratic; it was also anti-competitive and anti-meritocratic. Places in universities, civil-service jobs, and roles in government and industry did not go to the most industrious or the most capable. Instead, they went to the most loyal. People advanced because they were willing to conform to the rules of party membership. Though those rules were different at different times, they were consistent in certain ways. They usually excluded the former ruling elite and their children, as well as suspicious ethnic groups. They favored the children of the working class. Above all, they favored people who loudly professed belief in the creed, who attended party meetings, who participated in public displays of enthusiasm. Unlike an ordinary oligarchy, the one-party state allows for upward mobility: True believers can advance. As Hannah Arendt wrote back in the 1940s, the worst kind of one-party state "invariably replaces all first-rate talents, regardless of their sympathies, with those crackpots and fools whose lack of intelligence and creativity is still the best guarantee of their loyalty."
>
> –Anne Applebaum, *A Warning From Europe: The Worst Is Yet To Come*[242]

We describe the value of competition, in general and in each field, in Chapter 32.

Cherishing the Field of Government often entails sacrificing one's personal interests for the greater good. Doing this may lead to an increase in *yasa* (righteous fame). Yet to do what is honorable unobtrusively or even in the face of social pressure to the contrary, compounds the honor of the expert worker in the Field of Government.

23.4 Stewarding the Field of Ideas

For those in the Field of Ideas, dedication to the truth applied benefi-
cially is the key principle. As discussed previously, integrity is fundamental for every individual in society in order to carry out one's work.
Truth is the bedrock on which society rests. In this field we nurture
knowledge by finding it, updating it, and correcting it. We protect
knowledge by safeguarding it from corruption.

Workers in the Field of Ideas have a special duty to be neutral,
impartial, and objective. For example, in the United States, expert
witnesses called in jury trials often work in the Field of Ideas. However, they are hired and paid for their testimony by one side or the
other, the defense or the prosecution. If we are called as an expert
witness and slant the truth to favor whoever is paying us, then that
practice dishonors our own knowledge and endangers justice as well
as endangering victims or suspects in crimes. In a California murder
case hinging on DNA evidence that required sophisticated statistical
interpretation, the defense attorney protested to the judge regarding
the prosecution's expert witness:

> This man, she says, 'is willing to reach as far as he can go
> to serve [the prosecutor's] purpose.'
> –Chris Smith, *DNA's identity crisis*[243]

Such a perception, regardless of its accuracy, damages the functioning
of the Field of Ideas.* A 2003 paper by Daniel W. Shuman and Stuart
A. Greenberg offers a framework for psychologists testifying as expert
witnesses in court to remain professional, based on competence, relevance, perspective, balance, and candor. They elaborate how retaining high standards of neutrality, balance, breadth of view, and love
of truth are essential to function well as an expert witness.[244] Their
discussion can be extended to apply to the functioning of the Field of
Ideas more generally.

In general, it is especially important in this field to avoid being under the financial control of anyone who has a reason to distort truth or
its application in society. To avoid such situations may mean carefully
considering the nature of one's employer, sponsor, patron, or benefac-
tor. Because this field guides society's goals, values, and standards, it
is better for a person suited to the Field of Ideas to be willing to live

---

*A detailed analysis of this case is given in Chapter 5 of Leila Schneps and Coralie
Colmez's book *Math on Trial: How Numbers Get Used and Abused in the Courtroom.*

simply, even to the point of growing one's own food and living "off the grid," than to be in a position where one's integrity could possibly be compromised for one's maintenance.

More generally, protecting our knowledge means maintaining a certain degree of independence from those who are applying it in government and industry. At the same time, nurturing our knowledge entails sharing it with those who can benefit from it. This may require adding context-specific details, caveats, and exceptions, as well as personally offering guidance to those seeking to apply our knowledge in their fields.

Those in the Field of Ideas are often involved in training, educating, or advising others, in any of the fields of work. As we said previously, good stewardship includes mindfulness of the needs and capacities of those working under us. This includes our trainees, students, and advisees, who are especially vulnerable due to their lack of knowledge and experience, and who may be under our care for relatively long periods of time. Here's an example from the academic world:

> Graduate school in the sciences resembles a medieval apprenticeship. The graduate-student apprentice has virtually no rights or independence and no hope of advancement to the postdoctoral (journeyman) stage unless the adviser (the master) is satisfied with the student's progress and also willing to let the student go. If the apprentice is too valuable and the master too venal, the combination can delay graduation.
>
> –Leonard Cassuto, *How to Fire Your Adviser: Sometimes the only way forward is to start again*[245]

Stewarding our students also means ensuring that they themselves reach independence. This is our duty not only to them, but also to the greater society.

The Field of Ideas grows through connections and interactions among ideas. Often interactions among ideas that appear at first to clash can be the most fruitful. These can bring about truly enlarged understanding, forging syntheses that are greater than the sum of their parts. So part of stewarding the Field of Ideas includes encouraging, maintaining, and contributing to a diverse set of viewpoints. Nurturing the diversity of the field entails tolerating viewpoints with which we personally may disagree at a given moment. The ego shade of *sattva* embodies the contradiction of being open to ideas from many different people, and yet seeing ourselves as superior because of that very openness. Therefore, this apparent openness may end up transforming, in fact, into a type of prejudice. The true diversity of ideas that pervades the healthy Field of Ideas is comparable to diversity in the biosphere of plants and animals. Mono-cropping makes plants far more susceptible to disease and pests, and homogeneous thinking makes this field susceptible to stunting, withering, or blight. Answering questions stimulates the growth of knowledge. As many teachers know, we learn from our students, and the same applies more generally to those who question us sincerely, respectfully, and in good faith. When I share knowledge with you, I not only have the same knowledge I had before, my own knowledge may have deepened through the process of communicating it to you, so both of our bodies of knowledge have grown. Thus, knowledge grows by sharing, rather than hoarding or being excessively secretive.

Those who cherish the Field of Ideas remember that a love for learning, skill in thinking, and general reading do not substitute for academic training and knowledge in subjects other than one's own. Respecting those who have training and experience in their own subjects, and knowing the limits of one's own knowledge and experience, besides being essential to cherishing knowledge as we described in Chapter 21, are crucial to the health of this field overall.

Cherishing the Field of Ideas also includes appropriately respecting knowledge for which we personally can't take credit. Besides giving credit where it's due, this means we pursue the new ideas we generate when they seem to have a good chance of enlarging our understanding of truth, not simply because we can call them our own.

We've talked several times in this chapter about the importance of long-term thinking, which does not always come naturally. The long view is the special charge of those in the Field of Ideas, who have the responsibility to look out for what's coming over the horizon.

Having explored the ways to cherish our sources of wealth and the fields in which we work, in Chapter 25 we shall look at the importance of cherishing ourselves.

Chapter 24

Testimony: School Board Chair

By Rani Dasi, Chair Chapel Hill-Carrboro City Schools Board of Education, North Carolina, USA

A little girl sat near her mother intently staring at small shapes on a page that her mother suggested (insisted) could be deciphered into sounds and grow into stories. Her mother regularly pulled out the *We Adore Krsna* book, her finger gliding under the mysterious shapes that she translated into stories, until one day, the little girl started to recognize the shapes and how they translated to words, and her life was forever changed. That little girl was me, and the lady was my Mata (mother), and sharing her love for reading was the best gift.

Reading was my entrée to the world. Through books, I got to see other towns, countries, and cultures. I peeked into family dynamics, listened as people interacted, heard language, saw various structures people called home, and learned how choices drove actions, how limited choices constrained opportunities, how narrow opportunities often appeared as bad choices.

I learned to consider people in a deeper context, beyond how they present in the current moment. I learned the critical importance of getting to the root of the matter, digging beneath systems and structures that can make choices invisible. Most of all, I learned that so little of a story is what we think we see on the surface. This learning led to the understanding of how much we matter to each other, how we are all connected, how that requires me to consider how I engage, and how community success is my success. That is my inspiration.

As Tricia Hersey remarks in her book, *Rest is Resistance,*

> Nothing we accomplish in life is totally free of the influence of spirit and community. We do nothing alone.
> —Tricia Hersey, *Rest Is Resistance: A Manifesto*[246]

Along with her love of reading, my Mata, Krsnanandini, shared this spiritual foundation that guides my life and how I engage in the world. Spiritual awareness guides us to consider our responsibility to each other, and how individuals can support each other and build community health and wellness. We can realize our true capacity for love when we develop our relationship with God, and we do that by showing our care for each other. Ultimately, we're all parts of Krishna's energy.

As a young girl growing up in Cleveland, Ohio, I could not have imagined myself becoming involved in government. Making laws and setting policy seemed like something other people did, and, the furthest I could see into the future was what would be fun for me to do the next day. My visioning was not inclusive of my impact on others. Thankfully, education has always been important to my family.

Imagine the early 1970s. Millennials and Gen-Z reading this may think that was the stone ages, but the 1970s was a time of a growing introduction to technology; not the latest iPhone, but many homes seeing their first televisions, microwaves, and dishwashers. Widespread computer use was something people thought of as science fiction, and our telephones were rotary dial attached to a single outlet in the home. Women were more actively demanding rights and faced significant workforce gender discrimination. They could be fired or refused employment or promotion for becoming pregnant. Reproductive health choices were extremely limited, unmarried women were refused credit cards, and married women had to have their husbands' approval.

Many communities were highly segregated by race. Black people faced continued discrimination and experienced high levels of concentrated poverty, low investment in schools, and high unemployment.

In this environment, my mother, a Black woman determined to provide the best education to her children, decided to teach us at home, developing curricula, planning activities, and investing time to ensure we had deep understanding and mastery of subject areas ranging from math, reading, and science, to geography and others.

As the eldest of the ten children, I had the opportunity to see how different types of educational opportunities and exposure affect education outcomes.

Throughout college and beyond, I actively sought opportunities to mentor and tutor others. I also continued my personal learning journey, earning an MBA in Accounting and Finance at the University of Chicago after completing an undergraduate degree in Industrial Engineering and Management Science at Northwestern University.

So naturally, when my children were born, I prioritized their education. I decided to take some time away from my professional work in corporate finance and strategy and engaged in their schools, volunteering in the classroom, working with the PTA, and participating in local education advocacy. As I became more active in my children's schools, I began to see opportunities to make changes to improve foundations of learning and to leverage my experience to do so.

In 2015, I ran a successful campaign and was elected to the Chapel Hill-Carrboro City Schools Board of Education in North Carolina. In this position, I engage with other government officials to improve education outcomes for students.

As my children grew more independent, I was offered an opportunity to rejoin the workforce, with a nonprofit institute which has the mission to improve the human condition. They do this by partnering with governments on projects to improve systems and structures. They were looking for someone with financial expertise to help them with planning and budgeting. This work and the mission were so aligned with my beliefs, that I accepted the opportunity. My previous experience with for-profit companies had enabled me to make a living and support my family, but sometimes had less alignment with my values. Here was a chance to use my education, skills, and experience towards what really drew me most: building structural systems at scale, to enable people to have what they need to thrive.

Today, as I make policy and decisions that affect lives, my spiritual background guides me to center people and prioritize investments in resources that build structural solutions to address issues.

Chapter 25

No Egoism, No Lethargy

In addition to cherishing our field of work and sources of wealth, in the natural art of work we also cherish ourselves. Such cherishing involves six practical steps. Before detailing those, it's necessary to first examine our understanding of who we truly are.

The pleasure of real *rasa* (the essence of enjoyment and relationships), which is the result of spiritual richness, is the natural state of the self. It is already at the core of who we are. Such happiness is not exactly the result of any kind of work, as it does not need to be acquired from any separate source. Yet, working in a particular frame of consciousness makes us aware of the treasure we already have. As we've discussed, we can cover that awareness with the shades of *sattva*, *rajas*, and *tamas*, which are degrees of egocentric thinking and acting. The *Bhagavad-gita* suggests, instead, a reality-centric way of thinking and acting.

The *Bhagavad-gita* summarizes the egocentric approach to work[247] as the mistake of thinking we are the direct performers and creators of the results of our work. Rather, Krishna states that in mundane consciousness, the interplay of *sattva*, *rajas*, and *tamas* is taking place and we are merely the observer.[248][249] To use an analogy, think of people playing a video or computer game. The characters in the game and the actions they perform are, in one sense, happening according to the direction and desire of the players. Yet, the players are not really doing anything but pushing buttons, touching a screen, or the like. They are witnessing, and experiencing, emotions only through mental identification. The actual action in the game can be explained as electricity, circuits, metal, plastic, and glass, pixels, programming code, or ones and zeros. Are the players actually performing the characters' actions? In a concrete sense, no. Still, the players can become very absorbed. The accessible logic and apparent controllability of the game environment can lure players into abandoning the rich, natural world of reality, since the greater control exerted by the game designer on the gamer makes itself felt only indirectly, through systematic constraint and restriction of choice. The players' characters seem to acquire the six forms of riches, and the players manipulating the characters seemingly experience varieties of *rasa*. Yet, the entire experience is like a controlled dream. A similar thing happens when reading a book or watching a play, movie, or television. The reader or watcher identifies with characters and thus gets a vicarious experience of achieving some form of prosperity that leads to *rasa*, although there is less of a sense of personal agency when one is clearly reading or seeing someone else's story, as compared to electronic games, where there is an appearance of being the author and protagonist of the story.

In the *Bhagavad-gita*, we learn that we are as different from our present body and mind,[250] as video gamers are from their characters in the game. Our body and mind interact with the world and the bodies and minds of others according to a system of universal rules. According to our desires, the machines of the body and mind interact with material nature. The body and mind acquire (and lose!) *sri, yasa, aisvarya, virya, jnana,* and *vairagya,* which seem to bring *rasa* — friendship, romance, laughter, compassion, and so forth. But all these are not ultimately authentic experiences, just as looking through a window is not the same as experiencing being outside, and just as games and theater are imitations of life. Rather, the ego shades of *sattva, rajas,* and *tamas* combine to create temporary forms, and life scenarios, much as primary colors combine to form images on a screen. On a screen we see a story unfold with various characters, and we feel emotions and some level of *rasa*, but really there are just three colors combining. We sometimes get a sense that our real self is simply an observer and that authentic experiences are beyond shades of ego. For example, we may achieve something such as a new home, diploma, or a completed project, and find that we quickly return from the brief exaltation to our previous level of satisfaction, as if there had been no real change at all.

We obviously do have some influence on our work and its results, just as we have some kind of agency when we choose to become absorbed in a particular book, film, or electronic game. The *Bhagavad-*

gita lists five factors of action,[251] with one of them being our self.[*] As we experience over and over again in practical life, we as the doer are not sufficient to ensure a particular result, or even be 100% proactive. Of course, we have *some* degree of responsibility and agency. Thus, every society and tradition has rules of conduct with consequences. Yet, the *Bhagavad-gita* states[253] that actions, rewards, and punishment all arise from the pushing and pulling of *sattva, rajas, tamas,* and their combinations. The illusion of complete self-initiative draws us in such a way that we watch, desire, and identify with the illusion. To do egoless work, some may feel it's enough to contemplate the relationship between our real selves as observer and the illusion of ourselves as worldly actors. However, theory alone is generally not enough to bring most of us to the level we described in Chapter 12 of meaningful work and absolute increase.

The *Bhagavad-gita* lists four ways of gaining a direct experience of our real selves as observer. These are meditation, study of philosophy and sacred writings, detached work, and worship based on hearing from those who have fully realized these facts.[254] To be ultimately effective, each of the four needs to be done with a desire to connect with the ultimate source of all *rasa* and prosperity and can then be successful. In other words, meditation just to lower blood pressure, studying philosophy to impress others, detached work to relieve stress, or worship as social convention are not likely to help much. At the time of writing, many popular books, articles, and courses teach one of these paths, or a combination of them.[255][256][257]

It's ironic that much of the current instruction merely promises benefits in *sattva*'s ego shade, such as how to become peaceful and forgiving. Yes, in *sattva*, one will find peace, harmony, clarity of understanding, the ability to control our senses and mind, and inner joy. However, every shade of ego, including *sattva*, is ultimately unstable, being based on the illusion that we are at the center of reality. Fur-

---

[*]The other factors are the overall situation and environment, the means or instruments, the endeavor, and the Divine.

> The worker and the place, the worker's senses and the
> deed,
> and in the end, the Supersoul, determine what suc-
> ceeds.

–Kalakantha Dāsa, *Bhagavad-gītā: The Rap of God*[252]

Here "senses" refers to working senses such as hands, feet, and extensions thereof, such as tools.

thermore, seeing reality in *sattva* is through a framed clear window, not a full experience of reality. The ultimate benefit to aim for is this direct experience,[258] which gives us the ability to receive a constant flow of absolute increase from our prime source and thus work with real meaning. One's consciousness then goes beyond its usual states — wakefulness, dreaming, and deep sleep — to a transcendent kind of alertness and awareness.

Sometimes when we read or hear of our ultimate true spiritual state, we feel discouraged and think it sounds so lofty that it is impossible for us. However, we are discussing realization of our natural state — our default settings, in a sense. It is not a foreign imposition on us but our original state, and it comes quite easily with a little understanding and endeavor. If we practice egoless action, we experience it!

The *Bhagavad-gita* gives us six components to egoless action,[259] and guarantees[260] that such egoless action will free us from shades of ego and karmic law. Acting in these six ways can be increased gradually and incrementally.[261] Even a small effort is transcendent and frees us from the pitfalls of illusory identification.[262] These six components in verse 3.30 are:

- dedicate our work to the ultimate source;

- let go of desires to enjoy the six varieties of riches on the transactional plane;

- fill our consciousness with awareness of our spiritual self;

- let go of the ego of ownership;

- act externally according to our nature; and

- let go of lethargy born of "fever."

Three are positive and three are negative. The positive and negative are related because effort aimed toward the positive enables us to let go of the negative with little or no trouble. Let's explore them.

25.1 Dedicate Our Work to the Ultimate Source

Each field of work is like a system in the universal body, and thus is meant for the good of the entire body. The Field of Ideas is like the nervous system, the Field of Government like the immune and circulatory systems, the Field of Resources like the digestive and respiratory systems, and the Field of Artistry like the musculoskeletal system along with the subtle body of emotion and desires. An ordinary body there is considered healthy on both the cellular and aggregate level when each cell of each system dedicates its life and work to the entire body.* So, too, in the universal body.

Dedication to the source — whether we see it as the biosphere or universal body, the undifferentiated oneness, the Soul of the Universe, or the personal Supreme Being — is done both in deliberate periodic acts separate from activities of work as described in Chapter 17, and also at every other moment. The essence of this dedication is a mood and intention of: "This work is for the sake of the source from which all ultimately comes. My pleasure also comes from that primary source and fulfills me completely, just as a bodily cell is fulfilled when working for the pleasure of the body. Let my work be in harmony with the nature, wisdom, and happiness of this source." We briefly note that harmony with the source with the intention only to give ourselves inner peace is merely the ego shade of *sattva*. On the other hand, actual love and dedication brings us peace as a by-product. In the *Bhagavad-gita*, Krishna recommends using the mantra *om tat sat* to dedicate work.[263] (Note that the letters "a" in both *tat* and *sat* are pronounced like the "u" in "bus".)† *Om* indicates the source, the Supreme. *Tat* indicates the desire for such work to be on the plane of freedom (which we've been calling "reality outside," free from the shades of ego), and *sat* invokes that such work be proper, dedicated action.

While all of the four ways of understanding the source are given in the *Bhagavata Purana*, it's easiest for many people to dedicate their work to the source as the Supreme Person and ever-present well-wishing friend. Then, just as we may sometimes deal with one person in order to impress or please another, so we work with others and with objects of our work to please the Supreme Person. We thus experience a oneness or harmony of interest with the Divine and a full sense of connection, while remaining our own unique individual

---

*Cells that do not dedicate their life and work to the entire body are, by definition, malignant/cancerous.

†Each occurrence of the letter "t" in this particular mantra (and, for that matter, in the Sanskrit word *mantra* itself) is pronounced by pressing the tip of the tongue against the back of the upper front teeth, not upon the hard palate as for the English "t."

self. Acting in this way is natural, simple, and delightful. Such action removes our anxieties about others' views of us, and easily helps us to accomplish the next component.

> Oneness with Spirit is as much the destiny of a construction worker, teacher, salesperson, and engineer as it is the destiny of a spiritual leader. All aspects of earthly experience, including our career, can be a cup overflowing with peace and joy. Our professional life can be one more place where we experience life to the fullest.
> —Jim Rosemergy, *Even Mystics Have Bills to Pay: Balancing a Spiritual Life and Earthly Living*[264]

25.2 Let Go of Desires to Enjoy the Six Varieties of Riches on the Transactional Plane

All living beings seek to enjoy the richness of *yasa*, *virya*, *aisvarya*, *vairagya*, *jnana*, and *sri*, but when we try to do this separate from our source, we get only a shadow of these forms of prosperity. We get the transactional plane where none of the riches actually increase, as we described in Chapter 12, and where our claim to enjoyment stands on the false basis of positing our self as the ultimate cause of our actions and their results.

For a person who has dedicated work to the reservoir of *rasa*, the ability and desire to let go of small desires for worldly gain flows almost effortlessly. As discussed in Chapter 2, one may see all forms of riches as being truly experienced through Lakshmi, the goddess of prosperity. She is also the potency of pleasure, which gives *rasa* to the source and nourishes all those connected to that source. The following understanding is a bit esoteric and mysterious. Making it a core part of our work, however, allows us to go far beyond even egolessness. When we work for the pleasure of the original source of all life, we are, in a mystical sense, acting as the catalyst to unite our source with the spiritual energy of pleasure. That pleasure then nourishes us, who are part of the source. Analogously, if the hand puts food into the mouth, that food gets digested and becomes physical *rasa*, which pleases the body, including the hand, which could not have enjoyed the food separately. Through this system, the hand would feel fully satisfied. So, we let go of the desire for worldly riches when we have spiritual riches through dedication of our work to the ultimate source of everything.

25.3   Fill Our Consciousness with Awareness of Our Spiritual Self

Our direct experience of having a continuing sense of identity throughout our lives, regardless of how our body and mind change, suggests the possibility that we are spiritual, rather than merely a material body and mind.[*] This possibility comes to the fore when we encounter death: when the body of our loved one is in front of us, yet we mourn their passing. Whoever has passed away was, clearly, not the body. Our real self is spiritual, eternal, and an individual part of the whole, our source. Awareness of our spiritual self means to notice the very sense of being alive. In fact, it is only our spiritual self that is alive, temporarily animating our body.

Our real self, as part of the whole, is faultless and glorious. The more we become aware of who we really are spiritually, beyond body, mind, family, culture, nation, and so forth, the more we are filled with our birthright: joy. The *Bhagavad-gita* and *Bhagavata Purana* use phrases describing this awareness as "relishing the self," "rejoicing in the self," "being satisfied with the self," and "loving the self." However, we will not be able to have such a degree of "self" love for the clearly flawed body and mind we inhabit.

It can be helpful to note that understanding the infinite source of existence to be the personal, Supreme Being leads to a personal understanding of our own real identity, as we are part of that source and thus have the same characteristics, if to a small degree. Logically, it is only possible with a personal transcendent conception of this source, to understand it as having the six riches in infinite degree and kind, and an infinite depth and mixture of the various *rasas*. It is this theistic personal-ism that can accomplish this clarity and understanding.

Because the concept of ego is based on false identities of this world, when we live in consciousness of our real identity, it naturally leads us to drop all traces of confining ego. We naturally feel and know that we are observers of this world rather than controllers of it. We have a

---

[*]It may seem that this identity is based on memory, which is a function of the material mind. However, identity is more fundamental than memory. For instance, legally and medically, a person with amnesia continues to have the same identity. In many cases, amnesiacs recover their memories and return to their original understandings of their identities.

balanced perspective of our limited influence. Such a result is easiest when we have an individual and personal understanding of our real self. The next component of egoless work then flows effortlessly.

25.4 Let Go of the Ego of Ownership

As soon as our awareness of true self permeates our work, it is easy to let go of the ego of false ownership. All so-called ownership has to do with temporary identities related to the body and mind, neither of which we are.[*] In our state of illusion, we want to own the talents and abilities that we use in our work, the processes that we apply to our work, and the various riches and *rasas* that accrue from our work. Our anxieties revolve around whether or not we will get the desired objects of sense and mental pleasures. We become convinced that without all this sense of ownership, we will feel empty and unfulfilled. So, we grab tightly to the objects of our senses and mind. But, alas! Most of those objects fail to satisfy even when we have them in abundance. In fact, we then live in the following types of fear: will these objects satisfy us, and if so, for how long? How long will we keep them? Such fear causes us to cling tighter, and brings frustration or even anger when our ownership is threatened. A cycle of attachment, fear, and anger was not what we envisioned when we embarked on a career!

Instead, with full consciousness of our joyful spiritual self, and with work dedicated to the source of all, we can be filled to overflowing. We will then feel no need to own anything merely in order to fill an empty hole, as there is no emptiness. We will see the ever-changing needs of our limited, temporary body and mind as best filled correspondingly through ever-changing flows, so excessive accumulation will no longer appeal to us.[†]

Externally, on a practical level, this aspect of egolessness means working on the plane of giving, as explained in Chapter 15. But working on this plane goes beyond giving a portion of the richness of our

---

[*]It's important to note that the component of egolessness we're discussing here does not necessarily imply that all tangible goods or relationships are held in common communally — such is simply an expanded ego of ownership and carries with it the problems of individual ownership in an expanded way.

[†]For tangible objects, in supply-chain management terms, this attitude is analogous to "just-in-time inventory." However, rather than new things being manufactured and shipped "just in time," some of the things we need may be available in the community or environment just when we need them. For example, in many cities, renting bicycles, scooters, or small electric cars simply for the duration of one ride has become relatively easy.

life physically, and eventually expands to a total giving to the source emotionally. To the world, it will appear that we own so many things, but in our mind's eye we are merely caring for these things in temporary trust, as loving service.

25.5 Act Externally According to Our Nature

As we mentioned in Chapter 8, freedom from ego in work does not come from stopping work,[*] nor from doing others' work. Indeed, crossing fields of work generally damages us and society, as we explained in Chapter 5. It is true that a person motivated by ego does work according to his or her nature, because of feeling: "I love this and this is what I want to do in order to fully express myself for my own pleasure." Even on such an egoistic basis, it's much better to work according to one's nature than to ignore it. But, on the platform of egolessness, working according to one's nature takes place with a very different awareness.

As we've explained, real identity as a spiritual being includes a deep desire to serve our source, the infinite, with love and devotion. The best way to serve is to work in the way we are most suited and with what brings the greatest sense of connection to the all-inclusive whole, and therefore to our body and mind as well. Analogously, when heart muscles act like a heart, the body is happy, and the cells in the heart are also happy. Our pleasure then comes *through* our source rather than separately. We then are fully who we are, aligned and in harmony, working according to our expertise, in the service of the complete whole, which is greater than ourselves. Perfect.

25.6 Let Go of Lethargy Born of "Fever"

The word fever, *jvara* in Sanskrit,[265] is interesting in connection with egoless work. In the *Bhagavad-gita*, Krishna tells us that egoless work involves the giving up of feverish lethargy. In terms of illness, we know that fevers make us lethargic. The reason we have no energy to get out of bed, eat, or interact with anyone is that our energy is being taken up by enhanced immune activity, associated with the heightened body temperature, to fight the infection. However, fever is associated not only with lethargy due to depleted energy, but also

---

[*]Stopping work inappropriately can lead to ego in one's richness of *vairagya*, so the illusion is simply transformed.

with a kind of blind, frenzied energy and enthusiasm (which may precede or alternate with lethargy). Just as fever drains us of ability and will, so increased desires and feverish action to accomplish things in a mood of self-serving passion drain us of long-range vision and balanced, wholesome life. Intense fever may also involve hallucinations or other distorted thinking.

When we are in a feverish mood believing that we are the doer, and that our actions alone will increase our advantages in a transactional system, we invariably meet with disappointment and frustration. Our plans go awry, or fail to satisfy us over time. Others may fail to appreciate us. We sometimes stay up nights to finish a job, putting aside important tasks and relationships, yet our work may go unused or unnoticed. Feverish work can even eventually lead to such disappointment that we no longer care. We give up. We may go through the motions of work merely because we have to live. Or we may wax philosophical and think: if I am not the real mover and shaker, and I can't make a real difference, why bother doing anything at all? Thus, feverish ego work ultimately leads to lethargy as much as does physical fever. In terms of the shades of ego, we can see this problem as *tamas* following *rajas*, since each of the shades of ego is inherently unsustainable.[266]

However, when we work in concert with our source, without clinging to ownership or separate desires to enjoy the six kinds of richness, then we experience no lethargy. With dedication to our source, and consciousness absorbed in our real self, our sense of success fills us with a flow of that infinite *rasa*. We no longer identify success and failure on the external plane. Nor are we dependent on external situations in order to be fulfilled. Our enthusiasm and determination come from a grateful love for this source who is filling us with such *rasa*. In this egoless state, we do not fluctuate between feverish action and lethargy, but are steady in enthusiasm through what others may see as gain and loss, victory and defeat, success and failure.

When we practice the above six components of egoless action in the art of work, we are free from any bondage of work and feel our work to be a natural art.

Chapter 26

Testimony: Nursing Home Worker

Contributed by Damodar Prasad Roe

In the *Bhagavad-Gita*, Krishna teaches how one can work as a means to cultivate self-knowledge. He says that by work, one can even contact a supreme reality beyond cause and effect. I spent a lot of years overthinking what I want to do, but that was because deep down, I was afraid to start. Clarity about who I want to be, and what I want from my career, has come from following my heart's instinct and then learning from experience. I've volunteered at a suicide hotline, taken care of elders suffering from Alzheimer's and dementia, supervised troubled teenagers at a shelter, and offered life coaching for men. Somehow I've been blessed with some experiences of how work can become like Krishna describes, something touching a reality beyond my perception.

I remember one day I paused to watch an old woman with dementia walking down the hall. She took slow, two-inch steps while glancing ahead tentatively. There was something remarkable about it, almost like a presence I could feel but not see. It occurred to me that while the body — and especially the brain — is slowly deteriorating, within her remains the same conscious being as before, like when she was a young woman. Vulnerable people seem to lack power. But cultures all over the world have conceived of a conscious universe witnessing everything, reciprocating virtue with desirable results, and evil with the opposite. Assuming the existence of such a reality at the basis of cause and effect, the way I treat vulnerable beings determines the results of good and evil to a far greater degree. Therefore, some of the hidden power that they carry is in the potential effects of how I treat them.

It's so hard to be awake to my own suffering, and even more so to that of others. When I first began taking care of elders, my goal was to be compassionate. I was trying to help a man named Fred, because he had gone several days without a shower.

"I took one this morning!" he said to me, very annoyed. His face said it all, like I was some idiot invading his personal space.

It took over an hour-and-a-half just for a shower, with him hitting and cursing me angrily. Finally, as I sat him down in his chair all freshly showered, groomed, and dressed, I said:

"See? I was just trying to help you, but you were fighting me."

I was hoping he would come around. But instead, he looked me dead in the eye and said hatefully, "I should have hit you harder, you son of a bitch."

In that moment I felt how my own ego was getting in the way. Although I certainly did want to help Fred, a big part of it was wanting to be appreciated so that I could feel good about myself. I had been projecting a story on reality where all my patients were innocently needy and I was a compassionate hero. But more important than feeling a certain way is effectively delivering the service that is needed. I had a lot to learn.

I was losing my patience, as things were getting as hectic as they were disgusting. I kneeled on the bathroom floor to change someone's soiled pants. The poor guy had been sitting like that for too long while I was running around giving showers. I was trying to shift my mood from being frustrated. But I was suffering, and not being kindhearted while offering care.

I passed by the room of a patient who used to be a pastor. And when I heard him loudly praying, I instinctively entered the room to sit by him. He was expressing his gratitude over and over with a lot of feeling.

"It's just amazing how much the Lord has blessed me with all you taking care of me. Someone brought me lunch and I didn't even realize I was hungry before that. It's like you know what I need even before I do."

He was somewhat overwhelmed.

He began to thank me, while I was feeling rough and impure at heart. I was speechless because I felt undeserving of it. Here he was so full of gratitude, and here I was the opposite. He grabbed my hand, perhaps seeing my face betray my thoughts.

"When I say this I mean YOU. You've been a blessing to me many times. When I was a young man I used to look up to the church elders for guidance. Now I am just glad that young men like yourself are taking up the Lord's service. There are so many people out there in need of God's grace, and if you would tend to them like you do to me, then I would be relieved to know God's people are working today."

I searched my memory for times when I had helped him, wondering whether his dementia was confusing him about whom to thank. I remembered reading the Bible to him when he was upset, tossing a balloon back-and-forth for hours, and assisting him with his daily hygiene activities. The rest of the day, I chose to embrace being helpful. I made a point to ask my patients to say "Rama!" — a name of God meant for blessing. We all smiled, having a lot of fun with it.

Work trying to help others has offered me a lot more than money can buy. I've had the chance to realize that karma is more effective while dealing with vulnerable people. Yet while I find meaning in doing my best to make things better in this world, sometimes I get hints of a reality beyond what I perceive with my senses. Being alive is a precious gift that endures both suffering and enjoyment of the body. Sometimes we suffer and sometimes we are happy, but it is all part of a bigger plan — a plan where I have a role to play, and a lot to learn about the mysterious way God loves each one of us. The more I can check my ego and be grateful for the opportunities I have to serve, the more I may be allowed to enter into that inner current of reality.

Chapter 27

The Shades of Ego in the Workplace

In Part I, Chapter 8, we discussed how the shades of ego keep us from having completely satisfying freedom and prosperity, as well as permanent authentic experience of *rasa*. A shade of ego is known in Sanskrit as a *guna*. The word *guna* also means "rope" (as in a restrictive rope that binds us), and can also mean (neutral or positive) "quality." The following passage helps us review and get a deeper sense of the shades of ego:

> Let us now turn to the *gunas* per se (*sattva*, *rajas* and *tamas*), which the *Bhagavata* describes as underlying energies or potencies from which the temporal realm, in all its aspects, is derived. The *Bhagavata* defines *sattva* as *jnana-sakti*, the energy that manifests or illuminates things, *rajas* as *kriya-sakti*, the energy of motion and activity, and *tamas* as *dravya-sakti*, the energy that produces substances.[267] In the *Bhagavata*, the *gunas* are often described as energies[268] that possess certain dispositional qualities....
>
> *Sattva* and *tamas* are described as energies possessing opposite qualities: whereas *sattva* is bright and light, *tamas* is dark and heavy. These opposites coordinate with each other in the process of the temporal realm's maintenance (*sattva*) and dissolution (*tamas*). *Rajas*, the power of activity and motion, is described as predominating over *sattva* and *tamas* so as to bring about the temporal realm's creation (or manifestation). Although at every stage of creation one *guna* predominates over

the other two, they are never completely apart, nor is any one *guna* ever completely absent. Rather, all three continuously combine together in various unlimited proportions.

The *Bhagavata* states that just as the oil, wick, and flame of a lamp[269] work together to produce light, so do the three *gunas* combine in various ways to produce [the] fundamental substances that comprise the body and world.* These fundamental substances are produced from particular combinations of all three *gunas*, but each substance is classified under the *guna* that is predominant in that substance's generation and being.

–Gopal K. Gupta, Maya in the Bhagavata Purana:
Human Suffering and Divine Play[271]

We particularly related each of the four fields of work to tendencies for each of these shades to cover us. Throughout Part II, we referenced, among other topics, the shades of ego in relation to various individual arts of work. Here, we'll summarize the influence of the shades and how to gain freedom from them. Regardless of what field we work in, certain overall symptoms appear in workers veiled by each of the shades. These are as follows:

The *Bhagavad-gita* describes workers veiled by the shade of *tamas*:

> The worker who is disengaged, base, stubborn, deceitful, insulting to others, lazy, morose, and procrastinating is said to be veiled by the shade of *tamas*.
>
> — Bhagavad-gita 18.28

This doesn't sound either attractive or productive! Unfortunately, we may sometimes recognize ourselves beginning to fall into such a state.

What about the other shades? First, *rajas*:

> The worker who is attached, desiring to get the results of work, greedy, habitually envious and aggressive towards others, impure, and is constantly buffeted by waves of joy on success and misery on failure, is said to be veiled by the shade of *rajas*.
>
> — Bhagavad-gita 18.27

---

*This analogy of the oil, wick, and lamp is also found in the *Sankhya-karika*.[270]

314

Some of this may seem natural, and yet we can see that overall this is not a state we want to be in or encounter in others. Finally, *sattva*:

> The worker who performs his or her duty without attachment, without false identification, with great determination and enthusiasm, and without wavering in success or failure is said to be veiled by the shade of *sattva*.
>
> — *Bhagavad-gita* 18.26

That certainly sounds like a more pleasant and productive state to be in or around. (Let's keep in mind that it would be best not to be veiled at all — we'll come back to that point.) How would we get into such a state?

A benefit of recognizing these different states as symptomatic of different shades of ego, rather than as immutable character attributes, is that we don't identify ourselves (or others) as "lazy and procrastinating" or "greedy and aggressive." The symptoms of the worker veiled by the shade of *tamas* constitute a syndrome; the further we fall into this syndrome, the more of its symptoms we will exhibit, and likewise for the shade of *rajas*. These are not personality traits; they are signs that we have fallen into a trap. This perspective gives us several possibilities as to how to get ourselves out of the trap.

27.1   Shifting to a Lighter Shade of Ego

One thing we can do to get out of the ego trap is take actions associated with a lighter shade. Let's look at a real-life example:

> I remember being in this terrible funk once, and since I figured my clients would pick up on it anyway, the way I decided to deal with it was to stay home from work one day and escape by watching TV. I happened to catch one of those PBS fund-raising drives.[*] As I continued to watch, I became really moved by the participants' passion, and during one of the pledge breaks, I picked up the phone and pledged $300. Three hundred dollars seemed like quite a hefty amount to me at that time, but somehow I felt that was the right number.

---

[*]PBS is a public television station in the US, partly funded by direct donations from the viewing public.

> I can't tell you how good I felt when I hung up the phone. I got up, called a few friends, went back to work the next day. Later that week I was in my office, smiling, when Cliff, one of the brokers down the hall, came in and said, "Looks like you're in better spirits. What happened?" This made me stop and think for a moment. I really didn't know at first, but after retracing the few days before, I realized that my mood had switched right after I gave the money to PBS.
>
> –Suze Orman, *The 9 Steps to Financial Freedom: Practical and Spiritual Steps So You Can Stop Worrying*[272]

Orman goes on to explain that the switch she made was persistent: she made charitable giving a regular practice, and also saw a persistent benefit in her work with her clients. Her experience reminds us how in Chapter 15, we described charity veiled by the shade of *sattva* as charity "given at the right time and place, in the right circumstances, to the right person, without expecting a return, simply because it is right to give." In this story, Orman was not expecting any return from PBS (which broadcasts freely to everyone, regardless of whether they pay).

Here is another example. In the Field of Government, *rajas* tends to be a problem with its concomitant pull towards wanting fame and glory. Moving towards the lighter shade of *sattva*, a person feels inner satisfaction from being in a state of harmony with truth, rather than receiving accolades from others. One's work satisfaction, therefore, becomes less dependent on others' opinions of one's worthiness.

> Navy leaders chafed as Navy SEALs broke away from their "quiet professional" ethos, publicizing their participation in the raid into Pakistan that killed bin Laden, the al-Qaida leader responsible for plotting the 9/11 attacks. Two SEALs wrote books about the mission, prompting a rebuke form the Naval Special Warfare commander at the time, Rear Adm. Brian Losey. "A critical tenet of our ethos is 'I do not advertise the nature of my work, nor seek recognition for my actions,'" he said.
>
> –Lolita C. Baldor, *Navy SEALs to shift from counterterrorism to global threats*[273]

In this case, the action in the shade of *sattva* is rather inaction: keeping quiet about one's deeds, like the other Navy SEALS who did not write books or speak out publicly about the raid. Resisting a temptation can itself be a discipline that enhances *sattva*. As Krishna says in the *Bhagavad-gita,*

> One who sees inaction in action, and action in inaction,
> is truly wise and on the spiritual path, though doing all
> kinds of work.
> –Ranchor Prime, *Bhagavad Gita: Talks Between the
> Soul and God*[274]
>
> — *Bhagavad-gita* 4.18

In Chapter 17, we described sacred ceremony — regular, deliberate connection with the whole — veiled by the shades of *tamas* and *rajas* as being focused on others: at excluding them and feeling superior to them, in the former case; and at winning their praise and regard, in the latter case. So another way of lifting these veils is to attend to our regular practice of sacred ceremony as connecting us directly with the whole, rather than with trying to impress or manipulate other humans.

In Chapter 11, we mentioned how with the clarity of *sattva*, we can visualize the long-term results of what we are doing, whereas when we are veiled by the shades of *rajas* or *tamas*, we may rationalize away harming others for short-term benefits, or may not even see the harm in what we are doing. One practice that may help us lift these shades is to take a step back and evaluate how our work is affecting others and ourselves from time to time. Journaling can help us look at our work from a neutral point of view, and reviewing past journal entries weekly, monthly, or yearly may reveal trends or remind us of aspects of the big picture we may lose sight of when we're caught up in the day-to-day. Various forms of introspection can also help us with the self-discipline of speech:

> The self-discipline of speech consists in speaking words
> that are not agitating to others, true, pleasing, and beneficial, as well as self-study/recitation of sacred texts.
> — *Bhagavad-gita* 17.15

This self-discipline is of the nature of *sattva* and thus helps lift us out of the denser shades. If we try practicing this self-discipline in the course of speaking or interacting with others, we may find that it is sometimes tricky in the moment to satisfy all four of "not agitating to others," "true," "pleasing," and "beneficial" at once. It may appear that we have to trade one of these criteria for another. So another thing we can do while journaling is an easier version of this self-discipline: we can write down something we said during the day and see if it meets all these criteria. If not, we can try rewriting the sentence in different ways so that it better meets more of these criteria. We can do the same with things we plan to say in the future, where we anticipate the wording may be tricky. Workplace interactions provide many of the greatest opportunities for this practice. Gradually, this kind of journaling will help us speak this way in the moment. When our "speech" is written, such as in emails and forms of messaging, we can practice stopping and evaluating whether all the elements of *sattva* communication are present. Gradually our awareness will become more and more automatic. We can particularly become conscious of a tendency to "agitate others" when we are attached to getting a particular result and the other party seems to be opposing what we want. It's easy to fall into a habit of using emotionally manipulative language that is likely to disturb the mind of another when we are convinced only a particular response will satisfy us. Stepping back and evaluating our state of ego, and choosing to accept that others have the free will to respond as they like, give us the ability to communicate with respect such that others feel they can trust us.

On the other hand, sometimes people may be agitated simply by the way we live our own lives, even if we say nothing. They may assume that by adhering to particular practices, we are taking on an air of moral superiority even if such is not the case. This erroneous assumption can agitate them, and they may attempt to knock us off our supposed pedestal by finding fault with us. This phenomenon, called "do-gooder derogation," was elucidated by the psychologists Julia Minson and Benoît Monin.[275] Becoming aware of this general phenomenon can help us recognize when it is happening and maintain a sense of detachment. Our overall practice of *sattva* can also help us to remain unfazed and keep an even keel in these situations.

There is an important caveat regarding the criterion of our speech being "not agitating to others." When we are training or supervising others, it's sometimes necessary to speak sharply to our students or subordinates in the interests of being clear and firm. These situations may constitute exceptions in which those hearing us are agitated rather than pleased. (Speaking with people who have not entered into a training or supervisory relationship with us does not fall into this category of exception.) Sharp speech can be dulled by overuse, so if after some period it's not providing the desired benefit, it may be time to try something else. If our speech is coming from *sattva* or is free of the shades of ego, and if in general we are cherishing our subordinates (as described in Chapter 21) and letting them know how we cherish them, then any agitation from such occasional sharp speech will soon pass.

The timing of speech that may disturb others is crucial. Managers and leaders who feel the need to offer constructive, though painful, correction do well to become involved and speak up early in any project. There is a phrase to describe ill-timed criticism: "swoop and poop." That phrase brings to mind a bird that suddenly flies down and dumps its excrement on an unsuspecting head. Similarly, when a leader or employer waits to give input, or perhaps even attention, until a project or presentation is nearly completed, and then thoroughly denigrates the work, the subordinate has a similar emotional experience to suddenly finding bird poop on one's head, without having first even known a bird was in the vicinity. The subordinate may feel that the supervisor did not even spend due time and effort to understand the work (and its circumstances) before criticizing it. Of course, the subordinate also has some responsibility to keep the supervisor informed and not in the dark. However, supervisory responsibility entails fostering open communication through an overall context of cherishing subordinates.

As we get expert in practicing the self-discipline of speech, we can also apply it to our self-talk: how we talk to ourselves in our mind. As we explained in Chapter 25, our real self is beyond both the body and the mind. Indeed, the *Bhagavad-gita* tells us that our mind can be our worst enemy or our best friend.[276] We can treat our own mind as our cherished subordinate, practicing the self-discipline of speech with it, so eventually our mind becomes our friend. Then it will be our helpful ally, not only in the workplace but through the rest of life.

Another benefit of journaling is that as we look over our journal entries over a long period of time, we may get a real perspective on how the shades of ego have been playing out in our lives and the lives of those we interact with in our work. In Chapter 25, we described a metaphor of the interplay of three shades of ego creating the apparently infinite drama of life just as the combination of three colors on a screen creates the apparently infinite variety of pictures. With continued introspection, that metaphor will come to have practical meaning for us and aid our detachment. As *sattva*, *rajas*, and *tamas* are all simply shades of ego, we can engage in the sixfold practice described in Chapter 25 to get free of them altogether.

Another thing we can do to try to lighten our shades of ego is see what aspects of our life are veiling us with whatever shade of ego we have fallen into, and try to adjust or reduce those areas. The *Bhagavad-gita* and *Bhagavata Purana* describe many other aspects of life in terms of the shades of ego, besides the ones we've listed already in this book. For example, we might find that it is particularly our choices in food, or entertainment, dragging us into an ego shade and thereby taking us from our ideal life.

In *Mastering Life's Energies: Simple Steps to a Luminous Life at Work and Play*,[277] Maria Nemeth explains techniques for moving towards *sattva*, which she calles "luminosity," a state of "clarity, focus, ease, and grace." She distills deep insight into clear, simple explanations, and gives specific steps that can have a surprisingly big impact when practiced steadily over time.

In her book, Nemeth advises writing down "Life's Intentions." Among her suggested choices are some that pertain to specific fields of work, such as "to be a successful entrepreneur." The driving questions of each field of work can also be turned into Life's Intentions. For example, the driving question "Is it supportive?" of the Field of Artistry can be turned into a Life's Intention: "My intention is to be a contributor to the lives and work of people around me." The driving question "Is it beautiful?" of the Field of Artistry can be turned into a Life's Intention: "My intention is to be a contributor of beauty to the world around me."

Some of the more specific Life's Intentions she suggests may apply to more than one field of work. For example, "My intention is to be a successful author," might mean "My intention is to be a successful author, and in this way contribute to wisdom in the world around me," or it might mean "My intention is to be a successful author, and in this way contribute to beauty in the world around me," etc. While of course some authors may achieve both in some works, we are suggesting choosing one of these specifically as a Life's Intention, in accordance with our recommendation in Chapter 6 to choose one of the four fields of work suitable to one's nature. This more specific Life's Intention will bring greater clarity and focus, the ingredients of *sattva* or luminosity.

We can also aim to live a more balanced life overall. When describing the worker veiled by *tamas*, the *Bhagavad-gita* verse we quote at the beginning of this chapter uses the Sanskrit word *ayukta*, here translated as "disengaged." One way to help become more "present" and joyfully absorbed in our work is by adjusting how we meet our basic physiological functions:

> To be linked and engaged will be difficult if one eats too much or too little, or if one sleeps too much or not enough. For one who is linked and engaged during eating, sleeping, work, and recreation, the process of connection with the Divine becomes the destroyer of suffering.
>
> — *Bhagavad-gita* 6.16-17

These ancient writings are suggesting what modern science corroborates, namely that bringing our life into balance will make us better workers overall. Michael Breus, a doctor specializing in circadian rhythms, gives suggestions for balancing our sleeping and eating habits in his book *The Power of When*.[278] Each person falls into a particular chronotype (pattern of circadian rhythms), and Dr. Breus's recommendations are specifically tailored for each chronotype. Brad Stulberg and Steve Magness discuss balancing work and rest over periods shorter or longer than a day in their book *Peak Performance*.[279] If we've fallen into habits that impede our ability to balance our daily activity and inactivity, Kelly McGonigal's *The Willpower Instinct*[280] provides a variety of helpful advice for how to change these behaviors.

In terms of balance, we may also find it helpful to think of each day in terms of how much energy we have to spend, in addition to how much time. To get in touch with how much energy we have at a given time, we can make it a practice over a few days or weeks to note at set times of the day what we're doing and rating our energy on a scale of 1 to 10. This will help us gain or regain our psychophysical intuition. We can then consider what amount of energy we wish to allocate to various activities such as family, work, recreation, spiritual practices, bodily care, and so forth. We will likely find that energy is available for one of these activities even after it is exhausted for a different activity. Allocating energy in that way is something like budgeting money. A simple way to think about this concept is to imagine that one has, in cash, all the money that one can spend in a particular month. To budget, one puts specific amounts of cash into various envelopes, labeled with "food" or "clothes" or "recreation." When spending the money in a particular envelope, there need be no thought for the whole budget, as the entire contents of that envelope can be spent on the activity or goods at hand. In a similar way, if one has allocated, say, 20% of the day's energy for cooking, then while cooking one can "spend" the entirety of that 20%. Such a focus of energy assists one in giving one's actions, feelings, and thoughts fully to what one is doing, without distraction. This focus also means that we do not come to the end of the day too exhausted to give attention to our loved ones, as we have "set aside" energy for them that has not been spent on other activities. When one allocates energy in this way, it is wise to also consider that we have different kinds of energy. We have energy for physical tasks, energy for human interactions, and energy for mentally or intellectually stimulating activities.

Finally, the shades of ego are also contagious to some extent. We can try to be aware of how other people veiled by these shades of ego are affecting us, and avoid reacting in kind, which would veil us with the same shade of ego. For instance, if others around us are being quarrelsome, we can recognize that behavior as the shade of *rajas*, and avoid being drawn into the quarrel, however tempting it may be. If others around us are being hypocritical and dishonest, we can recognize that behavior as the shade of *tamas*, and not lower ourselves to that standard.

Many of us may be familiar with Reinhold Niebuhr's Serenity Prayer:

> God, give us grace to accept with serenity the things that cannot be changed, courage to change the things that should be changed, and the wisdom to distinguish the one from the other.
> —Reinhold Niebuhr & Elisabeth Sifton, *The Serenity Prayer: Faith and Politics in Times of Peace and War*[281]

Lao Tzu similarly wrote in the *Tao Te Ching*:

> Hold fast enough to Quietness,
> And of the ten thousand things none but can be worked
> on by you.[282]

Lifting the shades of ego can help us access the wisdom needed for this discernment, bringing us clearer vision of both the contours and the possibilities of our own work.

Overall, the more aspects of the natural art of work we apply, and the greater the degree to which we do so, the more we will get clear of the shades of ego.

27.2 Free from All the Shades

Of course, as we've emphasized several times in Part II, the shortcut to getting free from the shades of ego altogether is to connect with the biosphere, the source, the universal intelligence, or the Supreme Person. This connection directly fills us with enthusiasm and helps us transcend the shades of ego. We mentioned having that connection as the first element of the sixfold practice in Chapter 25. That connection is also the cornerstone that helps all the other elements of that practice fall into place.

The descriptions of the workers veiled in *rajas* and *tamas* quoted at the start of this chapter shed light on how these veils affect others with whom we interact in the course of our work. That the natural art of work helps lift these veils gives a hint of the ways in which those who practice this art would function together more smoothly.

Because practice right after learning something is the best way to solidify understanding, please turn now to Appendix E. In addition to going through these checklists now, you can also use them at various times to evaluate your position in the shades at that moment, as well as to get ideas for shifting the shades.

Chapter 28

Testimony: Fashion Designer and Retailer

By Janet Kaye

I have worked in the fashion industry for many years. When I first started it was just a job for me, but a job I really enjoyed. I enjoyed the beautiful textiles, the new styles and most importantly sharing it all with others. I was not fully satisfied though.

I moved away from fashion for some time, looking for the missing ingredient. I found it in Eastern teachings, in particular the *Bhagavad-gita*. It really helped me understand the connectivity of all things. How by working and living in a way, conscious of my eternal self and my relationship with the Supreme Divine, what before had seemed somewhat futile now became a rich, rewarding journey. Returning to the fashion world with this understanding, my experience was transformed.

I do not see it as a job any longer, I see it as a service of love. I do not see my staff as employees any longer, I see them as being sent to help and assist me. As much as I endeavor to be the best I can in the fashion world and am enthused by the success and growth of my business, I understand the temporary nature of all material things. I understand I have been given a gift to make fashion-savvy choices in purchasing and design, and I listen to my intuition in making these choices, rather than following the latest trends or what others are doing.

I feel very fortunate and grateful to be able to do this service and enjoy being able to use the profits in different ways to serve humanity.

Now my business is winding down and I embrace the end of this chapter and look forward to the next chapter of service in my life. The connectivity will remain regardless of the nature of my external activities. I understand that I am not the supreme controller, I do not get to choose what comes my way, but I do get to choose how to use it.

In the big picture of things, I am infinitesimal and insignificant, but I belong, I am connected to all things, I am loved and I love. It is not just a journey of the heart and body, it is a journey of the heart, body and soul. Whatever the journey may bring, I am cradled blissfully in that reality.

Chapter 29

Fields of Work and the Life Cycle

Career and work are intimately intertwined with the human physiological and psychological life cycle. While Shakespeare divides life into seven pathetic ages in *As You Like It*, the *Bhagavata Purana* divides life into four parts,[*] each with its own advantages and connection with career and society. As each of the four broad career fields we've discussed contains countless trees of specific careers, so the four ages of life now under discussion have subdivisions. This ancient view of aligning the biological stages of human existence with both work and overall spirituality could merit its own book. In this chapter, we will give only a brief sketch in order to show the most essential principles in relation to career.

---

[*]These four parts are a little different from Anne Bradstreet's "The Four Ages of Man". Interestingly, the stages described in the *Bhagavata Purana* are most similar to the division laid out by Peter Laslett:

> First comes an era of dependence, socialization, immaturity and education; second an era of independence, maturity and responsibility, of earning and of saving; third an era of personal fulfillment; and fourth an era of final dependence, decrepitude and death.
> –Peter Laslett, *A Fresh Map of Life: The Emergence of the Third Age*[283]

While Laslett did not consider the four ages as arriving on specific birthdays, academics currently place the Third Age at ages 55 to 75 and Gail Sheehy's 1995 book *New Passages* placed it at ages 50 to 80.[284] In the medical field, people older than 80 are termed the "older old," and even in those developed countries where life expectancy has been increasing significantly, *healthy* life expectancy has not increased to anywhere near the same extent.[285] Over the remaining courses of their lives, the "older old" face an increasing burden of non-communicable, age-dependent diseases that interfere to a growing extent with their abilities to carry out the activities of daily life.[286]

The four stages of life according to the *Bhagavata Purana* are 1) study and preparation, 2) home- and work-life, 3) gradual withdrawal, greater acceptance, and retirement, and 4) preparation for death. We will examine each in relation to the art of work and life in general.

29.1   First Stage: Study and Preparation

The first stage, study and preparation, begins even in the womb and ends with graduation from formal education. Of course, education may continue in many ways throughout adult life, long after any compulsory education is over. However, for our purpose here we can say that this study stage ends once a person is working his or her career full-time or enough to be financially self-sufficient. The kind of lifelong learning successful people do to keep career skills current would not be part of this earlier stage during which study and learning are primary.

The relationship between preparation and career is, to some degree, readily apparent. The majority of careers require both a framework of general knowledge and specific targeted training. Most societies today allow for many children and teenagers to receive knowledge and training without the responsibility of also having a job. Of course, preindustrial societies and many places even in the world today give children "on-the-job training" starting from a very young age. We discuss the advantages and disadvantages of this practice in Chapter 7. The main point, though, is that this life stage is one of preparation. Individual preparation is essential for the health of the entire workforce, so rather than seeing persons in this stage as parasites, the working part of society ideally looks at them with affection, as one might with younger family members.

In a society where the art of work is understood, the study and preparation stage would go beyond knowledge and skills. It would even go beyond what is often called "values education," most of which is frequently taught merely in the ego shade of *rajas*. What is needed in this state is training in the principles of the art of work we have discussed throughout this book. Let's go revisit some of the major principles discussed so far on an individual level, and see how a person would best get preparation and training in early life. (In Part III, we discuss these principles on a societal level.)

The first principle is to work according to one's nature. Ideally, in the study stage of life, application of this principle means that parents and teachers learn how to identify and nourish the natures of those in their care so that each person can continue to push the boundaries of mastery throughout life. We discussed this in more detail in Chapter 7. It's a shame that modern education in many countries delays practical vocational training until age eighteen or twenty, focusing until then on only general education. Many students are, therefore, bored or frustrated in schools, leading to discipline problems. If a young person's nature can be identified early then education can allow also for a high level of mastery at an early age, which encourages and motivates learning. It's important, however, that adults' own desires and prejudices not be projected onto the young person in the name of hastening their choice of specific vocational education or for the adults' vicarious enjoyment. It's best for adults to maintain a neutral, detached perspective and an attitude of curiosity and wonder while watching the young person unfold, and be prepared to deal with some false starts, graciously and with equanimity. One thing to keep in mind is that young people may feel like engaging in a pursuit because their friends or someone they admire does, or they may avoid a pursuit because someone they don't like engages in it. Adults who guide younger people in career choices do well to keep such social tendencies in mind. Of course, adults in all the fields of work can help avoid such situations by acting as positive role models.

Other principles of study deal with how to find genuine purpose and value in one's career. Youngsters can start to practice charity and regular times of inner connection with the bigger picture of life, such as daily meditation, prayer, wisdom research, and so forth. Charity and ways of connection are to be taught and practiced not ritualistically but so the young gain authentic experiences beyond ego-centralized thinking. Training to cherish our sources of wealth and joy is as important a part of study as are language and science. Outings to see the wonders of wild lands, forests, mountains, or star-filled skies, even if they may be rare in a particular child's life, can be quite valuable. Participating in community gardens or farm sanctuaries can be especially enriching experiences.

It is crucial to remember that to receive authentic increase from our unlimited source and to share that with others will require letting go of egocentric thinking in its various forms. To do so requires preparation for a life of service rather than self-centered sensuality. Service over sensuality does not mean deprivation, but real, deep joy in authentic sharing and harmony. Unfortunately, for many in today's world, the time of adolescent education has often involved quite the opposite in terms of irresponsible sexual behavior, misuse of easy parental money, mistreatment of those less fortunate, and neglect of the world's ecosystem. Those who have spent their early years in this way may have a harder time finding satisfaction in work later on, no matter how technically skilled they become, until they set aside time (which becomes more and more costly as life progresses) to reflect on and prepare for reaching their best selves. Indeed, ideally the first stage of life involves not just preparation for career but also preparation for responsible relationships that occur in the next stage of life. Learning how to have relationships of mutual respect and giving is crucial at this early stage if we want real meaning individually and collectively. The adolescent years at their best can involve strong integrity in seeking high ideals and pursuing them enthusiastically. It is in this stage that our vision of what we want to pursue may be clearest and our energy to pursue it may be highest, as we are less burdened by investment in or responsibility for our own previous decisions. Throughout the ages, it has been young people wholeheartedly pursuing what they believe in who have driven the most lasting progress in caring for the world's ecosystem, helping those less fortunate, and so forth in society at large.

For most of us, when we were young children, discipline was imposed upon us externally, by our parents and teachers. So the intrinsic value of disciplined habits may not really have been apparent to us, and once we get the opportunity to make our own decisions, we may easily discard these habits. Some time later, once the novelty of decision making has worn off and we've experienced enough consequences of our own decisions, some of us may naturally feel a bit more cautious about making new ones. So each decision we make takes mental energy. At this point, if we've lost our childhood habits of discipline, the decisions we constantly make become a low-level source of stress, which we may feel continuously without necessarily having any idea of the cause. In this case, we can try forming new disciplined habits of our own choosing, one at a time. In this way, instead of spending energy deciding how or when to do things that are to be done every day, week, or month, we can reserve our decision making energy for more consequential matters that will help us reach our best selves. Thus we have a strong foundation for the second stage, of home and work life.

Of course, people also vary in the degree of spontaneity they personally prefer, and many of us will settle on much less structure than we had as children.

As a side note, as we mentioned in Chapter 3 in regard to commensals, some people remain in the first stage as perpetual students for their entire lives, never getting involved with home and career. For these people, their entire life is one of seeking, studying, and learning. They may be associated with a university, getting one degree after another or doing research, preferably with one or more qualified mentors who have goodwill and their best interests in mind. Such voluntary perpetual students are to be distinguished from those who are forced, pressured, or misled into remaining students or trainees by supervisors who wish to exploit them. As voluntary perpetual students are not earning a livelihood with full adult autonomy (although they may do part-time work), they are not within the Field of Ideas or any Field of work at all. Some perpetual students may live in a monastery, convent, or *asrama* situation where their days are spent wholly in study and prayer. Others may travel without a destination, living by doing odd jobs, not to offer their talents and nature to society, but only to survive while on their quest. As we explained in Chapter 3, society can respect and honor the independence and autonomy of commensals.

29.2 Second Stage: Home and Work Life

The second stage, home and work life, is from the time of becoming adult until starting to retire. For most people, this stage of life is the main time for career as well as fulfilling desires for long-term romantic relationships and general independence. Here we encounter a principle discussed in Chapter 14 — that anyone who earns their living does not keep all the riches, in whatever form, for themselves alone. It is because of this principle that traditionally having a job has been connected with caring for family — spouse, children, and maybe extended family or aged parents. People may think that because they have a family they need to earn wealth, but the principle implies that the opposite is also true — because we want to earn wealth, we need to have someone with whom to share our wealth.[*] Without such sharing of wealth, it's almost impossible to avoid egotism in accumulating wealth. Therefore, career and family life complement one another.

Within the scope of this complementary relationship, it can often be challenging to carefully balance career, care of family members, and maintaining a residence. Very many books, articles, and courses have been written about successfully integrating home and career, children and career, and gender roles. Each person has an individual way of finding balance in this stage of life, but we can offer some ancient guidance that may assist.

One key to having balance is to be satisfied with the prosperity achieved with working for a set portion of time — for example, eight hours a day or forty to fifty hours a week. When we remember that there are six ways to be "rich" we can understand that working more hours to make more money may end up depriving us of the time and energy to have genuine wealth in ways truly enriching for us. Modern society with its labor-saving devices does not make us immune to the problem of overwork, whether for money, status (including managerial and peer pressure), or a sense of security, thus depriving ourselves of a balanced life.[288][†] In a 2004 report,[289] the US Department of Health and Human Services reviewed fifty-one research studies and one meta-analysis on the effects of overtime (defined as more than forty hours per week) and extended work shifts (defined as more than eight hours per day). They found that:

---

[*]The original Bengali is:

> *yauvaneyakhana, dhana uparjane, ha-inu vipula kami*
> *dharama smariya, grhinira kara, dharinu takhana ami*

> In my youth, when I had a great desire to earn money, I accepted a spouse, considering dharma.
> —Bhaktivinoda Thakura, *Saranagati*[287]

[†]Of course, not being able to get enough work hours to physically maintain oneself, despite one's ability and desire to work those hours, can also cause great difficulty. On a societal level, this can be the flip side of the same coin, when institutions prefer to increase the overtime of a smaller number of workers rather than to employ a larger number. An artificial dichotomy, between overtime work versus not enough work to get by, enables some institutions to pressure both sets of workers into accepting onerous or unhealthy conditions, as we illustrated in Chapter 16.

- Overtime led to decreased performance on tests of cognitive and executive function. Overtime also led to increased risk of automobile accidents and on-the-job injuries in certain industries.

- Extended shifts often resulted in greater proportionate risk of injury during later hours of the shift. Several studies reported deterioration in alertness and reasoning abilities during extended shifts. Some studies indicated these effects could be mitigated if workers were able to control the timing of their shifts and slow their pace of work during the later parts of their shifts. One study found that older workers were less able to maintain performance over extended shifts than younger ones.

Furthermore, beyond short bursts, excessive overtime provides only illusory benefits even as far as the work itself goes:

> Research that attempts to quantify the relationship between hours worked and productivity found that employee output falls sharply after a 50-hour work-week, and falls off a cliff after 55 hours — so much so that someone who puts in 70 hours produces nothing in those extra 15 hours, according to a study published [in 2014] by John Pencavel of Stanford University.
>
> ...
>
> "The simple reality is that work, both mental and physical, results in fatigue that limits the cognitive and bodily resources people have to put towards their work," said Ken Matos, senior director of research at the Families and Work Institute think tank. "When they are not thinking clearly or moving as quickly or precisely they must work more slowly to maintain quality and safety requirements."
>
> –Bob Sullivan, *Memo to work martyrs: Long hours make you less productive*[290]

In general, unsustainable overwork is a symptom of *rajas* (in the supervisors, the workers, or both).

When nature, career, and marriage partners are synchronized, it can also be much simpler for a couple to align career and home. Spouses who work together in the same career, with a balance of cooperation and sportive, supportive competition, gain an advantage of sharing a vital and significant part of their personality and time. The harmonizing of their individual energies and temperaments when working together in a livelihood has the potential to be deeply satisfying to each, and to enhance their relationship. For those already married who have, or discover, differences in career inclinations, honoring each person's nature is more important than trying to impose an artificial career partnership. As we discuss in Chapter 5, a person's nature cannot be successfully repressed, and harm comes to both individual and society when people try and work outside of their natural Field. As we described in Chapter 4 and especially in Chapter 6, the four fields of work in particular involve different outlooks on life that can often be at odds with each other, so if spouses are temperamentally suited to two different fields of work, these different outlooks can repeatedly cause friction and misunderstanding. What one person sees as his or her own strengths, the other person may see as the first person's weaknesses, and it may continually be difficult to find common ground for shared decision making.

Some may question how it is ideal according to ancient wisdom for spouses to work together in the same career if until recently only men had careers, and women only took care of household chores and child-raising. But such an understanding is historically inaccurate. In the *Bhagavata Purana* and other sacred writings from the Vedic tradition, both men and women have careers in the stage we call "home and work life," otherwise known as "the prime of life." Some of the evidence for this fact is in the great care taken in ancient times to have marriages between those of similar career propensity (though exceptions were also noted).[*]

In preindustrial days when women commonly had an average of six children,[291] they could work at their career from home, or near it, along with others in their family. These two great advantages — working from home, or close to home, being the norm instead of the

---

[*]Further evidence includes the great number of Sanskrit terms in ancient scriptures specifically denoting women of various professions; for example, *gopi*, "female dairy farmer," or *phalavikrayini*, "female fruit-seller." The professions of women in ancient Sanskrit scriptures were more eye-catching on the occasions when they engaged in them singly. Draupadi, queen of Arjuna and his brothers, took on the profession of *sairandri*, "female artisan," while all of them were incognito. (Each of them temporarily crossed fields during this time to maintain their disguise.) Queen Kaikeyi went with King Dasaratha into battle and, when he fell unconscious, rescued him from the battlefield while the enemies continued to attack. Maitreyi and Gargi each put forward their own positions in debates and discussions in assemblies of learned scholars.

exception, and extended family and community — were a practical help available to almost everyone. In many parts of the world, for instance, women worked to make textiles:

> Early on (thirteenth century), then, [European] merchants began to hire cottage workers....In the most important branch, the textile manufacture, peasant women did the spinning on a putting-out basis: merchants gave out (put out) the raw material — the raw wool and flax and, later, cotton — and collected the finished yarn....
>
> The [Inca] women spun thread while walking, and the story has it that the roads were built smooth to keep them from tripping; they were too busy to watch their feet....
>
> it was easier and more economical [in India] to hire...poor women for spinning....
>
> [In 19th-century Argentina], almost all such work fell to women — spinning and weaving, potting, soap-making, cooking oil, candle-making....
>
> [In Japan during the Meiji Restoration] Everything counted....Division of labor? Mother's time and work were too precious to waste on babies and self-indulgence — up after childbirth! Older children could care for younger; small children would learn early to perform light industrial tasks. The smallest threads, even lint, could be saved and sold to rag-pickers for a few sen (100 sen = 1 yen)....Such households were miniature textile factories, a mine of profit to the energetic merchant putter-out.
>
> –David Landes, *The Wealth and Poverty of Nations*[292]

Women carried out many responsibilities in agricultural work as well. In addition, one person was not responsible for all the childcare, cooking, cleaning, and other household duties, as these were shared with extended family and village friends:

> [In the Middle Ages], single-family households were uncommon in most of the world, and Western Europe became, around the 12th century, one of the first places where households were organized around monogamous couples and their children. But these households still

didn't look much like today's nuclear families. In addition to parents and their children, medieval households frequently included various townspeople, poor married couples, other people's children, widows, orphans, unrelated elderly people, servants, boarders, long-term visitors, friends, and assorted relatives.

...

By the 1500s, the idea of a household as a father, a mother, and their biological children caught on among Europe's new urban middle class, at least as something to strive for....For all its popularity as a comforting idea, [this kind of] household was hardly common 500 years ago. It was completely unrealistic for most people to find the time, money, and resources to run a household on their own. Even those who did usually had big households full of unrelated people; they relied on the larger community far too much to survive as a single-family unit.

...When societies were mostly agricultural, production was centered near the home, and families needed all the labor they could get to run the farm during busy seasons. But as industrialization took hold, people started leaving home to go to work, commuting to factories and, later, offices. Something communal was lost....

–Ilana E. Strauss, The Hot New Millennial Housing Trend Is a Repeat of the Middle Ages[293]

Many varieties of domestic groups, with different structures and different ways of dividing labor and arranging space, existed among various places and cultures.[294] It was largely because of industrialization that the conception of males being the sole breadwinner developed.[295] Industrialization pushed careers out of the home, starting with textiles.

A very important side note is that for some women — and increasingly today for people in general — homemaking itself is a combination of career and family in a literal sense. Such a situation can occur if someone's natural career is in the Field of Artistry, and the preferred trees of work deal with areas such as child care, food service, and cleaning.* For others, the stark separation of home from career in the

---

*Of course, even in this case, many may face situations like

early decades of industrialization forced women in particular to make a heart-wrenching choice between them. The biological realities of reproduction until the middle part of the 20th century, combined with rigid workplace policies and norms, practically forced most women to choose home over career — a choice women did not have to make previously.

Such a situation meant decades of frustration for half the human race. At least there was much to do at home, so women were busy, even if a large portion of their personalities and natures had little avenue for expression. With the automation of the home, and especially when that automation combined with varieties of chemical and physical ways to restrict childbearing, the situation reversed. Women started to join men in choosing career over home, a trend that continues to play out in different parts of the world. The situation is in flux and continues to pose many challenges on economic and emotional levels.

Overall solutions of mixing family responsibilities and career depend on circumstances and are far beyond the scope of this book. To summarize our observations here, having both a satisfying career and family life can often be easier through incorporating three time-tested strategies. These are: working on career from the home as much as possible, having extended networks of family and friends nearby to greatly relieve the isolation of the nuclear family, and, if possible, ensuring there is harmony between the natures of life partners' careers. Regarding the first strategy, one of the benefits of the information and technological revolutions is the increased option of work from home or close to home in all four fields, though of course many jobs do not support this option.*

---

the tragedy of women taking care of affluent American babies while their own children grow up, parentless, across an ocean or south of a border.
–Mona Simpson, *Love, Money and Other People's Children*[296]

We are referring instead to those whose homemaking career is dedicated to, or includes, their own families.

*We began writing this book in 2017, and these words were written before the pandemic of 2020. We were envisioning a gradual, self-initiated transition, with stable schooling situations, the ability to plan professionally, and access to social support. We do continue to believe that this option could be helpful in such a scenario, with adequate long-term planning and design.

29.3 Third Stage: Gradual Withdrawal, Greater Acceptance, and Retirement

> At some point, writing one more book will not add to my life satisfaction; it will merely stave off the end of my book-writing career. The canvas of my life will have another brushstroke that, if I am being forthright, others will barely notice, and will certainly not appreciate very much. The same will be true for most other markers of my success. What I need to do, in effect, is stop seeing my life as a canvas to fill, and start seeing it more as a block of marble to chip away at and shape something out of. I need a reverse bucket list. My goal for each year of the rest of my life should be to throw out things, obligations, and relationships until I can clearly see my refined self in its best form.
>
> –Arthur C. Brooks[297]

As we move into middle age, the third stage of the life cycle begins — gradual withdrawal from active involvement in work, greater acceptance of the limitations in life, and retirement. If we had children at the beginning of our reproductive years, they are now grown and making their own way in life. Our relationship with our spouse may have shifted from primarily lover to primarily friend, and our sexual desires may have abated to an extent. Ideally, we've used our nature in career in ways that resulted in meaningful work for ourselves and others. Or perhaps our work was marred by our being covered by the ego shades and the cycle of frustration. We may have failed to come to authentic meaning and found ourselves, instead, disappointed with knowing deep down that the apparent value of our work was not satisfying. Whether through satisfaction with a time of life completed well, or understanding the opportunity has passed, by mid-life most people are usually ready for a shift.

At this stage of human life, we ease away from being preoccupied with family, home, and work. Gradually, working for a livelihood winds down. People in this stage generally still have energy to be involved in life, but they have either come to a point where either they are so dissatisfied that they want a do-over (a mid-life crisis), or they happily accept that successful life is no longer about creating, doing, shaping, and changing the world as they expected when full of youthful idealism. Having experienced by this point in life how our own desires have changed, perhaps several times, we may view whatever desires come upon us with a degree of detachment, no longer identifying with them as strongly, or feeling such an urge to pursue them. In either case, it is time for a change.

While every human being must have an early life stage of study and preparation in order to know how to survive, some people never enter the stage of home, family, and career, nor do they remain lifelong seekers. Such persons go directly from the stage of preparation to the stage of retirement. They may make this shift in their twenties or in their fifties. For such persons, the change is from study and seeking to sharing wisdom and taking responsibility for society's spiritual upliftment, continuing as a commensal outside the fields of work.

The *Bhagavata Purana* suggests that in this stage of life we gradually move off center stage to make room for younger people to be the movers and shakers. We take time to travel, especially to places and situations of spiritual inspiration. We disentangle ourselves from our worldly responsibilities and sensual preoccupations, and we assimilate our life experiences. As we mature in this stage, moving through middle age and the start of old age, we become society's elders with wise counsel, regarding the field of work we've had and our family experiences. We delight more and more in the simpler things in life — not childishly, but as a wise person who has learned through the natural art of work what really matters. In this stage one may be a source of wisdom and helper mostly to one's family, or one may see the world as family.

There are several advantages for society when middle-aged people gradually withdraw from work life, moving into more of a mentoring role and less of a day-to-day role, or retire. First, younger people can gradually take over responsibility while the middle-aged workers are still around to give counsel and guidance. Second, younger people can gradually assume full responsibility while they are still young enough to be energetic and idealistic. Third, middle-aged people can continue to make important contributions to society just at the time when they may be starting to question their life and relevance. Fourth, middle-aged people can enjoy the freedom from responsibility they have earned, rather than trying to imitate and compete with youth. Fifth, such withdrawal facilitates a natural bridge to older old age.

In many countries today, the interplay of demographics, savings, and debt complicates the path to retirement for large portions of the middle-aged population. How societies can move toward better facilitating retirement depends on each specific context and is well beyond the scope of this book. Part of the path to sustainable prosperity may involve designing new financial instruments in tune with the life cycle. One of us is working on mathematical ecosociology (as we touch on briefly in Chapter 37), which can help inform such design. Overall, the natural art of work when done on a societal level can help facilitate retirement in the third stage for individuals. We explain how multiple individuals can practice the natural art of work together, up to a whole society, in Part III.

29.4   Fourth Stage: Preparation for Death

The fourth stage is older old age, another time of preparation. For many people, eventually the body slows down — sometimes the mind, as well — such that even traveling and sharing wisdom become difficult. The *Bhagavata Purana* suggests that a person does well to "die before dying" by letting go of worldly affiliation, sensuality, and responsibility other than that of sharing wisdom and insight as far as possible. When we let go voluntarily and prepare well for death, death is easy to accept when it arrives:

> In the last year of his life, William Jennings "Bill" Adams moved from darkness to light, from illusion to truth, and from death to immortality.
>
> ...Bill and his wife, Rosemary, were together for almost sixty years, until she passed away in April 2001....Her death was so crushing to Bill that when she was gone, he wrote poems about how his life had lost meaning, how all the familiar objects and pictures and photographs and things that seemed to matter were now just empty and hollow. He went through a great deal of existential despair — a very dark period.
>
> Kausalya and Anthony [Bill's daughter-in-law and son] lived in Los Angeles[*]....In December 2003 he phoned Anthony and Kausalya and asked if they could come and stay with him for a while. He hadn't revealed to them that he was ill, but he had been diagnosed with congestive heart failure nine years earlier.

---

[*]Los Angeles is a couple of hours' drive from San Diego, which is where Bill lived.

So Anthony and Kausalya went down to San Diego. The cardiologist informed them that Bill had one year to live. They were shocked. They decided to sell their house and move down and spend his last year with him.

"It was an amazing year," Kausalya told me. "When we first went down, he was very, very depressed and morose about everything — very sad. All of his poems — he was a writer, a poet — reflected this melancholy, this nihilistic worldview."

Soon after they moved, Anthony started working for Taylor Guitars, and Kausalya had a lot of time alone with Bill. She took him to the doctor and cooked for him, and they would talk about life.

…"With Kausalya remodeling the house and cooking him great *prasada* (sanctified food) and speaking with him," Anthony added, "and our always playing music and inviting friends over, he gradually regained his interest in life, and over the year he came to see that there was more to life than what met the eye. He became aware of the eternal.

"…he determined that he wanted to die peacefully at home. So we had the hospice people come over, and we were there when they told him, 'You have six months to live.' His eyes filled with tears; the cardiologist hadn't actually told him how long he had. For a few days he was depressed, and he didn't want to see anybody but us. But as he worked through it, he wanted to see everybody. He felt liberated. There was no sadness, and he would say, 'Everything is fine.' He made peace with it."

–Giriraj Swami, *His Darkness Ended with Light —
His Art Ended with God*[298]

Kausalya kept relating wisdom from the *Bhagavad-gita* and her own experiences to Bill:

…Bill's last poem was kind of a summation. One could track his change of consciousness from the early poems to the final one, from darkness to light, from death to eternal life. He had gone from being depressed, thinking, "What was my life worth? It is all over," to the final stage of his life, when he became joyous. He knew he was going to die, but he was joyous.

On what turned out to be the last night of Bill's life, [a couple of friends] came down from LA and spent the night. They and Kausalya and Anthony were up with Bill until midnight, playing music and talking. Kausalya made a wonderful meal, and Bill was happy and jubilant, and finally at midnight — everyone was laughing — he said, "That's all the hilarity I can stand for one night" and went to bed. That's the last thing he ever said. ...
Kausalya In that last poem, he wrote, "All matter is allowed to change, not die." So, he came to feel that death was not the end, that everything is eternal, in an endless journey of transformation. And he could release himself to that and feel that it was all wonderful.
Anthony He didn't feel the need to pin it down, to know exactly what was going to happen. He didn't really think any of us could know that, but he ended up feeling that he was eternal and that all life was eternal and that he was a part of it all. So it was all okay, and he could just surrender. He wasn't clinging to this body anymore; he was exhilarated, happy to be part of the mystery of life taking him where he was supposed to go next.

...On that last night, Bill's *prana* — his energy, his essence — was so strong, you wouldn't think he was about to die. He had a luminous quality and was up until midnight conversing and laughing and having fun with guests and friends.

I think he had finally accepted that it was time for him to go, that all things must pass, all forms must change, and he finally accepted it completely. And once he accepted it, he was filled with lightness of being, and joy. He wasn't struggling or fighting anymore — he was almost giddy, he could laugh. He was joyous and childlike and playful and writing poems and taking joy from talking to everybody and hearing news.

–Giriraj Swami, His Darkness Ended with Light —
His Art Ended with God[299]

So we see that preparing for death can make a great difference at the end of life. Of course, there's no guarantee that we'll get as much specific advance notice as Bill Adams got.

People preparing for death are fully commensals, totally outside the fields of work. Retired persons who are now in older old age, having gone through the stage of home and work life (and not directly from student life), can offer specific guidance and training about career and family, and so are making a clear contribution to the fields of work, though they no longer work there themselves. Even so, those in the last stage do well to gradually extricate themselves even from giving such advice. Though they may have knowledge in thousands of areas, and have figuratively fought on thousands of life's battlefields, the end of life is meant to fully fix our minds and our hearts on our Divine source, so that we can unite there with love and devotion, for doing so is the end goal of life.

29.5 Conclusion

To summarize the life stages in relation to career: the early part of life is for preparation for the natural art of work, the prime of life is for engaging in the natural art of work, the third stage is for consolidating and sharing the wisdom one has gained as well as allowing for succession in the natural art of work, and the fourth stage for complete renunciation of work. We note that only in the stage of the prime of life is one fully focused on career, and its concomitant responsibilities of stewarding the resulting riches, as we explain throughout this book. At the same time, we cherish the sources of wealth continuously throughout our lives in gratitude for how they sustain all of us, although we do so more actively in the prime of life.

Regarding the relationship between those in various life stages, those in the earlier stages do well to look to those in the later stages who were successful in their fields and in the types of relationships they wish to have, and then actively seek guidance and direction:

> When we do not intentionally cultivate the third and fourth stages, we lose their skills and fail to create the elders needed to understand the first and second stages and guide us through and beyond them.
> –Richard Rohr[300]

Too often those in the prime of life only rely on their friends who are at the same stage for direction. However, those peers aren't always the best source of information.[301] It's not particularly wise to take no guidance at all or to take only guidance from those on the same level or from those in later stages who have arrived at destinations different from what we aspire to.

Additionally, in a society where the natural art of work is the norm, those in the prime of life happily maintain those in the study stage, the retirement stage, and those in the preparation for death stage, when needed. In this way the natural art of work sustains and supports the whole life cycle.

In Part III, we turn to further principles of the natural art of work that describe interactions among pairs or larger groups of people, ranging up to society as a whole. While each of us only has control over our own actions, keeping this larger vision in mind can both encourage us and practically guide us in doing our part in making it manifest.

Chapter 30

Testimony: Interfaith Chaplain Educator

30.1   Introduction

My legal name is Robin Brinkmann. My initiated name is Rambhoru
Dasi ACBSP. I was initiated by A.C. Bhaktivedanta Swami in 1974 in
Cologne, Germany.

I have a BA in Religious Studies [Guilford College]; a Master's of
Divinity degree [Claremont School of Theology]; and a Masters of Patient Counseling degree [Virginia Commonwealth University]. I am
a Board Certified Professional Interfaith Chaplain;[302] and an ACPE
Certified Clinical Pastoral Educator,[303] which is the doctorate-level
of education in Pastoral Care. I have been certified in three different
methods of Grief Support Group Facilitation [Our House Grief Support Center, Grief Recovery Method, and Beyond Loss, Los Angeles,
CA].

30.2   My Story

After living within an *asrama* (religious community) for nearly thirty
years, I realized I could increase my capacity to care were I to embed
myself within the world at large.

As a child I had internalized the Christian notion of agape: offering unconditional care to others as a means of expressing my unconditional love for God. As a Vaishnava,* I understood my life's mission

---

*A practitioner of personal devotion to Krishna.

to be reciprocating God's unconditional love for me by extending it to others; more specifically, to assist God in His mission to relieve human suffering by awakening their natural loving relationship with Him.

As a Krishna devotee all those years, I had, for the most part, assumed I loved everyone unconditionally, because, well, that's what it means to practice *Bhakti* (devotion), right? To love and serve the Lord residing within my heart and the hearts of all others.

In my early *asrama* days, I had cooked for my religious community, and viewed my service to suffering humanity to be preparing delicious, healthy vegetarian food with love and devotion. There was nothing more gratifying to me than sharing such sacred food with others who ingested it in gratitude acknowledging it as *prasada (God's mercy)*.

At that time, my focus of concern was solely on my personal spiritual advancement to the exclusion of others. I eagerly engaged others in my mission to get vegetables cut, pots washed, and my kitchen cleaned so I could commence with yet another cooking venture in Krishna's mission of mercy. Besides the Hare Krishna mantra, my secret meditation was, "What will they eat, what will they eat?"

Stepping outside my religious community at age 46 was daunting. I had no marketable skills. I had given up chasing the dollar long before entering an *asrama*. Working only to survive went against everything I'd aspired for. Still, I was determined to find a way to do both; continue practicing love for God, and survive.

It wasn't until I took the opportunity to spend a year in Arizona on the Mexican border to pursue a chaplain residency that I experienced firsthand the depths of human suffering swirling all around me. Before I arrived in Yuma, I had taken a Pastoral Care course in seminary. My professor had asked our class to write down the most frightening population we thought we might minister to as ordained clergy persons. I wrote *"children who were burn victims"* on my paper, unaware of the assignment's goal. After she had all our responses in her hand, my professor instructed us to "physically spend time with whomever you wrote down, and write a paper reflecting on what your theology had to offer that would give a suffering person spiritual comfort."

The next day, I made an appointment with the woman who hosted visitors at the Los Angeles Shriner's Children's Burn Hospital. She agreed to meet me in the coming week. When I arrived, the woman I had spoken to on the phone came out and offered me her hand. It only had a thumb and forefinger, with scar tissue replacing where the remaining fingers once had been. The skin on her face sagged from severe scarring. One ear was gone.

Her hair was patchy. I winced to witness the impact of a trauma forever imprinted on her body. I wondered if she had been a patient in this hospital many years ago. She studied my face to see if it belied any feelings of repulsion. I'm sure I winced as I absorbed the magnitude of her history of pain.

My host's kind and gentle voice tone was pleasant as she escorted me to the balcony overlooking a large room where hospital staff were wheeling in what seemed like fifty severely burned children. Some lay on beds. Some were in wheelchairs. Some walked on crutches. Many had bandages covering their burns. Some were without arms, or legs, or ears, or eyes, or hair.

After sitting with me for a while, my host left to go about her business. But before turning to go, she said with melancholy in her voice, "Many of these children were abandoned by their families because they had no resources to take care of them." Hearing this, I felt my heart ache deeply for the endless days of despair and loneliness these children must have endured.

I pondered alone for the better part of an hour, searching for what spiritual comfort my theology had to offer in terms of comforting suffering persons such as these. Karma theory, the notion that our current reality is the consequence of our previous actions, seemed like just another form of victim-blaming unless tempered by the notion of a beneficent creator. Still, I was puzzled. What aspect of my theology would provide spiritual comfort to a suffering person? After the children were taken away, I went home, wrote a paper about my experience and thought little more about it.

Years later, as a chaplain resident in Yuma, I spent 40 hours of every week with all kinds of people suffering unimaginable distress like burns and disfigurement, amputation, and loss. Again, that seminary question returned… "What aspect of my theology could be drawn upon to provide spiritual comfort to a suffering person?"

As I made my daily rounds in and out of hospital rooms, I prayed with Christians in the name of Christ, with Muslims in the name of Allah, with Jews in the name of Yahweh. I shared a sacred moment of silence with Buddhists. And as I continued my ongoing journey with suffering people the answer to that nagging seminary question began to crystallize.

The one thing I was sure that people in pain needed to hear was, "Whatever is happening to you now, no matter how it looks to the world, no matter what you did or have had done to you, God is right here with you. He loves you as you are. You are not alone."

That was 15 years ago. And since that time my understanding of unconditional care has expanded as I've realized how many people suffer lives of quiet desperation, yearning for deeply meaningful, growth-fostering human connection.

In seminary, we studied the teachings of Martin Buber, a Jewish Rabbi who made famous the notion that God is present between people whenever they are engaged in heart-connecting communication. And in those sacred moments, God incarnates in the heartfelt words of other people.

As a chaplain I paid close attention to how the Lord within my heart and the hearts of those I provided care for spoke directly to me, revealing insights I might have missed had I allowed myself to be distracted. And when a person's grief was more than they could bear, I noticed the Lord showing up between us in long moments of silent solidarity.

At times like these, the words of St. Francis rang true for me: "Preach all the time, and if necessary use words," because he believed the best way to preach unconditional love was to embody it by caring for others. In this way, love is something a persons does; not just what they feel.

Psychologist Dr. David Richo explains love as an action word. It means to offer another person something he calls the "five A's; attention, acceptance, appreciation, affection and allowing or the freedom to choose."

Interestingly, this is also a central teaching in the *Bhakti* (devotional) tradition; to provide this sort of unconditional compassionate care to another person [suffering or otherwise] as an outpouring of our love for the Supreme Lord.

Becoming a chaplain was a radical shift from my life as a scholar who sat stiff-necked for hours on end studying theories of dead white guys in order to pump theory papers out of my computer. I was now on my feet or sitting bedside most of the day, joining suffering persons' journey of pain as they arrived despairing in the Emergency Department. Death, dying, illness, overdose, abuse, neglect, gunshot wounds, amputations, PTSD, and mental illness became my daily fare, particularly while holding the overnight on-call pager.

I cried that whole year in Yuma as I realized the pervasiveness of human suffering and how much my spiritual striving up till then had sorely missed the mark. I had excelled at following religious rules and regulations to the exclusion of tending to a person's human spirit. In college I had been busy with ideas. As a chaplain I encountered hearts so broken they seemed beyond repair.

I realized that whether a person professed a particular religious faith or no faith at all, every person had a meaning-making system that helped them find their unique place in the world. It was in that place that I joined them in their life's journey toward becoming all they were created to be. I learned that spirituality was a person's recognizing and celebrating that they were inextricably connected to others by a power greater than themselves and that their connection to that power and to others was grounded in love and compassion.

For me, becoming a chaplain was like entering a portal where heart-connecting relationships were the pathway into the heart of God; not in the pages of dry philosophies spun from the minds of those who were good at speculating but did not translate their ideas into practical action.

So what does a professional chaplain do exactly? Essentially, we don't "do" anything. We show up for people as a non-anxious, non-judgmental presence in others' lives, to catch their story and help them find meaning in it. We accompany persons in times of crisis, to assess their spiritual pain and respond in ways that empower them to solve their own problems. Sometimes we pray, read scripture, or perform a ritual for people. But, for the most part, we simply step into a person's world of suffering, stay present, and let them know they are not alone. We communicate our care by showing up and listening deeply for what gives their life meaning.

Chaplains train to read people as "living human documents," because at every given moment a person expresses who they are (or think themselves to be) through their attitudes, words, and behaviors. A seasoned chaplain has a well-tuned internal radar system that alerts them to a person's need for care.

Unlike a psychotherapist, clinical social worker, or professional counselor, a chaplain doesn't diagnose or prescribe anything, although they might refer a person to a professional to treat an organic issue in need of medication. Rather, we provide a heart-connecting relationship that accompanies and empowers people as they make their journey through pain.

I like to view chaplains as sages who wander around distributing wisdom and blessings to those who find themselves overwhelmed by their current life circumstances. In India's texts of sacred wisdom, the Sage Narada Muni comes to mind as an ideal role model for what a chaplain "does": they infuse a sense of hope in the lives of despairing persons.

Chaplains are often considered to be "crisis counselors" because we specialize in providing comfort to persons experiencing a sudden life change or loss that undermines what previously gave their life stability. Rather than a chronic mental or physical illness, a person's response to crisis is viewed as a normal response to loss.

This could be the sudden loss of a person's health, home, loved one, identity, job, money, trust, ability, limbs, etc., which are all places where a chaplain can be present to accompany and soothe a person's aching heart.

Chaplains provide compassionate care to anyone struggling to manage their current situation. They can be found in hospitals, hospices, prisons, psychiatric facilities, retirement homes, orphanages, homeless shelters, airport chapels, college campuses, family homes, religious institutions, or parking lots.

I personally have chaplain ID badges to serve in a hospital, juvenile prison, international airport, and the American Red Cross, where all expenses will be paid for me to deploy to the scene of a natural disaster, e.g., a flood, hurricane, earthquake, tornado, etc.

I continue to explore the depths of *Bhakti* and ways of translating it into practical acts of unconditional compassion. To the degree I can embrace God's love for me as unconditional (and by that I mean I don't need to earn it), I am capable of extending that same quality of care to others.

Love for God is a matter of the heart. By its very nature, it is a dynamic living force that is ever-expanding. For this reason, my quest for becoming an unconditionally caring presence in the lives of others will never be over. It is an eternal, moment-to-moment striving, despite my human limitations, to show up for those I share my world with as an emissary of God's unconditional loving care. For me, this is yoga: connecting with the source of all Life and Love (Krishna; the All-Attractive One) who resides in the core of my heart and the hearts of all others.

Part III

The Art of Work: Systems

Chapter 31

The Art of Work: Systems

Up to this point, we've examined work from an individual perspective. In Part III, we turn to career considerations from the viewpoint of the system as a whole. Some people may feel that systems thinking is the job of economists and government, and is thus of little concern to us as individuals as we embark on our career choices. While our own work is naturally our first priority and main focus, the tendency of individuals to be concerned *only* with their own work and not with the system as a whole can become a bit like medical specialists who focus only on the health of the organs of their specialty, without considering how treatment will affect the patient holistically. Knowing that a patient has kidney damage can affect what treatment to prescribe for arthritis, even though different bodily systems are involved and, similarly, having some perspective on the whole can help each of us in our own work. And, even if we are specialists who don't focus much on the whole system, we greatly benefit from working with those who do.

The individual principles of the natural art of work that we covered so far in Part II bring us a life of satisfaction in our career. While, in one sense, such satisfaction is "perfect" for an individual, the systems in the *Bhagavad-gita* and *Bhagavata Purana* are dynamic and interactive. In other words, "perfect satisfaction" can increase to become "more perfect" when the principles of the natural art of work are practiced in larger groups, culminating as "most perfect" when they are practiced throughout society.

One may legitimately ask to what extent we as individuals depend on a healthy economic system for our own happiness. It is certainly possible to achieve full personal fulfillment simply by applying individual principles of work even in a defective system, just as a person's lungs might function perfectly in an otherwise sick body. At the same time, it's essential to have members of society who extend their awareness beyond their own work in their own field, to how the fields can ideally relate to one another, and how we as individuals can ideally relate to larger groups and society as a whole. This next section is for such systems thinkers or those who aspire to be so. Hopefully we can all be gratefully appreciative of the systems thinkers in our communities, even if such an approach is not to our personal taste. Even for readers not inclined to systems thinking at the moment, the testimony in this section is particularly illustrative of the natural art of work, and the concluding chapter on a vision for society ties the ideas of the book together.

Chapter 32

Competition

32.1 The Value of Competition

Picture a soccer game for eight-year-old kids. Many parents put significant time and effort into taking their children to sports practice outside of school, arranging their own schedules so they can watch their kids' games. The outcome of the game — who wins or loses — does not, of course, have any intrinsic objective value for either side. Normally, a child on a team that wins every game in a season has not gained substantially more than a child whose team loses. Yet the way we prioritize these games demonstrates that we place a high value on these competitions.

We have our kids participate in these matches because we see that they gain something important from competing. While these gains might include fun, exercise, socialization, and fresh air, our kids could get all of these from less structured activities. The prospect of each upcoming match stimulates the kids to work hard at their practice. Each match is a set time and place where the kids are held to account for their work on their skills, and where the different skills that they work on come together in an integrated way.

The soccer match is also a key venue for kids to learn and practice cooperation: they cooperate with their teammates to get the ball into the opponents' goal and defend their own. It may be where they first learn how to be good sports. They learn that "It's not whether you win or lose, but how you play the game." Perhaps they learn the most important lesson when the two teams march by each other after the game, high-fiving the members of the other team and offering them congratulations for a "good game." In this way, children learn that competition is not about demonizing our opponents or considering them our personal enemies. Rather, it is through our opponents' willingness to compete honorably and intensely that these "good games" are possible.

Continuing into adult life, we can often rely on competition with well-matched opponents as a tried-and-true way to prevent complacency, or to jolt us out of a lull. Competition can lure us into opportunities we might miss otherwise. By spurring us to greater efforts and greater ingenuity, competition can energize us in ways that ultimately lead to personal growth.

Competition keeps us on our toes. While in theory doing our best is always worthwhile for its own sake, in practice having an opponent encourages us to do our best, focuses the mind, and invigorates our efforts. Seeing others do great things can remind us of our own potential, and inspire us to probe the edges of our own abilities.

When the well of motivation has run dry and our work is not challenging, competition keeps us from slacking off. We thus stay "in the game," gradually gaining skills and experience that will continue to serve us well. Additionally, when our work seems impossibly challenging, seeing others making an effort can induce us to try. When our mastery seems to have plateaued, a new surge of competition can get us over the hump to whole new levels of excellence.

32.2   Competition in Nature

Competition takes place continually throughout the natural world. Plants compete for sunlight, animals compete for territory and for mates, and bacteria compete to break down the food in our guts. We'll briefly turn to just a couple of specific examples.

Peacocks dancing

Picture a peacock displaying its tail. Hoping to mate with peahens, peacocks compete with each other by displaying their beautiful tails. They fan out all their tail feathers and shake them a bit so that they make a neat, pleasing shape. They dance and turn slowly, hoping to catch the eyes of nearby peahens (who often feign indifference — sometimes belied by their sidelong glances as they strut by). Even we humans can be the side beneficiaries of this aesthetic competition: if we're lucky, as we approach them the peacocks will display for us too.

T cells maturing

Great competitions occur within our own bodies over most of our lives. For example, T cells compete to survive within our thymus as they are maturing.

How does this competition help us? T cells attack various types of disease, yet have to not attack our own healthy cells. Because our body cannot know in advance every possible disease, it creates a wide variety of randomly configured T cells. These random cells go to the thymus (a small organ in our neck) where they need to attach to one part of our cells (the MHC — major histocompatibility complex), and not attach to another part (the "self" antigens). The T cells that can function in those two ways win the competition among one another and go on to become part of our body's "library" of cells available to fight disease.[i]

32.3 Economies of Agglomeration

In towns and cities, many similar businesses set up near each other. We might find clusters of clothing stores in the Garment District of New York City, or many shoe stores side by side along a street in Puebla, Mexico, or one jazz club after another along Fillmore Street in San Francisco. Why do businesses open near their competitors? Because then all the competitors benefit from economies of agglomeration: synergistic effects from many similar businesses in the same place. Customers are happy to find all these businesses in the same place, so more of them are attracted overall. The customers like having multiple choices, and feel the area as a whole is more likely to offer something that satisfies them. The businesses all compete to excel, and the whole area benefits.

32.4 Competition Versus Predation

Clearly, on the one hand, competition is valuable: in nature, as well as in our economies. On the other hand, "winner-take-most" competitions, leaving few survivors to compete again, are unhealthy in nature[304] as well as in economies.[305] When it comes to the natural art of work, it is vital to ensure that such competition is healthy. We often hear people justifying their engagement in no-holds-barred, all-out competition by saying that "it's a dog-eat-dog world." In fact, we may have heard this so often that we never stopped to think about it. It is not, in fact, a dog-eat-dog world. Dogs very rarely eat other dogs, and almost never prey on them (i.e., kill them in order to eat them).[j]

The reason many of us have accepted this idea as if it made sense is likely because in our minds we have confused competition — striving to outdo one another — with predation — striving to destroy and consume one another. Dogs certainly do compete and fight with each other. However, the usual result of a dogfight is simply to establish one dog as the winner on this particular day. The other dog acknowledges defeat and submits to the winner, perhaps to try again in a future contest. Similarly, stags lock horns until one pushes the other backward, establishing himself as stronger; the loser then runs away.[306]

Competition functions as part of the natural art of work when our competitors literally and figuratively survive to compete with us again another day. In this way, the competition can continue to provide all the above-mentioned benefits over the long term. It is no more natural or healthy for humans to prey on other humans, literally or figuratively, than it is for dogs to prey on other dogs.

Thus, even as we compete with one another, we accept restraints such as rules of fair play. These rules help ensure that many competitors enter and remain in the arena for match after match, continuing to yield the benefits of competition over the long run.

As it says in the *Bhagavad-gita*:

> The Lord is the strength of the strong, devoid of passion and desire.
>
> — *Bhagavad-gita* 7.11

Remembering these points can help us stay cool when competing and show compassion to those we defeat.

The Treaty of Versailles versus the Marshall Plan

As an example of helping our defeated opponents rebuild rather than continuing to punish them to the point of destruction, let's consider the Marshall Plan. After World War I, victorious Allies including France, Britain, and Italy formally ended the war with Germany by signing the Treaty of Versailles on June 28, 1919. This treaty required Germany to pay significant economic reparations to these Allied countries.

Over subsequent years, the German government's attempts to pay the reparations resulted in hyperinflation of the German mark, its currency at the time. In June 1922, the exchange rate was 314 German marks per US dollar, whereas in late 1924, the US dollar was worth over 4 trillion marks.[307] This situation caused great hardship for many Germans, whose fixed-income pensions or saved cash became worthless. The resentment and desperation that German people felt during the 1920s helped propel the Nazis to power in the 1930s, setting the stage for World War II.

On the other hand, after the Allies defeated Germany in World War II, the United States began spending large amounts of money to help reconstruct the war-torn economies of Western Europe. Former US President Herbert Hoover reported from Germany:

> The whole economy of Europe is interlinked with the German economy through the exchange of raw material and manufactured goods. The productivity of Europe cannot be restored without the restoration of Germany as a contributor to that productivity.
> –Herbert Hoover, *The President's Economic Mission to Germany and Austria, Report no. 3, Mar. 18, 1947.*[308]

Seeing the wisdom of this observation, the Truman administration proposed the Marshall Plan (named for Secretary of State George Marshall), to massively increase aid to Western Europe, including recently defeated West Germany. The United States Congress, with widespread backing from the American people, passed the Marshall Plan, which helped rebuild the economies of Western Europe from 1948 to 1952. The plan sped up Western Europe's recovery from the war and contributed to its growing prosperity over the following decades. As a result, Germany continues to live in peace with its European neighbors and to act as a linchpin in the European economy seven decades later.

Hoover's recognition of the interconnectedness of Germany with Europe is an example we can all remember when winning our own (smaller-scale) competitions. As mentioned in earlier chapters, we're all interdependent in the biosphere, we're all interconnected in the universal body, and we're all kindred issuing from the universal source.

32.5   Win-Win Games

When we think of "competition," many of us will imagine a zero-sum game: one with the losers' losses exactly offsetting the winners' gains. However, in this book we are looking instead for competition that is "win-win."

The plane of dedication, or charity, is where win-win situations bloom. While some of us may have heard the term "win-win" used in conversation, we may not have heard a clear definition or an explanation of its origins. The term originates in game theory, a branch of mathematics that studies the interactions among agents with combinations of shared and competing interests. We refer to bits of game theory throughout Part III. (Don't let the word "mathematics" scare you — games are fun!)

Many of us enjoy playing games such as soccer, checkers, or hearts with our family and friends. A game is a scenario in which two or more players interact, where each player has well-defined options as to what actions he or she can take, and the outcomes for all players depend on the actions each of the players choose to take (though perhaps the outcomes are not completely determined by the actions).

For example, in soccer, players can choose to run or kick the ball in different directions. Unless they are goalies (goalkeepers), they cannot choose to throw the ball. In other words, the set of actions a regular player can take includes running and kicking and does not include throwing. Depending on what all the players do, each team scores goals. Scoring more goals is a winning outcome for all the players on the winning team.

The game of soccer as we have just described it is what is called a zero-sum game, that is, a game in which a gain for any player (e.g., being on the winning team) is balanced exactly by a loss for another player (e.g., being on the losing team). It's worth noting two things very carefully. Firstly, it is this particular *framing* of the game of soccer that makes it a zero-sum game. We've described the game only in terms of winning and losing. We haven't described any additional benefits such as exhilaration, exercise, and so on. If we had included these, it would be a non-zero-sum game, that is, a game in which some of the possible outcomes result in a net gain or a net loss for all the players involved. A win-win outcome is an outcome in which none of the players experience a net loss. In the game of soccer, if the gains in terms of fun, exercise, skill, sportsmanship, and so forth are more important to all the players than who wins or loses the game, then soccer is a win-win game, while still competitive. The players' subjective values determine what kind of game it is. The effectiveness of advertising (to the tune of hundreds of billions of dollars yearly) demonstrates that people's subjective values are not fixed, but can be influenced. As we've discussed in this book, the shades of ego affect our subjective values. Lifting these veils clarifies our perception and makes it more likely that we can see much or all of life as win-win.

Mathematically speaking, zero-sum games are rare. The condition that every gain for one player must be balanced exactly by a loss for another player is a strong condition, which is hard to satisfy. So, in a strictly theoretical model, the chance that a game will be absolutely zero-sum is small.[*] Real-world experience tallies with theory, such that zero-sum games are uncommon in our lives. This rarity is because, in the real world, we often have an additional choice beyond those within the zero-sum framing of the game: namely, to walk away, i.e., not to play the game in the first place. Players may prefer to walk away from games in which their risk of loss is significant. When players make the choice to walk away from zero-sum games and towards non-zero-sum games, opportunities for win-win situations increase.[k]

We've barely scratched the surface of the theory of games here; we just want to give an idea of what we mean. A key takeaway is that win-win games are not limited to full cooperation; they can feature various degrees of competition. In other words, competition versus cooperation is usually a false dichotomy. Game theory is deep enough to provide fundamental underpinnings to mathematical statistics, to microeconomics, and to the behavioral sciences in general.

In order for us human beings to live, we need to do work that involves interacting with other people or at least other living beings, directly or indirectly. Unlike plants, we can't sustain ourselves solely on sunlight, and unlike lithotrophic microbes, we can't sustain ourselves solely on rocks! Sometimes, humans think of these other living beings merely as objects to exploit, and therefore act as predators in a zero-sum game. In contrast, the natural art of work is one in which our interactions with others are sustainable, and the theory of games provides a tool for assessing and even designing sustainable interactions.

---

[*] If you were sitting in a room and threw something on the floor completely randomly, the chance that it would land exactly at the edge of the wall is minute, and even the chance that it would land very close to the wall is very small. Mathematically speaking, the chance that a game is zero-sum is just as small.

32.6   Keys to Overall Gains from Competition

How do we gain the most from competing? The main key is fairness and honesty, in terms of with whom we compete, and how we compete.

The benefits of competition accrue when our competitors are on a nearly equal footing. If two competitors are at grossly unequal levels, there is generally no point in the competition as the result is a foregone conclusion. Even the winner will derive no satisfaction from besting a far weaker competitor, unless the winner is a bully — but that's bullying, not competing. Since bullying is neither wise, nor honorable, nor sustainable, nor supportive, anyone in any of the four fields of work who is bullying is not working according to their nature at all. Bullying purely indicates being covered by the shades of ego: the main illusion that one is at the center of reality.

Furthermore, competition spurs us into action and pushes us to excellence when we have a chance of succeeding: when the two or more sides are playing the same game by the same rules and have roughly matched skills. In regards to our career, competing with those in our same field of work meets these criteria.

We want the playing field on which we compete to be level and fair. Competing honestly builds up not only our skills but also our honor. A reputation for integrity and honest dealing is slow to build and can be destroyed in a moment. When we cheat, we are not only robbing ourselves of the opportunities for integrity, personal growth, and true accomplishment in the present competition; we are endangering the trust others have in us, and we risk being excluded from future opportunities. Doing this is extremely shortsighted. Cheating can only escape detection for so long; it's inherently unsustainable. Honor and integrity are by their very nature worth more than any more specific fruit from competition. Honesty is certainly the best policy.

We compete honorably by pushing ourselves to go higher, not by pushing our opponents down. If instead of climbing higher ourselves, we try to win by pushing others down, there is no net gain, except in terms of shallow win-loss calculations (which, as we've described, depend on a narrow framing). Pushing others down results in loss of our own character, and stagnation for the group of competitors as a whole. Proper competition benefits us by inducing us to stretch ourselves to our limits, and perhaps even to expand those limits. As each player is spurred to greater heights, all players gain from interaction and example. This kind of healthy competition is a non-zero-sum game.

32.7 Competitiveness Versus Envy

Envy sometimes arises in the context of competitions. The word "envy" is used in different ways. Here, by envy we mean the desire for others' misfortune. A close synonym would be "malice." Becoming happy at another's misfortune, and becoming unhappy at another's fortune, both constitute envy.

If we're competitive, we're doing our best to win. If we're competing for some scarce prize, then we most often want to get that prize. This is how competition works as an engine of motivation. From the definition of envy above, it sounds like envy might be an integral and inevitable part of competition. Is it?

Despite what one may think at first, it is not. There is a distinction between envy and a healthy competitive spirit. While envy sometimes arises during competition, it doesn't inevitably do so.

It's easiest to see this difference in games we play with those to whom we already feel connected — our friends and family. When we're playing a friendly game of Scrabble and someone comes up with an especially clever word, we all *ooh* and *aah* with admiration. When we're playing a friendly game of volleyball and someone makes an incredible save, we all admire it, whichever team we're on. These are the moments that make for a great game for all concerned.

By contrast, the spirit of envy derives from the shades of ego and is fundamentally unhealthy:

> One of the biggest problems in the workplace and in politics is that people feel they should be careful of what they say and do. They anticipate trouble, sensing they must watch their backs. Someone else is always envious of them. Afraid that a coworker might outshine them, they defensively guard their position. How many of us have lost jobs because a coworker sabotaged us? Real nonviolence means freedom from envy. Being envious means violence to the highest degree. It means desiring the demise of another. Not only do his achievements become a botheration to us, but we want his very existence to come to an end. No sane person envies a failure or a

> low achiever. We are envious of those who excel in some way. We view others' accomplishments as ones which should belong to us. In your own life, you may notice that if you are very envious of certain people, you do not want to see them, to hear about them, or to be around those who talk about them. The stronger the envy, the more we desire their annihilation.
>
> —B. T. Swami, *Surrender: The Key to Eternal Life*[309]

As described previously, what goes around comes around. Envying others always diminishes one's own excellence, whether or not it achieves diminution of others.

On the other hand, a healthy spirit of the game can continue to the highest professional levels. The sisters Venus and Serena Williams are both world-class tennis players. They compete intensely, including when they are playing against each other. Yet, even though they compete fiercely on the court, the two sisters are personally very close. While they each want to win their head-to-head matches, they bear no malice towards each other and indeed often play doubles together. They are each happy with the success of the other's career and certainly don't wish each other any harm.

When the stakes are high

Sometimes competition doesn't seem to be all fun and games. Often scarce prizes are awarded to winners of competitions. We might be competing for a contract to supply a large retailer or construct a huge building that could pay us and many of our employees for a long time. We might be trying out for roles in a Broadway show we've been dreaming about for years. We might be fighting to secure a crucial supply line for our comrades in arms. We might be competing for grants to research ideas for curing cancer.

When we lose in situations in which the stakes are so high, it may be easy for us to resent or envy the winners. Indeed, such feelings may eat at us.

It's at times like these that the practice of egolessness detailed earlier in this book can be especially helpful to regain our equilibrium. In regards specifically to competition, it's worth keeping in mind that the results of competition are never solely due to our own hard work, talents, intelligence, and so forth:

> The worker and the place, the worker's
> senses and the deed,
> and in the end, the Supersoul, determine
> what succeeds.

> –Kalakantha Dāsa, *Bhagavad-gītā: The Rap of
> God*[310]

> — *Bhagavad-gita* 18.14

Instead of personalizing what happened as being due to our opponent, we can stand back and look upon it as a neutral observer, seeing it as part of the workings of the universal body. It is the ego shades described earlier that bewilder us with resentment and envy. On the other hand, the *Bhagavad-gita* continues:

> The worker who performs his or her duty without attachment, without false identification, with great determination and enthusiasm, and without wavering in success or failure is said to be veiled by the shade of *sattva*.
> — *Bhagavad-gita* 18.26

Krishna describes going beyond even the ego shade of *sattva* in the *Bhagavad-gita*:

> The steadily devoted soul attains unadulterated peace because he offers the result of all activities to Me; whereas a person who is not in union with the Divine, who is greedy for the fruits of his labor, becomes entangled.
> –His Divine Grace A.C. Bhaktivedanta Swami Prabhupada, *Bhagavad-gita As It Is*[311]
> — *Bhagavad-gita* 5.12

32.8 Remembering Common Ground

Whether we win or lose, we can keep a healthy attitude by remembering how much common ground we have with our competitors. As mentioned earlier, they must be similar to us in many ways to even be competitors. Remembering how much we share in common can help enliven our spirit of kinship. We and our competitors are all interested in "the game" continuing, and we all have an interest in ensuring and maintaining the conditions that make this possible. We are all interested in growing to new heights of excellence. We can rejoice that we and our competitors are all inspiring one another to grow, turn by turn. And we can learn from one another.[*]

Indeed, when we compete within our field of work, this virtuous cycle of growth collectively promotes the excellence of the field as a whole. Competition within the Field of Artistry has led to the myriad inventions that ease and inspire our lives in so many ways. Artistic competition has also led to classic masterpieces of art, architecture, and music, as well as providing something to suit every taste, no matter how unusual. So, for instance, during the Renaissance, rulers of Italian city-states competed with one another to commission the finest pieces of art. This competition (originally between those in the Field of Government) spurred workers in the Field of Artistry to produce some of the greatest masterpieces the world has seen, competing with one another for patronage. Nowhere is this rivalry more apparent than in the direct competition between Leonardo da Vinci and Michelangelo to paint battle scenes in the Council Hall of the Palazzo Vecchio in Florence. Within the context of heated competition all across Italy, the ruler of Florence, Piero Soderini, set two of the most celebrated artists in history in direct competition, to produce works of art side by side. Although neither work was finished, the material that does survive has fascinated art historians ever since and is compelling evidence of the heights to which this era of competition pushed its artists.[312]

Competition within the Field of Resources is what has enabled the world's population to surpass eight billion, while supplying the physical needs of many of us. It has also resulted in efficient and effective ways of transporting supplies all over the world. Competition between firms such as Microsoft and Apple, or Epson and Canon, has led technology to jump forward rapidly in recent decades.

Competition within the Field of Government is what has enabled many of us, in many areas of the world, to live much of the time peacefully, safe from criminals and aggressors. It has also led to a variety of public services in various cities, states, and countries of the world, such as clean tap water, sanitation, universal health care systems, mass

---

[*] *The Art of Learning: An Inner Journey to Optimal Performance*, by chess champion and Tai Chi champion Josh Waitzkin, is all about learning from competition.

transit systems, and so forth. Such competition has also enabled different populations to experiment with different forms of government, adding to our collective knowledge about how well and in what ways these work for their people. For example, within the European Union, member states engage in friendly competition to provide for their citizens, while also working together cooperatively.

Competition within the Field of Ideas has led to sound and coherent philosophies, theories, worldviews, and religions that are available to each of us to guide our way through life. Scientists competing to characterize a phenomenon or advance a theory collectively enlarge our state of knowledge. For instance, the behaviorists, the humanists, and the cognitive school have all competed to make contributions in the field of psychology. Competition among religions and traditional groups has spurred some to enhance or revive the purity of their traditions, as well as to adjust to the changing circumstances of their constituents and the world they live in.

32.9 A Role for Cooperation

Of course, cooperation also plays a role within our own field of work. Workers in the Field of Artistry might cooperate to build a house or to perform a play. Workers in the Field of Resources might cooperate to run a business, taking various roles such as Chief Executive Officer, Chief Financial Officer, or Chief Operations Officer. Workers in the Field of Government might cooperate to inspect an industry or rescue people stranded by floods. Workers in the Field of Ideas may cooperate to educate children or to report on current events for a newspaper or magazine.[*]

Indeed, cooperation is widespread in human groups on many scales, and brings us much fulfillment in life. We discuss cooperation in the next chapter.

---

[*]Or for that matter, they might write a book together!

Chapter 33

Cooperation

33.1   The Whole World as One Family

> "Counting this one as a friend and that one as not — this is
> small-mindedness. But to those of noble character, the whole
> world is one family."
>
> *—Maha Upanishad 6.72*

Competition does not stand alone as a societal principle for a
healthy and sustainable economy of prosperity. Its seemingly[*] polar
opposite — cooperation — is also important. One form of cooperation that we previously discussed involves sharing our prosperity. In
Chapter 14, we talked about extending our circle of giving from our
family to our local community and beyond. The ultimate sharing
comes when we take in the fact that, as in the Maha Upanishad quote
above, the whole world is one family. We can make this conception
a practical reality in our interactions with other beings in the world
as we work, through sharing and other forms of cooperation. The
Bhagavata Purana describes the relativity of time, and recounts that
all life descends from a common ancestor who lived billions of earthly
years ago. We can now see this fact confirmed by genomic sequencing, whose pace has been growing exponentially since the year 2000,
when the first rough draft of the human genome became available.
The Book of Life written in our DNA confirms clearly that we are all
related.

---

[*]As we explained in Chapter 32, competition versus cooperation is a false dichotomy.

Figure 33.1: ATP Synthase, A Marvelous Molecular Machine

Rendering of the 3D molecular structure of ATP synthase by David S. Goodsell. © David S. Goodsell and RCSB Protein Data Bank. Used with permission.

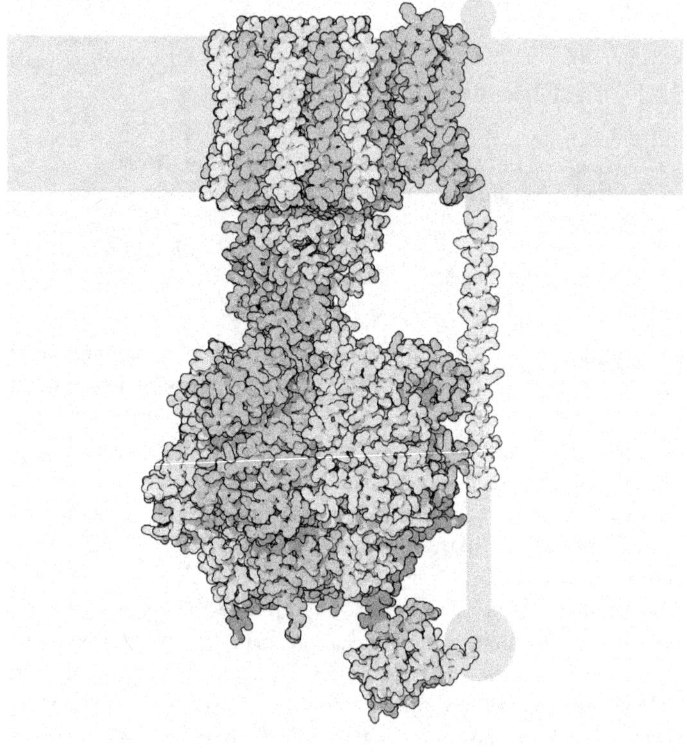

For example, the ATP (adenosine triphosphate) synthase molecule, pictured, is a marvelous molecular machine. It consists of two molecular motors connected in such a way that one motor turns the other into a generator. This machine stores energy in ATP molecules, the batteries of living cells. Genomic sequencing has shown us that this same molecule appears in the mitochondria of animals, plants, and fungi; in the chloroplasts of plants; and in bacteria. It's a mark of our kinship — one of many such marks. Detailed study of the interrelationships among all these molecules enables us to draw the Tree of Life, depicting the universal kinship of all beings.

The *Bhagavad-gita* says:

> All species born into this world come from the womb of nature, with me as their seed-giving father.
> > –Ranchor Prime, *Bhagavad Gita: Talks Between the Soul and God*[313]
> > > — *Bhagavad-gita* 14.4

It follows naturally that we are all one family, and indeed, elsewhere in the *Bhagavad-gita* it is said:

> The humble sages, by virtue of true knowledge, see with equal vision a learned and gentle educator, a cow, an elephant, a dog, and a pariah.[1]
> > — *Bhagavad-gita* 5.18

Furthermore, we are all living together on one planet:

> To see the earth as it truly is, small and blue and beautiful in that eternal silence where it floats, is to see ourselves as riders on the earth together, brothers on that bright loveliness in the eternal cold — brothers who know now they are truly brothers.
> > –Archibald MacLeish[314]

> Looking back at that spaceship we call earth, I was touched by a desire to convince man that he has a unique place to live, that he is a unique creature, and that he must learn to live with his neighbors....When you see the earth from the perspective of space, you don't see any evidence of the existence of man at all. The human problems do not seem overwhelming, they seem

insignificant and puny. All you see is the beauty of the
land and the water....That beautiful, warm living object
looked so fragile, so delicate, that if you touched it with
a finger it would crumble and fall apart.

> –James B. Irwin & William A. Emerson, Jr., *To Rule
> The Night: The Discovery Voyage of Astronaut Jim
> Irwin*[315]

The astronaut James Irwin saw the earth from space nearly half a
century ago. Now in the initial decades of the 21st century, we can use
Google Earth to view any place in the world, we can use Facebook to
video chat live with people from all over the world, and we can travel
to many of these places ourselves in no more than a day or two. In this
way we can see for ourselves that we're all interconnected.

The following prayer spoken by Prahlada in the *Bhagavata Purana*
is an emblem of how this vision of interconnection unfolds in one who
is pure of heart:

> May there be good fortune throughout the universe, and
> may all envious persons be pacified. May all living beings
> become calm by practicing the yoga of love, for by ac-
> cepting service in devotion they will think of each other's
> welfare. Therefore let us all engage in the service of and
> always remain absorbed in thought of the supreme tran-
> scendence.
>
> — *Bhagavata Purana* 5.18.9

We humans have the same biological needs — for water, food,
safety, and moderation of temperature for ourselves and our children —
as animals and other living organisms, So, if cooperation is beneficial
in human economic systems, we might expect to see some evidence of
it in the natural world.

33.2 Mutualism

In ecology, a mutualism is an interaction between two or more beings that benefits all of them. So mutualisms are cooperative win-win
games that occur naturally. Indeed, they're widespread in nature:

> [Mutualism's] influence transcends levels of biological
> organization from cells to populations, communities,
> and ecosystems....Mutualisms occur in every aquatic

and terrestrial habitat; indeed, ecologists now believe that almost every species on Earth is involved directly or indirectly in one or more of these interactions.
–Judith Bronstein, *Mutualism*[316]

Early in the development of the field of ecology, ecologists with notions of "nature, red in tooth and claw" tended to see predatory or competitive interactions everywhere, and overlooked the role of mutualisms. Such a view is an example of the fallacy of misleading vividness: overestimating the role of particularly dramatic phenomena. The ubiquity of mutualisms has become more and more apparent to ecologists in the last few decades, as surveyed in *Mutualism*. We're stressing the role of mutualism here because it's often overlooked, whereas the role of competition is widely acknowledged.

Of course, there are many examples of large-scale cooperation within species of social insects. We might dismiss these examples as exceptions in nature if we think in terms of the number of social insect species compared to the number of species as a whole. However, while these social insect species are extreme examples, a large number of species of mammals, birds, fish, plants, and even bacteria work cooperatively. Furthermore, when we consider the number of individual living beings rather than species, the count of insects living in large-scale cooperative communities is astronomical:

> If ever there was proof of the power of cooperation, ants, bees, and termites are it. There are probably ten thousand billion ants on the planet, weighing in aggregate as much as all the human beings put together. It has been estimated that three-quarters of all the insect biomass — and in some places one-third of all the animal biomass — in the Amazon rain forest consists of ants, termites, bees, and wasps....They are perhaps even more ubiquitous in deserts. Were it not for an inexplicable intolerance for cool temperatures, ants and termites would prevail in temperate climates as well....
>
> A single ant or honey bee is as feeble and doomed as a severed finger. Attached to its colony, though, it is as useful as a thumb. It serves the greater good of its colony, sacrificing its reproduction and risking its life on behalf of its colony. Ant colonies are born, grow large, reproduce, and die, just like bodies....

> As a result of their ecological holism, ants, termites,
> and bees can indulge in ecological strategies that would
> be impossible for solitary creatures....The ant, the bee,
> and the termite represent the triumph of collective en-
> terprise.
>
> –Matt Ridley, *The Origins of Virtue*[317m]

Based on the examples of social insects, some had overemphasized the role of relatedness (as siblings, offspring, cousins, etc.) in underpinning cooperation. In a 1975 paper, however, Hamilton showed that relatedness was not a necessary factor to stabilize cooperation.[318]

Indeed, mutualisms as defined by ecologists are usually between individuals of different species altogether.

Cooperation among unrelated beings is functionally, mathematically possible, exists in nature, and indeed can already be found widely in human society. We emphasize this fact because during the inevitable challenges of day-to-day work, it's sometimes the failures of cooperation that impinge most strongly on our consciousness. Keeping the strength and stability of cooperation firmly in mind can help us navigate challenges, seek common ground, and cooperate more effectively and more widely. The interactions among members of a functional family are generally mutualistic. In performing the natural art of work, we seek to extend this kind of relationship to those who are apparently divergent from us, taking to heart our universal kinship.

The *Bhagavata Purana* highlights an example:

> A saintly person as a student of the tree, should learn
> dedication to others.
>
> — *Bhagavata Purana* 11.7.38

Trees do indeed participate in some of the most well-studied examples of mutualisms. We'll look at a few of these next.

33.3 Trees Acting in Concert

Flowering trees provide nectar to pollinators such as bees and butterflies, attracting them through beauty and fragrance. The bees and butterflies reciprocate by carrying the trees' pollen to other trees, thus enabling the production of seeds. Fruit trees provide delicious fruit to a variety of animals. The animals reciprocate by spreading the trees' seeds in their scat, enabling the trees' offspring to sprout in distant locations.

Trees also cooperate with one another. When their leaves are chewed by insects, they communicate with their kindred trees in the neighborhood, who begin secreting defensive compounds to make their own leaves taste bitter or become poisonous. This cooperation coexists with the ways in which trees compete with one another for sunlight, to attract pollinators and fructivores, and in many other ways. Recall the cooperation of trees in beech forests to distribute sugar equitably, which we quoted from *The Hidden Life of Trees* in Chapter 23.

33.4   Cooperation Within Society

Mutualisms, relationships where beings cooperate to benefit one another, are thus widespread in nature, and tend to happen in human society. They occur most frequently when people work together in well-running teams, like Edith and Ruchira writing this book. As more of us practice the natural art of work, we will consciously seek out and engage in more and more such mutualisms. The practical experience of such connection in our lives not only increases our happiness with our work, but in our lives in general. A key to doing so is to combine competition that inspires with cooperation that invigorates.

In Chapter 32, we described win-win games: games in which all the players gain something from participating. We may not be consciously aware of the extent to which we're already participating in win-win games:

> ...the shirt I bought, although a simple item by the standards of modern technology, is a triumph of international cooperation. The cotton was grown in India, from seeds developed in the United States; the artificial fiber in the thread comes from Portugal and the material in the dyes from at least six other countries; the collar linings from Brazil, and the machinery for the weaving, cutting, and sewing from Germany; the shirt itself was made in Malaysia. The project of making a shirt and delivering it to me in Toulouse has been a long time in the planning, since well before the morning two winters ago when an Indian farmer first led a pair

of ploughing bullocks across his land on the red plains outside Coimbatore. Engineers in Cologne and chemists in Birmingham were involved in the preparation many years ago.

–Paul Seabright, *The Company of Strangers*[319]

In this example, each of the workers participates in the gains from trade: in a voluntary exchange, each participant gives something of which they have more than they need, in order to get something they need more. For instance, the cotton farmer gives surplus cotton to the weaver and gets money in return. At the end of the trade, both are better off: they have cooperated to make each other happier. So, at this surface level, they've both won. Here, the cotton farmer and the weaver are complements to each other: both are needed for the overall endeavor of producing the shirt, and the work of neither would be as valuable without the other.

Furthermore, in this example, although a casual observer might assume the workers are competing, closer inspection reveals they are cooperating. We might think of cotton farmers and producers of artificial fibers as substitutes for each other, because we might assume that the shirt would be made of only one or the other and the weaver would have to choose between them. In this case, it is a false choice; fabric that is a blend of the two sometimes turns out to be more desirable than either one alone.

Next, we shall explain how those in each field of work ideally cooperate with society in general, and with those in specific other fields. Again, we are describing what experts in the natural art of work would do, not necessarily what those in any particular society actually do.

Earlier in this book we've emphasized the distinctions between different fields of work in order to delineate them clearly. However, in fostering win-win interactions, the first step is often to bring common ground to mind. Those in different fields of work do tend to share some things in common.

After all, those in the Fields of Ideas and Artistry both value simplicity. Resources and Artistry both deal with highly practical and tangible societal benefits. Ideas and Government both focus on higher ideals. Government and Resources both involve an emphasis on practical leadership and expansion, as well as distribution of the means to meet human needs. Some of those in the Field of Ideas and those in the Field of Resources may share an inclination towards critical thinking and numeracy, as well as a lack of sentimentality that sometimes

Figure 33.2: Commonalities Between Pairs of Fields

Each pair of fields shares some things in common.

	Artistry	Resources	Government
Ideas	Liking for simplicity	Critical thinking, lack of sentimentality	Focus on higher ideals
Artistry		Practical, tangible societal benefits	Serving people directly
Resources			Practical leadership, expansion, distribution

is taken amiss by those in the Field of Government or the Field of Artistry. Government and much of Artistry tend to focus on serving people directly, often more so than Ideas and Resources.

How workers in the Field of Ideas cooperate with other fields

Workers in the Field of Ideas cooperate with those in every other field. Some of them teach students and trainees in many careers. It's workers in the Field of Ideas who specialize in religion and spirituality, and thus guide others in how to apply these in work. Others in the Field of Ideas work in the media, where they disseminate new ideas and discoveries widely. Workers in the Field of Ideas often practice contemplation and reflection, leading to a neutral, objective, detached perspective that integrates the big picture and encompasses the long term throughout all parts of society. This perspective is especially helpful to those in the Field of Government. In the US, for example, people in the Field of Ideas assist all three branches of government, working as legislative aides, on advisory councils and research arms of executive branch agencies, and as expert witnesses and career law clerks for the judiciary. In general, workers in other fields thus seek help from those in the Field of Ideas who act as counselors, coaches, and consultants, to help with challenges that can benefit from these broader perspectives.

How workers in the Field of Government cooperate with other fields

Government creates, maintains, and referees the arenas in which the rest of society peacefully interacts in many countries of the world. The government approves the licensing and accreditation for many jobs throughout society. While many licensing agencies consist of workers outside of government itself, it is government that acts as an outside referee and establishes standards for safety and social welfare. The government may also provide venues and facilitators to help launch, repair, or maintain cooperative endeavors, as well as keep their products available to society:

> Stake out the street grid; separate public from private space; and leave room for what's to come. Then let the free market take over. No market mechanism can ever create the road network that connects everyone. The government must do that first.
> —Emily Badger, *A Nobel-Winning Economist Goes To Burning Man*[320]

How workers in the Field of Resources cooperate with other fields

Workers in the Field of Resources organize, direct, and distribute the flow of money, materials, energy, and other finite resources that can be drawn on by people or groups throughout society in order to function effectively. They are experts at handling risk, which they assume by undertaking ventures or selling insurance, for example. By assuming such risks themselves, those in the Field of Resources help those in other fields to have a stable basis for their work.[*] They also cooperate

---

[*]It may be simplest to explain how this works in the case of insurance. The insurer (in the Field of Resources) charges premiums to a large number of policyholders, and makes money if the *mean* payout to each policyholder is less than the *mean* total premium

with others in society by distributing resources in the form of charity to the needy (which might include students, military veterans, artists, etc.). They also contribute to or influence a large portion of the tax base personally and through their enterprises.

How workers in the Field of Artistry cooperate with other fields

Careers in the Field of Artistry account for the greatest variety of trees of work. Many workers in Artistry are involved in joint endeavors with people in each of the other three fields. Here are just a few examples. They draft diagrams or run audiovisual equipment for people in the Field of Ideas. They act as court reporters and bailiffs, check paperwork, and disburse funds to wherever people in the Field of Government have allocated them. They transport resources and goods wherever people in the Field of Resources channel them. Workers in the Field of Artistry create and exhibit various kinds of functional and decorative objects, for sale in conjunction with the Field of Resources, for the public in conjunction with the Field of Government, for education or for spirituality in conjunction with the Field of Ideas, and so forth. The Field of Artistry also includes providers of various kinds of services such as child care, cleaning, tree trimming, and so forth. These people may provide their specific goods and services generally to all of society rather than in joint endeavors with specific fields.

Workers in this Field cooperate in making the communications of workers in other fields attractive, appealing, and memorable. Whether it's the proclamation and oratory of government, the marketing of resources, or the popularizing of the Field of Ideas, all benefit from the cooperation of workers in the Field of Artistry.

The Field of Artistry and the Field of Ideas working together

Workers in the Field of Artistry play a unique role when they join together with workers in the Field of Ideas. When ideas are expressed through the arts, such as painting, dance, drama, storytelling, and so

---

collected from each policyholder over the life of the policy. So individual policyholders can expect that, *on average*, they will pay more to the insurer then they will receive in claims. On the other hand, individual policyholders are minimizing the *variance* in what they spend. Whether some unusual catastrophe strikes them or not, they pay the same predictable premium, because it is the insurer who has assumed the risk. Minimal variance for the insured is what comprises the stable basis we mentioned, in this case. Of course, those in the Field of Resources often buy insurance themselves, as part of their sophisticated handling of risk.

forth, they often reach a wider audience and make a more profound, lasting impression than if they were expressed directly by people in the Field of Ideas. This phenomenon becomes particularly important when trying to improve society. Ideas expressed through those in Artistry tend to create memorable impressions that are more likely to move people to take action.

In the *Bhagavata Purana* and related scriptures, and in countries all across Asia, Artistry and Ideas are associated. Saraswati is the goddess of learning, speech, music, and the arts, and is associated with unseen currents. When thoughts and ideas flow together with *rasa* (the essence of enjoyment and relationship), their current becomes particularly potent.

All four fields working together

There is a poetic analogy about cooperation among the four fields in the *Bhagavata Purana*[321] in regards to charity. Those in the Fields of Resources and Artistry pay taxes to Government. Those in the Field of Resources make a profit from selling goods to the rest of society. The wealth thus accumulated by those in Government and Resources is compared to water-filled clouds ready to give charity that is compared to rain. Those in the Field of Ideas are compared to the wind that directs persons in Government and Resources to be equal and fair-minded in lavish giving of charity where excess wealth is distributed. Thus, those in the Field of Artistry flourish like the Earth that abounds in fruits and flowers after abundant rain.

33.5 Niches Within the Universal Body

Each of us as a unique individual has a special role to play within the
biosphere, the universal body.[*] When we work according to our nature, we fill the niche in the universal body in which we belong. As
more and more of us embody the natural art of work, the universal
body functions more and more healthily. Naturally, then, each of us
derives greater satisfaction in reciprocation with the universal body.
At a potluck, guests fills their niche by bringing a good amount of one
or two dishes that they make well. Through the magic of cooperation,
there is much more than enough food to go around and everyone experiences a tasty, balanced, varied, high-quality meal.

33.6 Enforcement Between Niches

Sometimes, those in some particular niche collude to corrupt the system or cheat the greater populace. Rather than competing with one
another to please the public, they band together in a cartel to exploit
the public:

> People of the same trade seldom meet together, even for
> merriment and diversion, but the conversation ends in a
> conspiracy against the public, or in some contrivance to
> raise prices.
>
> –Adam Smith, *An Inquiry Into The Nature and
> Causes of the Wealth of Nations*[322]

---

[*]Readers acquainted with sociology may be familiar with two major paradigms: conflict
theory and functionalism. Conflict theory emphasizes competition for resources between groups within society, whereas functionalism emphasizes how different parts of
society work together. The framework we are presenting appears more in tune with the
functionalist paradigm. However, please note carefully that the role of sociology is to
explain the past and present: how societies actually are or have been. The naturalistic
fallacy is to confuse an "is" with an "ought:" to think that because something is a certain
way, it should be that way. Conversely, it is also fallacious to confuse an "ought" with an
"is." We are describing in this book in general, and in Part III in particular, the healthy
condition of the social body. What we describe says nothing about whether any particular society at any particular time is in a healthy condition, or if not, how the unhealthy
condition came to be. Having a vision of how a healthy society would ideally work can
help guide a real society towards a better future (though, just as with a medical patient,
understanding an unhealthy condition in society and how it came to be also can play a
helpful role in healing that condition). Thus our framework is more future-oriented,
as compared to the sociological paradigms, which apply to the present and the past.

The main way to prevent such situations, and to disband such cartels once they appear, is through external oversight. That is, persons from outside the niche, acting as neutral auditors on behalf of the greater body, check that the members of a niche are acting lawfully according to their professional principles, or dharma. We have more to say about this in Chapter 35.

33.7   Cooperation Within the Universal Body

Although cooperation has a positive connotation and we've highlighted some of its advantages throughout most of this chapter, the drawbacks of cartels show that cooperation within limited contexts can be problematic. Here we elaborate on unhealthy and healthy cooperation within the universal body.

Tribalism and party spirit: the dangers

When we hear the word "cooperation," we may automatically associate the term with people helping each other in positive ways. But it sometimes happens that those in one field of work, or tending the same tree of work, even though they compete with one another from day to day, unite to present a common front against the enforcers from outside their field of work. This type of cooperation subverts the natural ways in which the workers in various fields regulate each other. As one well-documented example, towards the end of 1953, executives of five of the big six tobacco companies in the USA — the American Tobacco Company, Benson & Hedges, Brown and Williamson, P. Lorillard, Philip Morris, R. J. Reynolds, and U.S. Tobacco — met to coordinate their response to scientific discoveries about the health hazards of their product: cigarettes.[323]

While many people are aware that US tobacco companies tried to deny publicly that cigarettes cause cancer, what is less widely known is that shortly after tobacco company experiments demonstrated that tobacco is carcinogenic, on December 14, 1953, CEOs from the nation's leading tobacco companies got together at the Plaza Hotel in Manhattan to hatch their public relations strategy of spreading a haze of doubt and uncertainty about the tobacco-cancer link.

> From December 1953 forward, the tobacco companies
> would present a united front on smoking and health;
> more than 5 decades of strategic and explicit collusion
> would follow.
> —Allan M. Brandt, *Inventing Conflicts of Interest: A
> History of Tobacco Industry Tactics*[324]

Another example concerns makers of white lead (i.e., lead-based paint) in the US. Occupational physician Alice Hamilton, working in Chicago, began highlighting the toxicity of lead-based paint in 1910, and by 1912 it was well-established that white lead was poisonous. Starting in 1909, many countries across the world enacted bans on interior painting with white lead, and in 1922 the Third International Labor Conference of the League of Nations recommended banning white lead for interior use. The US refused to sign the ban, though a number of US physicians had started publishing articles about lead poisoning in children due to paint in 1917, which they continued to do through the 1920s. In 1928, US businesses involved in various aspects of lead, from mining to smelting, and refining to manufacturing lead pigments, banded together to form the Lead Industries Association (LIA). Felix Wormser, the LIA's secretary, stated in 1935 that combating negative publicity about the health effects of lead was a primary reason for the LIA's existence. Wormser led this battle from 1928 to 1947, seeking to cast doubt on all reports of white-lead poisoning as well as alternately threatening and attempting to buy the silence of their authors. The LIA vigorously countered any advertising by competitors — manufacturers of lead-free paint — that pointed out that lead-based paint was poisonous. Meanwhile, the lead industry launched a creative, multifaceted advertising campaign, targeting both children and parents, to convince the public that white lead was safe and hygienic for use on children's toys, furniture, and interior walls. In 1938, the LIA launched its White Lead Promotion Campaign, comprehensively soliciting farmers, real estate developers, public school superintendents, and hotel managers to paint their walls with white lead. In 1949, though the state of Maryland enacted a law forbidding the sale of children's toys and furniture painted with lead without a warning label, the LIA succeeded in getting this law repealed the very same year. It wasn't until 1971 that the US finally passed a federal law prohibiting the use of lead-based paint on interior walls.[325]

Actions that now seem questionable to us, decades later, may have felt natural to those in the midst of these situations. Both the tobacco industry and the lead industry included many people working on many different jobs. Reflecting on these examples from the past can draw each of us to take a closer look at what we ourselves are participating in or working on today. What would a person with a detached perspective decades from now say about us? When we collude with those in our own field of work to the detriment of others, we have extended our ego to include those within our field of work. We are identifying with those within the same field of work as part of our extended self, and we are trying to pull our extended self — our "tribe" — up at the expense of other tribes.

Of course, this scenario is only one of many ways in which we humans divide ourselves up into tribes and harm others. We might identify with our gender, or our firm, or our city, or our race, for example.

This "tribal tendency" exists because it's usually easier to see what we have in common with those of our own tribe than with those of other tribes, however we divide ourselves up. Earlier we described some of the temperamental particularities among people in different fields of work. These can lead us to enjoy similar kinds of recreation as people in the same field as us. Seeing each other often leads to familiarity. It simply becomes comfortable to spend time with people from our own field.

In a positive way, this party spirit can further a joint effort when those from our field are called upon to meet an urgent need in times of crisis. We may derive some satisfaction from reporting that "The X Tribe Is Here To Help!" This *esprit de corps* may inspire us to each pull our own weight and do our tribe proud. Historically, though, such a crisis has often come in the form of some external threat, such as a war. Sometimes this external threat is even manufactured, to evoke this *esprit de corps* and manipulate it.

The spirit of a party: beyond "tribalism"

Any cooperative effort among human beings is bound to run into frustration from time to time, no matter how well-intended participants are. Cooperation is a non-zero-sum game, an attempt to increase value overall. As we explained in Chapter 12, there is no way for a finite being to increase value alone. Similarly, no finite collection of finite beings can increase value either. If each of us depletes ourselves to contribute to the effort of a team, it may temporarily appear that something greater than ourselves has emerged. This entity may even last much longer than our own lifetimes. Yet, the added value of that entity comes into question once we account for the depletion of the individuals that make it up. We may end up wondering whether it's worth our personal struggles and sacrifice.

On the other hand, when each of us is connected with what is beyond the party or team spirit, the infinite source, our contribution does not deplete us. Rather, the current flowing through us from that infinite source enlivens us. While our bodies and minds may be engaged in strenuous effort, we ourselves are experiencing the bliss of connection. We enjoy being with team members as part of our universal family, with whom we've come together not for limited group benefits but for truly universal purposes.

33.8   Cooperation with God at the Center

In the *Bhagavata Purana*, Narada says:

> As by pouring water on the roots of a tree, its trunk, branches, and twigs are satisfied, and as by feeding the stomach, all the limbs and senses of the body are enlivened, so by sacrifice to the imperishable transcendence, all are honored.
>
> — *Bhagavata Purana* 4.31.14

Some of the most frustrating aspects of any team effort can come from human interactions, even, or perhaps especially, from those closest to us — those we consider family. We put our hearts into our work and we don't always get the reciprocation we expect. When our relationship is with a personal God, then this takes the strain off our personal interactions with individual human beings. We're cooperating with the aim of pleasing God, who is easily pleased and who always returns our affection. The side effect is that our efforts are sustainable, because of connection with the infinite. Then, regardless of apparent success or failure, we're happy to cooperate in another project another day.

Chapter 34

Testimony: Training My Son to be a Leader and Protector

By Hare Krishna Dasi

Just to give a perspective on training someone suited to the a role of leadership and protecting others, I want to offer a glimpse of factors that went into training my son Ashtottara-sata das. Ashto was two years old when I took him and his sister to live at Gita-nagari, an *ahimsa* dairy farm. I personally had hoped he would eventually be inspired to enter a career as an educator — but even as a child, it became clear that was not his nature. He was physically oriented, and also team oriented. So, over the course of years, I did the best I could to provide him with training to prepare him for a life of leadership and protection of others, encouraging his competitive spirit and his practical compassion for other people.

I encouraged him to notice and express appreciation for the work of others and their expertise. I wanted him to gain an insight into the position of the workers in society. I personally had gathered ideas from reading the works of Srila AC Bhaktivedanta Swami Prabhupada (Srila Prabhupada for short), a 20th-century commentator on the *Bhagavad-gita* and *Bhagavata Purana* who was my spiritual mentor's teacher. I shared these perspectives with Ashto.[*] I explained how Srila Prabhupada taught the value of full employment in society, and

---

[*]Editor's note: Srila Prabhupada's life is summarized in Joshua Greene's *Swami in a Strange Land*.[326]

how high unemployment makes it easy for workers to be exploited. I helped him study Mahatma Gandhi's writings, and to learn about Gandhi's teachings on swadeshi (self-sufficiency).

When he was in eighth grade, he came in thirteenth in a nation-wide competition for his National History Day presentation, "How Workers Lost the Industrial Revolution," which he based on the principles we had studied together. While Ashto was giving his presentation at the National History Day event in Washington, D.C., his classmates back in Maine held their annual "Superlatives" vote for fellow students who excelled in different areas. The students voted that Ashto was the "most creative thinker." In high school, he became class president his junior year, knocking down a traditional candy sales scheme (which he believed exploited the students by giving too large a percentage of the sales to the candy corporation) and replacing it with a far more profitable, well-focused bottle recycling drive.

After graduating from high school, Ashto attended Hampshire College, which offered studies in agriculture and economics. He worked on the school farm and majored in development economics. Even before he graduated from Hampshire, he took a semester to do an independent study in Uganda, where he worked at an Italian Catholic project called the Namalu Ox Training and Ox Hire Center. During the course of his stay in the region of Karamoja, he visited about eight different nonprofit projects in Uganda. He noted that they all depended on Western donations. When Western economies took a downturn, those projects — be they orphanages, hospitals, schools, or small businesses — all took a nosedive, and many ended.

He determined that he would establish a nonprofit that would promote economic independence for the people, so that they would not be victims of stock market fluctuations in the West. Before he graduated from Hampshire, he had incorporated Working Villages International, to be started in the war-torn Democratic Republic of Congo. He started with nothing. We are a poor family, so he could not even rely on relatives to help him.

Ashto practiced devotion to the Supreme Lord in the form of the ideal king, Rama, and he was determined to try to make his village prosper. He was also greatly inspired by the extensive leadership writings of another spiritual teacher, Bhakti-Tirtha Swami, whom he had met and briefly corresponded with, before Bhakti-Tirtha Swami passed away.[*]

---

[*]Bhakti-Tirtha Swami's life is summarized in Steven J. Rosen's *Black Lotus*.[327]

In his formal education, Ashto came in contact with many ideas which, for him, highlighted different teachings from the *Bhagavad-gita* and *Bhagavata Purana*. Thus, he developed his project using a different approach from that used by projects surrounding him. Congo was a dangerous and deadly place to work, but Ashto had a strong faith that the Supreme Lord would help him, one way or another.

From the *Bhagavad-gita*, Ashto learned to spot and value the talents of others in building his project. ("I am ability in human beings." Bg 7-8) He learned the importance of expressing appreciation for the work and ingenuity of others. On the other hand, from the *Bhagavata Purana* he learned to beware of treacherous individuals who pretend to be friends, but are actually seeking power. His skills at assessing personality were sharpened as he worked to develop his nonprofit in a very contentious region. At the same time, he learned the value of loyal and talented people that he found. He did his best to give them opportunities to expand their expertise, and to make sure they would not be lured away.

From teachers of ancient wisdom, Ashto learned that, as a leader, although he had plans of his own, he must solicit feedback from those under him, in this case the local farmers, and listen carefully to what they expressed as their needs. For example, he had envisioned an elaborate plan to build village housing, but what they really wanted from Working Villages was irrigation. In the end, throwing all his energy into their wishes for irrigation was what turned out to be the capstone for developing economic independence for the families of the Ruzizi Valley. (Interestingly, with the profits from their expanded crop sales, farmers employed artisans to manufacture bricks and build houses for them. About a dozen very simple brick-making factories were set up by artisans. Bricks were fashioned from clay found along the riverbanks, and then arranged into simple pyramids, interspersed with rice straw, which was ignited to cure the bricks.)

From his spiritual elders, Ashto learned the importance of establishing an economy based on grain production. In his later conversations with me, Ashto commented that it was doubtful that without that perspective, he would have thought of creating a grain-based economy. Certainly, none of the other nonprofit groups were trying to do anything like that. At best, they were trying to market handcrafts for Western boutique shops. But, under Ashto's leadership, the Working Villages project in the Ruzizi Valley quickly became the largest producer of rice in South Kivu province.

Ashto learned the exploitative nature of some capitalists such as financial speculators. "A picturesque scene of green paddy fields enlivens the heart of the poor agriculturalist, but it brings gloom to the face of the capitalist who lives by exploiting the poor farmers." (AC Bhaktivedanta Swami, *Light of the Bhagavata*, Text 9) He also learned that farmers and tradespersons should be independent land owners. "Ownership will turn land into gold."

Ashto was already on the lookout for dishonest exploitation by the grain buyers. They were monopsonists, the only buyers in the area. They also owned the crucial rice processing machines. Since they were the only buyers, they could force villagers to sell their rice at low prices. The grain buyers then processed the rice with their grain hullers, and sold it for high prices in the big city. Ashto went to work and raised the capital resources, so Working Villages could purchase its own grain hullers, and put the exploiters out of business.

From the *Bhagavata Purana* (7.11.14), Ashto had read that persons whose careers involve leading and protecting the society should not beg, but Ashto also knew he had to distribute land to make his farmers independent producers. He decided that following the principle of distributing land was more important than not begging, so he became a TED fellow and solicited donations from large foundations.

Thus, in the early years of the project, Ashto would report, "We employ 100 workers on our project," then, "We employ nearly 1,000 workers on our project," and so on. But, by the end, Ashto reported, "We employ zero workers on our project." Why? Because farmers and tradespersons should be self-sufficient. Such persons own the land, and they themselves should be able to employ any helpers such as artisans and laborers that they need.

From Srila Prabhupada, Ashto learned the importance of avoiding bureaucracy and centralization. (Letter to Karandhar from Srila Prabhupada, December 22, 1972) Better to promote local leadership and local self-sufficiency, rather than to foster dependence on a far away large-scale bureaucracy.

From his studies of ancient wisdom, Ashto was convinced of the importance of small-scale land ownership, the idea that a family could become self-sufficient with only four acres of land. Ashto did not encourage large-scale farming that had to be done with expensive large equipment, which would keep farmers in debt. Instead, he encouraged small-scale ownership and the use of small-scale-appropriate technology. Many of the farms were very small. Because of twenty years of fighting, a large percentage of the men had been killed. Thus, women were at the head of many farm families. They might have no more than 2 acres of land. But the Ruzizi Valley has volcanic soil, which is some of the richest in the world, and it is located at the equator. With irrigation built by Working Villages, farmers could plant 3 crops per year — so that production on just 2 acres was worth the same as production from 6 acres elsewhere in the world.

It turned out that small-scale land ownership had another benefit. Large corporations from South Africa colluded with corrupt government officials in Congo, so that the government in Congo would force large land owners in Congo to sell land to these corporations. The government did this by artificially increasing the land tax on large holders to exorbitant amounts, which the Congolese plantations could not pay. Then the South African firms would swoop in and purchase the land, and the corrupt Congolese government officials reaped kickbacks.

But they did not like the Working Villages farms, because there were so many small holders, owning just 2 to 10 acres. What that meant for the would-be land predators was that there would be a tangle of land titles to deal with. Better to take over the large plantations. Thus, holding firm to the ancient teachings saved the livelihoods of several thousand small farmers.

From his spiritual elders Ashto learned that unemployment is a key cause of violence. Thus, he was convinced that full employment would bring peace. From the *Bhagavad-gita* (3.14), he was convinced of the fundamental importance of food production. Although Ashto had a theoretical belief in what Krishna said in the *Bhagavad-gita*, even he was astounded to experience how true it was. From year to year, as the employment in Working Villages expanded, those villages involved became more and more peaceful. Sometimes when there were dangerous militias on the move, the militia leaders would instruct their soldiers, "Do not harm the Working Villages project — they are providing our food," or "Do not harm the Working Villages project — my cousin works there." This was not 100% effective. Sometimes the project's people actually were shot, but the rate of violence was far reduced compared with surrounding areas.

The most remarkable incident occurred when Working Villages was trying to construct a large-scale irrigation project in a very dangerous area. The region on one side of the river was controlled by the Kakamba militia group, and the region on the opposite side of the river was controlled by the Bwygera militia group. But the farmers on both sides longed to have the irrigation developed. At great expense, some heavy equipment was brought in to excavate the area, but soon the shooting started, and work had to be stopped. This went on for several days. Finally, Ashto and the project manager, Fiston Marc Malago Kashakere, talked to the heads of both militias. They requested them to stop shooting for just two weeks so that the irrigation could be completed. The militias agreed: no shooting until the irrigation was complete.

In a couple of weeks, the Kakamba-Bwygera irrigation project was complete. But, at that time all the farmers, and everyone who could possibly help, were needed to prepare fields to take advantage of the massive amount of water flowing through the irrigation canals. All the militia soldiers faded into the village population to help out. There was so much work that needed to be done immediately that they neglected to take up arms again when the crops were finally planted, because then they were needed to help cultivate the crops and regulate the amount of water flowing to different fields. The former militia members realized that a person could make more money working for the farmers than by trying to be a soldier in a ramshackle militia group, making only ten dollars per month.

When he began his project in Congo, Ashto told the people that his goal was for the people to become economically independent. He emphasized that Working Villages was not like a regular charity. They would pull out in ten years. In the end, Working Villages stayed for eleven years. By the end of the project in 2018, there was no one left who was employed by Working Villages. Everyone was an independent farmer, or employed by an independent farmer. The villagers — who had been actually starving in 2006 — were now economically independent. Photos show hard workers with robust, healthy bodies. Ten thousand families in the Ruzizi Valley were now out of poverty. They paid for their own teachers and schools and doctors, and they even set up their own credit unions. They were so satisfied with Working Villages' leadership and practical help that they persuaded the project manager, Fiston Marc Malago Kashakere, to run for office. He was elected by a huge margin, and has now become the Vice Governor of South Kivu Province.

Ashto maintained his own faith tradition of *bhakti* yoga with great conviction, but was disappointed that no reliable spiritual teachers or clergy from his own tradition could help him. There was one monk in that area of Congo, but he proved to be much more interested in cultivating wealthy donors among existing parishioners than in teaching self-sufficiency to starving villagers.

Nevertheless, with the surplus profits they were making, the villagers wanted to build a church, which they did. Ashto had conflicting feelings about this. On one hand, he hoped that the villagers would not follow the divisive path of so many Christian evangelical groups in Africa, some of whom spread hatred of other faiths; but on the other hand, he recognized their need for a spiritual brotherhood, and hoped that the Supreme Lord would guide them for the best.

The idea of this look at Ashto's project in Congo is to offer a practical glimpse of how training a person to lead and protect society, with a solid range of educational experience — balanced by pertinent and insightful instructions from the *Bhagavad-gita* and *Bhagavata Purana* — can provide the basis for community development.

This was just the attempt of one mother to provide her son with appropriate training to lead and protect society, to the best of her ability. The training could be so much more "magnificent." I wish there were more examples of people being trained in this way according to ancient principles of career dharma. Perhaps there are, and I don't know about them. Nevertheless, I hope this offers a glimpse of the powerful impact of this ancient wisdom, once it is put to practical application.

34.1 Conclusion

The question may be asked: who is best qualified to establish the organization of career dharma in a social context? And, the answer must be: those who are well trained in leadership and protection of citizens, because the job of the social organization of a society falls under the proper purview of those whose careers center on leadership, protection, and justice.[*] Certainly those who work as teachers and spiritual leaders have an important role, as consultants, but the actual work must be done by those whose nature and training qualify them as leaders and protectors governing society. Srila Prabhupada pointed this fact out in his commentary on Bhagavata Purana 9.11.5.

Furthermore, it must be stressed that without four fields of work — especially without those who provide leadership and protection in society — there can be no question of establishing career dharma organization on the societal level. There is certainly the

---

[*]Editors' note: As we've established in this book, individuals can adopt practices of career dharma on their own, either piecemeal or wholesale. What is being discussed is establishment at scale, in the whole of a society.

path of devotion connection, and one can certainly reach spiritual fulfillment without the institution of career dharma, just as one can develop and even advance in devotion connection without a temple. A temple is simply a building made of atoms.

Nevertheless, just as a material building (a temple or church) can greatly facilitate one's practice of spiritual life, similarly the system of psychosocial organization (career dharma) can greatly facilitate one's connection with the Supreme Person. There is a fine point in understanding that although a building made of stone and wood is just a material structure, when it becomes a church or temple and is used for service to the Supreme Lord, then it manifests a spiritual quality. Similarly, although the organization of career dharma is just a material psychosocial system in a social context, it takes on a critical spiritual dimension when it is used to glorify the Lord. The person to develop such a spiritualized social system is the well-trained protector of society, providing proper leadership and governance.

34.2 Resources

Elizabeth D. Samet, a professor of English at West Point, is the editor of *Leadership: Essential Writings by Our Greatest Thinkers: A Norton Anthology* (2015). Although the book is some 700 pages in length, it contains 100 small readings by notable authors, from ancient to contemporary. (Amazon's "Look Inside" feature includes the table of contents, and some sample readings.)[328]

Working Villages International – TED talks by Alexander Petroff[329][330]

Chapter 35

Checks and Balances Across Fields

In Chapter 32, we discussed some of the virtues of competition among those within a field. Competitors, for instance, help spur us to build and maintain a reputation for integrity and honest dealing. Overall, such competition helps ensure that workers in the field perform their service for the community with competence and integrity.

Each field contributes needed services (as described in Chapter 33) so that society as a whole can function smoothly. These services need to be provided reliably, something for which the competence and integrity of each field are critical. Similarly, as organs in our body work together, each must be competent to do its job (e.g., the heart to pump blood, the stomach to digest food, the lungs to exchange gases, and so forth). The cells of each organ must also communicate honestly with other cells of the body. Cancerous cells, for example, cheat other cells into helping them by communicating dishonestly (e.g., by mimicking wounded tissue that needs resources to heal). Furthermore, the parts of the body must be the right size relative to the others, and function to the extent required for the health of the whole body. Tumors, for example, grow beyond what is needed, and some kinds, such as endocrine tumors, may produce more hormones than required. The body as a whole has ways to *regulate* its parts, so that each works with competence and integrity, dynamically maintaining balance among one another and with the environment. Similarly, society needs ways of regulating the various fields of work.

As discussed, a field of work is regulated partly through competition among its members, which helps ensure the competence and integrity of the whole field. One way the cells of an organ of the body maintain the organ's appropriate size and shape is also through competition (e.g., for space, or for contact with cells of another type, such as blood vessels). However, competition is not the only means the body has to regulate itself; other means include the action of hormones, immune surveillance, and nervous signaling. Similarly, regulation of a field through competition is not completely sufficient in itself to ensure that the field as a whole does its best possible work.

Since those working in a particular field share similarities, they may develop collective blind spots with respect to concerns outside their experience. For example, take the efforts by the United States government to protect wild endangered species:

> Consider the Endangered Species Act (E.S.A.) of 1973, which protects flora and fauna as well as their physical habitats. The economists Dean Lueck and Jeffrey Michael wanted to gauge the E.S.A.'s effect on the red-cockaded woodpecker, a protected bird that nests in old-growth pine trees in eastern North Carolina. By examining the timber harvest activity of more than 1,000 privately owned forest plots, Lueck and Michael found a clear pattern: when a landowner felt that his property was turning into the sort of habitat that might attract a nesting pair of woodpeckers, he rushed in to cut down the trees. It didn't matter if timber prices were low.
>
> This happened less than two years ago in Boiling Spring Lakes, N.C. "Along the roadsides," an A.P. article reported, "scattered brown bark is all that's left of once majestic pine stands." As sad as this may be, it isn't surprising to anyone who has examined the perverse incentives created by the E.S.A. In their paper, Lueck and Michael cite a 1996 developers' guide from the National Association of Home Builders: "The highest level of assurance that a property owner will not face an E.S.A. issue is to maintain the property in a condition such that protected species cannot occupy the property."
>
> One notable wrinkle of the E.S.A. is that a species is often declared endangered months or even years before its "critical habitats" are officially designated. This allows time for developers, environmentalists and everyone in between to have their say at public hearings. What happens during that lag time?

In a new working paper that examines the plight of the cactus ferruginous pygmy owl, the economists John List, Michael Margolis and Daniel Osgood found that landowners near Tucson rushed to clear their property for development rather than risk having it declared a safe haven for the owl. The economists make the argument for "the distinct possibility that the Endangered Species Act is actually endangering, rather than protecting, species."

–Stephen J. Dubner & Steven D. Levitt, Unintended Consequences[331]

Here, the E.S.A. potentially did more harm than good. Those who drew the act up were well-intentioned, but lacked the foresight to realize the unintended consequences of their policy — a classic pitfall for policies where punishment for non-compliance is the primary implementation procedure.

By way of contrast, in Fort Hood, Texas, the US military together with the Department of Agriculture developed a system for trading credits with private landowners for species conservation actions. Through this Fort Hood Recovery Credit System, the Field of Government worked together with the Field of Resources to bring thousands of acres of habitat under conservation management.[332]

Another example, which is more insidious from a systemic viewpoint, is that individuals in a particular field may take advantage of their special roles and competencies to exploit those outside their field rather than cooperating with and serving them. Those outside the field may lack the expertise to detect and avoid these individuals, even if honest competitors are available. Members of the field who render service in good faith may be reluctant to point fingers at others, preferring to concentrate on their own work and let its quality and integrity speak for itself. They may also feel that if they point out the dishonest behavior, they may be accused of attempting to undermine the exploitative individuals simply to boost their own interests, and not be believed anyway. Whistleblowers are often branded as unjustly disgruntled, unfortunately. For example, Sherron Watkins, a certified public accountant, worked at Arthur Andersen, one of the "Big Five" accounting firms, which had been founded in 1913 and grew to acquire an international reputation. In 1993, Watkins left Arthur Andersen and joined Enron Corporation, where she became an executive. Several years later, Watkins noticed financial improprieties at

Enron, and raised concerns with the chairman of the company, Kenneth Lay. In 2002, Watkins testified before an investigative subcommittee of the US Congress:

> Watkins said that when she told Lay of her concerns, the chief financial officer, Andrew Fastow, wanted her fired and her computer seized.
> —Associated Press, *Enron executive Watkins says Fastow wanted her fired for going to chairman*[333]

So, was Watkins unjustly disgruntled, or a whistleblower? Ultimately, Enron was found to have committed fraud on a massive scale, went bankrupt, and was liquidated. Arthur Andersen had been Enron's main auditor, and this scandal led to its dissolution.

Another possibility is that exploitative groups may reach a critical mass within a field. The members of the field may identify more with others in the same field than anyone else. They may feel loyalty to those they consider "their own kind," and may feel little empathy or concern for those outside their field. Gradually exploitative behavior may become a norm in the field, defended with the phrase "Everybody does it." So, workers in that field may even lose awareness that it is unethical. Finally, in the worst situation, members of the field may actively collude to exploit those outside their field more effectively. In 2017, the EU fined eleven major air cargo carriers, including Air France-KLM, British Airways, and Lufthansa, for working together to fix prices to the detriment of their customers.[334] In this example, it was those in the Field of Government that sought to fix exploitative practices in the Field of Resources (something we shall turn to next).

In sum, in addition to competition within each field, society needs regulative feedback mechanisms between fields. Some of this feedback may come from other specific fields of work, while some may come from people in general.

35.1 How People Regulate Others Across Fields, Directly and Indirectly

Each of us indirectly regulates what other people do, through how we spend our time, money, and energy. Naturally, what people participate in and support grows stronger. Therefore, one way that people in different fields regulate each other is by choosing with whom to cooperate or not cooperate, and to what degree.

For example, competitive games are supported by competitors, referees, customers, spectators, and so on. Cooperative efforts are supported directly by those who advocate them and those who participate in them, and indirectly by those who report them. Those who benefit from cooperative efforts honestly also indirectly support them, since they are the impetus for these efforts being undertaken. On the other hand, those who benefit from cooperative efforts in a dishonest or exploitative way detract from them and over the long run may lead to their demise. The extraordinary success of cyclist Lance Armstrong, then his swift fall from grace once it was discovered he had cheated by using performance enhancing drugs, illustrates the way in which one individual's dishonesty can tar a sport's, and their own, reputation.

Intuitively, we associate power with the expenditure of energy, so we sometimes forget or underestimate the power we always have: namely, the power to not cooperate, not participate, and ignore. Yet while their effects may sometimes be subtle, they can be very powerful. Those on the receiving end notice. When our efforts to start or carry on something meet with little or no response, they soon run out of steam. Not cooperating, not participating, and ignoring are aspects of the richness of *vairagya* (detachment, being equipoised). The *Bhagavata Purana* and related scriptures often tell of how teja, fiery inner power, derives from *vairagya*. The power of walking away is a fundamental tactic in negotiation and bargaining. It leads to positive outcomes in one of the most famous problems in game theory, the prisoner's dilemma, which we have discussed in an endnote to Chapter 32.

Individual and Collective Responsibility

However, the above doesn't mean it's always an individual duty of every single member of each of these fields to take these actions to regulate others. Those are elective choices, and they occur by degrees in society as different individuals in each field make different choices. Furthermore, not everyone is in a position to make these choices to the same extent. Through acting by degrees, social regulation acts like a tuning knob rather than an on/off switch. For each field other than the Field of Government, regulating other fields is optional. Indeed, at the individual level, for a member of another field to take on the role of the Field of Government is dangerous, as we described in Part I in Chapter 6. An individual can undertake investigative reporting, withdraw charitable giving, go on strike, etc., and doesn't necessarily have to. It's contextual and conditional. Having said that, in a society where people in general apply the natural art of work, workers in each field do have specific ways in which they are are ideally situated to regulate the other fields and society as a whole. Let us examine the regulatory role each field can play in society.

How workers in the Field of Ideas regulate society

Workers in the Field of Ideas cooperate with government by giving advice, and also monitor the workings of the government itself. In *The Origins of Political Order*, Francis Fukuyama describes the importance of the rule of law in government rather than a society where one person or group rules arbitrarily. He specifically highlights the separation of the Field of Ideas from the Field of Government as key to supporting the rule of law.* Those in the Field of Ideas publicly and privately hold government leaders to the rule of law. For example, when Theodore Roosevelt was Police Commissioner of New York City, the journalist Jacob Riis showed him the plight of the poor in different parts of the city and helped him root out corruption in the police force, which had been contributing to that plight.[335]

Or, by way of another example, Julian Davis Mortenson, a professor of law at the University of Michigan, writes about the presidency of the United States:

> ...the presidency that leaps off the pages of the Founders' debates, diaries, speeches, letters, poems, and essays was an *instrument* of the law of the land, *subject* to the law of the land, and both morally and legally obliged to *obey* the law of the land. [Emphasis in original.]
> –Julian Davis Mortenson, *What Two Crucial Words in the Constitution Mean*[336]

In other words, presidents of the United States don't get to make up things as they go along, give any kind of orders they want, and have people do whatever they say. They are in place to carry out the law and get other people to carry it out. They follow the law themselves and get other people to follow it. The law is bigger than the president. Since laws are ideas put into words, it's people in the Field of Ideas who

---

*By "rule of law" we mean codes that are coherent, consistent, and designed to be applied equally even to government leaders and law enforcement persons.

see whether the actions of presidents, and other government leaders in the executive branch, match with those ideas. More generally, the principles of the natural art of work are bigger than the Field of Government or anybody in it. Those in the Field of Government follow the principles themselves and get others to follow them. Those in the Field of Ideas see that the principles are translated faithfully into action by those in the Field of Government.

To speak out without compromise, people working in the Field of Ideas need a wide base of support. One way of accomplishing this is by collecting charity from a wide range of sources, without strings attached. Ideally this collection would be without expectation of repetition at specific intervals or of specific amounts. Today's technology enables a number of ways of getting support from a wide base, such as donation buttons on one's personal website, crowd-funding for specific projects, or services such as Patreon that enable many people to support a particular individual.

Most people work in the Field of Artistry, and thus they form the widest base of support for those in the Field of Ideas. Conversely, people working in the Field of Ideas have a particular responsibility to speak out against exploitation or oppression of people working in the Field of Artistry, as they may be more vulnerable due to having less power or wealth.

People in the Field of Ideas regulate all other fields through their savvy advice. For example, former US President Theodore Roosevelt had thought everyone should serve in the military, and strongly advocated instituting a draft so that the United States could enter World War I right when it began in 1914. To the end of his life, Theodore's view persisted that his country could institute elective wars through conscription. His conviction was probably due, at least in part, to the fact that he did not have a trusted mentor in the Field of Ideas. Such a mentor could provide the insight that the best warriors are those who genuinely feel privileged to put their lives on the line in battle. As we mentioned, those in the Field of Government are constantly internally driven to ask the questions, "Is it just? Is it honorable?" Those without such a mood may not only compromise the standard of military ethics, but their combat experiences may subsequently damage their abilities to work according to career dharma in their natural field. Theodore did have a trusted mentor in the Field of Government, Henry Cabot Lodge. However, those in the same field of work tend to develop similar blind spots in some areas: he would have benefited most from having a mentor in the Field of Ideas.

Because workers in the Field of Ideas teach those in every other field, they pass on the standards (for each field) that define quality and ethical practices. For example, members of the press in the Field of Ideas bring to light dysfunction and corruption. Those in the Field of Ideas who specialize in religion and spirituality may address those who are not walking their talk as far as putting their values into their work. The pen is mightier than the sword! In general, people in the Field of Ideas can shift the values and thinking of groups of people through teaching, writing, and speaking. In one sense, such people can "create a public"[337] in the sense of creating a group of people who believe, think, and act in a way that didn't previously exist.

The purity, or unbiased integrity, of the speech of those in this field is what endows it with might. Therefore, in order to fulfill their role as a check and balance for the rest of society, those who are expert in the dharma of the Field of Ideas are willing to sacrifice everything for the sake of objective truth.

How those in the Field of Government regulate others

Regulating those in every field is most clearly and obviously one of the main functions of government, as these people make and enforce laws and dispense justice, though over-regulation can also be a problem. Therefore, the government ultimately guarantees that society runs smoothly and with integrity. Even if we don't see this often, the fact it exists plays a significant role in everyday life. This fact can easily be seen by comparison with regions where the state has failed and civil order has broken down. For instance, in the United States, the vast majority of citizens do not defraud one another in business agreements partly out of morality, but also because of the expectation that if they do there is a strong chance that they will face justice. This might not be true in a region where corruption is endemic.

In addition to implementing general laws and facilities for society to run peacefully and smoothly, those in the Field of Government act as enforcers to ensure that the workers of each field meet the standards within that field, often as set forth by those in the Field of Ideas. They may also penalize individuals who transgress these standards. These penalties might include suspending them from work for a period of time, placing specific restraints on parts of their field they are allowed to practice, or, in extreme cases, barring them from working altogether. Workers in the Field of Government also regulate other fields less directly, through speeches and announcements. Representing the Field of Government automatically carries weight, even when such acts do not have the force of law. Occasionally, workers in the Field of Government with the richness of *yasa*, (splendid fame through respect and admiration for their dharma) indirectly regulate society through their example.

One such leader was Nelson Mandela. South Africa endured decades of apartheid: oppression of nonwhites by whites, through laws put in place by whites. The overturning of apartheid could have led to widespread vindictive bloodshed. In fact, many whites who didn't necessarily support the continuation of apartheid in principle continued supporting it in practice out of fear that the only alternative was violent revolution. Instead, in 1996 South Africa established the Truth and Reconciliation Commission to investigate the crimes of apartheid. Here, the oppressed could speak the truth of what they had endured, coming face-to-face with their oppressors. The people of South Africa were encouraged to forgive, though not forget, these crimes.

Nelson Mandela, who had been imprisoned for decades for working to overturn apartheid, became the President of South Africa after apartheid ended. He set the example of reconciling with his oppressors, including the prosecutor who had sent him to prison. The people followed this example, enabling a peaceful transition that many had never dreamed possible. Mandela was elderly by the time he became president and left the day-to-day running of government to others. Yet the role he played as leader, exhibiting the inner strength he had cultivated through spiritual study and practice while in prison, continues to stand as an inspiring beacon in world history.[338]

Government also has a responsibility to balance the needs of those in various other fields. For example, the creation of the United States' Food and Drug Administration is evidence of "the government's often uneasy balancing act between supporting American business and protecting American citizens."[339] In the late 19th century, there was such adulteration of food that people often unknowingly ate highly toxic additives and fillers mixed with various food ingredients such as sawdust in "coffee." Since public health greatly suffered due to the abuses of those in the Field of Resources, eventually those in the Field of Government decided that the US needed to ensure the physical and mental well-being of its citizens, even if doing so meant fewer profits for business.

Although working in the Field of Government often brings *yasa*, some necessary policies may be misunderstood or unpopular with some segments of society. Therefore, workers who have dharmic expertise in the Field of Government are willing to sacrifice everything for the sake of justice, being an honorable person, and the public interest. It is only such an overriding concern that gives them the prerogative to make decisions affecting large groups and enables them to act effectively as a check and balance of the other fields.

How workers in the Field of Resources regulate others

The way workers in the Field of Resources set up their enterprises and distribution networks directly impacts how those in the Field of Artistry in general are able to do their work. Workers in the Field of Resources may also use their control of resources to set quality and ethical standards for their specific suppliers, contractors, and employees who are in the Field of Artistry.

The predominance of the Field of Resources in the tax base gives them power and influence with respect to those in the Field of Government and those who benefit from public works — in other words, everyone. In Chapter 23 we described Giovanni Impastato, who continued running his business while speaking out against the corrupt local government, namely the Mafia and those in league with them. Often, it is those in the Field of Resources who implement the social and economic theories of those in the Field of Ideas, thus moderating mere theory by eliminating what does not work in practice. The wealthy English financier Sir Thomas Gresham, who founded the Royal Exchange, stipulated in his will the founding of what became Gresham College, the first college in London. His bequest specified that professors should lecture in seven subjects including geometry, physics, and law. This benefaction played a key role in encouraging the application of mathematics.[340]

As those in the Field of Resources tend to be the main patrons of the arts and to fund artistic expression, they exercise some control over what ideas are expressed to the people in general through various media.

People working in the Field of Resources are particularly responsible for maintaining high integrity in their specific enterprises. Those practicing the natural art of work want all to prosper. Their dharma is to be honest in their livelihood; they would rather be poor than earn money dishonestly. Indeed, the trust they earn this way is an essential component of their capital, as we discussed in Chapter 21.

Besides this, as experts working in the Field of Resources have the best view of local concerns on the ground, they are responsible for ensuring that the flow of resources is sustainable. We discussed this earlier in Chapter 21. People with dharmic expertise in the Field of Resources are willing to sacrifice for the sake of preserving the flow of resources, and for the sake of maintaining high ethical standards in their livelihood. Thus they have the potency to act as a check and balance for those in the other fields.

How workers in the Field of Artistry regulate others

Most people work in the Field of Artistry. Thus, this field has power in numbers. So, whenever those who work in this field unite, they can reach a critical mass that the rest of society, whatever other kinds of power they may have, cannot ignore. When workers in the Field of Artistry organize themselves to protest, they not only communicate what they directly speak about, they also remind others of the power of solidarity. Since armies also depend on workers in the Field of Artistry, when these workers are truly united they can even overpower governments with armies on their side. For instance, the Romanian Revolution of 1989 was won not by a decisive military victory, but when the people won the Romanian Army over to their side against the dictator Nicolae Ceaușescu.

Cooperation and noncooperation are powers each of us have. The tactics of civil disobedience and nonviolent protest draw strength from numbers. Workers in the Field of Artistry can wield these tactics particularly effectively. Without these workers, nothing functions, quality of life immediately goes down dramatically, and all the other fields are crippled. On the positive side, when these same workers cooperate, things run smoothly and day-to-day life is beautiful.

Workers in the Field of Artistry are particularly influential in communicating information about corruption and social dysfunction to the public. While revealing corruption is a critical responsibility of the Field of Ideas, as well as regulating government in particular and the wider society from a detached, neutral perspective, it is often those in the Field of Artistry who "translate" from the Field of Ideas to society at large. For example, it is the writers of political protest songs, comedians, satirists, and caricaturists who perennially play crucial roles in bringing societal dysfunction to light and keeping it in the public consciousness, an essential ingredient in spearheading change. Without such people in the Field of Artistry, the insight and warnings of those in the Field of Ideas might never percolate beyond a small circle of like-minded people. Those who work with dharmic expertise in the Field of Artistry are willing to sacrifice by resisting pressure for artificially increased profits or expediency that would interfere with the integrity and quality of their work. Such dedication helps them to act as a check and balance for the rest of society.

How commensals regulate others

Any society can develop dysfunctions. Often these dysfunctions happen accidentally, for instance when environmental circumstances change and society does not adapt. Dysfunction can happen through shortsighted decisions that remain in place beyond the timeframe for which they were conceived. It can also happen when exploitative people put practices into place that benefit them at the expense of others. Such practices may even persist out of inertia long after the specific people who put them in place have departed.

When a society remains closed to outside influence over a period of time, then whatever dysfunctions it has or develops may become normalized. Dysfunctions become an ingrained part of the mental landscape. Society can become so habituated to the dysfunctions that it no longer knows any other way. Such dysfunction becomes "the way things are," about which people don't think twice.

Thus, remaining open to commensals, who don't participate in the main career stream of society but remain as neutral observers, is vital to the health of a society. When members of a society welcome these commensals and converse with them respectfully, they can learn from their divergent perspectives. The commensals are uniquely positioned to cast light on any dysfunctional norms that have arisen, serving to bring them to awareness, which is always the first step in fixing them. They can also bring novel ideas to the table, from their travels or their own creative insights, which can become ingredients in enhancing any field of work. Any field or any society that has been stagnating can be stirred up and stimulated to improve by exposure to these perspectives. It's important to remember that commmensals are not just lazy vagabonds. While it's not possible to demarcate the specific societal role or position in the universal body of commensals as a group in terms of the fields of work, their general "outsider" status, as explained previously, functions something like gut bacteria that keeps the body healthy without being part of the body itself.

An example is Joseph Brodsky, who received the Nobel Prize for Literature in 1987, primarily for his poetry. In 1964, the former Soviet Union had declared that his writing poetry and working odd jobs were an insufficient contribution to society and thus sentenced him to five years hard labor for "social parasitism." A transcript of his trial was quickly (and clandestinely) produced then sent abroad, something that helped launch the Soviet human rights movement.[341]

The book *The Way of a Pilgrim* is an autographical account by an anonymous pilgrim who travels through Russia in the early 19th century. The manuscript somehow made its way to the monastery at Mount Athos, where an abbot found it and had it published in 1884. The author does various odd jobs to maintain himself, and is absorbed in meditative prayer. He has no fixed residence and no career as such. Such a commensal contributes to society and the universal body by giving informal guidance and succor to those he meets on his journey.[342]

There are many examples in literature of fictional, and perhaps romanticized, commensals. They are intentional nomads with few possessions and no fixed career. They may plant trees, or assist law enforcement, or in some way be of assistance to those they meet on their journey.

35.2 The Importance of Enforcement

Some of the mechanisms of regulation we have described so far have been various sorts of pressure tactics. These are good for preventing problems in the first place or nipping them in the bud. These tactics maintain widespread social norms of cooperative behavior.

However, with the wide variation in human temperament, there will always be individuals who work in bad faith, pushing the envelope of what they can get away with, and who are not deterred by pressure alone. Allowing this misbehavior not only allows the direct bad consequences to accumulate but also leads to corruption in the fields of work as others see the lack of consequences and join in.

Government checks corruption and criminality in every field

Government provides protection from criminal elements, and provides laws that help smooth cooperation between fields of work. For example, government laws state what safety features those in the Field of Resources must provide for workers in the Field of Artistry. Competition alone can favor shortsighted skimping on worker safety. Government enforcement of mandatory standards means those in the Field of Resources can do the right thing without being at a competitive disadvantage.

The Field of Government is also responsible for monitoring what goes on in each field of work. Government is expected to look out for the new and creative ways people may come up with to get around lawful, ethical behavior. Government is, of course, responsible for devising and implementing means to deter and punish crime.

Government discourages parasitic lifestyles

Parasitism is an ecological relationship where one being benefits from another being and causes it harm in return (though not by completely consuming it, or even necessarily killing it). Parasitism is widespread in nature, and unfortunately humans may sometimes engage in it. Parasites keep devising clever new ways to find and invade susceptible hosts. Just as the human body has mechanisms for keeping parasitism within it under control, so society also needs active mechanisms to discourage parasitic lifestyles. At the same time, we need to be careful about jumping to the conclusion that a lifestyle is parasitic, and that our mechanisms for discouraging parasitic lifestyles don't cause greater harm than the parasitic lifestyles themselves. We describe specific instances below.

Within the body, microbes that are beneficial in some circumstances are harmful in others. In these cases, it isn't quite accurate to label the microbes as parasites since[*] they are parasitic only in certain circumstances. Similarly, in human society, it's not accurate to label any person as a parasite unless they are *willfully* and *chronically* so. Some people live lives that might be confused as being parasitic, but do not meet both of these two criteria. For example, when people are homeless, mentally ill, disabled, or for other reasons unable to

---

[*]For one thing, some of these microbes are bacteria. The definition of "parasites" in microbiology requires that they are eukaryotes, whereas the definition of "parasitism" in ecology has nothing to do with taxonomy.

support themselves in the prime of life, then a responsible society living by the principle of "the whole world is one family" gives them a helping hand rather than deeming them parasites. None of us knows when we might be in their shoes. These circumstances are often temporary, and a hand up at a crucial time can mean the difference between decades of entrapment in poverty versus moving on to live a full life.

One young English girl's family saw her imagination as "an amusing personal quirk that would never pay a mortgage, or secure a pension." (Recall how we described in Chapter 7 that children's natures can often be misunderstood by their families.) As she grew up, her life got off to a bit of a rocky start. Her mother died when she was 25. A couple of years later, she got married and had a daughter. However, when her daughter was only a few months old, the marriage ended. Now a single mother, she moved into a cramped apartment with her baby. During this time, she became deeply depressed and considered suicide. She says of that time, "An exceptionally short-lived marriage had imploded, and I was jobless, a lone parent, and as poor as it is possible to be in modern Britain, without being homeless....By every usual standard, I was the biggest failure I knew."

During this time, she was forced to rely on state benefits. A short-sighted, narrow-minded outlook might be to pigeonhole hers as a parasitic lifestyle. This young woman in the prime of life was being supported by the state along with her baby. Yet, her intention was to try as best she could in her current situation to move towards making a future contribution (and of course children themselves also comprise the future).

She was bringing her baby along to cafés and writing a book. The book was *Harry Potter and the Philosopher's Stone*, and the young woman was J.K. Rowling, now a multimillionaire. She has spoken out eloquently about why she continues to pay her full taxes in Britain:

> I chose to remain a domiciled taxpayer for a couple of reasons. The main one was that I wanted my children to grow up where I grew up, to have proper roots in a culture as old and magnificent as Britain's; to be citizens, with everything that implies, of a real country, not free-floating ex-pats, living in the limbo of some tax haven and associating only with the children of similarly greedy tax exiles.

> A second reason, however, was that I am indebted to
> the British welfare state; the very one that Mr. Cameron
> would like to replace with charity handouts. When my
> life hit rock bottom, that safety net, threadbare though it
> had become under John Major's Government, was there
> to break the fall. I cannot help feeling, therefore, that
> it would have been contemptible to scarper for the West
> Indies at the first sniff of a seven-figure royalty cheque.
> This, if you like, is my notion of patriotism.
> –J.K. Rowling[343]

While people in this situation will not all have the success of J.K. Rowling, her extraordinary example illustrates the importance of not automatically deeming people to be parasites.

All that being said, some people may willfully live in society as free riders, defrauding the government and taking advantage of the good-will of society by falsely claiming a disability. This is in fact a parasitic lifestyle, exploiting the kindness of strangers. There are a few ways for government to discourage this kind of fraud. The first is that those working in the Field of Government disburse benefits within a small local community to which they themselves belong and which they know well. Fraud is usually an effect and a symptom of impersonal interaction. The second is for aid not to consist merely of cash disbursements but also of help with the specific problems that are resulting in the situation. For instance, people in the Field of Government can provide homeless people with shelter, a place to clean up, a stable address, and so forth. They can arrange for mentally ill people to receive mental health care. They can arrange for people with disabilities to get appropriate therapies and care. A natural side effect of these caring interactions is that fraud will naturally diminish. Most people do respond and wish to reciprocate kindness with gratitude.

A tiny proportion of fraud may remain. It's not worth stamping out every last instance. Around the turn of the 20th century in Paris, the Russian zoologist Élie Metchnikoff noted the new discoveries of bacteria living in the gut and developed a theory that these were the cause of aging. (As we now know, helpful bacteria in our guts are key to many aspects of our physical and mental health.) Metchnikoff thought the solution was to surgically remove portions of the large intestines of some of his patients. This certainly did result in the removal of all the bacteria in those portions of the gut, but at what cost? Such a radical procedure demonstrated a complete lack of perspective on

410

the proportions of the putative problem. The lesson is that workers in the Field of Government, and society as a whole, need to maintain a balanced perspective regarding the tradeoffs of how much energy to spend pursuing every last possible instance of fraud, as well as the costs of denying help to those truly in need.

35.3 Conclusion

We've now seen how workers in the four fields would, in a perfect world, relate to one another within society. Within a field, while some workers in the same field may team up to head an endeavor, many such individuals or small teams will be competing with one another to excel, as we described in Chapter 32. Workers in different fields ideally collaborate, bringing their different emphases to bear, each with different roles to play, as we described in Chapter 33. On the other hand, workers in each field also have specific roles in keeping society as a whole running smoothly, as we described in this chapter. In the next chapter, we begin to describe how society as a whole can achieve sustainable prosperity through the natural art of work.

Chapter 36

Testimony: My Box

By Dave McWilliams

[Note from UEB and RSD: All footnotes are our editorial insertions to clarify, explain, or elaborate on what was written in the text.]

In life we often put people in boxes. We usually do so not to take away from the uniqueness or importance of the person but to give us a frame of understanding that we can build on. I've been given the title of "commensal" in this book. I find it difficult to write about my way of living, because so much of my life is normally confidential and intuitive. And I've rarely encountered someone with a patient enough ear to allow me to try and gently explain why and how I live the way I do.

A box has six sides. I've decided to divide this into six, and hopefully by the end you will have a nice little box to put me in.

36.1   On the surface.

Hi! I'm Dave McWilliams. I'm a musician who sometimes paints buildings. I'm a housekeeper who sometimes picks fruit. Finder of lost keys. Advisor. Dishwasher. River guide. Author. Dancer. Truck driver. Gardener. I can fix your laptop and take your mother to her dentist appointment. I can provide an alibi. I hold the door open for ladies and give my seat on the bus to senior citizens. I haven't gotten anywhere yet, but I got there by hard work. Cleaned out barns. Cycled thousands of miles. Walked the Pilbara[*] with an Alice pack.[†] Got enslaved by an avocado farmer. I'm a jeweler. Lived in mansions and tents. Slept on king-sized beds and behind dumpsters. If life experiences were ice cream, I've tried every flavor I'm interested in trying.

36.2   Meaningfulness

I'm a very confused person. There is so much I don't know and I'm often bewildered. There are some things, however, I have strong hunches about. I have a pretty strong feeling that most of what I'm seeing is an illusion. I think we have a lot of illusions as a result of our conditioning. Both material and conceptual illusions. An example of material illusions is the way you cannot see radio waves, yet they are all around you. The human eyes (like the mind) are very weak and subject to many limitations. Conceptual illusions are like societal conditioning, the "cult" in culture. Every country teaches the history of the world differently, yet all the while the history of the Earth herself has been going on all around us and we can't even perceive it. Imagine telling a giraffe he's a giraffe. He'd have no idea what a giraffe is, but he'd wonder why you act so strangely.

But I can say to myself with certainty that spiritual advancement and self-development are the most important things to me. I've been fooled many times in life, but those two things continue to remain true. So those are the two things I pursue.

36.3   Desire

I am completely hypnotized by desire. My biggest and most driving desire being love. As long as I remember, selfless love and security have been all I really wanted. But if I may quote the 90s artist Haddaway, "What is love?" I think that it's probably not romantic or conjugal. That's quite a strong attachment and a very powerful illusion, couples' love. It's also the leading cause of pain, depression, jealousy,

---

[*]The Pilbara is a large, dry, thinly populated region in the north of Western Australia. It is known for its Aboriginal peoples; its ancient landscapes; the red earth; and its vast mineral deposits, in particular iron ore. It is also a global biodiversity hotspot for subterranean fauna.

[†]A type of backpack. Alice is an acronym for All-purpose Lightweight Individual Carrying Equipment.

lust, anger and even murder. And anyway, it's always subject to conditions. "I love you, so long as you never do this and always do that." That's not love. Even familial love comes with terms and conditions, from the time of the womb.

I find true love within myself, and within the way I interact with other living beings, in the beauty of creation and in my quiet confidential time with God. So, my quest for love obliges me to live in ways that limit the time of separation there is between myself and love. This is fulfillment.

36.4 Security

Faith gives me a spiritual insurance policy. My faith isn't blind; I test it all the time. Actually, it's not faith but knowledge. It only becomes faith at times when I've become illusioned or forgetful as I'm so prone to do. Everything I've ever needed in life has always come to me. So often, I've been inexplicably in the right place at the right time to do, receive, or give something. My life has been full of small miracles. They happen so spontaneously. I feel that the universe uses me to fill in the little gaps here and there.

36.5 Interplay with reality

After a while of accruing skills and developing spiritual knowledge, a person can become quite detached from false reality. Seeing the world for what it is, and illusions for what they are. This is where the real fun starts. Interplay with reality. I see myself as embodied, serving a life sentence. But I'm not this body. I see that I'm not the experiencer, but the experience itself. So I'd better be a good one. I feel quite comfortable with going anywhere and doing anything I can think of that sounds interesting. The material world becomes a playground. Wealth of spirit and love actualized, fortified by divine protection through faith on a quest for spiritual advancement. It's instant retirement, and a life of play. I feel indifferent to most things, which enables me to be fine doing most things. I feel like a symptom of nature. This is steady peace.

36.6   Purpose

I can't stop anyway. Even if I tried (and I have), I would get sucked
back. It's too much to give up, too fun, too beautiful, too fulfilling. I
do it my way, and it's just right for me. This is how I know it's dharma.

Chapter 37

Sustainable Prosperity

A major stated aim of any society is for as many of its members as possible to experience prosperity, to flourish and thrive. Naturally, we would also like this prosperity to continue over time, that is, we want it to be sustained. Unfortunately, most current economic models contain a fundamental contradiction that makes sustainable prosperity impossible. However, we *can* have sustainable prosperity if we follow timeless principles and practices. In this chapter, we'll look at what problems come up when we try to talk about sustainable prosperity, and we'll also sketch out the solutions. In the process, we'll be tying together ideas from several of the earlier chapters.

37.1 Unsustainable Prosperity

Here is the main problem: when economists, politicians, and journalists talk about prosperity, they speak of "growth and prosperity" as if the two were inseparable. As economists Baumol, Litan, and Schramm wrote in 2007:

> …the importance of economic growth was assumed to be self-evident.…it was even on a par with the ideals of motherhood and apple pie.…only with more economic output can more people live a more enjoyable and satisfying existence.
> – William J. Baumol   Robert E. Litan   Carl J. Schramm , *Good Capitalism, Bad Capitalism, and the Economics of Growth and Prosperity*[344]

Why would conflating growth and prosperity render prosperity unsustainable? If we give it a moment's thought, we can immediately understand that any system for getting what we need for physical life — that is, any system of economics and work — is tightly tied to natural resources. All our food, clothing, building materials, medicine — indeed, everything we need for physical life — comes from the land and water as well as the plants and animals that depend on them. As natural resources are finite, economic growth can't continue forever, so the idea that the economy can or should just keep growing is obviously inconsistent with the natural world upon which we depend for prosperity. Surprisingly, however, this idea of continued growth is the standard view among economists today.

In the same 2007 book quoted earlier, Baumol, Litan, and Schramm dismissed the inconsistency we just explained by pointing out that economic growth had continued so far, even though "doomsayers" had previously predicted that it would run into limits imposed by natural resources. This dismissal is about as logical as saying that since one meteorologist predicted rain on Monday and it didn't come, and another meteorologist predicted rain on Tuesday and it didn't come, it will never rain. We all know that there are limited natural resources to supply our biological needs. Both common sense and considered reasoning tell us that this limitation will eventually emerge victorious over any trend of economic growth.

Surprisingly, only a few specialists in economics even write and speak about natural resources and their foundational role in economics. The connection between the two forms a very small part of the current science of economics. For example, from 1969 to 2007, articles about "Agricultural and Natural Resource Economics; Environmental and Ecological Economics" hovered steadily around 7% of all economics articles published in academic journals; on the other hand, by the end of this period, articles on "Financial Economics" or "Economic Development, Technological Change, and Growth" together made up 22% of all economics articles — nearly three times the percentage.[345]

Of course, economists cannot avoid references to finite products of the natural world, such as cotton, wood, and the like. But, by referring to any and all resources — whether directly from nature or synthesized from nature — as *goods*, an abstract term that brings to mind something anyone can pick up in a shop, it's possible to sidestep what would otherwise be an obvious limitation on the ability of any society to continuously produce more goods and services of greater value.

Was it always this way? No. For over 2,000 years, natural resources, often referred to collectively as "land" for short, were considered fundamental to economics, just as common sense would dictate. It's helpful to keep in mind that in 19th-century America, depopulated[*] land was abundant and seemed almost infinite. In 1862, the US government passed the Homestead Act, giving away 160 acres of land to any homesteader willing to pay a nominal sum and remain on the land for five years. That same year, the US government also began directly granting railroad corporations free land, eventually totaling 130 million acres. Because this land surrounded the new railroads, it soon became quite valuable.

It took some level of wealth to take advantage of either of these government programs, however, so many people remained landless and poor. In his 1879 book *Progress and Poverty*, Henry George, a journalist, advocated that since landowners didn't create their land, and since the value of their land depends on the surrounding community, they be required to pay a land value tax close to the amount of rent that would be derived from the unimproved land. His ideas became popular, threatening the wealth of large landowners such as the railroad tycoons.

To their rescue came college professor John Bates Clark, who opposed George vociferously. Clark argued that land (and other natural resources) are just one type of capital and have no special place in economics:

> Land, of course, has no cost value, since it is furnished by nature.
> —John Bates Clark, *The Distribution of Wealth: A Theory of Wages, Interest and Profit*[346]

A wealthy businessman, Columbia University's president, Seth Low, recruited Clark to become a professor of economics there. Businessmen were funding the formation of departments of economics in universities all over America, and those other professors fell under the sway of Clark's convenient ideas.[†] This influence that personally

---

[*]Regarding the previous population, see Charles C. Mann's book *1491*.
[†]When he was younger, John Bates Clark had been a proponent of the "Social Christian" school of socialism. The factors leading Clark's thinking to change over the course of his life are disputed among historians, and resolving them lies beyond the scope of this book.

motivated businessmen had over American economists also came to dominate the discipline of economics worldwide. In this way, "land" was practically banished from economics.[347]

This history of wealthy businesspeople controlling college professors provides a telling illustration of why, as we discussed in Chapter 6, it's best for people in the Field of Ideas to avoid becoming dependent on people in the Field of Resources. Additionally, knowing that the divorce of land from economics happened at a specific point in the not-too-distant past gives us hope for a solution: as we shall see, we can now correct this misstep.

After the shift away from discussing land as a key factor in economics, during the 20th century economists in the Field of Ideas — free from consideration of natural resources — taught that growth was always and everywhere the key to prosperity, thus compromising their integrity. Such theories of growth, growth, and more growth, with some occasional unwanted downturns, run the current economic policies of those in the Field of Government, and the practices of the stewards of nature — those in the Field of Resources. In short, the ego shade of *rajas* distorts the intelligence of those in the Fields of Resources and Government, who thus aim for unsustainable growth in their properties and possessions. And in turn, the people who work in the Field of Artistry are then urged to give up their natural contentment with expertise in their craft and told to shop, shop, and shop some more.[*]

---

[*]It may be argued that one consequence of the defeat of Henry George and banishment of land from economics has been a huge blind spot in the field of economics itself:

> a problem facing…neoclassical scholars more generally. That problem is the displacement of earlier, nineteenth-century preoccupations with illegitimate rent extraction, and the related absence of data tracking different forms of 'earned' versus 'unearned' income. Data in this case are not simply missing: they have never been of mainstream interest and never come into existence, thus remaining shadows of potential, unrealised research trajectories.
>
> —Linsey McGoey, *The elusive rentier rich: Piketty's data battles and the power of absent evidence*[348]

This blind spot is not just accidental, but self-reinforcing, as we also noted in Chapter 11:

> When value is determined by price (rather than vice versa), the level and distribution of income seem justified as long as there is a market for the goods and services which, when bought and sold, generate that income. All income, according to this logic, is earned income: gone is any analysis of activities in terms of whether they are productive or unproductive.

37.2 The Effects of Unsustainable Prosperity

What is particularly devastating is that any economy, regardless of theorizing, is based on finite natural resources. The urge towards eternal growth, therefore, induces humankind to push those natural resources beyond their limits. Artificial fertilizers are poured into the soil. Animals are filled with drugs and raised in horrific conditions, forcing quick and excessive weight gain to ready them for slaughter. Planes and boats use fossil fuel to ensure we have year-round what would normally be seasonal produce. We are forcing nature to grow and grow. What are the results?

British scientists have estimated that 180 million tons of nitrates from artificial fertilizers have accumulated in rock worldwide. They warn that these will inevitably seep into aquifers, causing blooms of algae and massive fish die-offs in lakes and rivers. The nitrates poisoning the water supply will cost billions of dollars per year in water treatment alone. Even if no new fertilizer were applied, the nitrates already there will persist for decades — as they call it, "the nitrate time bomb."[351]

Our treatment of animals induces another threat. Microbiologists say that if one wanted to design a system for cultivating antibiotic-resistant bacteria, one couldn't do better than a modern factory farm. The misuse of antibiotics has led to multi-drug-resistant "superbugs," for which modern medicine has few or no treatments. Melinda Wenner Moyer reported in a 2016 Scientific American article that scien-

---

> Yet this reasoning is circular, a closed loop. Incomes are justified by the production of something that is of value. But how do we measure value? By whether it earns income. You earn income because you are productive and you are productive because you earn income. So with a wave of a wand, the concept of *unearned income* vanishes. If income means that we are productive, and we deserve income whenever we are productive, how can income possibly be unearned?
> –Mariana Mazzucato, *The Value of Everything*[349]

> …the disappearance of the concept of value, this book argues, has paradoxically made it much easier for this crucial term 'value' — a concept that lies at the heart of economic thought — to be used and abused in whatever way one might find useful.
> –Mariana Mazzucato, *The Value of Everything*[350]

Thus the mixing of the Field of Ideas and the Field of Resources in the late 19th century that we described above, has continued to produce ramifications even in the 21st century.

tists have been unpleasantly surprised to find that antibiotic-resistant bacteria spread very quickly even to other farms where antibiotics are not used:

> Many researchers worry — and the new findings add fresh urgency to their concerns — that the abundant use of antibiotics on farms is unraveling our ability to cure bacterial infections....Stripped of the power of protective drugs, today's pedestrian health nuisances — ear infections, cuts, bronchitis — will become tomorrow's death sentences.
>
> —Melinda Wenner Moyer, *How Drug-Resistant Bacteria Travel From The Farm To Your Table*[352]

If our methods of production are unsustainable, then so are our methods of consumption. Transporting produce year-round to where it is out of season, along with the vast majority of people living away from farms, means that consumers in developed countries such as America are completely alienated from the process of how fruit and vegetables grow and ripen. Thus, such people become less aware of the value of food. According to a 2016 Guardian report, in the United States, 60 million tons of produce is thrown away each year at the retail and consumer levels — about one-third of all produce. If we also factor in food crops that are left unharvested in the field or left to rot in a warehouse, the total rises to nearly half of all produce:

> "There are a lot of people who are hungry and malnourished, including in the US. My guess is probably 5-10% of the population are still hungry — they still do not have enough to eat," said Shenggen Fan, the director general of the International Food Policy Research Institute in Washington. "That is why food waste, food loss, matters a great deal. People are still hungry." That is not counting the waste of water, land and other resources, or the toll on the climate of producing food that ends up in landfill. Within the US, discarded food is the biggest single component of landfill and incinerators, according to the Environmental Protection Agency. Food dumps are a rising source of methane, a far more powerful greenhouse gas than carbon dioxide.
>
> —Suzanne Goldenberg, *Half of all US food produce is thrown away, new research suggests*[353]

"In my mind, the desire for perfect produce came about in the 1940s as housewives adapted to widespread refrigeration and new CPG [consumer packaged goods] products," Eve Turow Paul, the author of A Taste of Generation Yum, writes in an email. "Suddenly, you could get a pineapple in Chicago in January. Wonderbread hit shelves a decade before. Perfection and manicured foods came to represent safety and new technology."
> –Adam Chandler, *Why Americans Lead The World In Food Waste*[354]

It's not just soil, plants, and animals that are forced to produce beyond the limits of nature. Economic models of growth, growth, growth divorced from a foundation of natural resources also force people beyond their limits. Better technology has not led to an increase in our leisure time; in fact US workers work more and more hours a week. Children see their parents less. And working adults are stressed:

In the last twenty years the amount of time Americans have spent at their jobs has risen steadily. Each year the change is…about nine hours.…[and] the accumulated increase over two decades is substantial.…[T]he rise of work…has affected the great majority of working Americans. Hours have risen for men as well as women, for those in the working class as well as professionals. They have grown for all marital statuses and income groups. The increase also spans a wide range of industries.…Nationwide, people report their leisure time has declined by as much as one third since the early 1970s. Predictably, they are spending less time on the basics, like sleeping and eating. Parents are devoting less attention to their children. Stress is on the rise.
> –Juliet Schor, *The Overworked American*[355]

Work-related technology can also contaminate leisure time and enjoyment. Ask anyone who has heard the buzz of a Blackberry during Saturday brunch. While it's theoretically very convenient to be able to instruct a San Francisco employee from Saturday brunch in Boston,

> being constantly "on-call" can pollute leisure time, according to [Ken] Roberts [a sociology professor at the University of Liverpool]. "You can feel that your time is never entirely your own. It's very difficult to switch off."
>
> –Taylor Gandossy, *Technology transforming the leisure world*[356]

As Schor puts it, the encroachment of work into leisure time is not what we expected from the rise of technology:

> Since 1948…[t]he level of productivity of the US worker has more than doubled. In other words, we could now produce our 1948 standard of living (measured in terms of marketed goods and services) in less than half the time it took in that year. We actually could have chosen the four-hour day. Or a working year of six months. Or, *every worker in the United States could now be taking every other year off from work — with pay.* Incredible as it may sound, this is just the simple arithmetic of productivity growth in operation.
>
> –Juliet Schor, *The Overworked American*[357]

So, we could have expected that better technology would mean that each worker would work fewer hours while maintaining the same standard of living. The main reason such a situation has not occurred, however, is that it runs completely counter to the growth mentality. Employers prefer instead to have fewer workers, each working for long hours, because then there will always be enough unemployed people in the population that the employers can say, "There are plenty of other people waiting for this job if you don't like it." When each worker in a firm is working long hours, it appears that the firm itself is firing on all cylinders and thus on a path to growth. Therefore, while some few people can have prosperity with less work, increasingly, Americans are finding they must work longer hours or more than one job.

The workers are also the consumers who purchase more and more goods and services, enabling firms to grow. Over the course of the 20th century, firms perfected the art of "manufacturing needs" through advertising. As we referred to in Chapter 11, this practice does not quite meet the definition of honest work. Having all the workers work long hours also has a side benefit for firms of forcing services to become commodities. Because everyone in the community works long hours, people no longer have time to help each other out on a friendly, neighborly basis, e.g., with child care or elder care. So people buy these services, provided by firms instead, and people then work even longer hours to make the money to do so. Through this vicious cycle, workers are locked onto a treadmill.

Such forcing of humans beyond their natural limits has psychological effects:

> Ever since the 1930s, young people in America have reported feeling increasingly anxious and depressed. And no one knows exactly why.
> —Jesse Singal, *For 80 Years, Young Americans Have Been Getting More Anxious and Depressed, and No One Is Quite Sure Why*[358]

> ...the age-adjusted suicide rate in the United States jumped 24 percent between 1999 and 2014, from 10.5 per 100,000 people to 13 per 100,000 people. The rate increased for both sexes and in all age groups from 10 to 74....Among white women ages 45 to 64, for example, the suicide rate jumped 80 percent.
> —Dan Keating & Lenny Bernstein, *US suicide rate has risen sharply in the 21st century*[359]

Why would economists, politicians, and businesspeople continue to push the very model that is destroying our planetary home and our very minds and bodies? For the answer, we turn again to the late 19th century, to British economist and skilled mathematician Alfred Marshall, who set out to introduce the use of mathematics into economics. Mathematics is the application of logic to the study of patterns, and thus is very powerful. Marshall knew very well that the foundation of economics was biology. It would then follow that the math needed for economics would be a special case of mathematical biology. But mathematical biology was in its infancy, whereas the math for physics was well-developed. So he borrowed mathematical models from physics — the kind of mathematics needed to prove a bridge would stay intact — and applied it to economics. To make such an application, his model had to treat people and other beings in nature like machines. Marshall hoped this situation would be temporary, and urged those who followed him to understand biological models, burning those mathematical models that were not in accordance with life. Instead, the field of economics during the first half of the 20th century did the opposite, expunging any trace of biology and building a more and more involved edifice of interlocking mathematical models treating people as automata and nature as inert and impossible to affect.

37.3 Towards an Ecosociological Model

Instead, we need an ecological and organic view of how beings with their own interests fulfill their material needs — ecosociology proposes that math can be used to establish an organic model. After all, if the basis of prosperity and economics is organic natural and human resources, then math that describes those resources would be perfectly suited to describe such a system of understanding. In more than a century since Marshall, the mathematics of ecology has already been developed extensively. And in the 21st century, the mathematics of social networks has been as well.

Ecosociology studies how populations of beings with their own interests interact with one another, treating human and non-human beings in an integrated way within one system:

> A more encompassing definition of sustainability would be in terms of an ecosystem being able to maintain its processes, functions, and biological diversity in the long term, with human interactions being seen as an *integral part of* that ecosystem....By taking a more ecocentric view and embracing an ecosociology that uses the language and metaphors of dynamic, open, interrelated systems, integrating biological embodiment and environmental embedment [situation in the environment], and extending the social to include the non-human, then true sustainability might arise almost as a side effect — an emergent property of a viably functioning ecosystem of which humans are...still a part.
> —Paul Stevens, *Towards an Ecosociology*[360]

Ecology is the study of the interrelationship of species with each other and with their environments. Sociology is the study of the development, structure, and functioning of human society. Ecosociology extends ecology to include the human. Mathematical ecosociology brings the power of mathematical modeling to bear on complex adaptive systems that include both humans and other beings.[*]

An important practice of mathematical ecosociology is to consistently communicate limitations in the scope of mathematical models, along with their intended use. Indeed, applied mathematicians and statisticians in general bear this responsibility.[362][363] As the statistician George Box wrote:

> All models are wrong but some are useful.
> –G. E. P. Box, *Robustness in the Strategy of Scientific Model Building*[364]

Mathematical models, like prescription drugs, need to come with instructions and contraindications (an explanation as to under what circumstances not to use them), and to be used in appropriate doses. People's misuse of mathematical models can have significant real-world consequences. Mathematicians have a habit of using regular English words and phrases to label mathematical concepts with new, technical definitions that have very little to do with their commonplace meaning. (Interested readers can try looking up the definition of a "simple group," for instance.) While such labels can be handy in pure mathematics, this habit poses a significant danger of misunderstanding and miscommunication in mathematical modeling.[†]

---

[*]Ruchira's previous work in noncooperative game theory allows the modeling of cooperation and competition at different levels within one system. This work defines within the framework of noncooperative game theory what it means to have a group with its own interests, distinct from those of its members, who may have any combination of shared and competing interests among one another. Ruchira is working on extending and incorporating this research into the new discipline of mathematical ecosociology.

In 2013, the International Integrated Reporting Council published a new framework for business accounting, involving six capitals: financial capital, manufactured capital, intellectual capital, human capital, social and relationship capital, and natural capital. Accounting for all six would be a big step towards surfacing hidden costs in one capital from measures that apparently save another.[361] However, mathematical ecosociology goes further, in that non-human beings are considered as agents with their own needs, rather than exclusively as "capital" belonging to some person, group, or organization.

[†]An example is the definition of "rationality" in noncooperative game theory. In an endnote to Chapter 32 we noted that the concept of "superrationality" alleviates the apparent paradox posed by the Prisoner's Dilemma. This concept was defined decades later and is still much less well-known than the game-theoretic concept of "rationality." The power of the positive connotation of the word "rationality" has outweighed the fact that it was chosen out of convenience and without due consideration of either such connotations and their likely impact, or what would actually constitute "rationality" at a

So another practice of mathematical ecosociologists is to choose jargon wisely, sparingly, and in collaboration with colleagues in other disciplines of ecosociology, to communicate clearly rather than confusingly.

To understand what kind of mathematical models would be applicable, we can consider that the mathematics used to model infectious disease across social networks can already handle all kinds of contagion in one framework. Therefore, such a model can be used for both the positive and negative ways in which humans spread behavior, ideas, and economic systems. For example, because humans communicate through language, social contagion (the spreading of ideas and behaviors among individuals connected in any number of ways), networking, and synergy is much greater between human beings than other beings. Mathematical ecosociology can apply this framework to analyze the problems in the current system. For example, the mathematical model can show how desires for "manufactured needs" spreads through a population of consumers, and reciprocally through a population of investors in firms, fueling speculative bubbles. In the perspective of this book, this is the way that the ego shade of *rajas* spreads through large parts of society. When the forced growth fueled in this way runs into the limitations of reality, then in turn these bubbles burst, leading to recession or even depression. This then means that the ego shade of *tamas* spreads through large parts of society. Firms and individuals under relentless pressure to grow will ultimately stop cherishing the sources of wealth and the fields of work, and finally face the consequences. These cycles of boom and bust continue repeatedly.

To create a sustainable economy, the organic mathematical model can map how ecosystems undergo cycles in response to natural variations such as times of day or seasons of the year, rather than volatile cycles based on speculation. With mathematical ecosociology treating humans as part of ecosystems, we will have a template for more stable fulfillment of human biological needs with less volatility, just as we see in healthy ecosystems without humans. This approach is one key ingredient of sustainable prosperity.

---

philosophical or practical level. As we noted there, the game-theoretic concept does not even subsume important aspects of the rationality of a well-raised eight-year-old child. (On the other hand, the game-theoretic concept is intractable even for high-powered computers, so its scope of applicability is doubly limited.[365])

A sustainable system of prosperity does not rule out all kinds of growth. As we explained in Chapter 4, especially people in the Field of Resources seek quantitative increase in some benefit. The kind of forced growth we have been talking about is in very crude and ultimately inaccurate measures of "benefit," namely, total output of goods and services. Mathematical ecosociology will use the tools of ecology and sociology to create more useful measures of increasing real benefit. For instance, ecologists have long studied the ways in which diversity can lead to resilience. People in the Field of Resources can seek to grow the diversity of their networks, including the number of different *kinds* of people and other creatures their enterprise interacts with, such as suppliers, employees, or customers.

Creatures, you may ask? Yes! For example, Birdsong Orchards (an organic farm in the US) includes a variety of flower and fruit trees (suppliers), goats, alpacas, and a llama (employees), and attracts a variety of birds (customers), forming a vibrant ecosystem. Of course humans are also involved in all these roles.[366] We are thinking about these organizations in a very broad sense.

Whether on a personal or on a corporate level, many of us feel the drive to increase our personal assets in order to feel secure against some unforeseen emergency. Both theoretically and practically, though, diversity provides a better hedge against risks than the growth of some single kind of capital. People in the Field of Resources can also seek to grow their resiliency through their capacity to deal with emergencies. For example, they can have more employees work fewer hours each. People in the Field of Resources as well as people in the Field of Artistry can also seek to increase the extent to which their regular interactions are win-win, or the number of different ways their interactions with a particular partner (a supplier, employee, or customer) are win-win. They can follow the goods they provide deeper into their life cycle, accounting for the hidden costs to any person, organization, creature, or population of sourcing raw materials or disposing of waste associated with their product. Reducing all these costs is another kind of benefit. All of these are different ways of cherishing the sources of wealth. While it might seem that the accounting would become complex, mathematical ecosociology will provide the computational tools to handle this complexity. People in the Field of Ideas will develop and teach these tools, and people in the Field of Government will promulgate standards and policies incorporating them. And, as we discussed in Chapter 11, a society that aims towards the spiritual can experience ever-expanding inner growth both individually and collectively.

As more people and enterprises increase more of these real measures of benefit, society as a whole will approach a steady-state, regenerative economy, the platform for sustained prosperity. Working together, people in all four fields will come up with ingenious ways to continue to increase these real measures of benefit, while keeping the economy sustainable and regenerative.

When we as individuals work in harmony with the principles of ancient wisdom we have explained, then our optimum self is expressed through our work and as a whole we experience satisfaction and fulfillment. The relation between satisfaction versus stress and its effects on health on the cellular level is well-established. So when such a major part of our life is running smoothly, the cells of our body also function more healthily. Similarly, when we collectively work according to the principles of the natural art of work, the economy that emerges is a healthy, natural functioning of the universal body. We stand in relation to the universal body as our cells stand in relation to our own bodies. Thus, part of our service to the Source is working together in such a way that the economy/ecosystem functions smoothly, naturally, and healthily, rather than being impeded by any of the shades of ego.

Chapter 38

Additional Thoughts: Case Study of a Mathematical Ecosociology Approach

In order to better understand mathematical ecosociology, we will present the concept of *ahimsa* milk, relating it also to society at large. Sometimes we'll discuss *ahimsa* milk in particular, and sometimes we'll discuss greater issues of mathematical ecosociology that apply to *ahimsa* milk.

Ahimsa generally means non-aggression.[*] *Ahimsa* milk is defined as milk produced without killing at any stage of dairy production (e.g., of bulls, or of cows who no longer produce milk), and without separating calves from their mother cows at birth.[†] In the US, for instance, small *ahimsa* dairies have existed for at least half a century, and the cows, bulls, and calves at these dairies are treated with as much affection and respect as people more commonly treat horses. Mathematical modeling can help with managing these dairies so that they remain steadily self-sustaining across generations, integrate with crop production, and scale to meet the needs of a larger community such as a village, town, or city. What distinguishes mathematical ecosociology from some other ecologically aware approaches is that the needs of the cows, the crops, the wildlife such as birds and insects, and so

---

[*] Readers familiar with yoga philosophy may know that *ahimsa* is the first of the five *yamas*, or abstentions, that form the first step of the eightfold yoga path[367]. The *Bhagavadgita* also lists *ahimsa* as an element of bodily self-discipline.[368]

[†] Also, *ahimsa* dairies generally don't euthanize animals who are ill. Some take the definition further, barring mechanization of various processes.

forth are taken into account in their own right, rather than primarily or exclusively deriving their value from services they provide to humans.

In the next section, we explain some benefits of *ahimsa* dairy farming. In the later section "Objections to the Concept of Ahimsa Milk," we address some possible objections that may arise against the whole concept of *ahimsa* milk.[*]

38.1 Integrating Ahimsa Milk into an Ecosystem

Ahimsa milk has several beneficial aspects. First and foremost, this approach to dairy farming treats the animals with respect and care in a way that follows the natural art of work. We described in Chapter 21 our responsibilities to cherish those who work under us, and those responsibilities extend to non-human beings such as bulls and oxen just as much as to human beings. But beyond this, there are a host of advantages for society at large, some of which can more clearly be discerned through the use of mathematical ecosociology. While we cannot outline all of these, we shall give just a few examples of the ways in which this method of modeling, when applied to just one relatively limited case study, can open us to a host of benefits across our society.[†]

Replenishing the soil

One beneficial aspect of *ahimsa* milk is the effect it can have on the health of the soil. Cattle can play a crucial role in replenishing the topsoil. Under rotational grazing, herders have cows graze some pastures intensely for periods of time, while leaving other pastures to recover over longer periods. In *Growing A Revolution*, David R. Montgomery describes the effects of rotational grazing on Neil Dennis's farm in Canada:

> Dennis was born and raised on the ranch his great-grandfather homesteaded. Much of his sixty-six years have been spent watching the soil degrade as conventional practices drove him broke....

---

[*]Those who find such objections coming to mind already, may want to read that section first, before returning here.

[†]Some of the benefits outlined here are not unique to *ahimsa* dairies and can apply across other types of farming. However, the choice of *ahimsa* milk reflects the values set out in this book, and the method can easily and naturally adopt the beneficial practices described here.

Dennis's wife, Barbara, hatched a plan to save the farm after she got a flyer in the mail about a course on holistic resource management, which involved rotational grazing methods....Dennis went home and did what the instructor said, determined to prove him wrong....He was surprised to find that by the next year the plant density on the paddock with the higher stocking density had increased. By the second year, it produced enough grass to graze twice as many cows.

As his pastures kept improving, he kept experimenting, increasing both his stocking density and the rest interval between grazing. By this time he started to realize that maybe the guy was right....

Frequent paddock rotation at higher stocking density also altered the grazing behavior of his cows. When they wandered a large paddock, they were more selective about what they ate, seeking out their favorite forage before chowing down. This left the less desirable plants in the field to set seed. In contrast, when cattle grazed in denser numbers, they were not selective about what they ate, grabbing all they could reach before their neighbor did....In the paddocks this helped eliminate weeds and less desirable forage. And when everything got grazed, the nutritious native prairie species bounced back faster.

The key conceptual change was the combination of short-duration, intense grazing followed by a long recovery time. Doing this, the native prairie came back on its own and grew better in dry years than in the wet ones. The trampling action at the higher stock densities created natural mulch on the soil surface, which helped keep soil moisture in place and foster regrowth. The longer Dennis followed this grazing system, the better his grass grew....

As Dennis's soil improved, the sugar and protein content of his grass increased. The better nutritional profile also saved him money. He reduced the amount of mineral supplements by 90 percent and cut his salt use in half. And so what was a vicious cycle became a virtuous one. As the soil regeneration continues, the higher sugar content grass pumps out more carbon-rich exudates [substances that ooze out, in this case from the roots] when grazed, which feeds more soil microbes that help grow more biomass. Over several decades, the carbon content of his soil rose from less than 2 percent to 6 percent, and he says some fields are now up to 10 percent. It seems that Dennis has brought his soil back to its native carbon content, as scientists in the 1890s reported organic matter contents of 5 to 11 percent for Canadian prairie soils. He says his molehills used to be gray — now they're coming up black. And he doesn't get any runoff anymore. The ground absorbs all the rain that falls onto his fields, even in big storms. He told me his fields now infiltrate as much as sixteen inches an hour, whereas his neighbors can absorb less than an inch an hour.

...Dennis has seen life come back to the ranch since he walked away from conventional practices. "We've got more birds and wildlife than ever," he said as a squadron of butterflies danced before us. Rotational grazing has opened up grassland beneath the trees in his forest patches, making overwintering habitat for deer. A lot more hawks visit and a fox even follows his cows around to clean up trampled snakes.

–David R. Montgomery, *Growing A Revolution: Bringing Our Soil Back To Life*[369]

Note that Dennis was grazing *non-milking* cattle. Milking cows do need to be selective about what they eat for proper nutrition to support lactation. However, an *ahimsa* dairy herd does include many other cattle besides the milking cows, including bulls and retired cows. Indeed, the milking cows form only a small proportion of the herd.[*] Therefore, much of what Dennis learned can apply to *ahimsa* dairies.

The increased fertility of Dennis's farm resulted from complex ecological interactions between the soil, the grass, the cattle, and herding practices. Mathematical ecosociology can be used to model such interactions to try to predict the effects of planned or unplanned changes, such as choice of cover crops for forage and soil fertility, changes in annual rainfall, or changes in availability of herders. As more data from *ahimsa* milk farms becomes available, mathematical

---

[*]We give a concrete picture of what *ahimsa* herd composition looks like, both initially and once the herd has stabilized, in the section "Objections Due To Population Conservation."

434

ecosociology can assess impacts of earlier practices on the health and quality of life of cows at later stages of the life cycle and post-retirement, as well as on bulls, steers, and oxen.

Integrating with polyculture

Monoculture, which is the practice of cultivating vast fields of a single crop and nothing else, has given rise to several unintended consequences. To name a few, monoculture generally requires massive applications of herbicides and insecticides, and any disease can spread easily among the neighboring plants, to devastating effect. By contrast, polyculture farms crops of multiple species in the same place at the same time, forming an ecosystem. By taking advantage of new developments, mathematical ecosociology can support polyculture, into which *ahimsa* dairy can also be integrated. The ecosystem includes creatures such as bees, birds, lizards, and butterflies; large animals such as dairy cows play key roles in whatever ecosystem they participate in.

In 2003, philosopher Mark Sagoff wrote in "The plaza and the pendulum: Two concepts of ecological science:"

> Last summer, I walked through the Luxembourg Gardens [in Paris] on a fine June day. The complexity and diversity of activity in that plaza reminded me of phenomena ecologists study. Competition, often important in natural communities, could be observed in the boisterous contests at the tennis courts and — next to them — in the quiet concentration at the chess tables. Tourists wary of pickpockets resembled prey alert to predators. Concepts ecologists use — such as "disturbance," "density-dependence," and "patch dynamics" — might describe the motions of people as they swirl and eddy in crowds about hawkers of trinkets, food vendors, street singers, and shops. The "discordant harmonies" (Botkin 1990) that attract ecologists to the places they investigate — savannas, forests, lakes, estuaries — may likewise attract tourists to places like the Luxembourg Gardens that similarly reflect free beauty and constrained variety.

> If you walk up residential streets a few minutes from the Luxembourg Gardens, as I did, you can visit the Pantheon, where in 1851, Jean Bernard Foucault hung a pendulum from the dome to demonstrate the rotation of the earth. A similar pendulum today metes out the hours by swinging straight back and forth as the floor — and the earth — rotate beneath it. Someone uninformed of the diurnal rotation of the earth and of the Newtonian principle of inertia might not discern the pattern but attribute the elliptical vagaries of the pendulum to contingent, historical, or haphazard events. We know that inertial forces that govern the largest phenomena also shape the behavior of smaller systems such as the path of a Foucault's pendulum. Mathematicians can model the motion of the pendulum, predict its behavior, and make its patterns intelligible and explicit.
>
> ...How can one tell whether the ecological goings-on in a lake, forest, or estuary exhibit the kinds of patterns or processes that warrant a theoretical top-down mathematical approach as contrasted with a case-based bottom-up inquiry?
>
> —Mark Sagoff, *The plaza and the pendulum: Two concepts of ecological science*[370]

Though Sagoff has described a dichotomy, new developments in the 21st century have taken mathematical modeling beyond "theoretical top-down approaches" so that it can make "patterns intelligible and explicit" even in complex systems of "free beauty and constrained variety." With computational models of stochastic (i.e., not entirely predictable, even in theory) processes, mathematics can help us perceive the patterns in the plaza. For instance, we can use a special technique, Approximate Bayesian Computation, to fit complex stochastic models to complex multi-dimensional data.[371]

These modern mathematical methods can help support polyculture farming of crops. Recall the diverse ecosystem described on Dennis's ranch. Polyculture extends such an ecosystem to crops. Charles Mann described one example of polyculture:

> [In ancient Mexico] maize became the center of an innovative agricultural system called the *milpa*. The term comes from the Aztec term for "maize field" but a *milpa*

itself is considerably more complex: it is a field, usually but not always recently cleared, in which maize, beans, squash, and other crops are grown at the same time. The diversity makes the *milpa* look untidy, but it has important ecological implications. Typical single-crop regimes, much less diverse than natural ecosystems, tend over time to exhaust the soil. In Europe and Asia, farmers try to avoid these difficulties by crop rotation; they plant wheat one year, for example, legumes the next, and let the field lie fallow in the year following. In a *milpa*, by contrast, prehispanic peoples planted a dozen or more crops simultaneously; multiple varieties of squash, bean, melon, tomatoes, chilis, sweet potato, jicama (a tuber), amaranth (a grain-like plant) and mucuna (a tropical legume) among them. "There are places in Mesoamerica that have been continuously cultivated for four thousand years and are still productive," says H. Garrison Wilkes, a maize researcher at the University of Massachusetts in Boston. "The *milpa* is the only system that would permit that kind of long-term use."

Maize and beans are agriculturally and nutritionally complementary. In the field, tall maize plants create a ladder for bean runners to climb; below ground, the beans' nitrogen-fixing roots provide nutrients needed by maize plants. As a food, maize lacks the essential amino acids lysine and tryptophan....Beans have both lysine and tryptophan, but lack the amino acids cysteine and methionine, which are provided by maize. As a result, beans and maize make a nutritionally complete meal; supplemented by avocado, the highest-calorie fruit, the meal is also incredibly filling.

–Charles Mann, *Diversity on the Farm*[372]

Also, Wes Jackson explains in *Becoming Native To This Place* how polyculture crops are more naturally resistant to disease and pests:

The prairie...counted on species diversity and genetic diversity within species, to avoid epidemics of insects and pathogens. The prairie maintains its own fertility, runs on sunlight, and actually accumulates ecological capital – accumulates soil. Observing this years ago I formulated a question: Is it possible to build an agriculture based on the prairie as standard or model? I saw a sharp contrast between the major features of the wheat field and the major features of the prairie. The wheat field features annuals in monoculture; the prairie features perennials in polyculture, or mixtures....Can perennialism and high yield go together? If so, can a polyculture of perennials outyield a monoculture of perennials? Can such an ecosystem sponsor its own fertility? Is it realistic to think we can manage such complexity adequately to avoid the problem of pests outcompeting us? At The Land Institute we have confronted these four key questions and have devoted all our research to answering them.

 –Wes Jackson, *Becoming Native To This Place*[373]

Subsequently Jackson quotes botanist Sir Albert Howard's foundational organic farming text, *An Agricultural Testament*, on the benefits of mixed farming:

Howard thought we should farm as the forest does for nature constitutes the "supreme farmers:" "The main characteristic of Nature's farming can therefore be summed up in a few words. Mother earth never attempts to farm without live stock; she always raises mixed crops; great pains are taken to preserve the soil and to prevent erosion; the mixed vegetable and animal wastes are converted into humus; there is no waste; the processes of growth and the processes of decay balance one another; ample provision is made to maintain large reserves of fertility; the greatest care is taken to store the rainfall; both plants and animals are left to protect themselves against disease."

 –Wes Jackson, *Becoming Native To This Place*[374]

Howard had derived his principles from his observations of traditional farming practices during his decades spent in India, where *ahimsa* farming had been ubiquitous.

A mathematical ecosociological approach would seek to integrate polyculture, to improve resiliency and consider the ecosystem holistically. In general, mathematical ecosociology aims to integrate models of different aspects of social and/or ecological systems, and different scales.[n] *Ahimsa* farming would naturally fit into the same approach.

Including cities and suburbs

An advantage of the holistic resource management practices described above is the potential for them to play some part in urban permaculture: sustainably producing some food on the outskirts of the city. Intensely grazing limited areas of land only for short periods means that some of these areas can be interspersed within urban and suburban environments, while the main base of the cows grazing these areas lies in the hinterlands of a town. These temporary paddocks may be part of reserved green space, which has many benefits for city-dwellers.[375] Manure and fertile topsoil can support urban community gardens and food forests. In 1826, Johann Heinrich von Thünen visualized a disc-like city ringed by a zone of intensive agriculture, such as dairies, orchards, and market gardens, ringed by another zone of extensive agriculture, such as grain, ringed by a zone for non-dairy livestock.[376] While his vision was a useful thought experiment in terms of shortening paths that need to be traveled more often, mathematical ecosociology can deal with more complexity, such as patches of green space interspersed within the city and used only occasionally. In this way, models of the dairy can interface with models of the human denizens of the city, in a multiscale modeling approach.

We feel it's important to note that scaling to meet the needs of a larger community of people near the farm does not necessarily entail making individual farms larger or more uniform. In the past, mathematical modeling tended to require uniform conditions. Allowing too much variation quickly became intractable. However, today's computational power, and the tools that go with it, can accommodate much more variability. Models can adapt to local conditions, rather than requiring extensive landscaping of locales to fit models.

Integrating food production, including *ahimsa* milk and polyculture crops, through small-scale operations throughout urban and suburban environments has multiple benefits. The most obvious benefit is a more resilient food supply. Another benefit is that how food is made will be more visible to everyone, not just those directly involved. Greater connection with this process can lead to more mindful consumption, better health, and less food waste. This sense of connection ties in with the benefits of sacred ceremony described in Chapter 17 and Chapter 19. Those who wish to can join such sacred ceremonies at many different points in the food production process, culminating in food festivals that all these people can participate in.

38.2   Objections to the Concept of Ahimsa Milk

These are just a few of the ways that mathematical modeling can work in conjunction with *ahimsa* milk. However, we also want to consider some of the possible arguments against the concept of *ahimsa* milk. Such arguments may come from concerns about animal rights, population conservation, or other environmental concerns. As mathematical ecosociology embraces all these areas of concern, it's important that we consider each of these arguments carefully.

Objections due to animal rights

From an animal rights perspective, there are those who question whether it can ever be moral to milk cows, and instead consider completely segregating bovine needs from human ones to be the only ethical practice.

To truly account for the needs of the cows in their own right, the first question we need to answer is whether to milk cows at all. What if we instead released all cows to roam over wild rangelands, and gradually turn feral? If that's a possibility, we would need to compare that scenario and its impact on all concerned — the cows, humans, and other wildlife and vegetation — with the *ahimsa* milk farm. A similar question could be asked about other animals that humans have domesticated, such as dogs, cats, horses, camels, chickens, pigs, goats, and sheep. Longstanding feral or wild populations of dogs[*], cats[†], horses[‡], camels[§], chickens[◇], pigs[¶], and goats[☆] exist. Feral populations of sheep can survive well if they are hair sheep

---

[*]Feral dogs roam many parts of the Americas, Europe, Australia, and Africa.[377]

[†]Many cat populations in Southern Europe may be considered feral or semi-feral, depending on how friendly they are towards humans.[378]

[‡]Feral horses roam large areas of the United States and Canada.[379]

[§]A large number of feral camels roam Australia.[380]

[◇]There are feral chickens in, for instance, Fitzgerald, Georgia, USA.[381]

[¶]Feral pigs are abundant in the United States.[382]

[☆]Numerous feral goat populations exist.[383]

(sheep not bred to produce excess wool)[*] or on certain islands[†]. That said, *ahimsa* wool, the ecological impacts of feral animals in general, and variations among breeds of these other animals are beyond the scope of this chapter (though within the purview of mathematical ecosociology). So what about cows?

There are feral populations of cows we can study. For instance, for more than thirty years, cattle from nearby ranches would break into Chino Hills State Park in California, and some would go feral.[387] However, after searching extensively, we could not find any feral populations of cattle worldwide that originate from dairy breeds. So, as the non-dairy breeds are outside the scope of this chapter, feral cows are not relevant for our purposes.

Is it necessary to milk dairy cows? In order to answer that question, let's look at the arithmetic of milk production.

The amount of milk that a calf needs to drink per day grows with its own weight and the amount of weight it gains per day. A daily gain of 800 g/day is on the high end for a dairy calf.[‡] Like human babies, calves drink milk exclusively only up to a certain age, when their digestive systems have developed. A weight of 75 kg is on the high end for a dairy calf still drinking only milk. The daily milk requirement of a calf can be found from the formula

$$R = 0.1M^{0.75} + (0.84M^{0.355})(G^{1.2})$$

where R is the milk requirement in Mcal per day, M is the calf's mass in kg, and G is the calf's rate of growth in kg per day.[388] Substituting $M = 75$ and $G = 0.8$, we get $R = 5.525$, i.e., a calf drinks at most 5.525 Mcal or 5525 kcal of milk per day. Whole milk contains about 149 kcal per 244 g serving,[389] which equates to 610 kcal per kg. So a calf needs to drink at most 5525 kcal/(610 kcal/kg)=9.06 kg of milk per day.

On the other hand, Swiss dairy cows managed according to organic practices[§] produce an average of more than 25 kg of milk per day.[390] These cows were likely being milked at the standard frequency, twice daily. A New Zealand study found that milking only

---

[*]E.g., a feral population of Texan Barbados sheep, also known as Barbados Blackbelly sheep, lived in the Sierra foothills in California for more than ten years.[384]

[†]E.g., feral sheep have long been established on Soay, an island off the coast of Scotland,[385] and in New Zealand.[386]

[‡]We exclude veal calves that are being fattened up for slaughter.

[§]Organic production prohibits the use of bovine growth hormones to stimulate milk production, as well as various other practices.

once daily would reduce total milk production by up to 32%, depending on the breed.[391] That would still result in dairy cows giving an average of 17.4 kg of milk per day, 93% more than even a large calf needs.

What happens if a cow is not milked every day? Many a small-scale dairy farmer who needed to miss a milking because of some unavoidable personal emergency can tell us: the cow's udder becomes swollen and painful, causing the cow a lot of discomfort. This can lead to mastitis, inflammation of the udder:

> Concerns over udder health when decreasing milking frequency are valid, but research indicates that if udder health is good and somatic cell counts are low, the once-a-day milking does not increase the occurrence of mastitis. If, however, animals have elevated SCC and decreased udder health, then decreasing milking frequency can increase the occurrence of mastitis. Given that one of the most effective treatments for mastitis is increasing the milking frequency — to keep the udder emptied of milk and bacteria — this is a logical conclusion.
>
> –Gnianaclis Caldwell, *The Small-Scale Dairy: The Complete Guide to Milk Production for the Home and Market*[392]

Such small-scale dairy farmers also report that cows remain annoyed with their humans about a missed milking for quite some time afterward. Cows, like smaller pets, have ways of communicating their feelings and can be quite vocal about them. So dairy farming is a serious responsibility, requiring steady, diligent work even during the heat of summer or in the cold of winter. Therefore, letting dairy cows go feral without milking them is likely to result in much disease and suffering for the herd.[*]

The argument may then be raised that these cows were bred to give excessive milk, which wouldn't have happened if cows hadn't been domesticated. Given that, as we shall see, *ahimsa* milk farms require restraint of breeding anyway, a question that may be asked is whether to keep the currently existing dairy cows on sanctuaries without breeding them, leading to the eventual extinction of these

---

[*]Regularity of milking is only one factor needed to keep cows and their udders healthy. Others include keeping everything clean and keeping the hands of the milkers smooth and without callouses.

subspecies once the current generation passes away.[*] However, mathematical ecosociology takes into account the interests not only of individual organisms, but also of populations. While extinctions may naturally happen in various times and places due to local dynamics, to advocate any specific extinction goes against the orientation of mathematical ecosociology. The trivial equilibrium of any set of interacting populations is for all of them to vanish. The role of mathematical ecosociology is to find and characterize other, more dynamic solutions.

Objections due to population conservation

So, mathematical ecosociology accepts that dairy cows continue to live and breed, and the fact that dairy cows need to be milked implies that humans need to be involved on a daily basis. Therefore, dairy cow habitats need to overlap with human habitats. However, an objection may arise that the dairy cow population would increase because of *ahimsa* practices. Because many human activities are incompatible with dairy cows, the dairy cow habitat would thus need to *extend* the human habitat. From the point of view of population conservation, however, many other species are already threatened by the spread of the human habitat all over the planet. So problems would arise, for humans as well as other species. To solve this problem, it might be thought that slaughter is necessary in order to control the dairy cow population.

To put it another way, any ecosystem has a limit to how many large ungulates (hooved mammals) it can support, and we want to leave room for other wild animals too. So sound stewardship entails restricting the movement of dairy cattle within a limited amount of land at any given time. Such a bounded space has a specific carrying capacity.

Is there an *ahimsa* way — without slaughter — to ensure that our population of dairy cattle remains within the limits that the available land can support? Fortunately, there is. We can use measures of the

---

[*]The moral philosopher Neil Levy wrote a thoughtful essay questioning why some people feel more sanguine about this kind of extinction than that of, say, pandas or wolves. He did not consider non-dairy cows going feral, however.[393]

Some *ahimsa* dairies have reported anecdotally that some cows gave milk without having calves or being pregnant, when the herders noticed that their udders were distended. However, in such instances those cows were around other cows and their calves, so that doesn't mean this kind of lactation would happen in sanctuaries with no calves present. Humans also sometimes lactate for babies they didn't give birth to.[394][395]

natural cow life cycle to simulate how the population of our farm will vary over time, depending on how often we breed the cows. Our aim is to reach a target steady-state population that is within the available capacity. This steady-state population includes a variety of dairy cattle: milch cows (milking cows) and their suckling calves; heifers (adolescent or adult cows that have never been pregnant) and bull calves; bulls, steers, and oxen; cows that are resting between lactations; and cows that are retired from milking. From the simulations we can see how, starting from a few cattle (e.g., a bull, a milking cow, and a calf), the herd would expand to include all these different demographics. We can restrict breeding to a frequency that both supports the individual health of the cows and will result in a steady-state population within bounds.

We can simulate how our *ahimsa* herd population will change over time. We shall describe one example simulation. In this example, each bull calf becomes a bull after one generation, and each heifer becomes a milch cow after one generation. Milch cows give birth to one calf per generation, for two generations. Then they retire. Both cows and bulls live out their natural lifespans of eight generations (assuming a generation of three years; we can vary the generation time to some extent). In the following tables, we show one such simulation run over twelve generations. Each 7x7 square represents one generation. Each position within the 7x7 square represents the same individual animal. The letters designate animals at different stages of the life cycle:

- H: heifer (or female calf);

- V: bull calf;

- M: milch cow;

- T: bull; and

- G: retired cow.[*]

Ahimsa Dairy Population over Twelve Generations

The simulation starts in Generation 1 with a bull (T), two milch cows (M), and their suckling calves: a heifer (H) and a bull calf (V).

---

[*]Letters were chosen to be visually distinct.

Generation 1

1	M	T	M	H	V		

Generation 2

2	M	T	M	M	T	H	H
	V						

In Generation 2, the heifer (H) in the middle of the top row turns into another milch cow (M), and the bull calf (V) next to it turns into another bull (T). All three of the milch cows give birth to calves: two heifers (H) and a bull calf (V).

Generation 3

3	G	T	G	M	T	M	M
	T	H	H	V			

In Generation 3, the two original milch cows turn into retired cows (G), having each given birth to two calves. The two heifers at the top right turn into two more milch cows (M), and the bull calf (V) turns into another bull (T). All three milch cows give birth to calves: two heifers (H) and a bull calf (V).

Generation 4

4	G	T	G	G	T	M	M
	T	M	M	T	H	H	V
	V						

In Generation 4, there are four milch cows: two who were born in Generation 2 and two who were born in Generation 3. The generations continue on in the same way.

Generation 5

5	G	T	G	G	T	G	G
	T	M	M	T	M	M	T
	T	H	H	V	V		

Generation 6

6	G	T	G	G	T	G	G
	T	G	G	T	M	M	T
	T	M	M	T	T	H	H
	V	V					

In Generation 8, the original bull and two cows at the top left, who were already one-generation old at the start, die naturally, so their positions are shown as blank from this generation forward.

Table A lists the counts of cattle of each type, and the number who were born or died, in each generation. Here we use the following abbreviations:

Generation 7

7	G	T	G	G	T	G	G
	T	G	G	T	G	G	T
	T	M	M	T	T	M	M
	T	T	H	H	V	V	

Generation 8

8				G	T	G	G
	T	G	G	T	G	G	T
	T	G	G	T	T	M	M
	T	T	M	M	T	T	H
	H	V	V				

Generation 9

9						G	G
	T	G	G	T	G	G	T
	T	G	G	T	T	G	G
	T	T	M	M	T	T	M
	M	T	T	H	H	V	V

Generation 10

10							
		G	G	T	G	G	T
		T	G	G	T	T	G	G
		T	T	G	G	T	T	M
		M	T	T	M	M	T	T
		H	H	V	V			

Generation 11

11							
					G	G	T
	T	G	G	T	T	G	G
	T	T	G	G	T	T	G
	G	T	T	M	M	T	T
	M	M	T	T	H	H	V
	V						

Generation 12

12							
		G	G	T	T	G	G
	T	T	G	G	T	T	G
	G	T	T	G	G	T	T
	M	M	T	T	M	M	T
	T	H	H	V	V		

- n: Generation #

- M: # Milch Cows

- T: # Bulls

- H: # Heifers

- V: # Bull Calves

- G: # Retired Cows

- B: # Born

- D: # Died

- S: Total #

From Generation 4 onward, there were four milch cows in the herd, giving birth to four calves. In Generation 12, the four calves who were born in Generation 4 died. From then onward, the population remains steady at thirty-two cattle, with four births and four

Table A: *Ahimsa* Dairy Demographic Counts over Twelve Generations

n	M	T	H	V	G	B	D	S
1	2	1	1	1	0	2	0	5
2	3	2	2	1	0	3	0	8
3	3	3	2	1	2	3	0	11
4	4	4	2	2	3	4	0	15
5	4	6	2	2	5	4	0	19
6	4	8	2	2	7	4	0	23
7	4	10	2	2	9	4	0	27
8	4	11	2	2	9	4	3	28
9	4	12	2	2	10	4	2	30
10	4	13	2	2	10	4	3	31
11	4	14	2	2	10	4	3	32
12	4	14	2	2	10	4	4	32

deaths in every generation.[*] We find in this simulation run that for each milking cow in the steady-state population, there are eight total cattle (i.e., seven additional cattle) from all demographics. Mathematical ecosociology would extend our example to stochastic simulations with many runs, including various events with various probabilities we would estimate from data.[†] For example, we would not expect exactly two heifers and two bull calves to be born each generation: sometimes cows have twins; some cows might only give birth once or not at all; some cattle might live for more or less than eight generations; and so forth. Over many possible runs, we would find the ranges within which the population count might vary. Then we can make sure that we can comfortably accommodate even the upper bound of that range within our available land. We could study the effect of resting cows for one generation between calves, or setting the generation time to four years, or of staggering the births.[○]

---

[*]To avoid inbreeding, *ahimsa* dairies can trade animals among one another from time to time.

[†]Astute readers may have noticed that in our example, there was an excess of heifers born in generations 2 and 3: four out of six calves born were heifers, rather than three out of six. Interested readers can try as an exercise to see what would happen if two bull calves and one heifer were born in Generation 3.

Figure 38.1: Three milking cow sisters, from left to right: Gopi Katyayani, Sriya, and Sita, in the Goshala milking barn (literally "cow shed").

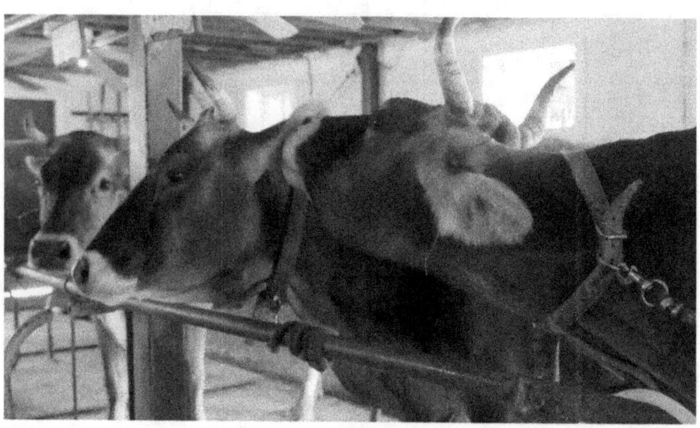

Large *ahimsa* dairy farms divide cows into several herds: the milking herd (milking cows and their suckling calves), the resting herd (heifers and mature cows between lactations), the retired herd (cows retired from milking), and the herd of bulls, steers, and oxen. These herds may occupy different, not necessarily contiguous, pieces of land (something that would play a role in how soil is replenished). This helps ensure that breeding is restrained. Grazing needs also differ at different stages of the life cycle.[*]

Pictured in Figures 38.1–7 is New Vrindaban, the oldest *ahimsa* dairy in the United States, herding cows continuously since 1969. Not pictured is Bahulaban, the barn where the resting herd stays. At the time pictured, New Vrindaban had sixty-seven cattle, eight of which were milch cows.

In this way, *ahimsa* practices can keep dairy herd sizes within limits. So the dairy cow habitats can remain restricted, leaving other habitats available for more wild animals. If the amount of land dedicated to agricultural purposes is kept to the least possible, then more is available for other purposes such as reforestation and biodiversity preser-

---

[*]Every large *ahimsa* farm that we are aware of neuters some of its bulls, turning them into steers. (Steers fully trained as draft animals are known as oxen.) Neutering is apparently needed to handle them in a limited territory. In any case, our simulation above treats bulls, steers, and oxen the same.

450

Figure 38.2: Milking cows: Vamsika with her head down and Jaya Radhe.

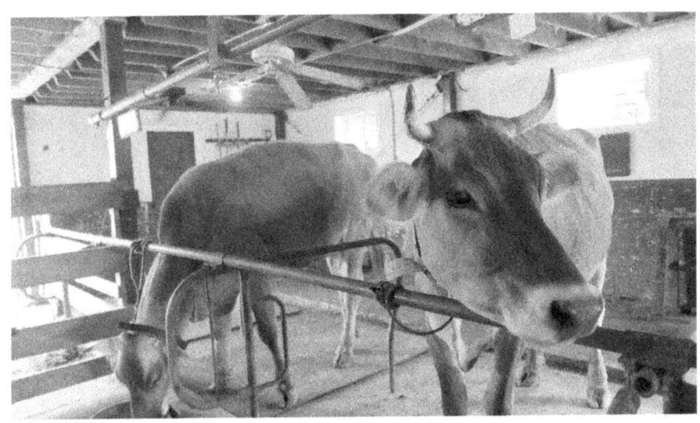

Figure 38.3: Cow herder Lalita Gopi milking Sita.

Figure 38.4: Three calves, from left to right: the heifer Yashoda, another heifer, and the steer Bhishma, in the yard next to the Goshala milking barn where their mothers stay.

Figure 38.5: Steers at Nandagram, outside their barn.

Figure 38.6: The cow herder Lalita Gopi, here with steers, guiding the tour.

Figure 38.7: The cow Parijata.

Figure 38.8: Parijata on a visit to Dharma the bull at The Valley Barn where he stays.

vation. Looking at humans and cows together, the more of them that can be fed by a given amount of land, the less land it would take to feed a fixed number of humans and cows.

On that note, a group of researchers found that the lacto-vegetarian diet (consuming dairy, honey, and plant-based foods, though not eggs or other animal products) results in the least land use by humans and cows put together. These researchers used a biophysical simulation model to calculate how many humans can be fed by US agricultural land, under ten diet scenarios, and found that carrying capacity was highest for the lacto-vegetarian diet, so this would be another aspect to include in our model.[396] Their model looked at sheer population sizes, however, and omitted per-capita environmental impacts, to which we turn next.

Objections due to other environmental impacts

So we've established that it's possible to limit the growth of the population of dairy cattle while practicing *ahimsa*. However, it may be argued that each individual cow has a significant impact on the climate. Let's look specifically into a frequently discussed way in which cows affect the atmosphere.

Cows, sheep, goats, camels, bison, deer, antelopes, giraffes, and buffalo are examples of ruminant animals. When these animals eat grass or hay, first they chew it roughly, shredding it, and then they swallow it, sending it to one compartment of their stomach, called the rumen. There, microbes start breaking it down and releasing nutrients, in a process called enteric fermentation. Just as when yeast ferments bread dough, the yeast releases gases, causing the dough to rise, so these rumen microbes also release gases. The fermented plant material, called cud, is sent back up to the ruminant animal's mouth to be chewed some more, and the gases are also sent up to be belched out. The ruminant spends a long time "ruminating," or chewing its cud, breaking it down physically and mixing it thoroughly with saliva, before sending it to another compartment, its true stomach (filled with acid, more like our own stomachs).[*] This intricate process is what allows ruminants to digest many kinds of plant material, such as seed coats and stems, that humans would otherwise waste.

Readers may be aware that sometimes the gases burped by cows include methane, a significant greenhouse gas. Cow manure also contains methane. However, the manure poses less of a problem than the burps, as the methane from manure can be captured in a methane digester and converted to biogas. While other ruminant animals may produce methane in the same or similar quantities, the argument is that the large numbers of domesticated cows inordinately add to detrimental greenhouse gases through their burping.

Dairies, including *ahimsa* dairies run by mathematical ecosociological principles, can solve this problem, because the extent to which cows burp methane depends on the specific species composition of the microbes in their rumens. That in turn depends on their diet. Feeding cows extruded linseed (flaxseed) can reduce their methane output by 38%.[397] An added benefit for humans, if the cows are being milked, is that the milk has more omega-3 fatty acids.[398] Feeding cows the seaweed *Asparagopsis armata* can reduce their methane emissions by 67%.[399†]

---

[*]Ruminants' stomachs actually have four compartments; we've broken down the process more simply here. Like the cows, we've also spent a long time ruminating on how to break down the material in the process of writing this book!

[†]*Ahimsa* milk farm practices are conducive to regularly feeding cattle these supplements. Practicing *ahimsa* entails actively watching over all cattle on the farm, not just those producing milk, each day, for the animals' own well-being as well as to modulate their impact on their surroundings. Non-dairy cattle, on the other hand, are often turned loose on large rangelands to fend for themselves throughout much of the year. *Ahimsa* herders interact personally with individual cows, calves, bulls, steers, and oxen.[400p] Indeed, the herders find each individual has a lot of personality!

Mathematical ecosociology would take an integrated approach to accounting for such additions as ground flaxseed or algae. For instance, since ancient times, bulls and oxen have turned grinding mills, which could be used for grinding the flaxseed. Aquaculture of algae can use gray water from the farm, so as not to use additional potable water resources. The same rotary action from bulls and oxen can charge batteries, supplying some of the energy needs of the farm. Bulls and steers also have individual natures, which may be more or less suited to different kinds of work, so this is something else to take into account. If the flax providing the seeds is grown on the farm itself, it also becomes a resource for human food and fiber needs, as well as having other value (linen is spun from flax).

Having looked at the benefits of *ahimsa* milk, and then seen how the objections can be overcome, we can now turn to how the example would fit into the wider framework of society.

38.3 *Ahimsa* in Place: One Health, One Ecosystem, One Society

So far, we've mostly written about ecosystems. In fact, however, mathematical ecosociology considers a single, unified, social-environmental system in any given place. The integrated ecosystem perspective of mathematical ecosociology includes and extends the One Health approach for people, animal, plants, and the environment.[401] Due to length considerations, we'll just briefly touch upon what additional aspects would be included.*† We'll highlight one intriguing possibility. Horses and certain other farm animals assist in counseling for a variety of conditions.[402] Whether cows or calves might assist in this way would be an interesting topic of investigation. People can already visit and hug cows at *ahimsa* dairies,[403] and the effects on people's sense of well-being may be researched in the future.

Persons who work in all four fields of work — Ideas, Government, Resources, and Artistry — would ideally participate in making *ahimsa* dairy possible. For instance, people in the Field of Artistry may focus on day-to-day milking and herding. People in the Field of Resources may focus on managing the feed and rotations as well as transporting and selling milk. They can fulfill their urge to optimize numbers by

---

*Multiscale modeling lets us put together different smaller models that cover specific aspects, such as restricted locales or subsets of species.

†Many of the social aspects of *ahimsa* dairies are shared in common with other types of farming, so for brevity's sake we've omitted them here. In the same way, prevention of infectious disease is similar between *ahimsa* and non-*ahimsa* dairies.

increasing the diversity of farm inputs and outputs. If they take our suggestion to integrate *ahimsa* dairy into a balanced farm ecosystem, then they can also target increasing the ecological diversity of residents and visitors to the farm (such as pollinators: butterflies, bees, and so forth), as well as increasing measures of soil health. People in the Field of Government may inspect *ahimsa* milk farms as third parties to ensure they are following the *ahimsa* milk practices that they advertise. They would also enforce boundaries and deal with disputes. People in the Field of Ideas may apply mathematical ecosociology, as well as provide counseling on the physical, mental, and organizational health of the people, animals, plants, and soil of the farm.

If *ahimsa* milk is sold outside the farm, its price would reflect the expenses of maintaining the entire herd, of which the milking cows form a fraction, at its steady-state size and composition. This higher price, reflecting the true costs, would naturally lead many consumers who switch to *ahimsa* milk and milk products to consume them at lower levels than current-day conventional milk, at least in the United States. Similarly, Fair Trade goods cost more than those produced by prison, slave, or otherwise coerced labor.

Equitable distribution of *ahimsa* milk could happen, as for other things, through charitable giving and at community festivals and ceremonies. People could also contribute any of the six kinds of richness in exchange for *ahimsa* milk. As readers may have noticed, a lot of labor is involved in running an *ahimsa* milk farm and there are many avenues to participate. The interactions of all these people can be modeled with network science and other aspects of computational social science, another discipline on which mathematical ecosociology draws.[*]

38.4 Conclusion

In this chapter, we've sketched how mathematical ecosociology can support an integrated, long-term approach to sustaining an *ahimsa* milk farm. In sum, mathematical ecosociology not only helps us to address various possible objections to the concept of *ahimsa* dairy in itself; the power of math can also help us to create a social-environ-

---

[*]Many creative and ingenious people have been coming up with alternatives to milk and milk products, such as oat milk, cashew cream, and almond cheese. Mathematical ecosociology can help with the production of these as well, and fair pricing will naturally lead to degrees of substitution among these products and *ahimsa* milk products.

mental system that is truly beneficial not just for dairy cows, but also for people, plants, and the planet as a whole. Mathematical ecosociology helps us to model the world holistically.

Next, in our concluding chapter, we return to the human dimension, outlining how career dharma leads to a vision for a whole society.

Chapter 39

Vision for a Whole Society

We've assembled the ingredients of the natural art of work. Now we can begin to see how a society where practicing the natural art of work is the norm would function as a system. Of course, individuals can find satisfaction in their work even within a system that does not support principles of fulfilling work. Yet, when society as a whole embraces these principles, the "rising tide lifts all boats." Let's envision such a society. Our vision isn't meant to include or map out every detail, nor to exactly align with any specific local situation that exists. Rather, the vision we delineate here will help us see the big picture of how the natural art of work fits together.

39.1   The Four Fields

In universities, teachers in the Field of Ideas would establish departments for the study of consciousness and spiritual practice. All departments and degrees would relate to one or more of the four fields of work, and would teach the principles and values of the natural art of work along with information and skills. (Education would also help children decide their preferred field, which is discussed below.) Teachers of primary- and secondary-school students would work with their students in multi-level, differentiated systems that facilitate each child or adolescent to learn according to their individual style and pace, and focus on their areas of interest. Workers in the Field of Ideas would guide those in the Field of Government so that the society-wide *systems* of the natural art of work are in place — competition within fields, cooperation between fields, and having appropriate checks and balances and an overall aim of sustainable prosperity rather than harmful "growth" models disconnected from the realities of the natural world. Leaders within the various religious traditions of the world would go to the roots of their faith and teach the essential principles of love of the Divine and all life, without personal motive. There would be no commercialization of spirituality. Cheating in the name of religion or spirituality would not be tolerated. Scientific research would aim towards advancing human knowledge and life in ways that add honest value individually and collectively, without commensurate harm. Medicine would combine surgery and chemical medicines with use of the natural world, mind-body connection, and holistic health. Those in the Field of Ideas would remain aloof from situations that could compromise their objectivity, for example by avoiding dependence for financial security on specific people in the Fields of Government or Resources. Workers in the Field of Ideas would establish the standards for all fields of work not just in terms of skills and knowledge, but also in terms of the values of the natural art of work — matching work to nature, doing work that is honest and of value, giving in charity, regularly connecting with the whole, cherishing one's sources of wealth and one's field of work, and working without ego or lethargy.

Those in the Field of Government would focus on the equal protection and care of all members of their domain — human, animal, and plant. They would use tax revenues, under the guidance of those in the Field of Ideas, to moderate risks at the societal level and facilitate people having all the material and spiritual necessities of life. Government leaders would support and encourage all citizens to love the Divine within their choice of spiritual path (including, as described previously, to see the universe or the biosphere as the body of God), and would discourage commercialization of religious functions. They would fund educational systems that facilitate people learning the natural art of work, and have policies that make it easy to live in extended families and work from home. They would learn the theory and practice of a sustainable and regenerative economy from those in the Field of Ideas and the Field of Resources, but they would remain aloof from becoming financially dependent or beholden to those with resources. Governments would provide broad, non-sectarian and non-discriminatory funding and support for the public to engage in spiritual celebration, and would connect national holidays with spiritual upliftment. Funding for libraries and the arts would be prioritized. The police would not use undue force. Prisons would focus on rehabilitation through spiritual upliftment and training in the principles of the natural art of work. Military action would take place away from civilian habitats and would involve combat where fighters face each other directly. The heads of state — the commanders-in-chief — would actually lead the charge. Thus, they would only start wars in which they themselves would be willing to sacrifice their own life and limb.

Government would regulate the manufacture and purchase of intoxicants and support prevention and rehabilitation based on genuine fulfillment through the natural art of work, as well as authentic means of reaching higher consciousness. Government would remove itself from the gambling industry, and allow gambling only in restricted areas. Sex work would be restricted and regulated, along with sex workers receiving protection and medical care.

Workers in the Field of Resources would ensure that all farming — for food, textile fiber, and medicine — is organic, sustainable, and regenerative. There would be a return in agriculture to working with animal power in humane ways that replenish the soil, and any machines used would rely on resilient, renewable energy. Mining would be done so as to preserve the earth and the health of the miners. Animal slaughter would not be a business, and animals who give their milk, wool, and honey would be cared for like family members. Many goods and services would once again be provided through loose, informal exchanges of favors in the community, and money would account for real wealth, including exergy (energy that is available to be used) and natural resources. People in the Field of Resources would distribute essential resources to people of all ages in society, through a combination of sales and charity. The recipients would also redistribute those resources to other people and animals. The poor, elderly, retired, and other people in need would be able to take excess resources, such as fruits and grain, which people in the Field of Resources would leave available for them. Leaders in this field would ensure that those in the Field of Artistry who work for them have a healthy work environment and enough compensation to be satisfied. Workers in Resources would focus on meeting people's real needs without commensurate harm and would completely avoid manufacturing needs. Leaders in this field would develop natural and sustainable energy sources. Wealthy workers in the Field of Resouces would channel their wealth into charity for the needy, as well as to the arts and causes for spiritual upliftment.

In the Field of Artistry, workers who have affinity for one of the other fields would work in a supportive capacity without crossing into that field. Those who are inclined only to the Field of Artistry would dedicate their work to having society function smoothly and with beauty. They would focus on their main service — that of providing all of society's members with varieties of sensory and emotional pleasures. They would use their talents and skills to create an egoless atmosphere of connection with our Divine Source, or at least with the ego shade of *sattva*. The focus in this field would be keeping alive human crafts and the development of new forms of both artistic expression and ways of fulfilling practical needs such as sanitation, plumbing, and so forth.

39.2 Education and Society

Throughout society, before marriage, couples would receive counseling and guidance on recognizing and nurturing their children's inclinations, interests, and overall nature in the direction of their career. Teachers would carefully observe each pupil to help identify strengths and proclivities, keeping in mind that untrained and misdirected tendencies often appear troublesome, especially in childhood. By early adolescence, pupils would choose, with the guidance of teachers and parents, apprenticeships where they would get impressions of the fields of work that interest them. The values of the natural art of work — honest work, work of value, dedication and charity, regular connection with the Source, cherishing our sources of wealth and our field of work, and working without ego or lethargy — would also be part of the virtues children imbibe directly and indirectly as they mature. Education from that point on would be practical and geared towards individual proclivity in terms of field of work and specific "tree" of work. Those in such apprenticeship programs would be able to switch to different programs, with the guidance of teachers who are trained in recognizing and developing persons' vocations.

From at least the time of entering school, children would be trained not only in general academic skills and specific vocations but also in practical life skills including communication and family relationships. Schools would frequently have pupils give various forms of charity in the areas of riches they enjoy and facilitate a variety of traditions and expressions for regular, deliberate connection with the whole. The practice of egolessness and the practice of working for absolute increase would be a regular part of school and student life.

Because most people would be able to maintain themselves before they are twenty years old, they would have the option to marry and start a family earlier, thus devoting the prime of their lives and their energies to providing the best possible environment for their children. Within society as a whole, this will enable demographic balance so that there are enough energetic working people to support others retiring at a reasonable age. Those retiring may also choose to help with child care for younger working parents close to them. Young people would consider harmony of career as a factor in their choice of marriage partner, and so, in many families spouses could more easily harmonize their family and their work. A return to an emphasis on working from home and extended family would assist parents — perhaps especially mothers — to have both career and family as part of a holistic life. Humans would live with the planet and its lifeforms as part of one ecosystem. People would have variety in the ways they balance work and life, with a continuous spectrum from spending most of their days working to spending most of their days on matters other than work. Those who spend most of their days not working for their own maintenance would live near each other as neighbors, cooperating in child care and elder care. People who maintain homes would also distribute resources from their homes, through their hospitality and by giving in charity. They would also consume goods and services and distribute them in a neighborly way to those nearby, sometimes in charity to those in need, sometimes through hospitality, and sometimes through simple neighborly exchanges such as barn raisings (when the community would collectively build or rebuild a house or barn for one of its members). Some retired people, and those who are easing into retirement and are so inclined, would also cooperate in the care of neighborhood children. By the time people are ready to retire, they would be satisfied with their contribution to society, and have a peaceful mind to allow them to dedicate the remainder of their lives to spiritual service. Such retired people, no longer in the working world, could live adequately yet lightly on savings or pensions, or have younger members of their extended families and intentional communities look after their care.

39.3 Benefits for Society

Most existing human societies involve some oppression, something that is reinforced by the way that we think. Such oppression begins when some person or group, influenced by *tamas*, tries to exploit others rather than following the principles of the natural art of work. This shading of ego then spreads. Thinking in terms of friend and enemy can sometimes result in a vicious cycle of greed, oppression, and exploitation, due to a mood arising in the oppressed of desiring the place of the oppressor, the place of the exploiter. This can happen not only between individuals, but among different groups in society. Thus, we sometimes see oppressed and oppressor changing places, rather than an overall culture of peace and prosperity emerging:

> But almost always, during the initial stage of the struggle, the oppressed, instead of striving for liberation, tend themselves to become oppressors, or "sub-oppressors." The very structure of their thought has been conditioned by the contradictions of the concrete, existential situation by which they were shaped. Their ideal is to be men; but for them, to be men is to be oppressors. This is their model of humanity….Liberation is thus a childbirth, and a painful one. The man or woman who emerges is a new person, viable only as the oppressor-oppressed contradiction is superseded by the humanization of all people. Or to put it another way, the solution of this contradiction is born in the labor which brings into the world this new being: no longer oppressor, no longer oppressed, but human in the process of achieving freedom."
> –Paulo Freire, *Pedagogy of the Oppressed*[404]

Indeed, the very problem of oppressed becoming oppressor has occurred historically in many societies. Seepe noted in 2001 with respect to South Africa, in reference to Freire's general observation:

> …[P]rogressive legislation and pious political pronouncements are rarely matched by a change of attitude or a new consciousness at both the personal and political level. Instead of the struggle achieving the liberation of both the oppressed and the oppressor, it has simply replaced the oppressor. The oppressed are assuming the role of the oppressor.

— The Oppressed Have Become the Oppressor[405]

In contrast, a society that embodies the principles of the natural art of work is classless in the sense of a mood of mutual appreciation, along with relative freedom from envy, exploitation, and prejudice. Thus the whole spiral of exploitation, accusation, and revenge is cut off at the root. As members of the four fields of work would pursue truth, justice, sustainability, beauty, etc. with less shading of ego, they would hear one another out receptively, redress, reconcile, and renew society, working together. Society and the world would be understood as a family where each person finds his or her own natural expression while contributing to the good of the whole. When people can directly get what they need in terms of the six types of richness, and they experience an absolute increase through connection with the whole, the entire ecosystem is in balance and good health.

39.4 Benefits for Individuals

People who have fields of work according to their tastes and inclinations, and who follow the principles of the natural art of work, tend to become more competent, have more integrity, and enjoy education more, as it is tailored to their practical needs. Their lives are more satisfying as they have much opportunity to connect ordinary life to transcendence and find deep meaning. Without the shades of ego, and with egolessness, relationships are more meaningful:

> Oneness with Spirit is as much the destiny of a construction worker, teacher, salesperson, and engineer as it is the destiny of a spiritual leader. All aspects of earthly experience, including our career, can be a cup overflowing with peace and joy. Our professional life can be one more place where we experience life to the fullest.
> —Jim Rosemergy, *Even Mystics Have Bills to Pay: Balancing a Spiritual Life and Earthly Living*[406]

On an individual level, we do well to discover our nature in terms of the ways in which we feel rich, and the field of work that energizes us. That nature needs nourishment, training, and strong impressions in order to display its glory. Individuals who match their field of work to their nature then apply the principles of finding absolute increase through connection with the whole, sharing their richness with others, having regular activities of connection with the Supreme, cherishing and protecting both one's field and one's sources of work, and working without egoism or lethargy.

Leaders who develop and guide society can encourage competition within fields and cooperation between fields, keep the system of checks and balances honest and functioning, and use systems thinking in terms of the whole ecosystem of work when guiding small groups or individuals.

In the non-human world, each creature and element plays its part instinctively, with little or no awareness of a greater contribution beyond self, family, or group. Humans, on the other hand, have the unique ability to choose our destiny and our role in the ecosystem. Let us choose wisely.

References

1. `https://digitalcommons.butler.edu/jhcs` (cit. on p.).

2. Gallup, *State of the Global Workplace: Employee Engagement Insights for Business Leaders Worldwide* (Washington, D.C.: Gallup, Inc., 2013), p. 12 (cit. on p. xviii).

3. Peter B. Myers, Isabel Briggs Myers with, *Gifts Differing: Understanding Personality Type* (Mountain View, California: Davies-Black Publishing, 2010), p. 150 (cit. on p. xix).

4. Lakoff, George, and Johnson, Mark, *Metaphors We Live By* (University of Chicago Press, 1980), 67 (cit. on p. xxii).

5. *Bhagavad-gita*, chap. 2.50 (cit. on p. xxiv).

6. Csíkszentmihályi, Mihályi, *Flow: The Psychology of Optimal Experience* (Harper Collins, 1991) (cit. on p. 3).

7. Kelly, Matthew, *The Dream Manager* (New York: Hachette Books, 2007), 16–7 (cit. on p. 4).

8. *Bhagavad-gita*, chap. 17.19 (cit. on p. 5).

9. Berg, A. Scott, *Max Perkins: Editor of Genius* (New York: New American Library, 2016), pp. 30–31 (cit. on p. 6).

10. J.K. Harter, F.L. Schmidt, T.L. Hayes, "Business-unit-level relationship between employee satisfaction, employee engagement, and business outcomes: A meta-analysis.", *Journal of Applied Psychology, 87(2)*, 268–79 (cit. on p. 7).

11. Gladwell, Malcolm, *Outliers: The Story of Success* (New York: Little, Brown and Company, 2008) (cit. on p. 7).

12. Peters, Shawn Francis, *The Yoder Case: Religious Freedom, Education, and Parental Rights* (Lawrence, Kansas: University Press of Kansas, 2003), p. 26 (cit. on p. 7).

13. Brown, Mick, "Inside the private world of London's ultra-Orthodox Jews", The Telegraph (February 25, 2011), `http://www.telegraph.co.uk/news/religion/8326339/Inside-the-private-world-of-Londons-ultra-Orthodox-Jews.html` (cit. on p. 7).

14. Shetty, Jay, *Extras:E225 Will You Choose Money OR Your Passion?*, `https://www.facebook.com/15578250057865287/videos/405084063439254` (cit. on p. 8).

15. Tibaldeo, Glen, "The Success Principles of Breaking Boards Bare-Handed", Psychology Today (Sep 16, 2013), `https://www.psychologytoday.com/us/blog/radical-sabbatical/201309/the-success-principles-breaking-boards-bare-handed` (cit. on p. 8).

16. Armstrong, Paul B, "Play and Cultural Differences", The Kenyon Review, new series, 13/1 (1991), p. 163 (cit. on p. 9).

17. *Bhagavad-gita*, chap. 4.11 (cit. on p. 9).

18. *Isopanishad*, chap. 8 (cit. on p. 9).

19. *Katha Upanishad*, chap. 2.2.13 (cit. on p. 9).

20. Larssen, Adrian Granzella, "25 Little Ways to Get Closer to Your Dream Career This Week", The Muse, `https://www.themuse.com/advice/25-little-ways-to-get-closer-to-your-dream-career-this-week` (cit. on p. 9).

21. Sher, Barbara, and Gottlieb, Annie, *Wishcraft: How to get what you really want* (New York: Ballantine Books, 2004) (cit. on p. 9).

22. Hicks, Esther, and Hicks, Jerry, *Ask and It Is Given: Learning to Manifest Your Desires* (Carlsbad, California: Hay House, 2004), p. 30 (cit. on p. 9).

23. Farber, Neil, "The Truth About the Law of Attraction", Psychology Today (September 18, 2016), `https://www.psychologytoday.com/blog/the-blame-game/201609/the-truth-about-the-law-attraction` (cit. on p. 9).

24. Covey, Stephen M.R., *The Speed of Trust: The One Thing That Changes Everything* (New York: Free Press, 2006) (cit. on p. 12).

25. Robinson, Ken, and Aronica, Lou, *Finding Your Element: How To Discover Your Talents and Passions and Transform Your Life* (New York: Penguin Books, 2013) (cit. on p. 13).

26. Gardner, Howard, *Frames of Mind: The theory of multiple intelligences* (New York: Fontana Press, 1993) (cit. on p. 14).

27. Wiseman, L., and McKeown, G., *Multipliers: How the best leaders make everyone smarter.* (New York: HarperBusiness, 2010), pp. 133–134 (cit. on p. 15).

28. *Vishnu Purana*, chap. 1.7.31 (cit. on p. 16).

29. Bloom, B. S., *Taxonomy of Educational Objectives, Handbook I: The Cognitive Domain* (New York: David McKay Co Inc., 1956) (cit. on p. 17).

30. Wiseman, L., and McKeown, G., *Multipliers: How the best leaders make everyone smarter.* (New York: HarperBusiness, 2010) (cit. on p. 17).

31. Seneca (cit. on p. 24).

32. Schwartz, Barry, *The Paradox of Choice: Why More Is Less* (New York: Ecco, 2004) (cit. on p. 24).

33. *Bhagavad-gita*, chap. 2.59 (cit. on p. 26).

34. *Bhagavata Purana*, chap. 2.10.25 (cit. on p. 28).

35. Hofstede, Geert, Hofstede, Gert Jan, and Minkov, Michael, *Cultures and Organizations: Software of the Mind* (New York: McGraw Hill, 2010) (cit. on p. 29).

36. Sonnenburg, Justin, and Sonnenburg, Erica, *The Good Gut: Taking Control of Your Weight, Your Mood, and Your Long-Term Health* (New York: Penguin, 2015) (cit. on p. 29).

37. Pasquaretta, Cristian, et al., "Exploring Interactions between the Gut Microbiota and Social Behavior through Nutrition", Genes, 9/11 (2018), p. 534 (cit. on p. 29).

38. Badger, Emily, "A Nobel-Winning Economist Goes to Burning Man", New York Times (Sept. 5, 2019), `https://www.nytimes.com/2019/09/05/upshot/paul-romer-burning-man-nobel-economist.html` (cit. on p. 31).

39. Drucker, Peter, *The Landmarks of Tomorrow* (Canada: Heineman, 1959) (cit. on p. 33).

40. Toledo, Isabel, *Roots of Style: Weaving Together Life, Love, and Fashion* (New York: Celebra, 2012) (cit. on p. 42).

41. *Bhagavata Purana*, chap. 11.9.13 (cit. on p. 43).

42. Csíkszentmihályi, Mihályi, *Finding Flow: The Psychology of Engagement with Everyday Life* (New York: Basic Books, 1998), 105 (cit. on p. 43).

43. Chokoisky, Simon, *The 5 Dharma Types* (Vermont: Destiny Books, 2014), p. 100 (cit. on p. 44).

44. Ericsson, Anders, and Pool, Robert, *Peak: Secrets from the new science of expertise* (Boston: Houghton Mifflin Harcourt, 2016), pp. 85–86 (cit. on p. 45).

45. Lefevre, Edwin, *Reminiscences of a Stock Operator* (Hoboken, New Jersey: John Wiley & Sons, 2012) (cit. on p. 46).

46. *Bhagavata Purana*, chap. 11.17.18 (cit. on p. 46).

47. Levinson, Marc, *The Great A&P and the Struggle for Small Business in America* (New York: Hill and Wang, 2011) (cit. on p. 47).

48. Mensching, Leah McBride, "Wind Energy Isn't A Breeze", Slate (August 24, 2017), `http://www.slate.com/articles/technology/future%5Ftense/2017/08/why%5Ffarmers%5Fin%5Fiowa%5Fhope%5Fwind%5Fenergy%5Fwill%5Fblow%5Fover.html` (cit. on p. 49).

49. Swami, AC Bhaktivedanta, Vrindavan, August 5, 1974 (cit. on p. 52).

50. Krakauer, Jon, *Where Men Win Glory: The Odyssey of Pat Tillman* (New York: Anchor Books, 2010), pp. 51–52 (cit. on p. 52).

51. Ludwig, Otto, *Gedanken Otto Ludwigs*, ed. Cordelia Ludwig (Leipzig: Eugen Diederich, 1903), 10 (cit. on p. 54).

52. Kovalevskaya, Sofya, *A Russian Childhood* (Berlin: Springer-Verlag, 2013), p. 215 (cit. on p. 55).

53. Frost, Robert, "Mending Wall", in *North of Boston* (New York: Henry Holt and Company, 1915), p. 12 (cit. on p. 63).

54. *A Simple Gita*, ed. Vraja Kishor (Scotts Valley, California: CreateSpace, 2013), p. 27 (cit. on p. 63).

55. Sher, Barbara, and Gottlieb, Annie, *Wishcraft: How to get what you really want* (New York: Ballantine Books, 2004) (cit. on p. 65).

56. Cowles, Charlotte, "My Degree Is Worthless and I Can't Make Enough Money", The Cut (Dec. 21, 2017), `https://www.thecut.com/2017/12/what-to-do-when-you-hate-your-job.html` (cit. on p. 66).

57. Dabrowski, Kazimierz, and Tillier, William, *Positive Disintegration* (Anna Maria, Florida: Mauryice Bassett, 2017) (cit. on p. 67).

58. Cohen, Mirit, July 30, 2021 (cit. on p. 68).

59. *Essential Sufism*, ed. James Fadiman and Robert Frager (San Francisco: HarperOne, 1997), 199 (cit. on p. 68).

60. Herzberg, F., Mausner, B., and Snyderman, B., *The Motivation to Work* (Transaction, 2004) (cit. on p. 69).

61. *Bhagavad-gita*, chap. 3.35 (cit. on p. 69).

62. *Bhagavad-gita*, chap. 4.11 (cit. on p. 69).

63. Truman, Harry (cit. on p. 76).

64. `http://web.archive.org/web/20151006142130/http://www.azcentral.com/news/articles/20110807arizona-prison-private-oversight.html` (cit. on p. 78).

65. Wilson, Reid, "Are governments incentivizing longer prison terms?", Washington Post (September 19, 2013), `https://www.washingtonpost.com/blogs/govbeat/wp/2013/09/19/are-governments-incentivizing-longer-prison-terms/` (cit. on p. 78).

66. Interest, In The Public, *Criminal: How Lockup Quotas and "Low-Crime Taxes" Guarantee Profits for Private Prison Corporations* (Washington, DC: In The Public Interest, September 2013) (cit. on p. 78).

67. "Anita Roddick: Cosmetics With A Conscience", Entrepreneur (October 10, 2008), `https://www.entrepreneur.com/article/197688` (cit. on p. 79).

68. Jacobs, Jane, *A Dialogue on the Moral Foundations of Commerce and Politics* (New York: Vintage Books, 1992) (cit. on p. 80).

69. Sinclair, Upton, *I, Candidate for Governor: And How I Got Licked* (cit. on p. 81).

70. Lewis, Michael, *Liar's Poker* (cit. on p. 82).

71. Hager, Thomas, *The Alchemy of Air* (New York: Broadway Books, 2008), pp. 260–1 (cit. on p. 82).

72. *personal communication*, Personal communication with Edith Best (2002) (cit. on p. 83).

73. Coddington, Mark, "The wall becomes a curtain: Revisiting journalism's news-business boundary", in *Boundaries of Journalism: Professionalism, Practices and Participation* (London: Routledge, 2015), chap. Ch. 4, pp. 93–100 (cit. on p. 85).

74. Westhoff, Ben, *Fentanyl Inc* (New York: Grove Atlantic Press, 2019), p. 57 (cit. on p. 88).

75. Bonsignore, Alessandro, et al., "MDMA Induced Cardiotoxicity and Pathological Myocardial Effects: A Systematic Review of Experimental Data and Autopsy Findings", Cardiovascular Toxicology, 19 (2019), pp. 493–9 (cit. on p. 88).

76. Iranpour, Abedin, and Nakhaee, Nouzar, "A Review of Alcohol-Related Harms: A Recent Update", Addiction and Health, 11/(2) (2019), pp. 129–137, https://www.ncbi.nlm.nih.gov/pmc/articles/PMC6633071/ (cit. on p. 88).

77. Petticrew, Mark, et al., "How alcohol industry organisations mislead the public about alcohol and cancer", Drug and Alcohol Review, 37/3 (March 2018), pp. 293–303, https://doi.org/10.1111/dar.12596 (cit. on p. 88).

78. Mencimer, Stephanie, "Did Drinking Give Me Breast Cancer?", Mother Jones (May 2018), https://www.motherjones.com/politics/2018/04/did-drinking-give-me-breast-cancer/ (cit. on p. 88).

79. MacFarquhar, Larissa, "Building a Prison-to-School Pipeline", The New Yorker (December 12, 2016), https://www.newyorker.com/magazine/2016/12/12/the-ex-con-scholars-of-berkeley (cit. on p. 91).

80. Dio, Cassius, *Roman History*, ed. Earnest Cary (London: Loeb, 1927), chap. 33, p. 58, https://penelope.uchicago.edu/Thayer/E/Roman/Texts/Cassius%5FDio/72*.html (cit. on p. 93).

81. Blight, James G, and Lang, Janet M, *The Fog of War: Lessons from the life of Robert S. McNamara* (2005: Rowman and Littlefield) (cit. on p. 94).

82. Dalberg-Acton, John Emerich Edward, *Historical Essays and Studies* (London: Macmillan, 1907), p. 504 (cit. on p. 95).

83. Juvenal, *Satire VI* (cit. on p. 95).

84. *Bhagavata Purana*, chap. 4.14.2-41 (cit. on p. 97).

85. Mintzberg, Henry, *The Structuring of Organizations* (Englewood Cliffs, New Jersey: Prentice-Hall, 1979) (cit. on p. 97).

86. Thomas J. Bouchard, Jr., et al., "The Minnesota Study of Twins Reared Apart: Project Description and Sample Results in the Development Domain", in Luigi Gedda, Paolo Parisi, and Walter E. Nance (eds.), *Intelligence, Personality, and Development*, iii (Twin Research) (cit. on p. 101).

87. Segal, Nancy L., *Born Together — Reared Apart: The Landmark Minnesota Twin Study* (Cambridge, Massachusetts: Harvard University Press, 2012) (cit. on p. 101).

88. Reiko, Lorna, *Identical twins who were separated at birth: Amazing similarities* (October 8, 2009), https://lornareiko.wordpress.com/2009/10/08/identical-twins-who-were-separated-at-birth-what-are-they-like/ (cit. on p. 102).

89. Research News (April 23, 2019), https://news.vanderbilt.edu/2019/04/23/gifted-kids-turn-50-most-successful-followed-heart-not-just-head/ (cit. on p. 103).

90. Kopelman, Richard E., Rovenpor, Janet L., and Guan, Mingwei, "The *Study of Values*: Construction of the fourth edition", Journal of Vocational Behavior, 62 (2003), 203–20 (cit. on p. 103).

91. Silverman, Linda Kreger, "The construct of asynchronous development", Peabody Journal of Education, 72 (1997), 36–58 (cit. on p. 103).

92. https://medium.com/s/story/a-culture-of-prestige-98c8671ceade (cit. on p. 103).

93. *Bhagavad-gita*, chap. 18.59-60 (cit. on p. 104).

94. Shipp, Josh, http://www.tedxmarin.org/josh-shipp/ (cit. on p. 104).

95. Pulver, Clint, https://clintpulver.com/about/ (cit. on p. 104).

96. Rodriguez, Richard, *Hunger of Memory* (David R. Godine, 1982) (cit. on p. 104).

97. Ericsson, A., and Pool, R., *Peak: Secrets from the New Science of Expertise* (New York: Eamon Dolan/Houghton Mifflin Harcourt, 2016), 233 (cit. on p. 106).

98. Simonton, Dean Keith, *The Origins of Genius* (Oxford: Oxford University Press, 1999), 78 (cit. on p. 107).

99. https://www.vanderbilt.edu/psychological%5Fsciences/bio/david-lubinski (cit. on p. 107).

100. https://my.vanderbilt.edu/smpy/ (cit. on p. 107).

101. http://www.peabody.vanderbilt.edu/ (cit. on p. 107).

102. Research News (April 23, 2019), https://news.vanderbilt.edu/2019/04/23/gifted-kids-turn-50-most-successful-followed-heart-not-just-head/ (cit. on p. 108).

103. Windhorst, Eric, http://www.ericwindhorst.ca/2018/01/03/growing-with-nature-part-2-naturally-inspiring/ (cit. on p. 110).

104. Ericsson, A., and Pool, R., *Peak: Secrets from the New Science of Expertise* (New York: Eamon Dolan/Houghton Mifflin Harcourt, 2016) (cit. on p. 111).

105. Zatorre, Robert J., "Absolute pitch: A model for understanding the influence of genes and development on neural and cognitive function", Nature Neuroscience, 6/7 (2003), 692–5 (cit. on p. 111).

106. Ericsson, Anders; Pool, Robert, *Peak: Secrets from the New Science of Expertise* (New York: Houghton Mifflin Harcourt, 2016), 196 (cit. on p. 112).

107. Kuhl, Patricia K., et al., "Phonetic learning as a pathway to language: new data and native language magnet theory expanded (NLM-e)", Philosophical Transactions of the Royal Society of London B: Biological Sciences, 363/1493 (2008 Mar 12), 981 (cit. on p. 112).

108. Bloom, B S, *Taxonomy of Educational Objectives, Handbook 1: The Cognitive Domain* (New York: David McKay Co Inc., 1956) (cit. on p. 113).

109. Pink, Daniel, *Drive: The Surprising Truth About What Motivates Us* (New York: Riverhead Books, 2009) (cit. on p. 113).

110. Herzberg, F., Mausner, B., and Snyderman, B., *The Motivation to Work* (Transaction, 2004) (cit. on p. 113).

111. Ericsson, Anders; Pool, Robert, *Peak: Secrets from the New Science of Expertise* (New York: Houghton Mifflin Harcourt, 2016) (cit. on p. 114).

112. Ericsson, A., and Pool, R., *Peak: Secrets from the New Science of Expertise* (New York: Eamon Dolan/Houghton Mifflin Harcourt, 2016), 98–100 (cit. on p. 114).

113. Rodriguez, Richard, *Hunger of Memory* (David R. Godine, 1982) (cit. on p. 115).

114. *Bhagavad-gita*, chap. 4.34 (cit. on p. 115).

115. Deresiewicz, William, *Excellent Sheep* (Free Press, division of Simon and Schuster Inc, 2014) (cit. on p. 116).

116. *Bhagavad-gita*, chap. 12.9 (cit. on p. 116).

117. Heath, Chip, and Heath, Dan, "Decisive: How to Make Better Choices in Life and Work", in (USA: Crown Business, 2013), chap. Ch. 7 (cit. on p. 117).

118. Brown, Peter C., RoedigerIII, Henry L., and McDaniel, Mark A., *Make It Stick: The Science of Successful Learning* (Cambridge, Massachusetts: The Belknap Press of Harvard University Press, 2014) (cit. on p. 118).

119. Stone, Douglas, et al., *Difficult Conversations: How To Discuss What Matters Most* (New York: Penguin, 2010) (cit. on p. 119).

120. Patterson, Kerry, et al., *Crucial Conversations: Tools for Talking When Stakes Are High* (New York: McGraw-Hill, 2012) (cit. on p. 119).

121. Senge, Peter M., *The Fifth Discipline: The Art & Practice of The Learning Organization* (New York: Doubleday, 1990) (cit. on p. 119).

122. *Bhagavad-gita*, chap. 7.14 (cit. on p. 125).

123. Porges, Stephen W., *The Pocket Guide to the Polyvagal Theory* (New York: W. W. Norton & Co., 2017) (cit. on p. 127).

124. Sullivan, Marlysa B., et al., "Yoga Therapy and Polyvagal Theory: The Convergence of Traditional Wisdom and Contemporary Neuroscience for Self-Regulation and Resilience", Frontiers in Human Neuroscience, 12 (February 27, 2018), 8, `https://www.frontiersin.org/articles/10.3389/fnhum.2018.00067/full` (cit. on p. 127).

125. *Yoga Sutras*, chap. 2.18 (cit. on p. 128).

126. *Sankhya-karika*, chap. 13 (cit. on p. 128).

127. *Bhagavud-gita*, chap. 14.6 (cit. on p. 128).

128. *Yoga Sutras*, chap. 2.18 (cit. on p. 128).

129. *Sankhya-karika*, chap. 13 (cit. on p. 128).

130. *Bhagavata Purana*, chap. 1.2.24pp (cit. on p. 128).

131. *Yoga Sutras*, chap. 2.18 (cit. on p. 129).

132. *Sankhya-karika*, chap. 13 (cit. on p. 129).

133. Belk, Russell W., "Possessions and the Extended Self", Journal of Consumer Research, 15/2 (Sep. 1988), pp. 145–6 (cit. on p. 129).

134. Hawkins, David R., *Letting Go: the Pathway of Surrender* (Sedona, Arizona: Veritas, 2012), 112–4 (cit. on p. 129).

135. *Bhagavad-gita*, chap. 18.47 (cit. on p. 133).

136. *A Simple Gita*, ed. Vraja Kishor (Scotts Valley, California: CreateSpace, 2013), p. 118 (cit. on p. 136).

137. *A Simple Gita*, ed. Vraja Kishor (Scotts Valley, California: CreateSpace, 2013), p. 118 (cit. on p. 136).

138. *Bhagavad-gita*, chap. 18.59 (cit. on p. 137).

139. `https://www.abcactionnews.com/news/national-politics/the-race-20` `20/growing-number-of-retirees-are-returning-back-to-work` (cit. on p. 141).

140. *Bhagavad-gita*, chap. 2.59 (cit. on p. 142).

141. Todd, Benjamin, *80,000 Hours: Find a fulfilling career that does good*, Kindle Locations 730–731 (cit. on p. 149).

142. Pink, Daniel, "Drive: The Surprising Truth About What Motivates Us", in (New York: Riverhead Books, 2009), chap. 6 (cit. on p. 149).

143. Pink, Daniel, *Drive: The Surprising Truth About What Motivates Us* (New York: Riverhead Books, 2009) (cit. on p. 150).

144. Achor, Shawn, et al., "9 Out of 10 People Are Willing to Earn Less Money to Do More-Meaningful Work", Harvard Business Review (November 6, 2018), `https://hbr.org/2018/11/9-out-of-1` `0-people-are-willing-to-earn-less-money-to-do-more-meaningful-work` (cit. on p. 150).

145. Herzberg, F., Mausner, B., and Snyderman, B., *The Motivation to Work* (Transaction, 2004) (cit. on p. 150).

146. Csíkszentmihályi, Mihályi, *Flow: The Psychology of Optimal Experience* (Harper Collins, 1991) (cit. on p. 150).

147. Auden, Wystan Hugh, *The Complete Works of W. H. Auden: Prose. 1939–1948.* Ed. Edward Mendelson (Princeton, New Jersey: Princeton University Press, 2002), 347 (cit. on p. 151).

148. Ariely, Dan, *Predicably Irrational* (HarperCollins, 2009), pp. 188–191 (cit. on p. 151).

149. Mazzucato, Mariana, *The Value of Everything* (New York: PublicAffairs, 2018), pp. 32–33 (cit. on p. 151).

150. `https://moralfoundations.org/` (cit. on p. 152).

151. Meegan, Dan, "Conservatives Have a Different Definition of 'Fair'", The Atlantic (April 30, 2019), `https://www.theatlantic.co` `m/ideas/archive/2019/04/why-conservatives-hate-warrens-loan-debt-re` `lief-plan/588322/` (cit. on p. 152).

152. Maslow, Abraham, "A Theory of Human Motivation", Psychological Review, 50/4, 370–96 (cit. on p. 152).

153. Rosenberg, Marshall, *Nonviolent Communication: A language of life* (Encinitas CA: PuddleDancer Press, 2003) (cit. on p. 152).

154. Matthew McDonald, Stephen Wearing, *Social Psychology and Theories of Consumer Culture: A Political Economy Perspective* (New York: Routledge, 2013), 8–9 (cit. on p. 153).

155. `https://www.theatlantic.com/international/archive/2015/02/how-an-ad-campaign-invented-the-diamond-engagement-ring/385376/` (cit. on p. 153).

156. `https://www.americangemsociety.org/page/diamondasengagement` (cit. on p. 154).

157. Cox, Lindsay Kolowich, *The Engagement Ring Story: How De Beers Created a Multi-Billion Dollar Industry From the Ground Up*, `https://blog.hubspot.com/marketing/diamond-de-beers-marketing-campaign` (cit. on p. 154).

158. "Tobacco Company Was Silent on Hazard", New York Times (May 7, 1994) (cit. on p. 154).

159. Tan, Chade-Meng, "Joy on Demand: The Art of Discovering the Happiness Within", in (New York: HarperCollinsPublishing, 2016), chap. 4 (cit. on p. 155).

160. *Bhagavad-gita*, chap. 18.48 (cit. on p. 156).

161. Duhigg, Charles, *The Power of Habit: Why We Do What We Do in Life and Business* (New York: Random House Publishing Group, 2012), 108 (cit. on p. 156).

162. *Bhagavad-gita*, chap. 9.15 (cit. on p. 157).

163. *Bhagavata Purana*, chap. 1.2.11 (cit. on p. 157).

164. Collins, Jim, *Good to Great: Why Some Companies Make the Leap... and Others Don't* (Williams Collins, 2001), 210 (cit. on p. 158).

165. Todd, Benjamin, "80,000 Hours: Find a fulfilling career that does good", in chap. 2 (cit. on p. 159).

166. Verhoeven, J.D., A.H.Pendray, and Dauksch, W.E., "The Key Role of Impurities in Ancient Damascus Steel Blades", Journal of Metallurgy, 50/9 (1998), pp. 58–64, `https://link.springer.com/article/10.1007/s11837-998-0419-y` (cit. on p. 161).

167. *Bhagavad-gita*, chap. 17.28 (cit. on p. 161).

168. *Bhagavad-gita*, chap. 8.20 (cit. on p. 162).

169. *Chaitanya charitamrta: Madhya-lila*, chap. 4.164-165 (cit. on p. 163).

170. *Bhagavad-gita*, chap. 3.27 (cit. on p. 164).

171. *The Bible, New Revised Standard Version*, chap. Matt.7.6 (cit. on p. 165).

172. *Padma Purana: Brahma-khanda*, chap. 25.17 (cit. on p. 165).

173. *Bhagavata Purana*, chap. 1.19.8 (cit. on p. 166).

174. Rosen, Steven J., *Krishna's Other Song: A New Look at the Uddhava Gita* (Santa Barbara, California: Praeger, 2010), pp. 13–14 (cit. on p. 183).

175. Dunn, Elizabeth W., Aknin, Lara B., and Norton, Michael I., "Spending money on others promotes happiness.", Science, 319, 1687–8 (cit. on p. 188).

176. Aknin, Lara B., et al., "Prosocial Spending and Well-being: Cross-Cultural Evidence for a Psychological Universal", Journal of Personality and Social Psychology, 104/4, 635–52 (cit. on p. 188).

177. `https://www.hillarys.co.uk/back-in-my-day/` (cit. on p. 189).

178. Edwards, Laura, *A Bit Rich: What the wealthy think about giving* (London: Institute for Public Policy Research, May 2002), 35 (cit. on p. 189).

179. Galbraith, John Kenneth, *The Age of Uncertainty* (Boston: Houghton-Mifflin, 1977), 192 (cit. on p. 189).

180. `https://www.washingtonpost.com/business/nelson-bunker-hunt-texas-oil-baron-who-lost-much-of-his-fortune-dies-at-88/2014/10/22/81739876-5a02-11e4-8264-deed989ae9a2%5Fstory.html` (cit. on p. 189).

181. `https://www.forbes.com/lists/2008/10/billionaires08%5FThe-Worlds-Billionaires%5FRank%5F7.html` (cit. on p. 190).

182. `http://www.bbc.com/news/uk-northern-ireland-15722053` (cit. on p. 190).

183. Edwards, Laura, *A Bit Rich: What the wealthy think about giving* (London: Institute for Public Policy Research, May 2002), 44 (cit. on p. 190).

184. Yamauchi, Kent T., and Templer, Donald I., "The Development of a Money Attitude Scale", Journal of Personality Assessment, 46/5 (1982), 522–8 (cit. on p. 191).

185. Curwen, Berni, Palmer, Stephen, and Ruddell, Peter, *Brief Cognitive Behaviour Therapy* (London: SAGE Publications, 2000) (cit. on p. 192).

186. *Bhagavata Purana*, chap. 3.29.26 (cit. on p. 194).

187. *Bhagavata Purana*, chap. 3.29.27 (cit. on p. 194).

188. Gosvami, Jiva, *Bhakti Sandarbha* (cit. on p. 194).

189. *Bhagavad-gita*, chap. 12.12 (cit. on p. 194).

190. Yamauchi, Kent T., and Templer, Donald I., "The Development of a Money Attitude Scale", Journal of Personality Assessment, 46/5 (1982), 522–8 (cit. on p. 195).

191. Rosemergy, Jim, *Even Mystics Have Bills to Pay: Balancing a Spiritual Life and Earthly Living* (Unity Books) (cit. on p. 197).

192. *Bhagavata Purana*, chap. 9.21.2-18 (cit. on p. 205).

193. Keats, John (cit. on p. 205).

194. Rosemergy, Jim, *Even Mystics Have Bills to Pay: Balancing a Spiritual Life and Earthly Living* (Unity Books) (cit. on p. 207).

195. *Bhagavad-gita*, chap. 9.2 (cit. on p. 208).

196. Bobo, Kim, *Wage Theft in America: Why Millions of Working Americans Are Not Getting Paid — And What We Can Do About It* (New York: The New Press, 2011) (cit. on p. 219).

197. *Bhagavad-gita*, chap. 6.20 (cit. on p. 227).

198. *Bhagavata Purana*, chap. 10.9.5 (cit. on p. 227).

199. *Bhagavad-gita*, chap. 9.2 (cit. on p. 227).

200. *Bhagavad-gita*, chap. 14.27 (cit. on p. 228).

201. *Bhagavad-gita*, chap. 9.18 (cit. on p. 228).

202. *Bhagavad-gita*, chap. 13.15 (cit. on p. 229).

203. *Bhagavad-gita*, chap. 3.18 (cit. on p. 229).

204. *Bhagavata Purana*, chap. 3.28.16-17 (cit. on p. 229).

205. *Bhagavad-gita*, chap. 12.11-12 (cit. on p. 230).

206. *Bhagavata Purana*, chap. 3.29.8 (cit. on p. 232).

207. *Bhagavata Purana*, chap. 11.2.47 (cit. on p. 233).

208. *Bhagavata Purana*, chap. 3.29.9 (cit. on p. 233).

209. *Bhagavata Purana*, chap. 3.29.10 (cit. on p. 233).

210. JimLoehr and Schwartz, Tony, *The Power of Full Engagement: Managing Energy, Not Time, is the Key to High Performance and Personal Renewal* (New York: Free Press, 2003) (cit. on p. 233).

211. *Bhagavata Purana*, chap. 3.29.11-12 (cit. on p. 233).

212. McGonigal, Kelly, *The Willpower Instinct* (New York: Penguin, 2012), p. 114 (cit. on p. 259).

213. Covey, Stephen M. R., and Merrill, Rebecca R., *The Speed of Trust: The One Thing That Changes Everything* (New York: Free Press, 2006), pp. 45–46 (cit. on p. 260).

214. Porath, Christine L., and Gerbasi, Alexandra, "Does Civility Pay?", Organizational Dynamics, 44/44 (2015), pp. 282 (cit. on p. 260).

215. Dasi, Devamayi, *A Life of Devotion: The Holy Biography of Om Visnupad Srila Bhakti Pramod Puri Gosvami Maharaj* (Berkeley: Nine Islands Press, 2002) (cit. on p. 263).

216. Hamermesh, Daniel, *BeautyPays: Why Attractive People are More Successful* (Princeton University Press, 2011) (cit. on p. 265).

217. Frevert, Tonya K., and Walker, Lisa Slattery, "Physical Attractiveness and Social Status", Sociology Compass, 8/3 (2014), p. 318 (cit. on p. 265).

218. Frevert, Tonya K., and Walker, Lisa Slattery, "Physical Attractiveness and Social Status", Sociology Compass, 8/3 (2014), p. 320 (cit. on p. 265).

219. Wiseman, L., and McKeown, G., *Multipliers: How the best leaders make everyone smarter* (HarperCollins, 2010) (cit. on p. 266).

220. Covey, Stephen M. R., and Merrill, Rebecca R., *The Speed of Trust: The One Thing That Changes Everything* (New York: Free Press, 2006), pp. 13–19 (cit. on p. 268).

221. Sloman, Steven, and PhilipFernbach, *The Knowledge Illusion: Why We Never Think Alone* (New York: Riverhead Books, 2017) (cit. on p. 268).

222. *Bhagavad-gita*, chap. 3.6 (cit. on p. 271).

223. *Bhagavata Purana*, chap. 11.4.11 (cit. on p. 271).

224. http://prabhupadaresearchinstitute.com/mission/ (cit. on p. 273).

225. Damerla, Venugopal R., et al., "Novice Meditators of an Easily Learnable Audible Mantram Sound Self-Induce an Increase in Vagal Tone During Short-term Practice: A Preliminary Study", Integrative Medicine: A Clinician's Journal, 17/5 (October 2018), https://www.heartmath.org/research/research-library/releva nt/novice-meditators-of-an-easily-learnable-audible-mantram-sound -self-induce-an-increase-in-vagal-tone-during-short-term-practice/ (cit. on p. 274).

226. Strasser, Susan, *Satisfaction Guaranteed* (Washington: Smithsonian Books, 1989), pp. 6–7 (cit. on p. 277).

227. Slade, Giles, *Made to Break: Technology and Obsolescence in America* (Cambridge, Massachusetts: Harvard University Press, 2006) (cit. on p. 277).

228. Wohlleben, Peter, *The Hidden Life of Trees: What They Feel, How They Communicate* (Vancouver: Greystone Books, 2016) (cit. on p. 279).

229. Montgomery, David R., *Growing A Revolution: Bringing Our Soil Back To Life* (New York: W. W. Norton, 2017), pp. 49–50 (cit. on p. 280).

230. George, Henry, *Progress and Poverty*, ed. Bob Drake (Plainfield, Indiana: The Henry George Institute, 2006), http://www.henryge orge.org/pcontents.htm (cit. on p. 282).

231. Ariely, Dan, *Predictably Irrational, Revised and Expanded Edition* (HarperCollins, 2009), pp. 267–268 (cit. on p. 282).

232. Yoder, Robert M., "Someday They'll Get Slick Willie Sutton", The Saturday Evening Post, 223/30 (January 20, 1951), p. 17 (cit. on p. 283).

233. https://www.aljazeera.com/indepth/features/2016/07/born-italian-maf ia-160718083907249.html (cit. on p. 283).

234. http://www.edizpiemme.it/autori/giovanni-impastato (cit. on p. 283).

235. Behan, Tom, *Defiance* (London: I.B. Tauris, 2008), pp. 184–5 (cit. on p. 284).

236. Behan, Tom, *Defiance* (London: I.B. Tauris, 2008), pp. 184–5 (cit. on p. 284).

237. Covey, Stephen R., *The 7 Habits of Highly Effective People: Powerful Lessons in Personal Change* (New York: Free Press, 2003), p. 196 (cit. on p. 285).

238. *Bhagavata Purana*, chap. 5.26.16 (cit. on p. 286).

239. Kohn, Isabelle, "The Secret Lives of Police Wives — and the Abuse They Suffer in Silence", MEL Magazine, `https://melmaga zine.com/en-us/story/the-secret-lives-of-police-wives-and-the-abuse -they-suffer-in-silence` (cit. on p. 288).

240. Kahneman, Daniel, *Thinking Fast and Slow* (New York: Farrar, Straus and Giroux, 2011) (cit. on p. 289).

241. `https://www.law.cornell.edu/cfr/text/5/part-2635/subpart-G` (cit. on p. 290).

242. Applebaum, Anne, "A Warning From Europe: The Worst Is Yet To Come", The Atlantic (October 2018), `https://www.theatl antic.com/magazine/archive/2018/10/poland-polarization/568324/` (cit. on p. 291).

243. Smith, Chris, "DNA's identity crisis", San Francisco Magazine (September 2008) (cit. on p. 292).

244. W.Shuman, Daniel, and Greenberg, Stuart A., "The Expert Witness, the Adversary System, and the Voice of Reason: Reconciling Impartiality and Advocacy", Professional Psychology: Research and Practice, 34/3 (2003), pp. 219 – 224 (cit. on p. 292).

245. Cassuto, Leonard, "How to Fire Your Adviser: Sometimes the only way forward is to start again", The Chronicle of Higher Education (February 28, 2016) (cit. on p. 293).

246. Hersey, Tricia, *Rest Is Resistance: A Manifesto* (New York: Little, Brown Spark, 2022), p. 20 (cit. on p. 296).

247. *Bhagavad-gita*, chap. 3.27 (cit. on p. 299).

248. *Bhagavad-gita*, chap. 5.8-9 (cit. on p. 299).

249. *Bhagavad-gita*, chap. 13.30 (cit. on p. 299).

250. *Bhagavad-gita*, chap. 2.13,20-25 (cit. on p. 300).

251. *Bhagavad-gita*, chap. 18.14 (cit. on p. 301).

252. *Bhagavad-gītā: The Rap of God*, ed. Kalakantha Dāsa (Gainesville, Florida: Sweetsong Publications, 2018), p. 105 (cit. on p. 301).

253. *Bhagavad-gita*, chap. 14.23 (cit. on p. 301).

254. *Bhagavad-gita*, chap. 13.25-26 (cit. on p. 301).

255. `https://yogainternational.com/article/view/become-your-own-inner-witness` (cit. on p. 301).

256. `http://www.consciouslifestylemag.com/negative-thoughts-getting-rid-of/` (cit. on p. 301).

257. Tan, Chade-Meng, *Joy on Demand: The Art of Discovering the Happiness Within* (New York: HarperCollinsPublishing, 2016) (cit. on p. 301).

258. *Bhagavad-gita*, chap. 9.2 (cit. on p. 302).

259. *Bhagavad-gita*, chap. 3.30 (cit. on p. 302).

260. *Bhagavad-gita*, chap. 3.31 (cit. on p. 302).

261. *Bhagavad-gita*, chap. 6.25 (cit. on p. 302).

262. *Bhagavad-gita*, chap. 2.40 (cit. on p. 302).

263. *Bhagavad-gita*, chap. 17.23-27 (cit. on p. 303).

264. Rosemergy, Jim, *Even Mystics Have Bills to Pay: Balancing a Spiritual Life and Earthly Living* (Unity Books) (cit. on p. 304).

265. *Bhagavad-gita*, chap. 3.30 (cit. on p. 307).

266. *Bhagavad-gita*, chap. 14.10 (cit. on p. 308).

267. *Bhagavata Purana*, chap. 2.5.24 (cit. on p. 313).

268. *Bhagavata Purana*, chap. 2.4.12 (cit. on p. 313).

269. *Bhagavata Purana*, chap. 12.5.7 (cit. on p. 314).

270. *Sankhya-karika*, chap. 35-6 (cit. on p. 314).

271. Gupta, Gopal K., *Maya in the Bhagavata Purana: Human Suffering and Divine Play* (Oxford, UK: Oxford University Press, 2020), pp. 58–60 (cit. on p. 314).

272. Orman, Suze, *The 9 Steps to Financial Freedom: Practical and Spiritual Steps So You Can Stop Worrying* (New York: Crown Business, 1997), 200 (cit. on p. 316).

273. Baldor, Lolita C., "Navy SEALs to shift from counterterrorism to global threats", AP News, `https://apnews.com/article/politics-osama-bin-laden-china-russia-government-and-politics-8f277ce1a284b227afcdcffabfb51ffc` (cit. on p. 316).

274. *Bhagavad Gita: Talks Between the Soul and God*, ed. Ranchor Prime (Glastonbury, UK: Fitzrovia Press, 2010), p. 46 (cit. on p. 317).

275. Minson, Julia A., and Monin, Benoît, "Do-Gooder Derogation: Disparaging Morally Motivated Minorities to Defuse Anticipated Reproach", Social Psychological and Personality Science, 3/2 (July 18, 2011), pp. 200–207, https://journals.sage pub.com/doi/abs/10.1177/1948550611415695 (cit. on p. 318).

276. *Bhagavad-gita*, chap. 6.6 (cit. on p. 319).

277. Nemeth, Maria, *Mastering Life's Energies: Simple Steps to a Luminous Life at Work and Play* (Novato, California: New World Library, 2007) (cit. on p. 320).

278. Breus, Michael, *The Power of When* (New York: Little, Brown and Company, 2016) (cit. on p. 321).

279. Stulberg, Brad, and Magness, Steve, *Peak Performance: Elevate Your Game, Avoid Burnout, and Thrive with the New Science of Success* (Emmaus, Pennsylvania: Rodale Books, 2017) (cit. on p. 321).

280. McGonigal, Kelly, *The Willpower Instinct: How Self-Control Works, Why It Matters, and What You Can Do To Get More of It* (New York: Penguin, 2012) (cit. on p. 321).

281. Niebuhr, Reinhold, and Sifton, Elisabeth, *The Serenity Prayer: Faith and Politics in Times of Peace and War* (New York: W. W. Norton, 2003), p. 7 (cit. on p. 322).

282. Tzu, Lao, "The Way and Its Power: Lao Tzu's Tao Te Ching and Its Place in Chinese Thought", in ed. Arthur Waley (New York: Grove Press, 1958), chap. Ch. XVI, p. 162 (cit. on p. 322).

283. Laslett, Peter, *A Fresh Map of Life: The Emergence of the Third Age* (Cambridge, Massachusetts: Harvard University Press, 1991), p. 4 (cit. on p. 327).

284. Sheehy, Gail, *That Vague, Crepuscular Time When Youth Has Passed: What Is It?* (Feb 1, 2012), https://www.nytimes.com/2012/02/ 02/books/in-our-prime-the-invention-of-middle-age-by-patricia-cohen .html (cit. on p. 327).

285. Rechel, B., et al., "Aging in the European Union", The Lancet, 381/(9874) (2013), pp. 1312–22 (cit. on p. 327).

286. Wymenga, A. N. M., Slaets, J.P. J., and Sleijfer, D. Th., "Treatment of cancer in old age, shortcomings and challenges", The Netherlands Journal of Medicine, 59 (2001), 259–66 (cit. on p. 327).

287. Thakura, Bhaktivinoda, "Saranagati", in Verse 1, chap. Dainya, Song 3 (cit. on p. 332).

288. Empson, Laura, *If You're So Successful, Why Are You Still Working 70 Hours a Week?*, https://hbr.org/2018/02/if-youre-so-successful-why-are-you-still-working-70-hours-a-week (cit. on p. 332).

289. Caruso, Claire C., et al., *Overtime and Extended Work Shifts: Recent Findings on Illnesses, Injuries, and Health Behaviors* (Cincinnati, Ohio: US Department of Health et al., April 2004) (cit. on p. 332).

290. Sullivan, Bob, *Memo to work martyrs: Long hours make you less productive* (Jan 26, 2015), https://www.cnbc.com/2015/01/26/working-more-than-50-hours-makes-you-less-productive.html (cit. on p. 333).

291. https://ourworldindata.org/fertility-rate (cit. on p. 334).

292. Landes, David, *The Wealth and Poverty of Nations* (New York: W. W. Norton, 1999), pp. 43, 43, 226, 316–7, 384 (cit. on p. 335).

293. Strauss, Ilana E., "The Hot New Millennial Housing Trend Is a Repeat of the Middle Ages", The Atlantic (September 26, 2016), https://www.theatlantic.com/business/archive/2016/09/millennial-housing-communal-living-middle-ages/501467/ (cit. on p. 336).

294. Segalen, Martine, *Historical Anthropology of the Family* (Cambridge, England: Cambridge University Press, 1986) (cit. on p. 336).

295. https://melmagazine.com/en-us/story/the-idea-that-men-should-be-the-sole-breadwinner-is-surprisingly-recent (cit. on p. 336).

296. Simpson, Mona, *Love, Money and Other People's Children* (July 13, 2012), https://www.nytimes.com/2012/07/15/magazine/nannies-love-money-and-other-peoples-children.html (cit. on p. 337).

297. Brooks, Arthur C., July 2019 (cit. on p. 338).

298. Swami, Giriraj, "His Darkness Ended with Light — His Art Ended with God", in id. (ed.), *Life's Final Exam: Death and Dying from the Vedic Perspective* (Badger, California: Torchlight Publishing, 2013), pp. 92–94 (cit. on p. 341).

299. Swami, Giriraj, "His Darkness Ended with Light — His Art Ended with God", in id. (ed.), *Life's Final Exam: Death and Dying from the Vedic Perspective* (Badger, California: Torchlight Publishing, 2013), pp. 92–97 (cit. on p. 342).

300. Rohr, Richard, `https://cac.org/stages-of-life-2018-08-15/` (cit. on p. 343).

301. Stanley, Andy, "The Principle of the Path: How to Get from Where You Are to Where You Want to Be", in (Thomas A Nelson, 2008), chap. 8 (cit. on p. 344).

302. `https://www.professionalchaplains.org` (cit. on p. 345).

303. `http://www.acpe.edu` (cit. on p. 345).

304. Duffy, J. Emmett, Godwin, Casey M., and Cardinale, Bradley J., "Biodiversity effects in the wild are common and as strong as key drivers of productivity", Nature, 549 (2017), pp. 261–4 (cit. on p. 357).

305. Philippon, Thomas, *The Great Reversal* (Cambridge, Massachusetts: Harvard University Press, 2019) (cit. on p. 357).

306. Clutton-Brock, T. H., et al., "The Logical Stag: Aspects of Fighting in Red Deer (*Cervus elaphus*L.)", Animal Behavior, 27 (1979), pp. 211–25 (cit. on p. 358).

307. Federal Reserve System (U.S.), 1935– Board of Governors of the, *Banking and Monetary Statistics, 1914–1941* (Washington, D.C.: Federal Reserve Board, 1943), p. 671 (cit. on p. 359).

308. Hoover, Herbert, "The President's Economic Mission to Germany and Austria, Report no. 3, Mar. 18, 1947.", in *Addresses upon the American road, 1945–1948* (New York: Van Nostrand, 1949), p. 84 (cit. on p. 359).

309. Swami, B. T., *Surrender: The Key to Eternal Life* (Washington, D.C.: Hari-Nama Press, 2013), p. 29 (cit. on p. 364).

310. *Bhagavad-gītā: The Rap of God*, ed. Kalakaṇtha Dāsa (Gainesville, Florida: Sweetsong Publications, 2018), p. 105 (cit. on p. 365).

311. Prabhupada, His Divine Grace A.C. Bhaktivedanta Swami, *Bhagavad-gita As It Is* (Los Angeles: Bhaktivedanta Book Trust, 1972) (cit. on p. 365).

312. `https://www.theguardian.com/culture/2002/oct/22/artsfeatures.higher education` (cit. on p. 366).

313. *Bhagavad Gita: Talks Between the Soul and God*, ed. Ranchor Prime (Glastonbury, UK: Fitzrovia Press, 2010), p. 147 (cit. on p. 371).

314. MacLeish, Archibald (cit. on p. 371).

315. Irwin, James B., and William A. Emerson, Jr., *To Rule The Night: The Discovery Voyage of Astronaut Jim Irwin* (Nashville: Holman, 1982), pp. 17, 24, 60 (cit. on p. 372).

316. Bronstein, Judith, *Mutualism* (cit. on p. 373).

317. Ridley, Matt, *The Origins of Virtue* (cit. on p. 374).

318. Hamilton, William D., *Innate social aptitudes of man* (cit. on p. 374).

319. Seabright, Paul, *The Company of Strangers* (cit. on p. 376).

320. Badger, Emily, "A Nobel-Winning Economist Goes To Burning Man", The New York Times (Sept. 5, 2019), `https://www.nytimes.com/2019/09/05/upshot/paul-romer-burning-man-nobel-economist.html` (cit. on p. 378).

321. *Bhagavata Purana*, chap. 10.20.24 (cit. on p. 380).

322. Smith, Adam, *An Inquiry Into The Nature and Causes of the Wealth of Nations* (Edinburgh: Thomas Nelson and Peter Brown, 1827), p. 54 (cit. on p. 381).

323. Glantz, StantonA., et al., *The Cigarette Papers* (Berkeley, California: University of California Press, 1998), p. 33 (cit. on p. 382).

324. Brandt, Allan M., "Inventing Conflicts of Interest: A History of Tobacco Industry Tactics", American Journal of Public Health, 102/1 (January 2012), pp. 63 – 71 (cit. on p. 383).

325. Markowitz, Gerald, and Rosner, David, *Deceit and Denial: The Deadly Politics of Industrial Pollution* (Berkeley, California: University of California Press, 2002), p. 12–105 (cit. on p. 383).

326. Greene, Joshua M., *Swami in a Strange Land* (San Rafael, California: Mandala Publishing, 2016) (cit. on p. 387).

327. Rosen, Steven J., *Black Lotus: The Spiritual Journey of an Urban Mystic* (Washington, DC: Hari Nama Press, 2007) (cit. on p. 388).

328. `https://wwnorton.com/books/9780393603668` (cit. on p. 394).

329. `https://youtu.be/K-cdsOuJjAI` (cit. on p. 394).

330.   https://youtu.be/UrRcA2kWoVA (cit. on p. 394).

331.   Dubner, Stephen J., and Levitt, Steven D., "Unintended Consequences", New York Times (January 20, 2008) (cit. on p. 397).

332.   Wolfe, David W., et al., "Regional Credit Market for Species Conservation: Developing the Fort Hood Recovery Credit System", Wildlife Society Bulletin, 36, pp. 423–431 (cit. on p. 397).

333.   Press, Associated, "Enron executive Watkins says Fastow wanted her fired for going to chairman", Arizona Daily Wildcat (Friday, Feb. 15, 2002), https://wc.arizona.edu/papers/95/101/05%5F1.html (cit. on p. 398).

334.   https://ec.europa.eu/commission/presscorner/detail/en/IP%5F17%5F661 (cit. on p. 398).

335.   Dalton, Kathleen, *Theodore Roosevelt: A Strenuous Life* (New York: Alfred A. Knopf, 2002), p. 151 (cit. on p. 400).

336.   Mortenson, Julian Davis, "What Two Crucial Words in the Constitution Mean", The Atlantic (June 2, 2019), https://www.theatlantic.com/ideas/archive/2019/06/executive-power-doesnt-mean-much/590461/ (cit. on p. 400).

337.   Robin, Corey, https://www.chronicle.com/article/How-Intellectuals-Create-a/234984 (cit. on p. 402).

338.   Graybill, Lyn S., *Truth and Reconciliation in South Africa: Miracle or Model?* (Boulder, Colorado: Lynne Rienner Publishers, 2002) (cit. on p. 403).

339.   Kelly, Kim, *These Men Ate Poison So You Could Have the FDA* (November 8, 2018), https://gizmodo.com/these-men-ate-poison-so-you-could-have-the-fda-1830069910 (cit. on p. 403).

340.   Clucas, Stephen, "'No small force': natural philosophy and mathematics in Gresham's London", in Francis Ames-Lewis (ed.), *Sir Thomas Gresham and Gresham College* (Abingdon: Routledge, 2016), p. 146 (cit. on p. 404).

341.   Gessen, Keith, *Joseph Brodsky and the fortunes of misfortune* (The New Yorker, May 23, 2011) (cit. on p. 407).

342.   *The Way of a Pilgrim and The Pilgrim Continues His Way*, ed. R. M. French (New York: Quality Paperback Book Club, 1998) (cit. on p. 407).

343. Rowling, J.K. (cit. on p. 410).

344. Baumol, William J., Litan, Robert E., and Schramm, Carl J., *Good Capitalism, Bad Capitalism, and the Economics of Growth and Prosperity* (Yale University Press, 2007) (cit. on p. 417).

345. Kelly, Michael A., and Bruestle, Stephen, "Trend of Subjects Published in Economics Journals 1969–2007", Economic Inquiry, 49/3, 658–73 (cit. on p. 418).

346. Clark, John Bates, *The Distribution of Wealth: A Theory of Wages, Interest and Profit* (1899), pp. 338–341 (cit. on p. 419).

347. Gaffney, Mason, et al., "Neo-classical Economics as a Stratagem Against Henry George", in *The Corruption of Economics* (Shepheard-Walwyn Ltd., 1994) (cit. on p. 420).

348. McGoey, Linsey, "The elusive rentier rich: Piketty's data battles and the power of absent evidence", Science, Technology, & Human Values, 42/2 (2017), 255–79, https://journals.sagepub.com/doi/abs/10.1177/0162243916682598 (cit. on p. 420).

349. Mazzucato, Mariana, *The Value of Everything* (New York: PublicAffairs, 2018), pp. 32–33 (cit. on p. 421).

350. Mazzucato, Mariana, *The Value of Everything* (New York: PublicAffairs, 2018), p. 28 (cit. on p. 421).

351. Harrabin, Roger, *Scale of 'nitrate time bomb' revealed* (BBC News: Science & Environment, November 10, 2017) (cit. on p. 421).

352. Moyer, Melinda Wenner, "How Drug-Resistant Bacteria Travel From The Farm To Your Table", Scientific American (December 1, 2016) (cit. on p. 422).

353. Goldenberg, Suzanne, "Half of all US food produce is thrown away, new research suggests", The Guardian (July 13, 2016) (cit. on p. 422).

354. Chandler, Adam, "Why Americans Lead The World In Food Waste", The Atlantic (July 15, 2016) (cit. on p. 423).

355. Schor, Juliet, *The Overworked American* (Basic Books, 1993) (cit. on p. 423).

356. Gandossy, Taylor, *Technology transforming the leisure world* (CNN, April 2, 2007) (cit. on p. 424).

357. Schor, Juliet, *The Overworked American* (Basic Books, 1993) (cit. on p. 424).

358. Singal, Jesse, "For 80 Years, Young Americans Have Been Getting More Anxious and Depressed, and No One Is Quite Sure Why", New York Magazine: Science of Us (March 13, 2016) (cit. on p. 425).

359. Keating, Dan, and Bernstein, Lenny, "US suicide rate has risen sharply in the 21st century", Washington Post (April 22, 2016) (cit. on p. 425).

360. Stevens, Paul, "Towards an Ecosociology", Sociology, 46/4, 579–95 (cit. on p. 426).

361. Gleeson-White, Jane, *Six Capitals, Or Can Accountants Save The Planet?* (New York: W. W. Norton, 2014), pp. 188–193 (cit. on p. 427).

362. Saltelli, Andrea, et al., "Five ways to ensure that models serve society: a manifesto", Nature, 582/7813 (June, 25 2020), pp. 482–4 (cit. on p. 427).

363. Fowkes, Neville D., and Mahony, John J., *An Introduction to Mathematical Modelling* (Chichester: John Wiley & Sons, 1994), pp. 2–3 (cit. on p. 427).

364. Box, G. E. P., "Robustness in the Strategy of Scientific Model Building", Mathematics Research Center Technical Summary Report, #1954 (March 29, 1979), pp. 2–3 (cit. on p. 427).

365. Datta, Ruchira S., "Universality of Nash Equilibria", Mathematics of Operations Research, 28/3 (August 2003), pp. 428–432 (cit. on p. 428).

366. https://birdsongorchards.com/pages/about-our-farm (cit. on p. 429).

367. *Yoga Sutras*, chap. 2.30 (cit. on p. 431).

368. *Bhagavad-gita*, chap. 17.14 (cit. on p. 431).

369. Montgomery, David R., *Growing A Revolution: Bringing Our Soil Back To Life* (New York: W. W. Norton, 2017), pp. 189–192 (cit. on p. 434).

370. Sagoff, Mark, "The plaza and the pendulum: Two concepts of ecological science", Biology and Philosophy, 18 (2003), pp. 529–531 (cit. on p. 436).

371. Sottoriva, Andrea, Barnes, Chris P., and Graham, Trevor A., "Catch my drift? Making sense of genomic intra-tumour heterogeneity", Biochimica et Biophysica Acta, 1867/(2) (2017 Apr), p. 98 (cit. on p. 436).

372. Mann, Charles, *Diversity on the Farm* (New York: Ford Foundation, 2004), pp. 8–9 (cit. on p. 437).

373. Jackson, Wes, *Becoming Native To This Place* (Berkeley, California: Counterpoint, 1996), p. 45 (cit. on p. 438).

374. Jackson, Wes, *Becoming Native To This Place* (Berkeley, California: Counterpoint, 1996), pp. 69–70 (cit. on p. 438).

375. Stuart-Smith, Sue, *The Well-Gardened Mind* (New York: Simon & Schuster, 2020) (cit. on p. 439).

376. Cronon, William, *Nature's Metropolis* (New York: W W Norton, 1991), pp. 48–50 (cit. on p. 439).

377. Green, Jeffrey S., and Gipson, Philip S., "Feral Dogs", in Scott E. Hygnstrom, Robert M. Timm, and Gary E. Larson (eds.), *The Handbook: Prevention and Control of Wildlife Damage* (Lincoln, Nebraska: University of Nebraska-Lincoln, 1994), p. C–78, https://digitalcommons.unl.edu/icwdmhandbook (cit. on p. 440).

378. Bradshaw, J. W., et al., "Feral cats: their role in the population dynamics of Felis catus.", Applied Animal Behaviour Science, 65/(3) (1999), p. 275 (cit. on p. 440).

379. Blitz, Matt, "The Best Places To See Wild Horses in North America", Smithsonian Magazine (September 17, 2015), https://www.smithsonianmag.com/travel/best-places-see-wild-horses-north-america-180956363/ (cit. on p. 440).

380. Saalfeld, W.K., and Edwards, G.P., "Distribution and abundance of the feral camel (Camelus dromedarius) in Australia", The Rangeland Journal, v.32/no. 1 (2010), p. 1 (cit. on p. 440).

381. Condan, Tomas, *Morphological Detection of Genetic Introgression in Red Junglefowl (Gallus gallus)*, Master's Dissertation (Statesboro, Georgia: Dept. of Biology, Georgia Southern University, 2012), p. 19, https://digitalcommons.georgiasouthern.edu/etd/762/ (cit. on p. 440).

382. Bevins, Sarah N., et al., "Consequences Associated with the Recent Range Expansion of Nonnative Swine", BioScience, 64/(4) (2014), p. 291 (cit. on p. 440).

383. O'Brien, P.H., "Feral goat social organization: A review and comparative analysis.", Applied Animal Behaviour Science, 21/(3) (1988), p. 209 (cit. on p. 440).

384. Rowell, T.E., and Rowell, C.A., "The Social Organization of Feral*Ovis aries*Ram Groups in the Pre-rut Period", Ethology, 95/3 (1993), p. 215 (cit. on p. 441).

385. Clutton-Brock, T.H., and Pemberton, J.M., "Individuals and populations", in *Soay Sheep: Dynamics and Selection in an Island Population* (Cambridge, UK: Cambridge University Press, 2004), p. 1 (cit. on p. 441).

386. Orwin, D. F. G., and Whitaker, A. H., "Feral sheep (*Ovis aries L.*) of Arapawa Island, Marlborough Sounds, and a comparison of their wool characteristics with those of four other feral flocks in New Zealand", New Zealand Journal of Zoology, 11/(2) (1984), pp. 201–207 (cit. on p. 441).

387. Scauzillo, Steve, "Cows gone wild: Feral cattle scaring hikers in Chino Hills State Park", San Gabriel Valley Tribune (October 22, 2013), `https://www.sgvtribune.com/2013/10/22/cows-gone-wild-feral-cattle-scaring-hikers-in-chino-hills-state-park/` (cit. on p. 441).

388. Council, National Research, *Nutrient Requirements of Dairy Cattle* (Washington, D.C.: National Academies Press, 2001), p. 215 (cit. on p. 441).

389. `https://fdc.nal.usda.gov/fdc-app.html%23/food-details/781084/nutrients` (cit. on p. 441).

390. Roesch, M., Doherr, M. G., and Blum, J. W., "Performance of Dairy Cows on Swiss Farms with Organic and Integrated Production", Journal of Dairy Science, 88/(7) (2005), p. 2467 (cit. on p. 441).

391. Clark, D.A., et al., "A Systems Comparison of Once- Versus Twice-Daily Milking of Pastured Dairy Cows", Journal of Dairy Science, 89/(5) (2006), p. 1858 (cit. on p. 442).

392. Caldwell, Gnianaclis, *The Small-Scale Dairy: The Complete Guide to Milk Production for the Home and Market* (White River Junction, Vermont: Chelsea Green Publishing, 2014), p. 66 (cit. on p. 442).

393. Levy, Neil, "So you're too ethical to eat meat; but should cows go extinct?", Aeon (January 29, 2018) (cit. on p. 443).

394. Hormann, Elizabeth, *Breastfeeding an Adopted Baby and Relactation* (Schaumburg, Illinois: La Leche League International, 2006) (cit. on p. 443).

395. Swaminathan, Nikhil, "Strange but True: Males Can Lactate", Scientific American (September 6, 2007) (cit. on p. 443).

396. Peters, Christian J., et al., "Carrying capacity of U.S. agricultural land: Ten diet scenarios", Elementa: The Science of the Anthropocene, 4/116 (2016) (cit. on p. 454).

397. Martin, C., et al., "Methane output and diet digestibility in response to feeding dairy cows crude linseed, extruded linseed, or linseed oil", Journal of Animal Science, 86/10 (October 01, 2008), p. 2642 (cit. on p. 455).

398. Isenberg, B.J., et al., "Production, milk fatty acid profile, and nutrient utilization in grazing dairy cows supplemented with ground flaxseed", Journal of Dairy Science, 102/2 (February 2019), pp. 1294–1311 (cit. on p. 455).

399. Roque, Breanna M., et al., "Inclusion of *Asparagopsis armata* in lactating dairy cows' diet reduces enteric methane emission by over 50 percent", Journal of Cleaner Production, 234 (2019), p. 134 (cit. on p. 455).

400. *Bhagavata Purana*, chap. 10.35.19 (cit. on p. 455).

401. Pappaioanou, Marguerite, and Spencer, Harrison, ""One Health" Initiative and ASPH", Public Health Reports, 123/(3) (2008 May-Jun), p. 261 (cit. on p. 456).

402. Chandler, Cynthia K., *Animal-Assisted Therapy in Counseling* (New York: Routledge, 2017), pp. 79–80 (cit. on p. 456).

403. Gormly, Kellie B., "Cow cuddling has become a thing for lonely hearts in the pandemic", Washington Post (March 8, 2021), https://www.washingtonpost.com/lifestyle/2021/03/08/cow-cudd le-sanctuary-covid/ (cit. on p. 456).

404. Freire, Paulo, "Pedagogy of the Oppressed", in (New York: Continuum International Publishing Group, 2000), chap. 1 (cit. on p. 464).

405. "The Oppressed Have Become the Oppressor", Mail and Guardian (November 9, 2001) (cit. on p. 465).

406. Rosemergy, Jim, *Even Mystics Have Bills to Pay: Balancing a Spiritual Life and Earthly Living* (Unity Books) (cit. on p. 465).

407. Michels, Robert, *Political Parties* (New York: Hearst's International Library Co., 1915) (cit. on p. 535).

408. Freeman, Jo, "The tyranny of structurelessness", Berkeley Journal of Sociology, 17 (1972), pp. 152–3 (cit. on p. 535).

409. Coddington, Mark, "The wall becomes a curtain: Revisiting journalism's news-business boundary", in *Boundaries of Journalism: Professionalism, Practices and Participation* (London: Routledge, 2015), chap. Ch. 4, pp. 93–100 (cit. on p. 536).

410. Mintzberg, Henry, *Structure in Fives: Designing Effective Organizations* (Englewood Cliffs, New Jersey: Prentice Hall, 1992) (cit. on p. 537).

411. Senge, Peter M., *The Fifth Discipline: The Art & Practice of The Learning Organization* (New York: Doubleday, 1990), pp. 264–5 (cit. on p. 538).

412. Kant, Immanuel, *Fundamental Principles of the Metaphysics of Morals*, ed. Thomas Kingsmill Abbott (Mineola, New York: Dover Publications, 2005), pp. 14–15 (cit. on p. 538).

413. Granovetter, Mark, "The Strength of Weak Ties", American Journal of Sociology, 78 (May 1973), pp. 1360–1380 (cit. on p. 539).

414. Abrantes, Roger, *Dog Language: An Encyclopedia of Canine Behavior* (Wenatchee, Washington: Wakan Tanka, 1997) (cit. on p. 540).

415. Axelrod, Robert, *The Evolution of Cooperation* (New York: Basic Books, 1984) (cit. on p. 541).

416. Vanberg, Viktor J., and Congleton, Roger D., "Rationality, Morality, and Exit", The American Political Science Review, 86/2 (June 1992), pp. 418–431 (cit. on p. 541).

417. Delahaye, Jean-Paul, and Mathieu, Philippe, "Complex Strategies in the Iterated Prisoner's Dilemma", in Alain Albert (ed.), *Chaos and Society* (Amsterdam: IOS Press, 1995), pp. 283–291 (cit. on p. 541).

418. Hofstadter, Douglas, *Metamagical Themas* (New York: Basic Books, 1985), pp. 737–755 (cit. on p. 541).

419. *Bhagavata Purana*, chap. 10.35.19 (cit. on p. 542).

420. Best, Urmila Edith, *Essence Seekers: A Quest Beyond the Forest of Enjoyment* (Hillsborough, North Carolina: Padma Inc., 2018), https://smile.amazon.com/Essence-Seekers-Beyond-Forest-Enjoyment-eb ook/dp/B07CKX49SW/ (cit. on p. 575).

421. Datta, Ruchira, Apr 1, 2002, https://groups.google.com/g/fa.caml/c/8A2JOT0sdp0/m/POUJfKcZnoAJ (cit. on p. 582).

422. Assange, Julian, Apr 2, 2002, https://groups.google.com/g/fa.caml/c/8A2JOT0sdp0/m/POUJfKcZnoAJ (cit. on p. 582).

Appendices

Appendix A

Exercises on Richness and Fields

This appendix includes exercises to be used for both Chapter 2 and Chapter 4.

Chapter 2
Read the description and then put a check mark next to the main form(s) of prosperity that the work provides for the worker — do not note what prosperity the work provides for others, or for society. The point is how this particular work bring richness into the life of the worker. Think of it as asking yourself, "Which of these forms of richness are a type of payment for the worker for the work being done?" For example, if Sam is a publicist or public relations worker, he is managing and creating *yasa* for someone else, but he may not be experiencing any for himself. Put a star next to any secondary forms of prosperity you feel this work gives to the person who is doing it. If you prefer to use a separate sheet of paper, write the name of the worker, "main," and the main form of prosperity, and then "secondary" and the secondary forms of prosperity, if any. After choosing the ways the work brings richness into the life of the worker, write a brief explanation of why you choose your answers. The answer key is in Appendix C.

Chapter 4
Write the field of work for each description. If you prefer to use a separate sheet of paper, write the name of the worker and then the field of work. The answer key is in Appendix D.

- **Aaron is an Air Traffic Controller.**

  He makes sure that aircraft are safe while landing and taking off as well as in the air. He tells the pilots what to do during landing and takeoff and is aware of where other aircrafts are, so as to prevent collisions. He lets pilots know important information and provides emergency information to his team members. He also communicates with other traffic control centers regarding incoming and outgoing flights. Aaron works on a tight schedule with constant supervision. It is a very high-pressure job, and many traffic controllers in busy hubs work only for a few years.

  - Virya — strength, power, and health
  - Yasa — meritorious fame and community
  - Sri — beauty, gracefulness; charismatic leadership
  - Jnana — knowledge
  - Vairagya — equanimity and freedom
  - Aisvarya — organizational leadership, money, and luxury

  Fields

  Government; Artistry; Ideas; Resources

- **Jose is an Event Planner.**

  He organizes business or private events. He works with clients, suppliers, caterers, and venue managers. He is the main supervisor of the set-up, execution, and clean-up of events. He has excellent communication skills, attention to detail, supervisory skills, and the ability to coordinate information on many subjects. He has to manage the client's finances, pick a suitable venue (which requires knowledge of available areas and buildings), and arrange for food, audiovisual equipment, hotels, transportation, and food, while keeping the clients satisfied. Jose has a small staff that work with him, and has regular consultants whom he hires for larger events. He runs his own event planning business.

  - Virya — strength, power, and health
  - Yasa — meritorious fame and community
  - Sri — beauty, gracefulness; charismatic leadership

- Jnana   knowledge
- Vairagya   equanimity and freedom
- Aisvarya   organizational leadership, money, and luxury

Fields

Government; Artistry; Ideas; Resources

- **Pavan is a Welder, or Brazer.**

  He assembles pieces of metal and repairs metal parts. He has to be able to read and understand blueprints before starting a project, find suitable materials for each project, measure and cut metal into the specific shapes needed, smooth cut metal into the appropriate shape, and smooth molten metal to remove creases.

  - Virya   strength, power, and health
  - Yasa   meritorious fame and community
  - Sri   beauty, gracefulness; charismatic leadership
  - Jnana   knowledge
  - Vairagya   equanimity and freedom
  - Aisvarya   organizational leadership, money, and luxury

Fields

Government; Artistry; Ideas; Resources

- **Susan is a Criminal Defense Attorney.**

  She gives advice and provides legal representation to people charged with crimes. She drafts motions and pleadings, and runs trials and motion hearings. Her main job is to make sure she is fair and unbiased in representing the accused, giving them the best possible representation. She often investigates the crime, interviews witnesses, puts together a legal strategy, researches the law as related to each case, fills out legal documents, and defends the accused in trials. She also tries to get cases dismissed or the accused charged with a lesser crime, or negotiate for lesser punishments.

  - Virya   strength, power, and health

- Yasa — meritorious fame and community
- Sri — beauty, gracefulness; charismatic leadership
- Jnana — knowledge
- Vairagya — equanimity and freedom
- Aisvarya — organizational leadership, money, and luxury

Fields

Government; Artistry; Ideas; Resources

- **Woo-jin is a Translator.**

  She translates texts from one language to another. She also edits others' translation work. She has to understand both the culture and meaning of each language and often has to consult with other experts. She often works to deadlines, and works for various organizations in the areas of business, education, healthcare, finance, and government. She needs expertise in word processing and other software.

  - Virya — strength, power, and health
  - Yasa — meritorious fame and community
  - Sri — beauty, gracefulness; charismatic leadership
  - Jnana — knowledge
  - Vairagya — equanimity and freedom
  - Aisvarya — organizational leadership, money, and luxury

Fields

Government; Artistry; Ideas; Resources

- **Farah is a Farm Warehouse Manager.**

  She is in charge of storing, shipping, and receiving agricultural materials. She supervises teams of workers, buyers, and purchasers, and oversees loading and unloading products and materials. She uses software and artificial intelligence to track inventory levels for agricultural products, controlling when to ship according to when inventory becomes too high or low. She is knowledgeable regarding government standards, which she applies for safe storage and transport of agricultural products.

— Virya   strength, power, and health

— Yasa   meritorious fame and community

— Sri   beauty, gracefulness; charismatic leadership

— Jnana   knowledge

— Vairagya   equanimity and freedom

— Aisvarya   organizational leadership, money, and luxury

Fields

Government; Artistry; Ideas; Resources

- **Adia is a Volunteer Program Coordinator.**

  She works in a charity organization that helps to provide basic needs for people displaced by war. She oversees volunteer activities within an organization. She interviews prospective volunteers and places them in appropriate roles, supervising and evaluating them, training them if needed, and keeping records. She also manages the volunteer schedule for regular and special events. She sometimes manages volunteer award programs and thank-you dinners. Sometimes her duties resemble that of an event planner.

  — Virya   strength, power, and health

  — Yasa   meritorious fame and community

  — Sri   beauty, gracefulness; charismatic leadership

  — Jnana   knowledge

  — Vairagya   equanimity and freedom

  — Aisvarya   organizational leadership, money, and luxury

Fields

Government; Artistry; Ideas; Resources

- **Hugo is an Audiologist.**

  He is a medical doctor who specializes in the diagnosis and treatment of balance disorders, hearing loss, and related issues. He often has to assess the psychological effects of hearing loss in addition to the physical when determining the proper treatment. He also generally educates his patients, both children and adults, on strategies for dealing with their condition and any medical equipment they use for treatment.

- Virya   strength, power, and health
- Yasa   meritorious fame and community
- Sri   beauty, gracefulness; charismatic leadership
- Jnana   knowledge
- Vairagya   equanimity and freedom
- Aisvarya   organizational leadership, money, and luxury

Fields

Government; Artistry; Ideas; Resources

- **Dimitry is a Biomedical Engineer.**

He develops biomedical equipment and medical devices, as well as software programs, for patients. He also trains healthcare professionals in the use of the equipment. He installs, troubleshoots, and maintains medical equipment, writes technical reports and research articles, and works with other scientists to study biological systems.

- Virya   strength, power, and health
- Yasa   meritorious fame and community
- Sri   beauty, gracefulness; charismatic leadership
- Jnana   knowledge
- Vairagya   equanimity and freedom
- Aisvarya   organizational leadership, money, and luxury

Fields

Government; Artistry; Ideas; Resources

- **Bintang is a Park Ranger.**

He protects wildlife, people, and the ecosystem within a state or national park. He takes people on tours, enforces park rules and laws regarding safety and fire codes, cares for the animals, and maintains the park. He regularly educates the public and has excellent communication skills. He gathers data about visitors, flora, and fauna, and uses the information to improve how the park is maintained. He occasionally helps with search and rescue, emergency care, and dealing with forest fires.

- Virya — strength, power, and health
- Yasa — meritorious fame and community
- Sri — beauty, gracefulness; charismatic leadership
- Jnana — knowledge
- Vairagya — equanimity and freedom
- Aisvarya — organizational leadership, money, and luxury

Fields

Government; Artistry; Ideas; Resources

- **Gabin is a Pipe Fitter.**

  He installs and manages the maintenance of various pipe equipment and systems. He reviews plumbing blueprints, fixing them and ensuring they meet the proper specifications. Sometimes he creates the materials from scratch and sometimes he creates a system from existing materials. He has to check that everything is effective, without leaks or blockages. He inspects and repairs pipes that run to various types of equipment. Gabin also works with customers to understand their needs, make recommendations, and provide estimates on work. He sources appropriate materials for each job.

  - Virya — strength, power, and health
  - Yasa — meritorious fame and community
  - Sri — beauty, gracefulness; charismatic leadership
  - Jnana — knowledge
  - Vairagya — equanimity and freedom
  - Aisvarya — organizational leadership, money, and luxury

Fields

Government; Artistry; Ideas; Resources

- **Sofia is a Bond Analyst.**

  She advises a company's management board in their financial investment decisions. She researches various investment opportunities and then counsels the board based on her calculations. She uses specialized software and stays up to date in her knowledge of statistics and economic trends. She has degrees in accounting and business administration and has excellent communication skills to explain trading agreements and investment terminology to business leaders.

– Virya	strength, power, and health
– Yasa	meritorious fame and community
– Sri	beauty, gracefulness; charismatic leadership
– Jnana	knowledge
– Vairagya	equanimity and freedom
– Aisvarya	organizational leadership, money, and luxury

  Fields

  Government; Artistry; Ideas; Resources

- **Bijoy is a Property Surveyor.**

  He oversees a survey team that measures property boundaries using special equipment, and then creates maps or charts of the measurements. He has to research government records of land titles and previous survey records and then submit his team's work to the government offices. Sometimes he helps with legal disputes.

– Virya	strength, power, and health
– Yasa	meritorious fame and community
– Sri	beauty, gracefulness; charismatic leadership
– Jnana	knowledge
– Vairagya	equanimity and freedom
– Aisvarya	organizational leadership, money, and luxury

  Fields

  Government; Artistry; Ideas; Resources

- **David is a Youth Pastor.**

  He trains youth volunteers to serve in the church he attends in coordination with parents and other family members. He also counsels the youth in the congregation, to help them achieve their spiritual goals. He plans and administers various youth programs, such as retreats and study seminars. He helps with the development and teaching of the Sunday-school curriculum. He participates in church staff meetings and helps young people to train for taking up leadership roles in the church and the congregation.

  - Virya   strength, power, and health
  - Yasa   meritorious fame and community
  - Sri   beauty, gracefulness; charismatic leadership
  - Jnana   knowledge
  - Vairagya   equanimity and freedom
  - Aisvarya   organizational leadership, money, and luxury

Fields

Government; Artistry; Ideas; Resources

- **Kyal is a Choreographer.**

  She creates dance routines. She works in theater, film, and music and for dance companies. She is a skilled dancer, and has experience in several types of traditional dance styles. She often works with the lighting and costume departments, as well as a play or film's director. She regularly demonstrates the dance moves to the dancers and so keeps her own dance skills honed.

  - Virya   strength, power, and health
  - Yasa   meritorious fame and community
  - Sri   beauty, gracefulness; charismatic leadership
  - Jnana   knowledge
  - Vairagya   equanimity and freedom
  - Aisvarya   organizational leadership, money, and luxury

Fields

Government; Artistry; Ideas; Resources

Appendix B

Self-Evaluation: the Six Kinds of Richness and the Four Fields

Can we take a self-test to find out what richness and fields suit us best? Well, yes and no. In order to have a test that gives accurate information and is reliable for many people from many cultures and situations, the test itself needs to be tested and then amended. A lot. And the tests have to be administered in various ways (oral, written, online, in person, etc.) to persons of various ages living in various countries. Really good tests are difficult to design, and even the most widely used tests always test not only the subject they are testing but also the familiarity one has with the format of the test, as well as familiarity with the language, references, etc. Charges of cultural bias hang over most tests that have been in wide use for decades.

The above problems with tests are not the whole story. As was explained in this book, it is extremely common for children to be told not to do the very things that indicate their nature. If children repeatedly hear that the tendencies and behaviors associated with their nature are wrong, then as adults they will often strongly deny that they, do, indeed, have that nature! People will then fill out a testing questionnaire with the answers they think are "good" and "right" rather than what really reflects who they are. Furthermore, if persons have not had strong impressions or training in line with their nature, they may lack awareness of what it is they love and can be very good at.

So, this self-evaluation will be different from what, perhaps, one might expect from the title. Its purpose is to give more definition and clarity to those for whom reading what we've written in the body of the text itself wasn't enough to induce sufficient self-awareness. It may also be helpful for those who did find those chapters themselves sufficient and would feel comfortable with further validation.

Some parts of this self-evaluation tool may be more or less useful for various people. We suggest that each person try to do all the parts and use what is most helpful.

B.1   Troubling tendencies

Try to recall what sorts of behavior kept getting you "in trouble" over and over again as a child that you never were able to really stop. Examples would be:

"Get your nose out of that book and be helpful."
"Mind your own business."
"Stop showing off."
"Be more assertive and make more friends."
"Stop drawing and do your homework."
"Stop taking all our appliances apart."
"Stop clowning around and get serious."

If you can't think of anything, ask your parents and/or your siblings if there was any type of repeated behavior you did that others found to be annoying or asked you to stop.

If you can identify something, try to match what you found to one or two types of prosperity and one of the four fields.

B.2   Enjoyable activities

Recall what sorts of activities you really enjoyed as a child and adolescent.
Think about activities that you would do for the joy of it, when you had extra time, or that you would sneak and do when you were supposed to be doing other things. These may be various core or extra-curricular school subjects, activities at youth groups, religious activities, and so forth. If you really enjoyed helping adults in some sort of occupational work, this is valuable information. For example, you may have helped in a shop, or with computer programming, or with accounting, or cloth-making, and so forth.

NOTE: In most cases, it's best not to consider things you tried, enjoyed for a while, and then abandoned, but rather activities you continued, perhaps in various forms. A few caveats are important when doing this exercise. One, is that many people who would not be happy in the Field of Artistry have hobbies similar to Artistry livelihoods that they do for relaxation. Such people love their hobbies and greatly look forward to doing them but would not enjoy doing something similar for their main working life, meeting the demands of customers, patrons, or bosses. Such hobbies include various forms of games, whether physical sports or mental games such as board games or computer games. Another caveat is that consuming entertainment of various kinds as a form of relaxation and recreation may be something pleasurable that one could spend much time at, but is not indicative of what would be an ideal career.

If you can identify something, try to match what you found to one or two types of prosperity and one of the four fields.

B.3 Times of satisfaction

Mentally go to times when you felt satisfied with your life and what you were doing.
It may help to talk to someone who knows you well to identify these times. Try not just to "remember" those times but to mentally and emotionally enter into your memories so that you come close to reliving them. Go through each of the ways of feeling rich and ask yourself which of those were present in your life in those times.

B.4 Questions on comparisons

Have someone take the list of the six ways of being rich, ask you the following, and note your answers.
This exercise works better if you have a friend ask rather than asking yourself. Your friend should ask for every possible pair of ways of being rich. There will be fifteen questions. Here are some examples:

- If you had to choose between having a life filled with beauty or health/strength, which would you choose?

- If you had to choose between having a life filled with beauty or organizational leadership (being the leader), which would you choose?

- If you had to choose between a life filled with organizational leadership (being the leader) and the love and praise of a community, which would you choose?

Your friend can then use your answers to make a list prioritizing which of the ways of being rich is most important to you.

B.5 Fundamental questions

For each field, ideal workers in each field continually examine their work in the light of a pair of fundamental questions:

- **Field of Artistry:**

  Is it supportive? Is it beautiful?

- **Field of Resources:**

  Is it sustainable? Is it regenerative?[*]

- **Field of Government:**

  Is it just? Is it honorable?

- **Field of Ideas:**

  Is it true? Is it wise?

Discuss with someone who knows you reasonably well which of these pairs of questions most represents the primary contribution you would like to make to the world in your lifetime, especially through your career. Keep in mind that if you cannot choose between Artistry and one other field — if those two sets of questions are equally important to you — then you may be most suited to a career in Artistry where you are assisting those in one of the other fields.

---

[*]Recall from Chapter 4 that the way we use these words in this book is much broader than just their current association with the environmental movement.

An alternative to a discussion would be to have a free-writing session yourself. Free-write for fifteen or twenty minutes about your ideal of what you would contribute to the world, especially through your work, and then see which set of questions is closest to what you have written.

B.6   If still mixed…

If through any of the above exercises you are getting a mix of fields other than Artistry and one other, then ask yourself which of the set of questions is more important if you had to choose only one set. If this still does not resolve the matter, you can consider that some careers are in one field but touch another. For example, there are people in the Field of Government who regulate those in the Field of Resources, and people who are in the Field of Ideas who are advisors to those in other fields, or specialize in teaching and/or research about them.

Appendix C

Exercises on Richness and Fields: Richness Answers

This appendix includes answers to exercises for Chapter 2.

- **Aaron the Air Traffic Controller**

  Primary: *yasa* secondary: *sri*

  Aaron gets a sense of "doing the right thing," "protecting people," and "saving people," which is an inner sense of meritorious, heroic, or righteous fame, from his work. He also regularly receives appreciation from his co-workers, the pilots, and other air traffic controllers. There is a community of air traffic controllers that give him a sense of belonging to an exclusive group who understand the unique challenges and stresses of this particularly intense job where the lives of thousands of people are in one's hands. He voluntarily takes on intense stress continually for the sake of protecting others, because one fraction of a second of inattention or a mistake can result in death and injury for hundreds. Aaron also gets a sense of beauty from his job, as he directs the patterns of planes in the sky and on the landing strip.

- **Jose the Event Planner**

  Primary: *yasa, aisvarya* secondary: *sri*

Jose gets the satisfaction of *aisvarya* in terms of leadership — managing and guiding others from his job. He receives the pleasure of the craft of organizing a wide variety of people, schedules, places, and jobs in a very complex environment. He also gains aisvarya in terms of luxury, as he gets to enjoy the food, music, elegant arrangements, and other luxuries that he provides for the group he serves. He also enjoys the prosperity of the praise of his community — both the ever-changing community of the people for whom he plans the event and the more stable but also changing community of caterers, building owners, florists, entertainers, cleaners, and so forth whom he engages for various events. Jose also receives the prosperity of charismatic leadership, as his authority is as much based on his personality as his managerial skills. He also takes pleasure in the various artistic arrangements and coordination that he provides for each event.

- **Pavan the Welder, or Brazer**

  Primary: *sri* secondary: *virya*

  Pavan primarily gets the satisfaction of *sri* from his work, as he is creating functional items of beauty and grace that require him to plan and picture his end product and the use of various materials, as an artist would do. As his work also sometimes involves strenuous physical labor, he gains physical health and strength from his work.

- **Susan the Criminal Defense Attorney**

  Primary: *yasa* secondary: *jnana, vairagya*

  The main type of prosperity that Susan gets from her job is the satisfaction of being righteous and doing meritorious work of protecting the rights of the citizens in her community. She regularly enjoys the appreciation of other lawyers and people in the justice system, which is her smaller community within the greater community that she serves. Her job also provides her with the satisfaction of constantly expanding and deepening her knowledge of the law and its application. Additionally, she gains the wealth of detachment and equanimity in the constant practice of doing her best to help accused persons without being overwhelmed by either joy or lamentation at the results.

This detachment comes from a focus on serving the law and justice above all else. She may also gain detachment from regularly interacting with suffering and the baser parts of human nature.

- **Woo-jin the Translator**

  Primary: *jnana* secondary: *sri*

  The primary type of prosperity that Woo-jin earns in her work is knowledge. She is constantly learning new vocabulary and the nuances of both language and culture, which enrich her intellectually. When her translations involve material other than that which is highly technical, she also gains the wealth of beauty in her reading of well-written prose and poetry and her creation of the equivalent in another language.

- **Farah the Farm Warehouse Manager**

  Primary: *aisvarya*

  Farah's work brings her the richness of leading and organizing a variety of people and products, with great attention to the ebb and flow of products. She gains the satisfaction of controlling and managing this complex variety.

- **Adia the Volunteer Program Coordinator**

  Primary: *yasa* secondary: *vairagya, aisvarya*

  Adia's work primarily gives her the richness of *yasa*, as she is mostly involved with managing a volunteer community for doing good work. She enjoys the feeling of being part of a team that is both a community in and of itself and is aiding the greater community. She enjoys both acknowledging the good works of the volunteers and being honored by them as well. Her work can also bring her the joy of leadership and the satisfaction of managing and controlling diverse people and projects. The pleasure of detachment can accrue from her work in the nature of volunteer work itself, where one does one's best to help others, but the results depend on many other factors involved with those one is helping. Detachment from materialistic life can also come from frequent interaction with suffering.

- **Hugo the Audiologist**

Primary: *jnana* secondary: *yasa sri*

The primary prosperity and satisfaction that Hugo gains from his work is *jnana*. He is constantly learning more about the nature of the ear as well as sound and balance — from his fellow doctors and from keeping current with research. He also gains in knowledge through the various ways he treats his patients and the feedback they give him. Additionally, he often enjoys the appreciation and praise from the communities he serves, both his patients and the fellow members of the healing profession. He may also enjoy beauty in his work as he marvels at the human body and all its workings and mysteries, the devices he works with, and the experience of restoring or augmenting hearing or balance.

- **Dimitry the Biomedical Engineer**

Primary: *sri, jnana*

The main type of prosperity Dimitry gains from his work is knowledge — he is constantly learning more about the body, disease, and wellness, as well as about software and hardware aids and solutions. He learns through his research, the rest of the medical community, and occasionally directly from patients. He also gains the satisfaction of the beauty and grace his devices and programs give to the ill and disabled.

- **Bintang the Park Ranger**

Primary: *virya, yasa, sri, vairagya* secondary: *jnana*

Bintang has a profession which gives him prosperity in strength and health, as it involves a lot of physical activity outdoors. He also regularly increases the beauty in his life through his nearly constant interaction with both landscaped and unspoiled nature and its splendor. His work regularly gives him the happiness of detachment and freedom by being away from general society and providing a lot of autonomy. The community he serves with tours, care, and rescue often acknowledges and praises his valuable contributions to society, thus bringing him *yasa*. His job may also contribute to his richness of knowledge, as he keeps learning about the ecosystem both on a macro and micro level. We might note that the job of Park Ranger is highly sought after. Most Park Rangers work at the same job for life, and there are a very limited number of openings. Perhaps this analysis of the types of prosperity inherent in this job are an indication of why the demand for working in this job regularly exceeds the supply of jobs available.

- **Gabin the Pipe Fitter**

Primary: *sri* secondary: *virya*

The main prosperity that Gabin gains from his work is *sri* because he creates and maintains a harmonious flow both of the pipes themselves and of the substances that flow through them. When his work requires physical labor, it can bring him the richness of health as well.

- **Sofia the Bond Analyst**

Primary: *aisvarya* secondary: *sri*

Sofia's work primarily brings her the prosperity of *aisvarya* as she gains the satisfaction of leadership and guiding others to manage the flow of money. Her work may also enrich her in the area of *jnana* because it involves continually learning and analyzing investment trends and explaining them to others. When she makes sound and ethical decisions, her work brings her the richness of *yasa*, as those she leads appreciate her guidance.

- **Bijoy the Property Surveyor**

Primary: *sri aisvarya*

The primary ways in which Bijoy's work enriches his life is through *aisvarya* and *sri*. In terms of *aisvarya*, he is managing and leading a team and its work, so he gains satisfaction when his coordination efforts make the jobs go smoothly and his team members do a job well. He gains the prosperity of beauty by constantly working with both the natural beauty of the land and the man-made beauty of construction, as well as in his own creation of charts and maps.

- **David the Youth Pastor**

Primary: *yasa, vairagya* secondary: *jnana*

David's work enriches him with the prosperity of *vairagya*, as he is constantly studying and teaching about spirituality, which aims (at least in part) for peaceful detachment from materialistic striving. He also gains *yasa*, as the community he serves — the youth themselves, their families, and those within the areas in which he helps place youth in service — all regularly praise his good works. He is likely to also gain in *jnana*, as his work involves study and research on scripture.

- **Kyal the Choreographer**

Primary: *virya, sri* secondary: *aisvarya*

Kyal's work brings her the satisfaction of health and strength due to its physically demanding nature. It also adds beauty to her life, as the focus of her work is on grace and symmetry. Because she directs and organizes people, she also gains the satisfaction inherent in leadership, though such is probably secondary.

Appendix D

Exercises on Richness and Fields: Fields Answers

This appendix includes answers to exercises for Chapter 2.

- **Aaron the Air Traffic Controller**

  Government

  His work is in the Field of Government because it is primarily concerned with the protection of people, and Aaron is constantly rushing into danger for the sake of saving others as he does his job.

- **Jose the Event Planner**

  Government

  Jose works in the Field of Government because he is providing people with their physical, emotional, and sometimes intellectual necessities. A cogent argument could also be made that he is more in the Field of Artistry as he provides beauty and functionality to society, but Government encompasses the sum total of his contributions.

- **Pavan the Welder, or Brazer**

  Artistry

  Pavan is in the Field of Artistry, as his work provides both beauty and functionality to society.

- Susan the Criminal Defense Attorney

  Government

  Susan's work is in the Field of Government because her career is directly involved with the protection of citizens, upholding the law, and doing work that aids honorable justice in society.

- Woo-jin the Translator

  Artistry

  Woo-jin works in the Field of Artistry because the main thing she contributes to society is beauty and functionality. She is not in the Field of Ideas because she does not generate knowledge or wisdom directly, but is rather an assistant to those who do.

- Farah the Farm Warehouse Manager

  Resources

  Farah's job is in the Field of Resources because she is generating wealth for society.

- Adia the Volunteer Program Coordinator

  Government

  Adia's work is in the Field of Government because volunteer organization generally provide government-type services (food, water, housing, education, health, etc.), although they do not act as an official government.

- Hugo the Audiologist

  Ideas

  Hugo's work is in the Field of Ideas as his primary job is the education and training of his patients (and others in the health profession). He brings people wisdom and hope.

- Dimitry the Biomedical Engineer

  Artistry

Dimitry's work is the Field of Artistry because he assists with people's basic functioning. He also adds grace to their life in terms of their physical mobility. While it might seem that such a person is in the Field of Ideas, his focus is on functionality rather than wisdom.

- **Bintang the Park Ranger**

Government

Bintang's work is in the Field of Government as he is directly protecting the land and animals, and sometimes the people, of the country in ways that sometimes require heroism, and always care and stewardship. He insures that the land, plants, and animals are treated in a just and honorable way.

- **Gabin the Pipe Fitter**

Artistry

Gabin's job is in the Field of Artistry, contributing functional beauty to society.

- **Sofia the Bond Analyst**

Resources

Sofia's work is in the Field of Resources as she is directing the flow of wealth, and helping others to gain wealth in sustainable and regenerative ways.

- **Bijoy the Property Surveyor**

Artistry

Bijoy's work is in the Field of Artistry because it primarily aids the function of society in terms of peaceful human relations and settlement of disputes. He assists the Field of Government but is not himself directly working in that field.

- **David the Youth Pastor**

Ideas

David's work is in the Field of Ideas because its main function in society is to increase wisdom.

- **Kyal the Choreographer**

  Artistry

  Kyal's work is in the Field of Artistry because her main contribution to society is beauty and pleasure.

Appendix E

Checklists on the Shades of Ego

Here is a little guide to the shades of ego as a way to understand how we
are personally affected. It's good to keep in mind that various shades,
or mixtures of the shades, can affect us at different times — even various times on the same day. Therefore, it might be useful to have
some photocopies rather than to write in the book or consider things
as "fixed."

For each category and each shade of ego, there is a list. A person
may exhibit only one or two items from a particular list in a particular
category. It is not necessary to exhibit every item on the list in order
for that shade of ego to be influencing someone.

For each category, check off the ones that apply to you. You can
then consider what you could do to come to a lighter shade or to rise
above the shades completely.

E.1   Overall

Above the shades of ego

- ☐ consciousness filled with attraction for the Source (according to
  one's understanding)

- ☐ various feelings of spiritual loving ecstasies

Sattva

- ☐ feeling health and vitality and clarity in all the senses

- ☐ an overall feeling of happiness and knowledge
- ☐ mostly doing "good" actions

Rajas

- ☐ unlimited desires and longings
- ☐ actions done for personal gain
- ☐ great attachment
- ☐ intense endeavor
- ☐ mixed happiness and distress
- ☐ mostly doing "good" actions

Tamas

- ☐ laziness
- ☐ procrastination
- ☐ oversleeping
- ☐ mental and emotional instability
- ☐ tendency towards doing "bad" actions, mostly distress

E.2   Religious or spiritual inclinations

Beyond the shades of ego

- ☐ natural attraction to hearing spiritual topics like a river flows to the sea
- ☐ wanting only spiritual love without obstructions

Sattva

- ☐ offering the results of one's activities to the Source in order to become free from materialistic entanglement

Rajas

☐ motivated by material enjoyment

☐ wanting fame

☐ wanting material things

Tamas

☐ pride

☐ envy

☐ violence

☐ anger

☐ thinking that oneself (or one's religion) is the most spiritual and "correct"

E.3 Food

Beyond the shades of ego

☐ same as *sattva*

☐ including some ceremony of sanctification, offering, or blessing

Sattva

☐ foods that increase the duration of life, purify one's existence, give strength, health, happiness, and satisfaction

☐ foods that are juicy, wholesome, and pleasing to the heart

☐ the food is bought with money earned honestly, cooked in a clean environment, and served in a clean and pure place by those with a satisfied mind

☐ the food is attractive to the stomach and eye

Rajas

☐ foods that are too bitter, sour, salty, hot, pungent, or dry, causing distress while eating, misery after eating, and disease later on

Tamas

- ☐ old food that is not fresh

- ☐ tasteless food

- ☐ food that is the product of violence

E.4 Religious or spiritual ceremonies and worship

Beyond the shades of ego

- ☐ like sattva for the pleasure of our Source

Sattva

- ☐ following scripture

- ☐ out of duty, not in the sense of "obligation" but in the sense of it being intrinsically the right and harmonious thing to do

- ☐ without desiring any worldly reward

Rajas

- ☐ for some material benefit

- ☐ out of pride

Tamas

- ☐ without regards for scriptures

- ☐ without distribution of sanctified food

- ☐ without songs of praise

- ☐ without offering remuneration to the priests (or equivalent)

- ☐ without faith

E.5   The types of self-discipline one has

Beyond the shades of ego

- ☐ fixed in consciousness because of having a higher taste

Sattva

- ☐ worship of God

- ☐ respect for teachers and elders

- ☐ cleanliness

- ☐ sexual regulation that will assist in spiritual realization (in some cases abstinence)

- ☐ speech that is truthful

- ☐ speech that is beneficial to ourselves and others

- ☐ speech that is pleasing

- ☐ speech that is based on sacred wisdom

- ☐ mental satisfaction

Rajas

- ☐ done out of pride

- ☐ done for the respect and honor of others

- ☐ unstable

Tamas

- ☐ foolish

- ☐ harmful to oneself or others

E.6 Charity

Beyond the shades of ego

- ☐ in *sattva* to please the Source

Sattva

- ☐ given at an appropriate time and place
- ☐ given to a worthy person or cause
- ☐ given without expecting return
- ☐ given simply because it is the right thing to do

Rajas

- ☐ given with expectation of return
- ☐ given in a grudging mood
- ☐ given with regret later
- ☐ given out of obligation
- ☐ given at the request of a superior

Tamas

- ☐ given at an inappropriate time or place
- ☐ given to an unworthy person or cause
- ☐ given without respect or attention

E.7 Detachment and renunciation

Beyond the shades of ego

- ☐ rejecting that which is spiritually harmful

Sattva

- ☐ doing one's work because it is the right and good thing to do

- ☐ giving up attachment to enjoying the fruits of one's work

Rajas

- ☐ rejecting good work if it's troublesome

- ☐ rejecting good work out of fear of bodily discomfort

Tamas

- ☐ capriciously not doing what one should be doing

E.8 Understanding

Beyond the shades of ego

- ☐ knowing how to connect with our Source with loving service

Sattva

- ☐ knowing what to do and what not to do

- ☐ knowing what is to be feared and what is not to be feared

- ☐ knowing what is binding and what is liberating

Rajas

- ☐ cannot distinguish between what is *dharma* and what is not

- ☐ cannot distinguish between what to do and what not to do

Tamas

- ☐ considers *dharma* to be not *dharma*

- ☐ considers what is not *dharma* to be *dharma*

- ☐ goes in the wrong direction

E.9 Wisdom

Beyond the shades of ego

- ☐ perceives a personal God and God's energies everywhere

Sattva

- ☐ perceives that all bodily forms are animated by a spiritual nature, all equal in value to one another

Rajas

- ☐ perceives that each type of body is ultimately a different type of being

Tamas

- ☐ has wisdom only in work and not much interest in truth

E.10 How one does one's work

Beyond the shades of ego

- ☐ with spiritual sense of self and unbounded bliss

Sattva

- ☐ without material identification
- ☐ with great determination and enthusiasm
- ☐ without wavering in success or failure

Rajas

- ☐ attached to the work and the results of one's work
- ☐ greedy
- ☐ envious
- ☐ moved by joy and sorrow

Tamas

- ☐ unethical

- ☐ obstinate

- ☐ deceitful

- ☐ expert in insulting others

- ☐ lazy

- ☐ prone to procrastination

- ☐ morose

E.11 Determination

Beyond the shades of ego

- ☐ uninterrupted and unmotivated

- ☐ only for love

Sattva

- ☐ unbreakable

- ☐ sustained by linking with the Source

- ☐ has self-control of mind and body

Rajas

- ☐ based on expecting favorable results in *dharma*, *artha*, and *kama*

Tamas

- ☐ fearful

- ☐ Lamentation

- ☐ morose

- ☐ illusory

E.12   Happiness

Beyond the shades of ego

- ☐ boundless

- ☐ experienced with spiritual senses

Sattva

- ☐ difficult at the beginning and pleasing at the end

- ☐ born of the satisfaction of having intelligence from the real self

- ☐ characterized by inner mental peace and satisfaction

- ☐ the process of purification to get there requires restraint

Rajas

- ☐ based on contact between the senses and sense objects

- ☐ pleasing at the beginning and painful at the end

Tamas

- ☐ asleep to the real self or any deliberate self-forgetfulness

- ☐ characterized by intoxication

- ☐ delusion from beginning to end

- ☐ based on sleep

- ☐ based on laziness

- ☐ based on illusion

Endnotes

a. Even groups that are ideologically pre-committed to not having anyone specially designated for these roles find that over time these functions naturally fall on the shoul-
ders of only a subset of people. German sociologist Robert Michels called this phenomenon "The Iron Law of Oligarchy."[407] Author Jo Freeman also elaborated on this
phenomenon.[408] The exceptions are generally very small societies, which often are not
self-sufficient but depend on a larger, encompassing society for these functions.

b. The following extract describes the boundary wall between journalism and advertising
in more detail:

> [The] wall, between the journalistic and business-oriented functions
> of a news organization, is one of the foremost professional markers of
> journalism, a principle that is reinforced most strongly in the central
> sites of its socialization — journalism schools, textbooks, and reviews,
> not to mention thousands of newsrooms large and small. Along
> with the principle of independence from political factions, the news-
> business wall is the cornerstone upholding American journalism's
> sense of autonomy, which allows it to function as a profession....
>
> ...scholars — at least the more critical ones who might be inclined
> to study journalistic discourse — tend to agree with journalists that this
> boundary should exist....
>
> The news-business boundary is based on a distinctive model of the
> modern news organization, with two sets of goals: financial viability,
> on the one hand, and public service or public influence on the other.
> These aims...can be traded off to varying degrees, but they cannot fun-
> damentally be made congruent....
>
> ...journalists have constructed and enshrined a border between
> themselves and their organizations' business operations primarily as a
> way to safeguard their professional autonomy, or journalists' ability to
> exercise judgment and control their work process....Journalists have
> worked exceptionally hard to maintain a strong boundary against
> commercial influence, making it a core element of their professional
> values....
>
> [During the 1800's] journalists decried...devotion to advertiser's
> desires and business concerns as unethical and polluting. As early as
> 1848, James Gordon Bennett's *New York Herald* banned puffs [promo-
> tional stories, bordering on ads disguised as news items] from its pages.
> In 1869, literary critic Richard Grant White called for the formation of
> what might be called a prototype of the news-advertising wall: "abso-

lute and without exception, that nothing in the interests of an advertiser, no matter what its importance, shall be admitted into the editorial columns for any consideration."...

Journalists have developed a variety of tools to defend their jurisdiction from commercial interests. Though boundary work is fundamentally a rhetorical process, one key strategy is more organizational than rhetorical — the distinctly bifurcated structure of news organizations described above, with the news and business departments operating independently from each other and often at odds....This organizational separation has historically manifested itself most materially in the physical separation between newsroom and advertising departments, an arrangement that reinforces the boundary both physically and symbolically. Longtime *Chicago Tribune* publisher, Robert McCormick, famously enforced this physical divide with separate elevators for journalists and those in the business operation, the latter of which did not stop on the newsroom floor....

Aside from organizational divides, most of the journalists' work in defining and defending the news-business boundary has been accomplished rhetorically. The professional values regarding independence from business are most formally encoded at the organizational level in news organizations' written guidelines and at the professional level in codes of ethics. These tools reify a set of professional norms to which journalists can appeal as their basis to a moral claim when their ethical rectitude is challenged....

The central metaphor used to maintain the news-business boundary is that of the wall — perhaps the most direct, forceful, and enduring metaphor in modern American journalism....

Journalists have widely employed two other rhetorical themes alongside that of the wall: Public service and trust. Journalists often set their public service and commercial goals in opposition to each other — and indeed they often conflict. Former *New York Times* executive editor Max Frenkel set up this distinction as the fundamental dividing line in the profession: "Serious journalists are not hard to define. Deep down, they think of packaging news not as a business but as a public service." The public-service argument is more than a way to claim social responsibility as a profession; as Squires notes, it is the basis on which journalists defend their First Amendment rights. If that claim is based on journalism's effectiveness as a business rather than its aim to serve democratic ends, journalists' moral case for expansive First Amendment rights — in essence, its formal autonomy from the state — crumbles.

While public service as a theme is meant to set up and defend professional journalism's idealized goals, trust is oriented toward its idealized assets. Like the wall, credibility is characterized...as an immense social assets for journalists — something they possess in enough quantity to drive virtually their entire social value...

—Mark Coddington, The wall becomes a curtain: Revisiting journalism's news-business boundary[409]

c. Here we mean "bureaucratic" in the sense of a machine bureaucracy. Henry Mintzberg identifies two types of bureaucracy, "machine" and "professional." A machine bureaucracy standardizes work processes, and people who set the rules for conduct are the key part of the organization. Members need little training or indoctrination; they simply have to follow the rules. This organizational type is for routine, formalized work. Informal communication is discouraged, authority is top-down, and people are often grouped together by what kind of work they do. This form aims for a set response to situations, with little or no individual consideration.

In a professional bureaucracy, it's the skills of the professional members that are standardized. The professionals get extensive training, both in theory and practice. Only selected persons are admitted to the training, and there is some sort of test upon completion of the training, although learning and improvement is expected to continue lifelong. The skills needed are well-defined but hard to learn. Fully trained specialists then control their own work. The specialists work closely with their "clients" — those they serve — but do not receive direct orders from administration, nor are they expected to always confer closely with peers. In these organizations, unlike a machine bureaucracy, there is not an extensive department to decide rules and procedures. The professionals learn those in the training situation. They are subject only to the collective control of colleagues who trained them and can censure them. Professionals join or create organizations so they can share resources, learn from each other, and help people who need a combination of experts.[410]

d. Here MacCarthy brings these department heads into dialogue, so they can see the needs of the company as a whole in an integrated way:

> **MacCarthy** I think we're onto something here. What we're saying is that the company in the past has been locked in. The only thing that made us great was product research and development. So we're having this incredible tension here….I think that the dilemma that you're [Grauweiler] helping us to see is that…we should be offering whatever products the customer fundamentally needs. But then there's the other side that says, "But if it comes out of DataQuest's research, it has to carry a DataQuest label." What you're saying is that's not true. That [what label to put on] ought to be a marketing decision based on what positioning you're trying to do. That's very helpful…because most of us have felt that if a product is not going to have a DataQuest label on it, you won't develop it in the first place.
>
> …
>
> **Smyth** There are two points I want to make from this. It looks to me like your efforts could be put to developing a product that could be manufactured outside…it looks to me that we've thrown away some development efforts that could have been licensed to other companies even….I've always thought it was crazy that, in order to get a product out of R&D, you had to put a DataQuest label on it.
>
> **Grauweiler** That's been a constraint on our program….
>
> **Smyth** Now, the other thing is that we're not communicating in any kind of rich way between marketing and R&D. As a matter of fact, it's getting more separate….If we're going to work on the total needs of the customer…there has to be a way that that's seen in a lot of different places in the company.

> –Peter M. Senge, *The Fifth Discipline: The Art & Practice of The Learning Organization*[411]

e. The interactive web tool https://www.hillarys.co.uk/back-in-my-day/, accessed on April 19, 2018, stated that it collated data from the Office for National Statistics, the Automobile Association, the Nationwide Building Society, and the National Archives, all in the UK, to draw up these figures.

f. The conversion from pounds sterling to dollars was done using the spot exchange rate according to the Bank of England. For some pairs of currencies, exchange rates do not reflect purchasing power, and "purchasing power parity" is used instead in some studies. However, the economies and financial systems of the US and the UK were sufficiently linked in 2002 that this is not a concern in this case.

g. In 1785, Immanuel Kant wrote:

> To be beneficent when we can is a duty; and besides this, there are many minds so sympathetically constituted that, without any other motive of vanity or self-interest, they find a pleasure in spreading joy around them and can take delight in the satisfaction of others so far as it is their own work. But I maintain that in such a case an action of this kind, however proper, however amiable it may be, has nevertheless no true moral worth, but is on a level with other inclinations, e.g., the inclination to honour....For the maxim lacks moral import, namely, that such actions be done from duty, not from inclination. Put the case that the mind of that philanthropist were clouded by sorrow of his own, extinguishing all sympathy with the lot of others, and that, while he still has the power to benefit others in distress, he is not touched by their trouble because he is absorbed with his own; and now suppose that he tears himself out of this dead insensibility, and performs the action without any inclination to it, but simply from duty, then first has his action genuine moral worth. Further still: if nature has put little sympathy in the heart of this or that man; if he, supposed to be an upright man, is by temperament cold and indifferent to the suffering of others, perhaps because in respect of his own he is provided with the special gift of patience and fortitude and supposes, or even requires, that others should have the same...would he not still find in himself a source from whence to give...a far higher worth than that of a good-natured temperament could be? Unquestionably. It is just in this that the moral worth of the character is brought out which is incomparably the highest of all, namely, that he is beneficent, not from inclination, but from duty.
>
> –Immanuel Kant, *Fundamental Principles of the Metaphysics of Morals*[412]

What Kant writes here is not always true. Acting out of duty can lead to a sense of inner harmony, or at least to relief from a sense of inner discomfort arising when one does not act out of duty. The difference between this feeling and "pleasure in spreading joy" is one of intensity, and does not make the feeling of acting out of duty categorically superior from a moral standpoint. We are not automata heartlessly following rules. This is a false self-conception, and every false self-conception itself springs ultimately from some, perhaps very subtle, egocentric motivation (e.g., pride in supposed lack of emotion — an oxymoron). The extinction of sympathy due to personal sorrow in Kant's first example of a philanthropist indicates the shading of *tamas*. That the philanthropist gives anyway indicates a mixture of the shade of *sattva*. However, this mixture is not superior to the purer *sattva* shading the joyful philanthropist. The extinction of sympathy in the second philanthropist is a subtle shading of *rajas*, one of the pitfalls of *vairagya* (detachment) that we discuss in Chapter 21.

h. If I used a search engine to arrive at this knowledge, that may contribute to this idea. Ruchira used to work in Google Search Quality, the core team responsible for providing search results. Using a search engine cannot replace deep study of or experience with a subject, which indeed was not the developers' goal. Search engines aim to *direct* users toward experts in a subject. However, they often direct people towards experts in "webspam," i.e., fooling search engines (and perhaps also the general public) instead. The battle between those developing search engines and the webspammers is continual, so as users of search engines, we must always remain on guard. Asking ourselves a few questions can sometimes help us detect webspam. How much effort would it take for me, or any random person who knows how to make webpages, memes, or videos (rather than the subject in question), to write a webpage, create a meme, or script a video like this myself? Is this site attempting to inflate my ego in any way? For example, is it suggesting that by viewing this site, I now have hidden knowledge to defeat evil people? (A one-two punch: I'm superior *both* because I now "know" what those foolish people don't *and* because I'm so good in comparison to those other, evil people.) What is this site trying to sell me? What proportion of the website is dedicated to either inflating my ego (especially, inflaming my *rajas*) or promoting a product, as opposed to neutrally conveying knowledge? The tricks of webspammers are one reason why, though search engines can be very useful, they are a supplement to, rather than a substitute for, getting knowledge from experts.

If I used Facebook to arrive at whatever knowledge I have, I do well to keep in mind that the stated mission of Facebook is to foster connection, rather than to organize information, and its main process is social reinforcement. The opinions of those most closely connected with me, or held by the greatest number of my friends, are not necessarily the most expert or the most useful. One effective way to use social networks to gain knowledge is to take advantage of the strength of weak ties: those who are less like us are more likely to know something we ourselves don't know.[413] Someone in our network may be able to refer us to the most expert person they know, who may be able to refer us to the most expert person they know, and so forth, until we arrive at the most useful expert resource to answer a particular question — or to help us undertake deeper study of a subject. While this process may be more time-consuming than haphazardly getting comments from whoever sees a Facebook thread, in many cases it is more likely to be more beneficial. We can save some time on each particular question by getting to know in which subjects each of our friends has seriously endeavored to become expert. (As explained above, this doesn't necessarily track with how much time they've spent using a search engine on the subject.) This way cherishing their knowledge goes together with cherishing our friends through respecting their efforts.

Incidentally, fast conversations on electronic media can often get *rajasic*. One way to break a feedback cycle of spreading *rajas* back and forth, or at least stop contributing to it, is to slow down one's own rate of response considerably, allowing a longer interval — perhaps even as much as a day — to elapse between one's own responses.

i. T cells are a particular kind of cell in our immune system. Some of them help to fight off certain kinds of infections and tumors by attaching to and killing the diseased cells of our own body. For instance, some kinds of viruses infect us by entering our own cells and turning them into factories for producing more of the virus. Tumor cells are cells of our own body that have gone rogue, going out of control recopying themselves so often that they impede bodily function instead of aiding it.

The cells of our bodies take small molecular fragments from inside themselves and hold them outside their surface. The holder is called the MHC, and the small molecular fragment is called an antigen. The T cells have to latch onto the diseased cells in at least two ways before they can kill them: by grabbing the MHC and by fitting a molecule on the T cell's surface called an antibody to the antigen being held out by the MHC. Different T cells display different antibodies. For a T cell to grab a diseased cell, its antibody has to fit with the diseased cell's antigen like a lock and key.

Within our bone marrow, our body makes immature T cells with many different kinds of antibodies, by mixing and matching different parts. Before these T cells can be ready to do their job, they have to migrate to the thymus. There all the T cells compete with one another to stay alive.

The T cells have to pass two tests to win the competition. First, they have to be able to latch onto the MHC of our cells. If they can't do this, they're useless for the job. Second, their specific antibodies must not attach to any of the antigens presented by our healthy cells. If they did, they would attack our own healthy cells, resulting in autoimmune disease. The antigens presented by our healthy cells are called "self" antigens. Our immune system must recognize that these healthy cells belong to the self — our whole body, of which the immune cells are also a part — and leave them alone. On the other hand, cells infected by a virus present antigens that are pieces of virus protein. The T cells recognize these as non-self. Tumor cells may also produce abnormal proteins, and so present tumor-specific antigens that T cells latch onto.

This competition is a key part of our adaptive immunity, which helps us fight off many kinds of infection. Also, within each of us, cells are continually going rogue and forming microscopic tumors. T cells find and kill off almost all of these tumors before they disturb our health. Training T cells to kill off full-blown cancers — cancer immunotherapy — is currently an exciting field of active research.

j. More specifically:

> …[cannibalism] does occur in canids, but only rarely. When it does happen, it is mostly as passive cannibalism, i.e., the individual that is eaten was already dead.
>
> –Roger Abrantes, *Dog Language: An Encyclopedia of Canine Behavior*[414]

k. Some readers may be familiar with the Prisoner's Dilemma, a classic lose-lose game between two players. The scenario is that two criminal accomplices have been arrested. There isn't enough evidence to convict either of them, and the police are questioning them separately. If neither of them confesses, i.e., they cooperate with each other as they had previously agreed, they will both be let go. If one of them confesses ("defects" from the agreement) and the other stays mum, the informant will be sentenced to one year in prison and the informant's accomplice will be sentenced to ten years. If they both confess, they will both be sentenced to five years. For the purposes of this scenario, if neither confesses and they are let go, then their loss is minimal: only the time they spent in detention being harangued by police. Although they would both be best off not confessing, if they think individualistically (rather than recognizing the symmetry of the situation), the dominant strategy for each of them is to confess. On the other hand, in another version of the game called the iterated Prisoner's Dilemma, there is a large arena of players and each player is repeatedly matched up with opponents: sometimes ones they've played against before, and sometimes new ones. In this scenario, a player can have a more complex strategy than either simply always confessing or always staying mum.[415] In a single match, players might seem to be worse off by "canceling" (i.e., walking away, refusing to play that match with that opponent). However, over the course of the tournament, those players who sometimes use the cancel option strictly outperform those players who never do.[416][417] If the prisoners realize that they're both in the same boat, and therefore should only look at strategies where they both play the same way, then they would both stay mum and would both be better off. "Superrational thinkers," as described by Douglas Hofstadter, do recognize when they're in the same boat as the other players and thus act so that they are all better off.[418] These are thinkers who have internalized the question that parents often ask their 8-year-olds, "What if everyone did that?" and regularly apply it in their decision making.

l. The Sanskrit word that we have rendered as "pariah" literally means "dog cooker;" in many cultures of the world, those who cook or eat dogs are generally looked down upon in society.

m. We might well doubt whether the behavior of such insects represents an ideal we could emulate from nature. There is a widespread misconception that, in general, cooperation is an unsound and unsustainable strategy in the natural world, and that nature is and must be founded on selfishness. This misconception often stems from an assumption that the prominent mathematical biologist W.D. Hamilton proved the selfish basis of nature. Even as late as 1997, Ridley, whom we quoted above, repeated this mistaken idea about Hamilton's conclusions in the same book. Some professional biologists today continue to be unaware that this idea is no longer the current consensus. However, biology, as a living science, often grows wiser as empirical evidence accumulates and better models are developed. The misconception derives from Hamilton's work of 1963 and 1964, in which he argued against the sustainability of cooperation in nature. By 1975, however, thanks to new data answering the empirical questions Hamilton had asked in his earlier papers, and through new models developed via the work of George Price, Hamilton revised his earlier skepticism about the viability of cooperation, and concluded that acting in the interests of groups at higher and higher levels can indeed lead to persistent success. The whole story is recounted by Elliott Sober and David Sloan Wilson in their 1999 book *Unto Others*. In 2006, the philosopher Samir Okasha brought further clear thinking to bear on the interplay of individual and group interests, dissipating confusion and stimulating subsequent developments in research. The dynamics of group interactions among those with a combination of shared and competing interests continues to be a field of active research.

n. For example, how a cow digests grass would be a smaller scale model, and how a herd of cows interacts with a pasture would be a larger scale model. Each of these models may impact the other. For instance, how many cows have been grazing and for how long may affect the nutritional quality of the grass and the microbes that are on it. That may affect how individual cows digest it, which in turn may affect how they fertilize the pasture.

o. While some people may appreciate the stability once the dairy reaches its equilibrium population, a threat to that stability may occur because when new and young managers take over a herd, they may want to innovate. The nature of those most suited for the Field of Resources is to thrive on a a thirst for something new and different. It is, therefore, a good idea to find ways for leaders of a dairy to innovate and expand without disrupting the equilibrium of the herd. We know that people in the Field of Resources often thrive on the challenges of optimizing resources. Once the *ahimsa* herd reaches a stable size, we can expect other kinds of challenges to continue. Besides dealing with unexpected events, persons in the Field of Resources may, therefore, use their natural inclination for expansion, innovation, and improvement to find enjoyment in diversifying feed and forage combinations, as well as diversifying milk products. Making freeze-dried milk powder may open up possibilities for storage and distribution. If the farm is implementing polyculture as we discussed above, new opportunities may arise for combining produce with milk products as the crop composition varies over time. Mathematical ecosociology can help map out these possibilities. With more data we could add other factors to the simple model above, or create additional linked models, to answer various questions for planning purposes, such as how much excess milk is produced at any given time over what the calves drink.

p. An example of this ideal of personal interaction is found in the *Bhagavata Purana*.[419] Viswanath Chakravarti, in his 17th-century commentary on this verse, wrote: "Thus being called by name, the cows are coming forward, and Krishna, thinking that when it is time to bring them back from the forest none should be forgotten, is counting them on his jewel-beads."

Glossary

ahimsa: Nonaggression.

aisvarya: Power and control.

ajna: Chakra of wisdom.

anahata: Chakra of care and compassion.

artha: Richness; something desireable.

asrama: A place of religious retreat; can be a monastery but can also be for families.

avadhuta: eccentric mendicant; commensal

bhakti: Devotional service (to a personal understanding of God).

brahman: The great formless luminosity in which there is absolute oneness.

commensal: A commensal is a person outside the four fields of work who derives benefits, but neither harms nor helps. Though commensals don't help society directly or in the short term, they do not harm it either. Sometimes society may benefit from their special viewpoint and skills as well.

daan: Giving in charity.

dharma: The intrinsic nature of something.

Field of Artistry: A large group of careers that provides the foundation of society and whose workers provide beauty, support, and functionality. This field includes most people called workers or labor, most of the service industry, most of the entertainment industry, and most athletes.

Field of Government: A group of careers that involve governing, whether or not the worker's pay comes from an official government agency. People in this field protect a social group from internal or external threats, or create and maintain rules and laws, or are responsible for overall stewardship to take care of the needs of a group of people.

Field of Ideas: A group of careers that provide wisdom, guidance, truth, and education to individuals, groups, or society in general. Such wisdom can be given, e.g., through language, math, or the fine arts. This field encompasses most careers in counseling, teaching, religion, science, and education.

Field of Resources: A group of careers that provide the resources for society, such as farming, business, finance, and trade. The essence of this field is directing the flow of raw materials from earth, water, air, fire, plants, and animals through the processes of harvesting and refinement to the people who finally use or consume them.

field of work: A grouping of many careers that share similarities in mood, disposition, values, and societal role.

jnana: Intelligence, philosophy, science (both hard and soft), and the process of learning and understanding.

kama: Desires, or even lust

kirtan: Call-and-response singing praise of the Lord

kirti: Spoken words of praise and honor

mantra: A pure sound vibration that when repeated over and over delivers the mind from its material inclinations and illusion. A transcendental sound or Vedic hymn, a prayer or chant.

mode of nature: *See* shade of ego

moksha: Living free of frustration; liberation.

occupational division: *See* field of work.

om: A name for the Source, the Supreme.

om tat sat: Dedicated action to the Supreme, free of the shades of ego.

rajas: Indicates a mood of energetic, external striving for bigger and better things of this world, both for the body and the mind. It is often translated as passion or attachment.

rajasic: Of the nature of *rajas*.

rasa/rasas: Flavor or taste. In Ayurveda, it is the liquid that nourishes us and allows us to have pleasure, as well as the various tastes (sweet, salty, etc) that our tongue can perceive; can also mean a state of emotion in relationships — feelings of friendship, joy, surprise, etc.

sat: Proper, dedicated action; literally "eternal" and "real"

sattva: That which is authentic, lasting, and beneficial. It is often translated as goodness, or illumination.

sattvic: Of the nature of *sattva*.

satya: Truth; knowing oneself.

saucha: Literally "cleanliness," and, in relation to business can mean to be honest and in compliance with legal standards; integrity.

seva: Service; generally service done for a religious or spiritual purpose.

shade of ego: Self-centered egotistical mindsets that exist on a continuum, which can be roughly divided into three forms.

sri: Often used synonymously with fortune or prosperity in general, *sri* is a name for a divine being, Lakshmi , who personifies fortune, prosperity, wealth, or resources. So, in one sense, *sri* is all-encompassing for all six types of wealth. Its core meaning has to do with giving off light or radiance, and can mean beauty, grace, and splendor. The word *sri* is often used as a title for both men and women in India, meaning respectable, and is also joined with various names of the Supreme, as in Sri Bhagavan, or Sri Rama.

tamas: Darkness, ignorance, and delusion. It is a kind of complacency. The *Yoga-sutras* describe *tamas* as "steadiness, immovability, or inertia" and the *Sankhya-karika* describes it as "heavy" and "enveloping."

tamasic: Of the nature of *tamas*.

tapasya: Effort, austerity, voluntarily taking up some difficulty for a higher purpose.

tat: The desire for our work to be on the plane of dedication to our Source, free from the shades of ego.

tree of work: A metaphor used in this book to refer to a particular career, comparing it to a particular kind of tree.

vairagya: Equanimity, peacefulness, literally "lack of attachment." *Vairagya* is not repression or suppression, but an inner state of equanimity and freedom from attachment and aversion.

virya: *Virya* literally means vitality and strength. It is closely associated with muscle strength. It can also mean sexual virility and potency for anyone, but particularly males. *Virya* is associated with strength, energy, determination, vigor, courage, and so forth.

yasa: Fame. This is the richness of honor, glory, renown, praise, and respect.

Index

Readers may need to follow the citations on the indexed page to see where the indexed entry occurs.

Index

Index of verses

Readers may need to follow the citations on the indexed page to see where the indexed entry occurs.

Bg stands for *Bhagavad-gita* and *BhP* stands for *Bhagavata Purana*.

Acknowledgments

We would like to thank all those who contributed guest chapters to this book, namely Charles Vishwambhar Towle, Srimati Dasi, Saradi and Catu, Dr. Venugopal Damerla, Rani Dasi, Damodar Prasad Roe, Janet Kaye, Dr. Rambhoru Brinkmann, Hare Krishna Dasi, and Dave McWilliams. We thank Ashto for letting Hare Krishna Dasi tell his story. We also thank Charles Eisenstein for permission to reprint his previously published essay.. We thank Mirit Cohen for permission to quote her story. We are very grateful to Dr. Michael Geary for kindly writing the foreword.

In the beginning stages of writing, the two of us worked together in person, at New Vrindaban for a month, then Denver, Colorado for two weeks, in Hilo, Hawaii for six weeks, and finally in Hillsborough, North Carolina for one week. We would like to thank our generous hosts at those respective locations, namely Jaya Krsna and Anuradha, Vrindasundari and Tusta Krishna, Murari and Nitya, and Krishnapriya. We also thank many others at each of those locations who went above and beyond the call of duty to welcome us hospitably and support our visits in many ways, big and small. Without their willingness to host us, this book would not have come into being.

Our deep gratitude extends to those who gave us feedback and helped us significantly improve the book. First to Gopavrindapala who commented extensively on our first rough draft, then Mahalakshmi (Ann V. Gray) who did some editing on part of an early draft, and then our test readers Caitlin Cameron and Ipek Tuncel who gave extensive detailed feedback on the penultimate draft. We would also like to thank other test readers who gave some feedback on partial or complete drafts. Jahnu Best gave us excellent feedback regarding the exercises. We are very grateful to Hari Parshad for occasional Sanskrit help. Mika Best entered some corrections. We also are grateful to the many people on social media such as Facebook, or in casual conversations, who helped each of us understand the subject better or gain insight on how to present it.

People on various forums and email lists helped us with technical issues preparing the manuscript. Dr. Deepak Sharma, and Nikhil, each took time out of their busy schedules to help. When we had seemingly impossible technical problems, Jagadguru cheerfully devoted his time and his software expertise to solve them.

We can hardly say enough to express our thanks to our editor, Dr. Michael A. French. We two authors remarked to each other on quite a number of occasions how his insightful feedback and suggestions reflected his deep engagement with our material, which significantly improved the book. He has been gracious and patient through our delays over the years we have been working together, and has even suggested a couple of the examples! Together with Dr. Vittorio Mattioli, he also did the final proofreading, and we are very grateful to both of them.

Although our book presented a few novel challenges, Virgina Kinniburgh indexed the book expertly. We appreciate her cheerfulness and competence.

Padma Gopi Walsh conceptualized and designed the cover, as well as creating all the original artwork. We are very grateful for her expert ability to turn ideas and concepts into beautiful and clear visuals.

We would like to thank the Protein Data Bank for permission to reprint the image of ATP synthase by Michael Goodsell. The original photographs in Chapter 38 were taken by Ruchira. Ruchira would especially like to thank Lalita Gopi for her guided tour of the *ahimsa* dairy at New Vrindaban and for spending several hours discussing the ins and outs of how the farm runs.

We each have taught small or large portions of this book in various classes. We thank the audiences for their responses, questions, and feedback, which have helped us improve our presentation.

We would like to acknowledge all the many sources that we quoted or referenced in this book. That includes those whose research, study, and insight provided evidence, explanations, and examples of concepts. And, it also includes the the great sages and saintly persons who contributed to the ancient sacred literature that provides the very foundation of the Career Dharma System, as well as our spiritual teachers and preceptors who brought the ancient wisdom to life for each of us personally.

Ruchira would like to thank Saheli Datta for her moral and emotional support during the writing of this book. Saheli also contributed very useful feedback at an early stage.

Urmila would like to thank Krishnapriya for hosting for several months in 2020 when travel was impossible, and also the managers of New Goloka, North Carolina, for providing a room for this work. She would also like to thank the many people over the years who urged her to write the book, and her children and adult grandchildren with whom she had illuminating discussions on many of the topics herein.

While various people mentioned above have contributed chapters, edited, provided feedback, and in other ways helped with our book, we two authors are fully responsible for any mistakes or omissions that may nevertheless remain.

Finally our debt of gratitude extends to the hundreds of people who have been asking since day one of our work when the book would be published, and who have expressed their eagerness to read it. Their enthusiasm certainly helped carry this work to fruition.[*][†]

[*]Colophon: The text face of *Career Dharma: The Natural Art of Work* is Agmena Pro, designed by Jovica Veljović in 2012 to be an ideal book font. The display face is Lydian, designed by Warren Chappell in 1938, inspired by the letter forms of calligraphy. The typewriter face is Iosevka Fixed, designed in 2015 by Belleve Invis (Renzhi Li) as an ideal programming font. The book was typeset in LaTeX using the memoir class and various other packages.

[†]Note to readers: If you would like to write to us regarding this book, please email feedback@careerdharma.net.

About the Author: Urmila Edith Best

Manhattan swarms with inhabitants from every culture and region. Growing up in this collage of humanity, I admired the Indian women above all, flowing down Fifth Avenue in their saris. By age four, I had traveled extensively, especially to Israel where my oldest sister lived. She was eighteen years older than me. There I was enchanted by the simple life of my brother-in-law's family. From Yemen, these religious people had an extended family that lived by planting crops and milking goats.

My mother, Esther Judith Manischewitz, had been born in Jerusalem to American parents and came to the United States as an infant. My father, Bernard Manischewitz, was born in the States and gradually took over the Manischewitz company that his father had run and his grandfather had started. His grandfather had been a rabbi, came to America to escape persecution, and started a Jewish foods business to fill a need.

Both my parents were dedicated to service. Although my father was a company president, and, by the time of my birth, a CEO, his view of the Manischewitz kosher foods company was that it was a spiritual vocation. He greatly increased both the company's product and profit line, for the purpose of serving his community.

He was also a highly compassionate and ethical person — I recall him refusing to bribe the truckers' union even though the consequences of his decision had a significant negative impact both for the company and him personally. He would take troubled employees under his wing and help them with both their personal and professional problems. As a president of synagogues, he helped lead congregations and manage practical matters.

He spent time with me each morning for hours before he went to work, teaching me stories, training me in right behavior and morality, discussing deep topics of life's meaning, and making me fresh orange juice. I saw him angry perhaps twice in my life. He was a person of great humor, reason, kindness, and love.

My mother had leadership roles in national and international religious charities. She gave much of her time, energy, and money to those less fortunate. She was also a connoisseur of the arts, and saturated my young life in Manhattan with art museums, libraries, science museums, theater, symphony concerts, ballet, and the like.

From the age of three, I attended New Lincoln School, which used individualized learning and had a highly diverse student body. With a wide range of exposure to ideas and ways of living from travel, preschool, and New York City itself, I started a search for truth before kindergarten. I wanted to find a truth whose reality had a base other than family and tradition. I said so, much to my mother's surprise.

While I was in preschool, at three years of age, my teachers complained to my parents that I was busier in trying to "teach the teachers how to teach" than in playing with the other students. So began the frequent admonishment from my parents and teachers along the lines of, "Stop teaching! You're not the teacher!" I grew up thinking that teaching was bad and that my tendency to want to teach, and to want to teach teachers how to teach, was something that needed to be destroyed or hidden in myself.

My second-oldest sister, who was sixteen years older than me, lived with her family on New York's Lower East Side during the 60s so she could attend Cooper Union Art School. I would often visit and walk around the neighborhood. One day, I noticed a new store, "The Krishna Shop." This store was managed by Mr. Coleman, who had recorded Hare Krishna chanting on the "Happening" Album. I regularly visited the shop, staying sometimes for an hour or more. The colorful Indian clothes decorated with mirrors deserved some passing interest. But the posters! I leafed through beautiful posters of Krishna. I was then about twelve years old.

The Jewish Theological Seminary, uptown near Columbia University, offered afternoon and weekend classes in Hebrew and the Bible. I studied there when I was fourteen. The Bible is full of references to a personal God, which both attracted and confused me, because in most of Judaism God is described as impersonal and without form. I read, "Moses spoke with God face to face, as a friend speaks with another friend." I wondered if that meant that, even in this body and on this earth, an exalted person could actually see God. And was that a finger the Lord used to write on the tablets of stone?

Playing the radio was part of my early-morning ritual, along with breakfast with my father and exercises. But one morning when I was fourteen, quite a different song was playing. It was heaven; no, it was Indian; no again, it was indescribable. Although I now hear this song daily, it is not difficult to bring back that first impression. The music swelled with known and unknown instruments in the background to a woman's rich voice singing another language. Soon she was joined by other voices which gradually melded together. I stopped brushing my hair, almost stopped breathing. What was this song?

I had a dream that I owned every album except this one. I looked for it frantically, but awoke dissatisfied. I only heard "Govinda" once more on the radio and finally purchased the Radha Krishna album at the largest record store in Manhattan. Inside the album were two pictures, which joined the other posters on my wall.

Soon after buying the album, which was produced by George Harrison and became a hit in Europe, I noticed a boy in the school library reading the Krishna Book, which had an identical cover to one of the pictures I had put on my wall. Borrowing it, I eagerly turned the pages, absorbing as much as possible before my next class. Upon returning it, I said, "This book is beautiful! And I have the cover picture on my wall. It was inside a record I bought."

"Really?" He looked up. "Would you like to come to the temple with me on Sunday?"

"Temple?"

"I go every Sunday. Would you like to come?" he repeated.

The Krishna temple was to the eyes, nose, ears, and mind what the record had suggested. I could not relate it to any other experience, but it seemed very comfortable and familiar. More pictures of Krishna went on my wall.

While starting my spiritual awakening, I traveled a road of material disillusionment that started at the beginning of high school when I joined the debating club. In the next two years I collected many trophies for public speaking, including the state and district championship. One year I made it to the quarter finals of the national competition.

In debate, one quickly learns that there are no absolutes. Every argument has a counter argument, every solution a problem. Winning is simply being cleverer than the next person in thinking on your feet and quoting authorities. The more I became expert, the more I became disgusted with material reasoning and solutions. My debating friends prepared for law school; I wanted a way out.

In terms of my life work, I didn't realize at the time how my training in debate and public speaking would be a great help in the realm of teaching, researching, and writing. At the time, I felt that other than law, my interests and talents could only be used on the stage. I never considered teaching because of how criticized I was for any such inclination. Therefore, both in high school and college, I studied drama and acting. I still love being in theater, though it remains an occasional hobby. In terms of research, my life's career got an accidental boost in high school thanks to the wisdom of one of my English teachers. As I already knew the class material, she allowed me to skip all classes except exams. Her only requirement was that I write a research paper every two weeks on any topic of my choice. I quickly realized that if I finished my work in two to three days I would have the rest of the time free. Thus, I learned how to be an effective and efficient researcher. I also wrote much poetry and had some published in the school newspaper. But my career path was still cloudy to me. My summer jobs as a nanny, and later, a chef in a Marriott Hotel, convinced me that I did not want to spend my life working simply to live.

Soon afterwards, while in college, I got a copy of the *Bhagavad-gita*. While I was an avid reader, this book was different from any other I had experienced. Reading it felt like someone knew my heart and inner mind, along with all my doubts and questions, and had perfect answers. After finishing the *Gita*, I read the Gospels of the New Testament for the first time. It was clear, to me at least, that Jesus was teaching basically the same message.

My college had a work term where students practically apply their studies. I got a job as a tour guide at the Museum of Science and Industry in Chicago. The museum job had many hours of boring guard duty when I would softly chant the mantras from the Radha Krishna album George Harrison had produced. Gradually the chanting changed my awareness and introspection. I could understand that despite my meditation, attempts to love my enemy, and discussions of deep philosophy, I had yet to realize anything close to enlightenment.

Deciding to move into an *asrama*, I gave notice that I would leave college at the end of the semester to dedicate my life to the practice of *bhakti* yoga in the Gaudiya Vaishnava tradition. Of course, this decision became the topic of discussion at home during vacations. My mother cried and couldn't see how naturally the path of my life led to this spiritual doorway. It would be many years before we became good friends and accepted each other's differences.

My father carefully examined the *Bhagavad-gita* and heard my story. He looked at me with the deep love of a relationship that is built on many frequent exchanges of shared conversation and adventures. "I'm so glad you are looking for God," he would say over and over during these months, "I just wish you could feel satisfied with our own faith. You know," he smiled, "I wanted to find spiritual truth when I was eighteen, but got distracted by marriage and business. I'm glad you are seeking a religious life."

Asrama life was communal, simple, and full of challenges to my pride and ego. It was also deeply intellectually and emotionally satisfying. I soon married a fellow *asrama* resident, and in 1973 became a disciple of A.C. Bhaktivedanta Swami Prabhupada. I delved into deep study of the *Bhagavad-gita* and *Bhagavata Purana*, along with meditation and kirtana. When the second of our three children was old enough for preschool, a mentor appeared in my life who was to greatly define the direction of my career. Jyotirmayi, who hailed from France, was an expert teacher, and she had a son the same age as my daughter. Her mood, determination, and expertise were focused on maximizing the children's fun, learning, and development in all areas, including the spiritual. I felt her to be a kindred spirit intellectually, spiritually, and emotionally. I became her apprentice and, at age twenty-four, all the long years of suppressed love and inclination for teaching finally burst forth from me. I had found my vocation and I was amazed that it had been there all along.

Seeking a good education for our three children when they became school-aged, I started taking professional courses in pedagogy and education in general and soon became a teacher of children in kindergarten through secondary school, as I gradually finished my undergraduate degree through distance learning. My husband and I lived in and out of various *asramas* for our first years of married life while he had successful jobs as a software engineer. By the time our third child was born, we owned a home and he had his own business custom designing and building home computers.

As a teacher of secondary-school students, I became interested in, and involved with, their career decisions. The *Bhagavad-gita* and *Bhagavata Purana* had much to say about having a satisfying and prosperous career, but there were few people who could translate those teachings into practical direction for my students. My interest in career and job satisfaction was also inspired by the fact that my husband and I opened two schools, and, in addition to teaching, I had become a school administrator, helping the teachers and staff in their own career development.

I was asked to write a regular column on spiritually based education for an international magazine, the renown of which resulted in my acting as a consultant to schools worldwide. Such consulting brought my interest in careers even more into focus. I wanted to help each member of the school staff and faculty gain happiness and prosperity from their work, as well as guide the students to a fulfilling life. I wrote a 500-page manual on starting a school, managing it, and the teaching of every subject at every level.

My husband and I had decided to take up separate lives of renunciation when our children were grown and starting their own families. In order to focus on writing curricula, I eventually resigned from teaching and school management. Shortly after my resignation, however, I was invited to London to teach *bhakti* yoga. Before that invitation, my training in, and love for, public speaking and debate had rusted for the decade after I had moved into an *asrama*; afterwards, I started getting invitations to deliver occasional lectures on *bhakti* yoga in my local community, first in Detroit, Michigan, and then in Hillsborough, North Carolina. But the London invitation turned out to be the start of teaching internationally. London is a type of "hub," and, while I was speaking there, many leaders from various countries came to my classes and extended further invitations.

Regardless of the door opening to international speaking engagements, I still wanted to produce curricula and, to that end, I decided to pursue graduate degrees at the University of North Carolina, Chapel Hill. In the master's of school administration program we gave much attention, again, to preparing students for working life, and creating a culture where school employees would find a rich life full of meaning and happiness. I wrote my doctoral dissertation on job satisfaction of teachers, and in the course of my overall study, delved into organizational culture, personality types, and the multi-faceted dimensions of what makes work satisfying or dissatisfying.

I completed my master's and doctorate together in 2006. Local newspapers ran an article celebrating the fact that our youngest son received his undergraduate degree in business from the same university on the same day as I received my graduate degrees. After graduating, my focus was on producing curricula, though I first helped to start a school system in London. My goal was an English literacy curriculum — a system that would teach beginner English reading skills with content from the *bhakti* yoga tradition.

While I had taught hundreds of children to read English and had produced some curriculum materials, and while I now had a master's and doctorate in education, producing a literacy program was daunting. Fortunately, I was tutored by the top experts in the UK government's Institute of Education in London, and in New Zealand by the top literacy expert and children's book writer for Nelson Thorne Publishing. While I can honestly say that I more or less followed the principles of career dharma my entire adult life, it was in the process of creating what came to be called *Dr. Best Learn to Read* that I came to appreciate the value of these principles in a very deep way. For each book, I would experience the interplay between letting go of ego while striving for excellence. Help would appear along the way as needed, whether financial or expert volunteers. The work was demanding and challenging, yet engrossing and thrilling, and I felt like I was completely in my element.

Once the work on the literacy program was progressing well, I responded to those speaking invitations and traveled the world numerous times, helping to start schools, assisting existing schools, training teachers and parents, and teaching the *Bhagavad-gita* and *Bhagavata Purana*. Along the way I continued to write magazine and journal articles, as well as books, such as the novel *Essence Seekers*[420] One of the greatest needs I encountered, whether in St. Petersburg, Cape Town, Sao Paulo, Shanghai, Dallas, Delhi, or Auckland, was the bewilderment of young people regarding what career to have and how to plan for it. I also met numerous adults already established in careers who rued their choices and felt stuck in them. And, of course, there were the many teachers and parents who ached to know how to guide those in their care. I also met many persons who were living the natural art of work in their own lives. Some had stumbled into the principles of career dharma through serendipitous quirks of life. A few intentionally studied their own nature, and wisdom both ancient and modern, in order to exemplify a truly prosperous livelihood.

On one of my journeys I met Ruchira and we quickly became friends. We discussed writing a small booklet on career dharma — maybe thirty pages we could finish in a few weeks. As we mapped out the chapters and started the work, it grew into a multi-year project with much research and testing. Writing this book with Ruchira has been a great joy. We started off by each writing chapters that moved us personally. We then edited and reedited each others' work to the point where we hope the book speaks in "one voice." Indeed, it is not easy for either of us to remember who wrote what!

I hope this labor of love helps you, those you love, and those you guide, to find the "live" in "livelihood" and to help make the world a place of satisfaction and prosperity.

About the Author: Ruchira S. Datta

My parents, Rabindra N. Datta and Debarati Datta, came from West Bengal, India. Each of them came from families connected with the Gaudiya Vaishnava tradition of *bhakti* yoga, or, as we call it in this book, devotional connection.

My paternal grandfather Dr. Nripendra Nath Dutta, a medical doctor, arranged to have learned persons come daily to the spacious family home to read from the *Bhagavata Purana*, one of the core sacred texts for Gaudiya Vaishnavas and a principal source for this book. In 1925, when my mother's paternal grandparents, Dr. Satyendra Nath (S. N.) and Nalini Ghosh, were a young couple, they became disciples of Srila Prabhupada Bhaktisiddhanta Saraswati Thakura, the visionary founder of a revivalist movement seeking to spread the teachings of *bhakti* yoga according to Chaitanya Mahaprabhu throughout India and beyond. My own views on charity are influenced by the fact that Dr. S. N. Ghosh, who had come to Calcutta as a poor orphan boy, would pay for the education of various people unrelated to him and also help poor students by giving them room and board in his home.

My parents met each other as graduate students in England, where my father was getting his PhD in rock mechanics. They decided to marry, and then spent a year back in India, where my father taught at a university. My mother's parents moved to Zambia, and my father got a job as a mining engineer in a nearby city there, so my parents also moved to Zambia, where I was born in June of 1973.

My father got a job in the US, when I was not yet two, and so we moved to Denver, Colorado. Our family used to attend the local Gaudiya Vaishnava temple there, associated with Srila Prabhupada A.C. Bhaktivedanta Swami.

Though I went to public school for kindergarten and first grade, in the spring of 1980 I began attending a private non-parochial school where I could learn at my own pace. When I was eight, I got an Apple II+ home computer, and delved into learning Applesoft Basic from the manual, teaching myself to program.

In late 1982, when I was nine, my maternal grandfather in England had a serious stroke. Our whole family flew there, and every day for three months we would visit my grandfather in the hospital, where my mother would spend hours in prayer, mantra meditation, and scriptural study. She asked me to read the *Bhagavad-gita*, a chapter a day, and talk with her about it. So it was at this time that I first read the whole book. The deep wisdom appeared to me to be luminous and intuitively true.

That same year, when I was nine, my mother gave me a popular book about Einstein and his theory of relativity. She had a lifelong love of science, which she instilled in me. I read the book and decided I wanted to be a physicist. When I was ten, I enrolled as a high school freshman at a private non-parochial college preparatory school. In my senior year, teachers tutored me to prepare me for the biology, BC calculus, and physics AP exams, which the school did not normally offer.

My mother flew to India for three months to formally take initiation into the practice of *bhakti* yoga from Srila Bhakti Rakshaka Sridhara Gosvami. My sister stayed with my father, who had moved to California for work. So that I could continue my senior year, my parents arranged for me to move into the *asrama* at the local Gaudiya Vaishnava temple for those three months, under the supervision of Mother Nidra. A classmate's mother drove me to and from school every day. It was under Mother Nidra's direction, at the age of thirteen, that I began my systematic study of the *Bhagavata Purana*.

My high school required all seniors to pursue a career internship experience in the final month of the school year. I chose to spend this month also at the local Gaudiya Vaishnava temple, as a volunteer. I computerized their financial records, which up till then were in paper ledgers, and also entered written recipes into a word-processing program.

At age thirteen, I was accepted by the AT&T Engineering Scholarship program. They would pay for four years of my college tuition, room and board, books, and fees at a college of my choice, as long as

I majored in electrical engineering, mechanical engineering, or computer science. Caltech accepted me with the stipulation that, unlike other freshmen, I must live at home with my parents.

The three local television news programs covered my high school graduation, and one of them came to the local Gaudiya Vaishnava temple. When they asked what I would like to achieve, I said I wanted to show the harmony of science and religion.

The AT&T scholarship included four years of summer internships at AT&T. So the day after my fourteenth birthday, on the first day I was eligible to work in Colorado, I started my first job, working for the summer as a programmer at AT&T Information Systems in Denver. That fall, my family moved from Denver. We had been deeply involved in the local Gaudiya Vaishnava temple, and they awarded my mother a plaque for her service. My family rented a small home in Pasadena, California, and I began my freshman year. The Los Angeles metropolitan area also had a local Gaudiya Vaishnava temple, though it was considerably further away, and my family became deeply involved in that community.

As a freshman, I chose to take epistemology and philosophy of science for two of my humanities and social sciences electives. I deeply engaged with these courses, and they made a profound impression on me. I have continued to study these subjects on my own, pondering how we know what we know, ever since.

In the spring of my freshman year I had to choose my major. Although I liked computers, Caltech did not have computer science as a major; it was merely a special emphasis of an engineering and applied science major. The AT&T scholarship program would not accept this emphasis. So I chose a double major in physics and electrical engineering.

In the summer of 1988, I did my second summer internship at AT&T in Denver. Again I stayed for three months in the *asrama* under the guidance of Mother Nidra, carpooling to work with a coworker. It was not until many years later that I came to appreciate how foundational my stays in that *asrama*, totaling six months, were to my spiritual life.

I also loved mathematics, so in my sophomore year, I started taking all the courses required for a triple major in mathematics, physics, and electrical engineering. Taking abstract algebra, I understood for the first time that mathematics was a living endeavor, and became enchanted. The winter quarter brought a crisis. I was not interested in electrical engineering, the triple major was not sustainable, and my studies collapsed.

After much discussion, the director of the scholarship program agreed to make an exception, allowing me to continue on the AT&T scholarship as a double major in mathematics and physics. While the attempt to fit a square peg into a round hole — namely, me into the electrical engineering major — turned out to be shortlived in practical terms, it darkened my mental outlook for years subsequently. This experience helped inform my conviction of the danger of crossing fields.

Fortunately, the gentle spiritual guidance of my Gaudiya Vaishnava teachers, including my mother, remained with me. I knew that I was not my mind, not my thoughts, not my memory, not my intelligence, and certainly not the results of any of my worldly endeavors. This knowledge helped ground me when any of the above was troubling me. I finished my first readings of the *Bhagavata Purana* and the *Chaitanya Charitamrita* when I was sixteen. This included the commentaries of Srila Prabhupada A.C. Bhaktivedanta Swami. Thanks to the thorough standards he had set for the publication of his books, I had also taught myself to read the Devanagari and Bengali scripts from them. In 1990 my father went on a trip to India, and became a disciple of Srila Bhakti Pramoda Puri Gosvami. On his return he moved to Las Vegas, Nevada, for another job.

I struggled with the laboratory requirements at Caltech, and I was not able to complete the advanced lab class required for the physics major. I realized it was mathematics that I loved, and what I liked about physics was the mathematics. So at the beginning of my senior year, I dropped the physics major, and became a mathematics major. Meanwhile, I had loved my humanities and social sciences classes, focusing especially on literature and political theory, rounded out with economics. I found it funny that our professor required us to buy his book *Game Theory and Political Theory*, although he never used it in class. Little did I know it would come in handy later. At seventeen I graduated as a math major from Caltech.

In the summer of 1991, our whole family traveled to India. I met Srila Bhakti Pramoda Puri Gosvami and Srila Bhakti Ballabha Tirtha Gosvami. Within a short time, I felt within my heart that Srila Bhakti Pramoda Puri Gosvami had the power to guide me to transcendence: he was the living embodiment of ideals, such as humility and tolerance, that I had only understood intellectually before. Srila Bhakti Pramoda Puri Gosvami accepted myself and my sister as disciples.

Upon our return, I began the PhD program in mathematics at UC Berkeley, receiving the National Need fellowship from the US government. Within two years I had completed all requirements except my dissertation. A professor agreed to accept me as his advisee in differential geometry. I also began teaching multivariable calculus discussion sections as a graduate research instructor for two years.

In the meantime, I had continued to take summer and part-time jobs doing programming. With the experience I had from my four summer internships, including the last two at the well-known AT&T Bell Labs in New Jersey, programming jobs were easy to get, especially in scientific computing or other applications of mathematics.

In the winter of 1997, our whole family travelled to India and had an extensive stay with Srila Bhakti Pramoda Puri Gosvami in Puri. He was 98 years old and it would turn out to be my last face-to-face visit with him. In November 1999, he left this world — my first deep experience of grief in this life.

A year later, my thesis advisor cautioned me against the use of computers in mathematical research in very strong terms, something that I wanted to do. He gave me the best advice he ever gave me: to find a different advisor. My new understanding, that I simply had my own perspective on mathematics that was different, enlivened me, and I felt like making a fresh start.

The 90s were the decade of the "dot-com boom," with many startups arising to take advantage of the new possibilities of the internet. This boom ended with the "dot-com bust." Very soon I encountered the changed landscape: in March 2001, I interviewed with an enterprise software company for a summer job. Everything went well, and the department leader asked me to contact their human resources division in a month or so to finalize the paperwork. In April, when I did so, I was informed that the entire department with whom I had interviewed had been eliminated. Instead, I got part-time work with the electrical engineering department at the university, writing software for self-driving cars.

One Saturday in March 2002, I got an email from Prof. Bernd Sturmfels, asking me to go to campus and pick up the paper he had left in my cubbyhole. "A Beautiful Mind" had recently won several Oscars, including Best Picture, and Bernd had discovered that game theory, which John Nash had worked on and received a Nobel prize for, involved polynomial systems! The paper was an early work of Nash, which Bernd wanted me to help prepare as an example for his class and book. When Bernd introduced game theory in class, his enthusiasm shone. "First the book, then the movie, then the Groebner bases!"

I found game theory itself quite fascinating. Through game theory we could link the behavior of people and groups, with mathematics! What could possibly be more interesting?

On April 1, 2002, I wrote a message to Caml-list, the mailing list dedicated to the Objective Caml programming language:

> It is my great pleasure to announce that the first fruits of the _Developing Applications with Objective Caml_ translation project are now online! Please go to
> `https://caml.inria.fr/pub/docs/oreilly-book/html/index.h` tmlhttp://caml.inria.fr/oreilly-book/
> where the preliminary version of the English translation of this seven hundred-odd page book is available for your viewing pleasure!
>
> This translation is the product of an unprecedented effort by roughly sixty volunteers worldwide...
> –Ruchira Datta[421]

The next day, one of the volunteers, Julian Assange, replied:

> We must also especially thank Ruchira Datta for the herculean task of booting and rebooting the 60-node translation machine over the past year ;)
> –Julian Assange[422]

It was a computer person's apt description of my first experience in leadership — a challenging, yet ultimately fulfilling task.

The next day, Bernd accepted me as his advisee, and shortly afterward we travelled to Texas A&M University for a week-long conference, where Bernd gave a series of ten lectures. It was an exciting gathering of mathematicians learning about and collaborating on different aspects of polynomial systems, both pure and applied. This was my first experience with the friendly, lively, and synergistic nature of mathematical collaboration. Perhaps because there is always such an abundance of new mathematics to be done, mathematicians can often be very sociable and collegial in their work.

During the conference, Bernd came up with a conjecture: the universality of Nash equilibria. To put it briefly, this means that every system of polynomial equations can be encoded into a game. After the conference, he suggested that I work on this conjecture. With his guidance, in the summer of 2002 I proved the universality of Nash equilibria! This major result answered some longstanding questions in complexity theory. I also made a connection with other work of Nash, the Nash-Tognoli Theorem, which had previously seemed unrelated to game theory. This theorem enabled me to prove a very general result. Speaking rather loosely for the sake of simplicity, I had proved that every shape arises in game theory, and that games with three or more players are fundamentally much more interesting than games with only two players.

Shortly afterward, Bernd called me into his office. He told me that at many universities, my proof of the universality theorem would be enough to get a PhD; but not at UC Berkeley, and not from him. He advised me to pursue game theory for my dissertation, since I already had a major result, which is what I did.

I also worked with Prof. Richard Fateman in the computer science department on a master's project related to game theory, and in December 2002, I received my master's in computer science. Soon afterwards, I came up with a new model of groups in noncooperative game theory, and, in December 2003, I received my PhD in mathematics. Working with Bernd had made a world of difference, which I gratefully appreciated. I dedicated my thesis to my guru, Srila Bhakti Pramoda Puri Gosvami, whose grace had made it possible, upholding and sustaining me through all the challenges and steering me toward the highest good at every step.

In January, I started commuting to Davis to teach classes two days a week, and working at Lawrence Berkeley the rest of the week. I took one day off to do a full day of onsite interviews at the growing company Google and shortly afterward received an offer of a permanent position there as a software engineer.

A Vice President of Research and Engineering spent an hour with me to answer any questions I might have. I asked him, why was I being offered the position of software engineer, why not research scientist? The VP told me that at Google they didn't want innovation to be limited to the Research department, they wanted everyone to innovate. He said research scientists were just people who didn't know how to program, and since I could program, why did I want to be a research scientist? I was left to ponder that question.

I decided to join Google. The mission statement, "to organize the world's information and make it universally accessible and useful," was very appealing. I accepted the position of software engineer, one of six hundred at the time.

It was an exciting time to join Google. The company was growing rapidly, and at the same time, it still retained a lot of its early, playful startup feel. Google was pioneering a fun and open workplace culture with many amenities, encouraging people from different teams to learn about one another's work.

I was working specifically in International Search Quality, focusing on users speaking non-English languages or in countries outside the US, and my starter project involved making a significant enhancement to the search engine itself. I consulted coworkers originally hailing from various countries as I was developing this enhancement. I helped identify the bugs in other parts of the search engine that temporarily prevented the launch and created a workaround, earning peer recognition. When my enhancement was finally launched properly, in May 2005, it turned out to have significant benefits for additional users even beyond the ones I had targeted. It was gratifying to have made a difference for so many people. Even at the time of this writing, from time to time opening a web browser and showing a new person my enhancement can be a bit of fun.

Shortly after joining Google, I had met a coworker, Eric. We got engaged, with the loving support of my family. However, some time later our relationship broke, though we remained friends. A few years later, when I learned that Eric had passed away, I grieved deeply.

While the potential for my work to have a large impact was fulfilling, in terms of management, Google was rather chaotic. As Search Quality had grown unwieldy, it was split, and the tech lead of International Search Quality became manager. However, he was more interested in engineering than managing. Our team members dispersed and I collaborated with another group, but was not really integrated with them.

There began to be talk of disbanding International Search Quality as a separate team, making each of its functions a responsibility of the respective functional divisions of Search Quality. I was asked where I might like to go next. I thought that now I would finally be able to work on research.

At this point, I was approached about a recruiting trip, the first of its kind for Google. While Google had an engineering office in Bangalore, India, it did not have enough engineers there to do enough interviews to grow the office at the desired rate. From Bangalore our interviewing team would fan out across India to conduct interviews at several IITs, or Indian Institutes of Technology, where the most promising computer science students could be found.

I jumped at the chance. In the past couple of years, my spiritual interests had been maturing, thanks to *sanga* (spiritual association) with practitioners, and I felt ready to take the next step. My guru had said that if we had any questions after his passing, we could ask Srila Bhakti Ballabha Tirtha Gosvami. So after the whirlwind recruiting engagement, I remained in India on vacation, and the rest of my family also came there. Srila Bhakti Ballabha Tirtha Gosvami gave me initiation into the Vaishnava *diksha* mantras (mantras for inner meditation) in January 2006.

Upon my return, I learned that International Search Quality had been disbanded. I had not been allowed to go into machine translation, since it was in Research, and they did not want engineers "leaking" into research. As I had mentioned Google Book Search in my alternative request to work on document summarization research, I had been transferred to Google Book Search, though not to work on that. Google Book Search was still a new product, and I was to work on web analytics.

During the next several months, much of my time was spent trying to get the infrastructure needed for the web analytics to work. From my present perspective as a data scientist (a term that had not yet become current), I was having to do both data science *and* data engineering. The latter was neither my interest nor my expertise, nor was I getting support. I ended up putting in long, unfulfilling, frustrating hours. Meanwhile, my mother, who had stayed back in India for an extended visit when the rest of us had returned, had fallen seriously ill, spent a month in intensive care, and nearly died. When she returned home, her health was still very precarious, with repeated hospitalizations. I would frequently undertake long commutes to visit her, and also learned to administer intravenous medicine when she was released at home. My schedule had become grueling. A rare high point was spending time with a patent lawyer describing my work in International Search Quality. This eventually resulted in four patents, two in which I was the sole inventor and two in which I had a single co-inventor. Otherwise, however, I was growing increasingly frustrated.

When I reminded the VP of Research and Engineering of what he had said to entice me about the prospect of doing research, he said that may have been true at the time. However Google had changed. Now Research would only accept well-established research scientists.

It had become apparent that there was actually no prospect of my becoming a well-established research scientist, or a research scientist at all, at Google. Moreover, the further I got from my PhD, the more difficult it would become to reenter research. So in the fall of 2006, I left Google.

I took some time to think about what to do next, becoming a Visiting Scholar at UC Berkeley. On the one hand, I could return to game theory. While at Google, I had read extensively about economics, and felt there were significant areas that needed improvement. My reading about experimental economics showed that even game theory itself made assumptions about human behavior that simply hadn't panned out. Over the course of friendly discussions with others at Google, I had seen that models in economics based on unrealistic assumptions were having severe real-world consequences on people's thinking, their policies, and ultimately their lives. I could also see that many of these problems stemmed from shoehorning scenarios into models that used particular mathematical techniques. While perhaps these were the best available at the time several decades before, I had much more flexible and powerful mathematical and computational techniques available, and had some directions in mind for better models. I felt it would take concentrated research.

On the other hand, I also had the opportunity to pursue mathematical and computational biology, which I had become interested in during graduate school. This continued to be a growing research field. Although I was doubtful about being able to enter this field without having published anything about it before, it turned out that the US federal research agencies had determined that there was a great need for such theoretical biologists. I did a lot of reading, and concluded that the choice between game theory and biology was a false one, since game theory was also relevant to biology. I started as a postdoc in the Berkeley Phylogenomics Lab in the summer of 2007.

That summer was also a time of great spiritual growth for me, due to favorable *sanga*. With my mother's help and encouragement, I began speaking from time to time in small gatherings of Gaudiya Vaishnava practitioners. I was able to experience the grace and purification of having divine speech pass through me, by sharing the wisdom that had been handed down by previous teachers.

My postdoc with the Berkeley Phylogenomics Lab gave me a firm foundation in computational biology. At first I felt very dull-witted and slow; I would look at research articles and could not make heads or tails of even the first page. The professor spoke to me extensively during the first few months, and it felt like suddenly arriving in a city where the only language spoken was foreign to me. After about nine months, however, I felt comfortable with biology, ready to learn whatever was required.

In mid-2011, it was time to move on to the next postdoc. My mother's health had never fully recovered, and I didn't want to leave the Bay Area. I did a Google search that I did not expect to have any results: ["evolution of cooperation" UCSF]. Fortunately, it did have a single result: a postdoc at the Center for the Evolution of Cancer at UC San Francisco, on cancer as an evolutionary and ecological process. A multicellular organism is the paradigm of cooperation — much more cooperative than most societies that we see — and cancer is the unusual failure of that cooperation. Just as we can learn about the functioning of the brain from the results of lesions in different areas, we can learn about the nature of cooperation from its failure in cancer, where I expected there to be lots of data. I started this postdoc in October 2011. I learned intensely about cancer, starting with the cancer section of medical school, attending all the lectures given to medical students (which took place in their second year).

Although I knew my mother's health was unstable, it still came as quite a shock when she passed away suddenly in April 2012.

The next several months were a time of immense spiritual growth as I processed my grief. I continued to go to work at UCSF, which I found to be an anchor that moored me (of course, every person is different). I also regularly saw a grief counselor in San Francisco.

In the summer of 2013, Sriman Rasavihari Dasa, one of the earliest disciples of Srila Bhakti Ballabha Tirtha Gosvami, visited the United States from India. We arranged gatherings where he could share the teachings of *bhakti* yoga. He encouraged me to share those teachings with the public myself, continuing to connect with some of those he had met during his visit. After he departed, I was invited to give a series of ten classes on *bhakti* yoga at a yoga studio. This was my first experience sharing Gaudiya Vaishnava philosophy and practice with those who were new to it. The response was deeply encouraging, and sharing with this kind of audience has become one of my favorite practices.

My postdoc with UCSF was ending in 2014. I had continued to delve deeply into cancer biology, and a special opportunity arose. The Mathematical Biosciences Institute, in central Ohio, would hold a special program on the mathematical modeling of cancer during the entire academic year 2014–2015. So I moved to Ohio for another postdoc there. In 2015, I took up the term "mathematical ecosociology" for my approach and orientation toward modeling social-ecological systems, and discussed it with a few other mathematicians at the Joint Mathematical Meetings in San Antonio.

In central Ohio, I found a very warm and dynamic Gaudiya Vaishnava *sanga*, and joined regularly multiple times per week. In 2015, I began speaking there from time to time when asked, and also began participating in a new group that shared *bhakti* yoga regularly with (new or longstanding) practitioners of postural yoga. It was here, in 2016, that I met Urmila Edith Best. We hit it off immediately, and a month later she invited me to start this book project with her.

At about the same time, my postdoc ended, and I decided to go into consulting about machine learning. This gave me plenty of unstructured time, which would enable me to delve into social and ecological theory, my deep and abiding research interest.

This unstructured time, as well as my personal inclination, led me to think deeply about career. Urmila and I began our book project in April 2017. The greater understanding of career dharma and how it fits with the yoga of devotion helped me to find and select my current full-time position, as a data scientist with CAS, a division of the American Chemical Society, a congenial work environment with a friendly group of colleagues. I do get to organize scientific information and make it accessible and useful through working on our search engine solutions. Furthermore, the ACS is a nonprofit learned society, so any "profit" from CAS's operations is contributed to the society at the end of each year, furthering its work in education and science. Integrating career and dharma through the ancient teachings has been immensely fulfilling for me personally. Urmila and I have also had a lot of fun along the way.